CW01660114

THE REST IS NOISE

LISTENING TO THE TWENTIETH CENTURY

(((. . .)))

ALEX ROSS

Farrar, Straus and Giroux
New York

Farrar, Straus and Giroux
19 Union Square West, New York 10003

Distributed in Canada by Douglas & McIntyre Ltd.
Printed in the United States of America

Portions of this book originally appeared, in different form, in *The New Yorker.*

Grateful acknowledgment is made for permission to reprint the following material:
Excerpt from "Art for Art's Sake" from *The Cradle Will Rock.* Used by permission of the Estate of Marc Blitzstein.
"Battle Cry" by Milton Babbitt. Used by permission of the author.
Excerpt from letter of September 1934 to Israel Citkowitz, by Aaron Copland.
Used by permission of the Aaron Copland Fund for Music, Inc.

ISBN-13: 978-0-7394-9777-7

Designed by Michelle McMillian

THE REST IS NOISE

For my parents
and
Jonathan

It seems to me . . . that despite the logical, moral rigor music may appear to display, it belongs to a world of spirits, for whose absolute reliability in matters of human reason and dignity I would not exactly want to put my hand in the fire. That I am nevertheless devoted to it with all my heart is one of those contradictions which, whether a cause for joy or regret, are inseparable from human nature.

—Thomas Mann, *Doctor Faustus*

HAMLET: . . . —the rest is silence.
HORATIO: Now cracks a noble heart. Good night, sweet prince,
And flights of angels sing thee to thy rest!
[*March within.*]
Why does the drum come hither?

CONTENTS

PART III: 1945–2000

PREFACE

In the spring of 1928, George Gershwin, the creator of *Rhapsody in Blue*, toured Europe and met the leading composers of the day. In Vienna, he called at the home of Alban Berg, whose blood-soaked, dissonant, sublimely dark opera *Wozzeck* had had its premiere in Berlin three years earlier. To welcome his American visitor, Berg arranged for a string quartet to perform his *Lyric Suite*, in which Viennese lyricism was refined into something like a dangerous narcotic.

Gershwin then went to the piano to play some of his songs. He hesitated. Berg's work had left him awestruck. Were his own pieces worthy of these murky, opulent surroundings? Berg looked at him sternly and said, "Mr. Gershwin, music is music."

If only it were that simple. Ultimately, all music acts on its audience through the same physics of sound, shaking the air and arousing curious sensations. In the twentieth century, however, musical life disintegrated into a teeming mass of cultures and subcultures, each with its own canon and jargon. Some genres have attained more popularity than others; none has true mass appeal. What delights one group gives headaches to another. Hip-hop tracks thrill teenagers and horrify their parents. Popular standards that break the hearts of an older generation become insipid kitsch in the ears of their grandchildren. Berg's *Wozzeck* is, for some, one of the most gripping operas ever written; Gershwin thought so, and emulated it in *Porgy and Bess*, not least in the hazy chords that float through "Summertime." For others, *Wozzeck* is a welter of ugliness. The arguments easily grow heated; we can be intolerant in reaction to others' tastes, even violent. Then again, beauty may catch us in unexpected places. "Wherever we are," John Cage wrote in his book *Silence*, "what we hear is mostly noise. When we ignore it, it disturbs us. When we listen to it, we find it fascinating."

Twentieth-century classical composition, the subject of this book, sounds like noise to many. It is a largely untamed art, an unassimilated underground. While the splattered abstractions of Jackson Pollock sell on the art market for a hundred million dollars or more, and while experimental works by Matthew Barney or David Lynch are analyzed in college dorms across the land, the equivalent in music still sends ripples of unease through concert audiences and makes little perceptible impact on the outside world. Classical music is stereotyped as an art of the dead, a repertory that begins with Bach and terminates with Mahler and Puccini. People are sometimes surprised to learn that composers are still writing at all.

Yet these sounds are hardly alien. Atonal chords crop up in jazz; avant-garde sounds appear in Hollywood film scores; minimalism has marked rock, pop, and dance music from the Velvet Underground onward. Sometimes the music resembles noise because it *is* noise, or near to it, by design. Sometimes, as with Berg's *Wozzeck*, it mixes the familiar and the strange, consonance and dissonance. Sometimes it is so singularly beautiful that people gasp in wonder when they hear it. Olivier Messiaen's *Quartet for the End of Time*, with its grandly singing lines and gently ringing chords, stops time with each performance.

Because composers have infiltrated every aspect of modern existence, their work can be depicted only on the largest possible canvas. *The Rest Is Noise* chronicles not only the artists themselves but also the politicians, dictators, millionaire patrons, and CEOs who tried to control what music was written; the intellectuals who attempted to adjudicate style; the writers, painters, dancers, and filmmakers who provided companionship on lonely roads of exploration; the audiences who variously reveled in, reviled, or ignored what composers were doing; the technologies that changed how music was made and heard; and the revolutions, hot and cold wars, waves of emigration, and deeper social transformations that reshaped the landscape in which composers worked.

What the march of history really has to do with music itself is the subject of sharp debate. In the classical field it has long been fashionable to fence music off from society, to declare it a self-sufficient language. In the hyper-political twentieth century, that barrier crumbles time and again: Béla Bartók writes string quartets inspired by field recordings of Transylvanian folk songs, Shostakovich works on his *Leningrad* Symphony while German guns are firing on the city, John Adams creates an opera starring Richard Nixon and Mao Zedong. Nevertheless, articulating the connection between music and the outer world remains devilishly difficult. Musical meaning is vague, mutable, and, in the end, deeply personal. Still, even if history can never tell us exactly what music means, music can tell us something about history. My subtitle is meant literally; this is the twentieth century heard through its music.

Histories of music since 1900 often take the form of a teleological tale, a goal-obsessed narrative full of great leaps forward and heroic battles with the philistine bourgeoisie. When the concept of progress assumes exaggerated importance, many works are struck from the historical record on the grounds that they have nothing new to say. These pieces often happen to be those that have found a broader public—the symphonies of Sibelius and Shostakovich, Copland's *Appalachian Spring*, Carl Orff's *Carmina burana*. Two distinct repertories have formed, one intellectual and one popular. Here they are merged: no language is considered intrinsically more modern than any other.

In the same way, the story criss-crosses the often ill-defined or imaginary border separating classical music from neighboring genres. Duke Ellington, Miles Davis, the Beatles, and the Velvet Underground have substantial walk-on roles, as the conversation between Gershwin and Berg goes on from generation to generation. Berg was right: music unfolds along an unbroken continuum, however dissimilar the sounds on the surface. Music is always migrating from its point of origin to its destiny in someone's fleeting moment of experience—last night's concert, tomorrow's solitary jog.

The Rest Is Noise is written not just for those well versed in classical music but also—especially—for those who feel passing curiosity about this obscure pandemonium on the outskirts of culture. I approach the subject from multiple angles: biography, musical description, cultural and social history, evocations of place, raw politics, firsthand accounts by the participants themselves. Each chapter cuts a wide swath through a given period, but there is no attempt to be comprehensive: certain careers stand in for entire scenes, certain key pieces stand in for entire careers, and much great music is left on the cutting-room floor.

A list of recommended recordings appears at the back, along with acknowledgments of the many brilliant scholars who assisted me and citations of the hundreds of books, articles, and archival resources that I consulted. More can be found at www.therestisnoise.com. The abundant, benighted twentieth century is only beginning to be seen whole.

Part I

1900–1933

I am ready, I feel free
To cleave the ether on a novel flight,
To novel spheres of pure activity.

—GOETHE, *FAUST, PART I*

1

THE GOLDEN AGE

Strauss, Mahler, and the Fin de Siècle

When Richard Strauss conducted his opera *Salome* on May 16, 1906, in the Austrian city of Graz, several crowned heads of European music gathered to witness the event. The premiere of *Salome* had taken place in Dresden five months earlier, and word had got out that Strauss had created something beyond the pale—an ultra-dissonant biblical spectacle, based on a play by a British degenerate whose name was not mentioned in polite company, a work so frightful in its depiction of adolescent lust that imperial censors had banned it from the Court Opera in Vienna.

Giacomo Puccini, the creator of *La Bohème* and *Tosca*, made a trip north to hear what "terribly cacophonous thing" his German rival had concocted. Gustav Mahler, the director of the Vienna Opera, attended with his wife, the beautiful and controversial Alma. The bold young composer Arnold Schoenberg arrived from Vienna with his brother-in-law Alexander Zemlinsky and no fewer than six of his pupils. One of them, Alban Berg, traveled with an older friend, who later recalled the "feverish impatience and boundless excitement" that all felt as the evening approached. The widow of Johann Strauss II, composer of *On the Beautiful Blue Danube*, represented old Vienna.

Ordinary music enthusiasts filled out the crowd—"young people from Vienna, with only the vocal score as hand luggage," Richard Strauss noted. Among them may have been the seventeen-year-old Adolf Hitler, who had just seen Mahler conduct Richard Wagner's *Tristan und Isolde* in Vienna. Hitler later told Strauss's son that he had borrowed money from relatives to make the trip. There was even a fictional character present—Adrian Leverkühn, the hero of Thomas Mann's *Doctor Faustus*, the tale of a composer in league with the devil.

The Graz papers brought news from Croatia, where a Serbo-Croat movement was gaining momentum, and from Russia, where the tsar was locked in conflict with the country's first parliament. Both stories carried tremors of future chaos—the assassination of Archduke Franz Ferdinand in 1914, the Russian Revolution of 1917. For the moment, though, Europe maintained the facade of civilization. The British war minister, Richard Haldane, was quoted as saying that he loved German literature and enjoyed reciting passages from Goethe's *Faust*.

Strauss and Mahler, the titans of Austro-German music, spent the afternoon in the hills above the city, as Alma Mahler recounted in her memoirs. A photographer captured the composers outside the opera house, apparently preparing to set out on their expedition—Strauss smiling in a boater hat, Mahler squinting in the sun. The company visited a waterfall and had lunch in an inn, where they sat at a plain wooden table. They must have made a strange pair: Strauss, tall and lanky, with a bulbous forehead, a weak chin, strong but sunken eyes; Mahler, a full head shorter, a muscular hawk of a man. As the sun began to go down, Mahler became nervous about the time and suggested that the party head back to the Hotel Elefant, where they were staying, to prepare for the performance. "They can't start without me," Strauss said. "Let 'em wait." Mahler replied: "If you won't go, then I will—and conduct in your place."

Mahler was forty-six, Strauss forty-one. They were in most respects polar opposites. Mahler was a kaleidoscope of moods—childlike, heaven-storming, despotic, despairing. In Vienna, as he strode from his apartment near the Schwarzenbergplatz to the opera house on the Ringstrasse, cab-drivers would whisper to their passengers, "*Der Mahler!*" Strauss was earthy, self-satisfied, more than a little cynical, a closed book to most observers. The soprano Gemma Bellincioni, who sat next to him at a banquet after the performance in Graz, described him as "a pure kind of German, without poses, without long-winded speeches, little gossip and no inclination to talk about himself and his work, a gaze of steel, an indecipherable expression." Strauss came from Munich, a backward place in the eyes of sophisticated Viennese such as Gustav and Alma. Alma underlined this impression in her memoir by rendering Strauss's dialogue in an exaggerated Bavarian dialect.

Not surprisingly, the relationship between the two composers suffered from frequent misunderstandings. Mahler would recoil from unintended slights; Strauss would puzzle over the sudden silences that ensued. Strauss was still trying to understand his old colleague some four decades later, when he read Alma's book and annotated it. "All untrue," he wrote, next to the description of his behavior in Graz.

"Strauss and I tunnel from opposite sides of the mountain," Mahler said. "One day we shall meet." Both saw music as a medium of conflict, a battlefield of extremes. They reveled in the tremendous sounds that a hundred-piece orchestra could make, yet they also released energies of fragmentation and collapse. The heroic narratives of nineteenth-century Romanticism, from Beethoven's symphonies to Wagner's music dramas, invariably ended with a blaze of transcendence, of spiritual overcoming. Mahler and Strauss told stories of more circuitous shape, often questioning the possibility of a truly happy outcome.

Each made a point of supporting the other's music. In 1901, Strauss became president of the Allgemeiner deutscher Musikverein, or All-German Music Association, and his first major act was to program Mahler's Third Symphony for the festival the following year. Mahler's works appeared so often on the association's programs in subsequent seasons that some critics took to calling the organization the Allgemeiner deutscher Mahlerverein. Others dubbed it the Annual German Carnival of Cacophony. Mahler, for his part, marveled at *Salome*. Strauss had played and sung the score for him the previous year, in a piano shop in Strasbourg, while passersby pressed against the windows trying to overhear. *Salome* promised to be one of the highlights of Mahler's Vienna tenure, but the censors balked at accepting an opera in which biblical characters perform unspeakable acts. Furious, Mahler began hinting that his days in Vienna were numbered. He wrote to Strauss in March 1906: "You would not believe how vexatious this matter has been for me or (between ourselves) what consequences it may have for me."

So *Salome* came to Graz, an elegant city of 150,000 people, capital of the agricultural province of Styria. The Stadt-Theater staged the opera at the suggestion of the critic Ernst Decsey, an associate of Mahler's, who assured the management that it would create a succès de scandale.

"The city was in a state of great excitement," Decsey wrote in his autobiography, *Music Was His Life*. "Parties formed and split. Pub philosophers buzzed about what was going on . . . Visitors from the provinces, critics, press people, reporters, and foreigners from Vienna . . . Three more-than-sold-out houses. Porters groaned, and hoteliers reached for the keys to their safes." The critic fueled the anticipation with a high-flown preview article acclaiming Strauss's "tone-color world," his "polyrhythms and polyphony," his "breakup of the narrow old tonality," his "fetish ideal of an Omni-Tonality."

As dusk fell, Mahler and Strauss finally appeared at the opera house, having rushed back to town in their chauffeur-driven car. The crowd milling around in the lobby had an air of nervous electricity. The orchestra played a fanfare when Strauss walked up to the podium, and the audience applauded stormily. Then silence descended, the clarinet played a softly slithering scale, and the curtain went up.

In the Gospel of Saint Matthew, the princess of Judaea dances for her stepfather, Herod, and demands the head of John the Baptist as reward. She had surfaced several times in operatic history, usually with her more scandalous features suppressed. Strauss's brazenly modern retelling takes off from Oscar Wilde's 1891 play *Salomé*, in which the princess shamelessly eroticizes the body of John the Baptist and indulges in a touch of necrophilia at the end. When Strauss read Hedwig Lachmann's German translation of Wilde—in which the accent is dropped from Salomé's name—he decided to set it to music word for word, instead of employing a verse adaptation. Next to the first line, "How beautiful is the princess Salome tonight," he made a note to use the key of C-sharp minor. But this would turn out to be a different sort of C-sharp minor from Bach's or Beethoven's.

Strauss had a flair for beginnings. In 1896 he created what may be, after the first notes of Beethoven's Fifth, the most famous opening flourish in music: the "mountain sunrise" from *Thus Spake Zarathustra*, deployed to great effect in Stanley Kubrick's film *2001: A Space Odyssey*. The passage draws its cosmic power from the natural laws of sound. If you pluck a string tuned to a low C, then pluck it again while pinching it in half, the tone rises to the next C above. This is the interval of the octave. Further subdivisions yield intervals of the fifth (C to G), the fourth (G to the next higher C), and the major third (C to E). These are the lower steps of the natural harmonic series, or overtone series, which shimmers like a rainbow from any vibrating string. The same intervals appear at the outset of *Zarathustra*, and they accumulate into a gleaming C-major chord.

Salome, written nine years after *Zarathustra*, begins very differently, in a state of volatility and flux. The first notes on the clarinet are simply a rising scale, but it is split down the middle: the first half belongs to C-sharp major, the second half to G major. This is an unsettling opening, for several reasons. First, the notes C-sharp and G are separated by the interval known as the tritone, one half-step narrower than the perfect fifth. (Leonard Bernstein's "Maria" opens with a tritone resolving to a fifth.) This interval has long caused uneasy vibrations in human ears; scholars called it *diabolus in musica*, the musical devil.

In the *Salome* scale, not just two notes but two key-areas, two opposing harmonic spheres, are juxtaposed. From the start, we are plunged into an environment where bodies and ideas circulate freely, where opposites meet. There's a hint of the glitter and swirl of city life: the debonairly gliding clarinet looks forward to the jazzy character who kicks off Gershwin's *Rhapsody in Blue*. The scale might also suggest a meeting of irreconcilable belief systems; after all, *Salome* takes place at the intersection of Roman, Jewish, and Christian societies. Most acutely, this little run of notes takes us inside the mind of one who is exhibiting all the contradictions of her world.

The first part of *Salome* focuses on the confrontation between Salome and the prophet Jochanaan: she the symbol of unstable sexuality, he the symbol of ascetic rectitude. She tries to seduce him, he shrinks away and issues a curse, and the orchestra expresses its own fascinated disgust with an interlude in C-sharp minor—in Jochanaan's stentorian manner, but in Salome's key.

Then Herod comes onstage. The tetrarch is a picture of modern neurosis, a sensualist with a yearning for the moral life, his music awash in overlapping styles and shifting moods. He comes out on the terrace; looks for the princess; gazes at the moon, which is "reeling through the clouds like a drunken woman"; orders wine, slips in blood, stumbles over the body of a soldier who has committed suicide; feels cold, feels a wind—there is a hallucination of wings beating the air. It's quiet again; then more wind, more visions. The orchestra plays fragments of waltzes, expressionistic clusters of dissonance, impressionistic washes of sound. There is a turbulent episode as five Jews in Herod's court dispute the meaning of the Baptist's prophecies; two Nazarenes respond with the Christian point of view.

When Herod persuades his stepdaughter to dance the Dance of the Seven Veils, she does so to the tune of an orchestral interlude that, on first hearing, sounds disappointingly vulgar in its thumping rhythms and pseudo-Oriental exotic color. Mahler, when he heard *Salome*, thought that his colleague had tossed away what should have been the highlight of the piece. But Strauss almost certainly knew what he was doing: this is the music that Herod likes, and it serves as a kitschy foil for the grisliness to come.

Salome now calls for the prophet's head, and Herod, in a sudden religious panic, tries to get her to change her mind. She refuses. The executioner prepares to behead the Baptist in his cistern prison. At this point, the bottom drops out of the music. A toneless bass-drum rumble and strangulated cries in the double basses give way to a huge smear of tone in the full orchestra.

At the climax, the head of John the Baptist lies before Salome on a platter. Having disturbed us with unheard-of dissonances, Strauss now disturbs us with plain chords of necrophiliac bliss. For all the perversity of the material, this is still a love story, and the composer honors his heroine's emotions. "The mystery of love," Salome sings, "is greater than the mystery of death." Herod is horrified by the spectacle that his own incestuous lust has engendered. "Hide the moon, hide the stars!" he rasps. "Something terrible is going to happen!" He turns his back and walks up the staircase of the palace. The moon, obeying his command, goes behind the clouds. An extraordinary sound emanates from the lower brass and winds: the opera's introductory motif is telescoped—with one half-step alteration—into a single glowering chord. Above it, the flutes and clarinets launch into an obsessively elongated trill. Salome's love themes rise up again. At the moment of the kiss, two ordinary chords are mashed together, creating a momentary eight-note dissonance.

The moon comes out again. Herod, at the top of the stairs, turns around, and screams, "Kill that woman!" The orchestra attempts to restore order with an ending in C minor, but succeeds only in adding to the tumult: the horns play fast figures that blur into a howl, the timpani pound away at a four-note chromatic pattern, the woodwinds shriek on high. In effect, the opera ends with eight bars of noise.

The crowd roared its approval—that was the most shocking thing. "Nothing more satanic and artistic has been seen on the German opera stage," Decsey wrote admiringly. Strauss held court that night at the Hotel Elefant, in a never-to-be-repeated gathering that included Mahler, Puccini, and Schoenberg. When someone declared that he'd rather shoot himself than memorize the part of Salome, Strauss answered, "Me, too," to general amusement. The next day, the composer wrote to his wife, Pauline, who had stayed home in Berlin: "It is raining, and I am sitting on the garden terrace of my hotel, in order to report to you that 'Salome' went well, gigantic success, people applauding for ten minutes until the fire curtain came down, etc., etc."

Salome went on to be performed in some twenty-five different cities. The triumph was so complete that Strauss could afford to laugh off criticism from Kaiser Wilhelm II. "I am sorry that Strauss composed this *Salome*," the Kaiser reportedly said. "Normally I'm very keen on him, but this is going to do him *a lot of damage*." Strauss would relate this story and add with a flourish: "Thanks to that damage I was able to build my villa in Garmisch!"

On the train back to Vienna, Mahler expressed bewilderment over his colleague's success. He considered *Salome* a significant and audacious piece—"one of the greatest masterworks of our time," he later said—and could not understand why the public took an immediate liking to it. Genius and popularity were, he apparently thought, incompatible. Traveling in the same carriage was the Styrian poet and novelist Peter Rosegger. According to Alma, when Mahler voiced his reservations, Rosegger replied that the voice of the people is the voice of God—*Vox populi, vox Dei*. Mahler asked whether he meant the voice of the people at the present moment or the voice of the people over time. Nobody seemed to know the answer to that question.

The younger musicians from Vienna thrilled to the innovations in

Strauss's score, but were suspicious of his showmanship. One group, including Alban Berg, met at a restaurant to discuss what they had heard. They might well have used the words that Adrian Leverkühn applies to Strauss in *Doctor Faustus*: "What a gifted fellow! The happy-go-lucky revolutionary, cocky and conciliatory. Never were the avant-garde and the box office so well acquainted. Shocks and discords aplenty—then he good-naturedly takes it all back and assures the philistines that no harm was intended. But a hit, a definite hit." As for Adolf Hitler, it is not certain that he was actually there; he may merely have claimed to have attended, for whatever reason. But something about the opera evidently stuck in his memory.

The Austrian premiere of *Salome* was just one event in a busy season, but, like a flash of lightning, it illuminated a musical world on the verge of traumatic change. Past and future were colliding; centuries were passing in the night. Mahler would die in 1911, seeming to take the Romantic era with him. Puccini's *Turandot*, unfinished at his death in 1924, would more or less end a glorious Italian operatic history that began in Florence at the end of the sixteenth century. Schoenberg, in 1908 and 1909, would unleash fearsome sounds that placed him forever at odds with the vox populi. Hitler would seize power in 1933 and attempt the annihilation of a people. And Strauss would survive to a surreal old age. "I have actually outlived myself," he said in 1948. At the time of his birth, Germany was not yet a single nation and Wagner had yet to finish the *Ring of the Nibelung*. At the time of Strauss's death, Germany had been divided into East and West, and American soldiers were whistling "Some Enchanted Evening" in the streets.

Richard I and III

The sleepy German city of Bayreuth is the one place on earth where the nineteenth century springs eternal. Here, in 1876, Wagner presided over the opening of his opera house and the first complete performance of the four-part *Ring* cycle. The emperors of Germany and Brazil, the kings of Bavaria and Württemberg, and at least a dozen grand dukes, dukes, crown princes, and princes attended the unveiling, together with leading composers of various countries—Liszt, Tchaikovsky, Grieg, Gounod—and journalists from around the globe. Front-page reports ran for three straight days in the *New York Times*. Tchaikovsky, not a Wagner fan, was captivated by the sight of the diminutive, almost dwarfish composer riding in a carriage directly behind the German Kaiser, not the servant but the equal of the rulers of the world.

Bayreuth's illusion of cultural omnipotence is maintained every summer during the annual Wagner festival, when the cafés fill with people debating minor points of the *Ring* libretto, the composer's visage stares out from the windows of almost every shop, and piano scores for the operas are stacked on tables outside bookstores. For a few weeks in July and August, Wagner remains the center of the universe.

Until the advent of movies, there was no more astounding public entertainment than the Wagner operas. *Tristan*, *Die Meistersinger*, and the *Ring* were works of mind-altering breadth and depth, towering over every artistic endeavor of their time. Notwithstanding the archaic paraphernalia of rings, swords, and sorcery, the *Ring* presented an imaginative world as psychologically particular as any in the novels of Leo Tolstoy or Henry James. The story of the *Ring* was, in the end, one of hubris and comeuppance: Wotan, the chief of the gods, loses control of his realm and sinks into "the feeling of powerlessness." He resembles the head of a great bourgeois family whose livelihood is destroyed by the modernizing forces that he himself has set in motion.

Even more fraught with implications is Wagner's final drama, *Parsifal*, first heard at Bayreuth in the summer of 1882. The plot should have been a musty, almost childish thing: the "pure fool" Parsifal fights the magician Klingsor, takes from him the holy lance that pierced Christ's side, and uses it to heal the torpor that has overcome the Knights of the Grail. But *Parsifal*'s mystical trappings answered inchoate longings in end-of-century listeners, while the political subtext—Wagner's diseased knights can be read as an allegory of the diseased West—fed the fantasies of the far right. The music itself is a portal to the beyond. It crystallizes out of the air in weightless forms, transforms into rocklike masses, and dissolves again. "Here time becomes space," the wise knight Gurnemanz intones, showing Parsifal the way to the Grail temple, as a four-note bell figure rings hypnotically through the orchestra.

By 1906, twenty-three years after his death, Wagner had become a cultural colossus, his influence felt not only in music but in literature, theater, and painting. Sophisticated youths memorized his librettos as American college students of a later age would recite Bob Dylan. Anti-Semites and ultranationalists considered Wagner their private prophet, but he gave impetus to almost every major political and aesthetic movement of the age: liberalism (Théodore de Banville said that Wagner was a "democrat, a new man, wanting to create for all the people"), bohemianism (Baudelaire hailed the composer as the vessel of a "counter-religion, a Satanic religion"), African-American activism (a story in W. E. B. Du Bois's *The Souls of Black Folk* tells of a young black man who finds momentary hope in *Lohengrin*), feminism (M. Carey Thomas, president of Bryn Mawr College, said that *Lohengrin* made her "feel a little like my real self"), and even Zionism (Theodor Herzl first formulated his vision of a Jewish state after attending a performance of *Tannhäuser*).

The English composer Edward Elgar pored over the Meister's scores with desperate intensity, writing in his copy of *Tristan*, "This Book contains . . . the Best and the whole of the Best of This world and the Next." Elgar somehow converted the Wagnerian apparatus—the reverberating leitmotifs, the viscous chromatic harmony, the velvety orchestration—into an iconic representation of the British Empire at its height. As a result, he won a degree of international renown that had eluded English composers for centuries; after a German performance of his oratorio *The Dream of Gerontius* in 1902, Richard Strauss saluted Elgar as the "first English progressivist."

Nikolai Rimsky-Korsakov, in Russia, rummaged through Wagner for useful material and left the rest behind; in *The Legend of the Invisible City of Kitezh*, the tale of a magical city that disappears from view when it comes under attack, *Parsifal*-like bells ring out in endless patterns, intertwined with a tricky new harmonic language that would catch the ear of the young Stravinsky. Even Sergei Rachmaninov, who inherited a healthy skepticism for Wagner from his idol Tchaikovsky, learned from Wagner's orchestration how to bathe a Slavic melody in a sonic halo.

Puccini came up with an especially crafty solution to the Wagner problem. Like many of his generation, he rejected mystic subjects of the *Parsifal* type; instead, he followed Pietro Mascagni and Ruggero Leoncavallo, composers of *Cavalleria rusticana* and *Pagliacci*, into the new genre of verismo, or opera verité, where popular tunes mingled with blood-and-thunder orchestration and all manner of contemporary characters—prostitutes, gangsters, street urchins, a famously jealous clown—invaded the stage. Almost nothing on the surface of Puccini's mature operas sounds unmistakably Wagnerian. The influence is subterranean: you sense it in the way melodies emerge from the orchestral texture, the way motifs evolve organically from scene to scene. If Wagner, in the *Ring*, made the gods into ordinary people, Puccini's *La Bohème*, first heard in 1896, does the opposite: it gives mythic dimensions to a rattily charming collection of bohemians.

The most eloquent critic of Wagnerian self-aggrandizement was a self-aggrandizing German—Friedrich Nietzsche. Fanatically Wagnerian in his youth, the author of *Thus Spake Zarathustra* experienced a negative epiphany upon delving into the aesthetic and theological thickets of *Parsifal*. He came to the conclusion that Wagner had dressed himself up as "an oracle, a priest—indeed more than a priest, a kind of mouthpiece of the 'in itself' of things, a telephone from the beyond—henceforth he uttered not only music, this ventriloquist of God—he uttered metaphysics." Throughout his later writings, most forcefully in the essay *The Case of Wagner*, Nietzsche declared that music must be liberated from Teutonic heaviness and brought back to popular roots. "*Il faut méditerraniser la musique*," he wrote. Bizet's *Carmen*, with its blend of comic-opera form and raw, realistic subject matter, was suggested as the new ideal.

By 1888, when Nietzsche wrote *The Case of Wagner*, the project of mediterraneanization was well under way. French composers naturally took the lead, their inborn resistance to German culture heightened by their country's defeat in the Franco-Prussian War of 1870–71. Emmanuel Chabrier presented his rhapsody *España*, a feast of Mediterranean atmosphere. Gabriel Fauré finished the first version of his *Requiem*, with its piercingly simple and pure harmonies. Erik Satie was writing his *Gymnopédies*, oases of stillness. And Claude Debussy was groping toward a new musical language in settings of Verlaine and Baudelaire.

Wagner himself wished to escape the gigantism that his own work came to represent. "I have felt the pulse of modern art and know that it will die!" he wrote to his comrade-in-arms Liszt in 1850. "This knowledge, however, fills me not with despondency but with joy . . . The monumental character of our art will disappear, we shall abandon our habit of clinging firmly to the past, our egotistical concern for permanence and immortality at any price: we shall let the past remain the past, the future—the future, and we shall live only in the present, in the here and now and create works for the present age alone." This populist ambition was inherent in the very technology of the music, in the vastness of the orchestra and the power of the voices. As Mahler later explained: "If we want thousands to hear us in the huge auditoriums of our concert halls and opera houses," he wrote, "we simply have to make a lot of noise."

Richard Strauss—"Richard III," the conductor Hans von Bülow called him, skipping over Richard II—grew up almost literally in Wagner's shadow. His father, the French-horn virtuoso Franz Strauss, played in the Munich Court Orchestra, which reported to King Ludwig II, Wagner's patron. The elder Strauss thus participated in the inaugural performances of *Tristan*, *Die Meistersinger*, *Parsifal*, and the first two parts of the *Ring*. Strauss *père* was, however, a stolid musical reactionary who deemed Wagner's spectacles unworthy of comparison to the Viennese classics. Richard, in his adolescence, parroted his father's prejudices, saying, "You can be certain that ten years from now no one will know who Richard Wagner is." Yet even as he criticized Wagner, the teenage composer was identifying harmonic tricks that would soon become his own. For example, he mocked a passage in *Die Walküre* that juxtaposed chords of G and C-sharp—the same keys that intersect on the first page of *Salome*.

Franz Strauss was bitter, irascible, abusive. His wife, Josephine, meek and nervous, eventually went insane and had to be institutionalized. Their son was, like many survivors of troubled families, determined to maintain a cool, composed facade, behind which weird fires burned. In 1888, at the age of twenty-four, he composed his breakthrough work, the tone poem *Don Juan*, which revealed much about him. The hero is the same rake who goes to hell in Mozart's *Don Giovanni*. The music expresses his outlaw spirit in bounding rhythms and abrupt transitions; simple tunes skate above strident dissonances. Beneath the athletic display is a whiff of nihilism. The version of the tale that Strauss used as his source—a verse play by Nikolaus Lenau—suggests that the promiscuous Don isn't so much damned to hell as snuffed out: ". . . the fuel was used up / The hearth grew cold and dark." Strauss's ending is similarly curt: an upward-scuttling scale in the violins, a quiet drumroll, hollow chords on scattered instruments, three thumps, and silence.

Don Juan was written under the influence of the composer and philosopher Alexander Ritter, one of many mini-Wagners who populated the Kaiser's imperium. Around 1885, Ritter had drawn young Strauss into the "New German" school, which, in the spirit of Liszt and Wagner, abandoned the clearly demarcated structures of Viennese tradition—first theme, second theme, exposition, development, and so on—in favor of a freewheeling, moment-to-moment, poetically inflamed narrative. Strauss also befriended Cosima Wagner, the composer's widow, and it was whispered that he would make a good match for the Meister's daughter Eva.

In 1893, Strauss finished his first opera, *Guntram*. He wrote the libretto himself, as any proper young Wagnerian was expected to do. The scenario resembled that of *Die Meistersinger*: a medieval troubadour rebels against a brotherhood of singers whose rules are too strict for his wayward spirit. In this case, the hero's error is not musical but moral: Guntram kills a tyrannical prince and falls in love with the tyrant's wife. At the end, as Strauss originally conceived it, Guntram realizes that he has betrayed the spirit of his order, even though his act was justifiable, and therefore makes a penitential pilgrimage to the Holy Land.

In the middle of the writing process, however, Strauss invented a different denouement. Instead of submitting to the judgment of the order, Guntram would now walk away from it, walk away from his beloved, walk away from the Christian God. Ritter was deeply alarmed by his protégé's revised plan, saying that the opera had become "immoral" and disloyal to Wagner: no true hero would disavow his community. Strauss did not repent. Guntram's order, he told Ritter in reply, had unwisely sought to launch an ethical crusade through art, to unify religion and art. This was Wagner's mission, too, but for Strauss it was a utopian scheme that contained "the seeds of death in itself."

Seeking an alternative to Wagnerism, Strauss read the early-nineteenth-century anarchist thinker Max Stirner, whose book *The Ego and Its Own* argued that all forms of organized religion, as well as all organized societies, imprison individuals within illusions of morality, duty, and law. For Strauss, anarchist individualism was a way of removing himself from the stylistic squabbles of the time. Near-quotations from *The Ego and Its Own* dot the *Guntram* libretto. Stirner criticizes the "beautiful dream" of the liberal idea of humanity; Guntram employs that same phrase and contemptuously adds, "Dream on, good people, about the salvation of humanity."

Guntram was a flop at its 1894 premiere, mainly because the orchestration drowned out the singers, although the amoral ending may also have caused trouble. Strauss responded by striking an antagonistic pose, declaring "war against all the apostles of moderation," as the critic and Nietzsche enthusiast Arthur Seidl wrote approvingly in 1896. A second opera was to have celebrated the happy knave Till Eulenspiegel, "scourge of the Philistines, the slave of liberty, reviler of folly, adorer of nature," who annoys the burghers of the town of Schilda. That project never got off the ground, but its spirit carried over into the 1895 tone poem *Till Eulenspiegel's Merry Pranks*, which is full of deliciously insolent sounds—violins warbling like fiddlers in cafés; brass instruments trilling, snarling, and sliding rudely from one note to another; clarinets squawking high notes like players in wedding bands.

In his songs, Strauss made a point of setting poets of questionable reputation—among them Richard Dehmel, infamous for his advocacy of free love; Karl Henckell, banned in Germany for outspoken socialism; Oskar Panizza, jailed for "crimes against religion, committed through the press" (he had called *Parsifal* "spiritual fodder for pederasts"); and John Henry Mackay, the biographer of Max Stirner and the author of *The Anarchists*, who, under the pen name "Sagitta," later wrote books and poems celebrating man-boy love.

Through the remainder of the 1890s and into the early years of the new century, Strauss specialized in writing symphonic poems, which were appreciated on a superficial level for their vibrant tone painting: the first gleam of sunrise in *Thus Spake Zarathustra*, the bleating sheep in *Don Quixote*, the hectic battle scene in *Ein Heldenleben* (*A Hero's Life*). Debussy commented presciently that *Ein Heldenleben* was like a "book of images, even cinematography." All the while, Strauss continued to pursue the underlying theme of *Guntram*, the struggle of the individual against the collective. The struggle always seems doomed to end in defeat, resignation, or withdrawal. Most of these works begin with heroic statements and end with a fade into silence. Latter-day Strauss scholars such as Bryan Gilliam, Walter Werbeck, and Charles Youmans assert that the composer approached the transcendent ideals of the Romantic era with a philosophical skepticism that he got from Schopenhauer and Nietzsche. Wagnerism implodes, becoming a black hole of irony.

There are, however, consoling voices in Strauss's universe, and more often than not they are the voices of women. Listeners have never ceased to wonder how a taciturn male composer could create such forceful, richly sympathetic female characters; the answer may lie in the degree to which Strauss submitted to his domineering, difficult, yet devoted wife, Pauline. His operatic women are forthright in their ideas and desires. His men, by contrast, often appear not as protagonists but as love interests, even as sexual trophies. Men in positions of power tend to be inconstant, vicious, obtuse. In *Salome*, Herod is nothing more than a male hysteric who hypocritically surrounds himself with Jewish and Christian theologians and pauses in his lust for his teenage stepdaughter only to comment on the loveliness of a male corpse. John the Baptist may speak in righteously robust tones, but, Strauss later explained, the prophet was really meant to be a ridiculous figure, "an imbecile." (The musicologist Chris Walton has made the intriguing suggestion that *Salome* contains a clandestine parody of the court of Kaiser Wilhelm, which was prone both to homosexual scandal and to censorious prudishness.) In a way, Salome is the sanest member of the family; like Lulu, the heroine of a later opera, she does not pretend to be other than what she is.

Strauss delivered one more onslaught of dissonance and neurosis: *Elektra*, premiered in Dresden in January 1909, based on a play by Hugo von Hofmannsthal in which the downfall of the house of Agamemnon is retold in language suggestive of the dream narratives of Sigmund Freud. The music repeatedly trembles on the edge of what would come to be called atonality; the far-flung chords that merely brush against each other in *Salome* now clash in sustained skirmishes.

But this was as far as Strauss would go. Even before he began composing *Elektra*, he indicated to Hofmannsthal, the poet-playwright who was becoming his literary guide, that he needed new material. Hofmannsthal persuaded him to go ahead with *Elektra*, but their subsequent collaboration, *Der Rosenkavalier*, was an entirely different thing—a comedy of eighteenth-century Vienna, steeped in super-refined, self-aware melancholy, modeled on Mozart's *Marriage of Figaro* and *Così fan tutte*. The same complex spirit of nostalgia and satire animated *Ariadne auf Naxos*, the first version of which appeared in 1912; in that work, an overserious composer tries to write grand opera while commedia dell'arte players wreak havoc all around him.

"I was never *revolutionary*," Arnold Schoenberg once said. "*The only revolutionary* in our time was Strauss!" In the end, the composer of *Salome* fit the profile neither of the revolutionary nor of the reactionary. There was constant anxiety about his de facto status as a "great German composer." He seemed too flighty, even too feminine, for the role. "The music of Herr Richard Strauss is a woman who seeks to compensate for her natural deficiencies by mastering Sanskrit," the Viennese satirist Karl Kraus wrote. Strauss was also too fond of money, or, more precisely, he made his fondness for money too obvious. "More of a stock company than a genius," Kraus later said.

And was there something a little Jewish about Strauss? So said the anti-Semitic French journal *La Libre Parole*. It did not go unnoticed that Strauss enjoyed the company of Jewish millionares. Arthur Schnitzler once said to Alma Mahler, with ambiguous intent: "If one of the two, Gustav Mahler or Richard Strauss, is a Jew, then surely it is . . . Richard Strauss!"

Der Mahler

Berlin, where Strauss lived in the first years of the new century, was the noisiest, busiest metropolis in Europe, its neoclassical edifices encircled by shopping districts, industrial infrastructure, working-class neighborhoods, transportation networks, and power grids. Mahler's Vienna was a slower, smaller-scale place, an idyll of imperial style. It was aestheticized down to its pores; everything was forced to glitter. A gilt sphere capped Joseph Olbrich's Secession building, a shrine to Art Nouveau. Gold-leaf textures framed Gustav Klimt's portraits of high-society women. At the top of Otto Wagner's severe, semimodernistic Post Office Savings Bank, goddess statues held aloft Grecian rings. Mahler provided the supreme musical expression of this luxurious, ambiguous moment. He knew of the fissures that were opening in the city's facade—younger artists such as Schoenberg were eager to expose Vienna's filigree as rot—but he still believed in art's ability to transfigure society.

The epic life of Mahler is told in Henry-Louis de La Grange's equally epic four-volume biography. Like many self-styled aristocrats, the future ruler of musical Vienna came from the provinces—namely, Iglau, a town on the border of Bohemia and Moravia. His family belonged to a close-knit community of German-speaking Jews, one of many pockets of *Judentum* scattered across the Austro-Hungarian countryside in the wake of imperial acts of expulsion and segregation. Mahler's father ran a tavern and a distillery; his mother gave birth to fourteen children, only five of whom outlived her.

The family atmosphere was tense. Mahler recalled a time when he ran out of the house in order to escape an argument between his parents. On the street, he heard a barrel organ playing the tune "Ach, du lieber Augustin." He told this story to Sigmund Freud, in 1910, during a psychoanalytic session that took the form of a four-hour walk. "In Mahler's opinion," Freud noted, "the conjunction of high tragedy and light amusement was from then on inextricably fixed in his mind."

Mahler entered the Vienna Conservatory at the age of fifteen, in 1875. He launched his conducting career in 1880, leading operettas at a summer spa, and began a fast progress through the opera houses of Central Europe: Laibach (now Ljubljana in Slovenia), Olmütz (now Olomouc in the Czech Republic), Kassel, Prague, Leipzig, Budapest, and Hamburg. In 1897, with seeming inevitability, but with behind-the-scenes help from Johannes Brahms, he attained the highest position in Central European music, the directorship of the Vienna Court Opera. Accepting the post meant converting to Catholicism—an act that Mahler undertook with apparent enthusiasm, having more or less abandoned his Judaism in Iglau.

Strauss, who had known Mahler since 1887, worried that his colleague was spreading himself too thin. "Don't you compose at all any more?" he asked in a letter of 1900. "It would be a thousand pities if you devoted your entire artistic energy, for which I certainly have the greatest admiration, to the thankless position of theatre director! The theatre can never be made into an 'artistic institution.'"

Mahler accomplished precisely this in Vienna. He hired the painter Alfred Roller to create visually striking, duskily lit stagings of the mainstream opera repertory, thereby helping to inaugurate the discipline of opera direction. He also codified the etiquette of the modern concert experience, with its worshipful, pseudo-religious character. Opera houses of the nineteenth century were rowdy places; Mahler, who hated all extraneous noise, threw out singers' fan clubs, cut short applause between numbers, glared icily at talkative concertgoers, and forced latecomers to wait in the lobby. Emperor Franz Joseph, the embodiment of old Vienna, was heard to say: "Is music such a serious business? I always thought it was meant to make people happy."

Mahler's composing career got off to a much slower start. His Symphony No. 1 was first played in November 1889, nine days after Strauss's *Don Juan*, but, where Strauss instantly won over the public, Mahler met with a mixture of applause, boos, and shrugs. The First begins, like Strauss's *Zarathustra*, with an elemental hum—the note A whistling in all registers of the strings. The note is sustained for fifty-six bars, giving the harmony an eternal, unchanging quality that recalls the opening of Wagner's *Ring*. There is a Wagnerian strain, too, in the theme of falling fourths that stems from the primeval drone. It is the unifying idea of the piece, and when it is transposed to a major key it shows an obvious resemblance to the motif of pealing bells that sounds through *Parsifal*. Mahler's project was to do for the symphony what Wagner had done for the opera: he would trump everything that had gone before.

The frame of reference of Mahler's symphonies is vast, stretching from the masses of the Renaissance to the marching songs of rural soldiers—an epic multiplicity of voices and styles. Giant structures are built up, reach to the heavens, then suddenly crumble. Nature spaces are invaded by sloppy country dances and belligerent marches. The third movement of the First Symphony begins with a meandering minor-mode canon on the tune "Frère Jacques," which in Germany was traditionally sung by drunken students in taverns, and there are raucous interruptions in the style of a klezmer band—"pop" episodes paralleling the vernacular pranks in Strauss's *Don Juan* and *Till Eulenspiegel*. Much of the first movement of the Third Symphony takes the form of a gargantuan, crashing march, which reminded Strauss of workers pressing forward with their red flags at a May Day celebration. In the finale of the Second Symphony, the hierarchy of pitch breaks down into a din of percussion. It sounds like music's revenge on an unmusical world, noise trampling on noise.

Up through the Third Symphony, Mahler followed the late-Romantic practice of attaching detailed programmatic descriptions to his symphonies. He briefly gave the First the title "Titan"; the first movement of the Second was originally named "Funeral Ceremony." The Third was to have been called, at various times, "The Gay Science," "A Summer Night's Dream," and "Pan."

With the turning of the century, however, Mahler broke with pictorialism and tone poetry. The Fourth Symphony, finished in 1900, was a four-movement work of more traditional, almost Mozartean design. "Down with programs!" Mahler said in the same year. Concerned to differentiate himself from Strauss, he wished now to be seen as a "pure musician," one who moved in a "realm outside time, space, and the forms of individual appearances." The Fifth Symphony, written in 1901 and 1902, is an interior drama devoid of any programmatic indication, moving through heroic struggle, a delirious funeral march, a wild, sprawling Scherzo, and a dreamily lyrical Adagietto to a radiant, chorale-driven finale. The triumphant ending was perhaps the one conventional thing about the piece, and in the Sixth Symphony, which had its premiere on May 27, 1906, eleven days after the Austrian premiere of *Salome*, Mahler took the triumph back. Strauss's opera had been called "satanic," and, as it happens, the same adjective was applied to Mahler's symphony in the weeks leading up to the first performance. Mahler, too, would see how far he could go without losing the vox populi.

The setting for the premiere of the Sixth was the steel town of Essen, in the Ruhr. Nearby was the armaments firm of Krupp, whose cannons had rained ruin on French armies in the war of 1870–71 and whose long-distance weaponry would play a critical role in the Great War to come. Unsympathetic listeners compared Mahler's new composition to German military hardware. The Viennese critic Hans Liebstöckl began a review of a subsequent performance with the line "Krupp makes only cannons, Mahler only symphonies." Indeed, the Sixth opens with something like the sound of an army advancing—staccato As in the cellos and basses, military-style taps of a drum, a vigorous A-minor theme strutting in front of a wall of eight horns. A little later, the timpani set forth a marching rhythm of the kind that you can still hear played in Alpine militia parades in Austria and neighboring countries: *Left! Left! Left-right-left!*

The first movement follows the well-worn procedures of sonata form, complete with a repeat of the exposition section. The first theme is modeled on that of Schubert's youthful, severe A-Minor Sonata, D. 784. The second theme is an unrestrained Romantic effusion, a love song in homage to Alma. It is so unlike the first that it inhabits a different world, and the entire movement is a struggle to reconcile the two. By the end, the synthesis seems complete: the second theme is orchestrated in the clipped, martial style of the first, as if love were an army on the march. Yet there is something strained about this marriage of ideas. The movement that follows, a so-called Scherzo, resumes the trudge of the opening, but now in superciliously waltzing three-quarter time. A sprawling, songful Andante, in the distant key of E-flat, provides respite, but Mahler's battery of percussion instruments waits threateningly at the back of the stage. (During the rehearsals in Essen, Mahler decided to switch the middle movements, and retained that order in a revised version of the score.)

As the finale begins, the march rhythm—*Left! Left! Left-right-left!*—comes back with a vengeance. No composer ever devised a form quite like this one—wave after wave of development, skirling fanfares suggesting imminent joy, then the chilling return of the marching beat. The movement is organized around three "hammerblows" (or, in the revised version, two), which have the effect of triggering a kind of collapse. For the premiere, Mahler had a gigantic drum constructed—"the hide of a fully grown cow stretched on a frame a meter and a half square," one critic wrote in sarcastic wonder—which was to have been struck with a mallet of unprecedented size. In the event, the drum produced only a muffled thump, to the amusement of the musicians. Like Strauss in *Salome*, Mahler is employing shock tactics on his audience, and he saves his biggest shock for the very end. The work is poised to die away to silence, with a three-note figure limping through the lower instruments. Then, out of nowhere, a *fortissimo* A-minor chord clangs like a metal door swung shut. Correctly performed, this gesture should make unsuspecting listeners jump out of their seats.

After the last rehearsal, Mahler sat in his dressing room, shattered by the power of his own creation. Alma reported that he "walked up and down . . . sobbing, wringing his hands, unable to control himself." Suddenly Strauss poked his head through the door to say that the mayor of Essen had died and that a memorial piece needed to be played at the beginning of the program. Strauss's only comment on the symphony was that the final movement was "over-instrumented."

Bruno Walter observed that Mahler was "reduced almost to tears" by the episode. How could Strauss have misjudged the work so completely?

Or was Strauss possibly right? That summer, Mahler lightened the orchestration of the Sixth's finale considerably.

After the events of May 1906, the friendship between the two men cooled. Mahler's envy of Strauss metastasized, affecting his conception of music's place in society. All along, in his letters to Alma and others, Mahler had recorded various indignities to which his colleague had subjected him, probably exaggerating for effect. "I extend to [Strauss] respectful and friendly solicitude," Mahler wrote to his wife on one occasion, "and he doesn't respond, he doesn't even seem to notice, it is wasted on him. When I experience such things again and again, I feel totally confused about myself and the world!" In a letter the very next day, Mahler described Strauss as "very sweet," which suggests not only that he had forgotten the snub of the previous day but that he had invented it.

In an essay on the relationship between the composers, the musicologist Herta Blaukopf cites the lopsided friendship of two young men in Thomas Mann's story "Tonio Kröger." Mahler is like the dark-haired Tonio, who thinks too much and feels everything too intensely. Strauss is like the fair-haired Hans Hansen, who sails through life in ignorance of the world's horror. Indeed, Strauss could never comprehend Mahler's obsession with suffering and redemption. "I don't know what I'm supposed to be redeemed from," he once said to the conductor Otto Klemperer.

Mahler was still trying to answer the question that he had pondered on the train from Graz: Can a man win fame in his own time while also remaining a true artist? Doubt was growing in his mind. Increasingly, he spoke of the insignificance of contemporary musical judgment in the face of the ultimate wisdom of posterity.

"I am to find no recognition as a composer during my lifetime," he told a critic in 1906. "As long as I am the 'Mahler' wandering among you, a 'man among men,' I must content myself with an 'all too human' reception as a creative figure. Only when I have shaken off this earthly dust will there be justice done. I am what Nietzsche calls an 'untimely' one . . . The true 'timely one' is Richard Strauss. That is why he already enjoys immortality here on earth." In a letter to Alma, Mahler spoke of his relationship with Strauss in terms borrowed from John the Baptist's prophecy of the coming of Jesus Christ: "The time is coming when men will see the wheat separated from the chaff—and my time will come when his is up." That last remark has been widely bowdlerized to "My time will come"—a statement of faith often quoted by composers who place themselves in opposition to popular culture.

With Mahler, though, the "untimely" stance was something of a pose. He cared mightily about the reception of his works, and danced on air if they succeeded, which they usually did. No Mahler myth is more moth-eaten than the one that he was neglected in his own time. The First Symphony may have baffled its first audience, but the later symphonies almost always conquered the public, if not the critics. "In his mature years," the scholar and conductor Leon Botstein writes, "Mahler experienced far more triumph than defeat and more enthusiasm than rejection by audiences." Even at the premiere of the "satanic" Sixth, a critic reported that the composer "had to return to the platform to receive the congratulations and thanks of the crowded audience."

In the summer of 1906, Mahler sought to cement his relationship with the public by sketching his life-affirming, oratorio-like Eighth Symphony, which he called his "gift to the nation." The first part was based on the hymn "Veni creator spiritus"; the second part was a panoramic setting of the last scene of Goethe's *Faust, Part II.* The Eighth inspired earthshaking applause on the occasion of its premiere, four years later. "The indescribable here is accomplished," hundreds of singers roar at the end; the storm of applause that followed might as well have been notated in the score.

The glowing optimism of the Eighth belied the fact that the composer was growing sick of Vienna, of the constant opposition of anti-Semites, of infighting and backstabbing. He announced his resignation in May 1907, conducted his last opera performance in October, and made his final appearance as a conductor in Vienna in November, bidding farewell with his own Second Symphony. To his ardent fans, it was as though he had been driven out by the forces of ignorance and reaction. When he left the city, at the end of the year, two hundred admirers, Schoenberg and his pupils among them, gathered at the train station to bid him farewell, garlanding his compartment with flowers. It seemed the end of a golden age. "*Vorbei!*" said Gustav Klimt—"It's over!"

The reality was a bit less romantic. Throughout the spring of 1907, Mahler had been negotiating secretly with the Metropolitan Opera in New York, and not the least of the management's enticements was what it called "the highest fee a musician has ever received": 75,000 kronen for three months' work, or, in today's money, $300,000. Mahler said yes.

The New World

There was no lack of music in the American republic at the beginning of the twentieth century. Every major city had an orchestra. International opera stars circulated through the opera houses of New York, Chicago, and San Francisco. Virtuosos, maestros, and national geniuses landed in Manhattan by the boatload. European visitors found the musical scene in the New World congenially similar to that in the Old. The orchestral repertory gravitated toward the Austro-German tradition, most musicians were immigrants, and many rehearsals took place in German. Operatic life was divided among the French, German, and Italian traditions. The Metropolitan Opera experienced a fad for Gounod, a cult of Wagner, and, finally, a wave of Puccini.

For the rich, classical music was a status symbol, a collector's delight. Millionaires signed up musicians in much the same way they bought up and brought home pieces of European art. Yet the appeal of composers such as Wagner and Puccini went much wider. In 1884, for example, Theodore Thomas led his virtuoso orchestra in a cross-country tour, playing to audiences of five, eight, even ten thousand people. And, as the historian Joseph Horowitz relates, Anton Seidl conducted all-Wagner concerts on Coney Island, his series advertised by means of a newfangled "electric sign" on Broadway. Enrico Caruso, who began singing in America in 1903, was probably the biggest cultural celebrity of the day; when he was arrested for groping the wife of a baseball player in the monkey house in Central Park, the story played on the front pages of newspapers across the country, and, far from ruining the tenor's reputation, it only augmented his already enormous popularity. In the *New York Times*, advertisements for classical events were jumbled together with myriad other offerings under the rubric "Amusements." One night the Met would put on John Philip Sousa's band, the next night the *Ring*. Elgar's oratorios rubbed shoulders with midget performers and Barnum's Original Skeleton Dude.

New technologies helped bring the music to those who had never heard it live. In 1906, the year of *Salome* in Graz, the Victor Talking Machine Company introduced its new-model Victrola phonograph, which, though priced at an astronomical two hundred dollars, proved wildly successful. Caruso ruled the medium; his sobbing rendition of "Vesti la giubba" was apparently the first record to sell a million copies. Also in 1906, the inventor Thaddeus Cahill unveiled a two-hundred-ton electronic instrument called the Telharmonium, which, by way of an ingenious if unwieldy array of alternators, broadcast arrangements of Bach, Chopin, and Grieg to audiences in Telharmonic Hall, opposite the Met.

The hall closed after two seasons; local phone customers complained that the Telharmonium was disrupting their calls. But the future had been glimpsed. The electrification of music would forever change the world in which Mahler and Strauss came of age, bringing classical music to unprecedented mass audiences but also publicizing popular genres that would challenge composers' long-standing cultural hegemony. Even in 1906, ragtime numbers and other syncopated dances were thriving on the new medium. Small bands made a crisp, vital sound, while symphony orchestras came across as tinny and feeble.

What classical music in America lacked was American classical music. Composition remained in the condition of cultural subservience that Ralph Waldo Emerson had diagnosed in his essay "The American Scholar" back in 1837: "We have listened too long to the courtly muses of Europe." American writers answered Emerson's call: by the turn of the century, libraries contained the works of Hawthorne, Melville, Emerson, Thoreau, Poe, Whitman, Dickinson, Twain, and the brothers James. The roster of American composers, on the other hand, included the likes of John Knowles Paine, Horatio Parker, George Whitefield Chadwick, and Edward MacDowell—skilled craftsmen who did credit to their European training but who failed to find a language that was either singularly American or singularly their own. Audiences saved their deepest genuflections for European figures who deigned to cross the Atlantic.

Strauss came to America in 1904. Notwithstanding his mildly dangerous aura—the American critic James Huneker labeled him an "anarch of art"—he was greeted almost as a head of state. Theodore Roosevelt received him at the White House, and Senator Stephen B. Elkins, a powerful operator in the pro-business Republican Party, invited him onto the floor of the Senate. In return, Strauss granted America the honor of hosting the premiere of his latest work, the *Symphonia domestica.* The program stirred controversy: it described a day in the life of a well-to-do family, including breakfast, the baby's bath, and connubial bliss. Despite some extended patches of note-spinning, the new work gave vigorous expression to Strauss's belief that anything could be set to music as long as it was felt intensely. Schopenhauer, in *The World as Will and Representation*, observed that music could find as much pathos in the disagreements of an ordinary household as in the agonies of the house of Agamemnon. There in one sentence was Strauss's career from *Domestica* to *Elektra.*

Demand for Strauss in New York grew so strong that two additional orchestral performances were arranged. They took place on the fourth floor of Wanamaker's department store, which was one of the original American superstores, occupying two blocks along Broadway between Eighth and Tenth streets. Wanamaker's felt that it had a duty to provide cultural uplift: its piano showroom, like the Steinway showroom uptown, regularly featured recitals by celebrated artists. "They do things sumptuously at the Wanamaker store," the *Times* wrote of the first Strauss concert. "There was, of course, an eager desire on the part of many people to hear the great German composer conduct his own compositions, and though there were fully five thousand people accommodated at the concerts last evening, there were many applicants who had to be refused, and every inch of space was occupied, many people standing." In the European press, however, Strauss was promptly pilloried as a moneygrubbing vulgarian who so desperately wanted to add to his coffers that he performed in supermarkets.

The *Symphonia domestica* entertained Manhattanites; *Salome* scandalized them. When the Metropolitan Opera presented the latter work in January 1907, there was a kerfuffle in the Golden Horseshoe, as the elite ring of boxes was known. Boxes 27 and 29 emptied out before the scene of the kissing of the head. J. P. Morgan's daughter allegedly asked her father to shut down the production; *Salome* did not return to the Met until 1934. A physician vented his disgust in a letter to the *New York Times*:

> I am a man of middle life, who has devoted upward of twenty years to the practice of a profession that necessitates, in the treatment of

> nervous and mental diseases, a daily intimacy with degenerates . . . I say after deliberation, and a familiarity with the emotional productions of Oscar Wilde and Richard Strauss, that *Salome* is a detailed and explicit exposition of the most horrible, disgusting, revolting and unmentionable features of degeneracy (using the word now in its customary social, sexual significance) that I have ever heard, read of, or imagined . . . That which it depicts is naught else than the motive of the indescribable acts of Jack the Ripper.

The greater part of the audience couldn't turn away. One critic reported that the spectacle filled him with "indefinable dread."

Giacomo Puccini arrived for his first American visit just a few days before the *Salome* affair. When his ship was trapped for a day in a fog bank off Sandy Hook, bulletins of his progress went out to opera-loving readers of the *New York Times*. Puccini's operas had lately become runaway hits in the city; during his five-week stay, all four of his mature works to date—*Manon Lescaut*, *La Bohème*, *Tosca*, and *Madama Butterfly*—played at the Metropolitan Opera, and *La Bohème* ran concurrently at Oscar Hammerstein's Manhattan Opera House.

Puccini was keen to write something for his American fans, and in the customary shipside press conference he floated the idea of an opera set in the Wild West. "I have read Bret Harte's novels," he said, "and I think there is great scope in your Western life for operatic treatment." He also looked into African-American music, or "coon songs," as the *Times* called them. Black musicians were summoned to the home of Dr. and Mrs. William Tillinghast Bull, so that the maestro could hear them.

Puccini returned to Italy with the plan of making an opera out of *The Girl of the Golden West*, by the playwright-showman David Belasco, who had also written the play on which *Butterfly* was based. The score branched out in a couple of new directions. On the one hand, Puccini demonstrated what he had absorbed from several encounters with *Salome*, as well as from a study of Debussy. Act I begins with blaring whole-tone chords, which must have alarmed the hordes who had fallen for *La Bohème*. Act II culminates in a "tritone complex" of the kind that had often appeared at climactic moments of *Salome* and *Elektra*—chords of E-flat minor and A minor in minatory alternation. At the same time, *The Girl of the Golden West* gamely tries to do justice to its classic American setting; intermittent strains of the cakewalk echo whatever it was that Puccini heard at Dr. and Mrs. Bull's, while a Native American Zuni song furnishes material for (oddly) an aria by a black minstrel. The most remarkable thing about the work is that a fearless, independent woman occupies the center of it; in an age when women in opera almost invariably came off as diseased and deranged, Puccini's Minnie is a bringer of peace, a beacon in a darkening world.

Mahler arrived in New York on December 21, 1907, taking up residence at the Hotel Majestic on Central Park West. His performances at the Met went splendidly, but trouble was brewing behind the scenes. Heinrich Conried, who had hired Mahler, was forced out, partly because of the *Salome* debacle, and the board expressed a desire to "work away from the German atmosphere and the Jew." Giulio Gatti-Casazza, of La Scala, became the new manager, bringing with him the firebrand conductor Arturo Toscanini. But another opportunity arose. The society figure Mary Sheldon offered to set Mahler up with a star orchestra, and the New York Philharmonic was reconstituted to meet his needs. Mahler believed that this arrangement would allow him to present his own works and the classics under ideal conditions. "Since [New Yorkers] are completely unprejudiced," he wrote home, "I hope I shall here find fertile ground for my works and thus a spiritual home, something that, for all the sensationalism, I should never be able to achieve in Europe."

Things did not turn out quite so rosily, but Mahler and America got along well. The conductor was no longer so addicted to perfection, nor did he hold himself aloof from society as he had done in Vienna. On a good night, he would take all seventy of his musicians out to dinner. He went to dinner parties, attended a séance, even poked his head into an opium den in Chinatown. When traveling to a concert, he refused the assistance of a chauffeur, preferring to use the newly constructed subway system. A Philharmonic musician once saw the great man alone in a subway car, staring vacantly like any other commuter.

A New York friend, Maurice Baumfeld, recalled that Mahler loved to gaze out his high window at the city and the sky. "Wherever I am," the composer said, "the longing for this blue sky, this sun, this pulsating activity goes with me." In 1909, at the beginning of his second New York season, he wrote to Bruno Walter: "I see everything in such a new light—am in such a state of flux, sometimes I should hardly be surprised suddenly to find myself in a new body. (Like Faust in the last scene.) I am thirstier for life than ever before . . ."

In his last New York season, Mahler ran into trouble with Mrs. Sheldon's Programme Committee. A streak of adventurous programming, encompassing everything from the music of Bach to far-out contemporary fare such as Elgar's *Sea Pictures*, met with a tepid response from traditional concertgoers, as adventurous programming often does. Meanwhile, Toscanini was ensconced at the Met, winning over New York audiences with, among other things, a Puccini premiere—the long-awaited *Girl of the Golden West*. For a time, it looked as though Mahler would return to Europe: the local critics had turned against him, as their Viennese counterparts had done, and he felt harried on all sides. In the end, he signed a new contract, and retained his equanimity of mood.

On the night of February 20, 1911, Mahler announced to his dinner companions, "I have found that people in general are better, more kindly, than one supposes." He was running a fever, but thought nothing of it. The following night, against his doctor's advice, he led a program of Italian works that included the premiere of Ferruccio Busoni's *Berceuse élégiaque*, a beautifully opaque piece that seems to depict a soul entering a higher realm. This was Mahler's final concert; a fatal infection, in the form of subacute bacterial endocarditis, was moving through his body. The remaining Philharmonic concerts were canceled. Mahler returned to Vienna, and died there on May 18.

European commentators made an anti-American cultural parable out of Mahler's demise, as they had in the case of *Symphonia domestica* at the Wanamaker store. The conductor was a "victim of the dollar," one Berlin newspaper said, of "the nerve-wracking and peculiar demands of American art." Alma Mahler helped to foster this impression, perhaps as a way of diverting attention from her affair with Walter Gropius, which had caused her husband more angst than any of Mrs. Sheldon's memos. "You cannot imagine what Mr. Mahler has suffered," she told the press. "In Vienna my husband was all powerful. Even the Emperor did not dictate to him, but in New York, to his amazement, he had ten ladies ordering him about like a puppet."

Mahler himself did not blame the dollar. "I have never worked as little as I did in America," he said in an interview a month before his death. "I was not subjected to an excess of either physical or intellectual work."

Resting on Mahler's desk was the manuscript of his Tenth Symphony, which must have been the work that he described to Maurice Baumfeld as "something entirely new"—a reflection of certain things he saw and felt in America. One American feature of the score is well known: the funeral march at the beginning of the finale—a dirge for tuba and contrabassoons, interrupted by thuds on a military drum—was inspired by the funeral procession of Charles W. Kruger, deputy chief of the New York Fire Department, who had died in 1908 while fighting a blaze on Canal Street.

There might also be an American impression in the symphony's first movement, the climax of which contains a dissonance of nine notes. This awe-inspiring, numbing chord is usually associated with the crisis in Mahler's marriage, but it may also point to a natural phenomenon, some craggy, sublime feature of the American continent. Like the chords at the beginning of Strauss's *Zarathustra*, it is derived from the overtones of a resonating string. The relationship becomes clear at the end of the movement, where the harmonic series is spelled out note by note in the strings and harp, like a rainbow emerging over Niagara Falls.

Stunned by his rival's death, Richard Strauss could barely speak for days afterward. He commented later that Mahler had been his "antipode," his worthy adversary. By way of a memorial he conducted the Third Symphony in Berlin. In a more oblique tribute, he decided to resume work on a tone poem that he had begun sketching some years before—a piece called *The Antichrist*, in honor of Nietzsche's most vociferous diatribe against religion. Mulling over this project in his diary, Strauss wondered why Mahler, "this aspiring, idealistic, and energetic artist," had converted to Christianity. Each man misunderstood the other to the end; Strauss suspected Mahler of surrendering to antiquated Christian morality, while Mahler accused Strauss of selling out to plebeian taste. The split between them forecast a larger division in twentieth-century music to come, between modernist and populist conceptions of the composer's role.

In the end, Strauss's last big orchestral work carried the more prosaic title *An Alpine Symphony*. It depicts a daylong mountain climb, complete with sunrise, storm, a magical moment of arrival at the summit, descent, and sunset. Beneath the surface, it may be partly "about" Mahler, as the critic Tim Ashley has suggested. In the section "At the Summit," the brass intone a majestic theme, recalling the opening of *Zarathustra*. At the same time, the violins sing a Mahlerian song of longing in which one pleading little five-note pattern—two steps up, a little leap, a step back down—brings to mind the "Alma" theme of the Sixth. The intermingling of Mahlerian strings and Straussian brass suggests the image of the two composers standing side by side at the peak of their art. Perhaps they are back in the hills above Graz, gazing down at the splendor of nature while the world waits for them below.

The vision passes, as joyful scenes in Strauss tend to do. Mists rise; a storm breaks out; the climbers descend. Soon they are shrouded in the same mysterious, groaning chord with which the symphony began. The sun has set behind the mountain.

(((2)))

DOCTOR FAUST

Schoenberg, Debussy, and Atonality

One day in 1948 or 1949, the Brentwood Country Mart, a shopping complex in an upscale neighborhood of Los Angeles, California, was the scene of a slight disturbance that carried overtones of the most spectacular upheaval in twentieth-century music. Marta Feuchtwanger, wife of the émigré novelist Lion Feuchtwanger, was examining grapefruit in the produce section when she heard a voice shouting in German from the far end of the aisle. She looked up to see Arnold Schoenberg, the pioneer of atonal music and the codifier of twelve-tone composition, bearing down on her, with his bald pate and burning eyes. Decades later, in conversation with the writer Lawrence Weschler, Feuchtwanger could recall every detail of the encounter, including the weight of the grapefruit in her hand. "Lies, Frau Marta, lies!" Schoenberg was yelling. "You have to know, *I never had syphilis!*"

The cause of this improbable commotion was the publication of *Doctor Faustus: The Life of the German Composer Adrian Leverkühn as Told by a Friend*. Thomas Mann, a writer peculiarly attuned to music, had fled from the hell of Hitler's Germany into the not-quite paradise of Los Angeles, joining other Central European artists in exile. The proximity of such renowned figures as Schoenberg and Stravinsky had encouraged Mann to write a "novel of music," in which a modern composer produces esoteric masterpieces and then descends into syphilitic insanity. For advice, Mann turned to Theodor W. Adorno, who had studied with Schoenberg's pupil Alban Berg and who was also part of the Los Angeles émigré community.

Mann self-confessedly approached modern music from the perspective of an informed amateur who wondered what had happened to the "lost paradise" of German Romanticism. Mann had attended the premiere of Mahler's Eighth in 1910. He had briefly met Mahler, and trembled in awe before him. Some three decades later, Mann watched as Schoenberg, Mahler's protégé, presented his "extremely difficult" but "rewarding" scores to small groups of devotees in Los Angeles. The novel asks, in so many words, "What went wrong?"

Leverkühn is an intellectual monster—cold, loveless, arrogant, mocking. His music absorbs all styles of the past and shatters them into fragments. "I have found that *it is not to be*," he says of Beethoven's Ninth Symphony, whose "Ode to Joy" once spoke for mankind's aspiration toward brotherhood. "It will be taken back. I will take it back." The illness that destroys Leverkühn is acquired in a curious way. He tells his friends that he is going to see the Austrian premiere of *Salome* in Graz. On a secret detour he sleeps with a prostitute named Esmeralda, whose syphilitic condition is visible on her yellowed face. Leverkühn contracts the disease deliberately, in the belief that it will grant him supernatural creative powers. When the devil appears, he informs the composer that he will never be popular in his lifetime but that his time will come, à la Mahler: "You will lead, you will strike up the march of the future, boys will swear by your name, and thanks to your madness they will no longer need to be mad." Since *Faustus* is also a book about the roots of Nazism, Leverkühn's "bloodless intellectuality" becomes, in a cryptic way, the mirror image of Hitler's "bloody barbarism." The cultish fanaticism of modern art turns out to be not unrelated to the politics of fascism: both attempt to remake the world in utopian forms.

Schoenberg was understandably incensed by this scenario, which gave a pathological veneer to his proudest achievements. The real-life composer could be a bit spooky at times—"I can see through walls," he was once heard to say—but he was hardly a cold or bloodless man. He set about revolutionizing music with high passion and childlike enthusiasm. As a born Viennese who venerated the Austro-German tradition, he could never have mocked Beethoven's Ninth. As a Jew, he divined the true nature of Nazism sooner than did Mann. Aloofness was not his style; he was, among other things, a galvanizing, life-changing teacher, dozens of whose students, from the operatic Berg to the aphoristic Anton Webern, from the Communist Hanns Eisler to the hippieish Lou Harrison, played conspicuous roles in twentieth-century music.

Yet Mann knew what he was doing when he put his composer in league with the devil. Faust's pact is a lurid version of the kinds of stories that artists tell themselves in order to justify their solitude. Eisler, when he read Mann's novel, connected it to the perceived crisis of classical music in modern society. "Great art, as the Devil maintains, can now only be produced, in this declining society, through complete isolation, loneliness, through complete heartlessness . . . [Yet Mann] allows Leverkühn to dream of a new time, when music will again to a certain extent be on first-name terms with the people." Other composers of the fin de siècle similarly conceived their situation as a one-man fight against a crude and stupid world. Claude Debussy, in Paris, assumed an antipopulist stance in the years before 1900 and not coincidentally broke away from conventional tonality in the same period. But Schoenberg took the most drastic steps, and perhaps more important, he set forth an elaborate teleology of musical history, a theory of irreversible progress, to justify his actions. The Faust metaphor honors the dread that Schoenberg's juggernaut inspired in early listeners.

At the beginning of the twenty-first century, Schoenberg's music no longer sounds so alien. It has radiated outward in unpredictable ways, finding alternative destinies in bebop jazz (the glassy chords of Thelonious Monk have a Schoenbergian tinge) and on movie soundtracks (horror movies need atonality as they need shadows on the walls of alleys). With the modernist revolution splintered into many factions, with composers gravitating back to tonality or moving on to something else, Schoenberg's music no longer carries the threat that *all* music will sound like this. Still, it retains its Faustian aura. These intervals will always shake the air; they will never become second nature. That is at once their power and their fate.

Vienna 1900

In his early stories Thomas Mann produced several lively portraits of a widespread turn-of-the-century type, the apocalyptic aesthete. The story

"At the Prophet's," written in 1904, begins with an ironic ode to artistic megalomania:

> Strange regions there are, strange minds, strange realms of the spirit, lofty and spare. At the edge of large cities, where street lamps are scarce and policemen walk by twos, are houses where you mount til you can mount no further, up and up into attics under the roof, where pale young geniuses, criminals of the dream, sit with folded arms and brood; up into cheap studios with symbolic decorations, where solitary and rebellious artists, inwardly consumed, hungry and proud, wrestle in a fog of cigarette smoke with devastatingly ultimate ideals. Here is the end: ice, chastity, null. Here is valid no compromise, no concession, no half-way, no consideration of values. Here the air is so rarefied that the mirages of life no longer exist. Here reign defiance and iron consistency, the ego supreme amid despair; here freedom, madness, and death hold sway.

In Mann's 1902 story "Gladius Dei," a young man named Hieronymus strides through Richard Strauss's hometown of Munich, scowling at the extravagance around him. He goes inside an art shop and berates its owner for displaying kitsch—art that is merely "beautiful" and therefore worthless. "Do you think gaudy colors can gloss over the misery of the world?" Hieronymus shouts. "Do you think loud orgies of luxurious good taste can drown the moans of the tortured earth? . . . Art is the sacred torch that must shed its merciful light into all life's terrible depths, into every shameful and sorrowful abyss; art is the divine flame that must set fire to the world, until the world with all its infamy and anguish burns and melts away in redeeming compassion!"

All over fin-de-siècle Europe, strange young men were tramping up narrow stairs to garret rooms and opening doors to secret places. Occult and mystical societies—Theosophist, Rosicrucian, Swedenborgian, kabbalistic, and neopagan—promised rupture from the world of the present. In the political sphere, Communists, anarchists, and ultranationalists plotted from various angles to overthrow the quasi-liberal monarchies of Europe; Leon Trotsky, in exile in Vienna from 1907 to 1914, began publishing a paper called *Pravda*. In the nascent field of psychology, Freud placed the ego at the mercy of the id. The world was unstable, and it seemed that one colossal Idea, or, failing that, one well-placed bomb, could bring it tumbling down. There was an almost titillating sense of imminent catastrophe.

Vienna was the scene of what may have been the ultimate pitched battle between the bourgeoisie and the avant-garde. A minority of "truth-seekers," as the historian Carl Schorske calls them, or "critical modernists," in the parlance of the philosopher Allan Janik, grew incensed by the city's rampant aestheticism, its habit of covering all available surfaces in gold leaf. They saw before them a supposedly modern, liberal, tolerant society that was failing to deliver on its promises, that was consigning large parts of its citizenry to poverty and misery. They spoke up for the outcasts and the scapegoats, the homosexuals and the prostitutes. Many of the "truth-seekers" were Jewish, and they were beginning to comprehend that Jews could never assimilate themselves into an anti-Semitic society, no matter how great their devotion to German culture. In the face of the gigantic lie of the cult of beauty—so the rhetoric went—art had to become negative, critical. It had to differentiate itself from the pluralism of bourgeois culture, which, as *Salome* demonstrated, had acquired its own avant-garde division.

The offensive against kitsch moved on all fronts. The critic Karl Kraus used his one-man periodical, *Die Fackel*, or *The Torch*, to expose what he considered to be laziness and mendacity in journalistic language, institutionalized iniquity in the prosecution of crime, and hypocrisy in the work of popular artists. The architect Adolf Loos attacked the Art Nouveau compulsion to cover everyday objects in wasteful ornament, and, in 1911, shocked the city and the emperor with the unadorned, semi-industrial facade of his commercial building on the Michaelerplatz. The gruesome pictures of Oskar Kokoschka and Egon Schiele confronted a soft-porn art world with the insatiability of lust and the violence of sex. Georg Trakl's poetry meticulously documented the onset of insanity and suicidal despair: "Now with my murderer I am alone."

If members of this informal circle sometimes failed to appreciate one another's work—the bohemian poet Peter Altenberg preferred Puccini and Strauss to Schoenberg and his students—they closed ranks when philistines attacked. There would be no backing down in the face of opposition. "If I must choose the lesser of two evils," Kraus said, "I will choose neither."

The most aggressive of Vienna's truth-seekers was the philosopher Otto Weininger, who, in 1903, at the age of twenty-three, shot himself in the house where Beethoven died. In a city that considered suicide an art, Weininger's was a masterpiece, and it made a posthumous bestseller of his doctoral dissertation, a bizarre tract titled *Sex and Character*. The argument of the book was that Europe suffered from racial, sexual, and ethical degeneration, whose root cause was the rampant sexuality of Woman. Jewishness and homosexuality were both symptoms of a feminized, aestheticized society. Only a masculine Genius could redeem the world. Wagner was "the greatest man since Christ." Strange as it may seem in retrospect, this alternately incoherent and bigoted work attracted readers as intelligent as Kraus, Ludwig Wittgenstein, and James Joyce, not to mention Schoenberg and his pupils. The young Alban Berg devoured Weininger's writings on culture, underlining sentences such as this: "Everything purely aesthetic has no cultural value." Wittgenstein, who made it his mission to expunge pseudo-religious cant from philosophy, was quoting Weininger when he issued his aphorism "Ethics and aesthetics are one."

The entire discourse surrounding the Viennese avant-garde demands skeptical scrutiny. Certain of these "truths"—fatuous generalizations about women, obnoxious remarks about the relative abilities of races and classes—fail to impress the modern reader. Weininger's notion of "ethics," rooted in Puritanism and self-hatred, is as hypocritical as anyone's. As in prior periods of cultural and social upheaval, revolutionary gestures betray a reactionary mind-set. Many members of the modernist vanguard would tack away from a fashionable solidarity with social outcasts and toward various forms of ultranationalism, authoritarianism, even Nazism. Moreover, only in a prosperous, liberal, art-infatuated society could such a determinedly antisocial class of artists survive, or find an audience. The bourgeois worship of art had implanted in artists' minds an attitude of infallibility, according to which the imagination made its own laws. That mentality made possible the extremes of modern art.

If the ethical justification of the modernist crusade rings false, composers did have one good reason to rebel against bourgeois taste: the prevailing cult of the past threatened their very livelihood. Vienna was indeed besotted with music, but it was besotted with *old* music, with the work of Mozart and Beethoven and the late Dr. Brahms. A canon was taking shape, and contemporary pieces were beginning to disappear from concert programs. In the late eighteenth century, 84 percent of the repertory of the Leipzig Gewandhaus Orchestra consisted of music by living composers. By 1855, the figure had declined to 38 percent, by 1870 to 24 percent. Meanwhile, the broader public was falling in love with the cakewalk and other popular novelties. Schoenberg's reasoning was this: if the bourgeois audience was losing interest in new music, and if the emerging mass audience had no appetite for classical music new or old, the serious artist should stop flailing his arms in a bid for attention and instead withdraw into a principled solitude.

After seeing *Salome* in Graz, Mahler doubted whether the voice of the people was the voice of God. Schoenberg, in his worst moods, completely inverted the formula, implying, in effect, that the voice of the people was the voice of the devil. "If it is art, it is not for all," he later wrote, "and if it is for all, it is not art." Did the split between the composer and his public come about as the result of such ferocious attitudes? Or were they a rational response to the public's irrational vitriol? These questions admit no ready answers. Both sides of the dispute bore some degree of responsibility for the unsightly outcome. Fin-de-siècle Vienna offers the depressing spectacle of artists and audiences washing their hands of each other, giving up on the dream of common ground.

Paris 1900

Schoenberg was not the first composer to write "atonal music," if it is defined as music outside the major- and minor-key system. That distinction probably belongs to Franz Liszt, erstwhile virtuoso of the Romantic piano, latter-day abbé and mystic. In several works of the late 1870s and early '80s, most notably in the *Bagatelle sans tonalité*, Liszt's harmony comes unmoored from the concept of key. Triads, the basic three-note building blocks of Western music, grow scarce. Augmented chords and unresolved sevenths proliferate. The diabolical tritone lurks everywhere. These profoundly unfamiliar works puzzled listeners who were accustomed to the flashy Romanticism of Liszt's *Hungarian Rhapsodies* and other favorites. Wagner muttered to Cosima that his old friend was showing signs of "budding insanity." But it wasn't happening only in Liszt's brain. Similar anomalies cropped up in Russia and France. The fabric of harmony was warping, as if under the influence of an unseen force.

Paris, where Liszt caused mass hysteria in the earlier part of the nineteenth century, was more or less the birthplace of the avant-garde as we now conceive it. Charles Baudelaire struck all the poses of the artist in opposition to society, in terms of dress, behavior, sexual mores, choice of subject, and style of delivery. The august Symbolist poet Stéphane Mallarmé defined poetry as a hermetic practice: "Everything that is sacred and that wishes to remain so must envelop itself in mystery."

The young Debussy took that attitude as gospel. To his colleague Ernest Chausson he wrote in 1893: "Music really ought to have been a hermetical science, enshrined in texts so hard and laborious to decipher as to discourage the herd of people who treat it as casually as they do a handkerchief! I'd go further and, instead of spreading music among the populace, I propose the foundation of a 'Society of Musical Esotericism . . .'"

Debussy shared with Schoenberg a petit bourgeois background. Born in 1862, the son of a shopkeeper turned civil servant, he studied at the Paris Conservatory, where he struggled for several years to write a cantata sufficiently dull to win the sinecure of the academically oriented Prix de Rome. He finally succeeded with *The Prodigal Son*, in 1884.

In his spare time, Debussy sampled the wares of Paris's avant-garde scenes, browsed in bookshops stocked with occult and Oriental lore, and, at the Bayreuth festivals of 1888 and 1889, fell under the spell of *Parsifal*. He attended Mallarmé's elite Tuesday gatherings from around 1892 on, and also delved into more obscure regions—cultish Catholic societies such as the Kabbalistic Order of the Rose-Cross and the Order of the Rose-Cross of the Temple and Graal. Alas, it does not seem to be the case, despite claims put forward in the bestselling books *Holy Blood, Holy Grail* and *The Da Vinci Code*, that Debussy served as the thirty-third grand master of the Prieuré de Sion, which, according to a fabricated legend, guarded the secret of the Grail itself.

All this was standard-issue post-Wagnerian mumbo-jumbo. But Debussy's honest quest for an unblemished, truthful musical language soon led him to other, distinctly un-Wagnerian sources. Just before his second trip to Bayreuth, in 1889, he attended the Paris Universal Exposition, which imported exotic sights and sounds from around the world, courtesy of a network of oppressive colonial regimes. It was here that Gauguin first became enamored of the tropical simplicity that eventually led him to take up residence in Tahiti. Debussy listened transfixed to the music of a Vietnamese theater troupe, with its effects of resonating gongs, and also to a Javanese gamelan ensemble, with its minimal scales of five notes, its delicate layering of timbres, its air of suspended animation. Gamelan music, Debussy wrote, "contained all gradations, even some that we no longer know how to name, so that tonic and dominant were nothing more than empty phantoms of use to clever little children."

Debussy also immersed himself in painting and poetry, working out musical analogies for his sharpest aesthetic impressions. Although he was later labeled a musical "impressionist," Renoir and Monet affected him little; he was influenced more by Anglo-American painters—by Turner's way of suffusing a landscape with light, by Whistler's way of subsuming a seascape into a single mood. He read the poetry of Paul Verlaine, whose *Fêtes galantes* he discovered on the shelves of his piano pupil and lover Marie-Blanche Vasnier. And Verlaine's perfectly simple and elusive images—the color of moonlight, the music of rustling leaves and falling rain, the unreadable beauty of the sea, the motion of ancient dances, the souls of marionettes—fired Debussy's musical imagination. To evoke the instrument of "Mandoline," he wrote strumming chords in which fifths accumulate in dreaming towers. To capture the plain mystery of the line "singing branches," he let common chords tumble over one another in defiance of textbook rules. In the midst of that kaleidoscopic rush of sounds, the whole-tone scale, one of Debussy's trademark devices, made an early appearance. This, in turn, brought the young composer to the threshold of so-called atonality.

Musicians and listeners had long agreed that certain intervals, or pairs of notes, were "clear," and that others were "unclear." The quoted words can be found on a cuneiform tablet from the Sumerian city of Ur. The clearest intervals were the octave, the fifth, the fourth, and the major third, which form the lower end of the harmonic series (see, again, the opening measures of *Thus Spake Zarathustra*). By contrast, the tritone had for centuries been considered a disturbing entity. The whole-tone scale, which had begun showing up as an exotic effect in mid-nineteenth-century Russian and Central European music, consists of six equal steps in succession; if one goes upward starting from any C on a piano, it is three white keys followed by three black keys. The scale has the interesting property of being "clear" and "unclear" in equal measure. It abounds in bright major thirds, which can be obtained by moving two steps from any note. It also abounds in tritones (three steps). In visual terms, the scale generates a palette at once luminous and unreal, bright and hazy.

Debussy also made use of pentatonic scales, which he encountered many times at the Paris Exposition—those ancient, elementary five-note scales that crop up in folk traditions all over the world, from Africa to Indonesia. And he continued using diatonic (major- and minor-key) scales, though often in a spirit of nostalgia or satirical play.

The composer thought deeply about the physical facts underlying harmony. Hermann von Helmholtz, in his 1863 treatise, *On the Sensations of Tone as a Physiological Basis for the Theory of Music*, had explained the physics of the natural harmonic series and attempted to define human perceptions of consonance and dissonance in relation to it. As the waveforms of any two simultaneous tones intersect, they create "beats," pulsations in the air. The interval of the octave causes a pleasant sensation, Helmholtz said, because the oscillations of the upper note align with those of the lower note in a perfect two-to-one ratio, meaning that no beats are felt. The perfect fifth, which has a three-to-two ratio, also sounds "clean" to the ear. Debussy may have known Helmholtz's work; he certainly knew the eighteenth-century speculations of Rameau, who had linked standard harmony to the overtone series. Debussy loved to plant octaves and fifths in the bass and let a rainbow of narrower intervals shimmer in the upper air.

Debussy's emblematic early work is *Prelude to "The Afternoon of a Faun,"* an orchestral narrative after a poem by Mallarmé, written and revised between 1892 and 1894. In the poem, a faun wonders how best to treasure the memory, or perhaps the dream, of two exquisite nymphs; he plays a song upon his flute, aware that music falls short of the viscerality of experience:

Long shall my discourse from the echoing shore
Depict those goddesses: by masquerades,
I'll strip the veils that sanctify their shades.

The score begins by summoning the very music that the faun plays—a languid melody on the flute, descending a tritone and going back up. The harmony, likewise, swings across the tritone and comes to rest on a richly resonant B-flat dominant seventh, which, in classical harmony, would resolve to E-flat. Here the chord becomes a self-sufficient organism, symbolic of unbounded nature. Then the flute repeats its melody while a new texture forms around it. Debussy thus resists the Germanic urge to develop his thematic material: the melody remains static while the accompaniment evolves. Cloudy whole-tone sonorities mark the horizon of the faun's vision, where shapes dissolve in mist.

All this suggestion eventually coalesces into a voluptuous, full-orchestral love song in D-flat major. The strings savor long, flowing unison lines, more akin to Indian ragas than to Wagner or Strauss. It is music of physical release, even of sexual orgasm, as Vaslav Nijinsky demonstrated in his undulating dance of the *Faun* at the Ballets Russes in 1912. "I hold the queen!" Mallarmé's faun exults. Yet the tritone lingers in the bass, a mystery ungrasped.

With the opera *Pelléas et Mélisande*, sketched in the early 1890s and then extensively revised before its 1902 premiere, Debussy created a new kind of interior music drama, using Wagner as raw material. The text is by the Symbolist playwright Maurice Maeterlinck, and, as Strauss would do in *Salome*, Debussy set Maeterlinck's play word for word, following its riddling prose wherever it took him. The love triangle of Pelléas, his half brother Golaud, and the inscrutable wandering princess Mélisande moves toward a grim climax, but most of the action takes place offstage; the score places the listener in a liquid medium into which individual psychologies have been submerged. Debussy's established resources—wholetone scales, antique modes, attenuated melodies that rise from wavering intervals—conjure an atmosphere of wandering, waiting, yearning, trembling.

Later come glimpses of a beautiful country on the other side. When Pelléas and Mélisande finally confess their love for each other—"I love you," "I love you, too," without accompaniment—the orchestra responds with a simple textbook progression moving from a tonic chord to its dominant seventh, except that in Debussy's spectral scoring it sounds like the dawn of creation. A similar transfiguring simplicity overtakes the prelude to Act V, in which we discover that Mélisande has given birth to a child.

At some point, Debussy's sense of himself as a sonic adventurer, a Faustian seeker, dissipated. By 1900 he was no longer calling for a Society of Musical Esotericism; instead, he prized classic French values of clarity, elegance, and grace. He was also listening intently to Spanish music—in particular, to the *cante jondo*, or deep song, tradition of Andalusian flamenco. His major works from the first decade of the century—*La Mer*; the Preludes, Book I, and *Estampes* for piano; and the cycles of *Images* for piano and for orchestra—intermingle familiar qualities of unearthliness with dancing movement and clean-cut lyricism. "Voiles" ("Sails"), in the Preludes, confines itself almost entirely to the whole-tone scale. "Steps in the Snow" revolves around hypnotic repetitions of a four-note figure. But "The Girl with the Flaxen Hair" has a melody of the sort that begs to be whistled in the street; many people would be surprised to learn that it had been "composed" at all. And the "Interrupted Serenade," a Spanish scene, intertwines flamenco guitar with Arabic scales suggestive of Moorish influence. Debussy did not learn to write such music in Faustian isolation; instead, he picked up clues from desultory nights at the opera, operetta, cabarets, and cafés.

Paris bohemia promoted an easy back-and-forth between occult esotericism and cabaret populism, not least because the two worlds were sometimes literally on top of each other. The Kabbalistic Order of the Rose-Cross met in a room above the cabaret Auberge du Clou, and as the cabal debated its arcane philosophy, the insinuating tunes of the café-concert would have floated up from below.

In such places, Debussy often encountered Erik Satie, another clandestine revolutionary of the fin de siècle, and, in some ways, the more daring one. Satie, too, dabbled in Rosicrucianism, serving briefly as the house composer for the Order of the Rose-Cross of the Temple and Graal, which the novelist Joséphin Péladan had founded in a *Parsifal* daze. Satie's music for Péladan's play *Le Fils des étoiles* (1891) begins with a totally irrational string of dissonant six-note chords—the next step beyond late Liszt. Yet a life of experiment was not to Satie's liking. The son of a publisher of music-hall and cabaret songs, he found deeper satisfaction in playing piano at the Auberge du Clou. He achieved liberation from the past in three piano pieces titled *Gymnopédies*, which discard centuries of knotted-brow complexity in favor of a language at once simple and new. In the first eighteen bars of the first piece, only six pitches are used. There is no development, no transition, only an instant prolonged.

The conductor Reinbert de Leeuw has written: "Satie was, in a manner of speaking, starting European musical history all over again." The same could have been said of Debussy, who, in 1901, remarked to his colleague Paul Dukas that too many modern works had become needlessly complex—"They smell of the lamp, not of the sun." Debussy was describing the motivation for his latest work, the *Nocturnes* for orchestra, and in particular for the movement "Fêtes," which depicted a festival in the Bois de Boulogne, replete with the sounds of soldiers' trumpets and the cries of the crowd. This was the germ of an alternative modernism, one that would reach maturity in the stripped-down, folk-based, jazz-happy, machine-driven music of the twenties. In essence, two avant-gardes were forming side by side. The Parisians were moving into the brightly lit world of daily life. The Viennese went in the opposite direction, illuminating the terrible depths with their holy torches.

Schoenberg

Schoenberg was born in 1874. His father, Samuel Schönberg, came from a German-speaking Jewish community in Pressburg, which is now Bratislava, in Slovakia. (Schoenberg dropped the umlaut from his name when he fled Germany in 1933.) Samuel Schönberg moved to Vienna as a young man to make a living as a shopkeeper. There he met and married Pauline Nachod, who came from a family of cantorial singers. The couple lived in modest circumstances and did not own a piano. Their son learned much of the classical repertory from a military band that performed in a coffeehouse on the Prater. Arnold taught himself several instruments and played in a string quartet that occupied a room set aside for messenger boys. He learned instrumental forms by subscribing to an encyclopedia, and waited for the *S* volume to arrive before composing a sonata.

One way or another, Schoenberg absorbed so much music that he had no need for formal instruction. He did take some lessons from Alexander Zemlinsky, a slightly older composer who wrote fine-grained, lyrically potent music in the vein of Mahler and Strauss. Zemlinsky's father was Catholic, his mother was the daughter of a Sephardic Jew and a Bosnian

Muslim. In 1901, Schoenberg married Zemlinsky's sister Mathilde, who, a few years later, would set off the central emotional crisis of his life.

After working for a time as a bank clerk, Schoenberg took on various odd musical jobs, conducting a workers' chorus, orchestrating operettas, and writing sentimental songs. In late 1901, he moved to Berlin to serve as a musical director for high-minded revues at the Überbrettl cabaret, or, as it was later called, the Buntes Theater. This organization was the brainchild of Ernst von Wolzogen, who hoped to import to Berlin the streetwise sophistication of Paris cabarets such as the Chat Noir and the Auberge du Clou. In the wake of financial difficulties, Wolzogen quit his enterprise in 1902, and Schoenberg, short on work, returned to Vienna the following year. Aspects of the cabaret reappeared in the 1912 song cycle *Pierrot lunaire*, where the soloist floats between speech and song. If Schoenberg later characterized his atonal music as a gesture of resistance to the popular mainstream, in the early days his stance was significantly more flexible.

Sharp-witted, widely cultured, easily unimpressed, Schoenberg made himself at home in the coffeehouses where the leading lights of fin-de-siècle Vienna gathered—the Café Imperial, the Café Central, the Café Museum. The great men in Vienna all had their circles of disciples, and Schoenberg quickly assembled his own. In 1904 he placed a notice in the *Neue Musikalische Presse* announcing that he was seeking pupils in composition. Several young men showed up as a result. One was Anton Webern, a stern young soul who may have seen the ad because it appeared directly beneath a report on the desecration of *Parsifal* in America. (The previous year, Heinrich Conried, Mahler's future employer, had staged *Parsifal* at the Met, breaking the rule that made Wagner's sacred opera exclusive to Bayreuth.) Another was Alban Berg, a gifted but feckless youth who had been working in the civil service.

The early works of Schoenberg always come as a pleasant shock to listeners expecting a grueling atonal exercise. The music exudes a heady, luxurious tone, redolent of Klimt's gilt portraits and other *Jugendstil* artifacts. Brash Straussian gestures mix with diaphanous textures that bear a possibly not coincidental resemblance to Debussy. There are spells of suspended animation, when the music becomes fixated on a single chord. The chamber tone poem *Transfigured Night*, written in 1899, ends with twelve bars of glistening D major, the fundamental note never budging in the bass. *Gurre-Lieder*, a huge Wagnerian cantata for vocal soloists, multiple choruses, and supersized orchestra, begins with a great steam bath of E-flat major, probably in imitation of the opening to Wagner's *Ring*. Yet all is not well in Romantic paradise. Unexplained dissonances rise to the surface; chromatic lines intersect in a contrapuntal tangle; chords of longing fail to resolve.

The young Schoenberg encountered opposition, but he also received encouragement from the highest musical circles. The Mahlers regularly invited him to their apartment near the Schwarzenbergplatz, where, according to Alma, he would incite heated arguments by offering up "paradox of the most violent description." Afterward, Gustav would say to Alma, "Take good care you never invite that conceited puppy to the house again." Before long, another invitation would arrive.

Mahler found Schoenberg's music mesmerizing and maddening in equal measure. "Why am I still writing symphonies," he once exclaimed, "if that is supposed to be the music of the future!" After a rehearsal of Schoenberg's First Chamber Symphony, Mahler asked the musicians to play a C-major triad. "Thank you," he said, and walked out. Yet he made a show of applauding Schoenberg's most controversial works, knowing how destructive the critics and claques of Vienna could be.

Strauss, too, found Schoenberg fascinating—"*very* talented," he said, even if the music was "overloaded." The two composers met during Schoenberg's first stint in Berlin—Wolzogen, the director of the Buntes Theater, had collaborated with Strauss on his second opera, the anti-philistine comedy *Feuersnot*—and Strauss helped his younger colleague locate other sources of income. When Schoenberg later founded the Society for Creative Musicians in Vienna, Strauss accepted an honorary membership, and expressed the hope that the new organization would "blessedly light up many minds darkened by decades of malice and stupidity."

Schoenberg withheld from Strauss the impertinence that he showed to Mahler. "I would like to take this opportunity to thank you, honored master," the future revolutionary wrote obsequiously in 1903, "once again for all the help you have given me at a sacrifice to yourself in the most sincere manner. I will not forget this for the whole of my life and will always be thankful to you for it." As late as 1912, Schoenberg still felt nervous and schoolboyish in Strauss's presence: "He was very friendly.

But I behaved very awkwardly . . . I stammered and surely left the impression of a servile devotion on Strauss." Schoenberg told himself that he should have been more of a "Selfian"—as proudly self-determined as Strauss himself.

In May 1906, the Schoenberg contingent had gone to see *Salome* in Graz. Beforehand, Schoenberg painstakingly studied the vocal score, which Mahler had given to him. It stood on his music stand, open to the first page. "Perhaps in twenty years' time someone will be able to explain these harmonic progressions theoretically," Schoenberg told his students. Aspects of *Salome*'s fractured tonality show up in the First Chamber Symphony, which Schoenberg wrote that summer. Yet this new piece was very different in tone and style from Strauss's opera. Its strenuous working out of brief motivic figures recalled Viennese practice in the Classical period from Haydn to Beethoven. In a deliberate rejection of fin-de-siècle grandiosity, it was scored for a mini-orchestra of fifteen instruments, its sonorities rough rather than lush. Schoenberg was throwing off excess baggage, perhaps in anticipation of lean years to come. The process of condensation led to *Pierrot lunaire*, in which the soloist is accompanied by an agile band of two winds, two strings, and a piano.

Just as Debussy imagined new sounds while perusing images in Verlaine and Mallarmé, Schoenberg let poetry guide him. He relished the erotic visions of Richard Dehmel, who furnished the story of *Transfigured Night*. He also investigated, at Strauss's suggestion, the plays of Maeterlinck; and in 1902 and 1903, he fashioned a large-scale orchestral tone poem on the subject of Maeterlinck's *Pelléas et Mélisande*, purportedly unaware that Debussy had just made a setting of the same text. But Schoenberg's most crucial literary encounter was with the poetry of Stefan George, then the leading Symbolist among German writers.

George stood apart from his compatriots on account of his ardent Francophilia; he had gone to Paris in 1889, attended Mallarmé's "Tuesdays" (the poet dubbed him "one of us"), and translated the major French poets into German. He might have met Debussy, though there is no evidence that he did. So determined was he to honor his French masters that he dropped capital letters from German nouns. A self-styled artist-prophet in the fin-de-siècle mode, George surrounded himself with a bevy of acolytes, among whom could always be found several beautiful adolescent boys. George's circle inspired Mann's satire "At the Prophet's"; minus the homosexual element, it might also have served as a model for Schoenberg, who treated his students as disciples and seldom appeared in public without them. More important, George showed Schoenberg a way out of the easygoing pleasures of Viennese aesthetics. The sheer density of the poet's imagery did not permit easy access, although sensual secrets resided in the labyrinth.

Schoenberg's voyage to the other side began on December 17, 1907, when he set a poem from George's collection *Year of the Soul*, much of which is concerned with an intense scene of farewell. It begins: "I must not in thanks sink down before you / You are the spiritual plain from which we rose." The music hangs by only the thinnest thread to the old harmonic order. It purports to be in B minor, yet the home chord appears only three times in thirty measures, once beneath the word "agonizing." Otherwise, it is made up of a ghostly flow of unrooted triads, ambiguous transitional chords, stark dissonances, and crystalline monodic lines, approximating the picture of an "ice-cold, deep-sleeping stream" with which the poem concludes. The date of composition is telling: eight days earlier, Schoenberg had bid farewell to Mahler at the Westbahnhof in Vienna. If, as seems possible, the fact of Mahler's departure impelled the choice of text, then it carries a double message: the young composer has been abandoned by a father figure, yet he is also liberated, free to pursue a different love.

The next leg of the journey took place in the midst of personal crisis. Schoenberg had admitted into his circle an unstable character named Richard Gerstl, a gifted painter of brutal Expressionist tendencies. Under Gerstl's direction, Schoenberg had taken up painting and found that he had a knack for it: his canvas *The Red Gaze*, in which a gaunt face stares out with bloodshot eyes, has come to be recognized as a minor masterpiece of its time and place. In May 1908 Schoenberg discovered that Gerstl was having an affair with his wife, Mathilde, and that summer he surprised the lovers in a compromising position. Mathilde ran off with Gerstl, then returned to her husband, whereupon Gerstl proceeded to stage a suicide that exceeded Weininger's in flamboyance: he burned his paintings and hanged himself naked in front of a full-length mirror, as if he wanted to see his own body rendered in Expressionist style. The suicide took place on November 4, 1908, on the night of a Schoenberg concert to which Gerstl had not been invited; evidently, that rejection was the final straw.

Schoenberg himself struggled with thoughts of suicide. "I have only one hope—that I will not live much longer," he wrote to his wife at the end of the summer. In a last will and testament that may have been an unused suicide note, he wrote, "I have cried, have behaved like someone in despair, have made decisions and then rejected them, have had ideas of suicide and almost carried them out, have plunged from one madness into another—in a word, I am totally broken." He warned that he would "soon follow the path, find the resolution, that at long last might be the highest culmination of all human actions." But, in an intriguingly vague turn of phrase, he could not foresee "whether it be my body that will give way or my soul."

Suicide was not Schoenberg's style. Just as Beethoven, in his Heiligenstadt Testament, resolved to forge ahead into a life of misery, Schoenberg pressed on. That same summer of 1908 he finished his Second Quartet, in which he hesitates at a crossroads, contemplating various paths forking in front of him. The first movement, written the previous year, still uses a fairly conventional late-Romantic language. The second movement, by contrast, is a hallucinatory Scherzo, unlike any other music of the time. It contains fragments of the folk song "Ach, du lieber Augustin"—the same tune that held Freudian significance for Mahler (or so Freud said). For Schoenberg, the song seems to represent a bygone world disintegrating; the crucial line is "*Alles ist hin*" (all is lost). The movement ends in a fearsome sequence of four-note figures, which are made up of fourths separated by a tritone. In them may be discerned traces of the bifurcated scale that begins *Salome*. But there is no longer a sense of tonalities colliding. Instead, the very concept of a chord is dissolving into a matrix of intervals.

In the final two movements of the Second Quartet a soprano voice joins the string players to sing two George poems, "Litany" and "Rapture." The texts come from a larger cycle that George wrote in memory of a handsome boy named Maximilian Kronberger, who died of meningitis one day after his sixteenth birthday, leaving the poet in spasms of grief. Schoenberg seems to identify not only with the poet's emotion but also with his urge to manipulate pain to expressive ends, in the name of self-abnegation and purification. "Litany" cries out for a quick end to sexual and spiritual agony: "Kill the longing, close the wound!" "Rapture," the culmination of George's "Maximin" cycle, presents the solution. It begins in a state of profound estrangement, with the alienation of the individual turning universal:

I feel the wind of another planet.
Growing pale in the darkness are the faces
Of those who lately turned to me as friends.

This Martian breeze is mimicked in soft, sinister streams of notes, recalling the episode in *Salome* when Herod hallucinates a chilly wind. Special effects on the strings (mutes, harmonics, bowing at the bridge) heighten the sense of otherness, as singing tones become whispers and high cries. Then comes the transformation:

I dissolve in tones, circling, weaving . . .
I am but a spark of the holy fire
I am but a roaring of the holy voice.

The soprano declaims her lines in a cool, stately rhythm. The strings dwell on sustained chords, most of which can be named according to the old harmonic system, although they have been torn from the organic connections of tonality and move like a procession of ghosts. At the climactic moment, under the word "holy," the composer's motto chord, the dissonant combination of a fourth and a tritone, sounds with unyielding force. Even so, Schoenberg is not ready to go over the brink. At the close the motto chord gives way to pure F-sharp major, which, in light of what has gone before, sounds bizarre and surreal. The work is dedicated to "my wife."

Schoenberg stayed in his Stefan George trance through the fall of 1908, when he completed a song cycle on the poet's *Book of Hanging Gardens*. The otherworldly serenity persists, together with vestiges of tonality. Then something snapped, and Schoenberg let out his pent-up rage. In 1909, as Mahler was sinking into the long goodbye of his Ninth Symphony and Strauss was floating away into the eighteenth-century dreamworld of *Rosenkavalier*, Schoenberg entered a creative frenzy, writing the

Three Pieces for Piano, the Five Pieces for Orchestra, and *Erwartung*, or *Expectation*, a dramatic scene for soprano and orchestra. In the last of the Three Piano Pieces, the keyboard turns into something like a percussion instrument, a battlefield of triple and quadruple *forte*. In the first of the orchestral pieces, "Premonitions," instrumental voices dissolve into gestures, textures, and colors, many of them derived from *Salome*: agitated rapid figures joined to trills, hypnotically circling whole-tone figures, woodwinds screeching in their uppermost registers, two-note patterns dripping like blood on marble, a spitting, snarling quintet of flutter-tongued trombones and tuba. *Erwartung*, the monologue of a woman stumbling through a moonlit forest in search of her missing lover, is distended by monster chords of eight, nine, and ten notes, which saturate the senses and shut down the intellect. In one especially hair-raising passage, the voice plunges nearly two octaves, from B to C-sharp, on a cry of "Help!" This comes straight from Wagner's *Parsifal*; Kundry crosses the same huge interval when she confesses that she laughed at the suffering of Christ.

Schoenberg's early atonal music is not all sound and fury. Periodically, it discloses worlds that are like hidden valleys between mountains; a hush descends, the sun glimmers in fog, shapes hover. In the third of the Five Pieces for Orchestra—the one titled "Farben," or "Colors"—a five-note chord is transposed up and down the scale and passed through a beguiling array of orchestral timbres. The chord itself is not harsh, but it is elusive, poised between consonance and dissonance. Such utterly original experiments in shifting tone colors came to be classified as *Klangfarbenmelodie*, or tone-color melody.

The same rapt mood descends over the Six Little Pieces for Piano, Opus 19, which Schoenberg wrote in early 1911, as Mahler lay dying. The second piece is nine bars long and contains about a hundred notes. It is built on a hypnotic iteration of the interval G and B, which chimes softly in place, giving off a clean, warm sound. Tendrils of sound trail around the dyad, touching at one point or another on the remaining ten notes of the chromatic scale. But the main notes stay riveted in place. They are like two eyes, staring ahead, never blinking.

Scandal

"I feel the heat of rebellion rising in even the slightest souls," Schoenberg wrote in a program note in January 1910, "and I suspect that even those who have believed in me until now will not want to accept the necessity of this development."

Nothing in the annals of musical scandal—from the first night of Stravinsky's *Rite of Spring* to the release of the Sex Pistols' "Anarchy in the U.K."—rivals the ruckus that greeted Schoenberg early in his career. In February 1907, his thornily contrapuntal, though not yet atonal, First String Quartet was heard against a vigorous ostinato of laughter, catcalls, and whistles. Mahler, leaping to Schoenberg's defense, nearly got into a fistfight with one of the troublemakers. Three days later, the First Chamber Symphony caused "seat-rattling, whistle-blowing, and ostentatious walk-outs," according to Schoenberg's student Egon Wellesz. When the Second Quartet had its premiere, in December 1908, the critic Ludwig Karpath couldn't wait until the following morning to make his feelings known, and shouted, "Stop it! Enough!" A critic friendlier to Schoenberg shouted back, "Quiet! Continue to play!"

The resistance to Schoenberg was deep-seated. It came not only from reactionaries and philistines but also from listeners of considerable musical knowledge. One early scandal, we are told, was fomented by pupils of Heinrich Schenker, a giant in the new discipline of musicology. Anti-Semitism played no significant role, despite some latter-day claims. (Two of Schoenberg's most vehement critics, Robert Hirschfeld and Julius Korngold, were Jews, and their colleague Hans Liebstöckl was a Prague-born German of antinationalist and pro-Debussy tendencies.) Even Mahler had trouble accepting the "necessity of this development," in Schoenberg's words. "I have your quartet with me and study it from time to time," Mahler wrote to Schoenberg in January 1909. "But it is difficult for me. I'm so terribly sorry that I cannot follow you better; I look forward to the day when I shall find myself again (and so find you)." When Mahler saw the Five Pieces for Orchestra, he commented that he could not translate the notes on the page into sounds in his head. Nevertheless, he continued to encourage his "conceited puppy" and, in his last days, was heard to say, "If I go, he will have nothing left."

Strauss, for his part, thought that Schoenberg had gone off the deep end. That reaction must have been especially disappointing, for Schoenberg had written the Five Pieces in answer to Strauss's request for some short works for his Berlin concert series. Schoenberg was so eager to show Strauss what he had done that he mailed off the Pieces before they were complete, and only ten days after the fourth of the set was finished. "There is no architecture and no build-up," Schoenberg explained in an accompanying letter. "Just a vivid, uninterrupted succession of colors, rhythms, and moods." Strauss politely wrote back that such "daring experiments" would be too much for his audience. Outwardly, he maintained his support, sending his colleague one hundred marks in 1911. But his true opinion surfaced three years later, when he made the mistake of writing to Alma Mahler that Schoenberg "would be better off shoveling snow than scribbling on music paper." Alma showed the letter to Schoenberg's student Erwin Stein, who decided that his teacher should be apprised of its contents. Schoenberg snapped that whatever he had learned from the composer of *Salome* he had misunderstood.

In the middle of these setbacks came a massive success, which, in the end, only magnified the composer's anger. This was the 1913 world premiere of *Gurre-Lieder*, which had been sketched ten years earlier and exhibited a late-Romantic style that Schoenberg had since abandoned. The setting was Vienna's Musikverein—the legendary hall where symphonies of Brahms and Bruckner had first been heard. The conductor was Franz Schreker, another Austrian composer who was moving through liminal realms of post-Wagnerian harmony. Signs of a triumph were already evident at intermission, as admirers crowded around the composer. But he was in a foul mood, and declined to receive new converts. When the performance was over, even the anti-Schoenbergians, some of whom had brought along whistles and other noisemakers in anticipation of a scandal, rose to their feet along with the rest of the crowd, chanting, "Schoenberg! Schoenberg!" The brawlers were weeping, one witness said, and their cheers sounded like an apology.

The hero of the hour failed to appear, even as the applause swelled. He was found, according to the violinist Francis Aranyi, "huddled in the most distant and darkest corner of the auditorium, his hands folded and a quiet, quizzical sort of smile on his face."

This should have been Schoenberg's hour of glory. But, as he recalled many years later, he felt "rather indifferent, if not even a little angry . . . I stood alone against a world of enemies." When he finally walked to the podium, he bowed to the musicians but turned his back on the crowd. It was, Aranyi said, "the strangest thing that a man in front of that kind of a hysterical, worshipping mob has ever done." Schoenberg had rehearsed this gesture; in 1911 he had made a painting titled *Self-Portrait, Walking*, in which the artist's back is turned to the viewer.

The scandal to end all scandals erupted on March 31, 1913, again in the storied Musikverein. The program mapped Schoenberg's world, past, present, and future. There were songs by Alexander Zemlinsky, Schoenberg's only teacher; if the police had not intervened, the audience would also have heard Mahler's *Kindertotenlieder.* Schoenberg was represented by his First Chamber Symphony. And new works by Berg and Webern offered up sonic phenomena that not even Schoenberg had yet imagined. The breaking point came during Berg's song "Über die Grenzen des All," or "Beyond the Limits of the Universe," a setting of a brief, tantalizing poem by Peter Altenberg, at the beginning of which the winds and brass play a chord of twelve separate pitches—as if all the keys between two Cs on a piano were being made to sound at once.

"Loud laughter rang throughout the hall in response to that squawking, grinding chord," one witness recalled. (It must have been a poor performance, because the chord is supposed to be very soft.) There were physical scuffles, and the police were called. A Dr. Viktor Albert complained that Erhard Buschbeck, the youthful organizer of the concert, had boxed him on the ears. Buschbeck responded that Dr. Albert had called him a "rascal," making physical retaliation necessary. A lawsuit followed. "The public was laughing," the operetta composer Oscar Straus testified in court. "And I openly confess, sir, that I laughed, too, for why shouldn't one laugh at something genuinely comical?" The sound of the scuffle, Straus quipped, was the most harmonious sound of the evening. The report of the trial took up almost an entire page of the *Neue Freie Presse*, pushing aside the murder trial of one Johann Skvarzil.

Atonality

The source of the scandal is not hard to divine; it has to do with the physics of sound. Sound is a trembling of the air, and it affects the body as well as the mind. This is the import of Helmholtz's *On the Sensations of*

Tone, which tries to explain why certain intervals attack the nerve endings while others have a calming effect. At the head of Helmholtz's rogues' gallery of intervals was the semitone, which is the space between any two adjacent keys on a piano. Struck together, they create rapid "beats" that distress the ear—like an irritating flash of light, Helmholtz says, or a scraping of the skin. Fred Lerdahl, a modern theorist, puts it this way: "When a periodic signal reaches the inner ear, an area of the basilar membrane is stimulated, the peak of which fires rapidly to the auditory cortex, causing the perception of a single pitch. If two periodic signals simultaneously stimulate overlapping areas, the perturbation causes a sensation of 'roughness.'" Similar roughnesses are created by the major seventh, slightly narrower than an octave, and by the minor ninth, slightly wider. These are precisely the intervals that Schoenberg emphasizes in his atonal music.

Psychological factors also come into play when the music is set in front of a crowd. Looking at a painting in a gallery is fundamentally different from listening to a new work in a concert hall. Picture yourself in a room with, say, Kandinsky's *Impression III (Concert)*, painted in 1911. Kandinsky and Schoenberg knew each other, and shared common aims; *Impression III* was inspired by one of Schoenberg's concerts. If visual abstraction and musical dissonance were precisely equivalent, *Impression III* and the third of the Five Pieces for Orchestra would present the same degree of difficulty. But the Kandinsky is a different experience for the uninitiated. If at first you have trouble understanding it, you can walk on and return to it later, or step back to give it another glance, or lean in for a close look (is that a piano in the foreground?). At a performance, listeners experience a new work collectively, at the same rate and approximately from the same distance. They cannot stop to consider the implications of a half-lovely chord or concealed waltz rhythm. They are a crowd, and crowds tend to align themselves as one mind.

Atonality was destined to raise hackles. Nothing could have been more perfectly calculated to cause consternation among the art-loving middle classes. But Schoenberg did not improve his situation when he set about answering his critics. He was a gifted writer, with a knack for turning out sharp-edged barbs: not for nothing was the acidulous Karl Kraus his literary hero. Starting in 1909, he issued a stream of commentaries, polemics, theoretical musings, and aphorisms. At times, he argued his case with charm and wit. More often, though, the fighter in him came out, and he summoned up what he called "the will to annihilate."

In a way, Schoenberg was most persuasive in justifying his early atonal works when he emphasized their illogical, irrational dimension. As far as we can tell, he composed them in something like an automatic state, sketching the hyperdense *Erwartung* in only seventeen days. All the while, the composer was in the grip of convulsive emotion—feelings of sexual betrayal, personal abandonment, professional humiliation. That turbulence may be sensed in some of the explanations that Schoenberg provided to friends in the period from 1908 to 1913. To Kandinsky he wrote: "Art belongs to the *unconscious*! One must express *oneself*! Express oneself *directly*! Not one's taste, or one's upbringing, or one's intelligence, knowledge or skill." To the composer-pianist Ferruccio Busoni he wrote: "I strive for: complete liberation from all forms, from all symbols of cohesion and of logic." And he instructed Alma Mahler to listen for "colors, noises, lights, sounds, movements, glances, gestures."

In public, however, Schoenberg tended to explain his latest works as the logical, rational outcome of a historical process. Perhaps because he was suspected of having gone mad, he insisted that he had no choice but to act as he did. To quote again his 1910 program note: the music was the product of "necessity." Instead of separating himself from the titans of the past, from Bach, Mozart, and Beethoven, he presented himself as their heir, and pointed out that many now canonical masterpieces had caused confusion when they first appeared. (That argument failed to impress some educated listeners, who felt with full justification that they were being treated like idiots. From the fact that some great music was once rejected it does not follow that any rejected music is great.) Schoenberg also cast himself in a quasi-political role, speaking of the "emancipation of the dissonance," as if his chords were peoples who had been enslaved for centuries. Alternatively, he imagined himself as a scientist engaged in objective work: "We shall have no rest, as long as we have not solved the problems that are contained in tones." In later years, he compared himself to transatlantic fliers and explorers of the North Pole.

The argument made a certain amount of sense. Levels of dissonance in music had been steadily rising since the last years of the nineteenth century, when Liszt wrote his keyless bagatelle and Satie wrote down the six-note Rosicrucian chords of *Le Fils des étoiles*. Strauss, of course, indulged discord in *Salome*. Max Reger, a composer versed in the contrapuntal science of Bach, caused Schoenberg-like scandals in 1904 with music that meandered close to the atonal. In Russia, the composer-pianist Alexander Scriabin, who was under the influence of Theosophist spiritualism, devised a harmonic language that vibrated around a "mystic chord" of six notes; his unfinished magnum opus *Mysterium*, slated for a premiere at the foot of the Himalayas, was to have brought about nothing less than the annihilation of the universe, whence men and women would reemerge as astral souls, relieved of sexual difference and other bodily limitations.

In Italy, where the Futurists were promoting an art of speed, struggle, aggression, and destruction, Luigi Russolo issued a manifesto for a "MUSIC OF NOISE" and began to construct noise-instruments with which to produce the roaring, whistling, whispering, screeching, banging, and groaning sounds that he had predicted in his pamphlet. In the United States, Charles Ives, a young New England composer under the influence of Transcendentalism, began writing music in several keys at once or none at all. And Busoni, in his *Sketch of a New Aesthetic of Music* of 1907, theorized all manner of extra-tonal experiments, and realized a few of them in his own works.

The teleological historian might describe all this activity as the collective movement of a vanguard, one that was bent on sweeping aside the established order. Yet each of these composers was following his or her own course (to take Scriabin's projected gender ambiguity into account), and in each case the destination was unique. Out of all of them, only Schoenberg really adopted atonality. What set him apart was that he not only introduced new chords but eliminated, for the time being, the old ones. "You are proposing a new value in place of an earlier one, instead of adding the new one to the old," Busoni observed in a letter of 1909.

Wagner, Strauss, and Mahler all counterbalanced their novel sonorities with massive statements of common chords; dissonance and consonance existed in mutually reinforcing tension. Debussy, likewise, populated his foggy harmonic terrain with quaint melodic characters. Scriabin maintained a feeling of tonal centricity even in the most harmonically far-out stretches of his later piano sonatas. Schoenberg was the one who insisted that there was no going back. Indeed, he began to say tonality was dead—or, as Webern later put it, "We broke its neck."

The first report of the death of tonality came in the pages of *Harmonielehre*, or *Theory of Harmony*, which Schoenberg published in 1911, with a dedication to the "hallowed memory of Gustav Mahler." From the start the author makes clear his detestation of the prevailing musical, cultural, and social order. "Our age seeks many things," he writes in the preface. "What it has found, however, is above all: *comfort* . . . The thinker, who keeps on searching, does the opposite. He shows that there are problems and that they are unsolved. As does Strindberg: 'Life makes everything ugly.' Or Maeterlinck: 'Three quarters of our brothers [are] condemned to misery.' Or Weininger and all others who have thought earnestly." A musical morality is introduced: the easy charm of the familiar on the one side, the hard truth of the new on the other.

Harmonielehre turns out to be an autopsy of a system that has ceased to function. In the time of the Viennese masters, Schoenberg says, tonality had had a logical and ethical basis. But by the beginning of the twentieth century it had become diffuse, unsystematic, incoherent—in a word, diseased. To dramatize this supposed decline, the composer augments his discourse with the vocabulary of social Darwinism and racial theory. It was then fashionable to believe that certain societies and races had corrupted themselves by mixing with others. Wagner, in his later writings, made the argument explicitly racial and sexual, saying that the Aryan race was destroying itself by crossbreeding with Jews and other foreign bodies. Weininger made the same claim in *Sex and Character*.

Schoenberg applied the concept of degeneration to music. He introduced a theme that would reappear often as the century went on—the idea that some musical languages were healthy while others were degenerate, that true composers required a pure place in a polluted world, that only by assuming a militant asceticism could they withstand the almost sexual allure of dubious chords.

In the nineteenth century, Schoenberg says, tonality had fallen prey to "inbreeding and incest." Transitional or "vagrant" chords such as the diminished seventh—a harmonically ambiguous four-note entity that can resolve in several different directions—were the sick offspring of incestuous relationships. They were "sentimental," "philistine," "cosmopolitan," "effeminate," "hermaphroditic"; they had grown up to be "spies," "turncoats," "agitators." Catastrophe was inevitable. "[T]he end of the system is brought about with such inescapable cruelty by its own functions . . . [T]he juices that serve life, serve also death." And: "Every living thing has within it that which changes, develops, and destroys it. Life and death are both equally present in the embryo." Weininger wrote in similar terms in *Sex and Character*: "All that is born of woman must die. Reproduction, birth, and death are inextricably linked . . . The act of coitus, considered not only psychologically but also ethically and biologically, is akin to murder." Moreover, Schoenberg's description of those rootless chords—"homeless phenomena, unbelievably adaptable . . . They flourish in every climate"—actually resembles Weininger's description of the effeminate, cosmopolitan Jew, who "adapts himself . . . to every circumstance and every race; like the parasite, he becomes another in every host, and takes on such an entirely different appearance that one believes him to be a new creature, although he always remains the same. He assimilates himself to everything."

The weird undercurrent of racial pseudoscience in *Harmonielehre* raises the question of Schoenberg's Jewish identity. He was born in Leopoldstadt, a section of Vienna that was heavily populated by former members of the eastern shtetl communities, many of whom had fled the pogroms. Like cultivated Austrian Jews such as Mahler, Kraus, and Wittgenstein, Schoenberg might have felt the need to distance himself from the stereotype of the ghetto Jew; perhaps this explains his conversion to Lutheranism in 1898, which, unlike Mahler's conversion to Catholicism the previous year, was not motivated by the offer of an official post. Later, as anti-Semitism became ever more unavoidable in Austro-German life, Schoenberg's sense of his identity underwent a dramatic change. By 1933, when he went into exile, he had returned to his faith, and remained intensely if eccentrically devoted to it thereafter.

In a way, Schoenberg's journey resembles that of Theodor Herzl, the progenitor of political Zionism, whose early attacks on self-satisfied assimilated urban Jews could be mistaken for anti-Semitic diatribes. The scholar Alexander Ringer has argued that Schoenberg's atonality may have been an oblique affirmation of his Jewishness. In this reading, it is a kind of musical Zion, a promised land in whose dusty desert climate the Jewish composer could escape the ill-concealed hatred of bourgeois Europe.

Schoenberg would prove uncannily alert to the murderousness of Nazi anti-Semitism. In 1934, he predicted that Hitler was planning "no more and no less than the *extermination* of all Jews!" Such thoughts were presumably not on his mind circa 1907 and 1908, yet to be Jewish in Vienna was to live under a vague but growing threat. Anti-Semitism was shifting from a religious to a racial basis, meaning that a conversion to Catholicism or Protestantism no longer sufficed to solve one's Jewish problem. Rights and freedoms were being picked off one by one. Jews were expelled from student societies, boycotts instituted. There were beatings in the streets. Rabble-rousers spouted messages of hate. Hitler himself was somewhere in the background, trying to make his way as an artist, building a cathedral of resentment in his mind. As the historian Steven Beller writes, Jews were "at the center of culture but the edge of society." Mahler ruled musical Vienna; at the same time, Jewish men never felt safe walking the streets at night.

All told, a Freudian host of urges, emotions, and ideas circled Schoenberg as he put his fateful chords on paper. He endured violent disorder in his private life; he felt ostracized by a museum-like concert culture; he experienced the alienation of being a Jew in Vienna; he sensed a historical tendency from consonance to dissonance; he felt disgust for a tonal system grown sickly. But the very multiplicity of possible explanations points up something that cannot be explained. There was no "necessity" driving atonality; no irreversible current of history made it happen. It was one man's leap into the unknown. It became a movement when two equally gifted composers jumped in behind him.

Disciples

"This book I have learned from my pupils," Schoenberg wrote at the top of the first page of *Harmonielehre*. With Webern and Berg he was able to form a common front, which eventually became known as the Second Viennese School—the first having supposedly consisted of Haydn, Mozart, and Beethoven. The notion of a "Viennese school," which another pupil, Egon Wellesz, put into circulation in 1912, had the effect of lending Schoenberg an air of historical prestige, not to mention guru-like status. But Berg and Webern quickly made clear their independence, even as they remained in awe of their teacher. Schoenberg confessed in his diary in 1912 that he was sometimes frightened by his disciples' intensity, by their urge to rival and surpass his own most daring feats, by their tendency to write music "raised to the tenth power." The metapor was apt: the modernist strain in twentieth-century music, as it branched out from Schoenberg, would complicate itself exponentially.

Webern was reserved, cerebral, monkish in his habits. The scion of an old Austrian noble family, he earned his doctorate at the Musicological Institute of the University of Vienna, writing a dissertation on the Renaissance polyphonic music of Heinrich Isaac. In his early works he drew variously on Wagner, Strauss, Mahler, and Debussy; the 1904 tone poem *Im Sommerwind* is a not exactly kitsch-free affair of lustrous orchestration, post-Wagnerian harmonies, and fragrant whole-tone chords. After entering Schoenberg's orbit, Webern enthusiastically changed course and joined in the search for new chords and timbres, and, it would seem, he sometimes moved ahead of his teacher in the expedition to the atonal pole. Webern later recalled that as early as 1906 he wrote a sonata movement that "reached the farthest limits of tonality."

In the summer of 1909, while Schoenberg was composing his Five Pieces for Orchestra and *Erwartung*, Webern wrote his own orchestral cycle, the Six Pieces, Opus 6. It is an incomparably disturbing work in which the rawness of atonality is refracted through the utmost orchestral finesse. Webern's pieces, no less than Schoenberg's, are marked by personal experience—here, lingering anguish over the death of the composer's mother, in 1906. We hear successive stages of grief: presentiment of disaster, the shock of the news (screaming, trilling flocks of trumpet and horns), impressions of the Carinthian countryside near where Amalie Webern was laid to rest, final memories of her smile.

In the middle of the sequence is a funeral procession, which begins in ominous quiet, with a rumble of drums, gong, and bells. Various groups of instruments, trombones predominating, groan chords of inert, imploded character. An E-flat clarinet plays a high, wailing, circling melody. An alto flute responds in low, throaty tones. Muted horn and trumpet offer more lyric fragments, over subterranean chords. Then the trombones rise to a shout, and the winds and the brass fall in line behind them. The piece is crowned with a crushing sequence of nine- and ten-note chords, after which the percussion begins its own crescendo and builds to a pitch-liquidating roar. The age of noise has begun.

The Six Pieces was arguably the supreme atonal work. After writing it, Webern forswore grand gestures and found his calling as a miniaturist. When he heard *Pelléas et Mélisande* in 1908, he was amazed at Debussy's ability to make so much from so few notes, and sought the same economy in his own music. The Five Pieces for Orchestra, Opus 10, show Webern's art of compression at its most extreme: most of the movements last less than a minute, and the fourth piece contains fewer than fifty notes. A smattering of *dolce* tones on mandolin; soft repeated tones on clarinet; a couple of high muted cries from the brass; more plucks and plinks of harp, celesta, and mandolin again; and, to conclude, a tiny song on solo violin, "like a breath"—this music is practically Japanese, like brushstrokes on white paper. By clearing away all expressionistic clutter, Webern actually succeeded in making his teacher's language easier to assimilate. He distributed his material in clear, linear patterns, rather than piling it up in vertical masses. The listener can absorb each unusual sonority before the next arrives.

Intellectuals of fin-de-siècle Vienna were much concerned with the limits of language, with the need for a kind of communicative silence. "Whereof one cannot speak, thereof one must be silent," Wittgenstein wrote in his *Tractatus Logico-Philosophicus*, marking a boundary between rational discourse and the world of the soul. Hermann Broch ended his novel *The Death of Virgil* with the phrase "the word beyond speech." The impulse to go to the brink of nothingness is central to Webern's aesthetic; if the listener is paying insufficient attention, the shorter movements of his works may pass unnoticed. The joke went around that Webern had introduced the marking *pensato*: Don't play the note, only think it.

Webern's works hang in a limbo between the noise of life and the stillness of death. The ease with which the one melts into the other is one major philosophical insight that arises from them. The crescendo in the funeral march in Opus 6 is among the loudest musical phenomena in history, but even louder is the ensuing silence, which smacks the ears like thunder.

• • •

Alban Berg was a debonair, handsome man, self-effacing and ironic in his attitude to the world. There was great empathy in his large, sad eyes; he was physically fragile, a chronic sufferer of severe bronchial asthma, and he identified strongly with all for whom life did not come easily. "Such a dear person," one friend said after his death—not a common eulogy at the funerals of geniuses. Yet, as the novelist and essayist Elias Canetti said, "[Berg] wasn't lacking in self-esteem. He knew very well who he was."

Blessed with a fine-tuned sense of the absurd, Berg stayed somewhat aloof from the utopian fantasies of the Schoenberg circle. On one occasion Berg had trouble keeping a straight face when his comrade-in-arms Webern, at a rehearsal of his Quartet for violin, clarinet, tenor saxophone, and piano, Opus 22, told the saxophonist to play a descending major seventh with "sex appeal." Berg feigned an asthma attack, fled the room, and burst into hysterical laughter.

Berg liked to think that he was descended from the aristocracy, cultivating the air of a dilapidated baronet who knows how far down in the world he has come. He was, in fact, a thoroughbred bourgeois, whose father, Conrad Berg, worked in an exporting firm and later went into business selling Catholic devotional items. (One of the family's regular customers was Anton Bruckner, who brought in a favorite crucifix for repairs.) Conrad Berg died suddenly in 1900, leaving the family in financial difficulties. Johanna Berg, the widow, considered sending the then fifteen-year-old Alban to New York, so that he could work alongside his brother Hermann at the toy distributor George Borgfeldt & Co., with which their father had been associated. At the last minute, an aunt stepped in to subsidize Alban's studies. Hermann, incidentally, later scored a sales coup by marketing the first teddy bears, three thousand of which he purchased at the 1903 Leipzig Toy Fair.

Berg had an unpromising adolescence. He fathered an illegitimate child with a family servant, suffered academic failures, and, in the wake of another love affair, attempted suicide. Although he had been writing songs in Romantic and impressionist styles since the age of fifteen, his talent was hardly prodigious.

Schoenberg molded Berg into a substantial musical force, but there was a price to be paid for the transformation. For much of his youth Berg was essentially subjugated to Schoenberg's will, sometimes functioning as little more than a valet. His tasks in the year 1911 included packing up a van when his teacher moved to Berlin, looking after bank accounts, engaging in fund-raising schemes, addressing legal problems, and proofreading and indexing *Harmonielehre*. After one barrage of demands, Schoenberg had the temerity to ask, "Are you composing anything?!?!" He dismissed as worthless several of Berg's finest early works. The student never ceased his adoration, although a proud determination grew in him, together with hidden resentments.

Like Schoenberg and Webern, Berg was incubated in the golden age of Mahler and Strauss. So ardent was his Mahler worship that he once trespassed on the Master's dressing room to steal a baton. Opulent, upward- and downward-lunging melodies of the Mahlerian variety appear in Berg's scores from beginning to end. Strauss's *Salome* made him swoon; he heard the opera in Graz, of course, and six more times in 1907, when the Breslau Opera brought its production to Vienna. "How I would like to sing to you *Salome* which I know so well," Berg wrote to an American friend. His Altenberg songs, which incited the climactic outbreak of violence at the "scandal concert" of 1913, are structured around a mildly dissonant collection of five notes—C-sharp, E, G-natural, G-sharp, B-flat—which appears throughout Strauss's opera and sounds as a single chord at the beginning of Salome's final monologue. Luxuriating in this ambiguous sonority, the young composer seems reluctant to give up the degenerate, inbred language that Schoenberg condemned in *Harmonielehre*. Berg would soon be labeled the approachable Romantic of the Schoenberg school, the one who, as the conductor Michael Tilson Thomas says, makes a turn toward the audience.

Yet it wasn't Berg's bent for nostalgia that worried Schoenberg. Instead, he chastised his pupil for displaying a "rather too obvious desire to use new means"—perhaps thinking of the twelve-note chord in the Altenberg songs. There were always two sides to Berg; he pined for sweet, kitschy sounds, but he also had a mathematical fetish, a love of complexity for complexity's sake.

Berg's contrary tendencies collided in the Three Pieces for Orchestra, which were written in 1914, five years after Schoenberg's Five Pieces and Webern's Six. They are fully symphonic in conception, Schoenbergian in content but Mahlerian in form. The final movement is a phantasmagoric

March for full orchestra, replete with thudding drumbeats and craggy brass fanfares. Notes blacken the page; instruments become an angry mob, spilling from the sidewalks into the streets. Right at the end comes a brief mirage of peace: phrases curl upward in the orchestra like wisps of cloud, and a solo violin plays a keening phrase. All the while, the harp and the celesta strike monotonous notes, which sound like the ticking of a bomb. It explodes in the last measures, with a booming trombone-and-tuba tone, a flailing, upward-spiraling movement of the brass, and a final percussive hammerblow in the bass.

The date of the completion of the March—Sunday, August 23, 1914—happens to be an infamous one in military history. The First World War had commenced at the beginning of the month; a million German troops had marched through Belgium and broached the French border. On the twenty-third, French armies began a humiliating withdrawal to the Marne, and the British Expeditionary Force fell back after the Battle of Mons. Hundreds of thousands were already dead. German soldiers were carrying out reprisals against civilians who resisted. That same Sunday night, German troops gathered the citizens of the town of Dinant and began firing into their midst, killing almost seven hundred people, including a three-week-old baby. Two days later the medieval library of Louvain was set on fire. In a few short weeks, Germany had done irreparable damage to its reputation as a cradle of modern civilization.

Wozzeck

"War!" Thomas Mann wrote in November 1914. "We felt purified, liberated, we felt an enormous hope." Many artists were exhilarated when the Great War began; it was as if their gaudiest fantasies of violence and destruction had come to life.

Schoenberg fell into the grip of what he would later call his "war psychosis," drawing comparisons between the German army's assault on decadent France and his own assault on decadent bourgeois values. In a letter to Alma Mahler dated August 1914, Schoenberg waxed militant in his zeal for the German cause, denouncing in the same breath the music of Bizet, Stravinsky, and Ravel. "Now comes the reckoning!" Schoenberg thundered. "Now we will throw these mediocre kitschmongers into slavery, and teach them to venerate the German spirit and to worship the German God." For part of the war he kept a diary of the weather, in the belief that certain cloud formations presaged German victory or defeat.

Berg, too, succumbed to the hysteria, at least at first. After finishing the March of the Three Pieces, he wrote to his teacher that it was "very shameful to be merely an onlooker at these great events."

The massacre at Dinant, the burning of Louvain, and other atrocities of August and September 1914 were not simply mishaps of the fog of war. They fulfilled the German General Staff's program of destroying the "total material and intellectual resources of the enemy." The notion of total war mirrored to an uncomfortable degree the apocalyptic mind-set of recent Austro-German art.

Not everyone fell victim to "war psychosis." Richard Strauss, for one, refused to join ninety-three other German intellectuals in signing a manifesto that denied German wrongdoing at Louvain. In public Strauss stated that as an artist he wished to avoid political entanglements, but in private he sounded a distinctly nonpatriotic tone. "It is sickening," he wrote a few months later to Hofmannsthal, "to read in the papers of the regeneration of German art . . . to read how the youth of Germany is to emerge cleansed and purified from this 'glorious' war, when in fact one must be thankful if the poor blighters are at least cleansed of their lice and bed-bugs and cured of their infections and once more weaned from murder!" The statement reads like a riposte to Mann's panegyric to violence. The next time Germany went to war, the two men would switch roles; Strauss would be the figurehead, Mann the dissident.

There are comical pictures of the Second Viennese School in the uniforms of the Austrian army. Schoenberg, plump and balding, looks like a village schoolmaster who has volunteered out of solemn duty. Webern, dwarfed by his helmet, is the picture of the student-soldier. Berg, leaning back in a chair with a half smile on his face and one leg crossed over the other, resembles an actor in a silent movie, perhaps a tale of a young soldier in love with an enemy maiden. None promises to pose much of a threat to the kitschmongers on the other side. Indeed, physical limitations prevented them from seeing action at the front. Schoenberg ended up playing in a military orchestra. Webern, extremely nearsighted, was attached to a reserve battalion of the Carinthian Mountain Troops. And Berg, after spending a month at a training camp in the fall of 1915, suffered a physical breakdown and had to be hospitalized. For the remainder of the fighting, he was confined to a desk job, where a beastly superior made his life miserable.

Largely unable to compose, Berg filled his notebook with instructions for the proper conduct of trench warfare and bureaucratic military parlance. But, as the scholar Patricia Hall notes, the same book is dotted with sketches for a work that would put the war in a different light: an opera based on Georg Büchner's play *Woyzeck*.

Büchner was a strikingly original literary talent who died in 1837 at the age of twenty-three. *Woyzeck*—Berg changed the *y* to *z* to make it easier to pronounce—was based on the true story of one Johann Christian Woyzeck, a soldier turned barber who had murdered his mistress in Leipzig in 1821. Despite Woyzeck's obvious signs of mental instability, the distinguished *Hofrat* Dr. Clarus—Felix Mendelssohn's doctor—declared him competent to stand trial. Büchner used transcripts of Woyzeck's psychological examinations as source material for the play; no writer had ever given such a matter-of-fact report on a murderer's mind. In Büchner's telling, Woyzeck is still a soldier when the action begins, and military discipline speeds his mental deterioration. He is subject to the whims of a fussy, pedantic captain; falls prey to a sadistically experimenting doctor, who puts him on an all-pea diet, with mutton to follow; and is demoralized by the callousness of his fellow soldiers, the mockery of tradespeople, and the diseased atmosphere of his ordinary-seeming town. After a time, he can no longer tell what is real and what is fantasy.

When Berg first saw Büchner's play, in May 1914, he immediately muttered aloud that someone had to make an opera out of it. His military experiences hardened his resolve. "There is a bit of me in [Wozzeck's] character," he wrote to his wife four years later, "since I have been spending these war years just as dependent on people I hate, have been in chains, sick, captive, resigned, in fact humiliated." All too well he knew real-life versions of the Doctor and the Captain (as Büchner named them); the sketchbook hints that a certain Dr. Wernisch furnished inspiration.

Berg set Büchner's play "raw," cutting and arranging the text himself rather than handing it off to a librettist. This was Debussy's procedure with *Pelléas*, and also Strauss's with *Salome*, and, in fact, Berg used both those operas as structural models. The project moved ahead in spite of Schoenberg, who pronounced the subject matter inappropriate. Berg went so far as to conceal his labors from his former teacher, at one point leading him to believe that he was working on an ostensibly more pressing task: a biography of Arnold Schoenberg.

Freud spoke of the "return of the repressed"; in *Wozzeck*, tonality will not be denied. When the curtain goes up, Wozzeck is administering a morning shave to his captain. The music scrapes like a razor: one abrasive five-note string chord slides down to another, comprising ten notes in all. But the top three notes in the first chord spell D minor; the second chord contains the notes of A-flat minor; the remaining four notes in the opening group form a diminished seventh. (Think of those paintings by Turner and Monet in which familiar forms are buried under layers of impasto paint.) The latent tonalities emerge more clearly in the following scene, where Wozzeck collects kindling with a comrade and hallucinates a world on fire. They come to the surface in the third scene, with the entrance of Marie, Wozzeck's common-law wife.

Marie is something more than a fin-de-siècle cartoon of instinctual Woman; although she stereotypically lusts for a muscular Drum Major, she is, on the whole, an independent, fully formed character, one who balances her sexual desires with strong religious feeling and dotes lovingly on her child. Marie's lullaby to her son is unabashedly Romantic, richly if eccentrically tonal. It begins with a familiar sound—the five-note *Salome* chord that Berg had already quoted in his Altenberg songs. Yet the music is also intimately related to Wozzeck's more dissonant gamut of sounds. The main motifs for husband and wife both contain the notes of a theme that is first heard in the opening scene, when Wozzeck sings of his desperate situation—"*Wir arme Leut*," or "We poor people." This signifies that both Wozzeck and Marie are victims of a larger injustice.

If there is one malign character in *Wozzeck*, it is the doctor, who does everything in his power to accelerate his patient's decline, in the belief that this "beautiful *aberratio mentalis partialis*" will guarantee his immortality. The Doctor dominates the fourth scene of Act I, which takes the form of a Passacaglia, or variations over a ground bass. The theme is a row of twelve notes, which serves to represent the character's ruthless rationality, his urge to reduce humans to data. The Doctor even sings a little aria to his intellect at the end: "Oh my theory! Oh my fame!" At one point there is a quotation from Schoenberg's Five Pieces for Orchestra. One wonders if the Doctor has a little Schoenberg in him. Berg loved to encode messages in his scores, and it may be no accident that when the doctor enters, the bass line moves from A to E-flat, or, in German lettering, A Es—Schoenberg's initials. Wozzeck answers with the notes B-flat and A, which in German are spelled B A—Berg, Alban. (When Berg wrote this music, Schoenberg had not yet announced his twelve-tone method, which is described in Chapter 6.)

By the last scene of Act I, when the brutish Drum Major forces himself on Marie to the tune of dissonated C-major chords and the strains of "We poor people," the method of the opera is clear. Strongly dissonant writing suggests the working of abstractions: the cruelty of authority, the relentlessness of fate, the power of economic oppression. Tonal elements represent basic emotions—a mother's love for her child, a soldier's lust for flesh, Wozzeck's jealous rage. The scheme contradicts Schoenberg's utopian notion that the new language could replace the old. Instead, Berg returns to the method of Mahler and Strauss, for whom the conflict of consonance and dissonance was the forge of the most intense expression. Consonance is all the sweeter in the moment before its annihilation. Dissonance is all the more frightening in contrast to what it destroys. Beauty and terror skirmish, fighting for Wozzeck's hollow soul.

Berg took pride in the fact that each scene in *Wozzeck* is based on a historical form: Suite, Passacaglia, Rondo, and so on. Act II is a five-movement symphony, and in the opening Sonata Allegro, Wozzeck's paranoia is developed like a classical theme. Once a level of maximum dissonance has been reached, there comes a sudden respite in the form of a C-major chord: this marks the moment that Wozzeck hands over to Marie the money he has earned for suffering through the sadistic games of the Captain and the Doctor. It is the last display of uncomplicated tenderness between the two.

In the second movement (Invention and Fugue on Three Themes), the Captain and the Doctor amuse themselves again by tormenting their charge, implanting in him the fatal idea that Marie has slept with the

Drum Major. Wozzeck confronts his wife in the slow Largo movement, accompanied by the same fifteen instruments that Schoenberg used in his First Chamber Symphony (Schoenberg's marital crisis of 1908 might be a subtext). The Scherzo of the "symphony" is set in an inn full of drunken revelers; a stage band plays a Mahlerian *Ländler* waltz, dissonantly distorted. Wozzeck's humiliation reaches its height in the Rondo marziale, the last movement, when he tries unsuccessfully to find rest in a barracks full of atonally snoring soldiers. The Drum Major barges in, bragging of his conquest of Marie. Wozzeck whistles at him derisively and is beaten to a pulp.

At the beginning of Act III, Marie reads aloud from the Bible to her child, her mind swaying back and forth between the calm glow of Christian verities and the virus-like action of fear and guilt. A heart-stoppingly beautiful horn theme—an extract from a piano piece that Berg had written during his studies with Schoenberg—is almost immediately scrubbed out by twelve-note patterns and other "difficult" features. When Wozzeck enters, the note B begins droning in various sections of the orchestra, sometimes high and sometimes low. The couple walks by a pond. The moon rises, and each of them comments on the apparition. "How the moon rises red," Marie says. "Like a bloody iron," Wozzeck adds. Büchner's writing here looks ahead to the Symbolist poetry of Wilde's *Salomé*, and, as if on cue, trumpets, horns, and violas play a transposition of Strauss's *Salome* chord, with its hint of outlaw sexuality on the brink of destruction.

Wozzeck takes out his knife as the timpani pound away at the fatal note. He kills Marie suddenly and unceremoniously, without much commentary from the orchestra. Once he rushes from the scene, though, the orchestra reenacts the death with an incredible succession of sounds. The B returns, humming almost inaudibly on a muted horn. Then instrument after instrument joins in on the same pitch, creating a super-bright beam of tone. As the composer and theorist Robert Cogan has demonstrated, by way of spectographic imaging of sounds, the scoring of this single note produces an exceptionally rich mass of overtones, with a chord of B major at its root. After a climactic dissonant chord and a shuddering death-rhythm on the bass drum, the crescendo begins again, now with a battery of percussion added, so that clean overtones give way to a toneless wash of noise. "Like the murder scene," Cogan writes, "this climactic passage reaches the ultimate in human limits, extending from the threshold of audibility to the threshold of pain."

As if with a rapid cinematic cut, the scene changes to a tavern, where an out-of-tune upright piano is playing a rickety polka, employing the same rhythm that has just been heard on the bass drum. Wozzeck is seated at one of the tables, blood dripping from his hand. The locals stop their wild dancing to accuse him of murder, and he rushes back to the pond to wash away the evidence. As the orchestra plays rippling transpositions of a six-note chord, he sinks beneath the waves. The Captain and the Doctor walk by a moment later, marveling at the uncanny stillness of the scene. It is as if they were studying a canvas at a Secession exhibition.

Now comes the masterstroke. At the end of the next-to-last scene, the orchestra delivers a kind of wordless oration, which, in Berg's own words, is "a confession of the author who now steps outside the dramatic action on the stage . . . an appeal to humanity through its representatives, the audience." There is a palpable break in the musical language, as Berg makes use of a piece that he wrote back in 1908 or 1909—a sketch for a Mahlerian Sonata in D Minor. (The composer associated this music with the singer Helene Nahowski, whom he married in 1911, and he apparently inserted it in the opera at her request.) Dissonance stages a counterstrike: trombones deliver a stentorian "We poor people," twelve woodwinds mass together in a twelve-note chord, and sheets of sound in the percussion replicate the terror of Marie's murder. Finally, the bass instruments pound out a rising fourth, and D minor crashes back in. All this sounds like something more than a lament for two human beings; it may be a tribute to what Thomas Mann called the "worldwide festival of death"—the Great War itself.

The ending is breathtakingly bleak. We see Wozzeck and Marie's child riding his hobbyhorse, oblivious to the fact that his mother is lying dead nearby. Berg, in a lecture on the opera, pointed out that the coda links up with the beginning; likewise, it is all too plausible that this child will grow up to be a replica of his father. A slow fade-out on an oscillating pair of chords points toward a despairing conclusion. As the chords rock back and forth, though, there are passing glimpses of G major, like transitory glimmerings of light.

Compare the ending of Debussy's *Pelléas*, where Mélisande dies within sight of her newborn baby while the serving women fill the room. "It's the poor little thing's turn now," says King Arkel. The onlooker is left to imagine the fate of these orphans of the fin de siècle: perhaps they will perpetuate the cycle of misery, breeding violence from violence, or perhaps they will escape to some great open city, where the children of unhappy families start anew.

(((3)))

DANCE OF THE EARTH

The *Rite*, the Folk, *le Jazz*

May 29, 1913, was an unusually hot day for Paris in the spring: the temperature reached eighty-five degrees. By late afternoon a crowd had gathered in front of the Théâtre des Champs-Élysées, on the avenue Montaigne, where Serge Diaghilev's Ballets Russes was holding its spring gala. "There, for the expert eye, were all the makings of a scandal," recalled Jean Cocteau, then twenty-three. "A fashionable audience in décolletage, outfitted in pearls, egret headdresses, plumes of ostrich; and, side by side with the tails and feathers, the jackets, headbands, and showy rags of that race of aesthetes who randomly acclaim the new in order to express their hatred of the *loges* . . . a thousand nuances of snobbery, super-snobbery, counter-snobbery . . ." The better-heeled part of the crowd had grown wary of Diaghilev's methods. Disquieting rumors were circulating about the new musical work on the program—*The Rite of Spring*, by the young Russian composer Igor Stravinsky—and also about the matching choreography by Nijinsky. The theater, then brand-new, caused a scandal of its own. With its steel-concrete exterior and amphitheater-like seating plan, it was deemed too severe, too Germanic. One commentator compared it to a zeppelin moored in the middle of the street.

Diaghilev, in a press release, promised "a new thrill that will doubtless inspire heated discussion." He did not lie. The program began innocuously, with a revival of the Ballets Russes' Chopin fantasy *Les Sylphides*. After a pause, the theater darkened again, and high, falsetto-like bassoon notes floated out of the orchestra. Strands of melody intertwined like vegetation bursting out of the earth—"a sacred terror in the noonday sun," Stravinsky called it, in a description that had been published that morning. The audience listened to the opening section of the *Rite* in relative silence, although the increasing density and dissonance of the music caused mutterings, titters, whistles, and shouts. Then, at the beginning of the second section, a dance for adolescents titled "The Augurs of Spring," a quadruple shock arrived, in the form of harmony, rhythm, image, and movement. At the outset of the section, the strings and horns play a crunching discord, consisting of an F-flat-major triad and an E-flat dominant seventh superimposed. They are one semitone apart (F-flat being the same as E-natural), and they clash at every node. A steady pulse propels the chord, but accents land every which way, on and off the beat:

> one two three four five six seven eight
> one *two* three *four* five six seven eight
> one *two* three four *five* six seven eight
> *one* two three four five *six* seven eight

Even Diaghilev quivered a little when he first heard the music. "Will it last a very long time this way?" he asked. Stravinsky replied, "Till the end, my dear." The chord repeats some two hundred times. Meanwhile, Nijinsky's choreography discarded classical gestures in favor of near-anarchy. As the ballet historian Lynn Garafola recounts, "The dancers trembled, shook, shivered, stamped; jumped crudely and ferociously, circled the stage in wild khorovods." Behind the dancers were pagan landscapes painted by Nicholas Roerich—hills and trees of weirdly bright color, shapes from a dream.

Howls of discontent went up from the boxes, where the wealthiest onlookers sat. Immediately, the aesthetes in the balconies and the standing room howled back. There were overtones of class warfare in the proceedings. The combative composer Florent Schmitt was heard to yell either "Shut up, bitches of the *seizième*!" or "Down with the whores of the *seizième*!"—a provocation of the grandes dames of the sixteenth arrondissement. The literary hostess Jeanne Mühlfeld, not to be outmaneuvered, exploded into contemptuous laughter. Little more of the score was heard after that. "One literally could not, throughout the whole performance, hear the sound of music," Gertrude Stein recalled, no doubt overstating for effect. "Our attention was constantly distracted by a man in the box next to us flourishing his cane, and finally in a violent altercation with an enthusiast in the box next to him, his cane came down and smashed the opera hat the other had just put on in defiance. It was all incredibly fierce."

The scene superficially resembled Schoenberg's "scandal concert," which shook up Vienna in March of the same year. But the bedlam on the avenue Montaigne was a typical Parisian affair, of a kind that took place once or twice a year; Nijinsky's orgasmic *Prelude to "The Afternoon of a Faun"* had caused similar trouble the previous season. Soon enough, Parisian listeners realized that the language of the *Rite* was not so unfamiliar; it teemed with plainspoken folk-song melodies, common chords in sparring layers, syncopations of irresistible potency. In a matter of days, confusion turned into pleasure, boos into bravos. Even at the first performance, Stravinsky, Nijinsky, and the dancers had to bow four or five times for the benefit of the applauding faction. Subsequent performances were packed, and at each one the opposition dwindled. At the second, there was noise only during the latter part of the ballet; at the third, "vigorous applause" and little protest. At a concert performance of the *Rite* one year later, "unprecedented exaltation" and a "fever of adoration" swept over the crowd, and admirers mobbed Stravinsky in the street afterward, in a riot of delight.

The *Rite*, whose first part ends with a stampede for full orchestra titled "Dance of the Earth," prophesied a new type of popular art—low-down yet sophisticated, smartly savage, style and muscle intertwined. It epitomized the "second avant-garde" in classical composition, the post-Debussy strain that sought to drag the art out of Faustian "novel spheres" and into the physical world. For much of the nineteenth century, music had been a theater of the mind; now composers would create a music of the body. Melodies would follow the patterns of speech; rhythms would match the energy of dance; musical forms would be more concise and clear; sonorities would have the hardness of life as it is really lived.

A phalanx of European composers—Stravinsky in Russia, Béla Bartók in Hungary, Leoš Janáček in what would become the Czech Republic, Maurice Ravel in France, and Manuel de Falla in Spain, to name some of the principals—devoted themselves to folk song and other musical remnants of a pre-urban life, trying to cast off the refinements of the city dweller. "Our slender bodies cannot hide in clothing," goes the text of Bartók's *Cantata profana*, a fable of savage boys who turn into stags. "We must drink our fill not from your silver goblets but from cool mountain springs."

Above all, composers from the Romance and Slavonic nations—France, Spain, Italy, Russia, and the countries of Eastern Europe—strained to cast off the German influence. For a hundred years or more, masters from Austria and Germany had been marching music into remote regions of harmony and form. Their progress ran parallel to Germany's gestation as a nation-state and its rise as a world power. The Franco-Prussian War of 1870–71 sounded the alarm among other European nations that the new German empire intended to be more than a major player on the international stage—that it had designs of supremacy. So Debussy and Satie began to seek a way out of the hulking fortresses of Beethovenian symphonism and Wagnerian opera.

But the real break came with the First World War. Even before it was over, Satie and various young Parisians renounced fin-de-siècle solemnity and appropriated music-hall tunes, ragtime, and jazz; they also partook of the noisemaking spirit of Dada, which had enlivened Zurich during the war. Their earthiness was urban, not rural—frivolity with a militant edge. Later, in the twenties, Paris-centered composers, Stravinsky included, turned toward pre-Romantic forms; the past served as another kind of folklore. Whether the model was Transylvanian folk melody, hot jazz, or the arias of Pergolesi, Teutonism was the common enemy. Music became war carried on by other means.

In Search of the Real: Janáček, Bartók, Ravel

Van Gogh, in his garden at Arles, was haunted by the idea that the conventions of painting prevented him from seizing the reality before him. He had tried abstraction, he wrote to Émile Bernard, but had run up against a wall. Now he was fighting to put the brute facts of nature on canvas, to get the olive trees right, the colors of the soil and the sky. "The great thing," he declared, "is to gather new vigor in reality, without any preconceived plan or Parisian prejudice." This was the essence of naturalism in late-nineteenth- and early-twentieth-century art. It surfaced in works as various as Monet's transcendent visions of train stations and bales of hay, Cézanne's hyper-vivid still lifes, and Gauguin's steamy visions of Tahiti. It also animated such late-nineteenth- and early-twentieth-century cultural phenomena as Zola's novels of miners and prostitutes, Maxim Gorky's exacting portraits of peasant life, and Isadora Duncan's free, antiformal dancing. In whatever medium, artists worked to dispel artifice and convey the materiality of things.

What would it mean for music to render life "just as it is," in van Gogh's phrase? Composers had been pondering that question for centuries, and, at various times and in different ways, they had infused their work with the rhythms of everyday life. The Enlightenment philosopher Johann Gottfried von Herder had proposed that composers find inspiration in *Volkslieder*, or folk songs—a phrase he coined. Countless nineteenth-century composers installed folkish themes in symphonic and operatic forms. But they tended to take their tunes from published collections, thereby filtering them through the conventions of musical notation—major and minor scales, regular bar lines, strict rhythm, and the rest. Toward the end of the nineteenth century, scholars in the nascent field of ethnomusicology began to apply more meticulous, quasi-scientific methods, and came to the realization that Western notation was inadequate to the task. Debussy, browsing through the multicultural sounds that were on display at the Paris Universal Exposition of 1889, had noticed how the music fell between the cracks of the Western notational system.

The advent of the recording cylinder meant that researchers no longer needed to rely on paper to preserve the songs. They could make recorded copies of the music and study it until they understood how it worked. The machine changed how people listened to folk music; it made them aware of deep cultural differences. Of course, the machine was itself helping to erase those differences, by spreading American-style pop music as a global lingua franca.

Percy Grainger, the Australian-born maverick pianist-composer, was among the first to apply the phonograph's lessons. In the summer of 1906, Grainger ventured out into small towns in the English countryside with an Edison Bell cylinder, charming the locals with his rugged, unorthodox personality. Back home, he played his recordings over and over, slowing down the playback to catch the details. He paid attention to the notes between the notes—the bending of pitch, the coarsening of timbre, the speeding up and slowing down of pulse. He then tried to replicate that freedom in his compositions. In 1908 he heard a Devon sailor sing the sea shanty "Shallow Brown," and later fashioned from it a symphonic song for soprano, chorus, and a unique chamber orchestra that included guitars, ukuleles, and mandolins. The ensemble creates a fantastic simulacrum of the sea, as pungent as any paragraph in Melville's *Moby-Dick*. String tremolos churn like surf, high woodwinds squawk like gulls, lower instruments hint at terrible creatures in the depths. The voice sails above, bursting outside bar lines to drive the emotion home: "*Shallow Brown, you're going to leave me . . .*" With each performance, John Perring, the man whom Grainger originally recorded with his cylinder, sings his song again, and the orchestra preserves the grain of the voice as a machine could never do.

The best way to absorb a culture is to be from it. Three great "realists" in early-twentieth-century music— Janáček, Bartók, and Ravel—were born in villages or outlying towns in their respective homelands: Hukvaldy in Moravia, Nagyszentmiklós in Hungary, and Ciboure in the French Basque country. Although they were trained in the cities, and remained city dwellers for most of their lives, these composers never shook the feeling that they had come from somewhere else.

Janáček's father served as *kantor*—schoolmaster and music master—of the remote hamlet of Hukvaldy. As Mirka Zemanová writes in her Janáček biography, he was hardly better off than the peasants he taught; the family lived in one room of the damp, rundown schoolhouse. At the age of eleven, Leoš received a scholarship to attend choir school in Brno, and his parents welcomed the award because they could not afford to feed all their children. He went on to study in Prague, Leipzig, and Vienna, compensating for his humble origins with a fierce work ethic. In the

1880s he founded the Brno organ school, which later became the Brno Conservatory, and began to enjoy local success as a composer in a Romantic-nationalist vein.

Then, on a trip home in 1885, Janáček experienced the street music of his village with fresh ears. In a later essay he recalled: "Flashing movements, the faces sticky with sweat; screams, whooping, the fury of fiddlers' music: it was like a picture glued on to a limpid grey background." Like van Gogh, he would paint the peasants as they were, not in their Sunday best.

When Janáček began collecting Czech, Moravian, and Slovakian folk songs, he wasn't listening for raw material that could be "ennobled" in classical forms. Instead, he wanted to ennoble himself. Melody, he decided, should fit the pitches and rhythms of ordinary speech, sometimes literally. Janáček did research in cafés and other public places, transcribing on music paper the conversations he heard around him. For example, when a student says "*Dobrý večer*," or "Good evening," to his professor, he employs a falling pattern, a high note followed by three at a lower pitch. When the same student utters the same greeting to a pretty servant girl, the last note is slightly higher than the others, implying coy familiarity. Such minute differences, Janáček thought, could engender a new operatic naturalism; they could show an "entire being in a photographic instant."

The oldest of the chief innovators of early-twentieth-century music, Janáček was almost fifty when he finished his first masterpiece, the opera *Jenůfa*, in 1903. Like *Pelléas* and *Salome*, written in the same period, *Jenůfa* is a direct setting of a prose text. The melodies not only imitate the rise and fall of conversational speech but also illustrate the characteristics of each personality in the drama. For example, there is a marked musical distinction between Jenůfa, a village girl of pure and somewhat foolish innocence who has a baby out of wedlock with the local rake, and the Kostelnička (sextoness), her devout stepmother, who eventually murders the baby in an effort to preserve the family reputation. In the opening scene of Act II, the Kostelnička sings in abrupt, acerbic phrases, sometimes leaping over large intervals and sometimes jabbing away at a single note. Jenůfa's melodies, by contrast, follow more easygoing, ingratiating contours. Behind the individual characterizations are pinwheeling patterns that mimic the turning of the local mill wheel, the meticulous operation of social codes, or the grinding of fate. The harmonies often have a disconcerting brightness, all flashing treble and rumbling bass. The coexistence of expressive freedom and notated rigidity in the playing suggests rural life in all its complexity.

Jenůfa seems destined to end in tragedy. The heroine's baby is found beneath the ice of the local river; the villagers advance on her with vengeful intent. Then the Kostelnička confesses that she did the deed, and they redirect their rage. Jenůfa is left alone with her cousin Laca, who has loved her silently while she has pursued the good-for-nothing Števa. Time stops for a luxurious instant: the orchestra wallows in elemental C major. Then, over pulsing, heavy-breathing chords, violins and soprano begin to sing a new melody in the vicinity of B-flat—a sustained note followed by a quickly shaking figure, which moves like a bird in flight, gliding, beating its wings, dipping down, and soaring again. This is Jenůfa's loving resignation as she gives Laca permission to walk away from the ugliness surrounding her. Another theme surfaces, this one coursing down the octave. It is Laca answering: "I would bear far more than that for you. What does the world matter, when we have each other?" The two sing each other's melodies in turn, the melodies merge, and the opera ends in a tonal sunburst.

Janáček, like Mahler, talked about listening to the chords of nature. While working on his cantata *Amarus*, he wrote: "Innumerable notes ring in my ears, in every octave; they have voices like small, faint telegraph bells." These natural sounds are linked to the opera's tough-natured emotional world, the hard-won love of a man and a woman in the wake of a terrible crime. No wonder audiences in Vienna and other European capitals were struck by *Jenůfa* when it finally made its way past Czech borders in the year 1918. Following the devastation of war, Janáček had unleashed the shock of hope.

Bartók's father, like Janáček's, was a teacher who worked with the rural population, running an agricultural school that aimed to introduce modern farming methods to the Hungarian countryside. He died young, and Bartók's mother supported the family by giving piano lessons in towns around Hungary. A shy and sickly child, Béla took refuge in music even before he could speak. By the age of four, apparently, he could play forty folk songs with one finger at the piano.

In 1899, at the age of eighteen, Bartók moved to Budapest to study at the Royal Academy of Music. He made his mark first as a pianist of fierce technique and fine expression; his early compositions emulated Liszt, Brahms, and Strauss, whose *Ein Heldenleben* he transcribed for the piano. But his musical priorities shifted when he read the stories of Maxim Gorky, in which peasants, long scorned or prettified in literature, become flesh-and-blood people. With another gifted young Hungarian composer, Zoltán Kodály, Bartók set about inventing a new brand of folk-based musical realism.

At first, the young Hungarians followed the established formula, collecting folk melodies and concocting handsome accompaniments for them, as if putting them in display cases. Then, after several expeditions into the countryside, Bartók acknowledged the gap between what urban listeners considered folkish—a professional Gypsy band playing a *csárdás* dance, for example—and what peasants were actually singing and playing. He decided that he had to get as far as possible from what he would later call the "destructive urban influence."

In his manipulation of folk material, Bartók went rather further than Janáček, who found authenticity in city and country settings alike. There was a certain fanaticism inherent in Bartók's philosophy; as the scholar Julie Brown observes, his diagnosis of the contaminating influence of cosmopolitan culture was only a step or two away from the noxious racial theorizing that was à la mode in Bayreuth. What saved Bartók from bigotry was his refusal to locate his musical truths in any one place; he heard them equally in Hungary, Slovakia, Romania, Bulgaria, Serbia, Croatia, Turkey, and North Africa. The mark of authenticity was not racial but economic; he paid heed mainly to the people on the social margins, those who had lived the toughest lives.

Bartók's most intense encounter with the Folk took place in 1907, when he went to the Eastern Carpathian Mountains, in Transylvania, to gather songs from Hungarian-speaking Székely villagers. Personal upheaval added urgency to the mission; the composer had fallen in love with a nineteen-year-old violinist named Stefi Geyer, who received his advances first with bemusement and then with alarm. Both the letters he wrote to Geyer that summer and his meticulous notes on Transylvanian songs give the impression that a fenced-off soul is opening itself to the chaos of the outer world.

Like Grainger in England, Bartók brought with him an Edison cylinder, and he listened as the machine listened. He observed the flexible tempo of sung phrases, how they would accelerate in ornamental passages and taper off at the end. He saw how phrases were seldom symmetrical in shape, how a beat or two might be added or subtracted. He savored "bent" notes—shadings above or below the given note—and "wrong" notes that added flavor and bite. He understood how decorative figures could evolve into fresh themes, how common rhythms tied disparate themes together, how songs moved in circles instead of going from point A to point B. Yet he also realized that folk musicians could play in absolutely strict tempo when the occasion demanded it. He came to understand rural music as a kind of archaic avant-garde, through which he could defy all banality and convention.

Emotional rejection can have a radicalizing effect, as Schoenberg's history in 1907 and 1908 suggests. Bartók, pining for the unavailable Stefi, swung away from Romantic tonality in those same two years. The Violin Concerto No. 1, his main work of this period, shows him still in thrall to a Richard Strauss aesthetic, with a five-note theme representing his beloved at the head of the piece. He planned but did not compose a third movement, which would have shown the "hateful" side of the unfortunate girl. Some of that negative energy spills out in the Fourteen Bagatelles for piano, written in the spring of 1908. A kind of substitution of love objects occurs: in place of Stefi's leitmotif there are now rusty shards of folk melody, showing the impact of the Transylvanian trip and other research expeditions. The Woman becomes the Folk.

The first Bagatelle begins with a radical harmonic break: the right hand plays roughly in C-sharp minor while the left plays in something like the key of C (in the Phrygian mode). This is "polytonality" or "polymodality," the juxtaposition of two or more key-areas, and it will play a significant role in early- and mid-twentieth-century music. Bartók probably derived the practice from Strauss and Debussy, but he also liked to attribute it to folk players, who periodically wandered free from their accompanying harmonies.

The Bagatelles, together with subsequent works such as the Two Elegies, *Allegro barbaro*, the First String Quartet, and the opera *Bluebeard's Castle*, veer close to atonality. They make frequent use of Schoenberg's searing motto chord of two fourths separated by a tritone. But Bartók's ardor for folk melodies prevented him from going over the brink. As the musicologist Judit Frigyesi observes, Hungarian modernists were not prone to annihilating rage of the Viennese type; instead, they sought higher unities, transcendent reconciliations. The philosopher and critic Georg Lukács put it this way: "The essence of art is form: it is to defeat oppositions, to conquer opposing forces, to create coherence from every centrifugal force, from all things that have been deeply and eternally alien to one another before and outside this form. The creation of form is the last judgment over things, a last judgment that redeems all that could be redeemed, that enforces salvation on all things with divine force." Bartók, likewise, talked about the "highest emotions," a "great reality." The artist in his loneliness need not bring about Vienna-style antagonism and scandal; instead, Frigyesi writes, he can stand in for all humanity, becoming a "metaphor for wholeness."

Bartók's quest led him both onward and inward. In the first days of June 1913, he boarded a steamer in Marseille, bound for Algeria. His ultimate destination was Biskra, on the northern edge of the Sahara, where, seven years before, Henri Matisse had found the inspiration for his raw, sensual *Blue Nude*. The trip lasted only two weeks: the composer fell ill with fever and had to retreat to Algiers. He hoped to return the following summer, and researched diets that would have allowed him to stay healthy. But the onset of the First World War put a stop to his plans. His wax-cylinder recordings of North African music remained a prize possession and led to a landmark ethnomusicological essay. They also furnished new compositional ideas, particularly in the area of rhythm. Bartók wrote from Algeria: "The Arabs accompany almost all their songs with percussion instruments; sometimes in a very complicated rhythm (it is chiefly varying accentuations of equal bar lengths that produce the different rhythmic patterns)." This could serve as a description of "The Augurs of Spring" in Stravinsky's *Rite*, whose first production was still playing to giddy Paris crowds as Bartók set out for Africa.

Maurice Ravel is a special case among turn-of-the-century "realists." He was a man both urban and urbane, disinclined to go wandering up a mountainside with an Edison cylinder on his back. Yet, during his brief and brilliant career, he drew on a sizable library of folk material—

variously, Spanish, Basque, Corsican, Greek, Hebrew, Javanese, and Japanese. He, too, was a phonographic listener, sensitive to microscopic details of phrasing, texture, and pulse. A gentleman flaneur with unusual powers of empathy, Ravel could spend his day as a man of the crowd, then reconstruct the experience in the privacy of his garret.

Commonly considered the most purely French of composers, Ravel was in fact something of a cultural mutt, part Basque and part Swiss. Although he was taken to Paris when he was four months old, his Basque origins held sway over his imagination, the connection maintained in the songs his mother sang for him. Manuel de Falla judged Ravel's Spanish-themed works "subtly authentic," which is a good general description of the composer's music as a whole. Ravel's father was a Swiss engineer who helped to pioneer, in unsung ways, the automobile; the Ravel prototype of a gas-powered car perished during the German bombardment of Paris in the Franco-Prussian War. In a sense, Ravel's music split the difference between his parents' worlds—his mother's memories of a folkish past, his father's dreams of a mechanized future.

In a series of piano works in the first decade of the new century, Ravel carried out a kind of velvet revolution, renewing the language of music without disturbing the peace. In *Jeux d'eau*, melody and accompaniment dematerialize into splashing, skittering lines, imitating the movement of water in a fountain. In "Valley of the Bells," from the cycle *Miroirs*, novel notation is used to enhance the impression of bell tones resonating in space: the music is spread over three rather than two staves, each line moving at an independent tempo. In "Le Gibet," from *Gaspard de la nuit*, ghostly figures rise and fall around a continuously tolling B-flat—a structure that was in itself a new kind of musical narrative, one of proto-minimalist repetition. Falla, in his writings on flamenco, points out that melodies of the "deep song" type often rotate around an obsessively repeated note, and pieces such as "Le Gibet" may allude to the great Andalusian dance, although the one-note pattern could just as well have come from Gregorian chant. Some years later, in the 1928 showpiece *Bolero*, Ravel would take the aesthetic of repetition to the extreme: for fifteen minutes the orchestra hammers away at a theme in the key of C.

Ravel put his Spanish-Basque heritage proudly on display in the orchestral suite *Rapsodie espagnole*, first heard in 1908. The *Rapsodie* calls to mind the explosive colors of Fauvist painting, especially the early work of

Matisse. Again, harmonic movement freezes on static sonorities; the narrative is driven by transformations of texture and rhythm. At the climax of "Feria," the festival finale of the *Rapsodie*, Ravel creates a dynamic effect of rhythmic layering, superimposing five separate pulses: two against three against four against six against twelve.

In the penultimate bar, in the midst of a quick rush of sound across the entire orchestra, the trombones make a gloriously rude noise—a glissando, a slide from one note to another. This effect was first popularized by Arthur Pryor, the virtuoso slide trombonist in John Philip Sousa's band, who featured it in such numbers as "Coon Band Contest" (1900) and "Trombone Sneeze" (1902). As it happens, the Sousa band toured all over Europe in 1900 and 1901, just before glissando effects spread through classical composition. Schoenberg and his brother-in-law Zemlinsky were the first to notate true trombone glissandos in orchestral works, in their symphonic poems *Pelleas und Melisande* and *Die Seejungfrau*, both from 1902–3.

In Schoenberg's Five Pieces for Orchestra the glissando is an expressionistic moan, a noise from the beyond. Ravel manages to have it both ways; his glissando in the *Rapsodie* has the exuberance of jazz to come, but it harbors a dangerous, drunken energy, as if the orchestra were about to be invaded by foreign hordes.

Stravinsky and the *Rite*

In the summer of 1891 French ships sailed into the Russian naval base at Kronstadt, to be greeted not by hostile fire but by ceremonial salutes. Tsar Alexander III, whose great-uncle had withstood the Napoleonic invasion, made a show of toasting the French sailors and listening to "La Marseillaise." These were the first public signs of the secret military convention between France and Russia, which was ratified the following year. The pact was kept hidden, but the friendliness between the two countries played out in the public eye. When Diaghilev began presenting concerts of Russian music, in 1907, his performances were quasi-official occasions, underwritten by money from the Romanov dynasty. By 1909, Diaghilev's relationship with the tsar's circle had deteriorated, but by then his Paris operation—now expanded to include ballet—had won an avid following in France. Nightly attendance at the Ballets Russes replaced pilgrimages to Bayreuth as the obligatory fad among the French aristocracy and upper bourgeoisie.

When the French ships arrived in Kronstadt, one German observer skeptically wrote that the civilized French would find "few points of sympathy with barbaric Russia." In fact, the sympathy already existed, and composers played a role in developing it. Debussy had visited Russia as early as 1881, in order to teach music to the children of the Russian music patron Nadezhda von Meck. It may have been on that trip that he first encountered the whole-tone scale, by way of the works of Mikhail Glinka. Eight years later, at a concert at the Paris Universal Exposition, Debussy fell under the spell of Rimsky-Korsakov, who was working with another novel mode, the octatonic scale of alternating semitones and whole tones. The speech-like vocal lines of Mussorgsky's *Boris Godunov* influenced Debussy's word setting in *Pelléas*. In the first decade of the new century, the latest French works began traveling east. Ravel's *Rapsodie espagnole*, which owed much to Rimsky's *Capriccio espagnol*, became a cult object among Rimsky's students, one of whom was the young Stravinsky. Then Stravinsky came west with his *Firebird*, *Petrushka*, and *Rite*, and the French were bewitched by the Russians once again.

In later years, Stravinsky preferred to describe himself as a deracinated modernist, a dealer in abstraction, and went to some lengths to conceal his early folkish enthusiasms. As Richard Taruskin documents, in his huge and marvelous book *Stravinsky and the Russian Traditions*, the composer actively suppressed information—"lied" is not too strong a word—about the source material of the *Rite*, claiming that there was only one folk song in the ballet. In the same vein, he derided Bartók's "gusto for his native folklore." In fact, the young Stravinsky steeped himself in Russian material, striving to become a vessel of primitive energies. On one occasion he described his homeland as a force of "beautiful, healthy barbarism, big with the seed that will impregnate the thinking of the world."

With his egg-shaped head, bulging eyes, and luxurious mouth, Stravinsky had a slightly insectoid appearance. His manners were elegant, his clothes impeccable, his jokes lethal. In every way, he personified Rimbaud's dictum

"*Il faut être absolument moderne.*" If there was something of the dandy or aesthete about Stravinsky, he did not create an artificial impression in person. His mind was in perfect sync with his body, which he kept in trim, gymnastic condition. His friend and fellow composer Nicolas Nabokov once wrote: "His music reflects his peculiarly elastic walk, the syncopated nod of his head and shrug of his shoulders, and those abrupt stops in the middle of a conversation when, like a dancer, he suddenly freezes in a balletlike pose and punctuates his argument with a broad and sarcastic grin."

Stravinsky was born in 1882. His ancestors were landowning aristocrats, members of the old Polish and Russian ruling classes who controlled much of western Russia. Young Igor spent many summers at his uncle's spacious country estate in Ustyluh, close to the present Polish-Ukrainian border. There he would have heard folk songs and dances of the region, which resembled to some extent the music that attracted Bartók and Janáček. Ustyluh lies about two hundred miles from Janáček's birthplace of Hukvaldy, and not too much farther from the Carpathian Mountains, where Bartók had his folk-music epiphany. But Stravinsky's sensibility was shaped equally by the sophisticated atmosphere of St. Petersburg, which, at the turn of the century, was experiencing a Silver Age, its artistic productions rivaling those of fin-de-siècle Vienna and Paris in luminosity of surface and intensity of feeling.

Stravinsky's father, Fyodor, was a noted bass-baritone at the imperial Mariinsky Theatre. Their home was comfortable, although Fyodor's cold, strict personality cast a shadow over it. Igor drew close to his brother Gury, who provided a measure of emotional warmth that was otherwise missing from the household. Although Igor read scores and improvised at the piano from an early age, he came late to composition, and began to display real ambition only after his father's death, in 1902. He took lessons from Rimsky starting that year, his student exercises mostly bland and imitative. The first flashes of genius came as late as 1907 and 1908, in the brief orchestral showpieces *Scherzo fantastique* and *Fireworks*, both of which blended French and Russian sounds. The works caught the attention of Diaghilev, impresario of the Ballets Russes, who was on the lookout for gifted young composers. In the 1910 season, Diaghilev planned to stun his Paris public with a multimedia fantasy on the folk legend of the Firebird, and when several more illustrious names turned him down, he took a chance on the novice.

The Firebird was a magical concoction: Russian musical sorcery, overlaid with French effects, lit up by the X-factor of Stravinsky's talent. The score is infested with references to Rimsky's works, and it leans heavily on the master's tone-semitone scale. But Stravinsky makes his mark in the zone of rhythm. In the climactic "Infernal Dance," in which the minions of the evil Kashchei are put under the Firebird's spell, the slashing Stravinsky accents make their first appearance. The timpani lays down a steady ostinato of rapid pulses. The bassoons, horns, and tuba play a jumpy theme whose accents fall between the beats. Then, at the end of the phrase, the accent shifts and now falls *on* the beat: the ear has been tricked into thinking that the offbeats are main beats and the main beat is a syncopation. The full orchestra sets the record straight with a whiplash triple *forte*. Such syncopations were not uncommon in nineteenth-century music, and Stravinsky may have heard something like them in rural Russian dances. But they also echo some of Ravel's favorite devices, and the last few bars of the "Infernal Dance" are basically lifted from the *Rapsodie espagnole*.

Overnight, under the spotlight of Diaghilev's patronage, an unknown became a phenomenon. Within days of his arrival for the *Firebird* premiere, Stravinsky met Proust, Gide, Saint-John Perse, Paul Claudel, Sarah Bernhardt, and all the major composers. "This goes further than Rimsky," Ravel wrote to a colleague after hearing *Firebird*. "Come quickly." Buoyed by the Paris atmosphere and by his impressive new fans, Stravinsky set to work on a second ballet, *Petrushka*, a tale of an animate puppet who performs at a Russian village fair. Unorthodox ideas emerged from his conversations with the intellectuals of the Ballets Russes. The choreographer Michel Fokine talked of a stage full of natural, flowing movement, the antithesis of academic ballet. Stravinsky responded with a score of exhilarating immediacy: phrases jump in from nowhere, snap in the air, stop on a dime, taper off with a languid shrug. The designer Alexander Benois had asked him to write a "symphony of the street," a "counterpoint of twenty themes," replete with carousels, concertinas, sleigh bells, and popular airs. Stravinsky answered with periodic explosions of dissonance and rhythmic complexity, which mimic the energy of the modern urban crowd.

The young sophisticates of Paris, for whom Debussy's music had always been a little too murkily mystical, rejoiced. It was as if all the lights had been switched on in the Wagnerian room. Jacques Rivière, the influential editor of the *Nouvelle Revue Française*, wrote of *Petrushka*: "It suppresses, it clarifies, it hits only the telling and succinct notes." The composer had succeeded in carrying out Wagner's "synthesis of the arts" without resorting to Wagnerian grandiloquence. Stravinsky could never be described as a humble man, yet there was something selfless in the way he made himself a collaborator among collaborators, exchanging ideas with Fokine, Benois, and Diaghilev, adapting his music to their needs. No prophet descending from the mountaintop, he was a man of the world to whom writers, dancers, and painters could relate. Ezra Pound once said, "Stravinsky is the only living musician from whom I can learn my own job."

One night in 1910, Stravinsky dreamed of a young girl dancing herself to death, and soon after he began to plan *Vesna svyashchennaya*, or *Holy Spring*. (The ballet's standard Western titles, *Le Sacre du printemps* and *The Rite of Spring*, miss the "holy" element, the pagan devotion.) Taruskin's *Stravinsky and the Russian Traditions* contains the definitive account of the ballet's gestation. For help in fleshing out the scenario, Stravinsky turned to Roerich, the painter and Slavic guru, who plotted out a sequence of historically accurate springtime rituals. Stravinsky delved into folkloric sources, drawing variously on a book of Lithuanian wedding songs, Rimsky's folk-song arrangements, and his own memories of peasant singers and professional balladeers at Ustyluh, where he had built his own summer house in 1908. He may also have seen the impeccably prepared folk collections of Yevgeniya Linyova, notated with the help of recording cylinders. Stravinsky hardly matched Bartók in the thoroughness of his research, but he thought carefully about which songs would be most appropriate, favoring geographical areas where paganism had persisted longest and emphasizing songs on the theme of spring.

Having assembled his folk melodies, Stravinsky proceeded to pulverize them into motivic bits, pile them up in layers, and reassemble them in cubistic collages and montages. As in Bartók's Bagatelles, the folk material enters the genetic code of the music, governing all aspects of the organism. Bartók was one listener who had no trouble figuring out what

Stravinsky was up to. In a 1943 lecture at Harvard, he called the *Rite* "a kind of apotheosis of the Russian rural music" and explained how its revolutionary construction was related to the source material: "Even the origin of the rough-grained, brittle, and jerky musical structure, backed by ostinatos, which is so completely different from any structural proceeding of the past, may be sought in short-breathed Russian peasant motives."

In a resonant phrase, Taruskin calls the *Rite* a "great fusion" of national and modern sounds. Its folkish and avant-garde traits reinforce each other. Consider that percussive, pungent chord in "The Augurs of Spring," the one that fuses a major triad with an adjacent dominant seventh. It is not unprecedented: something like it appears in *Salome*, at the line "You are truly your mother's child." But the aim of the gesture is not to outdo the Germans in the race toward total dissonance. Instead, it points up relationships among the simple folkish patterns that surround it. Immediately before the chords begin their stomp, the violins play a little figure that spells out the E-flat portion of the harmony. The winds resume that figure a little later. After several such back-and-forths, the ear can easily pick out the tonal components within any dissonance.

If other composers went further in revolutionizing harmony, none rivaled Stravinsky in the realm of rhythm. Off-the-beat accents had welled up in *Firebird* and *Petrushka*, although there the syncopations usually followed a set pattern. In "The Augurs of Spring," there is no way to predict where the accents will land next. As the composer-critic Virgil Thomson once explained, the body tends to move up and down in syncopated or polyrhythmic music because it wants to emphasize the main beat that the stray accents threaten to wipe out. "A silent accent is the strongest of all accents," he wrote. "It forces the body to replace it with a motion." (Think of Bo Diddley's "Bo Diddley," with its "*bomp ba-bomp bomp* [oomph!] *bomp bomp*.") In "Augurs" the positioning of the "bomps" and the "oomphs" changes almost from bar to bar, so that the main beat nearly disappears and the syncopations have the field to themselves.

In "Procession of the Sage," Stravinsky takes a different tack: in the climactic eight-bar section, each instrument plays a regular pattern, but almost every pattern is distinct. Tubas play a sixteen-beat figure three times; horns play an eight-beat phrase six times; a guiro plays eight pulses to the bar; the timpani play twelve pulses to the bar; and so on. This is

Rapsodie espagnole raised to the nth degree, and it rivals the most intricate structures of West African drumming. As in much African music, asymmetrical "time-line" patterns jostle against a hidden master pulse.

"*Une musique nègre*," Debussy called the *Rite*. There is no evidence that Stravinsky knew African music, although a few early ethnographic studies of that largely unknown realm, such as Henri-Alexandre Junod's *Les Chants et les contes des Ba-Ronga*, had circulated. Taruskin points out that irregular rhythms were also a long-standing feature of Russian folk music. But his notion of a "great fusion" in the *Rite* might ultimately be widened to mean something more than a thoroughgoing assimilation of folk motifs into modern music. These rhythms are global in reach, and at the time they were global in their impact. Jazz musicians sat up in their seats when Stravinsky's music started playing: he was speaking something close to their language. When Charlie Parker came to Paris in 1949, he marked the occasion by incorporating the first notes of the *Rite* into his solo on "Salt Peanuts." Two years later, playing Birdland in New York, the bebop master spotted Stravinsky at one of the tables and immediately incorporated a motif from *Firebird* into "Koko," causing the composer to spill his scotch in ecstasy.

The first part of the *Rite*, which ends with the sweat-inducing crescendo of "Dance of the Earth," is viscerally exciting, even celebratory. Part II is grittier, swaying between languor and violence. Debussy's influence is palpable at the outset: the crawling sextuplet figures in the winds and the ghoulishly bouncing string figures in the Introduction come from Debussy's *Nocturnes*, as does the snaking flute melody in "Ritual Action of the Ancestors." But Stravinsky has hardly run out of original ideas. At the end of the latter section the bass clarinet plays a soft, quick, spooky solo—the lower winds periodically show up in the score like black-clad cabaret hosts, ushering the next scandal onstage—and the final "Danse sacrale" begins. Another means of forward propulsion kicks in: in place of regular pulses in simultaneous layers there are variable rhythmic "cells" that expand or contract. As Bartók observed, these features are also ethnographically precise; severe rhythmic and metric asymmetries are common in Russian and Eastern European folk music. The cumulative effect is of exhaustion, not of intensification. The every-which-way pulsation leads to a feeling of stasis. The earth seems to be tiring itself out, just as the young girl is dancing herself to death. At the end comes a morbid spasm.

The notion of a female sacrifice was Stravinsky's special contribution. As Lynn Garafola points out, no pagan people except for the Aztecs demanded the sacrifice of young girls. Stravinsky was giving voice not to ancient instincts but to the bloodthirstiness of the contemporary West. At the turn of the century, purportedly civilized societies were singling out scapegoats on whom the ills of modernity could be blamed: Russian townspeople were enacting pogroms of Jews, white Americans were lynching young black men, and, closer to home, the denizens of the sixteenth arrondissement had cheered on the anti-Semitic campaign against the Jewish patriot Alfred Dreyfus. Against that backdrop, the urban noises in Stravinsky's score—sounds like pistons pumping, whistles screeching, crowds stamping—suggest a sophisticated city undergoing an atavistic regression.

More than a few people left the premiere both thrilled and chilled by the experience. Jacques Rivière, who took such joy from *Petrushka*, spoke no less rapturously of the *Rite*, but in the end he found himself falling into a despondent mood. "There are works that overflow with accusations, hopes, encouragements," Rivière wrote. "You suffer, regret, take confidence with them; they contain all the beautiful perturbations of the spirit; you give yourself to them as to the counsel of a friend; they have a moral quality and always partake of pity." The *Rite*, he admitted, was not among them.

War

When the guns began firing in August 1914, French, Russian, and English composers were swept away by the same patriotic fervor that had overcome their Austro-German counterparts. The long-standing resentment of Teutonic hegemony in the classical repertory blossomed into hate. In London, Strauss's *Don Juan* was taken off a Proms concert. The League for the Defense of French Music sought to ban "*infiltrations funèstes,*" or fatal infiltrations, of enemy composers. Manuel de Falla urged colleagues to reject any "universal formula," by which he presumably meant, as his biographer Carol Hess says, the "purely musical" ethos of the German canon. After the United States entered the war in 1917, Wagner disappeared from the Metropolitan Opera stage and Beethoven symphonies from programs in Pittsburgh. Karl Muck, the German-born conductor of the Boston Symphony, was thrown in prison on the spurious grounds that he had refused to conduct "The Star-Spangled Banner." Stories circulated that Muck had been communicating with U-boats from his cottage in Seal Harbor, Maine.

Absurd as this musical paranoia now seems, it was activated by deep shock at Germany's campaign of total war. Several significant composers lost their lives in ways that underlined the changing definition of combat. Albéric Magnard, composer of four eloquent Franckish symphonies, was burned alive along with a number of his works after he fired on marauding German soldiers from a window of his home. The refined Catalan composer Enrique Granados drowned in the middle of the Atlantic after a passenger vessel he was traveling on was torpedoed by a German submarine. England mourned the loss of George Butterworth, who worked alongside folkish composers such as Grainger, Gustav Holst, and Ralph Vaughan Williams. Butterworth's specialty was morris dancing, and on his expeditions into the countryside he made meticulous notes such as these:

> Both hands touch lower chest
> " " " upper "
> clap
> slap with opposite
> Then Hey

He was killed in August 1916, aged thirty-one, during an early-morning assault on a German trench in the Battle of Pozières Ridge.

Maurice Ravel nearly died at around the same time. The tiny-framed composer should have been barred from military service, but, enraged by the bombing of Reims, he enlisted as a truck driver. By the spring of 1916 Ravel was deployed just behind the front lines, and witnessed the ghastly aftermath of the Battle of Verdun. He often had to weave back and forth on pockmarked roads as shells fell all around him. Once he found himself in an abandoned town on a sunny day, walking through the empty, silent streets. "I don't believe I will ever experience a more profound and stranger emotion than this sort of mute terror," he wrote. Another time he entered an abandoned château, found a fine Erard piano, and sat down to play some Chopin.

Such unreal experiences provide clues to the piano cycle *Le Tombeau de Couperin*, Ravel's principal work of the war years. In the context of its time, *Le Tombeau* may seem a little precious, as if it were averting its gaze from the carnage. Not only the title but also the names of the movements—Prélude, Fugue, Forlane, Rigaudon, Menuet, and Toccata—look back to the French Baroque, paying homage to the harpsichord suites of Couperin and Rameau. But, as ever with Ravel, emotion smolders under the exquisite surface. Each piece is dedicated to a friend who died in battle; the old styles pass by like a procession of ghosts. There are also hints of muscle, glints of steel. Glenn Watkins, in his study of music during the Great War, argues that the metallic stream of tone in the Toccata is meant to suggest the twisting motion of a fighter plane. Ravel dreamed of being an aviator, a solitary hero in the sky.

Stravinsky spent the war in neutral Switzerland, urging humanity to resist "the intolerable spirit of this colossal and obese Germania," but otherwise immersing himself in musical business. The creator of the *Rite* was entering a period of experimentation, momentarily uncertain about what to do next. Never entirely secure in his reputation as the leader of the moderns, he glanced around to see what his rivals were doing. During a 1912 visit to Berlin, he attended one of the early performances of *Pierrot lunaire,* and came away impressed by the economy of Schoenberg's instrumentation, the use of a pocket orchestra of two winds, two strings, and piano. Next to the Wagner-sized orchestra of the *Rite*, the *Pierrot* band was like a motorcar speeding alongside a locomotive. Stravinsky effectively imitated Schoenberg in the second and third of his *Three Japanese Lyrics*, written after the Berlin visit.

If Richard Taruskin is right, Stravinsky drew lessons from the reviews of the *Rite*, both in Paris and back home in Russia. Parisians appreciated not just the wildness of the music but also its precision and clarity. Innately sympathetic to Stravinsky's anti-Romantic attitude, they applauded his prominent deployment of winds and brass and his relatively minimal use of strings. Jacques Rivière, in his review in the *Nouvelle Revue Française*, emphasized what the *Rite* was *not*—it lacked "sauce" and "atmosphere," it rejected "Debussysm," it refused to behave like a conventional "work of art." In the small-scale Cubist-Oriental opera *The Nightingale*, which Stravinsky began in 1908 and finished in 1914, Rivière heard the beginnings of a new kind of unsentimental, abstract music in which "each object will be set out apart from the others and as if surrounded by white."

Meanwhile, in St. Petersburg and Moscow, Russian critics and musicians dismissed the *Rite* as so much trendy noise. Taruskin suggests that the confluence of praise abroad and criticism at home essentially impelled Stravinsky to cut his ties to home and to become a Western European composer: "By imperceptible degrees, [he] came to resemble his hosts and exploiters."

The process of "progressive abstraction," as Taruskin calls it, governed Stravinsky's next big project, *Les Noces*, or *The Wedding*. The idea of a dance spectacle about a boisterous rural Russian wedding had first surfaced back in 1912. By the time Stravinsky began sketching the music, in the summer of 1914, he had lost interest in the lavish resources of the *Rite*, and was thinking in terms of a more limited orchestra of sixty players. As the years went by, even that ensemble came to seem too extravagant. In its final incarnation, which appeared in 1923, *Les Noces* was scored for singers, chorus, percussion, and four pianos. The critic Émile Vuillermoz called the result "a machine to hit, a machine to lash, a machine to fabricate automatic resonances." The sound of *Les Noces* is not inappropriate to the action: it suggests a harsh truth of pre-twentieth-century life, which was that most marriages were the result of a preconceived parental design, not of spontaneous romantic feeling.

The consummation of Stravinsky's hard-edged, steel-tipped style was *Symphonies of Wind Instruments* (1920)—a nine-minute sequence of lamenting cries, meandering chants, and chordal blocks. It was conceived as a memorial for Debussy, who had died before the end of the war. The dedication is ironic, for Debussy had disliked Stravinsky's first ventures in "objective" composition. Russians were losing their Russianness, Debussy had complained in 1915; Stravinsky was "leaning dangerously toward the Schoenberg side." Later that month, Debussy sent his colleague some pointed praise: "*Cher* Stravinsky, you are a great artist! Be, with all your energy, a great Russian artist! It is a good thing to be from one's country, to be attached to the earth like the humblest peasant!"

Stravinsky was determined to forsake his past. As Taruskin shows,

Symphonies of Wind Instruments is based on the Russian Orthodox funeral service, whose solemn chant may signify that the composer is ritualistically burying his old Russian self alongside the body of Debussy. A string of catastrophic events—the demise of tsarist Russia, the onset of the Russian Revolution, the early death of his beloved brother Gury—meant that by 1918 the world of Stravinsky's childhood had been effectively erased. The Ustyluh estate, where the polytonal chords of the *Rite* were hammered out, had passed into the hands of Polish farmers.

Debussy suffered much in his final years, both in body and in mind. He was afflicted with rectal cancer and could sometimes hardly move on account of the pain. Germany's conduct during the war angered him no end; in his 1915 letter to Stravinsky he declared that "Austro-Boche miasmas are spreading through art," and proposed a counterattack in terms borrowed from the new art of chemical warfare: "It will be necessary to kill this microbe of false grandeur, of organized ugliness." The last two phrases presumably signify Strauss and Schoenberg. A certain icy fury possesses Debussy's ultravirtuosic Études for piano, and also in his explicitly war-themed two-piano piece *En blanc et en noir*. Then came a remarkable turn. Abandoning his former opposition to the use of canonical classical forms, Debussy set to work on a cycle of six sonatas for diverse instruments, and lived to finish three—one for violin, one for cello, and one for flute, viola, and harp. They were couched in a taut, songful style, perfumed with the palmy air of the French Baroque. New beauty should fill the air, Debussy told Stravinsky, when the cannons fall silent.

On March 23, 1918, the day before Palm Sunday, the Germans opened a two-pronged campaign of terror against Paris. Gotha planes launched an audacious daytime air raid, killing several people in a church. Krupp's latest masterpiece, the Paris Gun, began firing on the city from seventy-five miles away. Paris was awash in noise—shells booming in the air every fifteen or twenty minutes; policemen beating warning signals on drums; church bells ringing and trumpets pealing as the planes approached; recruits chanting in the streets, schoolchildren singing "La Marseillaise," people defiantly shouting "*Vive la France!*" from windows. The death of Achille-Claude Debussy, on the following Monday, was hardly noticed.

Les Six and *Le Jazz*

In an absorbing study of war's effect on twentieth-century music, the composer Wolfgang-Andreas Schultz observes that feelings of "hyper-alertness, distance, and emotional coldness" often overcome the survivors of horrifying events. Just as the traumatized mind erects barriers against the influx of violent sensations, so do artists take refuge in unsentimental poses, in order to protect the self against further damage. Stravinsky's assumption of a "hard" aesthetic after 1914 exemplified a deeper shift that was taking place in the European mind—a turning away from the luxurious, mystical, maximalist tendencies of turn-of-the-century art. This was one aspect of the postwar reality. Another was the rise of popular music and mass technologies—cinema, the phonograph, radio, jazz, and Broadway theater.

Paris audiences got a foretaste of the Roaring Twenties in the spring of 1917, during one of the bloodiest periods of the war, when the Allies launched the ill-considered Nivelle offensive and the Germans responded with a lethal defensive strategy named Operation Alberich (after the master dwarf in the *Ring*). On May 18, six years to the day after the death of Gustav Mahler, the Ballets Russes again shocked the city by presenting an uproarious, circus-like production titled *Parade*. A scintillating array of personalities participated: Erik Satie wrote the music, Jean Cocteau created the libretto, Pablo Picasso designed the sets and costumes, Léonide Massine choreographed, Guillaume Apollinaire wrote the program notes (inventing the word "surrealism" in the process), and Diaghilev provided the scandal. As Francis Steegmuller recounts, the great impresario had conceived a brief passion for the Russian Revolution, and at a previous Ballets Russes evening he had unfurled a red flag behind the stage. Because the Bolsheviks were at that time pushing for a Russian withdrawal from the war effort, French patriots took umbrage at Diaghilev's revolutionary symbolism and showed up at *Parade* shouting, "*Boches!*"

The plot of *Parade*, such as it is, deals with relevance: how can an older art form, such as classical music or ballet, still draw an audience in the age of pop music, the cinema, and the gramophone? At a Paris fair, the managers of a traveling theater are deploying various music-hall performers—acrobats, a Chinese magician, a Little American Girl—in order to entice passersby. But the side acts prove so entertaining that the audience refuses to go inside. Low culture thus becomes the main attraction. Cocteau made some notes to Satie in which he described the pseudo-American aesthetic he had in mind:

> The *Titanic*—"Nearer My God To Thee"—elevators—the sirens of Boulogne—submarine cables—ship-to-shore cables—Brest—tar—varnish—steamship apparatus—the *New York Herald*—dynamos—airplanes—short circuits—palatial cinemas—the sheriff's daughter—Walt Whitman—the silence of stampedes—cowboys with leather and goatskin chaps—the telegraph operator from Los Angeles who marries the detective at the end . . .

Satie's score defines a new art of musical collage: jaunty tunes don't quite get off the ground, rhythms intertwine and overlap and stop and start, sped-up whole-tone passages sound like Warner Brothers cartoon music yet to come, bitter chorales and broken fugues honor the fading past. The "American Girl" episode contains a kooky paraphrase of Irving Berlin's "That Mysterious Rag," with one passage marked "outside and aching."

Francis Poulenc recalled the elation he felt as a teenager on attending *Parade*: "For the first time—it has happened often enough since, God knows—the music hall was invading Art with a capital A." Poulenc typified a new breed of twentieth-century composer whose consciousness was shaped not by the aesthetic of the fin de siècle but by the hard-hitting styles of the early modernist period. This young man had studied the *Rite*, Schoenberg's Six Little Pieces for Piano, Bartók's *Allegro barbaro*, and the works of Debussy and Ravel. He had also soaked up French popular songs, folk songs, music-hall numbers, sweet operetta airs, children's songs, and the stylish melodies of Maurice Chevalier.

Poulenc was one of a number of young composers who stormed onto the scene after the war, enacting a generational turnover in French music. Others were Darius Milhaud, Arthur Honegger, Louis Durey, Germaine Tailleferre, and Georges Auric. In 1920, they were dubbed Les Six. Satie was their godfather, or, more accurately, their funny uncle.

Cocteau appointed himself spokesman of the group and supplied a manifesto in his 1918 pamphlet *The Cock and the Harlequin*. The first order of business was to get rid of Wagner and Debussy. "The nightingale sings badly," Cocteau sneered, playing off the line "The nightingale will sing" in Verlaine's "En Sourdine," which Debussy had twice set to music. Stravinsky, who four years earlier had failed to respond to Cocteau's proposal for a ballet about David and Goliath, also came in for criticism; the *Rite* was a masterpiece, yes, but one that exhibited symptoms of "theatrical mysticism" and other Wagnerian diseases. "Enough of *nuages*, waves, aquariums, *ondines*, and nocturnal perfumes," Cocteau intoned, pointedly slipping in titles of pieces by Debussy and the no longer cutting-edge Ravel. "We need music on the earth, MUSIC FOR EVERY DAY. Enough of hammocks, garlands, gondolas! I want someone to make me music that I can live in like a house." For all his glib generalities, Cocteau succeeded in articulating the spirit of the moment: after the long night of war, composers were done with what Nietzsche called, in his critique of Wagner, the "*lie* of the great style."

Paris in the twenties displayed a contradiction. On the one hand, it embraced all the fads of the roaring decade—music hall, American jazz, sport and leisure culture, machine noises, technologies of gramophone and radio, musical corollaries to Cubism, Futurism, Dadaism, Simultaneism, and Surrealism. Yet beneath the ultramodern surface a nineteenth-century support structure for artistic activity persisted. Composers still made their names in the Paris salons, which survived the general postwar decline of European aristocracy, partly because so many wealthy old families had succeeded in marrying new industrial money.

The chief hosts and hostesses of Paris, such as the Comte de Beaumont, the Vicomte and Vicomtesse de Noailles, the Duchesse de Clermont-Tonnerre, and the American-born Princesse de Polignac, were eager, even anxious, to present new "looks" each season. The virtue of salon culture was that it illuminated connections among the arts; young composers could exchange ideas with like-minded painters, poets, playwrights, and jacks-of-all-trades like Cocteau. The disadvantage was that all this bracing activity happened at considerable distance from "real life." The members of Les Six were writing "MUSIC FOR EVERY DAY" that everyday people had little opportunity to hear.

The first great vogue was *le jazz*. Paris had taken a fancy to African-American music as early as 1900, when Sousa's band played the cakewalk during its first European tour and Arthur Pryor showed off his trombone glisses. Debussy responded with "Golliwog's Cakewalk," from the suite *Children's Corner* (1906–8), where rag rhythm was interlaced with a wry citation of the initial motif of *Tristan und Isolde*. In 1917 and 1918, American troops came to Paris, bringing with them syncopated bands such as Louis Mitchell's Jazz Kings and James Reese Europe's 369th Infantry Hell Fighters. In August 1918 the Comte de Beaumont hosted a jazz night at his town house; African-American soldier-musicians played the latest dance tunes while Poulenc presented his prankishly charming *Rapsodie nègre*, full of pseudo-African mumbo jumbo on the order of "Banana lou ito kous kous / pota la ma Honoloulou."

There is no need to belabor the point that *le jazz* was condescending toward its African-American sources. Cocteau and Poulenc were enjoying a one-night stand with a dark-skinned form, and they had no intention of striking up a conversation with it the following day. Baroque pastiches, Cubist geometries, or the music of machines could just as well express modern, urban, non-Teutonic values, which is why the craze quickly ran its course, at least among Paris composers. Yet they did learn significant lessons from jazz, even if their music only faintly resembled the real thing.

Among Les Six, the most alert practitioner of *le jazz* was Darius Milhaud, an ebullient man with a wide-open mind who wrote a memoir with the unlikely title *My Happy Life*. Milhaud had spent the last years of World War I on a diplomatic mission to Brazil, where he made regular excursions into the teeming nightlife of Rio de Janeiro and received a crucial education in how "art" and "pop" motifs could be reconciled. In these same years the young Brazilian composer Heitor Villa-Lobos was merging rhythmic ideas from Stravinsky with complex patterns that he had detected in Afro-Brazilian music. In neoprimitivist scores such as *Amazonas* and *Uirapuru*, Villa-Lobos wrote percussion parts of riotous intensity; Milhaud, likewise, used no fewer than nineteen percussion instruments in his brightly colored ballet *Man and His Desire*. He also produced two dazzling fantasies on Brazilian motifs, *Saudades do Brasil* and *Le Boeuf sur le toit*.

Because Latin American musicians had originated many of the tricky rhythms that figured in early jazz, Milhaud made an easy transition to jazz-based writing. When he returned to Paris, in 1919, he maintained the habit of ending his week with a night on the town. He would invite fellow composers and like-minded artists to his home for Saturday dinner, then lead them out into the wilderness of the modern city—"the steam-driven merry-go-rounds, the mysterious booths, the Daughter of Mars, the shooting-galleries, the games of chance, the menageries, the din of the mechanical organs with their perforated rolls seeming to grind out simultaneously and implacably all the blaring tunes from the music halls and revues."

When the Saturday-evening crowd grew too large to handle, Milhaud moved his soiree to a wine store on rue Duphot, in a room named Bar Gaya. The pianist Jean Wiéner, who had been working in nightclubs, set the tone by playing jazz-like music with an African-American saxophonist named Vance Lowry. Soon the audience got too big again, and the club settled on rue Boissy d'Anglas, where it took the name Le Boeuf sur le Toit, in honor of Milhaud's Brazilian showpiece. Virgil Thomson described it as "a not unamusing place frequented by English upper-class bohemians, wealthy Americans, French aristocrats, lesbian novelists from Roumania, Spanish princes, fashionable pederasts, modern literary & musical figures, pale and precious young men, and distinguished diplomats towing bright-eyed youths." Everyone from Picasso to Maurice Chevalier joined the hilarity. Cocteau sometimes sat in on drums.

In early 1923, Milhaud made his first trip to America. Paul Whiteman's plush orchestral jazz was at that time the sensation of American high society, but Milhaud avoided it; like Bartók in the Carpathian Mountains, he sought the genuine article. At a Harlem joint called the Capitol Palace, where the stride pianists Willie "The Lion" Smith and James P. Johnson were in residence and the young Duke Ellington would shortly be indoctrinated into the Harlem elite, Milhaud was stunned by the unadulterated power of the blues. Of the singers who were in town in this period, the great Bessie Smith best fits the description in the composer's memoirs: "Against the beat of the drums the melodic lines criss-crossed in a breathless pattern of broken and twisted rhythms. A Negress whose grating voice seemed to come from the depths of the centuries sang in front of the various tables. With despairing pathos and dramatic feeling she sang over and over again, to the point of exhaustion, the same refrain, to which the constantly changing melodic pattern of the orchestra wove a kaleidoscopic background."

The language is revealing: it could describe the *Rite*. Indeed, Milhaud is replicating, consciously or not, a phrase from Cocteau's 1918 description of the ballet: "Little melodies arrive from the depths of the centuries." Also revealing is the fact that Milhaud did not record the singer's name.

Milhaud summed up his exotic adventures in the African-chic spectacle *The Creation of the World*, which the Swedish Ballet presented in Paris in 1923, with a scenario by the Simultaneist poet Blaise Cendrars and sets and costumes by the Cubist innovator Fernand Léger. None of the participants knew anything about Africa, but Milhaud's score rises above *art nègre* stereotypes on the strength of its elegant intermingling of Bach and jazz: in the opening passage of the overture, trumpets dance languidly over a saxophone-laced Baroque continuo. On his Latin-American travels, Milhaud had encountered the music of the Cuban *danzón* composer Antonio María Romeu, who liked to frame syncopated dances in Bachian counterpoint. He may also have heard Villa-Lobos speculating about common ground between Brazilian folk music and the classical canon—an idea that would eventually generate Villa-Lobos's great sequence of *Bachianas Brasileiras*. Later, the notion of a pan-historical conversation between Bach and jazz would be taken up by the likes of Bud Powell, John Lewis, Jacques Loussier, and Dave Brubeck, the last of whom studied with Milhaud and drew inspiration from his work. Milhaud became a link in a long chain, connecting centuries of tradition with new popular forms.

Stravinsky, too, cocked an ear to jazz. His guide was the conductor Ernest Ansermet, who toured America with the Ballets Russes in 1916 and wrote excitedly to Stravinsky about the "*unheard-of music*" that he was encountering in cafés. (Just as the Ballets Russes was arriving for its tour, the Creole Band, pioneers and popularizers of New Orleans jazz, was playing at the Winter Garden in New York. Later that year, the jazz historian Lawrence Gushee reveals, both the Ballets Russes and the Creole Band played on the same night in Omaha, Nebraska.) Ansermet brought back to Switzerland a pile of recordings and sheet music, including, possibly, Jelly Roll Morton's "Jelly Roll Blues." Stravinsky played some of these for Romain Rolland, calling them "the musical ideal, music spontaneous and 'useless,' music that wishes to express nothing." ("Dance must *express nothing*," Cocteau had written to him back in 1914.) If nothingness wasn't really what Jelly Roll had in mind, it did explain why so many people responded to jazz during the last bloody years of the Great War: it offered a clean slate to a shellshocked culture.

In 1918, Stravinsky wrote a puppet-theater piece titled *Histoire du soldat*, or *Story of a Soldier*, which had a decisive influence on younger composers in France, America, and Germany. It is a down-to-earth Faustian tale of a soldier-fiddler who sells his soul to the devil in exchange for untold riches. Later, Stravinsky would tell the New York press that the instrumentation was copied from jazz ensembles, and, indeed, the combination of violin, cornet, trombone, clarinet, bassoon, double bass, and percussion resembles the makeup of the Creole Band (which had a guitar in place of a bassoon). The first scene of *Histoire* starts with a simple, plucked, one-two-three-four pulse. The violin breaks up and rearranges this beat, entering on a four, then on a three, then on a two, in a triplet motion, then in phrases of five and three, then in yet more complicated phrases of odd-numbered beats. The interplay between a pulsing bass figure and freewheeling solos suggests a café-band performance, if not of jazz as such.

As Stravinsky later confessed, *Histoire* was a Russian émigré's dream of jazz, rather than a reflection of the real thing. Of course, he had written the *Rite* the same way, assembling a fantasy world from scraps of evidence.

By official reckoning, *le jazz* lasted all of three years. Cocteau called it to a halt in 1920, announcing "the disappearance of the skyscraper" and the "reappearance of the rose." That same year Auric explained in the pages of the journal *Le Coq* that his piece *Adieu New-York*, a fox-trot for piano, was his farewell to jazz, which had served its purpose. Auric's new slogan was "*Bonjour Paris!*" By 1927, even Milhaud had lost interest in the mysteries of Harlem. "Already the influence of jazz has passed," he wrote, "like a beneficial storm that leaves behind a clear sky and stable weather."

What next? Lynn Garafola has introduced two useful terms to describe music and dance in the twenties: "period modernism" and "lifestyle modernism." Period modernism indicates the cultivation of pre-Romantic styles, notably the orderly and stylish Baroque. The trend was already well under way in turn-of-the-century Paris, when Debussy extolled Rameau, Satie revived Gregorian chant, and Reynaldo Hahn, Proust's lover, wrote neo-Handelian arias. But the retrospective impulse intensified after the war, perhaps as a way of escaping recent history. Diaghilev, not Cocteau, took the lead in promoting period modernism: he had collected tattered scores by the likes of Cimarosa, Scarlatti, and Pergolesi and began editing them for modern performance, hiring favorite composers to do the orchestration. In 1920, Diaghilev asked Stravinsky to arrange ballet music from a sheaf of scores attributed to Pergolesi. Stravinsky did more than arrange: by elongating and truncating notes here and there, by introducing discontinuities, irregularities, angularities, and anomalies, he emerged with *Pulcinella*, a new type of ultramodish Stravinsky confection.

A less celebrated guru had already nudged Stravinsky toward the classical past. This was the Princesse de Polignac, née Winnaretta Singer, heiress to the Singer sewing-machine fortune, whose story is chronicled in Sylvia Kahan's book *Music's Modern Muse*.

Singer's early passion was for Wagner, but she later developed a consuming love of Bach. In a turn of phrase that captures the inborn melancholy of period modernism, she wrote that a Bach chorale "reconstitutes the past, and proves to us that we had a reason for living *on this rock*: to live in the beautiful kingdom of sounds." At her salons, new works were often paired with Bach's, and the former began sounding like the latter. Oddly, the Princesse received inspiration from Richard Strauss, whose use of a thirty-six-instrument orchestra in *Ariadne auf Naxos* gave her the idea that "the days of big orchestras were over." She promptly asked Stravinsky for a score requiring thirty to thirty-six instruments, even specifying the instrumentation, though she wisely seems not to have mentioned the Strauss angle. (Decades later, Stravinsky snapped to Robert Craft, "I would like to admit all Strauss's operas to whichever purgatory punishes triumphant vulgarity.") Aloof, intellectual, secretly lesbian, Singer had the personality of an artist herself. She sat in a high-backed chair in front of the rest of the audience so that she would not be distracted. Much displeased her, nothing surprised her. When the instruments for *Les Noces* were delivered to her house on avenue Henri-Martin, a butler announced, in horrified tones, "Madame la Princesse, four pianos have arrived," to which she replied, "Let them come in."

If the Hôtel Singer-Polignac was the clearinghouse of period modernism, the racier salons—those of Étienne de Beaumont, Charles and

Marie-Laure de Noailles, Elisabeth de Clermont-Tonnerre, and the outrageous Natalie Barney—catered to lifestyle modernism, the spirit of high fashion, low culture, and sexual play. The rules of the game were laid down by the Ballets Russes, which in 1922 moved its center of operations to the playboy capital of Monte Carlo and began receiving support from the Société des Bains de Mer. The exemplary lifestyle production was *Le Train bleu*, which took its name from the train that conveyed the beautiful people from Paris to the Riviera. The action involved a gigolo, his flapper girl, a golfer, and a female tennis champion, all attired in sportswear by Coco Chanel. Milhaud, who wrote the music, was asked to tone down his polytonal harmonies so as not to ruffle the high-society audience. "*Le Train bleu* is more than a frivolous work," Cocteau said. "It is a monument to frivolity!" It was also a monument to the beauty of a boy, in the form of Anton Dolin. Diaghilev had long catered to a gay subculture, but he now became rather brazen, outfitting his favorite dancers in tight bathing suits or minuscule Grecian shorts.

In this giddy ambience, Poulenc came into his own. "What's good about Poulenc," Ravel said, "is that he invents his own folklore." Poulenc, too, was gay, and held a kind of coming-out party in his own Diaghilev ballet, *Les Biches*. It is easy enough to read between the lines of his subsequent description of the scenario—a "modern *fêtes galantes* in a large, all-white country drawing room with a huge sofa in Laurencin blue as the only piece of furniture. Twenty charming and flirtatious women frolicked about there with three handsome, strapping young fellows dressed as oarsmen." Bronislava Nijinska's original choreography, as Lynn Garafola describes it, made the innuendo fairly explicit: the strapping young fellows spent more time looking at one another than at the women, and the Hostess tried to revalidate her beauty by posing with the boys.

There must have been a menacing disconnect between Nijinska's dances of modern narcissism and Poulenc's aggressively antique genre pieces. Things go musically out of joint right at the start: first come two Stravinskyish signals, with jagged grace notes like catches in the voice; then a clear major third in clarinets and bassoons; and finally the cartwheeling main theme. Poulenc would write more substantial scores—he had the richest, most surprising career of any of Les Six—but *Les Biches* retains its nasty champagne kick after all these years.

• • •

Stravinsky reached the apex of his hipness. He wrote manifestos, gave inflammatory interviews ("Defend me, Spaniards, from the Germans, who do not understand and who have never understood music"), took homes on the Côte Basque and the Côte d'Azur, conducted, performed on the piano, met famous people, attended parties. There was a fling with Coco Chanel; there was a long affair with the bohemian émigré Vera Sudeykina, who eventually became his second wife. His premieres were A-list events at which luminaries of art and literature congregated. Joyce and Proust had their only meeting at a dinner following the 1922 debut of *Renard*, although they had trouble finding anything to talk about. Stravinsky's life took on a name-dropping Andy Warhol quality, as is evident in the questions that Robert Craft asked in the first of his "conversation books" with the composer:

> You were a friend of D'Annunzio's at one time, weren't you? . . . You knew Rodin, didn't you? . . . Wasn't there also a question of Modigliani doing a portrait of you? . . . I once heard you describe your meeting Claude Monet . . . You were with Mayakovsky very often on his famous Paris trip of 1922? . . . Would you describe your last meeting with Proust? . . . I often hear you speak of your admiration for Ortega y Gasset. Did you know him well? . . . How did Giacometti come to make his drawings of you?

The after-party for *Les Noces* took place on a barge in the Seine. Stravinsky jumped through a wreath, Picasso created a sculpture out of children's toys, and Cocteau went around in a captain's uniform saying, "We're sinking."

All the while, Stravinsky was writing rather little *music*. His output of major works from 1921 to 1925 consisted of the brief opera *Mavra*, the Octet, the Concerto for Piano and Winds, the Sonata for piano, and the Serenade for piano—less than ninety minutes in total. The composer seemed to spend as much time explaining his music as he did writing it, and amused himself by adopting the flat-toned, inexpressive jargon of a researcher defending his experiments to fellow experts:

> My Octuor is a musical object. This object has a form and that form is influenced by the musical matter with which it is composed . . . My Octuor is not an "emotive" work but a musical composition based on objective elements which are sufficient in themselves . . . My Octuor, as I said before, is an object that has its own form. Like all other objects it has weight and occupies a place in space . . .

Stravinsky further claimed that he had never done anything but create "objects" of this kind. "Even in the early days, in the 'Fire Bird,' " he told an English interviewer in 1921, "I was concerned with a purely *musical* construction." Some years later he declared, "I consider music by its very nature powerless to *express* anything: a feeling, an attitude, a psychological state, a natural phenomenon, etc." This chic formalism echoed Cocteau ("Dance must *express nothing*"), who probably got it from Oscar Wilde ("Art never expresses anything but itself"). The new objectivity was the old aestheticism.

Stravinsky had cast aside his old Russian self but had not yet hammered out a new identity. On the one hand, much of his writing in the twenties fell under the rubric of "period modernism." *Mavra* is a love letter to nineteenth-century Russian imperial style, especially Tchaikovsky. The Octet bustles through the antiquated arts of sonata form, theme and variation, and modulation through the major and minor keys. The becalmed slow movement of the Piano Concerto unfurls like an aria by Bach or Handel, replete with long, cantabile lines and stately, processional rhythms. Period modernism in music would come to be called neoclassicism, and it would hold sway well into the second half of the century. One early adherent was Manuel de Falla, who set aside his pursuit of flamenco in order to write a Harpsichord Concerto that equaled anything by Stravinsky in severity of method and austerity of tone.

Yet Stravinsky did not neglect the modern world. Better than almost any composer of his time, he understood how the radio, the gramophone, the player piano, and other media would transform music. When he first heard a pianola, in London in 1914, he was entranced by the thought that he could eliminate the unreliability inherent in human performers. Later, in Paris, he signed a contract with the Pleyel player-piano company to record his works, and for a time he even worked out of a studio in the

Pleyel factory. He also tailored a few of his works to the needs of the gramophone. During his first visit to New York, in 1925, he recorded some short piano pieces at the Brunswick Records studio, where, the following year, Duke Ellington would set down "East St. Louis Toodle-oo." Each movement of the Serenade in A fit on one side of a disc. One advantage of the neo-Baroque aesthetic was that its churning ostinatos and arpeggios readily suggested machines in action. For Stravinsky, as for many other composers, technology became a new kind of folklore, another infusion of the real.

The Politics of Style

In 1919, at the Peace Conference in Paris, Woodrow Wilson gave voice to the dream of a League of Nations—a harmonious new world order of "open covenants openly arrived at." One year later, at a festival of Gustav Mahler's music in Amsterdam, an international group of composers issued a manifesto welcoming the opportunity "to shake the hands of our brethren in art, irrespective of nationality and race," and "to rebuild the broken spiritual bridges between the peoples." To this end, they hoped for "a great international festival or congress of music . . . at which every musical nation of the world may present its last and best contributions to the art, and at which the workers in musical aesthetics and criticism may exchange their thoughts and the results of their studies." The idea of a musical League came to life two years later, with the formation of the International Society for Contemporary Music, or ISCM. The ISCM's festivals—in Salzburg in 1923, Salzburg and Prague in 1924, Prague and Venice in 1925, Zurich in 1926, and Frankfurt in 1927—were integral to music in the twenties, and the organization still exists today.

The postwar spirit of comity led to some odd alliances, none odder than the one that flourished briefly between Les Six and the Second Viennese School. "Arnold Schönberg, the six musicians hail you!" wrote Cocteau in 1920. Milhaud conducted part of *Pierrot lunaire* in December 1921, and presented the entire piece three times during the following year. Schoenberg, for his part, placed works by Debussy and Ravel on his series of "Private Musical Performances" in Vienna. When the two groups met face to face, Schoenberg called Milhaud "a nice person," while Poulenc pronounced Webern "an exquisite boy." As might be expected, this strained exchange of pleasantries didn't last. By the middle of the decade the ISCM was beginning to divide into opposing camps, one arrayed around Schoenberg and another around Stravinsky. The old Franco-German musical war resumed.

The twenties were years of runaway inflation, rampant stock speculation, and instant fortunes. The historian Eric Hobsbawm, in his book *The Age of Extremes*, writes that the economic boom was largely illusory, underwritten by a shaky network of international loans and undermined by widespread unemployment. Music, too, seemed trapped in a bubble economy; a composer could make his name with one or two attention-getting gestures but had a harder time sustaining a career. Publicity was guaranteed for any work that combined classical means with modern themes. Honegger proved adept at this trick, writing pieces titled *Rugby*, *Skating-Rink*, and the much-played *Pacific 231* (a steam locomotive with two front axles, three main axles, and one axle in the back). The young Czech composer Bohuslav Martinů produced works depicting a football match (*Half-Time*), crowds celebrating Lindbergh's flight (*La Bagarre*), jazz-dancing kitchen utensils (*La Revue de cuisine*), Satan as a Negro Cyclist (*The Tears of the Knife*), and a ballet about music itself (*Revolt*), in which classical music fights dance hits, gramophones rebel against their masters, critics commit suicide, Stravinsky escapes to a desert island, and a Moravian folk song saves the day.

The festivals of the twenties were the first great battleground of what the critic Bernard Holland has called the twentieth century's "politics of style." Composers weren't simply engaging in artificial games; they were asking mighty questions about what art meant and how it related to society. Yet, as in the salons of Paris, this discussion about music and modernity took place within an unreal ecosystem that was removed from daily life. The audience at the new-music festivals was a motley gathering of elites—culture-building captains of industry, American heiresses looking to acquire European status, snob aesthetes with no pressing responsibilities, members of the new leisure classes. Ordinary people could not book a hotel for a week in Venice or Zurich. The audience at the average symphony-orchestra subscription concert was more socially diverse; those in the upper galleries made modest wages and came out of a simple love of music. But most preferred to hear Brahms.

• • •

"That is no country for old men," William Butler Yeats cries in "Sailing to Byzantium." The youngest composers, the children of 1900, adapted most easily to the racing tempos of the twenties; they had the metabolism to digest fresh paradigms overnight. The older ones faced an agonizing adjustment—and to be old in that youth-mad time was to be over the age of forty. Bartók probably spoke for many when he wrote in a letter of 1926, the year of Yeats's poem: "To be frank, recently I have felt so stupid, so dazed, so empty-headed that I have truly doubted whether I am able to write anything new at all anymore. All the tangled chaos that the musical periodicals vomit thick and fast about the music of today has come to weigh heavily on me: the watchwords, linear, horizontal, vertical, objective, impersonal, polyphonic, homophonic, tonal, polytonal, atonal, and the rest . . ." Stravinsky let out a howl of disgust in a letter to Ansermet in 1922: "Here I am the *head of modern music*, as they say and so I believe, here I am forty years old—here I am being passed over in the grand prizes of the 'great international congress' in Salzburg . . . The committee reserved places of great importance on the program for Darius Milhaud, Ernest Blook [*sic*], Richard Strauss (probably Corngold [*sic*], Casella, Varese [*sic*], too)—all the musicians of 'international' stature . . . Oh, the *cons*."

Ravel's moment of crisis came when he played his new ballet score *La Valse* for Diaghilev in 1920. "Ravel, it's a masterpiece, but it isn't a ballet," the impresario told him. "It's a portrait of a ballet, a painting of a ballet." Evidently, Diaghilev was saying that Ravel's score lacked the pitiless spirit that the postwar era required.

The verdict was bizarre, for *La Valse* is both a dazzling incarnation of the twenties and a dazzling satire of it. It begins as a nostalgic journey in three-quarter time, Old Europe waltzing in the twilight. A stepwise intensification of dissonance and dynamics suggests the fury of the war just past, the wedding of aristocratic pride to the machinery of destruction. In the last moments, with trombones snarling and percussion rattling, the music becomes brassy, sassy, and fierce. Suddenly we seem to be in the middle of a flapper gin party—and there is no reason to feel any jolt of transition, since the Roaring Twenties were underwritten by the same fortunes that had financed the prewar balls. This is a society spinning out of control, reeling from the horrors of the recent past toward those of the near future.

Bartók's confusion went deeper than matters of style: his personal history had been largely obliterated by the cartographic fiats of the peace treaties. The reduction of Hungarian territory after the collapse of the Austro-Hungarian Empire meant that Nagyszentmiklós, the composer's birthplace, went to Romania, and that Pozsony, where his mother still lived, became Czechoslovak.

Nonetheless, Bartók remained loyal to the landscape of his dreams—that hidden empire of peasant music, which stretched as far as Turkey and North Africa. As Hungary moved toward fascism under the authoritarian government of Miklós Horthy, such multiculturalism attracted suspicion; nationalists perceived Bartók as lacking in true Hungarian spirit. At the same time, his allegiance to folklore made him a quaint, anachronistic figure on the international new-music circuit. He was too cosmopolitan at home, too nationalist abroad. He was, however, finding the balance he had always sought, between the local and the universal. Less concerned with policing the boundaries between genres, he stopped agitating against the supposed contaminations of Gypsy music; Hungarian Gypsy fiddling appears all over his two Rhapsodies for violin and his Second Violin Concerto. Occasionally, he even indulged in a bit of jazz. As Julie Brown has pointed out, Bartók responded to the rise of genocidal racism by extolling "racial impurity"—the migration of styles, the intermingling of cultures.

In the first years of the postwar period Bartók strove to establish his modernist credentials. When the Danish composer Carl Nielsen came to Budapest in 1920, Bartók asked him whether he thought his Second Quartet was "sufficiently modern." The ballet *The Miraculous Mandarin*, finished the previous year, matched the polytonal violence of the *Rite*, with a hint of Futurism in the honking cityscape of the prelude (" 'stylized' noise," Bartók called it). The strutting harshness of the two violin sonatas, the Piano Sonata, the piano suite *Out of Doors*, the First Piano Concerto, and the Third Quartet, all composed in the early and mid-twenties, won respect from the Schoenberg camp. But Bartók's melodies retained a folkish shape, and the harmony again stopped short of full atonality. These works use symmetrical scales that revolve around a "tonal center," a single pitch that sounds somehow "right" whenever it appears. In the wide-ranging Fourth Quartet, written in 1928, dissonant dances frame an ethereal slow movement that glides around the key of E major without quite touching it. In the final *tranquillo* section, the violin plays a sweet folkish melody, akin to the "Peacock Melody" of Magyar tradition. The composer has returned to first principles.

In several masterpieces of Bartók's last years—the Music for Strings, Percussion, and Celesta (1936), the Second Violin Concerto (1937–38), and the Concerto for Orchestra (1943)—the ceremony of homecoming is repeated. The final movement of each work brings a palpable feeling of release, as if the composer, who had observed peasants with shy detachment, were finally throwing away his notebook and entering the fray. Strings whip up dust clouds around manic dancing feet. Brass play secular chorales, as if seated on the dented steps of a tilting little church. Winds squawk like excited children. Drums bang the drunken lust of young men at the center of the crowd. There are no sacrificial victims in these neoprimitive scenes, even if some walk away with bruises. The ritual of return is most poignant in the Concerto for Orchestra, which Bartók wrote in American exile. Transylvania was by then a purely mental space that he could dance across from end to end, even as his final illness immobilized him.

Bartók and Janáček met twice in the twenties. The second time, in 1927, Janáček is said to have grabbed Bartók by the shoulders and dragged him into a quiet corner. Posterity would love to have a precise record of that conversation, but the eyewitness report is frustratingly impressionistic: "fascinating exchange . . . a fireworks of personalities . . ." Did Janáček urge Bartók to be true to his national, folkish self, as Debussy had urged Stravinsky?

By now well into his seventies, the Moravian master was more bemused than intimidated by the culture of the festivals; he liked to tell the story that when he tried to find his way to the stage to take a bow at the ISCM festival of 1925, he opened the wrong door and found himself out on the street. The belated international success of *Jenůfa* gave him the confidence to stay on the path that he had marked out before the turn of the century.

Janáček's creative Indian summer is often attributed to his infatuation with Kamila Stösslová, a young married woman whom he met in 1917. Richly imagined female characters populate his last works: the "dark-skinned Gypsy girl" who seduces a farmer's son in the song cycle *The Diary of One Who Disappeared*; Katerina, the tragic heroine of the opera *Katya Kabanova*, who throws herself into the Volga River to escape the tormenting rectitude of her mother-in-law; the female fox at the heart of the animal fable *The Cunning Little Vixen*, who finds love in the forest and then falls to the gun of a poacher; and the unlikely protagonist of *The Makropoulos Affair*, a 337-year-old opera singer who has achieved immortality at the price of being "cold as ice."

Janáček's late style is lean and strong. Melodies are whittled down but do not lose their grace. Rhythms move like a needle on a gramophone, skipping as if stuck in a rut or slowing down as if someone were fiddling with the speed. One signature sound is a raw pealing of trumpets, which ushers in both the rustic military Sinfonietta and the *Glagolitic Mass*, a setting of the Old Slavonic liturgy. In the mass, liturgical phrases such as "Lord have mercy," "Crucified for us," "I believe," and "Lamb of God" are linked to changing phases of rural weather: lashing rain, lightning, a clearing sky, a spell of moonlight, a pale sun the following day. Christianity and paganism are reconciled.

The Cunning Little Vixen, at once a charming children's tale and a profound allegory of modern life, may be Janáček's greatest achievement. It begins innocuously, as a folksy old forester—as a child Janáček dreamed of being a forester—captures a fox cub and brings her to his home. She runs amok, slaughters the chickens, and is banished to the woods. There she finds a handsome lover and woos him to music that parodies post-Wagnerian opera, notably Strauss in his kitschier moods. In Act III, the vixen is felled by a rifle shot, and the opera takes on an altogether different tone. In the final scene the forester steps out of his folk-tale role and meditates on the passage of time. He seems to be musing about the very opera that he's in: "Is this fairy tale or reality? Reality or fairy tale?" The forester falls asleep, and when he wakes the animals of the woods surround him. He sees fox cubs at play and realizes that they are the vixen's children. He then catches a little frog in his hand, thinking he's seeing the same "clammy little monster" whom he met in the first scene of the opera:

FORESTER: Where have you come from?

FROG: That wasn't me, that was grandpa! They told me all about you.

In other words, the animals of the forest have been telling stories about the forester over the course of their brief lives, as if he were a hero from long ago. In the disjuncture between human and animal time we see him—and ourselves—across an immense space. "Good and evil turn around in life afresh," Janáček wrote in his own synopsis.

The forester smiles and goes back to sleep. His gun slips from his hands. The vixen's music returns, raised to extraordinary vehemence by pealing brass and pounding timpani. A circular motif plays twice over chords of D-flat major, then modulates to E major; finally, as the harmony returns to D-flat, the melody clings to its E-major pitches, producing a rich modal sonority, a bluesy seventh chord. It recalls the ending of *Jenůfa*, the walk into paradise. "You must play this for me when I die," Janáček said to his producer. Which they did, in August 1928.

Stravinsky's moment of high anxiety arrived when he performed his Piano Sonata at the 1925 ISCM festival in Venice. Janáček was there; so, too, were Diaghilev, Honegger, the Princesse de Polignac, Cole Porter, Arturo Toscanini, and Schoenberg, with his red gaze. Many questioned Stravinsky's new neoclassical style; the rumor went around that he was no longer "serious," that he had become a pasticheur. Schoenberg reportedly walked out. Stravinsky must have been aware of the skepticism all around; insecurity, writes his biographer Stephen Walsh, was "the demon that lurked permanently in the inner regions of Stravinsky's consciousness." Emotional tensions preyed on him as well. Yekaterina Stravinsky, his wife, had suffered a breakdown, the result of a tubercular condition. Yekaterina's devotion to Russian Orthodoxy seemed a silent rebuke of her husband's dandyish lifestyle, not to mention his ongoing affair with Vera Sudeykina.

A few days before the concert, an abscess appeared on Stravinsky's right hand. Somewhat to his own surprise, he went to a church, got on his knees, and asked for divine aid. Just before sitting down to play, he checked under the bandage and saw that the abscess was gone. This sudden cure struck Stravinsky as a miracle, and he began to experience a religious reawakening. His official "return to sacraments" took place almost a year later, during Holy Week of 1926, when he reported to Diaghilev that he was fasting "out of extreme mental and spiritual need." Around the same time, Stravinsky wrote a brief, pungent setting of the Lord's Prayer in Old Slavonic. Over the next five years he wrote a trilogy of solemn-toned or explicitly sacred works: *Oedipus Rex*, *Apollo*, *Symphony of Psalms*. Religion was his new "reality," his new foundation; it gave substance to his devotion to the past and, not incidentally, direction to his mildly dissolute life.

In rediscovering religion, Stravinsky was, paradoxically, following fashion. The year 1925 was one of newfound sobriety in French culture. Many were pondering a valedictory essay by the recently deceased Jacques Rivière on the "crisis of the concept of literature"; the critic had proposed that the arts were becoming too disinterested, too "inhuman," and he listed Stravinsky's "music of objects" among the symptoms of an ethical and spiritual decline. Cocteau, having suffered the loss of his underage lover Raymond Radiguet, fallen into opium addiction, and experienced a hallucinatory epiphany in Picasso's elevator, returned to Catholicism in June of the same year. Cocteau's guru was the neo-Thomist philosopher Jacques Maritain, who believed that modern art could purify itself into an image of God's truth, into something "well made, complete, proper, durable, honest."

Stravinsky, too, fell under Maritain's influence, perhaps chastened when the philosopher criticized the notion of "art *for nothing*, for nothing else but itself." After considering the idea of an opera or oratorio on the life of Saint Francis of Assisi, Stravinsky elected to pursue a topic from ancient tragedy, and asked Cocteau to write a French-language adaptation of the story of Oedipus. He then had Cocteau's text translated into Latin. "The choice [of Latin]," Stravinsky later wrote, "had the great advantage of giving me a medium not dead, but turned to stone and so monumentalized as to have become immune from all risk of vulgarization." The score instructed: "Only their arms and heads move. They should give the impression of living statues." This marked a commitment to Rivière's project of spiritual rehabilitation, to Maritain's philosophy of art as sacred work.

Cocteau's involvement meant that *Oedipus* could go only so far in the direction of solemnity. The Latin declamations were strung together with a self-consciously, satirically pompous French-language narration. Cocteau's Speaker is so wrapped up in his literary dignity that he sometimes fails to notice what is happening onstage. "And now you will hear the famous monologue, 'The Divine Jocasta is dead,'" he proclaims—but no monologue ensues.

Such self-conscious gestures might have turned *Oedipus* into another panoply of camp. But Stravinsky was in earnest. "*Kaedit nos pestis*"—"Plague is upon us"—the chorus chants at the opening, over five booming chords in the key of B-flat minor. On its own, the core progression would sound a bit creaky and clichéd. What adds drama is the bass line, which sticks to the notes of the B-flat-minor triad but gnashes against the changing chords above. The impression, here and throughout the work, is of damaged, decaying grandeur—like acid streaks on cathedral marble. Yet *Oedipus* is a *living* statue, as the score instructs. Stravinsky's alertness to the rhythm of words puts bounce and thrust into the archaic Latin text. The word "*moritur*," coming at the end of the three opening gestures, sets in motion a purring triplet figure that propels the work to the end.

The ballet *Apollon musagète*, the second panel in Stravinsky's sacred triptych, is a serene spectacle of art in contemplation of itself: the young god Apollo matures and achieves mastery in the company of the muses Calliope, Polyhymnia, and Terpsichore. The scoring, for strings alone, reverses the post-*Rite* trend toward hard sonorities of winds and brass, which, in a typical feat of chutzpah, Stravinsky now chided his contemporaries for overexploiting. ("The swing of the pendulum was too violent," he wrote in his *Autobiography*, as if someone else had set the pendulum in motion.) *Apollo* floats by on straightforward major-key harmonies and draws on a vein of tender melody; collage-like cutting and layering give way to a smooth, unbroken surface.

In a prior Ballets Russes season, the airy conception of a "white ballet" might have been realized in an annoyingly precious way. With the arrival of George Balanchine, though, Stravinsky found his creative other half. Balanchine's project of recapturing the equipoise of classical dance through modern choreography—sometimes athletic, sometimes abstract—was the mirror image of Stravinsky's new style. The union of dance and music suggested a higher union of body and spirit. Boris de

Schloezer, who earlier in the decade had attacked the composer for perpetrating musical jokes, grasped the new Stravinsky when he wrote, "Logically, after *Apollo*, he ought to give us a Mass."

This Stravinsky more or less did, in an attitude of grief. In August 1929 the composer was stunned by the sudden death of Diaghilev, his discoverer, protector, and substitute father, and his distress was intensified by the fact that he had not had the chance to make proper farewells; the two men had lately bickered and fallen out. Meanwhile, Yekaterina grew sicker and more devout. Icons and candles filled the Stravinsky home, and there was talk of building a private chapel. Out of this fervid atmosphere arose the *Symphony of Psalms*.

The texts come from the Latin vulgate versions of Psalms 38, 39, and 150, but the music has something intangible in common with Russian Orthodoxy. For the American critic Paul Rosenfeld, it "called to our mind the mosaic-gilded interior of one of the Byzantine domes . . . from whose vaulting the Christ and his Mother gaze pitilessly down upon the accursed human race." The first chord fulfills Rosenfeld's cathedral metaphor: E-minor triads in the bass and treble are arranged around columnar Gs in the middle registers. Throughout, the habitually economical composer enlarges his sense of space. The setting of Psalm 150 ("Praise God in his holy place, praise him in the heavenly vault of his power") goes on for a relative eternity of twelve minutes.

The *Symphony* is not all frozen architecture. Stravinsky's trademark rhythms make subtle appearances. At one point in Psalm 150, the chorus lightly syncopates the phrase "*Lau-da-te do-mi*-nuumm," with the "*do*" falling between the second and the third beats and the last syllable prolonged to fill out the bar—almost like the Charleston. And in the raptly contemplative coda, the timpani repeat a four-note pattern over forty-two bars, the quasi-minimalist ostinato creating an almost imperceptible tension with the prevailing meter of three beats to a bar—a bounce of an ethereal, incorporeal kind.

Almost from the beginning, listeners worried that Stravinsky's wizardly creations were marred by an inner coldness. Ned Rorem, an American composer firmly committed to the "French" rather than the "German" politics of style, has asked himself: "Do I adore Stravinsky as I adore others who are perhaps less overwhelming—Ravel, for example, or Poulenc? I am dazzled by his intelligence and scared by his force, but my heart is not melted." If anything by Stravinsky can melt the heart, it is the *Symphony of Psalms*. The great nonexpresser and maker of objects lets down his guard, giving us a glimpse of his terrors and longings. Notice a telltale repetition of words in the first two psalms that Stravinsky chose to set: "Hear my prayer, O Lord, and give ear unto my cry . . . I waited patiently for the Lord; and he inclined unto me, and heard my cry." William James, in *The Varieties of Religious Experience*, wrote that a condition of desperate mental flailing is often the prelude to spiritual renewal: "Here is the real core of the religious problem: Help! help!"

Help for what? Stravinsky's biography provides plentiful fodder for speculation, but the underlying impetus may have been a growing discomfort with modernity itself—panic in the face of the speed and noise. Reality, into which so many artists yearned to plunge, turned out to be an engulfing medium. Young aesthetes went off to the trenches of the Great War hoping to acquire a manly finish; the survivors were shattered rather than invigorated by the ordeal. Perhaps for this reason, those who had earlier attempted to escape the temple of "pure music" now tried to find their way back in. In the end, the Germanic philosophy of musical universalism, according to which a few set forms and procedures would serve the composers of all nations, once more functioned as a bulwark against an increasingly indifferent culture. As in Yeats's poem, European composers embraced the sublimity of artifice, "to sing / To lords and ladies of Byzantium / Of what is past, or passing, or to come."

4

INVISIBLE MEN

American Composers from Ives to Ellington

To understand the cultural unease that gripped composers in the Roaring Twenties, you need only read the work of Carl Van Vechten, the American critic, novelist, and social gadfly who, in the 1920s, more or less defected from classical music to jazz and blues. The writer started out as a second-string music critic at the *New York Times*, dutifully chronicling the city's concert life in the years before the First World War. During an extended stay in Paris, he warmed to the European moderns and witnessed the riot of the *Rite* in the company of Gertrude Stein. By the end of the war, though, Van Vechten was getting his kicks chiefly from popular music, and in a 1917 essay he predicted that Irving Berlin and other Tin Pan Alley songwriters would be considered "the true grandfathers of the Great American Composer of the year 2001." Finally, he pledged his allegiance to African-American culture, writing off concert music as a spent force. In the controversial 1926 novel *Nigger Heaven*, he observed that black artists were in complete possession of the "primitive birthright . . . that all the civilized races were struggling to get back to—this fact explained the art of a Picasso or a Stravinsky."

The writings of Van Vechten, Gilbert Seldes, and other rebellious young American intellectuals of the twenties show a paradigm shift under way. They depict popular artists not as entertainers but as major artists, modernists from the social margins. In the twenties, for the first time in history, classical composers lacked assurance that they were the sole guardians of the grail of progress. Other innovators and progenitors were emerging. They were American. They often lacked the polish of a conservatory education. And, increasingly, they were black.

One nineteenth-century composer saw this change coming, or at least sensed it. In 1892, the Czech master Antonín Dvořák, whose feeling for his native culture had inspired the young Janáček, went to New York to teach at the newly instituted National Conservatory. A man of rural peasant origins, Dvořák had few prejudices about the social background or skin color of prospective talent. In Manhattan he befriended the young black singer and composer Harry T. Burleigh, who introduced him to the African-American spirituals. Dvořák decided that this music held the key to America's musical future. He began plotting a new symphonic work that would draw on African-American and Native American material: the mighty Ninth Symphony, subtitled "From the New World." With the help of a ghostwriter, Dvořák also aired his views in public, in an article titled "Real Value of Negro Melodies," which appeared in the *New York Herald* on May 21, 1893:

> I am now satisfied that the future music of this country must be founded upon what are called the negro melodies. This must be the real foundation of any serious and original school of composition to be developed in the United States . . . All of the great musicians have borrowed from the songs of the common people. Beethoven's most charming scherzo is based upon what might now be considered a skillfully handled negro melody . . . In the negro melodies of America I discover all that is needed for a great and noble school of music. They are pathetic, tender, passionate, melancholy, solemn, religious, bold, merry, gay or what you will. It is music that suits itself to any mood or any purpose. There is nothing in the whole range of composition that cannot be supplied with themes from this source.

At a time when lynching was a social sport in the South, and in a year when excursion trains brought ten thousand people to Paris, Texas, so that they could watch a black man being paraded through town, tortured, and burned at the stake, Dvořák's embrace of African-American spirituals was a notable gesture. The visiting celebrity didn't just urge white composers to make use of black material; he promoted blacks themselves as composers. Most provocative of all was his imputation of a "Negro" strain in Beethoven—a heresy against the Aryan philosophies that were gaining ground in Europe.

Black music is so intertwined with the wider history of American music that the story of the one is to a great extent the story of the other. Everything runs along the color line, as W. E. B. Du Bois wrote in *The Souls of Black Folk*. Still, it's worth asking why the music of 10 percent of the population should have had such influence.

In 1939, a Harvard undergraduate named Leonard Bernstein tried to give an answer, in a paper titled "The Absorption of Race Elements into American Music." Great music in the European tradition, young Bernstein declared, had grown organically from national sources, both in a "material" sense (folk tunes serving as sources for composition) and in a "spiritual" sense (folkish music speaking for the ethos of a place). Bernstein's two-tiered conception, which acknowledges in equal measure music's autonomy and its social function, makes a good stab at explaining why black music conquered the more open-minded precincts of white America. First, it made a phenomenal sound. The characteristic devices of African-American musicking—the bending and breaking of diatonic scales, the distortion of instrumental timbre, the layering of rhythms, the blurring of the distinction between verbal and nonverbal sound—opened new dimensions in musical space, a realm beyond the written notes. Second, black music compelled attention as a document of spiritual crisis and renewal. It memorialized the wound at the heart of the national experience—the crime of slavery—and it transcended that suffering with acts of individual self-expression and collective affirmation. Thus, black music fulfilled Bernstein's demand for a "*common* American musical material."

What Dvořák did not foresee, and what even the cooler-than-thou Bernstein had trouble grasping, was that the "great and noble school of music" would consist not of classical compositions but of ragtime, jazz, blues, swing, R & B, rock 'n' roll, funk, soul, hip-hop, and whatever's next. Many pioneers of black music might have had major classical careers if the stage door of Carnegie Hall had been open to them, but, with few exceptions, it was not. As the scholar Paul Lopes writes, "The limited resources and opportunities for black artists to perform and create cultivated music for either black or white audiences . . . forced them into a more immediate relationship with the American vernacular." Soon, jazz had its own canon of masters, its own dialectic of establishment and avant-garde: Armstrong the originator, Ellington the classicist, Charlie Parker the revolutionary, and so on. A young Mahler of Harlem had little to gain by going downtown.

Separateness became a source of power; there were other ways to get the message out, other lines of transmission. Black musicians were quick to appropriate technologies that classical music adopted only fitfully. The protagonist of Ralph Ellison's epochal novel *Invisible Man* sits in his basement with his record player, listening to "(What Did I Do to Be So) Black and Blue." He says, "Perhaps I like Louis Armstrong because he's made poetry out of being invisible." The invisible man broadcasts on the "lower frequencies" to which society has consigned him. Incidentally, Ellison once thought of becoming a composer. He took a few lessons from Wallingford Riegger, an early American admirer of Schoenberg. Then, like so many others, he stopped.

To tell the story of American composition in the early twentieth century is to circle around an absent center. The great African-American orchestral works that Dvořák prophesied are mostly absent, their promise transmuted into jazz. Nonetheless, the landscape teems with interesting life. White composers faced another, far milder kind of prejudice; their very existence was deemed inessential by the Beethoven-besotted concertgoers of the urban centers. They tried many routes around the intractable fact of audience apathy, embracing radical dissonance (Charles Ives, Edgard Varèse, Carl Ruggles), radical simplicity (Virgil Thomson), a black-and-white, classical-popular fusion (George Gershwin). For the most part, the identity of the American composer was a kind of nonidentity, an ethnicity of solitude.

Aaron Copland, whose story will be told in later chapters, once pointed out that the job of being an American artist often consists simply in making art *possible*—which is to say, visible. Every generation has to do the work all over again. Composers perennially lack state support; they lack a broad audience; they lack a centuries-old tradition. For some, this isolation is debilitating, but for others it is liberating; the absence of tradition means freedom from tradition. One way or another, all American composers are invisible men.

Will Marion Cook

The early history of African-American composition, at the end of the nineteenth century and the beginning of the twentieth, is full of sorrowful tales. Scott Joplin, the composer of "Maple Leaf Rag" and "The Entertainer," spent his last years in a futile effort to stage his opera *Treemonisha*, which vibrantly blended bel canto melody and rag rhythm. Syphilis invaded Joplin's brain, and he died insane in 1917. Harry Lawrence Freeman, the founder of the Negro Grand Opera Company in Harlem, wrote two Wagnerian tetralogies with black characters, only one part of which was ever staged. Saddest of all, perhaps, was the case of Maurice Arnold Strothotte, whom Dvořák singled out as "the most promising and gifted" of his American pupils. Arnold's *American Plantation Dances* was played at a National Conservatory concert in 1894 to much applause. The conductor-scholar Maurice Peress has shown that Dvořák's familiar *Humoresque* borrowed from an episode in Arnold's work. The conservatory concert was, unfortunately, the high-water mark of the young man's career. He continued writing music—an opera titled *The Merry Benedicts*, music for silent films, an *American Rhapsody*, a Symphony in F Minor—but performances were few. Instead, he made a living conducting operetta and teaching violin. Like the hero of James Weldon Johnson's *Autobiography of an Ex-Colored Man*, he apparently stopped identifying as black, living out his final years in the heavily German neighborhood of Yorkville. Oblivion engulfed him all the same.

Other stories had happier endings. The little-known life of the violinist, composer, conductor, and teacher Will Marion Cook serves as a useful case study in the development of African-American music from 1900 to 1930. If this charismatic, obstinate personality ultimately failed in his quest to conquer the classical realm, he did experience moments of triumph, and blazed a separate trail for many black artists who followed him. Among other things, he forms a direct link between Dvořák and Duke Ellington.

Cook's biography, sketchily documented, has been pieced together by the scholar Marva Griffin Carter. Born in 1869, Cook grew up in Washington, D.C., the son of middle-class parents. When his father died, he went to live with his grandparents in Chattanooga, where his arrogance created the sorts of disciplinary problems that are often noted in youngsters of unusual talent. He used to go to the top of Lookout Mountain, outside Chattanooga, to plot his future fame. In his unpublished autobiography, he wrote: "I would . . . remain there till late at night, planning my whole life, how I would study, become a great musician, and do something about race prejudice . . . Somehow I felt that such music might be the lever by which my people could raise their status. All my life I've dreamed dreams, but never more wonderful or more grandiose dreams than those inspired by Lookout Mountain."

Cook was then accepted into Oberlin, one of very few American colleges where black students could study alongside whites. A professor noticed his skill as a violinist and advised him to study with Joseph Joachim, who headed the Hochschule für Musik in Berlin. With some assistance from the slave-turned-orator Frederick Douglass, who belonged to Mrs. Cook's social circle, the boy gained admittance to Joachim's academy.

The Kaiser's Berlin proved surprisingly welcoming. According to the autobiography, titled *Hell of a Life*, Joachim took the young African-American under his wing, expressing a liking for his passionate playing and his untamed personality. "You are a stranger in a strange land," the violinist supposedly said. "We are going to become friends. Come to my house for lunch Sunday." At Joachim's gatherings Cook could have met or glimpsed many of the leading personalities of German music, including Hans von Bülow and the young Richard Strauss. In the winter of 1889, none other than Johannes Brahms came to the Hochschule to celebrate Joachim's fiftieth anniversary as a performer. In all, Cook seems to have enjoyed his time in Germany; the sight of a black violinist was apparently too exotic to arouse racial fears.

Compare the experiences of W. E. B. Du Bois, who began studying economics and history in Berlin just as Cook left. According to David Levering Lewis's biography, Du Bois "felt exceptionally free" during his Berlin sojourn—"more liberated . . . than he would ever feel again." On a train ride to Lübeck, Du Bois sang Beethoven's "Ode to Joy"—"All men will be brothers"—and dreamed of a better world. The young philosopher also became enamored of the Wagner operas, gaining from them an appreciation of how art could inflame national and racial spirit. In his story "Of the Coming of John," which appeared in *The Souls of Black Folk*, a Southern youth named John Jones attends a performance of *Lohengrin* and feels in it the contours of a better life: "A deep longing swelled in all his heart to rise with that clear music out of the dirt and dust of that low life that held him prisoned and befouled. If he could only live up in the free air where birds sang and setting suns had no touch of blood!" Then—here Du Bois reveals his "double-consciousness," his awareness of how even the most "cultured" black man is perceived—an usher taps John on the shoulder and asks him to leave.

That tap on the shoulder, metaphorical or not, Will Marion Cook came to know well when he returned to America. He tried to make his name as a violinist, advertising himself improbably as a "musical phenomenon performing some of the masterpieces upon his violin with one hand." Making little headway, he then formed the William Marion Cook Orchestra, with Frederick Douglass as honorary president. At around the same time, Cook wrote, or began writing, an opera based on Harriet Beecher Stowe's *Uncle Tom's Cabin*. Most significantly, in 1893, he went to Chicago to participate in the World's Columbian Exposition, a momentous event at which America declared its new status as a world power. In an effort to counteract the stereotypes of black savagery that figured in some of the fair's displays—crowds flocked to watch and hear the African drummers of Dahomey Village—Douglass organized a Colored People's Day, which aimed to affirm the nobility of the black American experience. Newspapers mocked Douglass by speculating that watermelons would be sold in bulk.

Colored People's Day was to have featured excerpts from Cook's *Uncle Tom's Cabin*, but the singer Sissieretta Jones failed to receive the travel advance that she needed to make the trip, and the performance was canceled. Yet the exposition wasn't a total waste for Cook. He obtained a letter of introduction to Dvořák, who evidently invited him to study at the National Conservatory. (Jeannette Thurber, the founder of the conservatory, had a policy of admitting Negro students free of charge.) There is little record of what Cook did during his first years in New York, but circumstantial evidence suggests that racism put a quick end to his dreams. One anecdote is cited in Duke Ellington's memoir, *Music Is My Mistress*. Cook makes his Carnegie Hall debut, and a critic hails him as "the world's greatest Negro violinist." Cook barges in on the critic and smashes his violin on the man's desk. "I am not the world's greatest Negro violinist," he shouts. "I am the greatest violinist in the world!" Marva Griffin Carter finds no evidence that such an incident took place, but yelling matches probably ensued as the temperamental Cook made the rounds of the concert halls.

Barred from the classical world, Cook got work where he could find it. In 1898 he collaborated with the poet Paul Laurence Dunbar on a musical revue titled *Clorindy; or, The Origin of the Cakewalk*, which opened on Broadway with an all-black cast. This was, at first glance, yet another self-denigrating minstrel show full of talk of "coons" and "darkeys." But, as Carter points out, the lyrics often have a hidden sting, making "confrontational jabs" at white listeners. The hit number "Darktown Is Out Tonight" delivers a prophecy of the coming sovereignty of black music:

For the time
Comin' mighty soon,
When the best,
Like the rest
Gwine a-be singin' coon.

When Cook's mother came to the show, she was distressed to see his Berlin education going to this end. A Negro composer should write just like a white man, she told him. Yet the composer could look back on *Clorindy* and its successor, *In Dahomey*, as examples of a black composer finally finding his own voice. "On Emancipation Day," *In Dahomey*'s big number, repeats the prophecy of "Darktown" in even starker terms:

All you white folks clear de way,
Brass ban' playin' sev'ral tunes
Darkies eyes look jes' lak moons . . .
When dey hear dem ragtime tunes
White fo'ks try to pass fo' coons
On Emancipation day.

The first chords of the overture, which recur at the beginning of "On Emancipation Day," echo the opening of the Largo of Dvořák's *New World* Symphony.

Cook's musicals, sophisticated in technique and assertive in tone, anticipated the spirit of the Harlem Renaissance, which came into its own around 1925. Since the beginning of the century, W. E. B. Du Bois had been calling for a "Talented Tenth" of black intellectuals and artists to lead the masses to a better place in society. The upsurge of artistic activity in Harlem in the twenties fulfilled Du Bois's prophecy, although the elitism implicit in the phrase "Talented Tenth" would prove problematic. Music was essential to the Renaissance spirit, and Du Bois, the philosopher Alain Locke, and the poet James Weldon Johnson all argued that black composers should avail themselves of European forms, even as they explored the native African-American tradition. Cook himself wrote in 1918: "Developed Negro music has just begun in America. The colored American is finding himself. He has thrown aside puerile imitations of the white man. He has learned that a thorough study of the masters gives knowledge of what is good and how to create. From the Russian he has learned to get his inspiration from within; that his inexhaustible wealth of folklore legends and songs furnish him with material for compositions that will establish a great school of music and enrich musical literature."

Still, Cook could not break into "straight" composition. In the second decade of the century, he became a bandleader, putting together a sharp group called the New York Syncopated Orchestra, which later toured Europe under the name Southern Syncopated Orchestra. Although Cook never felt comfortable with jazz—improvisation grated against his conservatory training—he highlighted the new sounds that were emerging from New Orleans, and hired the young clarinet virtuoso Sidney Bechet as his star soloist. The conductor Ernest Ansermet, who took an avid interest in jazz just as it was developing, heard Cook's orchestra play in 1919 and, with an alertness that has won him a place of honor in anthologies of jazz writing, acclaimed Bechet as a "genius" and Cook as a "master in every respect." Back in 1893 Anton Rubinstein had predicted that Negro musicians could form "a new musical school" in twenty-five or thirty years. Twenty-five years later, Ansermet perceived in Bechet's and Cook's performances "a highway that the world may rush down tomorrow."

Cook was hardly the only black musician to turn from classical study to a popular career. Many classically trained black musicians played significant roles in early jazz, giving the lie to the simplistic and racist idea that it was a purely instinctive, illiterate form. Will Vodery worked as a librarian for the Philadelphia and Chicago orchestras in his youth and showed promise as a conductor, but his career took off only when Florenz Ziegfeld, the master showman of Broadway, hired him to arrange music for his Follies. James Reese Europe trained on the violin but found no work when he arrived in New York in 1903; instead, he began playing bar piano, conducting theatricals, and leading bands. His all-black Clef Club Orchestra and Hell Fighters band introduced a broad audience to syncopated music that was a step or two away from jazz. Fletcher Henderson, Ellington's future rival for the crown of king of swing, started out as a classical piano prodigy; when he went to work with Ethel Waters in New York, he had to learn jazz piano by listening to James P. Johnson piano rolls. Johnson himself, Harlem's reigning stride pianist, had compositional aspirations that were only partly fulfilled. In a later generation, Billy Strayhorn, destined to win fame as Ellington's chief collaborator, shone as a composing prodigy in his youth and wowed his high-school classmates with a Concerto for Piano and Percussion.

The same scenario kept repeating. Middle-class parents would send their sons and daughters to Oberlin or Fisk or the National Conservatory, hoping that they could achieve the wonderful things that Dvořák had forecast for African-American music. Hitting the wall of prejudice, these young creative musicians would turn to popular styles instead—first out of frustration, then out of ambition, finally out of pride. The youngest players embraced jazz as their birthright; they gave little thought to Dvořák's old fantasy of Negro symphonies. Cook, however, never forgot the ambitions that he had nursed as a boy, when he stood on Lookout Mountain. He still dreamed of a "black Beethoven, burned to the bone by the African sun."

Charles Ives

Inscribed above the stage of Symphony Hall in Boston, one of America's great music palaces, is the name BEETHOVEN, occupying much the same position as a crucifix in a church. In several late-nineteenth- and early-twentieth-century concert halls, the names of the European masters appear all around the circumference of the auditorium, signifying unambiguously that the buildings are cathedrals for the worship of imported musical icons. Early in the century, any aspiring young composer who sat in one of these halls—a white male, needless to say, blacks being generally unwelcome and women generally not taken seriously—would likely have fallen prey to pessimistic thoughts. The very design of the place militated against the possibility of a native musical tradition. How could your name ever be carved alongside Beethoven's or Grieg's when all available spaces were filled? The fact that so many American composers still came forward is a tribute to the willfulness of the species.

Charles Ives was one such stubborn youth. He came from a distinguished New England family, the descendant of a farmer who arrived in Connecticut fifteen years after the voyage of the *Mayflower*. His grandparents George White Ives and Sarah Hotchkiss Wilcox Ives had connections to the Transcendentalists, the royalty of American intellectual life; Emerson himself supposedly once spent a night in their Danbury house. Ives's father was the bandleader George Ives, about whom little is known beyond Charles's not always reliable recollections. Whether the father really anticipated the son's experiments is impossible to determine, but one famous tale is corroborated by eyewitness testimony: the bandleader once marched two bands past each other for the simple joy of hearing them in cacophonous simultaneity. Ives also remembers that he and his brothers were directed to sing Stephen Foster's plantation tune "Old Folks at Home" in the key of E-flat while George played the accompaniment in C.

Charles attended Yale College, where he studied composition with Horatio Parker, under whose tutelage he produced an expert, Dvořákian four-movement symphony. In 1898 the young composer went to New York, where he worked a day job at the Mutual Life Insurance Company and played the organ and directed music at the Central Presbyterian Church. (He had been an expert organist since his teens, using the instrument to experiment with spatial effects and multiple layers of activity.) In 1902 Ives attracted positive attention with a cantata titled *The Celestial Country*. The *Musical Courier* detected "undoubted earnestness in study and talent for composition"; the *Times* called the new work "scholarly and well made," "spirited and melodious." Ives seemed poised for a distinguished career. First he would study with an important name in Europe, then he would find a position on an Ivy League faculty.

Just one week after the successful premiere, however, Ives suddenly resigned his church position, and subsequently vanished from the musical scene. Why he did so remains a mystery. Perhaps he had been expecting a more ecstatic reception to his debut; tellingly, he later scrawled the words "Damn rot and worse" over one of the reviews of *The Celestial Country*. Biographers have added speculation that this athletic young male, Yale's "Dasher" Ives, had a sort of macho hang-up with respect to American classical-music culture, which, to his eyes, appeared to be an "emasculated art," controlled by women patrons, effeminate men, and fashionable foreigners ("pussies," "sissies," "pansies," and so on). More prosaically, Ives may have lost faith when an acquaintance was picked to teach at Yale as Parker's heir apparent.

Instead, Ives chose to make his living in life insurance, at which he proved remarkably adept. He was a proponent of the hard sell, skilled at getting people to buy policies that they didn't know they wanted. He didn't go door-to-door himself; his job was to think up sales techniques that could be passed along to a network of freelance brokers. Ives codified his innovations in the pamphlet *The Amount to Carry*, which laid out a sales pitch "simple enough to be understood by the many, and complex enough to be of some value to all!" Ives told each salesman to plant himself firmly in front of a potential customer's door and "knock some BIG ideas into his mind."

In the evenings and on the weekends, Ives continued writing music, concealing his work from his business associates and making little effort to publicize it to the world at large. In almost total intellectual isolation, he launched an American musical revolution, either discarding the rules he learned at Yale or reinventing them on his own terms. At times, he unloosed dissonances that rivaled Schoenberg's. In more carefree moods, he delighted in popular sounds and miscellaneous Americana. His philosophy of music was almost diametrically opposed to his philosophy of insurance; he preferred to imagine a world in which music could somehow circulate without being bought or sold. "Music may be yet unborn," he wrote in *Essays Before a Sonata*, the companion volume to his piano masterpiece, the *Concord* Sonata. "Perhaps no music has ever been written or heard. Perhaps the birth of art will take place at the moment in which the last man who is willing to make a living out of art is gone and gone forever."

Once Ives finally launched himself in the public eye, with the publication of the *Concord* in 1920, a myth began to crystallize around him. Here was an American visionary who had discovered atonality in advance of Schoenberg. When, in 1939, the pianist John Kirkpatrick finally mastered that titanic score and played it in its entirety, Lawrence Gilman of the *New York Herald Tribune* hailed Ives as "one of those exceptional artists whose indifference to réclame is as genuine as it is fantastic and unbelievable." Schoenberg himself made an approving note: "There is a great Man living in this Country—a composer. He has solved the problem how to preserve one's self-esteem and to learn [*sic*]. He responds to negligence by contempt. He is not forced to accept praise or blame. His name is Ives." Later, the legend of Ives the innovator underwent skeptical scrutiny. The author Maynard Solomon wrote a paper alleging that Ives had backdated his scores in an effort to establish his precedence in the race toward atonality. Gayle Sherwood countered by proving that the composer had been tinkering with outlandish harmonies as early as 1898.

Whatever the outcome of that debate, Ives's originality really resides not in his outré chords but in his heterogeneous combinations of American sounds. Like Berg and Bartók, he ranged back and forth between folkish simplicity and dissonance. "Why tonality as such should be thrown out for good, I can't see," Ives once wrote. "Why it should always be present, I can't see."

In early experimental works such as *From the Steeples and the Mountains* and *The Unanswered Question*, Ives experimented with hyperrealistic reproductions of everyday sonic events. In the first piece, bells ring out from multiple village steeples and echo against the mountains. In the second, spells of nervous, dissonant activity are set against a serene, soft swell of strings, evoking the querulousness of stranded human voices amid the indifferent vastness of nature. In the Second Symphony, finished around 1909, Ives opens the old Teutonic form to what the musicologist J. Peter Burkholder calls "borrowed tunes": American hymns, marches, and ditties on the order of "Massa's in de Cold Ground," "Pig Town Fling," "Beulah Land," "De Camptown Races," "Turkey in the Straw," "Columbia, the Gem of the Ocean." These swirl together with quotations from Brahms, Wagner, Tchaikovsky, and Dvořák himself, provocatively leveling the European-American balance.

Finally, in mature large-scale works such as the *Holidays Symphony*, the *Concord* Sonata, and the Third and Fourth symphonies, Ives forges forms that could do justice to his all-American material. Rather than set forth musical ideas in orderly fashion at the outset of a piece, Ives follows a process that Burkholder names "cumulative form": themes materialize from a nebula of possibilities, then build toward a brief, blinding epiphany. In the Third Symphony the epiphany takes the form of the hymn tune "Woodworth" singing out crisply at the end. The tumultuous, magisterial Fourth concludes with a thick fantasia on "Nearer, My God, to Thee."

Three Places in New England, begun around 1914 and finished as late as 1929, is Ives's deepest meditation on American myth. Coincidentally or not, it is also the work in which the black experience matters most. Ives gave clues to his intentions in the autobiographical *Memos* and in the book *Essays Before a Sonata*, both of which touch on the relationship between black and white music. On first reading, the argument may seem predictably prejudiced. Rejecting Dvořák's program for a Negro-based American music, Ives insists that the spirituals had their origins in white gospel hymns and that the Negroes had "exaggerated" this white material. Ragtime, he writes in *Essays Before a Sonata*, "does not 'represent the American nation' any more than some fine old senators represent it." One cannot make music from ragtime any more than one can make a meal of "tomato ketchup and horse-radish."

Then the argument takes an interesting turn. A composer may make use of Negro or Indian motifs, Ives says, if he identifies deeply with the spirit burning in them—"fervently, transcendentally, inevitably, furiously." One must possess the same passion for truth that drove the abolitionist orator Wendell Phillips, who shouted down and shamed a pro-slavery faction at Boston's Faneuil Hall in 1837. Otherwise, the composer should look to his own heritage. What Ives seems to be saying is that the white hymns are no *less* fervent than the black; singers of all colors bend notes to express their spirit. In the end, Ives flatly states, "an African soul under an X-ray looks identically like an American soul."

Ives took pride in the fact that his family had long embraced African-American causes. His grandparents, outspoken abolitionists, had given support to the Hampton Normal and Agricultural Institute, an industrial school for Negroes and Native Americans. After the Civil War, George Ives and his parents more or less adopted a black boy named Henry Anderson Brooks and sent him to study at Hampton. Ives evidently heard ragtime early on, perhaps at the World's Columbian Exposition, which he attended during a summer off from high school. (He seems to have missed the fiasco of Colored People's Day by a day or two.) He often played spirituals on the piano. At one point he planned a set of pieces dealing with black America; it would have included *The Abolitionists*, a dramatization of Wendell Phillips's Faneuil Hall oration.

In the end, this material went into the first movement of *Three Places in New England*. "The 'St. Gaudens' in Boston Common (Col. Shaw and His Colored Regiment)" takes as its subject Augustus Saint-Gaudens's bas-relief sculpture of the Fifty-fourth Massachusetts Infantry, one of the Union's first African-American regiments, which lost more than one hundred men in an assault on the Confederate stronghold of Battery Wagner in 1863. At the head of the score Ives placed a poem of his own composition, in which he depicted "Faces of Souls" marching through pain toward freedom, led along by the "drum-beat of the common-heart." Whether any given tune in "St. Gaudens" represents the soul of a black soldier or a white officer is difficult to make out, but the fact that the composer sometimes called the piece his "Black March" suggests that he considered the Colored Regiment its protagonist.

The score of *Three Places in New England* is held at the Yale University Music Library. A bundle of revisions, additions, and last-minute corrections, it exemplifies the composer's unruly working methods. One inspiration occurred to Ives late in the game: he decided to insert a soft, cloudy, brooding chord of six notes at the head of the "St. Gaudens" movement. The chord fuses triads of A minor and D-sharp minor, and, as in *Salome* and the *Rite*, the tritone gap between them hints at unresolved and perhaps unresolvable conflict—in this case, perhaps the Civil War itself. Out of that mist of sound, a host of hymns and songs emerge, and tunes with African-American associations take precedence. Early on, two Stephen Foster songs, "Old Black Joe" and "Massa's in de Cold Ground," make appearances. Later come "The Battle Cry of Freedom," "Marching Through Georgia," a burst of ragtime, and "Deep River." The "white" tunes are given a relatively straitlaced setting, indicative of the Boston rectitude of Colonel Shaw. "Deep River," that mightiest of spirituals, sounds in noble, lonely tones on the horn.

The tunes converge in what the musicologist Denise Von Glahn has described as an orchestral reenactment of the Colored Regiment's suicidal siege of Battery Wagner. A C-major chord is pierced by a dissonant B:

Colonel Shaw is struck by a bullet as he cries, "Forward, Fifty-fourth!" The "rally round the flag" motif from "The Battle Cry of Freedom" blares out over a stumbling, collapsing march sequence: Sergeant William H. Carney, the first African-American to receive the Medal of Honor, carries the flag above the fray. In the hush that ensues, "Old Black Joe" and "Massa's in de Cold Ground" play once more, leading into a brief, bluesy lament for solo cello. At the end comes a hazy "Amen"—perhaps a funeral procession going up the steps of a church.

What are we hearing? Is Ives seriously suggesting that black soldiers in the Civil War sang "Hear dat mournful sound" as they went into battle? Presumably not. As the title indicates, the work is inspired not by the battle itself but by Saint-Gaudens's sculpture in honor of it. This is Shaw's regiment, as seen by Saint-Gaudens, as seen again by Ives. We are looking back through the eyes of a turn-of-the-century Yankee who cannot sing as the black soldiers sang. When he thinks "Negro," Foster tunes come to mind, as well as anachronistic strains of ragtime. Even so, by shattering these trite associations into fragments, Ives draws closer to the source. The movement seems to look ahead to black music of the near or distant future: the jagged country blues of Skip James, the dreaming chords of Ellington's symphonic jazz, John Coltrane's "sheets of sound." Such resemblances may be nothing more than accidents, but Ives's whole method was to plan accidents. He was incapable of asserting a monolithic point of view; instead, he created a kind of open-ended listening room, a space of limitless echoes.

The Jazz Age

Ives wisely waited until 1920 before trying seriously to publicize his modern Transcendentalist style. Ten years earlier, his work would have made little sense to listeners reared on the courtly values of the Gilded Age. But in the period of the Roaring Twenties there emerged what the scholar Carol Oja has called a "marketplace for modernism," an audience more receptive to disruptive sounds.

Cawing trombone glissandos defined the Original Dixieland Jazz Band's 1917 track "Livery Stable Blues," the first jazz record to capture national attention. Around the same time, audiences were cheering the immigrant Ukrainian pianist-composer Leo Ornstein, a.k.a. "Ornstein the Keyboard Terror," who offered up savage discords and slam-bang virtuosity. Ornstein's most startling effect, co-invented with the California experimentalist Henry Cowell, was the "cluster chord," in which three or more adjacent notes are struck with the hand, the fist, or the forearm. Somehow, Ornstein succeeded in generating an early form of the mass hysteria that would later greet Benny Goodman, Frank Sinatra, and the Beatles. One crowd was said to have "mobbed the lobbies, marched at intervals to the stage, and long clung there to walls, to organ-pipes, pedal-base, stairs, or any niche offering a view."

American music had grown from a well-behaved Eurocentric childhood into a rambunctious adolescence. Oja, in her book *Making Music Modern*, compares several leading composers of the period to "commuters who emerge baffled from the subway, peering in all directions to ground their location." Some adopted the strategy of avant-garde assault, firing off dissonances and percussive timbres that outdid the most unusual sound combinations of Stravinsky and the Viennese. They were dubbed the "ultra-moderns." Others aimed to ingratiate themselves with the concert-going public, garnishing opera and symphony with dollops of jazz. On the other side of the shaky popular-classical divide, young Broadway masters like Irving Berlin, Jerome Kern, Richard Rodgers, Cole Porter, and George Gershwin copped devices from grand opera and modern music, on their way to creating a new type of through-composed music theater. They, too, were part of Manhattan's "modernist marketplace," as Oja calls it. Meanwhile, Louis Armstrong, Duke Ellington, Sidney Bechet, Fletcher Henderson, Bix Beiderbecke, and Paul Whiteman, among others, were determining the fundamentals of the art of jazz. Almost all the above-named were born in the years just before or just after 1900, and they would dominate American music for decades to come.

Edgard Varèse, chieftain of the ultra-moderns, later recalled: "I became a sort of diabolic Parsifal, searching not for the Holy Grail but the bomb that would make the musical world explode and thereby let in all sounds, sounds which up to now—and even today—have been called noises."

Varèse, born in 1883, came to New York from the Paris avant-garde, where he patronized some of the same occult Rosicrucian gatherings that had intrigued Debussy and Satie. After writing for a time in a style that evidently fell somewhere between Debussy and Strauss—his early scores were subsequently destroyed in a fire—Varèse took an interest in Italian Futurism and its "art of noise." In 1915, having been released from the French army on medical grounds, he decided to try his fortunes in New York City. There, he fell in with a cosmopolitan group of artists, both native and expatriate, who were forging a distinctively American avant-garde, visceral in impact and exuberant in tone. Among them were Francis Picabia and Marcel Duchamp, who made art from everyday objects and eroticized the machine. The American critic Paul Rosenfeld, an orotund advocate of avant-garde music in the twenties and thirties, identified these artists as avatars of "skyscraper mysticism," by which he meant a "feeling of the unity of life through the forms and expression of industrial civilization, its fierce lights, piercing noises, compact and synthetic textures; a feeling of its immense tension, dynamism, ferocity, and also its fabulous delicacy and precision."

Varèse's music owes much to the cruel harmonies and stimulating rhythms of the *Rite*, but any trace of folklore or popular melody has been surgically excised. His first major American work was, appropriately, *Amériques*, or *Americas*, a gargantuan orchestral movement composed between 1919 and 1922. It echoed the sounds and rhythms of New York along the Hudson River and around the Brooklyn Bridge—the noise of traffic, the wail of sirens, the moaning of foghorns. The orchestra consisted of twenty-two winds, twenty-nine brass, sixty-six strings, and a vast battery of percussion requiring nine or ten players. Like Schoenberg in his early atonal period, Varèse broke down language and form into a stream of sensations, but he offered few compensating spells of lyricism. His jagged thematic gestures, battering pulses, and brightly screaming chords have no emotional cords tied to them, no history, no future.

An unexpected thing happened when Varèse offered his ultraviolent music to the public: the public liked it. Or at least was diverted by it. Leopold Stokowski, a conductor of insatiable curiosity and impeccable showmanship, presented *Amériques* with his deluxe Philadelphia Orchestra in 1926, and the following year he programmed the equally formidable *Arcana*. Those concerts took place at the Academy of Music in Philadelphia and at Carnegie Hall. There was much delighted press coverage of the New York Fire Department siren that appeared in the percussion section of *Amériques*. Cartoonists had a field day. Varèse acquired a patina of society glamour, becoming, in Oja's phrase, the "matinee idol of modernism." In fact, in a delightful twist of fate, the moodily handsome composer had already been cast in bit parts in several silent movies, including *Dr. Jekyll and Mr. Hyde*, in which he plays a nobleman who kills his wife with a poisoned ring.

Even bigger headlines greeted George Antheil, a native of Trenton, New Jersey, who made it his mission to become the next Stravinsky, or failing that, the next Ornstein. Antheil first won fame in postwar Paris, presenting works with such titles as *Airplane Sonata* and *Sonata Sauvage*. Ezra Pound, James Joyce, and other modernist writers admired him, although Stravinsky was unimpressed. One concert occasioned a *Rite*-style riot at the Théâtre des Champs-Élysées, although it turned out that the brouhaha had been staged for the benefit of the film director Marcel L'Herbier, who needed a wild crowd scene for his thriller *L'Inhumaine*.

In 1927 Antheil brought his act to Carnegie Hall, offering a program that managed to be jazzy and ultra-modern in equal measure: first, W. C. Handy's orchestra played *A Jazz Symphony* in front of a painting of a Negro couple dancing the Charleston, the man grabbing the woman's buttocks; then ten pianos, industrial-size electric fans, a siren, and assorted other noisemakers were rolled onstage for the *Ballet mécanique*, which aped *Les Noces*. Halfway through the latter piece, the composer-critic Deems Taylor caused universal merriment when he attached a handkerchief to the top of his cane and waved it in a gesture of surrender. "Expected Riots Peter Out at George Antheil Concert—Sensation Fails to Materialize" was the headline in one paper the next day. Antheil ended up making a living in Hollywood, writing scores for, among other films, Cecil B. DeMille's *The Plainsman* and *The Buccaneer*.

A gap had opened up between the ideal of modernism as the antithesis of mass culture and the reality of America as a marketplace in which absolutely anything could be bought and sold. Carl Ruggles, the most severe of the ultra-moderns, was tormented by that contradiction. He produced a limited number of works, each of them having the hardness and coarseness of granitic rock. His orchestral masterpiece, *Sun-Treader*, is one of the most tautly argued atonal works in the literature, as propulsive as Beethoven's Fifth. If Varèse is like early Stravinsky with the folk motifs removed, Ruggles is like Ives without the tunes.

Ruggles and Varèse joined ranks in founding the International Composers' Guild, which aimed to present difficult music without commercial restrictions. When someone happily observed that one of the concerts had drawn a full house, Ruggles accused his own organization of "catering to the public." As so often in the modernist saga, revolutionary impulses went hand in hand with intolerance and resentment. Ruggles and Varèse muttered between themselves about the consumerism and vulgarity that were ruining American culture, for which they tended to blame the Jews and the Negroes.

Notwithstanding the obnoxious racial views of the founders, the International Composers' Guild did make possible a rare breakthrough for a black composer. William Grant Still, a native of Mississippi who moved back and forth between classical activities and a day job at Okeh Records, studied for a time with Varèse, and his song cycle *Levee Land* appeared on an ICG program in 1926. Designed as a vehicle for the Harlem musical-theater star Florence Mills, *Levee Land* unfolds on two distinct but ingeniously coordinated tiers of activity: while the singer delivers vocal lines in classic blues style, the orchestra surrounds her with a seething, discordant harmonic field, including polytonal chords similar to those that Ives used in *Three Places in New England*. Five years later, Still's *Afro-American Symphony* had its premiere at the Rochester Philharmonic, and a black composer finally found a place of respect in classical America.

Virgil Thomson was a movement unto himself. A fastidious Harvard graduate with a Kansas City background, he moved through diverse spheres of modern music without becoming beholden to any of them. From 1925 until 1940 he was based in Paris, where he absorbed lessons from Stravinsky, Les Six, and, especially, Erik Satie. Thomson's destiny was to produce the American counterpart to Satie's deceptive naïveté. Where Satie used cabaret melodies and vaudeville dances, Thomson filled his scores with stock Americana—Sunday-school hymns, village-square marches, lazy waltzes suitable for a bandstand on a summer evening.

Thomson's aesthetic had something in common with that of Ives, but it lacked the chaotic, visionary element; America passed by at a dreamy distance. In Paris, the gregarious young composer befriended several leading modernist artists, and in 1927 he began collaborating with Gertrude Stein, another refugee from the heartland. Something lovely happened when Thomson's calculatedly simplified music was joined to Stein's calculatedly obscure images. Each half of the equation drew out unexpected qualities in the other—sensual strangeness in the music, elegiac warmth in the words.

In the Stein-Thomson opera *Four Saints in Three Acts*, there is no plot as such, only a succession of tableaux depicting in borderline-incomprehensible language the lives of Spanish saints:

To know to know to love her so
Four saints prepare for saints.
It makes it well fish.
Four saints it makes it well fish . . .

In Thomson's settings, such riddles become disarmingly concrete and everyday, as if they have been sung by schoolchildren for time out of mind. The harmonies are straight out of a basic textbook—John Cage, in a study of Thomson's music, counted 111 tonic-dominant progressions—but they are treated with an intellectual detachment that recalls Cubist sculpture and surrealist collage.

Four Saints had its first extended production in 1934, not in a salon or an opera house but on Broadway. What got everyone's attention on opening night was that the cast was entirely African-American. Thomson didn't conceive the score with black performers in mind; only in 1933, after seeing the black entertainer Jimmy Daniels perform at a Harlem club, did he decided to give his work a "Negro" veneer. Perhaps because of its exotic racial allure, *Four Saints* turned out to be a surprise hit, running for sixty performances. Sophisticated city dwellers went around singing such improbable tunes as "Pigeons on the Grass Alas." In *The New Yorker*, James Thurber penned a deadpan critique: "Pigeons are definitely not alas. They have nothing to do with alas and they have nothing to do with hooray (not even when you tie red, white, and blue ribbons on them and let them loose at band concerts); they have nothing to do with mercy me or isn't that fine, either." Yet, like Antheil before him, Thomson discovered that a spasm of press coverage was insufficient to launch a career. Once the *Four Saints* fad was over, he found to his dismay that he couldn't even get the score published. As a last resort he started writing music criticism to keep his name in front of the public.

In retrospect, Thomson's decision to use an all-black cast seems more a commercial calculation than a musical necessity. Some of the composer's explanatory comments were condescending, bordering on racist. "Negroes objectify themselves very easily," he later explained. "They live on the surface of their consciousness." African-American singers could make sense of Stein's nonsensical texts, Thomson stated, because they did not understand that they made no sense. Anthony Tommasini, Thomson's biographer, writes: "Thomson gave black artists an unprecedented opportunity to topple stereotypes and portray Spanish saints in what would be an elegant and historic production. However, the fact of their color was used to sully, in a sense, the rarefied white world of opera." No wonder *Four Saints* failed to resonate more deeply with a public that was falling seriously in love with African-American music. Perhaps Thomson was the one living on the surface of his consciousness.

"Jazz is not America," Varèse said in 1928. "It's a negro product, exploited by the Jews." Racist animus aside, the claim is not far off the mark: much of the music that white audiences of the twenties would have considered "jazz" came from the pens of Jewish composers. Jerome Kern, George Gershwin, Irving Berlin, and Richard Rodgers all came from Central European, Eastern European, and Russian Jewish backgrounds, and all made prolific use of African-American material. Scholars have tracked the surprising ways in which the modes and syncopations of Eastern European klezmer music and of African-American music overlap. *Pace* Varèse, the music of Kern and Gershwin was American precisely because it mixed cultures—and genres—in a creatively indiscriminate way.

Jewish Americans' identification with black music might have had something to do with inherited memories of European suffering. Old Testament metaphors appear all through the African-American spirituals: "Tell ole Pharaoh / Let my people go," "Ezekiel saw de wheel of time / Wheel in de middle of a wheel," "Deep river, my home is over Jordan." The composer Constant Lambert, in his 1934 book *Music Ho!*, was among the first to discuss what he called a "link between the exiled and persecuted Jews and the exiled and persecuted Negroes." Such racial essentialism easily turns ugly: Lambert goes on to say that the Jews had "stolen the Negroes' thunder," that they had robbed African-American material of its pure, primitive energy and endowed it with fake sophistication. African-Americans sometimes implied the same thing: Scott Joplin persisted in thinking that Irving Berlin had stolen "Alexander's Ragtime Band" from *Treemonisha*, and William Grant Still accused Gershwin of plagiarism. But these squabbles obscure the reality of the New York scene in the twenties and thirties—that Jewish, African-American, and even Caucasian composers were working shoulder to shoulder, trading ideas, borrowing themes, plundering the past, and feeding off the present.

When Kern's *Show Boat* opened at Ziegfeld's opulent new theater in New York, in December 1927, the audience was stunned into silence by the opening chorus, which was perilously far removed from the dancing girls and witty repartee for which Ziegfeld shows were famed. As the curtain rises, the showboat *Cotton Blossom* is stage left; stage right, black stevedores are loading bales of hay and singing, "Niggers all work on de Mississippi / Niggers all work while de white man play." If, as Marva Griffin Carter says, Will Marion Cook's musicals made "confrontational jabs" at white listeners back at the turn of the century, Kern and his librettist, Oscar Hammerstein II, delivered a slap in the face.

Even riskier is a sequence set at the World's Columbian Exposition of 1893. A group of threateningly attired black singers perform a deepest-Africa number called "In Dahomey"—the very name of Will Marion Cook's pioneering musical—and then reveal that they hail from Avenue A in New York. Frederick Douglass had complained that the organizers of the exposition imported African performers to "act the monkey"; Hammerstein's libretto spells out clearly how black culture was being used to satisfy white audiences' thirst for the exotic.

If these themes had been fleshed out more fully, *Show Boat* might have become a masterwork of social satire as well as a bewitching piece of theater. But, as the scholar Raymond Knapp points out, the creators could hardly address such an incendiary subject while they were keeping their black characters in subsidiary roles, on the margins of the drama. African-American suffering becomes a sort of background decor, an ambience of heartbreak.

Whatever its failings as a study in race relations, *Show Boat* provided a grand aerial view of the American musical scene. The first thing you hear is a blaring, minatory minor chord out of Verdi or Puccini. That operatic gesture quickly fades away into a rapid montage of popular styles: Tin Pan Alley melody, mass-market blues, banjo strummings, Gilbert and Sullivan ditties, Sousa marches, vaudeville patter, and hoochie-coochie music. The one song from *Show Boat* that everyone knows is, of course, "Ol' Man River," and they know it because of the way Paul Robeson sang it. *Show Boat* was not only the first major American musical but the first musical in which black performers were given showstopping moments. Robeson became, in effect, the co-composer of the song, transforming a resigned, melancholy number into a vessel of spiritual might. In later years he changed the lyric "Ah'm tired of livin' an' scared of dyin' " to "I must keep fightin' until I'm dyin'."

Humbly putting his music in the service of such august voices, Kern let white Americans know that there was more to black music than bouncing syncopation. Coursing under the zesty surface of *Show Boat* is the power of the blues.

Gershwin

"I frequently hear music in the very heart of noise," George Gershwin said, explaining the origins of *Rhapsody in Blue*. Epitomizing the Jazz Age in every pore of his suave being, Gershwin was the ultimate phenomenon in early-twentieth-century American music, the man in whom all the discordant tendencies of the era achieved sweet harmony.

Gershwin grew up on the Lower East Side of Manhattan, that superheated melting pot where Russian, Eastern European, Yiddish, African-American, and mainstream American cultures intermingled. He experienced what he called his "flashing revelation" in the schoolyard of P.S. 25; in the middle of playing ball with other kids, he was stopped cold by the sound of a fellow student playing Dvořák's *Humoresque*. There is a poignant historical symmetry here, because Dvořák had based his *Humoresque* on the *American Plantation Dances* of his young student Maurice Arnold, one of those would-be black composers who had dropped from sight.

Life on the Lower East Side could be tough for a middle-class kid who liked to play the piano. Gershwin's early biographers, wanting to establish their subject's all-American credentials, emphasized his boisterous, mildly delinquent escapades—roller-skating, skipping school, joining street brawls, dabbling in petty burglary. Gershwin stumbled into music by accident, it was said, and never had to work particularly hard. In fact, the boy spent endless hours practicing, and attended dozens of recitals at Cooper Union, Aeolian Hall, and the Wanamaker Auditorium (in the same department store where Strauss conducted his music in 1904). Gershwin's childhood scrapbooks, which can be seen in the music collection at the Library of Congress, are stuffed with pictures of favorite pianists and composers, pasted up where other boys might have featured sports heroes or pinup girls.

Gershwin's first significant teacher was Charles Hambitzer, who introduced him to the music of Debussy and Ravel and possibly to the early works of Schoenberg. Later came a thorough course of theory with the Hungarian émigré Edward Kilenyi, who told Gershwin that he had a better chance of winning an audience if he made his name in the popular arena rather than in the academic realm of composition. (Kilenyi, too, was familiar with Schoenberg, and apparently schooled Gershwin in the teachings of *Harmonielehre*.) While still a teenager, Gershwin began working as a pianist at Remick's publishing company, and with the help of Will Vodery, Ziegfeld's African-American arranger, he got some jobs on Broadway. His first songwriting success—what would remain his biggest hit, in terms of millions of copies sold—came in 1919, when the blackface singer Al Jolson took up the young composer's rollicking pseudo-Southern number "Swanee."

Early Gershwin classics like "The Man I Love," " 'S Wonderful," and "Fascinating Rhythm" trumpet the new sophistication of American popular song. Often, a simple repeating figure plays out against a cooler, more complex harmonic background. In " 'S Wonderful" the chorus melody consists simply of a falling third heard three times, followed by a falling fifth, spelling out a common chord. Nothing could be simpler—or, potentially, duller. It's a mere signal, like a ditty that plays when subway doors are closing. The wonderfulness is in the harmonization: that inert third becomes the pivot for a graceful merry-go-round of major, minor, dominant-seventh, and diminished-seventh chords.

"Fascinating Rhythm" is a study in aural sleight of hand. Over a foursquare beat, the melody unfolds in three helter-skelter phrases, each made up of six eighth notes plus an eighth-note rest. The fact that each phrase falls one eighth note short of a complete bar means that the vocal keeps slipping ahead of the main beat; four extra pulses are needed to make up the difference. So, a string of thirty-two pulses is divided into three sets of seven and one set of eleven.

Gershwin made his first serious foray into black music in 1922, with the vaudeville opera *Blue Monday Blues*. Set on 135th Street in Harlem, this brief one-acter tells of a woman who shoots the man who's done her wrong, or so she thinks. The arias lack the verve of the best Gershwin tunes, awkwardly shuffling among the conventions of European operetta, Yiddish musical theater, and black musicals like Cook's *In Dahomey*. The show had a whiff of minstrelsy about it: white singers performed in blackface, and Paul Whiteman's smooth-timbred jazz orchestra provided something other than an authentic Harlem sound. But Gershwin was learning as he went along, experimenting simultaneously with opulent vocal lines in the operatic mode and with rhythmically pliable melodic lines that imitated stride piano and the blues.

Curious about what the European moderns and Manhattan ultra-moderns were up to, Gershwin regularly attended International Composers' Guild concerts and other new-music events. In 1922 he heard the adventurous Canadian mezzo-soprano Eva Gauthier sing Ravel and Stravinsky, and in February 1923 he showed up at the American premiere of Schoenberg's *Pierrot lunaire*. That November, Gershwin made his official "highbrow" debut, accompanying Gauthier in contemporary songs by Kern, Berlin, and himself. He delighted the crowd—and showed off his classical knowledge—by inserting a phrase from Rimsky-Korsakov's *Scheherazade* into "Do It Again."

Gershwin now received a commission to write an orchestral work for Whiteman, who was preparing a program titled "An Experiment in Modern Music" for Aeolian Hall. The bandleader, who had played viola in the Denver and San Francisco symphonies, made it his mission to give jazz a quasi-classical respectability. The stated aim of the "Experiment," which took place at Aeolian Hall on February 12, 1924, was to show "the tremendous strides which have been made in popular music from the day of the discordant Jazz, which sprang into existence about ten years ago from nowhere in particular, to the really melodious music of today." The evening began with the raucous glissandos of "Livery Stable Blues," and ended, oddly, with Elgar's *Pomp and Circumstance* March No. 1. If, as Deems Taylor said in his review, the participants were engaged in the project of bringing jazz "out of the kitchen," evidently jazz ended up on the veranda, drinking Madeira and smoking cigars.

Planted in the middle, with one foot in the kitchen and one foot in the salon, was *Rhapsody in Blue*. The score famously begins with a languid trill on the clarinet, which turns into an equally languid upward scale, which then becomes a super-elegant and not at all raucous glissando. Having reached the topmost B-flat, the clarinet then saunters through a lightly syncopated melody, leaning heavily on the lowered seventh note of the scale. The tune dances down the same staircase that the opening scale shimmied up, ending on the F with which the piece began—a typical Gershwin symmetry.

A neat ambiguity becomes apparent: sometimes the lowered seventh is heard as a pitch-bending blue note, and sometimes it is interpreted as part of a straitlaced dominant-seventh chord, which has the effect of kicking the harmony into a neighboring key. The *Rhapsody* plays out as a dizzying sequence of modulations; the Rachmaninovian love theme at the center of the work ends up being in the key of E, a tritone away from the home B-flat. That theme, too, is strewn with extraneous blue notes, which give Rachmaninov a certain finger-snapping informality while propelling the harmony through a second string of modulations back to the point of departure.

When the last chord sounded, delirium ensued. In the audience at Aeolian Hall were such classical celebrities as Stokowski, Leopold Godowsky, Jascha Heifetz, Fritz Kreisler, and Rachmaninov himself, and they were practically unanimous in acclaiming Gershwin as the new white hope, so to speak, of American music. And when Gershwin went to Europe four years later, he met more high-level admirers: Stravinsky, Ravel, four of Les Six, Prokofiev, Weill, Schoenberg, and Berg. No American composer had ever gained such international notice.

Of the modern European masters, Berg fascinated Gershwin most. The legendary meeting between the two composers in Vienna—the one at which Berg said, "Mr. Gershwin, music is music"—perhaps gave Gershwin a glimpse of something new, of a deeper synthesis than what he had achieved to date. On the train from Vienna to Paris, he studied the score of the *Lyric Suite*, and at various parties held in his honor in Paris he had the Kolisch Quartet play the work several more times, no doubt to the puzzlement of the flapper crowds. Back in New York, Gershwin hung an autographed photo of Berg in a corner of his apartment, alongside a picture of the boxer Jack Dempsey and a punching bag.

European impressions bubbled up in the balletic tone poem *An American in Paris*, which Gershwin sketched during his 1928 tour and finished back home. If the *Rhapsody* had been predictable in form, alternating between plush tunes and busy transitional sections, *An American in Paris* showed a more confident use of a larger structure; the tunes undergo kaleidoscopic development and are stacked up in wickedly dissonant polytonal combinations. Yet the musical surface is kept shiningly clear, so that the listener can follow each jazz aria as it darts through the melee.

Gershwin had little left to learn, yet he still felt insecure about his education, and asked for advice and lessons from almost every accredited composer he met. Supposedly, he once approached Stravinsky, who asked after Gershwin's salary—$100,000 to $200,000—and then said, "In that case, I should study with you." (Alas, the story is probably legend: the same anecdote was told about Gershwin and Ravel.) As Howard Pollack shows in his authoritative biography, Gershwin kept trying to perfect his technique even after he had achieved fame. In 1932 he embarked on a new course of study with the émigré Russian composer-theorist Joseph Schillinger, who had created a system for symmetrically organizing rhythms, chords, and scales. Gershwin's notebooks from his sessions with Schillinger show him writing in multiple modes and deriving richly dissonant chords from the harmonic series.

Since the time of "Swanee" and *Blue Monday Blues*, Gershwin had been navigating among diatonic, blues, klezmerish, whole-tone, and chromatic scales. Now he had a coherent method with which to work—a grid on which he could plot large-scale designs. In those same notebooks, *Porgy and Bess* began to take shape.

The idea of writing a full-scale opera had preoccupied Gershwin for years. The arts patron Otto Kahn—chairman of the board of the Metropolitan Opera, prime mover of Jazz Age culture, old friend of Richard Strauss's—spurred him on, inviting him to write a "jazz grand opera" for the Met. Gershwin concluded, however, that the Met's staff singers could never master the idiom; a true jazz opera could be sung only by a black cast.

DuBose Heyward's novel *Porgy* had long interested Gershwin as a subject. After a long delay related to questions of rights, he set to work on the opera in early 1934. The story is of a crippled beggar with an indomitable urge to make his dreams come true. He falls in love with Bess, who returns his love but is prey to the affections and manipulations of other men. The story ends on a note of mingled hope and dread: Bess goes off to New York with the drug-dealing ne'er-do-well Sportin' Life, and Porgy resolves to follow. Gershwin later said that he liked the story because of its mix of humor and drama; it allowed him to shift between Broadway-style song-and-dance numbers and vocal-symphonic writing in the style of *Wozzeck.* Although his aim was to "appeal to the many rather than to the cultured few," the work far exceeded the average Broadway revue in ambition. Gershwin spent eighteen months writing it, notating every note of the final orchestral score in his own hand, as he felt compelled to prove when journalists came calling.

Porgy begins with an introductory orchestral and choral explosion in which Gershwin shows off what he has learned from his experiments in modern music. First comes a typical rhapsodic flourish, an upward scale followed by a trill. This gives way to a hard-driving two-chord ostinato, which sounds like a honky-tonk version of the quivering alternation of chords at the end of *Wozzeck*. The orchestra then drops out and the ostinato is carried on by an out-of-tune barroom piano—a feat of cross-cutting that imitates the tavern scene in *Wozzeck*. Next comes a great crescendo: the chorus launches into a neoprimitivist chant of "Da-dooda" while the orchestra adds layer upon layer of dissonant harmony. The climax brings shrill harmonic complexes of seven or eight notes, split between a G dominant seventh in the bass and C-sharp-major arpeggios in the treble. Gershwin probably assembled this music from overtone rows, as he had done in his Schillinger notebooks.

The texture then subsides toward a summery, humid kind of stillness. A new ostinato gets under way, one of alternating half-diminished sevenths, recalling *Wozzeck* again—Marie's song of "Eia popeia" to her child. Gershwin even uses his chords for the same scenic purpose, to accompany a mother's soothing lullaby. If the kid from the Lower East Side seems in danger of losing himself in European arcana, there is no reason to worry. We are listening to one of the best-loved melodies of the twentieth century: "Summertime, and the living is easy . . ."

The entire score is structured around such fusions of complexity and simplicity, although the simple always wins out in the end. In his notebooks Gershwin wrote down some rules that would never have sufficed for Berg: "Melodic. Nothing neutral. Utter simplicity. Directness."

What sets *Porgy* apart from every classical theater work of the time is that the score invites considerable freedom of interpretation. Once the chords of "Summertime" start rocking, they become a steady-state environment in which a gifted performer can move around at will. She can bend pitches, add ornaments, shift the line up and down. Billie Holiday and Sidney Bechet made "Summertime" their own; Miles Davis, on his *Porgy and Bess* album of 1958, actually discarded Gershwin's chords and kept only the melody. The same freedom of expression is permitted in the opera's other set pieces, such as "Bess, You Is My Woman Now," "My Man's Gone Now," and "It Ain't Necessarily So." When, at the premiere, John W. Bubbles sang the last-named number with devil-may-care pizzazz, he irritated the trained singers in the cast, but Gershwin defended him.

Glowing with confidence, Gershwin offered *Porgy* to the public in the fall of 1935. To his surprise—he was accustomed to being loved—it met with critical opposition and commercial disappointment. *Porgy* ran on Broadway for 124 performances, a large number by operatic standards but not enough to recoup expenses. People had trouble deciding whether Gershwin had written an opera or a musical show: some theatergoers complained that the orchestral passages and turbulent recitatives got in the way of the hit numbers, while classical-music intellectuals found the showstoppers bewildering. There was fuss over how the work should be labeled—"opera," "folk opera," "musical," or something else.

Virgil Thomson, smarting over the disappearance of *Four Saints*, wrote a thoroughly incoherent review for *Modern Music* in which he proposed that Gershwin was "not a very serious composer" who had nonetheless produced an important work: "Gershwin does not even know what an opera is; and yet *Porgy and Bess* is an opera and it has power and vigor." Thomson was, in fact, paying Gershwin a compliment—the highest that he could offer to a composer who lacked the correct credentials and could never be considered "one of us."

Gershwin's racial ambiguities, his miscegenating mixture of Western European, African-American, and Russian-Jewish materials, also caused trouble. The black singers were generally overjoyed by what Gershwin had written for them; J. Rosamond Johnson, James Weldon Johnson's brother, who sang the part of Lawyer Frazier in the premiere, went so far as to describe the composer as the "Abraham Lincoln of Negro music." African-American critics were more cautious, though generally positive. A few commentators on the political left attacked what they perceived to be white exploitation of black material. Unexpectedly, Duke Ellington, who seldom had a bad word to say about anyone, led the critique. "Grand music and a swell play," Ellington was quoted as saying, but "it does not use the Negro musical idiom. It was not the music of Catfish Row or any other kind of Negroes." As it turned out, some of Ellington's remarks had been fabricated by an overeager Marxist journalist, although in a subsequent clarification Ellington stated once more that *Porgy* was not a true Negro opera.

Thomson picked up on this leftist critique of *Porgy* when he wrote, "Folk-lore subjects recounted by an outsider are only valid as long as the folk in question is unable to speak for itself, which is certainly not true of the American Negro in 1935." In the end, the racial debate around *Porgy* (was it a real Negro opera?) bled into the aesthetic debate (was it an opera at all?). Thomson concluded thus: "I don't mind his being a light composer and I don't mind his trying to be a serious one. But I do mind his falling between two stools."

Falling between two stools was, in fact, the essence of Gershwin's genius. He led at all times a double life: as music-theater professional and concert composer, as highbrow artist and lowbrow entertainer, as all-American kid and immigrants' son, as white man and "white Negro." *Porgy* performed the monumental feat of reconciling the rigidity of Western notated music with the African-American principle of improvised variation. In the end, Gershwin reunited two sides of the composer's job that should never have been separated to begin with, and he came as close as any composer of the day—his chief rival was Kurt Weill—to the all-devouring, high-low art of Mozart and Verdi.

Tragically, Gershwin did not live to fulfill his entire vision. Not long before his sudden death in 1937, of a brain tumor, he told his sister: "I don't feel I've really scratched the surface of what I want to do."

The Duke

The Harlem Renaissance, insofar as W. E. B. Du Bois and others defined it, aspired to create an African-American version of "high culture." By the early thirties, that mission was becoming more difficult to sustain. A terrible riot in 1935 exposed the misery and rage behind the illusion of an upwardly mobile black culture.

As Paul Allen Anderson explains in his book *Deep River*, a split opened between the original leaders of the Renaissance and younger artists such as Langston Hughes and Zora Neale Hurston, who disavowed what Hughes called the "Nordicized Negro intelligentsia" and sought a less status-conscious, less politely affirmative definition of black culture. Du Bois and his colleagues had dreamed, in Anderson's words, of a "hybridic fusion" of African-American, mainstream-American, and European ideas. Alain Locke, in his musical commentaries, remained suspicious of commercial jazz and saved his highest praise for the symphonies of William Grant Still, William Dawson, and Florence Price. By contrast, the young rebel Hughes—whose great-uncle John Mercer Langston had been a good friend of Will Marion Cook's father—celebrated the authenticity of "hot" jazz and rural blues. "We build our temples for tomorrow, strong as we know how," Hughes wrote, in a widely quoted 1926 essay, "and we stand on the top of the mountain, free within ourselves."

The split between the Harlem Renaissance elders and the new radical Negroes formed the backdrop for Duke Ellington's career. Like Gershwin, Ellington had a flair for ambivalence. He partook of Du Bois and Locke's cosmopolitanism, their rhetoric of uplift and transcendence. Yet he also adopted Hughes's slogans of resistance and subversion.

There's a wonderful scene in a 1944 *New Yorker* profile in which Ellington is shown deflating the expectations of an Icelandic music student who tries to nudge him toward the "classical," "genius" category. The student keeps peppering the master with questions about Bach, and, before answering, Ellington makes an elaborate show of unwrapping a pork chop that he has stowed in his pocket. "Bach and myself," he says, taking a bite from the chop, "both write with individual performers in mind." With that pork-chop maneuver, Ellington put distance between himself and the European conception of genius, though without rejecting it entirely. Another time he addressed the issue head-on: "To attempt to elevate the status of the jazz musician by forcing the level of his best work into comparisons with classical music is to deny him his rightful share of originality."

Black musicians had to work fast and hard to escape appropriation. The great early jazz records, from Louis Armstrong's Hot Fives and Hot Sevens onward, show an art form developing at blinding speed. As the composer Olly Wilson has said, jazz composers compensated for the limitations of the three- or four-minute track by exploiting a "heterogenous sound ideal": multiple rhythms, call-and-response patterns, and diverse timbres conspire to create "a high density of musical events within a relatively short musical time frame." Albert Murray writes in his classic book *Stomping the Blues*: "The phonograph record has served as the blues musician's equivalent to the concert hall almost from the outset. It has been in effect his concert hall without walls, his *musée imaginaire* . . ." European harmonies were one more ingredient added to the mix.

Dvořák had assumed that American music would come into its own when it succeeded in importing African-American material into European form, but in the end the opposite thing happened: African-American composers appropriated European material into self-invented forms of blues and jazz.

When Duke Ellington set about making his name, he went for advice to Will Marion Cook. The grand old man of African-American music would give him informal lessons in the course of extended horse-and-buggy rides around Central Park. "I'd sing a melody in its simplest form," Ellington recalled, "and he'd stop me and say, 'Reverse your figures' . . . Some of the things he used to tell me I never got a chance to use until years later, when I wrote the tone poem *Black, Brown, and Beige*." Cook was expounding Brahmsian principles of variation and development: "Reverse your figures" suggests the notes of a theme spelled in inversion or retrograde. Cook also directed Ellington to discover his individual voice: "You know you should go to the conservatory, but since you won't, I'll tell you. First you find the logical way, and when you find it, avoid it, and let your inner self break through and guide you. Don't try to be anybody else but yourself."

Ellington's "inner self" is present in his first original recording, "East

St. Louis Toodle-oo," from 1926. The piece is distinctive because it creates a distinctive tension between a blues theme on solo trumpet and a straitlaced accompaniment in the band. The lead tune, written and played by the master trumpeter Bubber Miley, depicts an old man shuffling in wearily from the cornfield. The minor-key accompaniment, Ellington's work, takes the form of a hypnotic string of closely voiced chords, circling around like a cool crowd of onlookers.

An improvising soloist was, of course, hardly a novelty in musical history; Mozart's and Beethoven's concertos offered spells of cadenza freedom, and opera singers had freely ornamented their parts for centuries. The difference in Ellington's jazz pieces—as in Armstrong's and Fletcher Henderson's—was that the distinction between the composed and the improvised broke down at an almost subatomic level. Players moved in and out of the improvisatory circle, taking their solos. They burst into exhilarating runs that sounded spontaneous but were in many cases intricately rehearsed beforehand. The entire ensemble was in a state of flux. Yet it all came out sounding like Ellington.

What distinguished Ellington from most of his contemporaries was that he set himself the goal of expanding the time frame of the jazz piece, stretching it well beyond the limits of the 78-rpm side and into the realm of the large-scale classical work. *Rhapsody in Blue* was the obvious model, a jazz-based work that had grown into symphonic dimensions. In a 1931 article titled "The Duke Steps Out," Ellington announced that he was writing "a rhapsody unhampered by any musical form in which I intended to portray the experiences of the coloured races in America in the syncopated idiom." It would be "an authentic record of my race *written by a member of it*"—the italics are Ellington's. In the same year he wrote *Creole Rhapsody*, which required two record sides. Whether or not this is the work described in "The Duke Steps Out," *Creole Rhapsody* has clear ties to *Rhapsody in Blue*, and at one point it alludes directly to Gershwin's opening flourish—the upward scale that turns into a glissando. In essence, Ellington was declaring that he would follow Gershwin in uniting jazz and classical procedures, but that he would do it his own way.

Gershwin and Ellington were friendly on a personal level, appreciative of each other's work. Ellington liked the fact that Gershwin stood around backstage at his shows dressed like a stagehand, as incognito as a celebrity composer could be. Gershwin, for his part, listened intently to Ellington's records, reportedly filing them separate from the rest of his collection at home. There were, however, moments of tension between the two, as the dispute over *Porgy and Bess* showed. Ellington flatly rejected the idea that a white composer could be hailed as the composer of a "Negro opera."

Right around the time of *Porgy*'s premiere, Ellington set down initial ideas for his own opera, which was to have been called *Boola*, and which would presumably have shown how Negro opera should really be done. The title character was imagined as a mythic being who would sum up the entire African-American experience, from his crossing to America on a slave ship, to his experiences as a soldier in the Civil War, to his emancipation and emigration north, and on to his arrival in the renaissance city of Harlem—where, Ellington once reminded the *New York Times*, churches outnumber cabarets.

Boola never got past the sketching stage. While Gershwin would happily spend month after month tinkering with his material, Ellington had a fundamentally collaborative temperament, and composition on the operatic scale defeated him. He did use his sketches in two extraordinary instrumental works, both of which mix jazz and classical devices. *Ko-Ko*, written in 1939, evokes the drum-and-dance ceremonies that slaves once performed on Sunday afternoons in New Orleans. Anticipating the postwar modal jazz of Miles Davis, it is derived almost entirely from an E-flat-minor Aeolian scale. A driving four-note figure echoes the Morse-code rhythm of the opening of Beethoven's Fifth, as the Ellington scholar Ken Rattenbury points out. Ellington takes a long solo in the middle, dancing between thick Romantic harmonies and Debussyan whole-tone chords. The piece works up to a towering six-note dissonance that sets an F-flat dominant seventh against B-flat, not unlike the "Da-doo-da" chords in *Porgy and Bess*. But Ellington doesn't use modernist harmony to connote conflict, crisis, and collapse. Instead, he makes it the deep background from which solos emerge and into which they disappear. It's the way things are. In an interview, Ellington pointed out a discord in one of his latest compositions. "That's the Negro's life," he said. "Hear that chord!" Ellington played it again. "That's us. Dissonance is our way of life in America. We are something apart, yet an integral part."

The other spin-off from *Boola* was the forty-five-minute swing symphony *Black, Brown, and Beige*, first presented at a historic 1943 concert at Carnegie Hall that marked Ellington's twentieth anniversary as a bandleader. On that night the future that Will Marion Cook had pictured on Lookout Mountain became real: a black composer conquered the haughtiest of concert stages.

The occasion is palpable in the music. The first movement, *Black*, begins with drums pounding out a slow, martial pattern. Trumpets and saxophones declaim the opening theme, "Work Song," while a trio of trombones hold an E-flat-major triad in first inversion. It has a Richard Strauss quality to it—Thus Spake Boola. Yet the fanfare represents, in Ellington's words, "not a song of great Joy—not a triumphant song—but a song of Burden—a song punctuated by the grunt of Heaving a pick or axe." The drums might be tom-toms beating in the jungle, warning of invaders. Proud Africa is under threat from the white West. In keeping with symphonic procedure, Ellington presents a contrasting theme, "Come Sunday," which, in the never-to-be *Boola* opera, would have depicted slaves congregating, listening, and humming outside the doors of a steepled church. The soaring hymnal melody, as played by Johnny Hodges, is one of Ellington's finest inspirations, and words were later added for Mahalia Jackson to sing. Throughout *Black*, these two themes undergo rigorous variation ("Reverse your figures," as Cook said). The remaining two movements have their lulls—Ellington finished the score in his usual rush, with an assist from Billy Strayhorn—but in the end the work outshines every symphonic jazz piece of the time.

The reception of *Black, Brown, and Beige* exposed many of the same anxieties over the mixing of races and genres that had shadowed *Porgy and Bess*. Aesthetic policemen on both sides of the classical-jazz divide effectively united in casting doubt on this latest attempt at "hybridic fusion." The composer, critic, and future novelist Paul Bowles, writing in the *New York Herald Tribune*, called Ellington's piece "formless and meaningless . . . a gaudy potpourri of tutti dance passages and solo virtuoso work." He concluded that "the whole attempt to fuse jazz as a form with art music should be discouraged." The producer and critic John Hammond, speaking for jazz purists, complained that Ellington had deserted "hot" jazz and fallen under highbrow influence.

Disappointed by the criticism, Ellington nonetheless persisted in employing extended forms. He and Strayhorn later put together a masterpiece of a film score for *Anatomy of a Murder* and a commanding series of jazz suites. *Such Sweet Thunder*, a twelve-movement 1957 work, took its title from some lines in *A Midsummer Night's Dream*, and they nicely sum up Ellington's aesthetic: "I never heard / So musical a discord, such sweet thunder."

In the 1967 television documentary *On the Road with Duke Ellington*, the grand old man of jazz was asked why he still toured the country with his band. Sitting in the back of a limousine on the way to the next date, Ellington replied: "Anyone who writes music has got to hear his music . . . There used to be days years ago when people would come out of conservatory, after investing the greater part of their lives, maybe ten years, and many times more, and . . . mastered all the devices of the masters and they've written symphonies, concertos, rhapsodies, and never got to hear them." When he said this, Ellington might have been thinking of Will Marion Cook, or of Will Vodery, or of the "ex-colored" composer Maurice Arnold, or of any of the other invisible men. Cook dreamed of a "black Beethoven"; Ellington carved out his own brand of eminence, redefining composition as a collective art. Carnegie Hall was a hoot, but he didn't need it.

Once, when the critic Winthrop Sargeant expressed the hope that jazz composers might rise to classical eminence, the Duke issued a gently devastating riposte, saying, in essence, thanks but no thanks: "I was struck by Mr. Sargeant's concluding statement, that given a chance to study, the Negro will soon turn from boogie woogie to Beethoven. Maybe so, but what a shame!"

5

APPARITION FROM THE WOODS

The Loneliness of Jean Sibelius

Composing is a difficult business. "Desperately difficult," says the devil in *Doctor Faustus*. It is a laborious traversal of an imaginary landscape. What emerges is an artwork in code, which other musicians must be persuaded to unravel. Unlike a novel or a painting, a score gives up its full meaning only when it is performed in front of an audience; it is a child of loneliness that lives off crowds. Nameless terrors creep into the limbo between composition and performance, during which the score sits mutely on the desk. Hans Pfitzner dramatized that moment of panic and doubt in *Palestrina*, his "musical legend" about the life of the Italian Renaissance composer. The character of Palestrina speaks for colleagues across the centuries when he stops his work to cry, "What is the point of all this? *Ach*, what is it for? What for?"

Jean Sibelius may have asked that question once too often. The crisis point of his career arrived in the late 1920s and the early '30s, when he was being lionized as a new Beethoven in England and America and dismissed as a kitsch composer in the taste-making Austro-German music centers. The contrasts in the reception of his music matched the manic-depressive extremes of his personality—an alcoholic oscillation between grandiosity and self-loathing. Sometimes he believed that he was in direct communication with the Almighty—"For an instant God opens his door," he wrote in a letter, "and *His* orchestra plays the Fifth Symphony"—and sometimes he felt worthless. In 1927, when he was sixty-one years old, he wrote in his diary, "Isolation and loneliness are driving me to despair . . . In order to survive, I have to have alcohol . . . Am abused, alone, and all my real friends are dead. My prestige here at present is rock-bottom. Impossible to work. If only there were a way out."

Sibelius spent the last part of his life at Ainola, a rustic house outside Helsinki, Finland. On his desk for many years lay the Eighth Symphony, which promised to be his summary masterpiece. He had been working on it since 1924, and had indicated several times that it was almost ready for performance. A copyist transcribed twenty-three pages of the score, and at a later date Sibelius's publisher may have bound the manuscript in a set of seven volumes. There were reportedly parts for chorus, as in Beethoven's Ninth. But the Eighth never saw the light of day. The composer finally gave in to the seduction of despair. "I suppose one henceforth takes me as—yes!—a 'fait accompli,'" he wrote in 1943. "Life is soon over. Others will come and surpass me in the eyes of the world. We are fated to die forgotten. I must start economizing. It can't go on like this."

Aino Sibelius, the composer's wife, for whom the house was named, recalled what happened next: "In the 1940s there was a great auto da fé at Ainola. My husband collected a number of manuscripts in a laundry basket and burned them on the open fire in the dining room. Parts of the *Karelia Suite* were destroyed—I later saw remains of the pages which had been torn out—and many other things. I did not have the strength to be present and left the room. I therefore do not know what he threw on to the fire. But after this my husband became calmer and gradually lighter in mood."

Ainola stands much as Sibelius left it. The atmosphere of the house is heavy and musty, as if the composer's spirit were still pent up inside. But you get a different feeling when you walk into the forest that stretches out on one side of the house. The treetops meet in an endless curving canopy, tendrils of sunlight dangling down. The ground is uncluttered: many paths fork among the trunks. Venturing a little farther into the wood, you lose sight of all human habitation. A profound stillness descends. The light begins to fail, the mists roll in. After a while, you may begin to wonder if you will ever find your way back. Many times in Sibelius's music the exaltation of natural sublimity gives way to inchoate fear, which has less to do with the outer landscape than with the inner one, the forest of the mind.

In his 1993 essay collection *Testaments Betrayed*, Milan Kundera anatomizes the more peripheral of the European cultures, taking his native Czechoslovakia as a specimen. "The small nations form 'another Europe,'" the novelist writes. "An observer can be fascinated by the often astonishing intensity of their cultural life. This is the advantage of smallness: the wealth in cultural events is on a 'human scale'; everyone can encompass that wealth." Kundera warns, however, that the familial feeling can turn tense and constricting at a moment's notice. "Within that warm intimacy," he says, "each envies each, everyone watches everyone." If an artist ignores the rules, the rejection can be cruel, the loneliness crushing. Even those who rise to fame may experience isolation at the summit—the burden of being a national hero.

Each of the "small nations"—a category into which Western European music experts have tended to dispose not only Scandinavian and Eastern European countries but also Great Britain, formerly known to Germans as the "land without music"—had its retinue of locally famous composers. A few of them broke out to wider renown, becoming standard-bearers of patriotic feeling. Edvard Grieg, in the late nineteenth century, wrote the "song of Norway." Karol Szymanowski established a Polish modernist tendency. Edward Elgar, Gustav Holst, Ralph Vaughan Williams, Arnold Bax, and William Walton built up a modern British repertory just as the glory of empire was fading. And Carl Nielsen, in Denmark, wrested music of brilliance and violence from rough-hewn folk melodies. Sibelius, the great composer of the small nation of Finland, set the pace for many others, not only because he forged a vital relationship with his native land but because he succeeded in stamping his own voice on seemingly worn-out, antiquated symphonic forms. Both Bax and Vaughan Williams revered the Finnish master and dedicated works to him; Walton opened his First Symphony with a nod to Sibelius's Fifth.

As the twentieth century rumbled on, composers with strong national ties were haunted by feelings of obsolescence. Many twentieth-century symphonies, concertos, oratorios, and chamber works of the so-called conservative type were rich in lamentations for a lost world, elegies for the golden age, forebodings of disaster. Some found it difficult to keep writing: Elgar, who died in 1934, failed to finish another large-scale piece after his supremely elegiac Cello Concerto of 1918–19, and Rachmaninov, whom Tchaikovsky had anointed his heir apparent, produced only five major works from 1917 until his death in 1943.

"I feel like a ghost wandering in a world grown alien," Rachmaninov wrote in 1939. "I cannot cast out the old way of writing, and I cannot acquire the new. I have made intense effort to feel the musical manner of today, but it will not come to me. Unlike Madame Butterfly with her quick religious conversions"—this is presumably Stravinsky—"I cannot cast out my musical gods in a moment and bend the knee to new ones." Sibelius felt the same pang of loss. "Not everyone can be an 'innovating genius,'" he wrote one day in his diary. "As a personality and '*eine Erscheinung aus den Wäldern*' [apparition from the woods] you will have your small, modest place."

And yet the so-called regional composers—for whom Sibelius speaks in this book as a representative—left behind an imposing body of work, which is integral to the century as a whole. Their music may lack the vanguard credentials of Schoenberg or Stravinsky, at least on the surface, but some words from Nielsen's book *Living Music* make a good counterargument: "The simplest is the hardest, the universal the most lasting, the straightest the strongest, like the pillars that support the dome." Precisely because these composers communicated general feelings of mourning for a pretechnological past, or, more simply, yearning for vanished youth, they remained acutely relevant for a broad public.

Mainstream audiences may lag behind the intellectual classes in appreciating the more adventurous composers, but sometimes they are quicker to perceive the value of music that the politicians of style fail to comprehend. Nicolas Slonimsky once put together a delightful book titled *Lexicon of Musical Invective*, anthologizing wrongheaded music criticism in which now canonical masterpieces were compared to feline caterwauling, barnyard noises, and so on. Slonimsky should also have written a *Lexicon of Musical Condescension*, gathering high-minded essays in which now canonical masterpieces were dismissed as kitsch, with a long section reserved for Sibelius.

• • •

Born in 1865, Sibelius was not merely the most famous composer Finland ever produced but the country's chief celebrity in any field. He played a symbolic but active role in the drive toward Finnish independence, which was finally achieved in 1917. Asked to characterize their culture, Finns invariably mention, alongside such national treasures as the lakeside sauna, Fiskars scissors, and the Nokia cellular phone, "our Sibelius." Before the advent of the euro, Sibelius's monumental head graced every hundred-markka banknote. Mostly because of him, classical music has retained a central role in modern Finnish culture. The country's government invests enormous sums in orchestras, opera houses, new-music programs, and music schools. The annual Finnish expenditure on the arts is roughly two hundred times per capita what the U.S. government spends on the National Endowment for the Arts.

In a certain sense, Finns are strangers in the European family. Belonging to the Finno-Ugrian category, they speak a language largely unrelated to the Indo-European group. For centuries they were governed by the kingdom of Sweden; then, in 1809, they became a semi-autonomous grand duchy of tsarist Russia. In the late nineteenth century, the Swedish influence remained strong, with a minority of Swedish speakers forming the upper crust of society. Sibelius belonged to this Swedish elite; his father spoke no Finnish, and he himself learned it as a second language. Yet, like many of his generation, he avidly joined in the independence campaign, whose cultural apparatus blended traces of ancient tribal ritual with invented mythologies in the Romantic vein. The nationalist movement became more urgent after Tsar Nicholas II introduced measures designed to suppress Finland's autonomy.

The national legends of Finland are contained in the *Kalevala*, a poetic epic compiled in 1835 by a country doctor named Elias Lönnrot. Cantos 31 through 36 of the *Kalevala* tell of the bloodthirsty young fighter Kullervo, who "could not grasp things / not acquire the mind of a man." While collecting taxes for his father, Kullervo has his way with a young woman who turns out to be his sister. She commits suicide, he goes off to war. One day he finds himself again in the forest where the rape occurred, and strikes up a conversation with his sword, asking it what kind of blood it wishes to taste. The sword demands the blood of a guilty man instead of an innocent one, whereupon Kullervo rams his body on the blade. In 1891 and 1892, Sibelius used this rather dismal tale as the basis for his first major work, *Kullervo*, an eighty-minute symphonic drama for men's chorus, soloists, and orchestra.

Kullervo anticipates the folk realism of Stravinsky and Bartók in the way it heeds the rhythm and tone of a *Kalevala* recitation. In 1891, shortly after completing two years of study in Berlin and Vienna, Sibelius traveled to the old town of Porvoo to hear runic songs chanted by the folksinger Larin Paraske. The Finnish epic has a meter all its own: each line contains four main trochaic beats, but vowels are often stretched out for dramatic effect, so that each line has its own pattern. Instead of smoothing out the poetry into a foursquare rhythm, Sibelius bent his musical language in sympathetic response. In the setting of the passage below—from "Kullervo and His Sister," the third movement of *Kullervo*—the orchestra maintains a pattern of five beats in a bar while the chorus elongates its lines to phrases of fifteen, ten, eight, and twelve beats, respectively.

Kullervo, Kalervon poika,	Kullervo, Kalervo's offspring,
sinisukka äijön lapsi,	With the very bluest stockings
hivus keltainen, korea,	And with yellow hair the finest
kengän kauto kaunokainen	And with shoes of finest leather

The harmony, meanwhile, drifts away from major- and minor-key tonality. The runic melodies, with their overlapping modes, twine around the chords that lie beneath them; at moments, the accompaniment amounts to a rumbling cluster, a massing together of the available melodic tones.

Kullervo had a decisively successful first performance in Helsinki in 1892. For the remainder of the decade, Sibelius worked mainly in the tone-poem genre, consolidating his fame with such works as *En Saga*, *The Swan of Tuonela* (part of the symphonic *Lemminkäinen* Suite), the *Karelia* Suite, and *Finlandia*. Sibelius's mastery of the orchestra, already obvious in *Kullervo*, became prodigious. *The Swan of Tuonela*, which was initially conceived as the overture to an unfinished *Kalevala* opera, begins with the mirage-like sound of A-minor string chords blended one into the next over a span of four octaves. Sibelius's early works, like contemporaneous works of Strauss, obey a kind of cinematic logic that places disparate images in close proximity. But where Strauss—and later

Stravinsky—used rapid cuts, Sibelius preferred to work in long takes.

Sibelius finished his first two symphonies in 1899 and 1902, respectively. On the surface, these were typical orchestral dramas of the heroic soul, although Sibelius's habit of breaking down themes into murmuring textures sounded strange to many early listeners. Finns quickly appropriated the Second as an emblem of national liberation; the conductor Robert Kajanus heard in it "the most broken-hearted protest against all the injustice that threatens at the present time," together with "confident prospects for the future." In other words, the symphony was understood as a gesture of defiance in the face of the tsar. Although Sibelius rejected this interpretation, images of Finnish struggle may well have played a role in his thinking. In the finale of the Second, a slowly crawling, rising-and-falling pattern in the violas and cellos shows a distinct likeness to a figure in the second scene of Mussorgsky's *Boris Godunov*—the scene in which Pimen the monk records the villainies of Tsar Boris.

At a time when verbal declarations of national feeling were censored by tsarist overseers—at one performance *Finlandia* had to be presented under the title *Impromptu*—the Second served as the focus of clandestine patriotic demonstrations. It was thus the first in a series of politically charged twentieth-century works; secret programs would, of course, later be attached to Shostakovich's symphonies.

No such messages were detected in Sibelius's other "hit" scores of the period, the brilliantly moody Violin Concerto and the affectingly maudlin *Valse triste*, but they cemented his international reputation and therefore increased his stature at home. It was around this time that Sibelius's alcoholism became an issue. He would fortify himself with liquor before conducting engagements and afterward disappear for days. A widely discussed painting by the Finnish artist Akseli Gallen-Kallela, *The Problem*, showed Sibelius in the middle of a drinking bout with friends, his eyes rolled back in his head. Although the composer was now supported by a state pension, he ran up large debts. He was also beset by illnesses, some real and some imagined. Cracks were appearing in the facade that "Finland's hero" presented to the world.

In 1904 Sibelius tried to escape the multiplying embarrassments of his Helsinki lifestyle by moving with his family to Ainola. There he set to work on his Third Symphony, which was itself a kind of musical escape. In contrast to the muscular rhetoric of *Kullervo* and the first two symphonies, the Third speaks in a self-consciously clear, pure language. At the same time, it is a sustained deconstruction of symphonic form. The final movement begins as a quicksilver Scherzo, but it almost imperceptibly evolves into a marchlike finale: the listener may have the feeling of the ground shifting underfoot.

It was in the wake of composing this terse, elusive work that Sibelius got into a debate with Gustav Mahler on the nature of the symphony. Mahler came to Helsinki in 1907 to conduct some concerts, and Sibelius presented his latest ideas about "severity of form," about the "profound logic" that should connect symphonic themes. "No!" Mahler replied. "The symphony must be like the world. It must be all-embracing."

Sibelius kept a close eye on the latest developments in European music. On visits to Germany, he made the acquaintance of Strauss's *Salome* and *Elektra* and Schoenberg's earliest atonal scores. He was variously intrigued, alarmed, and bored by these Austro-German experiments; more to his taste was the sensuous radicalism of Debussy, whose *Prelude to "The Afternoon of a Faun,"* *Nocturnes*, and *La Mer* revealed new possibilities in modal harmony and diaphanous orchestral color. In general, though, he felt ill at ease in the fast-moving environs of Berlin and Paris. He resolved to stay true to his *Alleingefühl*, his feeling of aloneness, to play his role as "apparition from the woods."

In his next symphony, the Fourth, Sibelius presented his listeners with music as forbidding as anything from the European continent at the time. He wrote it in the wake of several risky operations on his throat, where a tumor was growing. His doctors instructed him to give up drinking, which he agreed to do, although he would resume in 1915. The temporary loss of alcohol—"my most faithful companion," he later called it—may have contributed to the claustrophobic grimness of the music, which, at the same time, bespoke a liberated intellect. The first few bars of the symphony extrapolate a new dimension in musical time. The opening notes, scored darkly for cellos, basses, and bassoons, are C, D, F-sharp, and E—a harmonically ambiguous whole-tone collection. It feels like the beginning of a major thematic statement, but it gets stuck on the notes F-sharp and E, which oscillate and fade away. Meanwhile, the durations of the notes lengthen by degrees, from quarter notes to dotted quarters and then to half notes. It's as if a foreign body were exerting gravitational force on the music, slowing it down.

The narrative of the Fourth is circular rather than linear; it keeps revisiting the same unresolved conflicts. An effort at establishing F major as the key of the initially sunnier-sounding second movement founders on an immovable obstacle in the form of the note B-natural, after which there is a palpable shrug of defeat. The third movement dramatizes an attempt to build, note by note, a solemn six-bar theme of funerary character; the first attempt falters after two bars, the second after five, the third after four, the fourth after three. The fifth attempt proceeds with vigor but seems to go on *too* long, sprawling through seven bars without coming to a logical conclusion. Finally, with an audible grinding of the teeth, the full orchestra plays the theme in a richly harmonized guise. Then uncertainty steals back in.

The finale thins out as it goes along, as if random pages of the orchestral parts have blown off the music stands. This is music facing extinction, a premonition of the silence that would envelop the composer two decades later. Erik Tawaststjerna, Sibelius's biographer, reveals that the middle section of the movement is based on sketches that Sibelius made for a vocal setting of Edgar Allan Poe's "The Raven," in a German translation. It is easy to see why a student of the *Kalevala* would have savored Poe's mesmerizing repetition of images—and also easy to see how a man of Sibelius's psychological makeup would have been drawn to its melancholia:

> *"Leave my loneliness unbroken!—quit the bust above my door!*
> *Take thy beak from out my heart, and take thy form from off my door!"*
> *Quoth the Raven, "Nevermore."*

The German version duplicates the rhythm of Poe's original, so the curious listener can correlate lines of "The Raven" with corresponding material in the Fourth's finale. A softly crying flute-and-oboe line in the coda exactly fits the words "Quoth the Raven, 'Nevermore.'" The symphony closes with blank-faced chords that are given the dynamic marking *mezzo-forte*, or half-loud. That instruction is surprising in itself. Most of the great Romantic symphonies end with *fortissimo* affirmations. Wagner operas and Strauss tone poems often close *pianissimo*, whether in blissful or tragic mood. Sibelius ends not with a bang or a whimper but with a leaden thud.

When the Fourth Symphony had its first performance, in April 1911, Finnish audiences were taken aback. "People avoided our eyes, shook their heads," Aino Sibelius recalled. "Their smiles were embarrassed, furtive or ironic. Not many people came backstage to the artists' room to pay their respects." This was a *Skandalkonzert* in Scandinavian style, a riot of silence.

"A symphony is not just a composition in the ordinary sense of the word," Sibelius wrote in 1910. "It is more a confession of faith at different stages of one's life." If the Fourth is a confession, its composer might have been on the verge of suicide. Yet, like so many Romantics before him, Sibelius took a perverse pleasure in surrendering to melancholy, finding joy in darkness. "*Freudvoll und leidvoll*," he wrote in his diary—"Joyful and sorrowful." In his next symphony, he set himself the goal of bringing to the surface the joy inherent in creation.

Joy is not the same thing as simplicity. The Fifth begins and ends in crystalline major-key tonality, but it is an unconventional and staggeringly original work. The schemata of sonata form dissolve before the listener's ears; in place of a methodical development of well-defined themes there is a gradual, incremental evolution of material through trancelike repetitions. The musicologist James Hepokoski, in a monograph on the symphony, calls it "rotational form"; the principal ideas of the work come around again and again, each time transformed in ways both small and large. The themes really assume their true shape only at the end of the rotation—what Hepokoski calls the "*telos*," the epiphanic goal. The method is similar to the one that J. Peter Burkholder, in his studies of Ives, calls "cumulative form." Music becomes a search for meaning within an open-ended structure—a microcosm of the spiritual life.

At the beginning of the Fifth, the horns present a softly glowing theme, the first notes of which spell out a symmetrical, butterfly-like set of intervals: fourth, major second, fourth again. (Fifty years later, John Coltrane used the same configuration in his jazz masterpiece *A Love*

Supreme.) Sibelius's key is heroic E-flat major, but the melody turns out to be a rather flighty thing, never quite touching the ground. A rhythmic trick adds to the sense of weightlessness. At first it sounds as if we're in a standard 4/4 meter, but after a syncopated sidestep it turns out that we're in 12/8. A rotation process begins: the material is broken into fragments and reshaped. In the fourth rotation an electrifying change occurs: the tempo accelerates by increments until the music is suddenly hurtling forward. Sibelius achieved this effect by way of an exceptional feat of self-editing. After the premiere of the first version of the symphony in 1915, he decided to rework it completely, and one of the things he did was to cut off the ending of the first movement, cut off the beginning of the second, and splice them together. The accelerating passage becomes a cinematic "dissolve" from one movement to another.

The second movement of the Fifth provides a spell of calm, although beneath the surface a significant new idea is coming to life—a swaying motif of rising and falling intervals, which the horns pick up in the finale and transform into the grandest of all Sibelian themes. The composer called it his "swan hymn"; he recorded it in his notebook next to a description of sixteen swans flying in formation over his Ainola home. "One of my greatest experiences!" he wrote. "Lord God, that beauty! They circled over me for a long time. Disappeared into the solar haze like a gleaming, silver ribbon . . . That this should have happened to me, who have so long been the outsider." The swans reappeared three days later: "The swans are always in my thoughts and give splendor to [my] life. [It's] strange to learn that nothing in the whole world affects me—nothing in art, literature, or music—in the same way as do these swans and cranes and wild geese. Their voices and being."

The swan hymn transcends the depiction of nature: it is like a spiritual force in animal form. When the horns introduce it, in the midst of a flurry of action in the strings, they seem always to have been playing it and we have only begun to hear it. A moment later, a reduced version of the theme is heard in the bass register of the orchestra at one-third the tempo, creating another hypnotic Sibelian effect of layered time. Then the winds launch into their own melody—a wistfully circling figure that bears an odd resemblance to Satie's *Gymnopédies*.

This is not "masculine" heroism on the order of Beethoven's *Eroica*, also in the key of E-flat major. As Hepokoski suggests, Sibelius's later music implies a maternal rather than a paternal logic—God-given themes gestating in symphonic form. Only by way of wrenching dissonances does the music break loose of its endlessly rocking motion and push toward a final cadence. The swan hymn, now carried by the trumpets, undergoes convulsive transformations and is reborn as a fearsome new being. Its intervals split wide open, shatter apart, re-form. The symphony ends with six far-flung chords, through which the main theme shoots like a pulse of energy. The swan becomes the sun.

Sibelius was at the height of his powers. Yet he had precious little music left in him: the Sixth and Seventh symphonies, the tone poem *Tapiola*, incidental music for Shakespeare's *Tempest*, a smattering of minor pieces, and the phantom Eighth. His pursuit of a final symphonic synthesis made the process of composition almost impossibly arduous. Suddenly dissatisfied with the fluid form that he had evolved in the Fifth, he began to dream of a continuous blur of sound without formal divisions—symphonies without movements, operas without words. Instead of writing the music of his imagination, he wanted to transcribe the very noise of nature. He thought he could hear chords in the murmurs of the forests and the lapping of the lakes; he once baffled a group of Finnish students by giving a lecture on the overtone series of a meadow. Whatever he succeeded in putting on paper seemed paltry and inadequate. As the revisions of the Fifth show, he looked at his own creations with a merciless eye, slashing away at them as if they were the scribblings of an inept student.

Harbingers of silence proliferate in Sibelius's last works. As Hepokoski writes, the teleological narratives end not in a blaze of victory, as in the Fifth Symphony, but in "dissolution," "decay," "liquidation." The Sixth Symphony echoes the sober, neoclassical spirit of the Third, with antique modes underpinning the harmony; it's as if the composer were trying to flee into a mythic past. Yet brutal choirs of brass keep slicing into the gossamer string textures and through the neat ranks of dancing winds. The final movement is stopped in its tracks by a traumatic episode: in Hepokoski's account, nature motives representing the pine trees and the wind rip the stately rotational design to pieces. The process continues for another minute or two, but the motives crumble before one's ears, and the music retreats into the thin, unreal string music with which it began.

The Seventh Symphony expands on the formal innovation of the Fifth, the telescoping of two movements into one. Contrasting episodes are fused into one continuous structure, so that Adagio hymns become Scherzo dances by imperceptible degrees. In emotional terms, the symphony unites the dark and the light sides of the composer's personality, the worlds of the Fourth and the Fifth. The piece is anchored on a grand theme for solo trombone, which sounds three times against a mercurially changing background. Like Strauss's Zarathustra motif, it is made up of "natural" building blocks, thirds and fifths and octaves. On its first appearance, it is couched in summery C major. The second time, the harmony slips into the minor, and a grim, nocturnal mood descends. (One early sketch for the theme is marked "Where the stars dwell.") Finally, the theme returns to the major, generating such a heat of elation that it teeters on the edge of chaos. Growling runs in the low strings and winds recall the funeral-march movement of Beethoven's *Eroica*, and the expected catastrophe looms. It takes the form of a metallic smear of dominant-seventh chords in chromatic sequence followed by a high, exposed line in the violins. When the main key of C returns in the coda, it comes by way of a halting, ambivalent cadence that manages to sound at once radiant and resigned. In the last bars, the note B aches for six slow beats against the final C-major chord, like a hand outstretched from a figure disappearing into light.

Tapiola, a twenty-minute tone poem picturing the Finnish forest, was Sibelius's last big orchestral work, at least that the rest of the world got to hear, and his most severe statement in any form. The connection to traditional tonality grows ever more tenuous, although the work is anchored on a half-diminished seventh, a standard Wagnerian chord. The British composer Julian Anderson has highlighted a passage in *Tapiola* in which a whole-tone interval in multiple registers generates "deep acoustic throbbing"; this is dissonance of a deeper order, the kind that alters your consciousness without assaulting your ears. In a central section depicting a physical or mental storm, whole-tone harmony crumbles into near-total chromaticism, upward- and downward-slithering patterns of notes. Like a wanderer lost in the woods, the listener struggles to find a path through the thicket of sound. When the home chord of B minor is finally reasserted in the brass, it has a hollow ring, its middle note pushed deep into the bass. We are apparently back where we started, no exit in sight.

Finally came the music for *The Tempest*, written on commission from the Danish Royal Theatre in 1925. As if liberated from the burden of symphonic thought, Sibelius abandons his familiar Nordic austerity and indulges the more playful side of his personality. Some sections of the score are deliberately archaic in style, partaking of the rarefied manner of the Sixth Symphony. Others are sweetly nostalgic dance and song pieces, tailored to the needs of the stage. The "Storm" Overture takes up where the most adventurous sections of *Tapiola* left off: the strings play restlessly swirling lines while the brass carve out whole-tone chords. The setting of the lines "Full fathom five" suggests all too realistically the image of a body twisting gently in the deep. An A-minor chord is gradually deformed and transformed by the whole-tone scale with which it partly overlaps, in a kind of musical parallel to the "sea-change" of Ariel's song:

Full fathom five thy father lies,
Of his bones are coral made;
Those are pearls that were his eyes . . .

Perhaps Sibelius felt some conscious or unconscious identification with the figure of Prospero, who, at the end of the play, decides to set aside his magic powers and resume a semblance of normal life:

I have bedimmed
The noontide sun, called forth the mutinous winds,
And 'twixt the green sea and the azured vault
Set roaring war. To the dread rattling thunder
Have I given fire, and rifted Jove's stout oak
With his own bolt; the strong-based promontory
Have I made shake, and by the spurs plucked up
The pine and cedar; graves at my command
Have waked their sleepers, oped, and let 'em forth
By my so potent art. But this rough magic
I here abjure. And when I have required
Some heavenly music—which even now I do—

To work mine end upon their senses that
This airy charm is for, I'll break my staff,
Bury it certain fathoms in the earth,
And deeper than did ever plummet sound
I'll drown my book.

Sibelius wrote no music for this tremendous speech, but its rhetoric carries over into the cue for "solemn music" that follows. The harmony at the outset recalls the submersion music of "Full fathom five," except that the dissonances now sound at earsplitting volume, semitone clashes in full cry. Then the chaos melts away into a clean open fifth, which sounds alien in context. All this evokes Prospero dimming the sun, setting sea and sky at war, waking the dead. A quiet hymn for strings follows, in which the chromaticism of the storm is woven back into classical harmony. It is "heavenly music," but also sweet, ordinary music, dispelling the rage and pain that fuel Prospero's art.

Did Sibelius, like Prospero, think about abjuring his magic and drowning his book? If so, he gave no sign of it in the late 1920s and early '30s. The Eighth Symphony was under way, and the composer seemed happy with it. He is known to have worked on the piece in the spring of 1931, while staying alone in Berlin. Writing home to Aino, he said that the symphony was "making great strides," although he was puzzled by the form it was taking. "It's strange, this work's conception," he told his wife. That is all we know about it.

Fame can confuse any artist, and it had an especially disorienting effect on Sibelius. Since the turn of the century he had enjoyed international celebrity, but in the twenties and thirties he became something like a pop-culture phenomenon. Why his symphonies struck such a chord with Jazz Age audiences is difficult to explain. Perhaps they achieved mass popularity precisely because they were foreign to the neon light and traffic noise of contemporary urban life. In any case, no composer of the time caused such mass excitement, especially in America. Celebrity conductors vied for signs of favor from Ainola. New York Philharmonic listeners went so far as to vote Sibelius their favorite living symphonist. His name even cropped up as a plot point in Hollywood movies. In Otto Preminger's chic 1944 thriller *Laura*, a detective played by Dana Andrews interrogates a shady Southern gentleman portrayed by Vincent Price:

DANA ANDREWS: You know a lot about music?

VINCENT PRICE: I don't know a lot about anything, but I know a little about practically everything.

DANA ANDREWS: Yeah? Then why did you say they played Brahms's First and Beethoven's Ninth at the concert Friday night? They changed the program at the last minute and played nothing but Sibelius!

"Nothing but Sibelius" comes close to summing up orchestral programming of the period. Serge Koussevitzky, the conductor of the Boston Symphony, presented a complete cycle of the Sibelius symphonies in the 1932–33 season, and he hoped to cap the series with the world premiere of the Eighth.

Crucial to Sibelius's American reputation was Olin Downes, who from 1924 to 1955 served as music critic of the *New York Times*. The son of Louise Corson Downes, a crusading feminist and Prohibitionist, Downes believed that classical music should appeal not just to elites but to common people, and from the bully pulpit of the *Times* he loudly condemned the obscurantism of modern music—in particular, the artificiality, capriciousness, and snobbery that he perceived in the music of Stravinsky. Sibelius was different; he was "the last of the heroes," "a new prophet," who would rescue music from cerebral modernism. At heart, Downes's motives were good; he wished to celebrate the music of the present and saw in Sibelius a serious figure of mass appeal. But his attacks on Stravinsky were merely tendentious. It would have been more productive to show what the two composers had in common, rather than using one as a stick to beat the other.

Downes traveled to Finland in 1927 to meet Sibelius on his native ground. The composer had fallen into one of his periodic bouts of depression—it was at this time that he wrote, "Isolation and loneliness are driving me to despair." Meeting Downes temporarily lifted his spirits, although, in the long term, Downes's devotion may have had a deleterious effect. Glenda Dawn Goss, in a book-length study of this singular composer-critic relationship, suggests that Sibelius was in some way crushed by the attention that Downes heaped on him.

In the early thirties, just as Koussevitzky was expecting to conduct the premiere of the Eighth Symphony in Boston, Downes pestered the composer for the completed score. In 1937 the critic wrote a follow-up letter in which he passed along the sentiments of none other than Louise Corson Downes: "My mother and I often speak of you and she asked me again about his Eighth Symphony . . . 'Tell Mr. Sibelius that I am not concerned or anxious so much about his Eighth Symphony, which I know he will complete in his own good time, as about his *Ninth*. He must crown his series of works in this form with a ninth symphony which will represent the summit and the synthesis of his whole achievement and leave us a work which will be worthy of one of the elected few who are the true artistic descendants and inheritors of Beethoven.'"

As if pressure from music critics' mothers were not enough, Sibelius was also brooding over the reception he encountered in Europe. Paris had no time for him. Berlin, before Hitler came to power, viewed him with condescension bordering on contempt. In neither city did expansive symphonies and evocative tone poems have much intellectual market value. The critic Heinrich Strobel, future impresario of the Donaueschingen Festival, referred to Sibelius's Violin Concerto as "boring Nordic dreariness." Sibelius was tormented by these characterizations, and also annoyed by the cult of Stravinsky. He happened to be in Berlin at the time of a performance of *Oedipus Rex* in 1928, but decided that he "could not afford to throw away three or four hundred marks." He later said of Stravinsky: "When one compares my symphonies with his stillborn affectations . . . !"

In America, Downes's pugilistic praise of Sibelius aroused resentment among American Stravinsky admirers. In 1940, Virgil Thomson became the music critic of the *New York Herald Tribune*, and in his debut review he tore lustily into the Sibelius myth, calling the Second Symphony "vulgar, self-indulgent, and provincial beyond all description." Equally venomous attacks emanated from the Schoenberg camp. Theodor Adorno prepared a dire analysis of the Sibelius phenomenon for a sociological think tank called the Princeton Radio Research Project: "The work of Sibelius is not only incredibly overrated, but it fundamentally lacks any good qualities . . . If Sibelius's music is good music, then all the categories by which musical standards can be measured—standards which reach from a master like Bach to most advanced composers like Schoenberg—must be completely abolished." Adorno sent his essay to Thomson, who, while agreeing with its sentiments, sagely advised that "the tone is more apt to create antagonism toward yourself than toward Sibelius."

Sibelius's confidence was by that time already gone. You can see it slipping away in his correspondence with Koussevitzky, which is preserved at the Library of Congress. The conductor sends letters and telegrams on an almost monthly basis, pleading for the Eighth. Sibelius replies in an elegant, slanting hand on parchment-like paper, tantalizingly mentioning a symphony that is almost finished but not quite.

In January 1930 Sibelius reports, "My new work is not nearly ready and I cannot say when it will be ready." In August he is more sure: "It looks as though I can send you a new work this season." But he is worried about American copyrights, which do not protect his music. Koussevitzky reassures him that the symphony will be safe from pirates. In the end, it does not appear. Then, in August 1931, in the wake of his productive stay in Berlin, Sibelius writes, "If you wish to perform my new Symphonia in the spring, it will, I believe, be ready." In December the information is leaked to the *Boston Evening Transcript*, which publishes an item: "Symphony Hall has received an important letter from Sibelius, the composer, about his new Symphony, the Eighth. It is completed, and the score will soon be on the way to Boston." A telegram from Finland arrives two weeks later, saying that the current season wouldn't work. Sibelius probably got wind of the *Transcript* article and panicked.

The following June, the Eighth is back on its feet: "It would be good if you could conduct my new symphony at the end of October." Then comes a fresh panic. "Unfortunately I have named October for my new symphony," the composer writes just one week later. "This is not certain, I am very disturbed about it. Please do not announce the performance." Eventually, it is promised for December 1932. Koussevitzky sends a "restless" telegram on New Year's Eve, as if he has been checking the mailbox every day that month. Two weeks later he receives yet another terse telegram, yet another postponement. There are a couple more tentative mentions of the Eighth in subsequent correspondence, then nothing.

In the late thirties, Sibelius again hoped to set the Eighth free from its forest prison. By that time he knew better than to say anything to the garrulous Koussevitzky. Then, in 1939, Hitler invaded Poland, and Finland became part of a chess game between Nazi Germany and the Soviet Union. Early in the war, Finland was applauded in the West for its hardy stand against the Soviets, and Sibelius was more popular than ever; Toscanini took him up with a passion. In 1941, Finland aligned itself with the Germans, partly to avoid undergoing a hostile occupation and partly to regain territory lost to the Soviet Union in the previous conflict. Sibelius went from being a symbol of freedom to serving as an apparent Nazi stooge. As a Nordic, "Aryan" composer, he had enjoyed glowing notices in Nazi Germany, and won the Goethe Prize in 1935. Now he became almost an official German artist, receiving as many performances as Richard Strauss. The Sibelius Society held a gala concert at the Berlin Philharmonic in April 1942. In a message to Nazi troops in the same year he allegedly said: "I wish with all my heart that you may enjoy a speedy victory."

Privately, Sibelius was tormented by the promulgation of race laws in Nazi Germany. In 1943 he vented in his diary, "How can you, Jean Sibelius, possibly take these 'Aryan paragraphs' seriously? That is a great advantage for an artist. You are a cultural aristocrat and *can* make a stand against stupid prejudice." But he made no stand. As the culture god of the Finnish state he had long since ceased to see a difference between music and history, and with the world in flames his music seemed destined for ruin. At the same time, obscure agonies consumed him. The diary again: "*The tragedy begins*. My burdensome thoughts paralyze me. The cause? Alone, alone. I never allow the great distress to pass my lips. Aino must be spared." The final page of the diary, from 1944, contains a shopping list for champagne, cognac, and gin.

Sibelius lived to the age of ninety-one. Like his contemporary Strauss, he made wry jokes about his inability to die. "All the doctors who wanted to forbid me to smoke and to drink are dead," he once said. In a more serious mood, he observed, "It is very painful to be eighty. The public love artists who fall by the wayside in this life. A true artist must be down and out or die of hunger. In youth he should at least die of consumption." One September morning in 1957, he went for his usual walk in the fields and forest around Ainola, scanning the skies for cranes flying south for the winter. They were part of his ritual of autumn; back when he was writing the Fifth Symphony, he had noted in his diary, "Every day I have seen the cranes. Flying south in full cry with their music. Have been yet again their most assiduous pupil. Their cries echo throughout my being." When, on the third-to-last day of his life, the cranes duly appeared, he told his wife, "Here they come, the birds of my youth!" One of them broke from the flock, circled the house, cried out, and flew away.

There is a curiously moving photograph of Igor Stravinsky kneeling over Sibelius's grave, which takes the form of a horizontal metal slab on the grounds at Ainola. The visit took place in 1961, four years after Sibelius's death. The master of modern music had practical reasons for making the pilgrimage: the Finnish government had promised him the Wihuri Sibelius Prize, which came in the generous amount of twenty-five thousand dollars. But the gesture had a certain gallantry. In the past, Stravinsky had belittled Sibelius, and on the occasion of the old man's death he had slammed down the phone when a reporter called for comment. In his last years, though, Stravinsky warmed to a few Sibelius scores, and made an arrangement for octet of the Canzonetta for strings.

The notion that there might be something "modern" about Sibelius was risible to self-styled progressives of the immediate postwar era. The Schoenbergian pedagogue René Leibowitz summed up the feelings of many new-music connoisseurs when he published a pamphlet with the title *Sibelius: The Worst Composer in the World*. Surveys of twentieth-century music labeled the composer a peripheral figure in the central drama of the march toward atonality and other intellectual landmarks. At least two texts—Joan Peyser's *The New Music* and Glenn Watkins's *Soundings*—failed to mention him at all. Yet performances of Sibelius's music continued unabated; conductors and audiences had it right all along.

In the last decades of the century, the politics of style changed in Sibelius's favor. The composer began to be understood in terms of what Milan Kundera called, in another meditation on the culture of small nations, "antimodern modernism"—a personal style that stands outside the status quo of perpetual progress. Suddenly, composers and scholars were paying heed to Sibelius's effects of thematic deliquescence, his ever-evolving forms, his unearthly timbres. New-music luminaries such as Brian Ferneyhough, Wolfgang Rihm, Tristan Murail, Gérard Grisey, Per

Nørgård, Peter Maxwell Davies, John Adams, and Thomas Adès all cited him as a model. A generation of upstart Finns—Magnus Lindberg, Kaija Saariaho, and Esa-Pekka Salonen—found new respect for the national hero after having rejected him in their punkish youth. Lindberg made his name with a gripping piece called *Kraft* (1983–85), whose orchestra is augmented by scrap-metal percussion and a conductor blowing a whistle. At any given point, it sounds nothing like Sibelius—Lindberg cites the influence of noise-rock bands such as Einstürzende Neubauten—but the accumulation of roiling processes from microscopic material feels like a computer-age reprise of *Tapiola*.

In 1984, the great American avant-garde composer Morton Feldman gave a lecture at the relentlessly up-to-date Summer Courses for New Music in Darmstadt, Germany. "The people who you think are radicals might really be conservatives," Feldman said on that occasion. "The people who you think are conservative might really be radical." And he began to hum the Sibelius Fifth.

6

CITY OF NETS

Berlin in the Twenties

One day in 1932, during the last months of Germany's first attempt at democracy, Klaus Mann, Thomas Mann's son, walked into a room and saw the corpse of the young actor Ricki Hallgarten, his friend and sometime lover. Hallgarten had shot himself through the heart, splattering blood on the wall. Klaus wrote, "The blood stains looked like the scattered fragments of a mysterious pattern—a last message, a warning, the writing on the wall." That phrase, from the book of Daniel, became the leitmotif of Klaus Mann's recollections of Germany in the 1920s, and, lest anyone miss the allusion, he went on to quote the biblical text itself: "MENE, MENE, TEKEL, UPHARSIN . . . God hath numbered thy kingdom . . . Thou art weighed in the balance, and art found wanting . . . Thy kingdom is divided."

The Weimar Republic, as embodied in the culture of Berlin, invites melodrama. Every violent act or image seems to foreshadow the catastrophe to come. But it is too easy to write the story of German culture from 1918 to 1933 as the prelude to the next chapter. Berlin was a city of possibilities, of myriad outcomes, glowing with promise as well as threat. It played host to Communists, Nazis, Social Democrats, nationalists, New Objectivists, Expressionists, Dadaists, and straggling Romantics. Its spirit spoke in the meeting of opposites. In the wake of the humiliation of defeat, Berlin shook off its imperial past and reinvented itself as the prototype of media-saturated urban cultures to come—the first all-night city, the city without shame.

The young composers of Berlin—among them Kurt Weill, Paul Hindemith, Ernst Krenek, Hanns Eisler, and Stefan Wolpe—happily joined in the frenzy. Like their counterparts in Paris and New York, they picked up the rhythms of jazz, the noise of industry, the fashionable clutter of twenties life. They not only gained entry to popular culture but at times took control of it: Weill's *Threepenny Opera* charmed Germany as *Show Boat* charmed America. Weill and company seemed on the verge of solving the ultimate mystery—how to break the divide between classical music and modern society. "Music is no longer a matter of the few," Weill proclaimed in 1928. "The musicians of today have made this sentence their own. Their music, therefore, is simpler, clearer, and more transparent . . . Once musicians obtained everything they had imagined in their most daring dreams, they started again from scratch."

Historians of Weimar debate whether German democracy was preordained to fail, or whether Hitler's rise to power was a freak event. Music historians face a similar problem. Was Weimar a kind of fever dream, its arts programs destined to fall victim to the vagaries of commercial culture? Or might Weimar have given artists a permanent safe haven? As so often, the pessimists seem to have the force of history behind them. Schoenberg, who lived in Berlin from 1926 on, warned his colleagues against a futile chase after popularity, and in this period he devised a new way of working—a "method of composing with twelve notes"—that would protect the serious composer from vulgarity.

Back in Vienna, Alban Berg went his own way; his second opera, the opulent and terrifying *Lulu*, reconciled his teacher's latest ideas with Weimar rhythms and Romantic chords. *Wozzeck* conquered Berlin in 1925; in an alternate universe, *Lulu* might have had the same reception. But Berg did not live to finish it, and by the time of his death, in 1935, Klaus Mann's "writing on the wall" had become reality.

Ministry of Enlightenment

When Kaiser Wilhelm II abdicated his throne on November 9, 1918, Germany fell into a political disorder from which it never fully recovered.

Leaders of the Social Democratic Party proclaimed a republic from the windows of the Reichstag. Karl Liebknecht hailed a Communist revolution while standing on the steps of the Royal Palace.

Kurt Weill, an eighteen-year-old student at the Hochschule für Musik, was in the streets that day; he heard Liebknecht's speech and watched the skirmishes around the Reichstag. "I've had indescribable experiences the last few days," he wrote to his parents. What he saw on the ground led him to make a perceptive comment, which historians of the Weimar period have confirmed: the moderate elements lacked power and influence, so the extremes of the left and the right were setting the tone and the agenda. This was an ominous note on which to inaugurate a republic.

Still, the school stayed open and musical life went on. Cafés were full and the trams were running. Even as the revolution began, the Ufa film studio held a champagne reception for Ernst Lubitsch's film of *Carmen*. The previous night Richard Strauss had conducted *Salome* at the Court Opera, which promptly shook off its royal title and became the State Opera.

The brief life of the Weimar Republic is usually divided into three periods: chaos, stabilization, and the devolution toward Nazism. Chaos lasted a full four years, bringing with it various coups and counterrevolutions and an astonishing total of four hundred political murders. (One victim was Gustav Landauer, commissar for people's enlightenment of the short-lived Soviet Republic of Bavaria, whose wife, Hedwig Lachmann, translated *Salome* into German.) Most damaging to the country's psychological security was the hyperinflation of 1923, at the height of which the mark was valued at several trillion to the dollar. "Nothing was so mad or so atrocious that it could have caused any awe in people anymore," Thomas Mann wrote of the inflation. "[Germans] learned to look on life as a wild adventure, the outcome of which depended not on their own effort but on sinister, mysterious forces."

The "stabilization" period, which lasted from 1924 to 1929, unfolded under the guiding hand of the master politician Gustav Stresemann, who, first as chancellor and then as foreign minister, restored economic order and led Germany back into the world community. Stresemann's death in 1929 removed from the scene the most powerful personality who might have stopped Hitler.

Directing the "stabilization" of music was a man named Leo Kestenberg, who in December 1918 assumed the post of musical adviser to the Prussian Ministry of Science, Culture, and Education. He had studied piano with Ferruccio Busoni before becoming active in the Social Democratic Party. In the spirit of that well-meaning organization, he aimed to clear away the cobwebs of elitist culture and promote the creation of "art for the people." One of his flagship institutions was the Kroll Opera, which presented antitraditional stagings to a working-class audience. Half the seats were made available to the Volksbühne, the socialist theater, at prices appropriate to the salary of a manual worker. The conductor was Otto Klemperer, a Mahler protegé, who at this early stage of his long career specialized in subversive productions of classic repertory. Kestenberg also gave Berlin's new-music scene a shot of adrenaline by appointing two leading progressives to teach at the conservatories: Busoni at the Prussian Academy of Arts and Franz Schreker at the Hochschule für Musik. When Busoni died, Schoenberg moved from Vienna to take his place. Schreker and Schoenberg brought with them bristling cohorts of students, who quickly took over the limelight.

Inconvenient realities soon intruded on Kestenberg's arts utopia. As the critic John Rockwell has shown in his study of Weimar musical politics, Kestenberg never really figured out who the People were or what they wanted to hear: the working classes whom the Kroll Opera hoped to serve were often confounded by the company's revisionist take on the classics. At the same time, Kestenberg lacked the political skill to placate the right wing, which deplored all avant-garde doings. While Weimar's bohemians and leftists had their time in the sun, the reactionary, xenophobic strain in German culture was never far below the surface. One night in 1928, Joseph Goebbels walked around the Tauentzienstrasse cabaret district and returned home to write: "This is not the true Berlin . . . The other Berlin is lurking, ready to pounce."

Music for Use

During the Great War, Paul Hindemith banged the bass drum in a military band, racing back and forth a mile or so behind the front lines, playing marches and dances for soldiers who were recovering from their spell in the trenches. He also performed in an all-soldier string quartet, at the behest of a cultured commanding officer, Count von Kielmannsegg, who adored Debussy. The group happened to be playing the Debussy Quartet when news of the composer's death came over the radio. The count himself died in action a few months later. Such surreal juxtapositions of music and war left their mark on Hindemith's imagination, and he, more than anyone, set the pace for postwar German music.

A no-nonsense man with a bulbous face and a machine-gun manner of speech, Hindemith had nothing aristocratic or bourgeois in his background. He was the son of a small-town manual laborer, and attended the Hoch Conservatorium in Frankfurt with the help of a full scholarship. In the first months of the peace, he declared his independence from German Romanticism by completing a series of six sonatas for stringed instruments, crisply constructed pieces in which the influence of Debussy and Ravel was pervasive; few German composers of the preceding fifty years had written music of such uncomplicated grace. The young composer also showed a deep feeling for pre-Romantic traditions, for the stately forms of the Renaissance and the Baroque, although he modernized them relentlessly.

"Beauty of sound is beside the point," Hindemith instructed the player in his Second Sonata for Solo Viola. He was considered the musical personification of what Gustav Hartlaub called the New Objectivity—a form of expression "neither Impressionistically vague nor Expressionistically abstract, neither sensuously superficial nor constructivistically introverted." The archetypal Hindemith piece takes the form of a fast, furious, off-kilter march, with fanfares in multiple tonalities and bass lines bent off course. The music is intense, but it does not take itself particularly seriously, or seriously at all. The "Ragtime" movement of Hindemith's *Suite 1922* for piano is inscribed with the placard-like notice "*Mode d'emploi*—Directions for Use!!" in which the performer is told to "look on the piano as an interesting kind of percussion instrument and act accordingly." The *Kammermusik No. 1*, also from 1922, opens with an homage to Stravinsky's *Petrushka* and ends with a squealing siren out of a Dada cabaret. All this resembles the up-to-date, streetwise music that Milhaud was writing in Paris, except that Hindemith's constructions had a rougher, rowdier edge.

There was something bracingly un-German about this new German talent. Strauss, even in his merriest prankster mood, could never have perpetrated something like *The Flying Dutchman Overture as Sight-Read by a Bad Spa Orchestra by the Village Well at Seven in the Morning*, in which a string quartet plays Wagner's overture horribly out of tune. Hindemith was anything but visionary in his preoccupations; he was practical, efficient, down-to-earth. Another catchword that became attached to him was *Gebrauchsmusik*, or music for use. If, say, a bassoonist and a double-bass player were looking for something to play, then Hindemith would dash off a Duet for Bassoon and Double Bass and not worry what posterity might make of it. He worked fast and to order; on one occasion he wrote two sonata movements in the buffet car of a train and performed them on arrival. As violist of the Amar Quartet, he energetically promoted his colleagues' music as well as his own. He helped to organize festivals and "new-music weeks" in Donaueschingen, Salzburg, Baden-Baden, and eventually Berlin, where, in 1927, he became a teacher at the Hochschule für Musik.

The idea of "music for use" quickly took root in the Weimar musical scene. The Munich-born Carl Orff, who would find everlasting fame as the composer of *Carmina burana*, cultivated it assiduously. If Hindemith, like Stravinsky, found rejuvenation in the curt forms and sharp timbres of the Baroque, Orff went much further back in time, to the music theater of ancient Greece. The austere aesthetic of Stravinsky's *Les Noces* and *Histoire du soldat* metamorphosed into a timeless ritual language, tuneful, percussive, and hypnotically repetitive. In his early years Orff tended to the political left, setting poems by Bertolt Brecht. But his most singular achievement was a massive cycle of pieces for children, the *School Work* project, which, by way of infectious musical invention, instructed youngsters in the basics of mode, harmony, form, and rhythm. Kestenberg took notice, and by the early thirties he was proposing to give Orff control of the entire German music education system. The Nazi takeover in 1933 ended that prospect.

"Music for use" and educational music went hand in hand with what Peter Gay has called Weimar's "hunger for wholeness": its obsessive pursuit of arts-and-crafts projects, physical culture, back-to-nature expeditions, youth movements, sing-alongs, and so on. After the war, Theodor Adorno professed to see proto-Fascist tendencies in Weimar's communitarian music making, playing off the fact that both Hindemith and Orff had become entangled, to a greater or lesser degree, in Nazi culture. Yet the denunciation rests on specious logic. There is nothing intrinsically fascistic about the longing to connect music to a community; it can just as easily serve as a vehicle for the propagation of democratic thought. Untold millions of children would learn the basics of musical language by tapping out notes on the mallet percussion instruments that Orff had constructed to his purposes. The man himself may have been politically duplicitous, but his passion for teaching was profound, and it probably touched more lives than any music described in this book.

Now Opera

A publicity photo issued by the music publisher Universal Edition in 1927 shows the twenty-seven-year-old Austrian composer Ernst Krenek in a vaguely druggy double exposure, an endless cigarette holder dangling from his mouth. With his sharp suit and unlined face, he looks like a baby gangster gone legit. Another photomontage from that year puts the young artist together with two other celebrities of the moment: the boxer Max Schmeling and the aviator Charles Lindbergh.

For a little while in the late twenties, Krenek acquired certifiable, almost Gershwin-like celebrity; his opera *Jonny spielt auf*, or *Jonny Strikes Up*, was enshrined as one of those pop-culture artifacts that every Central European had to know. Fame came Krenek's way because he dared to bring jazz—or what passed for jazz—onto the hallowed opera stage. Like George Antheil in Paris and New York, he was an ambitious young man seeking to make a splash, although there was a serious side to his enterprise as well; like so many young Austrians and Germans, he yearned to break out of the hothouse of Romantic and Expressionist art, to join the milling throngs in the new democratic street.

Jonny exemplified a new subgenre that came to be called *Zeitoper*, or Now Opera. Composers working in this mode set works in factories, or on board ocean liners, or, in one case, on "Fiftieth Avenue" in Manhattan. Typical was the plot of Max Brand's *Maschinist Hopkins*, memorably described by Nicolas Slonimsky in his reference work *Music Since 1900*: "A cuckolding libertine pushes the husband of his mistress to his death in the cogs of a monstrous machine and strangles her when he finds out that she has become a promiscuous prostitute, whereupon the foreman, Maschinist Hopkins, dismisses him from his job ostensibly for inefficiency." Now Operas almost always contained a scene in which one or another of the characters throws off his or her inhibitions to dance a Charleston, a *Fox-Trott*, a shimmy, or a tango. Composers thereby liberated themselves.

Several *Zeitoper* composers, Krenek and Brand among them, studied with the once celebrated and now unfairly neglected Austrian opera composer Franz Schreker, who, back in 1912, had unveiled a remarkable work titled *Der ferne Klang*, or *The Distant Sound*. The story of that opera is essentially the story of this book: the cultural predicament of the composer in the twentieth century. An ambitious young musical dramatist named Fritz decides to abandon his middling career and his adoring fiancée in order to find a new style—a "mysterious distant sound," a "high, sublime goal." He produces a work that people call "something really new," "spine-chilling." It causes a Schoenbergian scandal, replete with stamping and whistling. Meanwhile, Grete, Fritz's fiancée, sinks low in the world, ending up as a prostitute. In the opera's final scene they meet again, and Fritz, dying of an unspecified illness, tragically realizes that the sound he has been seeking has been around him all this time, in the multifarious textures of modern life, and in Grete's voice.

The magic of Schreker's opera is that from the first bars we have been hearing the music that Fritz cannot grasp—buoyantly lyrical vocal writing, more Italian than German in style; a golden blur of orchestral sound, more Debussy than Wagner in timbre; a cosmopolitan sensualism, incorporating, in the "grand bordello" sequence of Act II, Gypsy bands, barcaroles, and choral sernades.

Jonny tries to replicate Schreker's achievement, but with more modern means. The title character is a Negro jazz violinist on a European tour, a sort of Austrian cartoon of Will Marion Cook. He crows in triumph: "Across the sea comes New World brilliance / Inheriting old Europe with dance." The cast also features a composer named Max, who, at the beginning of the opera, is seen sitting at the side of a grim glacier, which he addresses as "*Du schöner Berg*" ("you beautiful mountain"). Like Fritz in *Der ferne Klang*, Max cannot forgo the pursuit of a distant sound, presumably of the Schoenbergian variety. The subtext becomes amusingly obvious when Max says of the glacier, "Everyone loves it once they have got to know it," as if quoting from propaganda literature of the Second Viennese School. The glacier eventually instructs Max, through the medium of an invisible choir of women's voices, to "return to life." In a climactic railway-station scene Max catches up with his beloved Anita as she rides off into the unknown. Jonny jumps up on top of the station clock and the chorus reprises his song of triumph. According to Krenek's original notes, the opera was to have ended with the image of a 78-rpm recording spinning on a phonograph, the composer's name inscribed upon it.

The entire plot was autobiographical. Before discovering a taste for jazz and other popular materials, Krenek had gone through his own wild-eyed semi-atonal phase, with Schoenberg and Bartók his guides. In writing *Jonny*, he was trying to live out Max's epiphany, exposing his own glacier world to the warmth of Jonny's violin. Furthermore, the character of Anita was based on Anna Mahler, Gustav and Alma's daughter, to whom Krenek was briefly and tempestuously married. Not long after the relationship ended, the composer went to see Sam Wooding's jazz revue *Chocolate Kiddies*, which was the rage of Europe in the mid-twenties, and he seized on Wooding's polite jazz arrangements as a lifeline that would lead him out of the abysses of Central European despair. Interestingly, the revue contained at least one early Duke Ellington song, "Jig Walk," and that tune bears a slight resemblance to Jonny's big number. Alas, Krenek's engagement with African-American music went about as deep as the blackface painted on the singer playing Jonny.

Zeitoper drew sharp criticisms from both ends of Weimar's hyper-extended political spectrum. The Nazis attacked it as degenerate art. The Communist composer Hanns Eisler, meanwhile, wrote of *Jonny* in *Die Rote Fahne*: "Despite the infusions of chic, this is exactly the same mushy, petit bourgeois stuff that other contemporary opera composers produce." Eisler was equally unkind to Hindemith's "music for use," dismissing it as a "relative stabilization of music" (a wry echo of German economic lingo). All modern music lived a *Scheindasein*, an illusory existence bereft of meaning or community. In 1928 Eisler wrote: "The big music festivals have become downright stock exchanges, where the value of the works is assessed and contracts for the coming season are settled. Yet all this noise is carried out in the vacuum of a bell glass, so to speak, so that not a sound can be heard outside. An empty officiousness celebrates orgies of inbreeding, while there is a complete lack of interest or participation of a public of any kind."

What Germany needed, Eisler said, was music that told deeper truths about human society. Open the window when you compose, he instructed his colleagues. "Remember that the noise of the street is not mere noise, but is made by man . . . Discover the people, the real people, discover day-to-day life for your art, and then perhaps you will be rediscovered." By that time, the revolution had begun; *The Threepenny Opera* was playing to packed crowds at the Theater am Schiffbauerdamm.

Gestic Music

Kurt Weill's schoolmates probably never imagined him as the cynosure of a decadent city. The son of a Jewish cantor in the town of Dessau, about seventy miles from Berlin, Weill grew up a shy, serious boy, devoted to music. Like Krenek, he admired Schoenberg in his youth, and yearned to study with the Master himself in Vienna, but the family's limited finances prevented him from going. Instead, in the last weeks of 1918, Weill journeyed to revolutionary Berlin, where he ended up enrolling in Busoni's master class at the Prussian Academy of Arts.

His first reactions to Weimar culture were skeptical. After a visit to the 1923 Frankfurt Chamber Music Festival, he reported to Busoni that "Hindemith has already danced too far into the land of the fox-trot." Yet his ears were opening to a broader gamut of sounds: Mahler's catchall symphonies, Stravinsky's pop-tinged *Histoire du soldat*. The latter work appeared on the Frankfurt programs, and Weill was moved to admit—his snobbery was on the wane—that its "pandering to the taste of the street is bearable because it suits the material."

As Krenek followed Schreker's path out into the wider world, Weill followed Busoni, a magus-like musician who hovered over the early twentieth century like a spider in his web. A Tuscan of Corsican descent, a resident variously of Trieste, Vienna, Leipzig, Helsinki, Moscow, New York, Zurich, and Berlin, Busoni was a cosmopolitan in a nationalist age, a pragmatist in an era of aesthetic absolutism. In 1909, Busoni reprimanded Schoenberg for rejecting the old while embracing the new; as Busoni saw it, you could do both at once, and in the *Sketch of a New Aesthetic of Music* he called simultaneously for a reinvention of the "tonal system" and for a return to Mozartean, classical grace. Like so many Romantics and modernists before him, Busoni idolized the figure of Faust, but he delighted more in the science of magic than in the theory of heaven and hell. *Doctor Faust*, his unfinished operatic masterpiece, circumnavigated the globe of musical possibility, incorporating diatonic, modal, whole-tone, and chromatic scales, Renaissance polyphony, eighteenth-century formulas, operetta airs, and flurries of dissonance.

Perhaps the most effective lesson that Busoni imparted to Weill was a single sentence: "Do not be afraid of banality." For a young German who had been raised to think that "banality" included almost everything Italian and French, this advice had an enlightening effect. Busoni showed how the great operas of Mozart and Verdi interwove naive tunes and sophisticated designs. He talked about the *Schlagwort*, the "hit word" or catchword, which can sum up in one instant an intricate theatrical situation—for example, the scalding cry of "*Maledizione!*" ("The curse!") in Verdi's *Rigoletto*. In a 1928 essay, "On the Gestic Character of Music," Weill elaborated the related idea of *Gestus*, or musical gesture. The literary critic Daniel Albright defines *Gestus* as the dramatic turning point "in which pantomime, speech, and music cooperate toward a pure flash of meaning." Bertolt Brecht, Weill's principal literary collaborator, would give the concept of *Gestus* a political cast, describing it as a revolutionary transfer of energy from author to audience. For Weill, though, it always had a more practical meaning, one to which politics might or might not be attached.

Weill's first efforts at music theater were one-act operas: *The Protagonist*, a neat little shocker in which an Elizabethan actor, unable to distinguish between art and life, murders his own sister onstage; *Royal Palace*, in which a socialite throws herself into a lake rather than pursue a spiritually empty Jazz Age existence; and *The Tsar Has Himself Photographed*, in which a female anarchist posing as a society photographer plots the assassination of the tsar. Each of these works contains a pivotal moment—"gestic" in the musical if not political sense—when a popular, everyday sound grabs the listener's attention. In *The Protagonist* it is an oompahing wind-and-brass octet, which intrudes on the dissonant ruminations of the orchestra. In *Royal Palace* it is the blast of an auto horn and the jangling of a honky-tonk piano, which illustrate an innovative film interlude in the center of the piece. And in *The Tsar* it is the effortlessly slinky "Tango Angèle" that plays as the tsar and his would-be *assassine* dance and fall in love. Weill asked that this last piece be executed not by the orchestra but by an onstage Victrola, and, to this end, a 78-rpm record was included with the score. Something interesting happened after the premiere, which took place in February 1928: Weill's publisher, Universal Edition, began selling the Tango in stores, and it became a hit.

The transformation of Weill's style was quickened by two crucial meetings, one with Lotte Lenya and one with Bertolt Brecht. Weill become romantically and professionally involved with Lenya starting in 1924, and was never the same afterward. If Weill had a "cool, withdrawn" nature, as Busoni observed, Lenya was in every sense a woman of the world. The product of a poor background and an abusive father, she found employment variously as a dancer, a singer, an actress, a stage extra, an acrobat, and, briefly, a prostitute—a profession that ensnared countless German and Austrian women during the years of chaos and inflation. Weill met her through the playwright Georg Kaiser, who wrote the texts for *The Protagonist* and *The Tsar*. His music began to resemble Lenya's voice—that famously unpolished, cutting, wearily expressive instrument. "She can't read music," Weill wrote in 1929, "but when she sings, people listen as if it were Caruso."

Brecht barged into Weill's life in early 1927. Scholars are still trying to capture the dynamic of their collaboration, which Brecht obfuscated for many years by telling arrogant, self-serving lies; the playwright used to say that he had written all the best tunes of *The Threepenny Opera* and *Mahagonny* and that Weill, a "composer of atonal psychological operas," had merely transcribed them. Subsequent investigations have shown that it was Brecht who relied quite often on the work of others—touching up translations of foreign plays and calling them his own, borrowing indiscriminately from the literature of several centuries, playing down or covering up the contributions of co-writers such as Elisabeth Hauptmann, his sometime lover. All the same, Brecht had an utterly distinctive style—his sentences say what they have to say and then snap shut—and with a modicum of editing he could stamp his voice on anyone's writing. On Weill, Brecht had as electric an effect as Lenya did: he further toughened the composer's image, pushing him in the direction of hard-left politics and giving him words with teeth and bite.

Weill asserted his musical personality not just in the large structures that contained his "hits" but in the interstices of the songs themselves. Consider the "Alabama-Song," from *Mahagonny Songspiel*, the first collaboration between Weill and the firm of Brecht. The title, an Americanization of the old German genre of the popular *Singspiel*, signals the creators' intentions to appropriate modern pop, and the lyrics, by Hauptmann, are couched in a delightfully eccentric version of the English language: "Oh show us the way to the next whisky bar / Oh don't ask why, oh don't ask why." A steady rhythm chugs under the almost entirely monosyllabic text, but subtle irregularities complicate the song's progress. The vocal line keeps plunking down a minor third, and then drops a minor third again, like a drunk whose legs buckle under him as he staggers forward. Extraneous notes creep into what seems to be a C-minor key, and by the seventh bar ("Oh don't ask why") the harmony has tilted across the tritone into the area of F-sharp before veering back again. The chorus—"Oh! Moon of Alabama"—comes as a relief, its arching tune shaking off the churlishness of the verse. But one of the inner voices descends by half steps, like the chromatic bass of a Renaissance lament, and a bare fifth drones dully and menacingly in the bass. Berlinish world-weariness is woven into the fabric of the score.

Mahagonny Songspiel had its first performance at Hindemith's Baden-Baden Festival in 1927, where it was an instant smash. At the party after the performance, Lenya felt a huge hand on her shoulder and turned to see the looming figure of Otto Klemperer, who grinned and sang a line from the "Benares Song": "Is here no telephone?" Everyone in the bar joined in. Thrilled at the impact that this spontaneous little work had made on the new-music elite, Weill and Brecht decided to create an evening-length opera based on the *Mahagonny* material; this would become *Rise and Fall of the City of Mahagonny*.

Before that project came to fruition, however, composer and playwright took a detour into the criminal underworld of eighteenth-century London. And in the process they escaped the paradox that had encircled the jazzy, poppy ventures of Paris composers, as well as Leo Kestenberg's state-funded modernist theater; they produced "art for the people" that the people heard and liked.

The Threepenny Opera

Brecht loved outlaws, thugs, men of no principles. In his adolescence, he idolized the turn-of-the-century Austrian playwright Frank Wedekind, who shocked Vienna with his scabrous, criminal appearance—"ugly, brutal, dangerous, with close-cropped red hair," in Brecht's words. Brecht had his hair shorn in the same style and, like Wedekind, took to strumming on a guitar during poetry recitations.

How Brecht's infatuation with antisocial hooligans can be reconciled with the strict Marxist doctrine that the writer adopted after 1926 is something that scholars have long struggled to comprehend. In a 1930 article, Walter Benjamin proposed that Brecht's thugs should be understood as promising material for revolutionary transformation, and used a Faustian metaphor to describe the hoped-for process: "Just as Wagner [Doctor Faust's assistant] produced a homunculus in a test tube from a magic brew, Brecht hopes to produce the revolutionary in a test tube from a mixture of poverty and nastiness." But Brecht seemed to relish the nastiness more than the promise of socialist redemption to follow.

Macheath, a.k.a. Mackie, the antihero of *The Threepenny Opera*, is the nastiest of Brecht's homunculi. He is based on the character of Captain Macheath in John Gay's eighteenth-century ballad opera *The Beggar's Opera*, which served as the main source for Brecht and Hauptmann's libretto. In the original, Macheath is a master criminal with a dashing style who stands in metaphorically for the corrupt politicians of Gay's time. Benjamin, in a later essay on *The Threepenny Opera* and its sources, observed how "intimately the countermorality of beggars and rogues is intertwined with the cant of the official morality." Brecht and Weill's Macheath is at once more charming and more menacing than Gay's, mainly because of the musical number that introduces him: "Die Moritat vom Mackie Messer," otherwise known as "Mack the Knife." This most famous of Weimar songs takes the form of a "murder ballad," a catalog of killings. Macheath is revealed not merely as a high-living highwayman but as an apparent psychopath who kills as much for pleasure as for financial gain. Schmul Meier has disappeared, along with many rich men; Jenny Towler is found with a knife in her breast; seven children die in a great fire in Soho; a young girl is raped.

Weimar culture exhibited an unhealthy fixation on the figure of the serial or sexual killer. The German press gave comprehensive coverage to such homicidal lunatics as Georg Karl Grossmann, the "Bluebeard of the Silesian Railway"; Karl Denke, the "Monster of Münsterberg"; Fritz Haarmann, the boy killer of Hannover; and Peter Kürten, the "Vampire of Düsseldorf." The artists George Grosz and Otto Dix depicted the bloody corpses of prostitutes in pitiless fashion; Grosz went so far as to have himself photographed acting out the crimes of Jack the Ripper (also a character in Wedekind's prewar play *Pandora's Box*). Peter Lorre portrayed a child killer in Fritz Lang's film *M.* Macheath has something in common with all these bloodthirsty types. At the same time, he fits the profile of the detective-story archcriminal, a figure like Arthur Conan Doyle's Professor Moriarty and Lang's Dr. Mabuse—and the Weimar fascination with masterminds is also unsettling in retrospect, given how Hitler would blame everything on the hidden machinations of the Jews. In one way or another, Macheath seems to be the agent of all that is insoluble and unspeakable behind the scenes of the Western city.

Weill encased Brecht's hymn to Macheath in insidiously hummable music. A simple tune circles around and around, coming to rest repeatedly on an added-sixth chord—a C-major triad plus the note A—which was a favorite device of Debussy. That "sweetened" harmony would become a standard device in jazz, but there is something desperate and bedraggled about Weill's use of it here. In the first verse, the main chord is wheezed out on a solo harmonium; thumping bass notes give the melody heavy feet; and, throughout, the almost obsessive stress on the note A tends to darken rather than lighten the mood, nudging the music toward the minor mode. "Mack the Knife" is a song chained to one chord. It's a pop tune with no exit.

Everything about *The Threepenny Opera* is ambiguous; in the words of the scholar Stephen Hinton, it practices a "style of willful and relentless equivocation on absolutely every level." The ambiguity reaches down to the fundamental level of musical identity: like Jerome Kern's *Show Boat*, which opened the previous year, and like Gershwin's pre-*Porgy* musicals, *Threepenny* sits on the border between classical and popular genres, combining "hit" numbers with modernistic textures and socially critical themes. Weill's most ingenious move was to score his breakthrough theater piece not for a symphony orchestra but for a sleek, mutable band of seven musicians, who were asked to play no fewer than twenty-three different instruments. (The drummer, for example, plays second trumpet for a couple of numbers, and the banjo player at one point picks up the cello.) And, by asking his performers to take on so many roles, Weill guarantees that the playing will have, in place of soulless professional expertise, a scrappy, seat-of-the-pants energy.

The singers were liberated, too. Just as John W. Bubbles and other performers were allowed to improvise their way through parts of *Porgy and Bess*, Lenya and the rest of the *Threepenny* cast had the opportunity to freight Weill's deceptively simple vocal lines with varying degrees of knowingness, sarcasm, ennui, and despair. That freedom of expression became a performing tradition that continues to evolve today.

In the 1950s, "Mack the Knife" began a second life as an American pop standard, and new variations were rung on the tune. When Louis Armstrong sang it, he warmed up Brecht's hard-bitten lyrics with the husky humanity of his voice, and jokingly added Lenya's name to the list of Mackie's victims: "Sukey Tawdry, Jenny Diver / Lotte Lenya, sweet Lucy Brown." Frank Sinatra turned the song into a display of Rat Pack braggadocio: "When I tell you all about Mack the Knife, babe / It's an offer you can never refuse." Weill's song thus became a showbiz tour de force, although its sting remained. Armstrong and Sinatra, both children of the streets, understood what the text was about: Armstrong said that Mack the Knife reminded him of characters he had encountered in New Orleans, while Sinatra knowingly grafted on a line from Francis Ford Coppola's *Godfather* films, which exposed American politicians as gangsters of a higher order.

Weill's influence did not end there. In 1962 Lenya appeared in the revue *Brecht on Brecht* at the Theater de Lys in New York's Greenwich Village. A young Minnesota-born singer-songwriter named Bob Dylan came to see the show and found himself mesmerized by Lenya's singing of "Pirate Jenny," in which a prostitute fantasizes revenge on the men who exploit her. "The audience was the 'gentlemen' in the song," Dylan wrote in his autobiography, *Chronicles*. "It was their beds she was making up . . . It wasn't a protest or topical song and there was no love of people in it." What especially intrigued Dylan was the cryptic repetition of the chorus—"And a ship with eight sails and fifty cannon . . ." The line reminded him of the foghorns on Lake Superior, next to his childhood home in Duluth: "Even though you couldn't see the ships through the fog, you knew they were there by the heavy outbursts of thunder that blasted like Beethoven's Fifth—two low notes, the first one long and deep like a bassoon."

In the spirit of Brecht and Weill, Dylan proceeded to carve his own *Gestus*-like phrases into the minds of late-twentieth-century listeners:

"The answer is blowin' in the wind," "A hard rain's a-gonna fall," "The times they are a-changin'." The last was a direct quotation from one of Brecht's lyrics for Hanns Eisler. The spirit of Berlin played on.

Twelve-Tone Music

In October 1928, while *The Threepenny Opera* was still enjoying its first run, Arnold Schoenberg, resident in Berlin since 1926, began work on a libretto for an opera titled *Moses und Aron*. Like Stravinsky's *Symphony of Psalms*, *Moses* would display new religious conviction in a morally uncentered time. In the face of anti-Semitism, Schoenberg was rediscovering his Jewish roots, and, in telling of Moses's struggle to bring the Word of God to his recalcitrant people, he aligned himself with the prophetic tradition. By the time Hitler came to power, Schoenberg had completed the second act, which features the dance around the golden calf—that orgy of idol worship in which the people indulge themselves while Moses goes up the mountain to receive the Tables of the Law. The scene has many sardonic echoes of twenties styles—some stamping Stravinskyan cross-rhythms here, some bustling Hindemithian counterpoint there, a few woeful Weill-like tunes. Schoenberg had been inveighing against Weimar culture in his prose writings, and there is a congruence between those jeremiads and Moses's thunderings in Act III of the libretto: "You have betrayed God to the gods, the idea to images, this chosen folk to others, the extraordinary to the commonplace."

Schoenberg had unveiled his own new law in 1923, in the form of the "method of composing with twelve tones which are related only with one another." Pupils and friends were summoned to his house in Mödling, outside Vienna, to hear news of the breakthrough. Schoenberg had hit on the notion of twelve-tone music after enduring an extended period of creative confusion. The "extreme emotionality" of atonal composition, in his own words, had exhausted him, and he needed a less fraught, more orderly way of working. From 1912 to 1915 he had labored on a choral symphony, which was to have depicted modern man's struggle to find a realistic form of faith. One section was titled "The bourgeois God does not suffice." The symphony never made it past the sketching stage, but some of its ideas passed into another project, the oratorio *Jacob's Ladder*. This, too, was never finished, but an impressive beginning was made. At the outset, Archangel Gabriel gives direction to the hapless denizens of modernity: "Whether right or left, forward or backward, uphill or downhill—one must go on, without asking what lies ahead or behind." This titanic utterance is backed up by an equally titanic prelude in which a six-note ostinato grinds beneath a ladderlike ascending sequence of six other notes, making up a total of twelve.

Twelve is the number of steps it takes to go from middle C on a piano to the next C above or below. Twelve consecutive notes make up what is called the chromatic scale, so named because it suggests all the colors of a spectrum. Over the course of the nineteenth century, composers made increasingly free use of the complete set of chromatic notes, depending on it to create a turbulent, even devilish atmosphere. Liszt's *Faust Symphony* begins with a nonrepeating series of twelve, an emblem of Faust's ceaseless striving after knowledge. Strauss's *Thus Spake Zarathustra* employs a twelve-tone theme to mock the workings of the scientific mind. *Salome* and *Elektra* have several such episodes of chromatic saturation. Likewise, the first atonal works by Schoenberg and his students tend to run through the set of twelve in a few bars. Twelve-tone writing simply made official the tendency to "run the gamut."

A particular arrangement of twelve notes is called a series or row. The idea is not to consider the row a theme in itself but to employ it as a kind of fund of notes, or, more precisely, of relationships among notes, or intervals. Schoenberg added some concepts from the old art of counterpoint to maximize the possibilities of thematic play. The composer can run the row in *retrograde* (go backward from the last note). Or he can use an *inversion* (turn it upside down). For example, if the original begins by moving up three half steps and down two, the retrograde row will end with that same pattern in reverse, while the inverted row begins by going down three half steps and up two. The *retrograde inversion* goes back to front and upside down. The composer can also *transpose* the row by moving it up or down the scale. All told, the chromatic scale contains a huge number of permutations—to be exact, 479,001,600, the factorial of 12.

The great discovery made Schoenberg happy. Through the early and mid-twenties he composed with a fluency that he had not experienced since 1909. A set of Five Pieces and a Suite for piano, a Serenade, a Wind Quintet, a Septet-Suite, and a set of Variations for Orchestra appeared in quick succession. Nearly all of Schoenberg's early twelve-tone works are couched in established forms, usually from the Baroque and Classical periods. Formal rules are observed, dance rhythms replicated, ideas clearly spelled out and rigorously developed. Schoenberg has almost entirely abandoned the mystical mind-set of his early atonal period, when he wished to dissolve form and leap into the unknown.

Along the way, a peculiar thing happens: the tonal building blocks that Schoenberg formerly disavowed begin popping up on occasion. One may even find that rootless cosmopolitan, the diminished seventh: the Variations starts with one. The Swiss composer Frank Martin later noted that the twelve-tone idea never forbids the use of tonal materials; in fact, one must manipulate the system to *avoid* producing them. Schoenberg did not always make the correction: the groundbreaking twelve-note sequence in *Jacob's Ladder* culminates in a C-sharp-major triad in the horns, followed by a hint of G—harmonies that follow logically from the intervals contained in the opening corkscrew figure.

Many of Schoenberg's pupils loyally adopted the new method. Anton Webern, it turned out, had been tinkering with his own form of twelve-tone writing for some time; as far back as 1911, while working on his Bagatelles for String Quartet, he had made a chart of the twelve chromatic notes and crossed them off one by one as he composed. "When all twelve notes have gone by," he would tell himself, "the piece is over." In a manuscript dated 1922, some months before the ceremonial unveiling of dodecaphony in Mödling, Webern copied out rows in retrograde and inversion. Schoenberg later complained that his former student had "used twelve tones in some of his compositions—*without telling me*."

Webern's twelve-tone music is of a piece with his atonal music, with its spare construction and haiku strokes. In 1927 he completed his first extended instrumental piece in the new medium, the word "extended" being understood in a relative sense; the String Trio, the product of nine months' labor, lasts nine minutes. Its second and final movement contains an old-fashioned repeat sign, in a seeming nod toward neoclassical practice; yet the gestures are so evanescent that the listener may have a hard time noticing when the repeat commences. A ten-minute Symphony followed in 1928, and, in 1930, the Quartet for violin, clarinet, tenor saxophone, and piano (this is the work for which Webern demanded "sex appeal," to Berg's amusement). The composer kept whittling down his materials, employing twelve-tone rows that were really elaborations of smaller, three-note segments. Works of later years, notably the Piano Variations of 1936, have the abstract beauty of ice crystals or snowflakes, their structures made up of symmetrical patterns. Joseph Auner points out that there was an element of nature-mysticism to Webern's method. On a hiking trip in 1930 the composer wrote ecstatically of the experience of being lost in a snowstorm, of walking into a whiteness that was like a "completely undifferentiated screen." His music offered a similar experience for the ears.

In the mad year of hyperinflation, Schoenberg offered a kind of stabilization—the conversion of a chaotic musical marketplace to a planned economy. There was a nationalistic thrust, too, to Schoenberg's return to order; at a time when Russian, French, and American composers were seizing headlines with their Jazz Age antics, Schoenberg was reasserting the primacy of Austro-German composition, its ancient arts of counterpoint and thematic development. Supposedly, he once declared that he had ensured the supremacy of German music for the next hundred years. In the end, however, twelve-tone writing turned out to be an impeccably cosmopolitan method, almost a lingua franca in the post–World War II period. Already, in the late twenties and early thirties, scattered young composers were feeling the pull of Schoenberg's intervallic games: Nikos Skalkottas in Greece, Luigi Dallapiccola in Italy, Roberto Gerhard in Spain, Fartein Valen in Norway, and young Milton Babbitt of Jackson, Mississippi.

Despite the occasional scandal—a Berlin Philharmonic audience registered its unhappiness when Wilhelm Furtwängler conducted the Variations for Orchestra in 1928—the late twenties were the happiest years of Schoenberg's life. He felt vindicated by the esteem that the appointment at the Prussian Academy of Arts bestowed. "Recognition does one good," he wrote to Leo Kestenberg. There was unprecedented stability in his personal life; in 1923, the unfaithful Mathilde had died after a long illness, and less than a year later Schoenberg married Gertrud Kolisch, the daughter of a Viennese doctor and the sister of the violinist Rudolf Kolisch, whose Kolisch Quartet would do much to advance Schoenberg's cause.

Yet the cultural antics of the Weimar era irritated the composer no end. "Art is from the outset naturally not for the people," he wrote in 1928. "But one wants to force it to be. Everyone is supposed to have their say. For the new bliss consists of the right to speak: free speech! Oh God!" He derided his more faddish colleagues variously as window dressers, restaurateurs, and purveyors of greaseproof paper and neckties. The satirical song cycle *Three Satires*, from 1925–26, took potshots at Stravinsky:

But who's this beating the drum?
Why, it's little Modernsky!
He's had his hair cut in an old-fashioned queue,
And it looks quite nice!
Like real false hair!
Like a wig!
Just like (or so little Modernsky likes to think)
Just like Papa Bach!

In an essayistic introduction to the *Satires*, Schoenberg widened his attack to include folkloristic composers, who "want to apply to the naturally primitive ideas of folk music a technique that only suits a complicated way of thinking" (this would presumably be Bartók), and certain "middle road" composers who mingle dissonance and tonality (Krenek, possibly Berg). In another essay from 1926, Schoenberg wrote, "Many modern composers believe they are writing tonally if they occasionally introduce a major or minor triad, or a cadence-like turn of phrase, into a series of harmonies that lack, and must lack, any terms of reference." He added cryptically: "They betray their God, but remain on good terms with those who call themselves His attorneys." Here is a pre-echo of the *Moses* libretto: "You have betrayed God to the gods . . ."

Curiously, even as Schoenberg vented against the popular styles of the day, he not so subtly assimilated them in his music. The *Serenade*, for example, originally had movements titled "Jo-Jo-Foxtrot," "Film Dva," and "Tenn Ski." There is a sort of jazz episode, or at least a burst of syncopation, in the eighth of the orchestral Variations. The comic opera *From Today Until Tomorrow*, undertaken in the wake of *The Threepenny Opera*, portrays an agitated married couple in a modern setting, replete with ringing telephone, ringing doorbell, three saxophones, and a guitar. The couple is trying to decide whether to become "up-to-date" by entering into an open marriage. The wife racily contemplates taking an array of lovers, "one after the other or two at the same time, but just not a system!" In the end, husband and wife resolve their differences, spurn modernity, and reaffirm traditional roles. So sure was Schoenberg of the opera's success that he had it published at his own expense, figuring that he could reap all the profits when it became a runaway hit. For all its spiky charms, it did not.

In a way, Schoenberg's resentment of Weimar's young composers was a personal affair. As the *Satires* said, it was a question of betrayal. Those who had formerly embraced atonality as the one true path were being tempted in more outwardly fashionable directions. Krenek ventured to criticize a certain unnamed brand of contemporary music as "the self-gratification of an individual who sits in his studio and invents rules according to which he then writes down his notes." Schoenberg took offense at this masturbatory metaphor and snapped in an unpublished commentary that Krenek "wishes for only whores as listeners." Eventually, Krenek came back to the fold: at the beginning of the thirties, he abandoned the jazz airs of *Jonny spielt auf* and took up twelve-tone writing, discovering a gritty new voice in his historical opera *Charles V*.

Hanns Eisler, too, disavowed his teacher's methods. By 1926, he could no longer reconcile modernist complexity with his leftist politics, as he said in a characteristically blunt letter to Schoenberg: "Modern music bores me, it does not interest me, I hate much of it and even despise it. I will in fact have nothing to do with the 'modern.' If possible I try to avoid hearing it and reading it." Schoenberg accused Eisler of committing "treason"—not so much because he wished to go his own way as because he insisted all along that he remained loyal to Schoenberg's cause.

The most infuriating apostasy was that of Kurt Weill. In this case, there could be no question of personal disloyalty, since the two men barely knew each other. Perhaps it was the similarities in their backgrounds—both were descended from synagogue cantors—that prompted Schoenberg to look on Weill as something of a prodigal son, or, closer to the allegory of *Moses und Aron*, as a wayward younger brother.

The Schoenberg-Weill dispute began in October 1927, when Weill wrote an article drawing a pointed contrast between those composers "who, filled with disdain for the public, work toward the solution of aesthetic problems as if behind closed doors" and those who "open up a connection with any kind of public." The following year Weill called on composers to end all elitist pursuits and start "from scratch." Schoenberg got hold of the second article and annotated it furiously. Where Weill wrote, "You want to hear music you can understand without special explanations," Schoenberg put an "X" next to the word "understand." And where Weill imagined a theater in which "operatic figures become once again living human beings who speak a language understandable by all," Schoenberg put a wavy line under "understandable." His conclusion was harsh: "In the end, those communally oriented artists will have addressed their idiocies only to each other." He began to take pride in the fact that his music attracted so few listeners. When, in 1930, he was asked to describe his public, he said, "I do not believe I have one."

The textual evidence suggests that Schoenberg's critique of Weill carried over into *Moses und Aron*. In the final scene of Act II of the opera the prophet argues with his brother Aron—Schoenberg having changed Aaron to Aron in order to avoid an unlucky thirteen-letter title, or so the legend goes—over whether and how God should be represented. Aron says his mission is to "make [Moses] understandable to the people in their own accustomed way." He uses the same word—"*verständlich*"—that Schoenberg had underlined skeptically in Weill's essay. And as Aron sings of his urge to reach out to all the people the music keeps slipping into quasi-tonal patterns. Schoenberg probably did not know Weill's music well enough to imitate it, but this may be *The Threepenny Opera* as he heard it in his head. Moses, reciting nonmelodious *Sprechstimme* over strict atonal harmonies, declares his loyalty to the "unrepresentable," the "inexpressible."

Weimar polemics aside, *Moses* stands as Schoenberg's most awesome achievement. It is a profound meditation on faith and doubt, the difficulty of the language commensurate with the difficulty of the subject; no doubt the God of the Old Testament would speak through atonal hexachords. At the same time, Schoenberg's parodies in the "Dance Around the Golden Calf" give the work a stylistic diversity that helps to sustain the ordinary operagoer's interest. (The scene is a little like the moralizing politician's trick of waving pornography while he condemns it.) Yet Schoenberg does not exempt himself from judgment. Moses, his alter ego, ends Act II in abject despair, crying out, "O Word, you Word that I lack!" Admittedly, this aura of frailty dissipates in Act III (never set to music), where the prophet regains his confidence and wreaks vengeance on all who misunderstood him. Aron falls dead. The people cannot be saved, there is no promised land. Moses is destined to roam the desert in the company of his soldier-acolytes. "In the desert," he tells them, "you shall be invincible."

Battle Music

In the summer of 1929, Gustav Stresemann, the foreign minister of the Weimar Republic, attended a performance by the La Scala opera company of Milan. The event was part of an extraordinary festival of music, dance, and theater involving all the leading German musicians (Strauss, Furtwängler, Klemperer, and so on) as well as Arturo Toscanini's Italian company and Diaghilev's Ballets Russes. It turned out to be Berlin's last hour of cultural glory before the decline and fall. Many who bought tickets for that La Scala gala were worried to see Stresemann in poor health; they knew that he was almost single-handedly providing a semblance of a steady center in German politics. When he died that October, German intellectuals had a sinking feeling. "It's the beginning of the end," the author Bruno Frank said to Klaus Mann. That same month the American stock-market crash brought on a worldwide depression, putting a quick end to "relative stabilization" and thus to the merrymaking spirit of what Germans still call the "Golden Twenties."

German music entered a new period of sobriety. Many young composers abandoned notions of entertaining a mass public and instead began writing music of aggressively political character, in anticipation of a coming battle with the right.

Far-left musical agitation had been stirring since the first days of the republic. One early locus of activity was the Novembergruppe, a cross-disciplinary artistic organization that took its name from Liebknecht's aborted revolution of November 1918. At first, musical leftists hoped to use avant-garde methods to overthrow bourgeois values. Stefan Wolpe, one of very few Berlin-in-the-twenties luminaries who were actually from the city, became the prime musical mover of the Novembergruppe movement; on one occasion he organized a kind of happening at which eight phonographs played recordings of Beethoven's Fifth Symphony at different speeds. Even fellow Novembergruppists were aghast at Wolpe's

First Piano Sonata, which had its premiere at a 1927 evening of "Stationary Music." Among the most extreme works of the time, it mixed whiplash mechanical gestures with serpentine, gamelan-like patterns on the white keys of the piano. Later, Wolpe would write an absurdist *Zeitoper* titled *Zeus und Elida*, in which the god of the Greeks tries to rape Europa in the middle of a jazz-filled Potsdamer Platz. A narrator tells the audience to think of Zeus as Hitler. Had the opera been performed, it would have been one of very few musical works of the period to attack Hitler by name.

Wolpe's brand of avant-garde agitation failed to satisfy Hanns Eisler, who thought that composers should communicate as directly as possible with the working classes and other potential revolutionary elements. By 1928, Eisler had developed a genre that he called *Kampflieder* (songs of struggle), which was intended strictly for proletarian audiences and their intellectual allies. Fiercely trudging marches, usually in a minatory minor mode, and modernized Bachian chorales served to focus the emotion of the crowd. Eisler's right-hand man was the actor-singer Ernst Busch, whose riveting voice, a blunt instrument of righteous anger, seemed to compel some decisive, brutish act on the part of the listener. Busch's postwar recordings of *Kampflieder* preserve the desperate passions of the Weimar era; in Eisler's song "Der heimliche Aufmarsch," or "Secret Mobilization," originally written in 1930, the singer barks out the line "The attack against the Soviet Union is a stab in the heart of the revolution" with a palpable tone of wounded pride.

Schoenberg claimed that the populists of Weimar were talking mostly to each other. Eisler, though, found a real mass following. The German Worker-Singers Union, with which he was closely associated, had 400,000 members. He and Busch would venture into halls and bars in Berlin's working-class districts, whipping up fervor with the force of their performances; the composer drew shouts of approval whenever he banged the piano keys with a balled-up fist. Unlike other parties on the political spectrum, German Communists did not stand idle as the Nazi Party gathered strength. The problem was that they, too, were in thrall to a totalitarian ideology; Germany faced a choice between tyrannies. Eisler soon began to involve himself not only in German politics but in the Soviet cultural bureaucracy, taking a role in a Comintern (Communist International) organization called the International Music Bureau. Eisler could have been under no illusions about the nature of the emergent Stalinist regime, which tolerated no dissent or diversity of opinion. Pitilessness was in the air; sentimental humanist values would have to be sacrificed at the altar of action. In a way, German Communists were most effective against the Nazis because they shared the will to violence.

On such issues the alliance between Brecht and Weill foundered. The two were still uneasily conjoined in the summer of 1929, during that last spell of freedom. They appeared once again at the Baden-Baden Festival, where the *Mahagonny Songspiel* had struck a nerve two years before. This time they presented a didactic cantata describing Charles Lindbergh's solo flight across the Atlantic. In the face of a looming deadline, Weill persuaded Hindemith to write several of the numbers. Hindemith was also the sole composer of Brecht's other music-theater project of the summer, *The Baden-Baden Learning Play About Acquiescence*. This instantly notorious piece explored, by way of interrelated stories, the question of "whether man helps man." In one scene a clown named Herr Schmidt complains that his limbs hurt, whereupon two other clowns tear them off his body one by one. While blood gushes from the stumps, a "Clown March" plays in the orchestra. A summary placard is held up, reading, "Better to make music than to hear it." Hindemith found the material revolting, and reacted by moving to the aesthetic and political right during the remaining years of the Weimar Republic.

"Acquiescence"—the German word *Einverständnis* also implies "thinking as one"—became Brecht's favorite leitmotif. Stephen Hinton paraphrases it as an individual's "willingness to act in the interests of the community, even to the point of sacrificing his own life." That idea dominated the "school opera" *The Yes-Sayer*, for which Weill wrote the music in early 1930. The text was adapted by Hauptmann and Brecht from the Japanese play *Taniko* (in an English-language version). Four young people go on a hazardous mountain journey, and when the youngest of them falls sick the others face the possibility of having to turn back. The boy agrees that the mission must go on and that he should be thrown over the side of the mountain. "With closed eyes, none guiltier than another," the others toss the boy off the cliff.

Brecht secularizes this Buddhistic parable of self-sacrifice, thereby converting it into agitprop. The politics may be antithetical to Hitler's, but there is the same mythologizing of the community, the same disregard for the sanctity of life. Weill may have had a more conflicted attitude—his music audibly mourns for the boy, a brief allusion to the funeral march from Beethoven's *Eroica* sending him off with a tinge of Romantic grandeur—but the hard-heartedness at the core of the scenario overpowers any countervailing humanistic messages. The opera both begins and ends with the thought "Above all it is important to learn acquiescence." *The Yes-Sayer* was performed hundreds of times in schools in Berlin and elsewhere, and it inadvertently prepared German children for a time when they would have to do the unthinkable for the sake of the Führer.

With both Weill and Hindemith proving insufficiently ruthless, Brecht finally turned to Eisler, his perfect political match. At the end of 1930 Brecht and Eisler collaborated on a supremely vicious theater piece titled *Die Massnahme*, or *The Measures Taken*, which had its premiere on the same night as Stravinsky's *Symphony of Psalms*. The scenario of *The Measures Taken* recalls that of *The Yes-Sayer*, but the pretense of literary allegory is dropped in favor of something like an instruction manual for international espionage—and it may have been directly inspired by secret assignments that Eisler's brother, the mysterious Gerhart Eisler, apparently carried out for Soviet intelligence in China.

The plot is this: covert Communist operatives in China have in their midst a Young Comrade who compromises their mission by reaching out to the oppressed. After a string of mistakes, he is told that he must die, and he not only acquiesces in his own death but plans it. "What shall we do with your body?" the Agitators ask. "You must cast me into the lime-pit," the Young Comrade replies. "In the interests of Communism in agreement with the progress of the proletarian masses of all lands." Eisler responds with music of blistering directness, again using Bachian chorales to ennoble the bloodlust inherent in the material. The journalist Ludwig Bauer could have been thinking of *The Measures Taken* when he lamented that political fanaticism on both the right and the left was devaluing the life of the individual. "The I is disappearing," Bauer wrote. "Individuals count only as part of the whole."

By 1931, Brecht and Weill were hardly speaking. The divergence of their worldviews incited bitter arguments; Brecht famously shouted that he would throw this "phony Richard Strauss" down the stairs. Still, one more Brecht-Weill masterpiece had made its way into the world. *Rise and Fall of the City of Mahagonny* was the culmination of everything that Weill sought in his most recent phase, and it was more his opera than Brecht's—a many-layered entertainment, critical of social norms but unburdened by dogma. The songs of the original *Mahagonny Songspiel* become part of a three-act drama about the founding, heyday, and decline of a semi-American "paradise city," otherwise known as the "city of nets."

At the beginning of the opera, the Widow Begbick and her cronies are on the run from the law, guilty of swindling and procuration. When their truck breaks down in the middle of the desert, they decide to found a city—Brecht's uncanny prophecy of Las Vegas. A solemn drumbeat beneath Begbick's proud manifesto, again reminiscent of the funeral music of Beethoven's *Eroica*, signals that Mahagonny is destined for a bad end. As the "Alabama-Song" plays, the sharks move in—the prostitute Jenny and her steely-eyed cohorts. Vice prospers, fortunes are made, rules laid down. Jim Mahoney, a lumberjack, realizes that "there is something lacking." After a hurricane nearly destroys the city, he proclaims a new rule, which is that all should do as they please. A bacchanal follows, very Berlinish in its herky-jerky, every-which-way rhythm—Weill's version of the "Dance Around the Golden Calf." The philosophy of self-gratification has the eventual effect of ruining Jim, who is put on trial for failing to pay his bills. He is sentenced to death, over music of bone-chilling relentlessness, and Mahagonny likewise goes to its doom. The slow marching song that ends the opera is nothing short of apocalyptic, with the Beethovenian rhythm thundering on the drums and a death motif descending like Mahler's hammer blows of fate. The libretto was widely understood as a protest against rampant capitalism, although it reads just as well as a critique of the fake utopia of the Soviet Union.

The performance history of *Mahagonny* dovetails with the disintegration of the Weimar Republic. The opera should have had its premiere at the Kroll, but Klemperer, losing political support, declined to perform it. (The "people's opera" closed its doors the following year; its last new production was, appropriately, Janáček's *From the House of the Dead*.) Instead, *Mahagonny* made its debut on March 9, 1930, in Leipzig, where right-wing agitators greeted it with a riot. Three weeks later, the last Social Democratic government dissolved, and that summer Heinrich Brüning began governing by emergency decree, delivering a fatal blow to the democratic process. Performances of *Mahagonny* in Essen, Oldenburg, and Dortmund were canceled. The elections of September showed the

Nazis in ascendance, and the Brownshirts made their presence felt when the opera came to Frankfurt the following month. The first performance went off smoothly, but the second dissolved into bedlam. A hundred and fifty Nazis swarmed into the hall, shouting, "*Deutschland erwache!*" Stink bombs were thrown, fireworks set off. In a subsequent brawl, a Communist acquiesced to death by a beer stein to the skull.

Lulu

"The great retaliation has begun, the revenge of a man's world which has the audacity to punish its own guilt." Karl Kraus, the unforgiving satirist of Vienna, idol of Schoenberg and Berg and a hundred other modernist youths, said these words at a lecture back in May 1905. He was describing the world of Wedekind's plays *Earth Spirit* and *Pandora's Box*, in which a bewitching young singer named Lulu descends from the heights of society to the depths of prostitution, meeting her death at the hands of Jack the Ripper. She is, to some extent, a grotesque caricature of the lethal female, fit for the misogynistic pages of Otto Weininger's *Sex and Character*. Yet, as Kraus points out, Wedekind reserved his utmost contempt for the haute bourgeoisie, which hypocritically encourages its men to seek sexual satisfaction from prostitutes while condemning those same women as bearers of disease and degradation. If the woman is a monster, men are responsible. Lulu "became the destroyer of all," Kraus says, "because she was destroyed by all."

In the audience at Kraus's lecture was Alban Berg. The novice composer stayed transfixed through the ensuing performance of *Pandora's Box*, in which Wedekind himself took the role of Jack the Ripper. Whether Berg imagined a Lulu opera at that time is not known. *Wozzeck* became his chief obsession, and after finishing it, he weighed various options for his next stage piece, including an adaptation of Gerhart Hauptmann's play *Und Pippa tanzt!* (about a blind ocarina player who wanders Austria in search of his lost love). Only in the summer of 1928 did he finally settle on *Lulu*, as he titled his synthesis of the two Wedekind plays. (The subject was in the air: G. W. Pabst's silent film of *Pandora's Box*, starring the flapper icon Louise Brooks, opened the following year.) Berg had not yet completed the orchestration of Act III at the time of his death, but his intentions were clear enough that the Austrian composer Friedrich Cerha was later able to put together a three-act version, which had its premiere in 1979. By turns hyper-Romantic and avant-garde, stately and brutal, empathetic and inhumane, *Lulu* embodies all the raging contradictions of Central European culture on the eve of the Hitler catastrophe.

Although Berg lived his entire life in Vienna, Berlin was the scene of his greatest success—the premiere of *Wozzeck*, on December 14, 1925. Before that night, Berg had been an obscure member of the Schoenberg circle; afterward, he joined the ranks of the most illustrious composers of the day. Ovation upon ovation greeted him when he walked onstage at the Staatsoper on Unter den Linden. If Theodor Adorno is to be believed, Berg was upset by the response. "I was with him until late into the night," Adorno recalled, "literally consoling him over his success. That a work conceived like Wozzeck's apparitions in the field, a work satisfying Berg's own standards, could please a first-night audience, was incomprehensible to him and struck him as an argument against the opera." Schoenberg, on his side, was jealous. "Schoenberg envied Berg his successes," Adorno observed, "while Berg envied Schoenberg his failures."

Berg dutifully took up twelve-note composition, although his use of it was quirky, to say the least. In a letter to Adorno he brazenly announced that what interested him most about Schoenberg's method was its capacity to generate new kinds of tonality. For example, the row for the first movement of the *Lyric Suite*—the work that spellbound Gershwin—splits into white-key notes (from the scale of C major) and black-key notes (from F-sharp major). This arrangement almost guarantees a resurgence of turn-of-the-century harmony in the vein of Strauss and Mahler. Because of the rapid rotation of pitches, no chord can stay in place for long: thus, late-Romantic harmony becomes a flickering mirage.

In a way, twelve-tone composition gave Berg the best of both worlds. It imposed discipline on an unruly spirit, and, at the same time, it allowed for the smuggling in of forbidden pleasures. The game reached its zenith in the Violin Concerto, which Berg wrote in the summer of 1935, as a memorial for Alma Mahler and Walter Gropius's daughter, Manon. The main tone row allows not only the usual tonal allusions but a living fragment of the music of the past—the first notes of Bach's chorale "Es ist genug." The work ends in unambiguous B-flat major, with the violin soaring toward a stratospheric G and the harp strumming sympathetically.

It sounds like nothing so much as the first chords of Debussy's *Prelude to "The Afternoon of a Faun."*

Berg's works of the twenties are double layered in another sense: they allude to the latest twists in the composer's always complex emotional life. The *Lyric Suite* makes coded references to Berg's hopeless affair with a woman named Hanna Fuchs-Robettin, who is represented in the work by the notes B and F (H and F in German notation). Those notes and their related triads can be found all over Berg's later works. A psychoanalyst might say that such romantic skulduggery was the unsuccessful self-sabotage of a fundamentally innocent, isolated nature. Berg was unfaithful to his wife in the same sense that he was unfaithful to Schoenberg: he followed the letter but sinned in spirit. Helene Berg knew of the situation. After her husband's death she wrote to Alma, "Alban invented an excuse to keep his poetic passion within *those* boundaries which he himself desired. *He himself constructed obstacles* and thereby created the romanticism which he required." These words apply equally well to Berg's manipulation of the twelve-note method.

"*Hereinspaziert!* Step right up, lively ladies and distinguished gentlemen, into the menagerie." *Lulu* opens with an allegorical Prologue, in which an animal trainer tries to entice passersby into his circus act. The most captivating creature in the menagerie turns out to be Lulu, whom the trainer is carrying on his back. His bid for the audience's attention is typical 1920s stagecraft: think of Cocteau's Speaker in *Oedipus Rex* ("*Spectateurs!*"), or the alienating announcers in Brecht, or the grimacing hosts of the Berlin cabarets.

As the curtain rises on the first act proper, Lulu is having her portrait done by a painter, who pledges his undying devotion. Her husband, a hapless doctor, walks in on the two of them, shouting, "You dogs!" He falls dead of a heart attack. By the second scene, Lulu is married to the painter, who, upon learning of various irregularities in his wife's sexual history, elects to slash his own throat. By the end of Act I, the man in Lulu's life is Dr. Schön, an editor, who has known her long enough to know that he should have stayed away. In Act II, Scene I, Schön makes an unexpected visit to his home in the middle of the day and finds his new wife in the company of his son Alwa, an emotionally scattered operetta composer. (As in *Der ferne Klang* and *Jonny spielt auf*, there is an autobiographical dimension to the composer character: when Alwa remarks that one could write an interesting opera about Lulu, the orchestra plays the first chords of *Wozzeck*.) Also in the room are an acrobat, a schoolboy, and a lesbian countess, all besotted with the woman of the hour. Schön gives her a revolver and instructs her to commit suicide. When she refuses, he prepares to do the job himself. More or less in self-defense, Lulu kills him.

We jump forward a year (here *Earth Spirit* gives way to *Pandora's Box*). Alwa, the acrobat, and the countess have conspired to effect Lulu's escape from prison, where she was sent for the killing of Schön. When she reappears, she gives herself to Alwa, and as they press their bodies together, she asks the immortal question "Isn't this the couch on which your father bled to death?" Lulu still has her wits about her, but her social trajectory is heading downward. She starts off Act III in high style, consorting with her menagerie in the gaming room of a Paris salon. The illusion of glamour collapses when the acrobat and a disreputable marquis both threaten to denounce her to the police. Amid a stock-market panic, she escapes again, but, being a Wedekind character, she has no choice but to go to London to become an East End prostitute. Berg here introduces an inspired stroke of dramaturgy: the singers who portrayed Lulu's "victims" in the first two acts return as her "customers." The doctor becomes a mute professor. The painter becomes an African prince, who bludgeons Alwa to death. And Dr. Schön becomes Jack the Ripper. When Lulu retires with her final client, there is an awful shriek. Jack emerges, stabs the countess, and leaves. The countess sings that she will be with Lulu into eternity.

As in *Wozzeck*, the various acts and scenes are built around classical forms. The third act also takes in operetta, vaudeville, and jazz; ever the good student, Berg studied a how-to manual called *Das Jazzbuch* to get his orchestration right. There are possible echoes of Weill's *Rise and Fall of the City of Mahagonny*, which Berg saw in Vienna in 1932. At the same time, *Lulu* is, like *Wozzeck*, circular in design, churning through a tight configuration of tone rows, leitmotifs, and harmonic relationships. In a way, it is a gigantic palindrome, the midpoint of which is the interlude that ties together *Earth Spirit* and *Pandora's Box*. Borrowing a trick from Weill's *Royal Palace*, Berg calls for the showing of a short silent film, illustrating Lulu's trial, escapades in prison, and escape. Right in the middle of the interlude, the music literally begins running in reverse.

From then on, the opera is saturated in déjà vu. Motifs, passages, even entire sections are repeated from earlier parts of the opera. Adding to the uncanny atmosphere is the fact that most of the motifs relate to a single twelve-note row. As in the *Lyric Suite*, the master row carries tonal implications, dividing into white-key and black-key areas that correspond to C major and F-sharp major. Indeed, sketchbooks reveal that Berg looked at his rows as funds for keys, noting the triads that could be extracted from each.

Wozzeck plays like a film by Sergei Eisenstein or Orson Welles, its musical images running together in a virtuoso montage. *Lulu*, by contrast, brings to mind a coolly observed social satire by Jean Renoir or Stanley Kubrick, the sort of film in which the camera dissects the complexities of human relations in gliding movements. Opera's camera can pass in and out of souls, and when it looks into the hearts of the people of *Lulu* the effect is almost overwhelming. The most powerful epiphany comes in the music that expresses the impossible love of Dr. Schön and Lulu. Schön is the one man in Lulu's life for whom she has any sort of reciprocal feeling; the floodgates of emotion open when she speaks the words "If I belong to one man in this world, then I belong to you." The grandiose leaps of Dr. Schön's series, strongly implying D-flat major, define the initial shape of the theme. But from the third bar on, Schön's and Lulu's series unfold simultaneously—Lulu's in a rapid stream, Schön's at a more deliberate pace. The result is a supersaturated harmony that feels like a fifty-bar Mahler theme compressed into minimum space.

Whenever the theme of Lulu and Dr. Schön reappears, it dramatizes a new stage in the plunge of the characters' fortunes. It is bellowed out at the end of Act I, as Schön, having witnessed the painter's end, realizes that he is next in line: "Now comes the execution!" By then, the theme's dreaming grandeur is gone; Schön's characteristic upward leap is undermined by the sudden immobility of the harmony beneath him. The theme is heard again after Schön's death, when Lulu repeats that he was the only man she ever loved. Beneath the sentimental phrase is a disquieting subtext: Lulu has not only killed Schön but subsumed him. Berg provides a musical metaphor for this process of depersonalization: in Schön's last moments the lovers' two rows are again heard in tandem, now arranged so that we can clearly hear how the notes of the one come from repeating cycles of the other. As Schön gasps, "Oh God, oh God," Lulu's row plays one more time, alone. The man no longer has a self.

Schön's chilly demise is nothing next to the soul-freezing mood that descends when Jack the Ripper enters. The most disturbing thing about the scene is that, in keeping with the repetitive structure of the opera, the Schön-Lulu theme plays in the orchestra as Lulu and Jack bicker over the evening's price. What does it mean, to have such unabashedly romantic music unfurling as the soundtrack to an act of prostitution that leads to murder? Perhaps Berg is suggesting, in a faintly positive vein, that sympathy and ardor live on even amid total degradation. Or perhaps he is perpetuating the *Lustmord* chic of the Weimar era, the obsessive focus on sexual killings and other revolting acts. That magnificent theme out of Mahler and Strauss is unmasked as the love song of Jack the Ripper. To quote Otto Weininger, whom Berg read so intensely, love is murder.

When Lulu is killed, the orchestra plays a monstrous chord of twelve tones. It is built up out of fourths and fifths, not unlike the chords that underpin the Doctor's aria in *Wozzeck* ("Oh my theory! Oh my fame!"). There, twelve-note harmony symbolized social cruelty; here, Jack the Ripper may represent, per Kraus's lecture of 1905, the collected malevolence of the male species. The death chord is a prolonged assault on the senses, overkill in every way. In contrast, though, to Wedekind, who could be accused of reveling in the role of Jack the Ripper, Berg's music has the effect of putting us in Lulu's place: the chord falls with terrible swiftness, stabbing at our ears. This is in keeping with the composer's nature. Many witnesses noted his exceptional ability to register the pain of other people. "I always had the impression," Schoenberg said after Berg's death, "that he had experienced beforehand what people close to him were going through, as though he had already suffered with them when they were suffering, so that when they came to tell him of it it did not catch him unawares but rather on the contrary reopened old wounds. Wounds that he had already inflicted on himself by his powerful sympathy."

Countess Geschwitz has the last word: "Lulu! My angel! Show yourself one more time! I am near you! I am always near! Into eternity!" In delivering this eulogy, she picks up a lyrical fragment from the debris of the dissonant detonation. As the curtain comes down, the implacable twelve-tone machinery takes over: three trombones play three fateful chords, taken respectively from Dr. Schön's, Alwa's, and the countess's rows. The last chord is an ambiguous entity, a chord of nowhere. It is the same chord that sounds in *Wozzeck* as Marie's life ebbs away. Berg called it his chord of waiting, of expectation. Every time it is played, it rotates in the air, searching for the music that will complete it.

In the climactic scene of *Doctor Faustus*, Adrian Leverkühn stands in front of a group of friends, who are expecting him to demonstrate his final work, *The Lamentation of Doctor Faustus*. Speaking in medieval dialect, he proceeds to confess his pact with the devil. Only a few people remain in the room when he finally begins to play. Serenus Zeitblom, the composer's long-suffering Boswell, reports: "We saw tears trickle down his cheeks and fall on the keys, which, though wet, were now struck in a strongly dissonant chord. At the same time he opened his mouth as if to sing, but from between his lips there emerged only a wail that still rings in my ears." It is like *Lulu*'s death shriek, now issuing from the artist's throat.

Thomas Mann often thought of Berg while he worked on his musical novel. He attended the 1937 premiere of *Lulu* in Zurich—where the first two acts were performed together with the orchestral music of the final scene—and he probably had the opera's ending in mind when he wrote of Leverkühn's descent into madness. Also, Mann apparently based his account of the final bars of *The Lamentation of Doctor Faustus* on Adorno's description of the *Lyric Suite*. "One instrument after another falls silent," Adorno had written. "The viola alone remains, but it is not even allowed to expire, to die. It must play for ever; except that we can no longer hear it." Mann converted those sentences into one of the most affecting passages in twentieth-century literature, in which the icy-minded composer seems finally to grasp a sliver of hope: "One instrumental group after the other steps back, and what remains as the work fades away is the high G of a cello, the final word, the final sound, floating off, slowly vanishing in a *pianissimo fermata*. Then nothing more. Silence and night. But the tone, which is no more, for which, as it hangs there vibrating in the silence, only the soul still listens, and which was the dying note of sorrow—is no longer that, its meaning changes, it stands as a light in the night."

Part II

1933–1945

Along the legendary embankment
The real—not the calendar—
Twentieth Century draws near.

—ANNA AKHMATOVA, *POEM WITHOUT A HERO*

7

THE ART OF FEAR

Music in Stalin's Russia

On January 26, 1936, Joseph Stalin, the general secretary of the All-Union Communist Party (Bolshevik), went to the Bolshoi Theatre in Moscow for a performance of Dmitri Shostakovich's opera *Lady Macbeth of the Mtsensk District.* The Soviet dictator often attended opera and ballet at the Bolshoi, where he made a show of being inconspicuous; he preferred to take a seat in the back row of Box A, just before the curtain rose, and positioned himself behind a small curtain, which concealed him from the audience without obstructing his view of the stage. Phalanxes of security and a general heightening of tension would signal to experienced observers that Stalin was in the hall. On this night, Shostakovich, the twenty-nine-year-old star of Soviet composition, had been officially instructed to attend. He sat facing Box A. Visible in front were Vyacheslav Molotov, Anastas Mikoyan, and Andrei Zhdanov, all of them members or candidate members of the Politburo. According to one account, they were laughing, talking among themselves, and otherwise enjoying their proximity to the man behind the curtain.

Stalin had lately taken an interest in Soviet opera. On January 17 he had seen Ivan Dzerzhinsky's *The Quiet Don*, and liked it enough to summon the composer to his box for an interview, commenting that Soviet opera should "make use of all the latest devices of musical techniques, but its idiom should be close to the masses, clear and accessible." *Lady Macbeth*, the tale of a vaguely Lulu-like Russian housewife who leaves a string of bodies in her wake, did not meet these somewhat ambiguous specifications. Stalin left the hall either before or during the final act, taking with him Comrades Molotov, Mikoyan, and Zhdanov. Shostakovich confided to his friend Ivan Sollertinsky that he, too, had been hoping to receive an invitation to Box A. Despite vigorous applause from the audience, the composer left feeling "sick at heart," and he remained so as he boarded a train for the northern city of Arkhangel'sk, where he was scheduled to perform.

Two days later, one of the great nightmares of twentieth-century cultural history began riding down on the nervous young composer. *Pravda*, the official Communist Party newspaper, printed an editorial with the headline "Muddle Instead of Music," in which *Lady Macbeth* was condemned as an artistically obscure and morally obscene work. "From the first moment of the opera," the anonymous author wrote, "the listener is flabbergasted by the deliberately dissonant, muddled stream of sounds." Shostakovich was said to be playing a game that "may end very badly." The last phrase was chilling. Stalin's Terror was imminent, and Soviet citizens were about to discover, if they did not know already, what a bad end might mean. Some would be pilloried and executed as enemies of the people, some would be arrested and killed in secret, some would be sent to the gulags, some would simply disappear. Shostakovich never shook off the pall of fear that those six hundred words in *Pravda* cast on him.

A few weeks before "Muddle Instead of Music" was published, a familiar face appeared again in Moscow. Sergei Prokofiev, who had been living outside Russia since 1918, arrived with his wife, Lina, to celebrate New Year's Eve. According to Harlow Robinson's biography, Prokofiev attended a party at the Moscow Art Theatre and remained there until five in the morning. Since 1927, the former enfant terrible of Russian music had returned many times to his native land; now he decided to live in Moscow full-time. He was well aware that Soviet artists were subject to censorship, but he chose to think that such restrictions would not apply to him. He was, at this time, forty-four years old, at the height of his powers and in good health. He, too, would endure a long string of humiliations, and was not granted the satisfaction of outliving

Stalin. In a twist that would seem too heavy-handed in a novel, Prokofiev died on March 5, 1953, about fifty minutes before Stalin breathed his last.

The period from the mid-thirties onward marked the onset of the most warped and tragic phase in twentieth-century music: the total politicizing of the art by totalitarian means. On the eve of the Second World War, dictators had manipulated popular resentment and media spectacle to take control of half of Europe. Hitler in Germany and Austria, Mussolini in Italy, Horthy in Hungary, and Franco in Spain. In the Soviet Union, Stalin refined Lenin's revolutionary dictatorship into an omnipotent machine, relying on a cult of personality, rigid control of the media, and an army of secret police. In America, Franklin D. Roosevelt was granted extraordinary executive powers to counter the ravages of the Depression, leading conservatives to fear an erosion of constitutional process, particularly when federal arts programs were harnessed to political purposes. In Germany, Hitler forged the most unholy alliance of art and politics that the world had ever seen.

For anyone who cherishes the notion that there is some inherent spiritual goodness in artists of great talent, the era of Stalin and Hitler is disillusioning. Not only did composers fail to rise up en masse against totalitarianism, but many actively welcomed it. In the capitalist free-for-all of the twenties, they had contended with technologically enhanced mass culture, which introduced a new aristocracy of movie stars, pop musicians, and celebrities without portfolio. Having long depended on the largesse of the Church, the upper classes, and the high bourgeoisie, composers suddenly found themselves, in the Jazz Age, without obvious means of support. Some fell to dreaming of a political knight in shining armor who would come to their aid.

The dictators played that role to perfection. Stalin and Hitler aped the art-loving monarchs of yore, pledging the patronage of the centralized state. But these men were a different species. Coming from the social margins, they believed themselves to be perfect embodiments of popular will and popular taste. At the same time, they saw themselves as artist-intellectuals, members of history's vanguard. Adept at playing on the weaknesses of the creative mind, they offered the seduction of power with one hand and the fear of destruction with the other. One by one, artists fell in line.

Untangling composers' relationships with totalitarianism is a tricky exercise. For a long time discussion of Shostakovich revolved around the issue of whether he was an "official" composer who produced propaganda on command or a secret dissident who encoded anti-Stalinist messages in his scores. Likewise, people have pondered whether Prokofiev knowingly aligned himself with Stalinist aesthetics in order to advance his career or returned to the Soviet Union in a state of unknowing naïveté. Similar questions have been posed about Richard Strauss's murky, unheroic behavior in the Nazi period, but they are the wrong ones to ask.

Black-and-white categories make no sense in the shadowland of dictatorship. These composers were neither saints nor devils; they were flawed actors on a tilted stage. In some extra verses for "Die Moritat vom Mackie Messer," Bertolt Brecht wrote, "There are those who dwell in darkness, there are those who dwell in light." Most dwell in neither place, and Shostakovich speaks for all.

Revolution

Lenin, the prototype of the twentieth-century dictator, had favorite authors and composers, but he was too rigorous a materialist to bother much with art. He had little patience for the avant-garde, and once had a fit when futurists painted May Day colors on the trees in the Aleksandrovsky gardens. Music he regarded as a bourgeois placebo that covered up the sufferings of mankind. In a conversation with Maxim Gorky, he extolled the power of Beethoven, but added, "I can't listen to music too often. It affects your nerves, makes you want to say stupid nice things, and stroke the heads of people who could create such beauty while living in this vile hell." Nevertheless, he tolerated the activities of various avant-garde factions, which lent a veneer of sophistication to the thuggery of Bolshevism in its early days.

Lenin's chief artistic functionary was Anatol Lunacharsky, who from 1917 to 1929 headed the Commissariat of Enlightenment. Lunacharsky was not unlike Leo Kestenberg in Berlin—a peculiarly smart and broad-minded bureaucrat with a poor understanding of political reality. A philosopher by training, an observant critic of Dostoevsky and other authors, something of a mystic, Lunacharsky believed that a revolution in society should go hand in hand with a revolution in art. Communism, in his view, was a new kind of secular rite, for which art should supply the chant, icons, and incense. The poet Vladimir Mayakovsky, among the first to join Lunacharsky's crusade, joined him in believing that Communism could wipe out the "old aesthetic junk." Mayakovsky's poetry railed against bourgeois art in all its manifestations: "Spit on rhymes and arias and the rose bush and other such mawkishness from the arsenal of the arts . . . Give us new forms!" The epoch-making actor and director Vsevolod Meyerhold, who had dismantled the artifice of naturalistic theater shortly after the turn of the century, hoped that the revolution would breathe life into his dream of a "people's theater." As in Weimar, artists embraced Communism because it promised to cut the throat of a common enemy, the decadent bourgeoisie.

To lead Muzo, the music section of the Commissariat of Enlightenment, Lunacharsky appointed Arthur Lourié, a bohemian composer who was writing dissonant, spiritually charged music in the manner of Alexander Scriabin. Under the aegis of these two unlikely bureaucrats, a period of "anything goes" ensued. Russian composers of the twenties produced some of the wildest sounds of the time, in many cases out-cacophonizing their Western European counterparts. Alexander Mosolov's orchestral sketch *The Iron Foundry* used grinding beats and layered rhythms to mimic the action of a factory. Nikolai Roslavetz composed according to a "new system of tone organization," building dense chromatic textures from "synthetic chords." Lev Theremin pioneered the eerily wailing electronic instrument that later bore his name. Georgi Rimsky-Korsakov, grandson of the great Rimsky, formed the Society for Quarter-Tone Music. The pièce de résistance of the era was Arseny Avraamov's *Symphony for Factory Whistles*, which achieved a memorable performance in the port of Baku in 1922: "The Internationale" and "La Marseillaise" were sounded by an orchestra of factory sirens, artillery, machine guns, bus and car horns, shunting engines, and the foghorns of the Caspian Fleet.

Lunacharsky's notion of Communism as an artistically enhanced mass religion violated Leninist thought, and the Bolshevik arts utopia inevitably ran into difficulties. Experimentalism proved to have no propaganda value, except when it came to advertising Soviet culture to the West. Various factions of self-styled proletarian artists attacked the modernist tendency and demanded simple, popular entertainment in its place. Lunacharsky pleaded for multiple perspectives and freedom of expression—"Let the worker hear and evaluate everything, the old and the new"—but he steadily lost ground as the twenties went on. The Commissariat of Enlightenment crumbled into a morass of competing bureaucracies, and the Party eventually shunted the arts apparatus into the ideology and propaganda section.

When Stalin assumed sole power in 1929, artists found themselves in a more conspicuous and also more dangerous position. Recent biographies, such as Simon Sebag Montefiore's, have emphasized Stalin's intelligence and charm alongside his well-known cunning and brutality. He was a well-read man with a taste not only for canonical literature but also for the modern satires of Mikhail Bulgakov and Mikhail Zoshchenko. Although Stalin detested the radical styles that had prospered during the Lunacharsky period, he promoted the idea of a "Soviet modernism," a school of art that would embody the power and prowess of the new proletarian state. His musical tastes were narrow but not vulgar. He patronized the Bolshoi, listened to classical music on the radio, and sang folk songs in a fine tenor voice. He monitored every recording made in the Soviet Union, writing judgments on the sleeves ("good," "so-so," "bad," or "rubbish"), and accumulated ninety-three opera recordings.

Stalin liked to use the telephone, and had an unnerving habit of calling artists in the middle of the night. Sometimes, like a Roman emperor in an indulgent mood, he would grant his petitioners an extraordinary favor. Others would be told to expect a call that never came, and they would interpret the silence as an omen of disaster. Soon might come the dreaded knock at the door—"sharp, unbearably explicit," wrote Nadezhda Mandelstam, in her great memoir *Hope Against Hope*—which heralded the arrival of the NKVD. Stalin's manipulations created a new species of fear. "The fear that goes with the writing of verse has nothing in common with the fear one experiences in the presence of the secret police," Mandelstam wrote. "Our mysterious awe in the face of existence itself is always overridden by the more primitive fear of violence and destruction." As her husband, Osip, used to say, in the Soviet era the second kind of fear was all that was left.

Young Shostakovich

Dmitri Shostakovich made a nerve-racking first impression. His face was ashen in hue, his eyes darting furtively behind thick glasses. His body constantly twitched, as if something were struggling to escape from it. When he talked, his speech doubled back on itself, phrases repeating themselves like anxious mantras. In intimate gatherings, with the aid of a favorite vodka, Shostakovich showed another side of his personality—antic, caustic, passionate. He was capable of puppy-dog-like tenderness and also of forbidding anger.

Laurel Fay, in her authoritative Shostakovich biography, quotes a verbal portrait that Zoshchenko made of the composer in the early 1940s: "It seemed to you that he is 'frail, fragile, withdrawn, an infinitely direct, pure child.' That is so. But if it were only so, then great art (as with him) would never be obtained. He is exactly what you say he is, plus something else—he is hard, acid, extremely intelligent, strong perhaps, despotic, and not altogether good-natured (although cerebrally good-natured) . . . In him, there are great contradictions. In him, one quality obliterates the other. It is conflict in the highest degree. It is almost a catastrophe."

Shostakovich was born on September 25, 1906. From an early age he showed an astounding aptitude for music, grasping basic theory and notation almost without formal instruction. In 1919, at the age of thirteen, he enrolled in what was then called the Petrograd Conservatory, where his abilities mesmerized Alexander Glazunov, the alcoholically dilapidated but still formidable head of the institution. Glazunov made sure that the young man stayed well fed during the lean years of Lenin's New Economic Policy. In exchange, Shostakovich's father supplied Glazunov with beverages illegally obtained from the Bureau of Weights and Measures.

There was a history of radical-left commitment in Shostakovich's family, and his parents welcomed the Russian Revolution in its initial stages. But they were not Bolsheviks, and took fright when Lenin's forces swept aside the more liberal government of Alexander Kerensky. Shostakovich, then eleven, imitated his parents' politics. In the early weeks of the revolution he wrote a Funeral March in honor of fallen anti-tsarist fighters, but the following year he either renamed that piece or wrote a new one in memory of two early victims of Bolshevik terror. Even in prepubescence, it seems, he was ambiguous.

As a teenager, Shostakovich developed a taste for the iconoclastic poems of Mayakovsky, but not necessarily for the politics behind them. Only toward the end of his studies at the conservatory did Shostakovich finally come face-to-face with the absurdities of Soviet ideology: when a fellow student was asked to explain the socioeconomic dimensions of the music of Chopin and Liszt, Shostakovich burst out laughing. Later, once he had become a prominent figure in the music-education system, Shostakovich would go out of his way to help students who flailed about when confronted with the political portions of the syllabus. At one oral exam, Shostakovich found himself sitting beneath a large poster that said, " 'Art belongs to the People.'—V. I. Lenin." With a helpful upward tilt of the head, he posed the question "To whom does art belong?"

Shostakovich was never politically naive. While still a student in Petrograd, or Leningrad, as it was renamed in 1924, the composer gained an influential ally in Mikhail Tukhachevsky, a Red Army hero who was infamous in Tambov Province for having employed poison gas against anti-Bolshevik peasants. According to Shostakovich's friend and chronicler Isaak Glikman, Tukhachevsky was "a man of great education and intelligence" who assiduously attended concerts, played violin, and made instruments by hand. He offered to find the young composer a room and a job in Moscow. Fortunately, perhaps, in view of Tukhachevsky's eventual fate in the Terror, Shostakovich elected to remain in his home city.

Shostakovich's youthful assurance blazed forth in his First Symphony, which the Leningrad Philharmonic introduced to frenetic applause on May 12, 1926. It is a work of unusually gripping narrative drive, careening from one vertiginous climax to the next. The musical language is mobile and flexible, making intermittent use of a system that the Russian theorist Boleslav Yavorsky had set forth in his 1908 book, *The Construction of Musical Speech*, whereby various modes, ranging from the familiar diatonic scale to Rimsky's octatonic scale, and so forth, are played off each other. The symphony quickly found an international audience, and none other than Alban Berg wrote the composer a congratulatory letter.

By way of reward, Shostakovich received a well-paying commission from the Department of Agitation and Propaganda of the State Publishers' Music Section for a grand choral-orchestral work to honor the tenth anniversary of the October Revolution. The piece was initially titled *To October*, and later became the Second Symphony. The opening section evokes prerevolutionary days with a snapshot of economic chaos: the strings are divided into seven parts, each moving in an independent rhythm. A little later nine caterwauling winds go every which way, perhaps representing the Silver Age intellectuals. Then a factory whistle (F-sharp) signals the arrival of Bolsheviks, and high-modern complexity gives way to elemental hymns. Although the text is banal, Shostakovich whips up a militant frenzy that anticipates the most potent of Hanns Eisler's "battle songs." The Third Symphony, subtitled "The First of May," follows the same template, redeeming abstraction with bombast.

Despite the slow decline of Lunacharsky's system, the Soviet musical scene remained varied and vibrant throughout the twenties. Without leaving Russia, Shostakovich was able to soak up various foreign influences, because the West came to him. Hindemith, Krenek, Berg, and Milhaud all paid visits to the new Soviet paradise; *Der ferne Klang*, *Wozzeck*, and *Jonny spielt auf* were staged; and Sam Wooding's Negro revue *Chocolate Kiddies* toured Russia in 1926, giving Soviet avant-gardists a taste of jazz. On a brief visit to Berlin the following year, Shostakovich experienced the magic of Weimar culture firsthand. He was soon echoing the antisentimental, "objectivist" tone of Hindemith, Weill, Bartók, and middle-period Stravinsky. Shrill winds, curt brass, and jangling xylophones cut through the traditional luxuriousness of Russian strings.

Shostakovich also absorbed the unconventional narrative strategies of Soviet artists and theorists of the period, delighting in effects of discontinuity, montage, parody, self-conscious artificiality, and the "estrangement" of familiar styles and forms. Meyerhold, the titan of radical theater, recognized the young composer as a kindred spirit and asked him to write music for several of his productions—notably for his 1929 staging of Mayakovsky's play *The Bedbug*.

In the same year, Shostakovich began what would turn out to be a lifelong collaboration with Grigori Kozintsev, who, together with Leonid Trauberg, had launched an avant-garde theater and film collective called Factory of the Eccentric Actor, or FEKS. In typical twenties fashion, FEKS aped the madcap pacing of the circus, the variety theater, and American movies, and Shostakovich followed suit. His score for Kozintsev and Trauberg's silent film *New Babylon*, a politicized love story set in the period of the Paris Commune, avoided direct illustration of on-screen action and jarred the viewer with bizarre juxtapositions. For example, when the Communards are killed by firing squad at the end, Shostakovich responds with a distorted version of the high-kicking can-can from Offenbach's *Orpheus in the Underworld*. Such paradoxes fulfilled an idea that Sergei Eisenstein and colleagues had advanced in the summer of 1928: "The first experiments in sound [in film] must aim at a sharp discord with the visual images."

Shostakovich's radical period culminated in the opera *The Nose*, based on Nikolai Gogol's story of an appendage that walks away from its owner and assumes an exalted social rank. Percussion interludes, trombone glissandos, and grotesque dance rhythms are deployed in what purports to be a mockery of bourgeois values, although the composer's dependence on the stock devices of the Western avant-garde undercuts the message. If Shostakovich had moved to Berlin at this time, he might have had trouble standing out from the general throng of spiky young composers.

It was after the premiere of *The Nose*—in concert form, in June 1929—that Shostakovich found himself first accused of "formalism." The word was Soviet shorthand for any style that smacked too strongly of Western modernism. The strike came from the Russian Association of Proletarian Musicians (RAPM), which had made it its mission to extirpate all remnants of bourgeois musical culture. *The Nose* vanished from Soviet stages, not to be seen again on Russian soil until 1974. Shostakovich buried himself in film and theater work, dutifully using his music to portray the eternal battle between good Soviets and their "class enemies." The ballets *The Golden Age* and *The Bolt* expose, respectively, the decadence of Western competitors at a football match and the nefarious activities of "slackers," "tipplers," and "saboteurs." The films *The Golden Mountains* and *The Counterplan* unmask capitalist bosses and wreckers of industry. Kozintsev and Trauberg's film *Alone* follows a Leningrad schoolteacher into farthest Siberia, where landowning peasants are obstructing the Soviet experiment. Stalin approved these films for wide release in late 1931, and Shostakovich's name probably first came to his attention at the screenings. The dictator is known to have loved "The Song of the Counterplan," which went on to become one of the iconic melodies of the Soviet age.

In November 1931, Shostakovich made what seemed a brave move.

Fed up with the agitations of the proletarians, he issued a manifesto, "Declaration of a Composer's Duties," stating that demands for songfulness in Soviet music and theater were having a ruinous effect on composers. In fact, as Shostakovich may well have been aware, the Party was about to disavow the proletarian line; the following April, RAPM was dissolved, and the new Union of Soviet Composers took its place. You can sense a certain cackling quality in the music that Shostakovich wrote for Nikolai Akimov's irreverent 1932 production of *Hamlet*, which opened in Moscow a month after the demise of RAPM. In Act III, Scene 2, Hamlet accuses Rosencrantz and Guildenstern of trying to play him like a pipe, and in the Akimov production the prince dramatized his contempt by lowering a flute to his buttocks. At that moment, Shostakovich had a piccolo in the orchestra pipe out Alexander Davidenko's mass song "They Wanted to Beat Us, to Beat Us," a favorite of the proletarian faction.

After years of collectivization, industrialization, and famine, the Soviet populace was feeling rebellious, and in the early thirties Stalin tried to placate his subjects by promising new comforts and freedoms. Artists were deputized to broadcast the message that "life is getting better," as Stalin eloquently put it. To this end, artists' lives were made better, at least in the material sense. The Union of Soviet Composers supplied composers with health plans, sanatoriums, and a cooperative building in Moscow. At an October 1932 gathering at Maxim Gorky's Moscow mansion, Stalin mused aloud that writers should be "engineers of human souls," and the writers debated among themselves what he meant. From the meeting emerged the concept of socialist realism, according to which Soviet artists would depict the people's lives both realistically and heroically, as if from the standpoint of the socialist utopia to come. Established nineteenth-century forms such as the novel, the epic drama, the opera, and the symphony were deemed suitable vehicles of expression, although they required thorough renovation in line with Soviet thought. The Party theorist Nikolai Bukharin, at the Writers' Congress of 1934, offered a more elaborate definition of socialist realism, calling for stories of "tragedies and conflicts, vacillations, defeats, the struggle of conflicting tendencies."

Shostakovich's first contribution to the new phase in Soviet art was *Lady Macbeth of the Mtsensk District*. The libretto, based loosely on a story by Nikolai Leskov, tells of Katerina Ismailova, a strong-willed woman in a provincial town in 1860s Russia. Variously bored and oppressed by the men in her life, she finds it convenient to dispose of them. She first kills her father-in-law, Boris, whom Shostakovich identified as a "typical master kulak," or wealthy landowning peasant, in order to save herself from his repulsive advances. She then connives with her lover, Sergei—a "future kulak"—to kill her jealous, abusive husband, Zinovi. The last act takes place in a Siberian prison camp, to which the lovers have been consigned. When Sergei's eyes wander to another woman, Katerina drowns herself in a river, taking her rival with her.

What made this scenario politically timely was that in 1929 Stalin had launched a genocidal campaign of "liquidating the kulaks as a class," whether by execution, imprisonment, or deportation. Shostakovich himself gestured toward the subtext: "In *Lady Macbeth* I wanted to unmask reality and to arouse a feeling of hatred for the tyrannical and humiliating atmosphere in a Russian merchant's household." These "petty," "vulgar," "cruel," "greedy" merchants are Soviet counterparts to the hook-nosed banker Jews who appeared in Nazi cartoons of the same period. Robert Conquest estimates that three million people died as a result of the "dekulakization" program.

Seen from one angle, then, *Lady Macbeth* is nearly an opera in the service of genocide. In other ways, however, it is anything but a propaganda work. The composer called it a "Tragedy-Satire," and that ambiguity sets the tone; nothing can be taken entirely at face value. Extending Eisenstein's notion of discord between sound and image, Shostakovich uses cartoonish musical stereotypes to undermine rather than illustrate the action onstage. The attempted rape of Katerina's cook, Aksinya, for example, plays out against a manic galop worthy of Walt Disney's Silly Symphonies. Boris's lust for Katerina is represented by a drunken Viennese waltz. As the opera goes on, hard-hearted grotesquerie gives way to spells of confession and lamentation. When Boris is killed in Act II, the musical reaction is at first icily unsympathetic, but after a priest offers to say a requiem for the merchant, the orchestra takes the stage with a grandiose dirge in the form of a passacaglia, rather plainly modeled on the D-minor threnody in Berg's *Wozzeck*. The dramatic function of this music is obscure. Is it, unexpectedly, a statement of sympathy for the awful Boris? Does it express internal turmoil on the part of Katerina? The general grinding operation of fate? Whatever it means, it fails to advance the stated program of stirring hatred for the kulaks.

The opera makes more sense as a fable of the madness of love, of the disorienting power of sexuality. It was written under the spell of the physicist Nina Varzar, whom Shostakovich married in 1932; the soprano Galina Vishnevskaya thought that Katerina was an exaggerated depiction of Nina's passionate nature. But the madness may really have been Shostakovich's own; two years later, he would fall in love with the young translator Elena Konstantinovskaya, precipitating a crisis in his marriage, and his romantic life would display tragicomic aspects ever after. The writer Galina Serebryakova recalled: "[Shostakovich] was thirsting to re-create the theme of love in a new way, a love that knew no boundaries, that was willing to perpetrate crimes inspired by the devil himself, as in Goethe's *Faust*." Katerina is too consumed by her desires to register the absolute corruption around her; instead, like Salome, she exposes the insanity of her world by embodying it to excess. In this sense, the opera becomes an altogether darker kind of monument to Stalin's world.

Terror

Shostakovich was not the first Soviet composer to be censured by the state. In 1935, Gavriil Popov, a greatly gifted artist who had studied alongside Shostakovich at the Leningrad Conservatory, unveiled his First Symphony, an immensely forceful hour-long work to which Shostakovich's subsequent symphonies owe a more than minor debt. After the premiere, a censorship board denounced Popov's symphony as a work of "class-enemy character" and banned further performances. With Shostakovich's support, Popov succeeded in having the ruling overturned. But the renewed assault on musical and artistic formalism in 1936 meant that the piece was taken out of circulation again. Popov began a long descent into alcoholism and mediocrity. The difference between his fate and Shostakovich's says much about the latter's power of endurance, his ability to preserve his musical self under potentially annihilating pressure.

Shostakovich's own crisis did not stem solely from Stalin's dislike of *Lady Macbeth*. Certainly, the general secretary had no fun that night at the Bolshoi; at a Kremlin conference on the role of music in film, which was held one day after the publication of "Muddle Instead of Music" in *Pravda*, the dictator bemoaned Shostakovich's cacophonies, his "rebuses and riddles." But the Central Committee had probably already selected

Lady Macbeth—it had been playing for two years before Stalin went to see it—as a jumping-off point for a campaign against waywardness in the arts.

The American Communist sympathizer Joshua Kunitz, who covered Soviet affairs for *New Masses* magazine, later asked a *Pravda* editor why the composer had been targeted. "We had to begin with somebody," the editor told Kunitz. "Shostakovich was the most famous, and a blow against him would create immediate repercussions and would make his imitators in music and elsewhere sit up and take notice. Furthermore, Shostakovich is a real artist, there is the touch of genius in him. A man like that is worth fighting for, is worth saving . . . We had faith in his essential wholesomeness. We knew that he could stand the shock . . . Shostakovich knows and everyone else knows that there is no malice in our attack. He knows that there is no desire to destroy him."

When the *Pravda* editorial appeared, Shostakovich had a curious reaction. He rang up his friend Glikman and instructed him to subscribe to a newspaper clipping service, so that he could monitor all mentions of his name. Within three weeks he had accumulated seventy-eight pages of invective, which he studied in silence. Glikman accused him of masochism, but the composer insisted that the exercise had a constructive purpose. "It has to be there, it has to be there," he said. (Schoenberg, by the way, also kept a scrapbook of critical abuse, recording the malice of the age for posterity.) Among the items in the collection was a second broadside from *Pravda*, this one accusing his collective-farming ballet, *The Limpid Stream*, of being *too* simple.

The "Shostakovich 'Affair,'" as Kunitz called it, served mainly as the test run for a new mode of cultural control. Creative artists who displayed too much independence would be subject to vilification and reorientation, with the threat of censorship, imprisonment, or death offered as an incentive. Furthermore, when one artist was criticized, the authorities could observe how the others behaved. Around the time of "Muddle Instead of Music," there was much public discussion of Stalin's new constitution, which promised a host of personal liberties. Artists were told that they could speak freely on the subject of "formalism" and other matters. Informers for the NKVD monitored the results, and some of their reports have been published in Russia. The following excerpts show that the editorial aroused vigorous opposition, even though Shostakovich himself was not widely liked:

ISAAC BABEL: There's no need to make a lot of noise over know-nothings. Why, no one has taken this seriously. The People keeps silent, and, in its soul, quietly chuckles . . .

L. SLAVIN: I don't love S., and don't know a thing about music, but I'm afraid that the blow to S. is a blow to anyone trying to work outside the template . . .

P. ANTOKOLSKY (poet): . . . Kaverin told me that S.'s mother called Zoshchenko (I think they live near each other) and asked, despairingly, "What, now, will become of my son?" This sounds like a Jewish joke, but it isn't funny.

VICTOR SHKLOVSKY (man of letters): . . . What does it mean to say that we don't need "petty-bourgeois innovations"? It's very thoughtlessly written.

A. LEZHNEV (writer): The horrible thing about any dictatorship is that the dictator does whatever his left leg tells him to do. We are like Don Quixote, always dreaming, until reality tells us otherwise. I view the incident with S. as the advent of the same "order" that burns books in Germany . . .

A. GATOV (poet and translator): . . . I view this attack on S. as a pogrom . . .

ANDREI PLATONOV (writer): . . . It's clear that someone from the ranks of the strong wandered into the theater, listened for a bit, understood nothing of music, and strongly criticized . . .

K. DOBRONITZKY (Party member, man of letters): . . . I'm not a devotee of S.'s, but he's searching for something new . . .

VS. MEYERHOLD: . . . S. *should* have been rewarded, so that he could get down to work, instead of writing whatever it falls to him to write . . . S. is now in very bad shape. He was called by my theater, to write new music for *The Bedbug*, but he said he was incapable of doing anything . . .

The composer SHAPORIN: . . . The opinion of "one" person—this isn't the thing to determine the course of art. S. will be driven to suicide . . .

The composer MIASKOVSKY: I'm afraid that music will now be overwhelmed by wretchedness and primitivism.

The composer KOCHYOTOV V.N.: The last straw—this article kills S.

Most of the remarks are nonpolitical, simply protesting the imposition of official taste on the artistic sphere. But those of the literary critic Abram Lezhnev take the form of a direct swipe at Stalin. A footnote in the NKVD reports tells us that someone circled Lezhnev's name and put two check marks next it. On account of various ideological errors, he was shot in 1938.

Several leaders of Soviet art spoke out on Shostakovich's behalf. Meyerhold, who, according to one account, had been sitting next to Shostakovich on the night which Stalin attended *Lady Macbeth*, defended Shostakovich at a lecture in March. Gorky wrote—or perhaps only drafted—a letter to Stalin that said: "All that the *Pravda* article provided was the opportunity for a pack of mediocrities and hacks to persecute Shostakovich in every possible way." Stalin, in his much-quoted "Talk with the Metal Producers," had advised the Party to treat each individual carefully, "as a gardener cultivates a favorite fruit tree." Gorky threw those words back in Stalin's face: "What was expressed in *Pravda* cannot be described as a 'careful regard.' "

On February 7, Platon Kerzhentsev, the chairman of the Committee for Artistic Affairs, met with Shostakovich and assured him that he would survive the crisis if he followed certain suggestions. Kerzhentsev reported back to Stalin: "To my question, 'does he fully accept the criticisms of his works,' [Shostakovich] said that he accepted most, but not all, of them." Shostakovich, for his part, asked to speak to Stalin in person. He thus had to perform the familiar ritual of waiting by the phone. On February 29 he wrote to Ivan Sollertinsky: "I am living very quietly here in Moscow, sitting at home and not going anywhere. I am waiting for a phone call. I don't have much expectation of being received, but have not entirely given up hope."

The phone did not ring. Performances dwindled. Shostakovich's income dried up, just as Nina Shostakovich was bearing their first child. Shostakovich went to see Tukhachevsky, the violin-making Red Army hero, who sat down to write a letter to Stalin on his behalf, sweating profusely as he worked.

The climate in Stalin's domain was turning chillier by the day; the commencement of the show trials in August signaled that the campaign against formalism in the arts was widening into purges and Terror. Many close to Shostakovich or favorable to his cause were disappearing. Elena Konstantinovskaya, the translator who had caused a separation in his marriage in 1934, was arrested and briefly imprisoned in 1935. Galina Serebryakova, who had observed Shostakovich at work on *Lady Macbeth*, was sent into the gulags the following year, not to return for almost two decades. Shostakovich's brother-in-law, mother-in-law, sister, and uncle were all imprisoned at around this time. Maxim Gorky died mysteriously in June 1936. Bukharin's name was mentioned many times during the August show trial—a sign that his days were numbered. Isaac Babel, who had advised that "Muddle Instead of Music" shouldn't be taken seriously, found in 1937 that his books could no longer be published. He had three years to live, as did Meyerhold.

Most ominous of all was the fate of Tukhachevsky. Despite the sterling work that he had done in liquidating the anti-Bolshevik opposition, Stalin saw him as a dangerous rival—too independent, too charismatic. He was arrested in May 1937, and in the torture chamber he confessed his part in a nonexistent conspiracy to overthrow Stalin, evidence of which Hitler's SS helped to fabricate. When the text of the confession was retrieved decades later, there were bloodstains on several pages.

Of the artists and intellectuals who were pilloried as "enemies of the people" in the late thirties—Bukharin, Meyerhold, Mandelstam, Babel—Shostakovich was one of the few who lived to tell the tale. As other members of Tukhachevsky's circle were rounded up, including the composer Nikolai Zhilyayev, it might have looked to Shostakovich as if people around him were being plucked away in systematic fashion. This was the psychological elegance of the Terror; although it was impersonal, even random, in its logic, it always seemed to be closing in unswervingly on any given individual.

At the time that *Pravda* delivered its judgment, Shostakovich was writing his Fourth Symphony, by far the most ambitious of his symphonies to date. In this work he came to terms with the influence of Gustav Mahler, and in particular with Mahler's conception of the symphony as a form of untrammeled psychological theater. The Mahler symphony that Shostakovich's work most resembles is the Sixth—both in the militaristic thrust of its opening and in the drawn-out anguish of its close. In later years Shostakovich encouraged the view that the Fourth had in some way been a statement of defiance in the face of what he had undergone in the first months of 1936. "The authorities tried everything they knew to get me to repent and expiate my sin," he told Glikman. "But I refused. I was young then, and had my physical strength. Instead of repenting, I composed my Fourth Symphony."

Yet the chronology doesn't fit; Shostakovich had already written two of the symphony's three movements when the edict against him was handed down. As the musicologist Pauline Fairclough points out, for much of its length the Fourth could be considered an energetic realization of socialist realism as articulated by Bukharin—"the struggle of conflicting tendencies." Scored for a mammoth orchestra of up to 130 players, the symphony begins with intimations of industrial might: a phalanx of fifteen high winds move in lockstep, a squadron of eight horns bear down, an ostinato of lower winds and strings pump like a piston. The Soviet listener of 1936 might have tried to picture—if a performance had taken place—the laborers who built the Dnieper Dam, or the "shock brigaders" of collective farming, or the overachieving Stakhanovites.

After the mighty opening, Bukharin's vacillations and defeats take over. The first theme fritters away its momentum in overextended transitional passages; the second theme is a slow, pale, lurching string of notes on the bassoon, which wanders here and there, strikes an unconvincing heroic attitude, is blown into jagged fragments, then falls in with a ragtag wind-band version of the first theme. Stranger events ensue, including a madcap fugue and a screaming twelve-note chord. The second movement is a pseudo-Scherzo that supplies little comic relief and ends with a skeletal rattling of percussion. Much of the final movement is given over to a dreamlike succession of genre pieces—puppet-show music, madcap polka, hurdy-gurdy waltz, and so on—which Fairclough hears as a clandestinely nostalgic portrait of prerevolutionary Russia, although there must be characteristic Shostakovichian sarcasm here as well.

If this were a model socialist realist work, all these conflicts would eventually be resolved in a conclusive affirmation. Toward the end of the third movement, cellos and basses play an excitedly murmuring sequence of notes (as in the finale of Mahler's *Resurrection* Symphony), the timpani strike up a grandiose pattern along the interval of the fourth, and utopia seems imminent. But the would-be triumph goes haywire, shattering repeatedly against a dissonant chord. A quotation underlines the sense of internal failure: as Richard Taruskin points out, the entire sequence imitates the "Gloria" of Stravinsky's *Oedipus Rex*, in which Jocasta is mordantly praised as queen of "*pestilentibus Thebis*" ("disease-ridden Thebes"). After the crack-up comes a long recessional in the orchestra, taking up 234 hushed, dismal bars. The final chord is marked *morendo*, dying away—an instruction that appears at the end of at least twenty other Shostakovich scores.

Shostakovich set to work on the finale of the Fourth shortly after "Muddle Instead of Music" appeared. Did he already have a tragic ending in mind? Or did the events of early 1936 send him into a spiral of despair? Either way, it was clear from the start that the Fourth would not suffice as a response to *Pravda*'s attack. The Leningrad Philharmonic began rehearsals for the premiere in the autumn of 1936, and word quickly spread through the music community that Shostakovich had rejected criticism and written music of "diabolical complexity." Apparatchiks appeared and spoke to the director of the orchestra, who called Shostakovich into his office. The composer came out wearing a downcast look. After walking silently for a while, he told Isaak Glikman that the symphony would not be played. "I didn't like the situation," Shostakovich later recalled. "Fear was all around. So I withdrew it."

For nearly two years Shostakovich placed no major works before the public. Finally, on November 21, 1937, in the Great Hall of the Leningrad Philharmonic, he unveiled his Fifth Symphony. The change in style was dramatic. The Fifth followed an ordinary four-movement pattern: Moderato, Allegretto, Largo, Allegro non troppo. Like Beethoven's same-numbered symphony, it proceeded from tragic minor to exultant major. Here was a work that the ordinary music lover—Stalin, for example—could comprehend.

A subsequent article, which appeared under Shostakovich's signature, advertised the symphony as "My Creative Response" and described it as an apology for *Lady Macbeth* and the unperformed Fourth: "If I have really succeeded in embodying in musical images all that I have thought and felt since the critical articles in *Pravda*, if the demanding listener will detect in my music a turn toward greater clarity and simplicity, I will be satisfied." Although Shostakovich may not have written these words, they contain ambiguities that are characteristic of his mental process. "All that I have thought and felt" might denote personal suffering and defiance. Musical simplicity does not rule out emotional complexity. And note the "if": nothing about this great work is simple or clear.

Beethoven's "hero" symphonies, the *Eroica* and the Fifth, tell stories of conflict and resolution, of protagonists overcoming obstacles to win victory. Maxim Shostakovich, the composer's son, indicates that his father's Fifth follows much the same plan: "The Fifth Symphony is his 'Heroic' Symphony. [The novelist Alexander] Fadeyev once said that he was scolding someone in the finale. My father replied: it was not just scolding. The hero is saying: 'I am right. I will follow the way I choose.'" The first movement sets out the grim landscape in which the hero will have to make his way. The second theme alludes, surprisingly, to a phrase from the Habanera in Bizet's *Carmen*—the notes to which Carmen sings the phrase "Amour, amour." The Russian musicologist Alexander Benditsky has discovered that the symphony is in fact riddled with references to *Carmen*, and they are probably connected to Shostakovich's lingering love for the translator Elena Konstantinovskaya, who, after her time in prison, had gone to Spain and married the Soviet photographer and filmmaker Roman Karmen. As in *Lady Macbeth*, personal layers lie beneath the surface of what appears to be a public, political work.

The heart of the symphony is the slow movement, the Largo. Sounds like sobs, lonely cries in the night, calls for help, even a kind of insistent begging for mercy—four loud repeated notes high on the violins—fill the air. Over a bank of tremolo violins, one woodwind instrument after another comes forward to sing a plaintive song, which falls a fourth and then a major second, as the sorrow chorus in Jerome Kern's "Mis'ry's Comin' Aroun'." (The neuroscientist Jaak Panksepp has investigated the phenomenon of the "musical chill," a tremor that runs down the body and raises the hairs on the skin. A passage in which a solo instrument steps in front of a softer background is especially prone to cause this effect; Panksepp compares it to "the separation call of young animals, the primal cry of despair to signal caretakers to exhibit social care and attention.") Adding to the funereal tone is an apparent allusion to Mussorgsky's *Boris Godunov*, the ultimate pageant of Russian suffering. The first five notes of Mussorgsky's setting of the words "Flow, flow, bitter tears, weep, weep, O soul of the Orthodox faithful" overlap with the last five notes of Shostakovich's main Largo theme. They are heard again at the end of the movement, plucked out on harp and celesta, like a music box winding down. The two final chords are a kind of "Amen"—a significant gesture from an atheist composer.

A brassy blast of D minor shoves us into the finale. The change is so wrenching that listeners may learn to dread its arrival. The pivotal notes D and A, which sounded pensively in the first movement, now thunder on the drums, setting the stage for a martial, declamatory theme in the trumpets, trombones, and tuba. The barreling energy of this theme and the motorized quality of its accompaniment nearly replicate the opening of the Fourth Symphony. The possibility that Shostakovich may in some way be rewriting his earlier work gives added meaning to a self-quotation that appears in the quiet contrasting section of the movement. Just before he set to work on the Fifth, Shostakovich made a setting of Pushkin's poem "Regeneration," which reads as follows:

An artist-barbarian with a drowsy brush
Blackens over the painting of a genius
And senselessly draws on top of it
His own illegitimate designs.
But over the years the foreign paint
Flakes away like old scales,
And the genius's work appears again
Before us in its former beauty.
Thus do delusions vanish
From my worried soul,
And in their place visions arise
Of pure, original days.

In the Fifth's finale, a yearning phrase from this song appears high in the strings and in the harp, suggestive of some luminous, angelic sphere. It floats up until it is out of reach, and a tapping of the timpani marks the return of the martial mood. There may be a whole series of repaintings going on here: motifs from the Fourth reworked, a song for voice and piano orchestrated but stripped of the voice, the song itself blotted out by a drumbeat. From here on, the symphony is all crescendo. The timpani pound relentlessly. Trumpets turn the main theme into a fanfare-like statement, an emblem of power.

The question arises: Who or what is triumphing? Is this the work of the artist-barbarian—the blackening of the work of genius that was the Fourth? Or, by the end, has the illicit drawing been erased, revealing Shostakovich's intentions in their original purity?

Even before the reference to "Regeneration" became known, the brutalism of the finale caused confusion and consternation among listeners. Some opponents of Stalin's regime took it as a sign that Shostakovich had joined the ranks of the conformists. Vladimir Shcherbachev, who had spoken up for the composer during the *Pravda* crisis, called the Fifth "remarkable, but sickeningly depressing." Nikolai Miaskovsky, himself a composer of turbulent, pessimistic symphonies, said the ending was "bad," a "D-major formal reply"; Osip Mandelstam called it "tedious intimidation." On the other side, some officials believed that Shostakovich was defying *Pravda*'s wise counsel. The well-connected critic Georgiy Khubov complained that the Largo was "an expressionist etching depicting 'numb horror,'" the finale "severe and threatening."

But the better part of the audience seemed to identify strongly with the symphony's assertion of will—what Maxim Shostakovich called "the determination of a strong man to BE." Many listeners had already lost friends and relatives to the Terror, and were in a numbed, terrified state. Gavriil Popov said to Lyubov Shaporina, the founder of the Puppet Theater: "You know, I've turned into a coward. I'm a coward, I'm afraid of everything, I even burned your letters." The Fifth had the effect of taking away, for a little while, that primitive fear. One listener was so gripped by the music that he stood up, as if royalty had walked into the room. Others began rising from their seats. During the long ovation that followed, Yevgeny Mravinsky, the conductor, held the score above his head.

Shaporina wrote in her diary: "Everyone kept saying: 'That was his answer, and it was a good one.' D.D. came out white as a sheet, biting his lips. I think he was close to tears."

Prokofiev Returns

Shostakovich and Prokofiev, the two giants of Soviet music, never understood each other particularly well. They met only occasionally, and often traded criticisms in front of colleagues and in haphazard correspondence: Prokofiev would comment on Shostakovich's supposed melodic deficiency, while Shostakovich would chide Prokofiev for his habit of farming out orchestration to colleagues.

In some ways their relationship recapitulates, in a cooler key, the rivalry between Mahler and Strauss, with similar psychological motifs in play. Like Mahler, Shostakovich pictured himself as a perennial victim of fate, yet he had total confidence in his abilities. For both men, the attitude of martyrdom may have been something of a pose. Prokofiev, like Strauss, presented a phlegmatic, devil-may-care exterior. Where Shostakovich was cagey, Prokofiev was forthright, even blatant in his opinions—"a kind of big baby who must tell the truth on all occasions," said his friend Nicolas Nabokov. A colleague overheard the following historic exchange between them:

> PROKOFIEV: You know, I'm really going to get down to work on my Sixth Symphony. I've written the first movement . . . and now I'm writing the second, with three themes: the third movement will probably be in sonata form. I feel the need to compensate for the absence of sonata form in the previous movements.
>
> SHOSTAKOVICH: So, is the weather here always like this?

Shostakovich, like Mahler, had an exceptional ability to dramatize his inner life; he saw no difference between his own fate and the fate of his country and the world. Prokofiev and Strauss, by contrast, were "Selfians," struggling to maintain their poise as the world spun around them. They had a more practical, pragmatic relationship with the craft of composition, and both have been underrated as a result.

Prokofiev was a tall, imposing man. One American critic, on first viewing him, described him as a blond Russian football guard; another claimed that he was made entirely of steel. Born in the Ukraine in 1891, Prokofiev became the prodigy and enfant terrible of the St. Petersburg

Conservatory in his teens. On December 18, 1908, three days before the premiere of Schoenberg's Second Quartet in Vienna, he caused a sensation with a recital of his piano music at the Evenings of Contemporary Music in Petersburg; the highlight of the program was a brief, savagely dis-sonant piece titled *Suggestion diabolique*. He would also show a knack for sensuous, Rachmaninov-like lyricism (the opera *Maddalena*); brooding chromatic fantasies at the outer edges of the tonal (the piano piece "Despair"); and a pioneering essay in neoclassical, back-to-Mozart style (the *Sinfonietta*). In all, Prokofiev had a gift for what the Russian literary theorist Mikhail Bakhtin called the "carnivalesque"—farce, parody, irresponsible merrymaking, mock grandeur.

The ten days that shook the world did not shake Prokofiev. In February 1917 he was anticipating the first performance of *The Gambler*—a ferociously effective adaptation of Dostoevsky's novella about a young man riding the roulette wheel to ruin—and much of his correspondence in the following months concerned his fruitless attempts to have the premiere rescheduled. Springtime found him on a leisurely trip up the Kama River, in the Volga region. In the summer he put the finishing touches on two works of untroubled lyricism, the First Violin Concerto and the *Classical* Symphony. Sviatoslav Richter compared the concerto to "the sensation you get when you first open your window in spring and are assailed by the sounds rising up from the street."

By the time of the Bolshevik takeover, in October, Prokofiev was on a hiking expedition in the Caucasus. (That aristocratic excursion had to be edited out of Soviet-era histories, as David Nice notes in the first volume of his Prokofiev biography.) Later that fall Prokofiev composed the apocalyptically noisy cantata *Seven, They Are Seven*, based on ancient Akkadian incantations as adapted by Konstantin Balmont. Again the composer seemed peculiarly disconnected:

They bring us sorrows. They bring us hatred.
They are heralds proclaiming the plague.
Seven gods of infinite worlds!

One day Prokofiev showed up at the Commissariat of Enlightenment, saying that he needed fresh air to develop his art. Lunacharsky protested that "in Russia we also have a lot of fresh air," but sent him away cordially, with a Soviet passport in case he wished to return. Prokofiev's subsequent adventures played out like a picaresque tale along the lines of *Around the World in Eighty Days*. He set off on the Trans-Siberian Express toward Japan, intending eventually to go to Buenos Aires. Instead, he wound up in San Francisco. When the American authorities detained him as a suspect alien, he claimed to hate the Bolsheviks because they had taken all his money.

The better part of the years 1918 to 1922 was spent in America, where audiences applauded Prokofiev's virtuosic piano playing but struggled to make sense of his compositions. During the Pacific Ocean voyage, Prokofiev had begun writing an opera libretto based on Carlo Gozzi's deliciously absurd commedia dell'arte play *The Love of Three Oranges*, using an adaptation that Meyerhold had made for his experimental studio in the years before the revolution. This was "estrangement" in a lighthearted vein: in the Prologue, Tragedians, Comedians, Romantics, Eccentrics, and Empty-Heads debate among themselves what genre of entertainment should be performed, and as the fairy-tale plot plays out, they periodically intrude to offer observations and criticisms. The soprano Mary Garden, a famous exponent of the roles of Mélisande and Salome, arranged a successful staging of *The Love of Three Oranges* at the Chicago Opera Company in 1921, but a subsequent New York run flopped, curtailing dreams of American fame. The country left one major mark on Prokofiev, though; he fell under the influence of Mary Baker Eddy's Christian Science movement, according to which people can overcome sickness, sin, evil, even death itself if they achieve the right spiritual understanding.

By 1923, the adventurer had settled in Paris, where he had to contend with the politics of style. For all his compositional virtuosity, Prokofiev could not rival Stravinsky and Les Six in their rapid invention and assimilation of musical trends. Stravinsky, Prokofiev commented, "frightfully desires his creativity to adhere to modernity. If I want anything, it's that modernity should adhere to my creativity." Circa 1908 the teenage Prokofiev would have been perceived as the more modern of the two; Stravinsky, at that time, had barely made a mark on the Petersburg scene. In the twenties it was Prokofiev who was struggling to keep up, and after several years of frustration he decided to go his own way.

Although composers in the Diaghilev circle went around proclaiming that opera was defunct, Prokofiev devoted much of the twenties to the composition of *The Fiery Angel*, a comparatively old-fashioned drama of sexual obsession and demonic possession in which Faust and Mephistopheles have supporting roles. It was an extravagant, alluring, floor-rattling affair, recalling the Symbolist door-to-the-beyond mentality that prevailed before the war, and, not surprisingly, it failed to arouse interest in Stravinsky's Paris. Prokofiev then turned his attention to Berlin, where, he hoped, one of Leo Kestenberg's state-supported theaters would stage the opera. A production of *The Fiery Angel* was scheduled for 1927, but the conductor Bruno Walter peremptorily canceled it when the orchestral parts arrived late. Prokofiev's biggest work to date was effectively dead.

Prokofiev had no trouble satisfying Diaghilev's demand for propulsive, percussive, machine-age ballets—in the mid-twenties he produced *The Step of Steel*, an aestheticized and eroticized Ballets Russes fantasy of life in the Soviet Union—but he was tiring of the bludgeoning, dissonant manner that he had perfected in his youth. Instead, he wished to give free rein to his melodic gift—one area in which Stravinsky could not rival him. He drew on a seemingly inexhaustible supply of long-breathed melodies that start with a voluptuous upward reach and then graciously sink down. As in Shostakovich, the diatonic scale is so richly ornamented with added tones—the lowered fifth, the lowered second, and so on—that the harmonies constantly float away from their home key. In the harshest passages of early Prokofiev scores such as *The Gambler*, those extra tones are like symptoms of spreading infection. The same air of corruption, of a world gone wrong, floats through much of Shostakovich's music. But the mature Prokofiev is striving for lyrical release, and "wrong notes" become a play of light and shadow around a shapely form.

By the early thirties, Prokofiev had committed himself to what he called, in an interview with the *Los Angeles Evening Express*, a "new simplicity"—a conservative modernism rooted in Classical and Romantic tradition. Since socialist-realist ideology was demanding the same, Prokofiev concluded that the Soviet worldview magically coincided with his own. In fact, he had been carefully primed to think so. Stalin placed a priority on bringing illustrious cultural exiles back into the fold, and the project of seducing Prokofiev was supervised by the OGPU, as the secret police were known at the time.

When the composer came back to Russia in 1927, he saw a panorama of Soviet life that was controlled in every detail. Hardly blind to the OGPU's presence, he noted in his diary the shady characters lurking in restaurants, the mysterious clicks on the phone line, the personal searches, and other signs of surveillance. Hearing that a cousin had "taken ill," he understood at once that she had been arrested. Nonetheless, he chose to focus on the improvements that the regime had brought about in some sectors of society—the increase of literacy in the rural population, the shiny new high-rises in the cities, the nationwide project of electrification, the paving of roads, and so on. As a Christian Scientist, he may have believed that he could will the evil away—although there was certainly also personal calculation in his decision to return, a sense that the Soviet Union would give him due attention and support.

The final stage of Sovietization was accomplished by a simple trick: Prokofiev didn't need to "become" a Soviet composer, because he had been one all along. He still had his Soviet passport; his works had been published by the official Soviet house; many of his recent premieres had taken place on Soviet soil; and his style already fulfilled the mandate for simplicity. All that remained was a bureaucratic matter of changing his address.

Prokofiev's first "official" Soviet work, the dance epic *Romeo and Juliet*, showed him at his optimistic peak. In his autobiography he identified five main lines in his writing: the classical, the modern, the motoric, the lyric, and the grotesque. In *Romeo* these modes find equilibrium, with the lyric at the center. Prokofiev's extended tonal language achieves maximum sophistication: the lovely opening melody of the work is interspersed with just enough passing semitone clashes and lowered or raised pitches that it acquires a grainy, acidic finish, avoiding sentimentality or kitsch. The ballet was written at high speed in the summer of 1935, in the last months before the onslaught of the Terror. It had the makings of an instant classic, yet inexplicable obstacles appeared in the way of the first performance. Members of the Bolshoi Ballet declared the music undanceable. Soviet officials, reversing their usual stance on the inadvisability of tragic endings, said that Prokofiev had betrayed Shakespeare by letting the lovers live happily ever after. Even with a new ending of ardent heartbreak, *Romeo* did not reach a Russian stage until 1940. What Prokofiev could never understand was that these difficulties had nothing to do with the notes he put on paper; they were the ritual of humiliation that every Soviet composer had to undergo.

Perplexed by the indifferent reception of *Romeo*, Prokofiev now tried his hand at propaganda. In contrast to Shostakovich, who dispatched his official duties as efficiently and soullessly as possible, Prokofiev worked painfully hard at such projects as the *Cantata for the Twentieth Anniversary of October*, *Songs of Our Days*, and *Zdravitsa* (*Toast to Stalin*). The ten-part *Cantata*, with its two large choruses and four distinct orchestras, including an ensemble of accordions, was too raucous to gain approval. *Songs of Our Days*, in which a mother reassures her child,

There is a man behind the Kremlin walls
And the entire land knows and loves him
Your joy and happiness come from him
Stalin! That is his great name!

also failed to please, this time on the grounds that Prokofiev had simplified *too* much and ceased to be himself—the same mind game that commentators had played with Shostakovich in the reviews of *The Limpid Stream*.

With *Zdravitsa*, Prokofiev finally hit the mark. The text is a paean to the loving attentions of the man in the Kremlin, who, it is claimed, brings sunshine, nourishes meadows, and whitens the cherry orchards. Prokofiev took the idea of Stalin's love at face value, writing surreally beautiful music in the vein of *Romeo and Juliet*. Indeed, as Philip Taylor points out, the opening melody has more or less the same lilting accompaniment as in the ballet's balcony scene. *Zdravitsa* was considered sufficiently true to life that it was broadcast from loudspeakers on the Moscow streets. Oleg, the composer's younger son, ran into the house one day and said, "Daddy! They're playing you outside!"

Official applause also greeted Prokofiev's score for Sergei Eisenstein's film *Alexander Nevsky*, a celebration of the thirteenth-century prince who routed the Teutonic Knights on the ice of Lake Peipus. Few experiences in Prokofiev's checkered career gave him more satisfaction than his collaboration with Eisenstein, who treated his composers not as hired hands but as creative equals. The tour-de-force scene in *Nevsky*, the battle on the ice, was filmed only after the music had been sketched out, and the resulting integration of sound and image rivals anything in the animated creations of Walt Disney, whom both director and composer admired. In other scenes Eisenstein implied rhythm in the sequence of images. Watching in the screening room, Prokofiev would tap his fingers in time to the footage. He would deliver a finished piece by noon the following day, and Eisenstein would use the music to finalize his edit. This almost unprecedented vision of film as spoken-word opera was one that Stalin did not fail to appreciate. When, in 1941, the first Stalin prizes were handed out, *Alexander Nevsky* was among the winners.

By the time Eisenstein's film received that honor, however, Prokofiev had begun to understand the dimensions of his velvet prison. In 1938 and 1939, the composer labored away on his first Soviet opera, *Semyon Kotko*, which told of a young man's transformation into a socialist hero and his concomitant defeat of various class enemies. The libretto is alternately fatuous and vicious, but Prokofiev lavished on it some of the strongest dramatic music of his career, including a German invasion sequence of malevolent splendor. What most excited him was the opportunity to work with Meyerhold, whom he had long idolized.

Meyerhold was readying *Semyon Kotko* for rehearsal at the Stanislavsky Opera Theater when, on June 15, 1939, he made some ill-advised remarks on Soviet arts policy, the precise nature of which remains a matter of debate. On June 20, he was arrested, his fate probably having been sealed long before. Meyerhold's wife was later found stabbed to death. The opera's premiere was, of course, postponed. Prokofiev was still recovering from these events when a change in Soviet foreign policy forced a revision of the opera's libretto. The signing of the Hitler-Stalin pact in August 1939 meant that Germans could no longer be depicted as villains. Hasty cosmetic changes failed to save *Semyon Kotko* from obsolescence, and it disappeared from Soviet stages soon after its premiere. On January 16, 1940, Stalin signed 346 death sentences, Meyerhold's and Babel's among them.

Throughout the late thirties Prokofiev continued to make trips to the West, waving his passport at the border. Talking to his friends outside Russia, he kept to a pro-Soviet line, but close acquaintances thought they could see the strain. Nicolas Nabokov, in his book *Old Friends and New Music*, reported that "behind this mask of optimism and official praise, one could detect a feeling totally contradictory to the very nature of

Prokofiev's character: the feeling of profound and terrible insecurity." According to the Russian-American composer Vernon Duke, a Hollywood studio offered Prokofiev the huge salary of twenty-five hundred dollars a week. Duke himself conveyed the offer and watched the reaction—momentary excitement turning to truculent dismissal. "That's nice bait," Prokofiev said, "but I won't swallow it. I've got to go back to Moscow, to my music and my children."

Dostoevsky's story *The Gambler*, which formed the basis for Prokofiev's great early opera, has a line that may pinpoint the major weakness in the composer's personality. Alexei, the protagonist, is looking back at the moment when he might have turned away from the roulette wheel and overcome his compulsion. "I ought to have gone away," he says, "but a strange sensation rose up in me, a sort of defiance of fate, a desire to challenge it, to put out my tongue at it." Prokofiev's diary of his first Soviet tour records a similar turning point. "Should I forget the whole thing and stay here?" the composer asked himself as he boarded the train to Moscow. "Can I count on coming back or will they stop me?" Again, during a change of locomotives at the Latvian border, he said to himself: "This is our last chance, it's still not too late to turn back." But he brushed aside his misgivings and stayed on the train. A little over ten years later, upon returning from his 1938 American tour, Prokofiev handed in his foreign-travel passport, as per Soviet procedure. He never got it back, and never set foot outside the Soviet Union again.

The Great Patriotic War

"A blizzard is raging outside the windows as 1944 approaches," Shostakovich wrote to Isaak Glikman on New Year's Eve. "It will be a year of happiness, of joy, of victory, a year that will bring us all much joy. The freedom-loving Peoples will at last throw off the yoke of Hitlerism, peace will reign over the whole world, and we shall live once more in peace under the sun of Stalin's Constitution. Of this I am convinced, and consequently experience feelings of unalloyed joy." This quintessentially Shostakovichian utterance exemplifies the composer's penchant for talking through a mask of Soviet doublespeak. Indeed, he appears to be echoing, for comic effect, Stalin's own wearyingly repetitive prose style; the threefold use of the word "joy" (*radost'*) is a typical Stalinist tic. Yet the repetition is also a private code. Glikman informs us that whenever Shostakovich repeats himself unnecessarily, or emphasizes some stale phrase, he means the opposite of what he appears to be saying. Thus, when he writes, "Everything is so fine, so perfectly excellent, that I can find almost nothing to write about," he is in fact saying that things are too awful to be described in correspondence that is being monitored by the NKVD. Glikman says that Shostakovich used this code even in conversation. "I'm feeling fine" had a variety of implications.

But did Shostakovich *always* mean the opposite of what he said? Did he take no joy at all in the prospect that "freedom-loving Peoples will at last throw off the yoke of Hitlerism"? Even in the grip of totalitarian terror, life goes on. People are able to feel joy, rage, sorrow, love. Music is, in fact, better at communicating these primal emotions that it is at managing anything as tricky as irony. Irony, in the standard definition, is saying something other than what one appears to be saying. To talk about musical irony, we first have to agree on what the music appears to be saying, and then we have to agree on what the music is really saying. This is invariably difficult to do. We can, however, learn to be wary of any interpretation that displays too much certitude about what the music is "really saying," and stay alert to multiple levels of meaning. Shostakovich's Fifth Symphony becomes a rich experience when heard in this way. So does his Seventh Symphony, or *Leningrad*, which for many years was dismissed as an exercise in wartime propaganda.

Shostakovich displayed patriotic fervor from the start of the war. In late June 1941, immediately after the Nazi invasion began, he reported to the civil defense headquarters with his pupil Veniamin Fleishman and volunteered for duty. Rejected on account of his poor eyesight, he joined the Leningrad Conservatory fire brigade and moved into a barracks in the building. A famous photo shows him wearing a fireman's helmet on the conservatory roof. The image was staged for propaganda purposes; colleagues made sure to keep the prize of Soviet music out of harm's way.

In July, Shostakovich set to work on the Seventh Symphony, in which he planned to record, in almost stenographic fashion, the emotions of battle. In mid-September he announced on Leningrad radio that he had finished the first two movements. "Our art is threatened with great danger," he said. "We will defend our music." German artillery shells were by then landing in the city, marking the onset of the nine-hundred-day siege.

For several composer friends Shostakovich played through at the piano what he had written so far, and continued playing even as the air-raid sirens went off and anti-aircraft fire all but drowned him out. Against his own wishes, he was evacuated from the city on October 1, and spent the winter in Kuybyshev, formerly Samara, in the Volga region.

The *Leningrad* had its premiere in Kuybyshev in March 1942. It then made its way around the world, its progress complicated by wartime. As *The New Yorker* reported in a Talk of the Town item, the score was transferred to microfilm, put in a tin can, flown to Tehran, driven by car to Cairo, flown to South America, and finally flown to New York. Toscanini beat out Koussevitzky and Stokowski for the rights to conduct the Western premiere, which took place on July 19, 1942. *Time* magazine put Shostakovich on the cover, in his firefighting regalia, with the caption "Amid bombs bursting in Leningrad he heard the chords of victory." The composer became a propaganda symbol for the Allied cause, a profile in courage.

Besieged Leningrad heard the symphony on August 9, 1942, under the most dramatic circumstances imaginable. The score was flown in by military aircraft in June, and a severely depleted Leningrad Radio Orchestra began learning it. After a mere fifteen musicians showed up for the initial rehearsal, the commanding general ordered all competent musicians to report from the front lines. The players would break from the rehearsals to return to their duties, which sometimes included the digging of mass graves for victims of the siege. Three members of the orchestra died of starvation before the premiere took place. The opposing German general heard about the performance in advance and planned to disrupt it, but the Soviets preempted him by launching a bombardment of German positions—Operation Squall, it was called. An array of loudspeakers then broadcast the *Leningrad* into the silence of no-man's-land. Never in history had a musical composition entered the thick of battle in quite this way: the symphony become a tactical strike against German morale.

For the benefit of his vast international audience, Shostakovich drew up a program for the first three movements of the Seventh. "The exposition of the first movement tells of the happy, peaceful life of people sure of themselves and their future," the composer wrote. "This is the simple, peaceful life lived before the war . . . In the development, war bursts into the peaceful life of these people. I am not aiming for the naturalistic depiction of war, the depiction of the clatter of arms, the explosion of shells, and so on. I am trying to convey the image of war emotionally." Later, in conversations with friends, Shostakovich hinted that he was not thinking only of German Fascism; he had in mind "all forms of terror, slavery, the bondage of the spirit."

As official, unofficial, and rumored meanings multiply, the music itself grows elusive, even as it invites decoding with its charged musical signals. The attention-getting event in the first movement is the "invasion episode," as Shostakovich himself called it. It falls where one would expect to find a development section in a sonata-form movement. In place of elaboration and variation of the first and second themes, the orchestra begins repeating one rather simpleminded idea over a span of 350 bars, with a snare-drum rhythm rapping continuously underneath. If this music is meant to suggest the Germans marching in, it does not sound particularly Teutonic. The tune is based on the operetta aria "Da geh' ich zu Maxim," from Franz Lehár's *The Merry Widow*, known to have been one of Hitler's favorites. The snare-drum ostinato is inspired by Ravel's *Bolero*, as is the structure of unending crescendo. It begins as a kind of Pied Piper march, a picaresque procession. It ends as a gargantuan, vulgar rant, with one figure sounding like a child's chant of "nyah-nyah."

What to make of this Austrian-French-Spanish mishmash? One of the keener interpretations comes from Eisenstein, who was reminded of a scene in Dostoevsky's antirevolutionary masterpiece *The Demons*. At one point in the novel, the leftist agitator Lyamshin, who is also a pianist and composer, entertains his friends by improvising a piano piece titled *The Franco-Prussian War*, in which "La Marseillaise" is overrun by the German folk song "Ach, du lieber Augustin." That famous tune—which haunted both Mahler and Schoenberg—enters "somewhere on one side, from below, from some corner," Dostoevsky writes, then grows in power until it sweeps "La Marseillaise" aside. "One had a feeling of countless barrels of beer, the frenzy of self-glorification, demands for milliards, expensive cigars, champagne and hostages: *Augustin* passed into a wild roar." Eisenstein adds, "Surely it is this page of the great Russian writer's work that lies at the heart of [the *Leningrad*]."

Anna Akhmatova, too, heard the *Leningrad* as a kind of mad carnival. At the end of the original version of her wartime cycle *Poem Without a Hero*, she presents a complex of images to conjure up her flight from

Leningrad under siege. One inspiration is Mikhail Bulgakov's novel *The Master and Margarita*, written in secret in the 1930s and not published until 1966. In that Russian-Soviet version of the old Faustian tale, the devil and his anarchic-surrealist retinue expose the madness of Stalin's society by way of violent farce. In particular, Akhmatova has in mind a scene Margarita, after discovering that she possesses witchlike powers, flies to a Walpurgis Nacht ball. The fact that Shostakovich flew out of Leningrad on a small plane shortly after Akhmatova did, taking with him the manuscript of the first three movements of the *Leningrad*, leads the poet to picture the symphony as a witch's broomstick, carrying the spirit of Petersburg through the night:

And over forests full of the enemy
Like that one, *possessed by the devil,*
Flying to the Brocken at night, I soared.
And after me, sparkling with a mystery
And having named herself the Seventh
She rushed to an unprecedented feast . . .
Pretending to be a musical score,
The famous Leningrader
Returned to her native ether.

All this amends the image of the *Leningrad* as a bluntly propagandistic exercise. The score has a countervailing element of fantasy, which resurfaces from time to time as the massive four-movement structure unfolds. A hint of the snare-drum rhythm slices through the symphony's final bars, beneath mechanized sonorities of Soviet glory. Another demonic procession might be ready to begin.

Prokofiev responded to the Nazi invasion with a characteristically idiosyncratic gesture: he made an opera out of Tolstoy's *War and Peace*. Up to a point, the project seemed relevant to the historical situation: Tolstoy's scenes of the Napoleonic invasion of 1812—the Battle of Borodino, the occupation of Moscow, Marshal Kutuzov's crafty turning of the tide, the downfall of the French army during the long Russian winter—resonated with the ongoing struggle against Hitler. Prokofiev was careful to end the opera not with Tolstoy's meditations on man's insignificance before the forces of history but with a rousing nationalist pageant. Yet the composer was at his best in sketching portraits of the old Russian aristocracy—in particular, the character of young Natasha Rostova, the pure-hearted but woefully unfocused daughter of an impoverished landowning family. The centerpiece of Part I of the opera is a grand ballroom scene, drenched in longing for a lost world. "*Valse! Valse! Valse! Mesdames!*" cries the host of the ball, over a sinister vamp in the bass. It is a heartbreaking mirage of splendor, with the pistons of modernity churning in the background.

Then came a second film collaboration with Eisenstein, whose montage style may have influenced the innovative flow of semi-independent scenes in *War and Peace*. Eisenstein had undertaken the tricky task of making a multipart film about the life of Tsar Ivan IV, otherwise known as Ivan the Terrible, Stalin's idol. If Eisenstein produced a hagiography of Ivan, he would be issuing an apologia for the worst of Stalin's Terror; if he offered a "warts and all" portrait, he would offend the leader. He split the difference by making Part I more festive in tone and Part II more critical. Prokofiev's music, likewise, played both sides. The swordlike motto theme—four horns and two trumpets in B-flat major, grazed by G-flat major in the lower brass—creates a nimbus of dark glory around Ivan, a kind of super-major harmony. But the music for the "orgy scene" in Part II, where the Oprichniks are shown wallowing in blood and drunkenness, has a mocking tone, oompah notes in the tuba rendering Ivan's henchmen ridiculous rather than fearsome. Stalin reacted predictably. Part I received a Stalin prize, shared by Eisenstein and Prokofiev. Part II never made it to the theaters. "Ivan the Terrible was very cruel," Stalin said to Eisenstein, after viewing the second part. "You can show he was cruel. But you must show why he *needed to be cruel*."

Prokofiev faced no such problems when he worked in instrumental forms, at least for the time being. A trio of vehement, hard-driving piano sonatas—Nos. 6, 7, and 8—drew praise for their evocation of the Soviet war effort, although they had been conceived in peacetime, in the summer of 1939. His Fifth Symphony, likewise, was hailed as an inspirational "war symphony," though it lacked a program along the lines of the *Leningrad*. This was Prokofiev's first attempt at a large-scale, Beethovenian utterance, his previous symphonies having been more in the nature of orchestral suites. Shostakovich almost certainly served as a model. The plan follows that of Shostakovich's Fifth: a measured, somber opening movement, hinting at massive forces in motion; a diverting, lightly acerbic Scherzo; a slow movement with funereal overtones; and an up-tempo, faintly militaristic finale.

As in the case of Shostakovich's Fifth, a question mark hangs over the ending. The final movement is marked Allegro giocoso, and seems determined to marshal its energies into a jocular, brassy close. In the coda, however, a bitingly dissonant kind of machine music takes over, harking back to the insolent, *diabolique* manner of Prokofiev's youth. Eleven bars before the end, there is a sudden diminuendo, followed by a sound like the whirring of gears. Possibly this passage was meant to echo Stalin's image of Soviet citizens as cogs in a great machine, but it makes for a strangely icy close to an ostensible victory narrative.

The Fifth Symphony gave Prokofiev perhaps his finest hour as a Soviet composer. He conducted the premiere himself, in the Great Hall of the Moscow Conservatory, on January 13, 1945. As at the first Leningrad performance of Shostakovich's Seventh, the sound of cannons shook the hall beforehand, but this time the guns were being fired in ceremonial salute, to mark the Red Army's advance across the Vistula River in Poland. Sviatoslav Richter, who was in the audience that night, basked in the composer's aura of power: "When Prokofiev stood up, it seemed as though the light poured down on him from on high. He stood there, like a monument on a pedestal." Later that month, the composer had an attack of dizziness, fell to the ground, and suffered a severe concussion. He never recovered fully from the consequences of the injury. The last stage of his misfortune was beginning.

The Zhdanov Affair

"A very pleasant place, indeed," the American newspaperman Harrison Salisbury wrote in 1954, when he visited Shostakovich in his dacha in Bolshevo, outside Moscow. "There is a big garden. There is room to play volleyball, and the Klyazma River is convenient for swimming." Shostakovich was given his first country retreat in 1946. In the same year he received a new five-room apartment in Moscow, one equipped with no fewer than three pianos—two for the composer in his study and one for his son. Shostakovich promptly wrote a thank-you note to Stalin: "All of this made me extraordinarily happy. I ask you to accept my most heartfelt gratitude for the attention and concern. I wish you happiness, health, and many years of life for the good of our beloved Motherland, our great people."

In the wake of the *Leningrad*, then, Shostakovich had recovered his standing as the chief composer of the Soviet Union. One positive sign from above came in 1943, when he and Aram Khachaturian jointly submitted a draft of a new Soviet national anthem, as part of a composers' competition that Stalin personally supervised. Although their entry failed to win, Shostakovich somehow wound up with the largest monetary reward. He also received the Order of Lenin, became a deputy to the Supreme Soviet of the Russian Federation, became the head of the Leningrad composers' group, served on the Stalin Prize committee, advised the Ministry of Cinematography, and most notably, took over Maximilian Steinberg's composition class at the Leningrad Conservatory. He therefore occupied the podium at which Rimsky-Korsakov, Stravinsky's teacher, once had stood.

A new round of muttering began. The rank and file of the Composers' Union, especially the former members of the proletarian-music movement, had grown envious of the dachas, prizes, posts, interest-free loans, complimentary automobiles, and other perks that the elite composers were arranging for one another. Meanwhile, indications of a new wave of repression could be seen in all the Soviet arts; a campaign against "art for art's sake," "formalist," and "individualist" tendencies in the writings of Akhmatova and Zoshchenko set the stage.

All through 1946 and 1947, independent-minded Soviet composers received sharper criticism, from which Shostakovich was not immune. He had already lost a little ground with his Eighth Symphony, which had appeared in 1943 and struck some listeners as excessively gloomy and harrowing. Officialdom expected him to respond to the defeat of Hitler with a great Soviet "Victory Symphony," replete with chorus and soloists, à la Beethoven's Ninth. Shostakovich promised to write such a work and made a start on the first movement in the last winter of the war. But he broke off in the middle, for reasons that remain unclear. In its place he dashed off a kind of anti-Ninth, an alternately satiric and melancholic five-movement suite, which occasioned intense debate after its November 1945 premiere. Shostakovich had gone on vacation from his great duties, one critic proposed the following year.

Prokofiev, too, came under renewed scrutiny. On October 11, 1947, thirty years to the day after the Central Committee of the Bolshevik Party resolved to overthrow Kerensky's Provisional Government, Prokofiev's Sixth Symphony had its premiere, and it failed to strike the affirmative note that the occasion demanded. As in the composer's previous symphony, a kind of malfunction seems to happen in the finale. The movement begins in deceptively buoyant, up-tempo fashion, with vaudeville-like ditties prevailing. The brass kick in with Sousa-esque march music, replete with baton-twirling piccolos. Then a grinding, machinelike noise is heard, and the merrymaking mood vanishes into a slow procession of towering dissonant chords and cruelly blaring major triads. This unambiguously tragic ending was an apt prelude to what happened next.

The second nightmare began in earnest on January 5, 1948, with another trip to the opera. This time Stalin and other members of the Central Committee went to the Bolshoi to see *The Great Friendship*, a saga of the postrevolutionary Caucacus by the undistinguished Georgian composer Vano Muradeli. Again the members of the committee failed to enjoy themselves, and various reasons were given for their displeasure—something to do with the incorrect representation of the political orientation of the Northern Caucasian peoples, something to do with the improper use of a folk dance. But that was all pretext. Muradeli took the heat because he could be trusted to grovel in public and shift the blame to more significant targets—namely, the bigwigs in the Union of Soviet Composers, who had been consuming excessive state resources in pursuit of self-indulgent ends.

The driving force behind the campaign was Andrei Zhdanov, the Leningrad Communist Party chief, who had risen to become Stalin's apparent second-in-command. "The Pianist," Zhdanov was called, in honor of his modest abilities on that instrument.

In mid-January, Zhdanov called a number of composers to the Central Committee offices for a three-day conference. He criticized Muradeli's hapless opera, recited from the *Pravda* editorial of 1936, and stated that "muddle instead of music" was alive and well. Several yes-men got up to say no to formalism. "Shostakovich's Seventh, Eighth, and Ninth symphonies are supposed to be considered as works of genius abroad," said the song composer Vladimir Zakharov. "But who considers them as such?" Tikhon Khrennikov, a younger composer of minor abilities and major political gifts, delivered a carefully calibrated critique of Shostakovich, aimed not so much at the composer himself as at the supposed cult around him. The *Leningrad*, Khrennikov said, "was described as a work of stupendous genius besides which Beethoven was a mere pup."

Some of the composers were not afraid to fight back. "You don't know what you are talking about," someone called out in the middle of Zakharov's disquisition. Lev Knipper protested, "You can't start standardizing everything." Vissarion Shebalin warned that sweeping statements about cacophony in Soviet music were creating an atmosphere of panic in which "servile idiots . . . might cause a lot of trouble."

Prokofiev is said to have walked in late and shown obvious disdain for what Zhdanov was saying. Depending on which story you believe, he either chatted away loudly with his neighbors or fell asleep, and eventually got into an argument with a high-ranking Party official who accused him of not paying proper attention. These stories may be apocryphal; voluminous lore has accumulated around Soviet composers over the decades, and scholars are still trying to sift out the truth. What is certain is that Prokofiev did not address the gathering, by way of either self-justification or apology.

Shostakovich swallowed his pride. Although he complained about the more extreme criticism—"Comrade Zakharov was not very thoughtful in what he said about Soviet symphonies," he said—he took a generally self-abasing tone, admitting that some of his works may have been defective. Old fears probably caused him to act in this way: the situation must have stirred memories of the late thirties, when so many people near him disappeared. Another death got Shostakovich's attention. On the last day of the conference he learned of the sudden passing of the actor Solomon Mikhoels, the founder of the Moscow Jewish Theatre. Although the cause of death was not yet known, Mikhoels had been killed at Stalin's behest. Shostakovich went directly from the meeting at the Kremlin to the Mikhoels household. "I envy him," he said.

On February 10, 1948, the Central Committee issued what became known as the "Historic Decree." Four days later, forty-two works by "formalists"—including Shostakovich's Sixth, Eighth, and Ninth symphonies, Prokofiev's Sixth and Eighth sonatas, and Popov's unlucky First Symphony—were banned. Another conference, a General Assembly of composers, followed, at which Khrennikov delivered a stem-winder of a speech denouncing half the major works of the early twentieth century.

This time Prokofiev claimed to be too sick to attend, and sent a seemingly apologetic letter whose insincerity was obvious to many observers, Shostakovich included. Prokofiev essentially congratulated Soviet aestheticians for having arrived at a concept of musical simplicity that he had formed independently, even if he had "unwittingly" diverged from his chosen path and occasionally indulged in the "mannerism" of atonality.

Behind the nonchalant facade lay a shattered spirit. Despite years of effort, Prokofiev had been unable to bring about a complete performance of his masterpiece, *War and Peace*. Part I was staged in Leningrad in 1946, but a production of Part II the following year was halted after a dress rehearsal, its libretto disparaged for supposed historical errors. "I am prepared to accept the failure of any of my works," Prokofiev said to a colleague, "but if only you knew how much I want *War and Peace* to see the light of day!" He never saw the entire opera performed.

More bad news followed in the days after the Historic Decree. On February 11, one day after the decree came down, Eisenstein, Prokofiev's favorite collaborator, died of a heart attack at the age of fifty. On February 20, Lina Prokofiev, the composer's first wife, was arrested on trumped-up charges of spying against the state and sent into the camp system, from which she would not return for eight years. Because Prokofiev had recently entered into a second marriage, with his longtime lover, Mira Mendelson, he might have concluded that Lina's arrest was some sort of sadistic manipulation, although documents recently unearthed in the Soviet Union suggest that it was nothing more than a chilling coincidence.

Shostakovich's conduct in the wake of the decree should come as no surprise. He addressed the General Assembly in the following terms:

> All the resolutions of the Central Committee of the All-Union Communist Party (Bolshevik) regarding the art of recent years, and

> particularly the Resolution of 10 February 1948 in regard to the opera *Great Friendship*, point out to Soviet artists that a tremendous national uplift is now taking place in our country, our great Soviet nation. Some Soviet artists, and among them myself, attempted to give expression in their works to this great national uplift. But between my subjective intentions and objective results there was an appalling gap. The absence, in my works, of the interpretation of folk art, that great spirit by which our people lives, has been with utmost clarity and definiteness pointed out by the Central Committee of the All-Union Communist Party (Bolshevik). I am deeply grateful for it and for all the criticism contained in the Resolution. All the directives of the Central Committee of the All-Union Communist Party (Bolshevik), and in particular those that concern me personally, I accept as a stern but paternal solicitude for us, Soviet artists. Work—arduous, creative, joyous work on new compositions which will find their path to the heart of the Soviet people, which will be understandable to the people, loved by them, and which will be organically connected with the people's art, developed and enriched by the great traditions of Russian classicism—this will be a fitting response to the Resolution of the Central Committee of the All-Union Communist Party (Bolshevik).

We know Shostakovich to have been a fluent speaker of Soviet officialese, with its ponderous jargon, empty clichés, and numbing repetition. If he wrote this speech himself, he produced a masterpiece of the genre—prose so awful that it now has a comic effect when read aloud. No one, of course, was laughing at the time.

By April 1948, the wily Khrennikov had assumed the post of general secretary of the Composers' Union. The formalists were invited to deliver their apologies at the First All-Union Congress of Composers. Most failed to show up; the sickness that allegedly overcame Prokofiev in February had spread. It was a "conspiracy of silence," one participant said. Shostakovich, alas, went to the podium to deliver one more mea culpa, which, he later claimed, a Party operative had thrust into his hands at the last moment. Afterward, his colleagues avoided looking him in the eye. In his own words: "I read like the most paltry wretch, a parasite, a puppet, a cut-out paper doll on a string!" He is said to have shrieked the last phrase and repeated it maniacally. The novelist Boris Pasternak, among others, was crestfallen at Shostakovich's show of acquiescence. "O Lord, if only they knew at least how to keep silent!" the novelist exclaimed. "Even that would be a feat of courage!"

All the while, Shostakovich continued to work. In early 1948 he was writing his First Violin Concerto, and after attending each day of the musicological inquisition he would pick up where he had left off the previous night. The second movement marks the first appearance of what would become his signature motif—the notes D, E-flat, C, and B, which in German notation spell out D S C H, or Dmitri SCHostakowitsch. When the Zhdanov affair commenced, Shostakovich was working on the third movement, in which a furiously sorrowing Passacaglia is joined to a scalding solo cadenza. Once, he showed the composer Mikhail Meyerovich what point in the score he had reached when the "Historic Decree" was published. "The violin played semiquavers before and after it," Meyerovich recalled. "There was no change evident in the music."

Dance of Death

On March 16, 1949, Shostakovich answered the telephone and was told that Stalin was coming on the line. "Thank you, everything is fine," Shostakovich was heard to say. This was in answer to a series of questions about his health. The topic changed to America. Shostakovich had reluctantly agreed to travel to the United States the following month as part of a Soviet cultural and scientific delegation, but he had trouble understanding how he could represent Soviet culture abroad when so many of his compositions were forbidden at home. Boldly, he put the issue to Stalin. "How do you mean forbidden?" Stalin asked in turn. "Forbidden by whom?" Shostakovich named the responsible authority—Glavrepertkom. Stalin told him there must have been a mistake and that nothing prevented performances of his music.

Later that day, the Council of Ministers of the U.S.S.R. not only rescinded the ban on "formalist" works but reprimanded Glavrepertkom for its mistake. The document was signed by Stalin himself. Shostakovich wrote another letter of thanks, saying, "You supported me very much." He could breathe again, he told one of his students.

Yet Shostakovich achieved this sense of security only by splitting his creative persona down the middle. In his propaganda works, he assumed an optimistic mask, though the smile was halfhearted. Already in 1948, Khrennikov was sufficiently impressed by Shostakovich's film score for *The Young Guard* that in a year-end review of the activities of the accused formalists he placed Shostakovich in the "most successful" category. (Prokofiev, on the other hand, was condemmed for his latest, last, and worst opera, *Story of a Real Man*.) Even more humiliatingly effective was the music for *The Fall of Berlin*, which one film scholar has called the "ultimate Stalinist film." One can only guess what passed through the composer's head when he sat down to score a scene of Stalin cultivating trees in his garden—an image that was possibly intended to recall God walking in Eden.

In a slew of patriotic cantatas and mass songs, Shostakovich kept recycling gestures from the Fifth Symphony's finale. The ending of *Song of the Forests* (1949) catalogs the glories of the motherland, Stalin chief among them: at the words "Glory to the wise Stalin" the timpani begin pounding in fourths while the brass play a stepwise rising fanfare. In *The Sun Shines Over Our Motherland* (1952), the timpani fourths are cued to the word "*Communisti*." Shostakovich almost certainly felt shame at having to parody himself in this fashion. According to his pupil Galina Ustvolskaya, after the premiere of *Song of the Forests* he collapsed on a bed and burst into tears.

The "other Shostakovich" was a gnomic, cryptic, secretly impassioned figure who spoke through chamber music (twelve string quartets from 1948 on), piano music (the epic cycle of Twenty-four Preludes and Fugues), and songs. The string quartet became his favorite medium: it gave him the freedom to write labyrinthine narratives full of blankly winding fugues, near-motionless funeral marches, wry displays of folkish jollity, off-kilter genre exercises, and stretches of deliberate blandness. One of the composer's favorite modes might be called "dance on the gallows"—a galumphing, almost polka-like number that suggests a solitary figure facing death with inexplicable glee. Just such an image appears in Robert Burns's poem "McPherson's Farewell," which Shostakovich set to music in the 1942 cycle *Six Romances on Texts of W. Raleigh, R. Burns, and W. Shakespeare*. The setting of Shakespeare's Sonnet 66 comes close to delivering a direct commentary on the situation of art under Stalin:

And art made tongue-tied by authority,
And folly doctor-like controlling skill,
And simple truth miscall'd simplicity,
And captive good attending captain ill . . .

Interestingly, four years before the Nazi invasion, the German writer Lion Feuchtwanger visited the Soviet Union and produced a tract titled *Moscow 1937*. It contained an apologia for the purge trials, and Stalin had it reprinted in mass quantities. In one section, though, Feuchtwanger ventured mild criticism of Soviet censorship of the arts. Among other things, he wrote, "an extraordinarily good opera was banned." Set off in the margins were the words "And art made tongue-tied by authority."

Only after Stalin was gone did Shostakovich try to reunite his divided selves. The Tenth Symphony, written in the summer and fall of 1953, in the months following Stalin's death, might communicate, like the Fifth, all that the composer had "thought and felt" in recent years. In the last movement, Shostakovich seems to be trying to talk himself into writing a positive, life-goes-on conclusion, but the celebration becomes hysterical and overwrought. The self-referential D S C H theme sounds so often that it becomes a cliché, an obnoxious jingle. Rapid up-and-down flourishes in the winds and strings echo the march movement of Tchaikovsky's *Pathétique*, another somber-minded composer's attempt at joy. Underneath, the timpani punch out D S C H one last time, the tones dissolving in a blur.

The musicologist Marina Sabinina linked this ending to Shostakovich's account of his speech at the 1948 conference, in which he compared himself to a "cut-out paper doll on a string." She writes, "This motif sounds strange and mechanical, lifeless but persistent, just as if the composer had, with terror and revulsion, seen himself as a puppet." She connected that scene to an anecdote about Gogol—the author's "habit of long and continuous self-contemplation in front of a mirror, when, completely self-absorbed, he would repeatedly call out his own name with a sense of alienation and revulsion." Still, the puppet survives, even enjoys a kind of victory. Perhaps this is how Shostakovich felt when the news of Stalin's death reached him.

The long-awaited announcement was made on the morning of March 6, 1953. Moscow promptly dissolved into chaos: thousands of people swarmed around the Hall of Columns, where Stalin's corpse was on view, and several hundred were trampled to death. So momentous was the news that *Pravda* did not bother to report for another five days the fact that Sergei Prokofiev had also passed away. Sviatoslav Richter heard the news of Prokofiev's death while flying back to Moscow to perform at Stalin's funeral; he was the only passenger on a plane filled with wreaths.

About thirty people showed up to bid Prokofiev farewell. The Beethoven Quartet was instructed to play Tchaikovsky, although Prokofiev never liked Tchaikovsky; the quartet then disappeared into the mob to play the same music for Stalin. The hearse was not allowed near Prokofiev's house, so the coffin had to be moved by hand, through and around streets that were blocked by crowds and tanks. As the masses moved toward the Hall of Columns along one avenue, Prokofiev's body was carried in the opposite direction down an empty street.

Shostakovich was among the mourners. He and Prokofiev had grown closer in the preceding years, especially since 1948. Prokofiev's final scores, more tentative in construction but still pulsing with lyric power, fascinated Shostakovich as he set about finding new paths for his own music. In October 1952, after the premiere of Prokofiev's Seventh Symphony, a gentle, wistful withdrawal from the world, Shostakovich sent along a touching and unusually direct letter of congratulation: "I wish you at least another hundred years to live and create. Listening to such works as your Seventh Symphony makes it much easier and more joyful to live." Five months later, he was photographed standing over Prokofiev's body, his face inscrutable and blank.

8

MUSIC FOR ALL

Music in FDR's America

In 1934, Arnold Schoenberg moved to California, bought a Ford sedan, and declared, "I was driven into Paradise." By the beginning of the forties, when the Soviet Union, Nazi Germany, and their respective satellites controlled Europe from Madrid to Warsaw, crowds of cultural luminaries sought refuge in the United States, and they were greeted by a significant irony. Europeans had long depicted America as a wilderness of vulgarity; the cult of the dollar had driven Gustav Mahler to an early grave, or so his widow claimed. Now, with Europe in the grip of totalitarianism, America had unexpectedly become the last hope of civilization. The impresario and Zionist activist Meyer Weisgal, in a telegram to the Austrian director Max Reinhardt, put it this way: "IF HITLER DOESN'T WANT YOU I'LL TAKE YOU." Many leading composers of the early twentieth century—Schoenberg, Stravinsky, Bartók, Rachmaninov, Weill, Milhaud, Hindemith, Krenek, and Eisler, among others—settled in the United States. Entire artistic communities of Paris, Berlin, and the former St. Petersburg reconstituted themselves in neighborhoods of New York and Los Angeles. Alma Mahler was herself among the refugees; she escaped the German invasion of France by hiking across the Pyrenees with her latest husband, Franz Werfel, and by the end of 1940 she was living on Los Tilos Road in the Hollywood Hills.

That such disparate personalities as the White Russian Stravinsky and the hard-core Communist Eisler could feel temporarily at home in America was a tribute to the inclusive spirit of Franklin Delano Roosevelt, who served as president from 1933 until his death in 1945. A patrician with a populist flair, Roosevelt embodied what came to be known as the "middlebrow" vision of American culture—the idea that democratic capitalism operating at full tilt could still accommodate high culture of the European variety.

Back in 1915, the critic Van Wyck Brooks had complained that America was caught in a false dichotomy between "highbrow" and "lowbrow," between "academic pedantry and pavement slang." He called for a middle-ground culture that would fuse intellectual substance with communicative power. In the thirties, the middlebrow became something like a national pastime: symphonic music was broadcast on the radio, literary properties furnished plots for Hollywood A pictures, novels by Thomas Mann and other émigrés were disseminated through the Book-of-the-Month Club.

The influx of European genius coincided with an upsurge of native composition. Pay no heed to the muses of Europe, Ralph Waldo Emerson had told American artists and intellectuals in 1837; by the 1940s the muses were studying for U.S. citizenship exams, and young American composers had found their voice. Aaron Copland wrote music in praise of the Wild West, Abraham Lincoln, rodeos, and Mexican saloons. Alongside Samuel Barber, Roy Harris, Marc Blitzstein, and other more or less like-minded colleagues, Copland reached out to a new mass public with the aid of radio, recording, and film, and, surprisingly, the U.S. government itself. The Works Progress Administration, inaugurated in 1935, launched an ambitious scheme of federal arts projects, and some ninety-five million people were said to have attended presentations by the Federal Music Project over a two-and-a-half-year period. The democratic masses were evidently taking hold of an art that had long been the property of the elite.

Hence the exhilaration that Blitzstein felt in 1936, when he wrote an article titled "Coming—the Mass Audience!" for the magazine *Modern Music*: "The great mass of people enter at last the field of serious music. Radio is responsible, the talkies, the summer concerts, a growing appetite, a hundred things; really the fact of an art and a world in progress. You can no more stop it than you can stop an avalanche."

The mass audience came, but it did not remain. No sooner had classical music entered the mainstream arena than it began to face insurmountable obstacles. One problem was political. Populists of Blitzstein's type subscribed not just to the vaguely social-democratic rhetoric of Roosevelt's New Deal but also to the semi-Communistic doctrines of the Popular Front. When the New Deal came under political attack in 1938, Roosevelt promptly retreated, letting the federal arts projects collapse, and suddenly the picture was a lot less pretty.

There was the deeper problem of classical music's true place in American culture. At some level Americans did not seem to believe that a Europe-based art form could speak for their condition; to most, Duke Ellington or Benny Goodman was a more convincing musical answer to Emerson's demand for an American Scholar. Yet Copland and others of his generation succeeded in forging sounds so charged with patriotic feeling that they endure in movies and the media today. During the Depression and the Second World War, classical music, whether in the form of Beethoven symphonies or Copland ballets, encapsulated America's we're-all-in-this-together spirit; it showed how individual efforts could be pooled together in a "common discipline," as Roosevelt said in his inaugural speech of 1933. That music has not lost its binding power. Whenever the American dream suffers a catastrophic setback, Barber's Adagio for Strings plays on the radio.

Radio Music

Three major technological advances altered the musical landscape from the twenties onward. First, electrical recording allowed for sound quality of unprecedented richness and dynamic range. Second, radio transmission allowed for the live broadcast of music coast to coast. Third, sound was added to motion pictures. Common to all these breakthroughs was the innovation of the microphone, which had the effect of freeing classical music from the elite concert halls in which it had long been confined, and, consequently, from the domain of city dwellers and the wealthy. The millions whom Beethoven longed to embrace in his "Ode to Joy" showed up in the Hooper ratings—up to ten million for Arturo Toscanini's broadcasts with the NBC Symphony, and millions more for the Metropolitan Opera broadcasts.

Electrical recording set off a rush to rerecord the classics of the orchestral repertory. Leopold Stokowski and his Philadelphia Orchestra led the way with a disc of Saint-Saëns's *Danse macabre* in July 1925. Toscanini was not far behind, and with the publicity machine of the radio-recording conglomerate of NBC and RCA behind him he would go on to sell some twenty million records. NBC's first nationwide radio broadcast took place in November 1926; it carried a concert by the New York Symphony under the direction of Walter Damrosch, a genial conductor and lecturer who was to become a radio star in his own right. A rival network, CBS, inaugurated its existence in 1927 with Deems Taylor's opera *The King's Henchman*. Sound film created new careers for a host of composers, who fleshed out on-screen action with orchestral brouhaha. Contrary to legend, Al Jolson's cry of "Wait a minute! You ain't heard nothin' yet!" was not America's first experience of the power of sound film; in 1926, Warner Brothers created a nationwide sensation by releasing a film of *Don Juan* with rousing synchronized accompaniment by the New York Philharmonic.

To some extent, the radio vogue for classical music was imposed on the American public from above. One reason for the trend was utilitarian: the networks feared a government takeover of the radio industry, and by broadcasting classical music they could make a gesture toward "public service" and thus stave off the threat. Another reason was cultural: radio and record-company executives were naturally inclined to support classical programming, whether or not audience surveys demanded it. Many were émigrés or the first-generation offspring of immigrant families, and they considered Beethoven and Tchaikovsky a birthright. The radio pioneer David Sarnoff, who grew up in the same New York Russian-Jewish communities that produced George Gershwin, had declared back in 1915 that one of the advantages of the "radio music box" was that rural listeners would be able to enjoy symphonies by the fireplace. By 1921 Sarnoff had become general manager of the Radio Corporation of America, and five years later he created NBC. All along, he insisted that radio should aspire to class and culture. "I regard radio as a sort of cleansing instrument for the mind," he once said, "just as the bathtub is for the body."

Yet, even without the prompting of the radio executives, Americans of the period avidly sought the cultural improvement that classical music was presumed to provide. The middlebrow ideal was to be sophisticated without being pretentious, worldly but not effete, and classical music with an American accent fit the bill. NBC's "Blue" network might carry Ohio State versus Indiana one afternoon and a Lotte Lehmann recital the next. Benny Goodman recorded both Mozart and swing. The classically trained composer Morton Gould appeared on radio as the star of the *Cresta Blanca Carnival*, and Harold Shapero switched between swing arrangements and neoclassical composition. Alan Shulman, a cellist in the NBC Symphony, composed "serious" works, joined an NBC jazz ensemble called New Friends of Rhythm ("Toscanini's Hep Cats," they were called), and mentored the master pop arranger Nelson Riddle.

There was no bigger star of radio than Toscanini himself, whom Sarnoff introduced to the national NBC audience on Christmas Day 1937. At the close of the first season, the *New York Times* editorialized ponderously that "Wagner, Beethoven, Bach, Sibelius, Brahms are made manifest in many a remote farmhouse and in many a plain home." Sarnoff's radio idyll was complete.

The trouble was that Toscanini could not make classical music American. As the *Times*'s list of names suggested, the Maestro's canon was focused on European composers and stopped short of the present, Sibelius having fallen silent. During his tenure with the New York Philharmonic, from 1926 to 1936, Toscanini had ignored American music week after week, conducting only six native works in ten years. He evinced little interest in living composers of any nationality, apart from a few Italians whom he knew personally. At NBC, his taste broadened slightly, and a smattering of American pieces—Roy Harris's Third Symphony, Copland's *El Salón México*, Barber's Adagio for Strings, and Gershwin's *An American in Paris*, among others—appeared on his programs. On a typical night, though, Beethoven and Brahms prevailed.

Two other celebrity conductors—Leopold Stokowski, who served briefly as co-conductor of the NBC Symphony, and Serge Koussevitzky, who led the Boston Symphony—treated new and American works far more respectfully. "Dee next Beethoven vill from Colorado come," Koussevitzky declared. By the end of his twenty-five-year reign in Boston, the Russian émigré had hosted an astounding 85 premieres of American scores and 195 American works altogether. He also commissioned such international masterpieces as Stravinsky's *Symphony of Psalms*, Bartók's

Concerto for Orchestra, Benjamin Britten's *Peter Grimes*, and Olivier Messiaen's *Turangalîla Symphony*. Stokowski, who had promoted Edgard Varèse and other ultra-moderns back in the twenties, introduced two big new Schoenberg works, the Violin Concerto and the Piano Concerto. Between them, Stokowski and Koussevitzky created much of the core repertory of the mid-twentieth century. Yet they failed to stimulate the radio executives and the corporate heads who bought advertising. Stokowski's advocacy of new music reportedly alarmed the higher-ups at General Motors, which had begun sponsoring the NBC Symphony. A few months after the premiere of Schoenberg's Piano Concerto, it was announced that Stokowski's contract would not be renewed, and composers lost their most forceful advocate.

Theodor Adorno and Virgil Thomson, the same dyspeptic duo who tried to stamp out Sibelius, mocked the cult of Toscanini, Walter Damrosch's music-appreciation lectures for children, and other instances of classical hype in the thirties. If their diatribes were egregiously snooty in tone—"It is highly doubtful," Adorno sniffed, "if the boy in the subway whistling the main theme of the finale of Brahms's First Symphony actually has been gripped by that music"—the critique of the middlebrow mentality sometimes hit home. The classical conglomerates, Thomson noted, confined themselves to a repertory of fifty masterpieces, because they were the easiest to sell. Yet the failure to support the new led inexorably to the decline of classical music as a popular pastime, for nothing bound it to contemporary life. A venerable art form was set to become one more passing fad in a ravenous consumer culture.

Young Copland

Aaron Copland hardly looked the part of the Great American Composer. He was a tall, wiry man with an angular, bespectacled face, resembling an awkward office clerk in a Hollywood genre picture. He was the son of Russian-Jewish immigrants; he was an ardent leftist; he was gay. Yet he had a plausible claim to the evanescent mythology of the frontier and the Wild West. In the late nineteenth century, his maternal grandfather, Aaron Mittenthal, operated an emporium in Dallas, near such outfits as W. R. Hinckley's tin shop and Ott & Pfaffle's gun store. According to family legend, Mittenthal once hired the outlaw Frank James, brother of the famous Jesse James.

Copland heard stories of the West, but he spent his childhood in Brooklyn. His father ran a department store at the corner of Dean Street and Washington Avenue, and the family lived above it. Copland later described the neighborhood as "simply drab" and claimed that he had received no musical stimulus from it, although he could hardly have been unaffected by the diverse clamor of popular and classical airs that enlivened any Brooklyn or Manhattan block at the turn of the century.

Copland's background was, as it happens, very similar to George Gershwin's. Both were Brooklyn-born, a little over two years apart. Both were Russian-Jewish in origin. Both studied composition with a man named Rubin Goldmark. And they haunted the same locales in their youth; Gershwin attended recitals at Wanamaker's department store, while Copland made his debut there in 1917. Copland noted some of the similarities in his memoirs, but said that no personal bond formed between them: "When we were finally face to face at some party, with the opportunity for conversation, we found nothing to say to each other!" Each may have envied the other's advantages—Copland's intellectual acclaim, Gershwin's fame and wealth.

While Gershwin developed his craft in the back rooms of Tin Pan Alley, Copland followed more conventional avenues of European study. In 1921, at the age of twenty, he attended the American Conservatory in Fontainebleau, outside Paris, and plunged into the carnival of twenties styles. Walking through the city on his first day, he saw a poster for the Swedish Ballet and found himself sitting through Cocteau's absurdist ballet *Les Mariés de la Tour Eiffel*, with music by five of Les Six. Over the next three years he showed impeccable taste in concertgoing, attending the first nights of Milhaud's *Creation of the World* and Stravinsky's *Les Noces*, Koussevitzky's performances of Stravinsky's Octet and Honegger's *Pacific 231*, and the Paris premiere of *Pierrot lunaire*. At the Shakespeare and Company bookstore he timidly approached James Joyce to ask about a musical passage in *Ulysses*. All told, he was very much in the middle of the action, although he observed more than he participated; it was his fellow student Virgil Thomson who danced all night at Le Boeuf sur le Toit.

Copland's teacher was the organist, composer, and pedagogue Nadia

Boulanger, who honed the compositional skills of half the major American composers of the rising generation—Copland, Thomson, Harris, and Blitzstein, among others. Through Boulanger, Copland absorbed the aesthetics of the twenties—the revolt against Germanic grandiosity, the yen for lucidity and grace, the cultivation of Baroque and Classical forms. She preached, in other words, the gospel according to Igor Stravinsky. If you were to take a Stravinsky score such as the Octet or the *Symphonies of Wind Instruments*, loosen up the tightly controlled structure, and insert a few melodies of the New England hymnal or urban-jazzy type, you would have the beginnings of a Copland work such as *Billy the Kid* or *Appalachian Spring*. The entire style is implicit in the "Pastorale" of *Histoire du soldat*.

In 1923 Boulanger did Copland the gigantic favor of introducing him to Koussevitzky, who, she had heard, would be taking over the Boston Symphony the following season. After hearing Copland bang out his *Cortège macabre* on the piano (Prokofiev happened to be in the room as well), Koussevitzky proposed that Copland write a work for organ and orchestra, with Boulanger as soloist. Walter Damrosch also promised the young composer a place on his New York Symphony concerts. Thus, Copland's Organ Symphony was booked for performances in both New York and Boston—a sensational send-off for a composer aged twenty-four. The symphony begins in an atmosphere of spacious mystery, with a sweet, ambiguous flute melody unfolding over sustained notes on the viola. The ending is all action and gesture and dancing motion; the solo instrument begins to sound less like the voice of God and more like an organ at a fairground. The journey from nocturnal meditation to communal celebration brings to mind Ives's American idylls, but Copland executes his design with a clarity and an economy that do credit to his French training.

Copland showed an uncommon flair for the lowlier arts of organization and publicity. He recognized that composers would make little headway with the public unless they formed a common front, as Les Six had done in Paris. "The day of the neglected American composer is over," he wrote in 1926. The announcement had been made before, but Copland made it stick. He helped design Koussevitzky's epoch-making American programming in Boston and also became the dominant figure in the League of Composers, which had formed as an alternative to the modernist-minded, racially bigoted International Composers' Guild. (Carl Ruggles promptly dubbed the league a "filthy bunch of Juilliard Jews.") With Roger Sessions, another Brooklyn-born music fiend, Copland developed the Copland-Sessions Concerts, which tried to bridge the gap between modernist and populist camps. A spirit of camaraderie and derring-do broke out among younger American composers. Virgil Thomson later fondly called this group Copland's "commando unit."

Copland acquired a degree of notoriety with two jazz-inflected works, the *Music for the Theatre* of 1925 and the Piano Concerto of 1926. Although his comprehension of jazz went not too much deeper than that of his Parisian contemporaries ("It began, I suppose, on some negro's dull tomtom in Africa," he wrote), he did send a strong rhythmic jolt into American concert music. The jabbing, bluesy riffs of the Piano Concerto point the way to Leonard Bernstein's *West Side Story*, while the climactic theme of *Music for the Theatre*'s "Burlesque" sounds like Jerome Kern's "Ol' Man River," written two years later. As Copland's biographer Howard Pollack observes, the racy hint of striptease in the title can also be felt in the raucous, how-ya-doin'-honey orchestration.

Having "done" jazz, Copland moved on to the dissonant high modern. His *Piano Variations* of 1930 is a monolithic masterpiece that threatens to surpass the ultra-modern school of Varèse and Ruggles in the relentlessness of its attack. It is based on a broadly gesticulating four-note motif—E, C, D-sharp, C-sharp an octave above—that Copland probably extracted from the slow movement of Stravinsky's Octet. The theme is subjected to an astringent sequence of permutations that at times approaches twelve-tone writing. By the end, the music is heading in a tonal direction: grand triads of A major and E major ring out in the treble, though with sharp dissonances attached. A new American harmony, brash and bluesy, grows from primordial chaos.

Copland's early works won raves from progressive critics. Paul Rosenfeld, Varèse's celebrant, called them "harsh and solemn, like the sentences of brooding rabbis." But brooding did not pay the bills. In 1938, Pollack tells us, the composer's checking account contained $6.93, and he was asking himself whether he should seek refuge in academia. He continued to struggle with feelings of spiritual hollowness, of social irrelevance. "I might force myself a little," he wrote in his diary in 1927, contemplating the possibility of getting drunk. "My everpresent fear is that by thinking that I know myself, i.e. my normal self completely, I may circumscribe whatever latent possibilities I may have." On Christmas Day of 1930 he wrote: "How does one deepen one's experience of life. That is a problem that interests me deeply. Would serving as dish washer for a week help—or doing a term in prison? Or the Gurdjieff Method?" Copland soon found an answer to these nagging questions: his spiritual plunge, his drunken adventure, would take the form of leftist politics.

Popular Front Music

On October 24, 1929, Wall Street posted nine billion dollars of losses in a few hours, and the Great Depression began. The economic collapse staggered America's urban elites, but it came as no great shock to farmers and agricultural workers, who had remained ungilt during the Gilded Age and had not roared during the Roaring Twenties.

Most rural Americans were still part of an agrarian society, functioning largely without indoor plumbing and electricity. Back in the final years of the nineteenth century, resentment against the powers that be had spawned the People's or Populist Party, which mixed utopian socialism with religious revivalism and old-fashioned demagoguery. Populism was the first effective progressive movement in American politics, even though it never caught fire at the national level. Crucial to its rhetoric was a sacralization of the heartland and the Wild West, where, it was thought, a pure American spirit had resisted the encroachments of industrial capitalism. Populism entered the mainstream with the onset of the Depression, altering the vocabulary of urban intellectuals and Democratic politicians. Roosevelt, in his first inaugural speech, mimicked Populist jargon when he decried the "practices of the unscrupulous money changers" and demanded "a better use of the land for those best fitted for the land."

According to polls, one quarter of the American people wanted a socialist government and another quarter had an "open mind" about the prospect. Such statistics gave Moscow the idea that America was ripe for the plucking. In the 1932 presidential campaign, William Foster and James Ford ran as the first serious Communist Party candidates. Ford was also the first African-American to appear on a presidential ticket, the Communist International having determined that blacks were instrumental to the cause. Many in the Harlem Renaissance intelligentsia, Duke Ellington included, committed themselves to Communism to a greater or lesser degree. But the Communist vote in 1932 was meager; for America, Roosevelt was radical enough.

In the mid-thirties a new directive went forth from Moscow: Western Communists should find common ground with other leftist groups, the better to insinuate themselves into positions of power. From the order stemmed the Popular Front, which bound together various parties of the left around a limited set of pro-union, anti-fascist, anti-racist positions. The American Communist Party, under the leadership of Earl Browder, adopted the slogan "Communism is twentieth-century Americanism." Such formulations charmed the gentler spirits in the Popular Front coalition—those who envisaged a gradual interpenetration of Soviet and American values rather than an overthrow of the government. Michael Denning, in his book *The Cultural Front*, argues that Popular Fronters manipulated the Soviets as much as the Soviets manipulated them. Americans are said to have drawn on the intellectual resources of the Soviet cause—and on its finances—while pursuing their own agenda.

Still, the Popular Front was in many ways a shut-in, fanatical world, faithfully replicating the worst of the Soviet mind-set. Ideologues encouraged conformity and discouraged dissent, even if it meant denouncing yesterday's conformity as dissent and vice versa. Most American Communists refused to acknowledge the violence of Stalin's regime, even when evidence of it was placed in front of them. After Shostakovich was denounced in 1936, the *New Masses* reporter Joshua Kunitz quoted the soothing words of a young Communist: "Don't worry. There'll be no blood, no prisons, no ruin and no darkness. The fellows who deserve it will be criticized—that's all." (Kunitz retailed these rationalizations in a lecture to New Yorkers that May: "The Truth About Shostakovich," followed by refreshments and dancing.) Others knew of the violence and chose simply to accept it. Back in 1933, *New Masses* had invited its readers to ask themselves this ominous question: "Based not on my words, or thoughts, but on the day-to-day acts of my life, would the working-class leaders of the future American Soviet Government be justified in putting me in a responsible job—or in a prison camp for class enemies?" At its most frightening, American Communism exhibited a kind of voluntary self-repression.

The man in charge of coordinating international Communist activity in the musical area was Hanns Eisler. The firebrand of pre-Nazi Berlin was now hailed by the *Daily Worker* as the "foremost revolutionary composer . . . beloved of all the masses of every country." As chairman of the International Music Bureau of the Comintern, Eisler visited America twice in 1935, lecturing in New York at the New School for Social Research and at Town Hall. The latter appearance shook up the local composers, Copland and Blitzstein included. Eisler informed them that modern composers had become nothing more than luxury tools of the capitalist system—"dealers in narcotics"—and that if they wished to break out of their prison they would have to fulfill a new social function. They were told to abandon purely instrumental music for more "useful" forms—workers' songs, workers' choruses, socially critical theater pieces. In another lecture Eisler stated bluntly that "the modern composer must change *from a parasite into a fighter*."

Charles Seeger and his wife Ruth Crawford, two exemplary leftist composers, so feared the sin of formalism that they nearly barred themselves from composing altogether. Seeger, who came from old New England stock, began as an Ivesian modernist, formulating a method of "dissonant counterpoint" that spread widely among the ultra-modern composers. His best disciple was Crawford, a young Chicago-based composer, who began studying with him in late 1929 and fell in love with him not long after. This earnest, self-deprecating woman went on to write some of the most fabulously byzantine music of her time. In *String Quartet 1931*, orderings of pitch, rhythm, durations, and dynamics anticipate avant-garde music of the post–World War II era; in *Chant 3*, a women's chorus is divided into twelve parts, each assigned a separate chromatic note and shifting through a variety of polyrhythms. Even as she indulged in these experiments, Crawford gave strong narrative shape to her material. The slow movement of the Quartet unfurls as a continuous wave of sound, its complexities concealed behind a softly shimmering exterior.

Ruth and Charles were married in 1932, and around the same time they fell under the influence of Communist ideology. Charles helped to found a new organization called the Composers' Collective, wrote a column for the *Daily Worker*, and penned a song titled "Lenin! Who's That Guy." Most important, he undertook to collect American folk songs in league with the father-son team of John and Alan Lomax, who were in the process of recording traditional music in the South and West.

Judith Tick's biography of Ruth Crawford Seeger movingly records the stages by which this gifted composer gave up her urge to create. She worked for a while on a second quartet, which was to have blended modern techniques with folk sources in a "combination of simplicity and complexity," but it never materialized. Her confidence sapped by her husband's neolithic belief that "women can't compose symphonies," she devoted herself instead to meticulous folk-song transcriptions. Her work appeared in two Lomax anthologies, *Our Singing Country* and *Folk Song USA*, which became bibles of the postwar folk-song revival (one of whose leaders was her stepson Pete). Only after the war did she regain interest in composition, completing in 1952 a Suite for Wind Quintet. But cancer claimed her the following year. Thus ended the career of one of the few major women composers of the early twentieth century.

Copland had been leaning leftward since his days playing piano at the Finnish Socialist Union. On European trips in 1927 and 1929 he encountered *Mahagonny Songspiel* and *The Threepenny Opera*, and fell to thinking about how a composer could combine social critique with mass appeal. Later, in 1930 and 1931, he attended the first meetings of Harold Clurman's Group Theatre in New York, which included among its regular collaborators such theater notables as Clifford Odets, Maxwell Anderson, Lee Strasberg, Stella Adler, and Elia Kazan. Copland, who had been Clurman's roommate back in the Paris days, became a stalwart of the Group Theatre, finding space for meetings, identifying potential donors, and offering financial support from his own almost empty pockets.

There was a Communist cell within the Group Theatre, but most members understood the project in largely aesthetic terms, as a corrective to the intellectual flight from society. Odets, who made his breakthrough with the pro-union play *Waiting for Lefty* in 1935, was obsessed with the figure of Beethoven, who represented for him not only the triumph of genius but also the tragedy of isolation. "[Beethoven] was the first great individualist in art," Odets wrote. "Today we are locked in a death grip with our individualities and coming back to a social thing again. Call it Communism, call it Group Theatre, call it the life of farms, but artists are coming back to the truth of root things, fundamentals again."

Political themes infiltrated Copland's scores in the early and mid-thirties. The ballet *Hear Ye! Hear Ye!* (1934) uses a distorted version of "The Star-Spangled Banner" to convey, in Copland's words, "the corruption of legal systems and courts of law." Clurman plausibly heard the orchestral piece *Statements* (1935) as a portrait of Depression-era America, with a Shostakovich-like scherzo movement ("Jingo") mocking the shallow chauvinism of the Roaring Twenties. The movement "Dogmatic" quotes the *Piano Variations*, blasting out the main motif as if it were a slogan in a demonstration. Around this time, Charles Seeger observed happily that Copland had moved "from ivory tower to within hailing distance of the proletariat." During a trip to Minnesota in the summer of 1934, Copland walked into the proletariat's midst, speaking at a full-blown political rally for the Communist Party of the U.S.A. As he described it in a letter to a friend:

> We learned to know the farmers who were Reds around these parts, attended an all-day election campaign meeting of the C.P. unit, partook of their picnic supper and made my first political speech! If they were a strange sight to me, I was no less of a one to them. It was the first time that many of them had seen an "intellectual." I was being gradually drawn, you see, into the political struggle with the peasantry! I wish you could have seen them—the true Third Estate, the very material that makes revolution . . . When S. K. Davis, Communist candidate for Gov. in Minn. came to town and spoke in the public park, the farmers asked me to talk to the crowd. Its [*sic*] one thing to think revolution, or talk about it to ones [*sic*] friends, but to preach it from the streets—OUT LOUD—Well, I made my speech (Victor says it was a good one) and I'll probably never be the same!

This tale has a quality of make-believe. It is an extravagant fulfillment of Copland's old notion of "getting real" by washing dishes. The exhortation of the peasantry reeks of big-city condescension; the "people" remain an airy abstraction. All the same, Copland emerged from such political dabblings charged with purpose.

Crucial to Copland's transformation were his adventures south of the border, in Mexico. He first went there in 1932, at the invitation of the Mexican composer Carlos Chávez, and appreciated the adulation that Chávez and others offered him. "At last I have found a country where I am as famous as Gershwin!!" he wrote to the Koussevitzkys. The National Revolutionary Party, which held power, was hardly a paragon of democratic thought, but its cultural departments did advance the socialist program of bringing art to the masses, along the lines of Kestenberg's initiatives in Berlin and Lunacharsky's in Russia. José Vasconcelos, the Mexican minister of public education from 1921 to 1924, commissioned Diego Rivera and other Mexican painters to create murals of workers, peasants, and other real-life heroes. Their counterparts in composition were the crisply disciplined Chávez, who based his laconic modal melodies on Amerindian folk music, and his more disorderly colleague Silvestre Revueltas, who fell victim to alcoholism just as he was attaining mastery. Revueltas's 1939 work *La noche de los Mayas*, originally conceived as a film score, has found a second life as a Mahlerian symphonic canvas, moving from purposefully kitschy dance episodes to stretches of openhearted Romantic lamentation and on to a scary Mayan bacchanal that spills over into polyrhythmic mayhem.

Galvanized by the Mexican scene, Copland began sketching the tone poem *El Salón México*, which, six years later, gave him his long-sought popular breakthrough. *El Salón* is richly stocked with Mexican melody and dance rhythm. At the same time, it retains the rhetorical punch of the composer's early modernist scores. As Michael Tilson Thomas has pointed out, the jaunty, upward-leaping figures at the beginning of *El Salón* look back to passages in the *Piano Variations*. Similarly, oratorical quarter-note utterances for the trombones and horns in the closing pages recall the craggy fanfares that set in motion the late-twenties *Symphonic Ode*. Such gestures serve to defamiliarize folkish material, take it out of the realm of rearranged cliché. As the historian Elizabeth Crist writes, *El Salón* is a utopian attempt to synthesize pre- and postindustrial cultures, "rural peasants and the urban proletariat." Crist adds that when the music is divorced from its political context it devolves into a simplistic essay in musical exoticism, which is how it now sounds at pops concerts.

Back in New York, Copland edged into more direct forms of musical activism. He hung around the edges of the Composers' Collective and tried his hand at Hanns Eisler–style "workers' music." In 1934, in response to a competition sponsored by *New Masses*, he set a poem by Alfred Hayes titled "Into the Streets May First," which contained the lines "Shake the midtown towers / Crash the downtown air." The Daily Worker Chorus essayed the song at the second American Workers' Music Olympiad, alongside performances by the Pierre Degeyter Symphonietta and orchestras of balalaikas and mandolins. The olympiad was organized by the American chapter of the International Music Bureau, Eisler's outfit.

This was as far as Copland would go. He never joined the Communist Party, and advised his younger colleague David Diamond not to do so. He rejected the idea that a good leftist American composer should be a "plain unpretentious person," as Seeger put it, accompanying himself on a banjo. In a 1935 essay in the Communist-funded periodical *Music Vanguard*, Copland showed that his interest lay more in finding a clear, communicative musical style than in transmitting political content: "Those young people who just a few years ago were writing pieces filled with the *weltschmerz* of a Schoenberg now realize that they were merely picturing their own discontent and that the small audience which existed for Schoenberg's music could never be stretched to include their own. Let these young people say to themselves once and for all, 'No more Schoenberg.'" That last slogan had little chance of seizing the attention of the workers of the world. Copland was conducting a conversation with himself in public, and, tellingly, his flirtation with radical activism ended when he found the style—and the deeper experience of life—that he had long been seeking.

The first section of the ballet score *Billy the Kid* is called "The Open Prairie," a phrase that has become synonymous with Copland's populist or Americana style. Woodwind figures in rough-hewn parallel fifths cut across an emptied-out musical space, conjuring the picture of a wagon train moving across some long, dusty valley of the West. Yet the music comes straight out of the Parisian Stravinsky. Keening lines for high clarinets and low oboe echo the "Spring Rounds" section of the *Rite of Spring*, as do some folkish grace notes that are added later. Copland delighted in pointing out that "The Open Prairie," or "The Open Prairee," as he initially spelled it, was written in an apartment on the rue de Rennes. Indeed, there is nothing intrinsically American about such sounds; they could just as well be used to suggest the English countryside or the Russian steppes. Still, they do create the illusion of a wide expanse, American or otherwise. Later, a liberal sprinkling of cowboy melodies—"Great Granddad," "Whoopee Ti Yi Yo, Git Along Little Dogies," "The Old Chisholm Trail," and so on—makes the Wild West association explicit.

Billy the Kid commemorates the legendary outlaw William Bonney, who, it was said, stole from the rich, befriended the poor, charmed the ladies, and killed twenty-one men. Earl Browder, the Communist Party chief, liked to portray the America of the revolutionary period as a kind of proto-socialist utopia; the first pages of *Billy the Kid*, likewise, evoke America in a prelapsarian state, before the loss of innocence under capitalism. When the cowboy melodies are first heard, they meet up in out-of-whack polyrhythms: Copland's West sounds rather like his Mexico. Yet this prairie Eden is threatened by the westward movement of city-building settlers, whose grand designs already glimmer in the brassy climax of the introductory "processional." Eugene Loring, the choreographer, based his scenario on a semimythical chronicle by the Chicago journalist Walter Noble Burns, who painted Billy as a good-hearted outlaw in rebellion against ruthless capitalist values. The first chapter of Burns's book contrasts Billy's bygone world with a modern America covered in asphalt. Copland hints at the paving of the West at the end of his ballet; after Billy falls victim to Pat Garrett, the pioneer march becomes a juggernaut in three-quarter time, accented by cymbals and bass drum. A new key-area of E major clashes with remnants of the heroic E-flat of the opening. Skycrapers are rising on the prairie, their hard forms glinting in the sun.

Leftist politics runs through other Copland works of this period—the school opera *The Second Hurricane*, which teaches the Brechtian virtue of acquiescing in the common good (though without the scary dogmatism); the CBS commission *Music for Radio: Saga of the Prairie*, which may contain a concealed program about the Scottsboro Boys (nine black youths imprisoned in 1931 on unsubstantiated charges of rape); and the heart-catching *Lincoln Portrait*, which arranges quotations from Lincoln's writings into a vaguely socialistic narrative ("As I would not be a slave, so

I would not be a master"). But the radicalism implicit in these pieces never comes all the way to the surface. Hence, they have been appropriated by all manner of political and nonpolitical parties over the years. Innumerable films, television commercials, news broadcasts, and political campaign ads have used Copland music or Copland-esque imitations to convey the innate goodness of small-town life—elderly couples sitting on porches, newsboys on bicycles, farmers leaning on fences, and so on. By the time of the presidential campaign in 1984, Copland's open-prairie sound had become such a universal quantity that a kitschy version of it was piped into Ronald Reagan's "Morning in America" commercials.

Copland probably never lost sleep over the uses and misuses to which his music was put, although he might have relished the irony of a gay leftist of Russian-Jewish extraction supplying the soundtrack for the Republican Party platform. Pragmatic rather than radical at the core, he wanted to speak for the entire country, even at the expense of diluting his message. In this sense, he was the perfect musical counterpart of the thirty-second president of the United States.

New Deal Music

Culture ranked low among Franklin Delano Roosevelt's priorities. Music hardly registered at all. To the extent that the president supported the arts, it was with an obligatory aristocratic air. As Richard McKinzie has written, "Roosevelt was willing to do the noble thing, and support painting, theater, and other creative arts in the same way he supported them as the 'lord' of Hyde Park manor." Alert to all twitches of the political web, Roosevelt knew the dangers inherent in federal funding of the arts. Only with the support of Eleanor Roosevelt, the adamantly liberal First Lady, did the experiment last as long as it did.

From the beginning Mrs. Roosevelt pushed the idea that the government had "responsibility toward art, and toward artists," as she put it in 1934. Her most significant intervention in music came in 1939, when she resigned from the Daughters of the American Revolution in protest of that organization's refusal to host a concert by the black singer Marian Anderson. That gesture set the stage for Anderson's legendary concert at the Lincoln Memorial, where the program included an arrangement of "Gospel Train" by Dvořák's old associate Harry T. Burleigh.

The New Deal had a mighty impact on the arts for the simple reason that it had a mighty wad of money to spend. Roosevelt dispensed $4.9 billion to relief projects in 1935, whence came the Works Progress Administration, or WPA; of that amount, some $27 million went to the Federal Arts Projects, also called Federal One, and, of this amount, $7,126,862 funded the Federal Music Project, or FMP. At its peak the FMP supported sixteen thousand musicians and operated 125 orchestras, 135 bands, and 32 choral and opera units. Harry Hopkins, the architect of the WPA, hoped that Federal One would become a permanent agency. Eleanor, in her column "My Day," wrote: "When the arts flourished in the old days it was sufficient for an artist to have a rich patron and then to develop under the protection of his important sponsor. All nobles had their pet artists . . . Today, for the most part, this method of developing and protecting art has passed out of existence and I am wondering if the WPA art projects may not take their places."

The challenge for any arts bureaucracy is to make sound decisions about which artists to promote. Federal One, lacking a precedent, tended to fall back on the Ivy League old-boy network and its attendant cultural connections. The earliest New Deal arts initiative, the Public Works of Art Project, came about when Roosevelt's Harvard classmate George Biddle, a left-leaning artist who had consorted with Diego Rivera in Mexico, asked the newly elected president to fund an artistic homage to the New Deal's "social revolution," in the style of the Mexican muralists. Roosevelt showed immediate interest and even laid out some aesthetic precepts in remarks at an exhibition in the spring of 1934. The president said that none of the paintings exhibited a "despondent theme," that they generally avoided "both slavery to classical standards and decadence common to much European art." Stalin and Hitler would have agreed with these sentiments completely; the difference, of course, is that FDR lacked the means, the will, or the desire to enforce them.

The Federal Music Project got under way in July 1935. "Through the program of instruction carried on by the Federal Music Project," a press release for an education program said, "a tremendous, unsuspected hunger for musical knowledge has been disclosed among the children of the underprivileged and the relief population from which the classes are enrolled." In Boston, opera was thrown open to the masses, and a reporter pictured it as a storming of the Bastille: "This was opera for the 4,000,000 and the sign warning, 'Drivers, chauffeurs, footmen not allowed to stand in the vestibule,' might just as well have been draped, for the drivers, chauffeurs, and footmen were occupying the seats of the master and the madame at 83 cents per chair." The New York Police Athletic League reported that singing classes had proved surprisingly popular among juvenile delinquents; the boys were suspicious at first of this "sissy stuff," but soon were singing out at full strength.

Big cities were not the only beneficiaries of the FMP. Live music spread out to rural towns, such as Anadarko, Chickasha, and El Reno in Oklahoma. "For the first time in the history of the state these smaller cities have been able to have symphony concerts at home," wrote the Oklahoma state director. "I wish that I could portray for you a picture of hundreds of school children from rural districts sitting in breathless suspense at a school concert." Another report summons up a scene out of Charles Ives, or, more appositely, Will Marion Cook's "On Emancipation Day":

> The highlight of Music Week Observation for the teaching project was the statewide negro music festival which was held at Boley, the negro metropolis of Oklahoma. An outstanding feature of this festival was a musical parade in which over one thousand pupils participated. Flags, banners, placards and gay streamers added color to the parade which was made doubly interesting by musical selections which were dramatized by choruses and class groups as they marched to the music of three bands.

Large numbers of women played in orchestras for the first time. Dean Dixon, an African-American, was featured in *Time* magazine as a rising WPA conductor.

The FMP also took up the cause of new music, setting up a series called the Composers' Forum-Laboratory, where composers could interact with the public and thus break away from their presumed artistic isolation. A press release explained: "A technic has been perfected by which the writer of music has opportunity to amend or change his composition in the experience of audience reaction. Following the program the composer answers any questions addressed to him from his hearers." The Composers' Forum-Laboratory was directed by Ashley Pettis, an active

Popular Fronter and music critic for *New Masses*. The first event in New York was dedicated to the young composer Roy Harris, who used the occasion to call for "a very great virile music . . . music which moves in its vastness at a very rapid rate, music of great color, music of great mass, music which could only come out of an American civilization."

Harris was another model New Deal musician. His background might have been dreamed up by Great American Composer central casting: he was born in the oil-boom town of Chandler, Oklahoma, in a log cabin, no less, on Lincoln's birthday. *Time* further noted that the log cabin had been "hewed by hand" and that the young composer had driven a truck. The implication was that Harris was no classical sissy or bourgeois darling. The work that won Harris nationwide attention was his Third Symphony of 1938—an all-American hymn and dance for orchestra in which strings declaim orations in broad, open-ended lines, brass chant and whoop like cowboys in the galleries, and timpani stamp out strong beats in the middle of the bar. Such a big-shouldered sound met everyone's expectations of what a true-blue American symphony should be. When Toscanini deigned to conduct the piece in 1940, the owner of the Pittsburgh Pirates wrote to the composer: "If I had pitchers who would pitch as strongly as you do in your Symphony, my worries would be over."

If the Federal Music Project was a well-meaning, hardworking organization that never quite defined its purpose, the Federal Theatre Project (FTP), toward which politically engaged composers gravitated, was *too* clear about its goals. A few weeks before the first Composers' Forum-Laboratory concert in New York, Hallie Flanagan, the head of the FTP and an authority on Russian experimental theater, gave a speech with the title "Is This the Time and Place?" in which she set out her vision of a federally funded radical theater along the lines of Meyerhold's studios in Russia and Brecht's projects in pre-Nazi Berlin. The occasion was the first meeting of the regional directors of the FTP, which took place in Evalyn Walsh McLean's mansion in Washington, D.C. Flanagan said that this palatial setting—whose owner wore the Hope Diamond—represented "the conception of art as a commodity to be purchased by the rich, possessed by the rich." She was reminded, she said, of scenes that she had witnessed on a trip to the Soviet Union ten years before:

> During the first days in this house I was haunted by a sense of having gone through this experience before; gradually that memory became focused upon golden palaces of Soviet Russia now turned into offices and orphans' homes and theatres for the Russian proletariat. I remembered a theatre meeting in the great Hall of Mirrors in Leningrad where reflected from every side in those mirrors which once gave back the image of the Empress and later the execution of her officers, I saw the faces of Stalin, Litvinov, Lunachaisky [*sic*], Petrov and other leaders of political, educational and theatrical life. They met to discuss their mutual problem: how the theatre could serve in educating the people and in enriching their lives.

That last image—Stalin's face staring from a mirror—marked an unpromising beginning for an American arts bureaucracy.

Flanagan's projects had an obvious socialist realist flavor. Artists were encouraged to create strong, simple scenarios in which working people played heroic roles and moneyed interests were the villains. In the "Living Newspaper" play *Triple-A Plowed Under*, which criticized the Supreme Court for striking down the farm-subsidy system of the Agricultural Adjustment Act of 1933, one actor played the role of Earl Browder, the head of the American Communist Party. The ghost of Thomas Jefferson also chimed in, appearing to give credence to Browder's ideas. This revisionist picture of the Founding Fathers matched Browder's "Communism is twentieth-century Americanism" philosophy. At the same time, *Triple-A Plowed Under* was a brief on behalf of Roosevelt, who was sparring with the Supreme Court. The Republican Party properly took umbrage at the use of a federally funded theater program to generate propaganda on behalf of an embattled president in an election year. By engaging in such blatant activism, Flanagan's playwrights, directors, and composers almost single-handedly doomed the entire arts program to oblivion.

The FTP's most legendary production was Marc Blitzstein's pro-union musical *The Cradle Will Rock*. The scion of a wealthy Philadelphia family, Blitzstein received a first-class musical education from the likes of Alexander Siloti, a pupil of Liszt's; Nadia Boulanger, in Paris; and Schoenberg, in Berlin ("Go ahead, you write your Franco-Russian pretty music," Schoenberg told him). Early on, Blitzstein disdained radical politics and dismissed Kurt Weill's music as "little more than drivel." But disgust for the conventional classical world took hold of him, and he was drawn politically to the left by the Berlin-born novelist Eva Goldbeck, whom he married in an effort to disguise his homosexuality. He went on to join the Communist Party. In 1935, through Goldbeck, he met Bertolt Brecht, who challenged him to "write a piece about all kinds of prostitution—the press, the church, the courts, the arts, the whole system."

Cradle was Blitzstein's attempt to follow through on Brecht's command. It told of the union's fight for freedom in an abstract place called Steeltown, the villain of the piece being a Brechtian capitalist named Mister Mister, an art-snob robber baron. The satires of upper-class circles and the artists who aim to please them are the most successful passages in the work; in general, the workers' struggle in *Cradle* is probably best understood as a metaphor for the artists' struggle in the American marketplace. At one point, Dauber the artist and Yasha the violinist, in thrall to the patronage of Mrs. Mister, sing an ironic paean to the ghetto in which American musicians had long dwelled:

Be blind for art's sake
And deaf for art's sake
And dumb for art's sake
Until for art's sake
They kill for art's sake
All the art for art's sake.

There follows a menacing quotation from the main theme of Beethoven's *Egmont* Overture—which, we earlier learned, plays on Mrs. Mister's car horn. Blitzstein is sneering at the upper-class cult of imported European art, which covers up the machinery of exploitation and oppression.

The Broadway premiere of *The Cradle Will Rock* was scheduled for June 16, 1937, with the prodigiously gifted twenty-two-year-old Orson Welles directing. A few days before opening night, the WPA temporarily shut down all theater productions for budgetary reasons; the unsubstantiated rumor in the theater world was that the administration wished to suppress *Cradle* because it feared outbreaks of violence in steel towns across the country. Literally at the last minute, Welles heard of a vacant theater twenty blocks to the north, and most of the company marched there dramatically on foot. To get around the WPA ruling, the singers performed from seats around the auditorium while the composer played his score at the piano. *Cradle* was an immediate sensation among New York leftists, and a sell-out run of performances followed. But Blitzstein wanted more than press coverage and controversy. According to Welles, the composer believed that his work could become a conduit for revolutionary energies on American soil. "You can't imagine how simple he was about it," Welles said. "They were going to hear it, and that would be it!"

The unlikeliest of Federal Theatre revolutionists was the Parisian expatriate Virgil Thomson. Already in *Four Saints in Three Acts* Thomson had shown a knack for exploiting musical Americana, and his plaintively powerful *Symphony on a Hymn Tune* of 1926–28 anticipated aspects of Copland's populist style. In 1936, Thomson served as musical director for Orson Welles's production of *Macbeth*, which came courtesy of the Negro Theatre Project, one of Flanagan's more commendable initiatives. Much of the music was supplied by a group of African drummers, and at one point Thomson took it on himself to tell them how proper voodoo music should be played. "It don't sound wicked enough," he said to the group's director, who happened to be the dancer, choreographer, singer, and composer Asadata Dafora, a pioneer in the dissemination of West African tribal culture. The same year, Thomson wrote violently percussive music for the "Living Newspaper" play *Injunction Granted*, which was so strident in its denunciation of capitalism and the courts that even Flanagan criticized it as "hysterical."

Thomson also scored two federally funded film documentaries, *The Plow That Broke the Plains* (1936) and *The River* (1938). Both were commissioned by the Resettlement Administration, which was relocating displaced farmers to model communities around the country. Resettlement even had a Special Skills Division, designing a model culture for model towns, with Charles Seeger as musical adviser. *The Plow That Broke the Plains*, beautifully directed by Pare Lorentz, depicts the devastation wrought by soil erosion on the Great Plains. Thomson's score, interweaving hymns, ballads, fugues, and jazz, creates subtle counterpoint to the images on-screen, showing the grasslands in their primal state—the Edenic mood again—and then the incursion of capitalist misuse. The excellence of the product could not hide the dubiousness of the enterprise; as in the case of *Triple-A Plowed Under*, a government agency was using an art form to defend itself against political criticism and hostile judicial rulings. The narration of *The River*, likewise, makes an aesthetically and ethically jarring transition from Whitmanesque rhetoric ("The water comes downhill, spring and fall; / Down from the cut-over mountains") to bureaucratic boilerplate ("Down in the Valley, the Farm Security Administration has built a model agricultural community").

Anthony Tommasini, Thomson's biographer, paraphrases the position taken by Roosevelt's foes: "The German Führer had his Leni Riefenstahl; now FDR had his Pare Lorentz."

Circa 1936, Copland's "commando unit," his crack squad of young American composers, consisted of five men: Thomson, Harris, Sessions, the elegant neoclassicist Walter Piston, and Copland himself. By the early forties, with the addition of Blitzstein, Paul Bowles, Samuel Barber, Morton Gould, and David Diamond, it had grown to battalion proportions. For a time, these composers seemed to be writing almost with one voice. Fast movements jumped along with jazzy syncopations; slow movements cried out plaintively in empty spaces. Scoring was brassy and brilliant. Climaxes transpired in high Shostakovich style, all pealing trumpets and precisely pounding timpani, the better to punch through the fuzz of radio static.

American composers had apparently worked out a common practice, a lingua franca. Behind the scenes, though, the old style wars continued. In a 1938 article, Thomson divided music into three types of audiences, with three types of composers to serve them:

> 1) The luxury-trade, capitalist Toscanini public riding with sedate satisfaction in streamlined trains from Beethoven to Sibelius and back. 2) The professor-and-critic conspiracy for internationalist or "contemporary" music which prizes hermetism and obscurantism and makes a cult out of the apparent complexities in systematically discordant counterpoint. 3) The theatre-public of the leftist-front, a public of educated, urban working people who want educated, urban spokesmen for their ideals.

Exhibit A in category 1 was Samuel Barber—cultivated Italophile, son of a Pennsylvania surgeon, nephew of the Met contralto Louise Homer. He studied composition and voice at the newly founded Curtis Institute in Philadelphia, whose officials promoted him vigorously. In 1935 he appeared on NBC, singing his own easefully beautiful setting of Matthew Arnold's "Dover Beach." None other than Arturo Toscanini was listening; and when the Maestro decided to conduct *two* of Barber's works, the *Essay for Orchestra* and the Adagio for Strings, a minor media sensation ensued. Two years later Artur Rodzinski led both the New York Philharmonic and the Vienna Philharmonic in Barber's First Symphony, which owed a debt to the Sibelius Seventh. While so many of his generation favored lean textures and brief motifs, Barber produced long melodic lines and rich orchestral textures, leaving audiences with the feeling that they had consumed a high-protein meal.

Barber's rise stirred resentment among some musical operatives of the Popular Front, who saw him as a useless bourgeois. R. D. Darrell, in *New Masses*, called the First Symphony a "grotesque harlequinade of specious modernity (which, it goes without saying, is about as 'modern' as Richard Strauss)." Ashley Pettis, of the Federal Music Project, dismissed the Adagio as " 'authentic,' dull, 'serious' music—utterly anachronistic as the utterance of a young man of 28, A.D. 1938!" But Copland himself, rarely doctrinaire or petty in his reactions to colleagues' work, came to admire the spellbinding quality of Barber's creation, and later said that it had the virtue of absolute sincerity. The time-suspending atmosphere of the piece derives from a metrical trick that Barber might have picked up from Sibelius: although the music streams by in a steady flow, the ear has trouble detecting where the bar lines fall. The result is something like a modern form of Gregorian chant, and it is no more or less anachronistic than anything else written in A.D. 1938.

The university-intellectual composers, in Thomson's category 2, resisted Copland's demand for "no more Schoenberg." Their most articulate spokesman was Sessions, who absorbed some of the values of the Schoenberg circle during a Berlin sojourn that lasted from 1931 to 1933. In his Violin Concerto, finished in 1935, Sessions pivoted from neoclassicism toward free atonal expressionism, producing a Bergian mood of ambiguity and loss. He emerged from his European years with the conviction that American composers should obey only an inner creative urge—an "*essential innerlich notwendig* [inwardly necessary] musical impulse," as he put it in a letter to Copland—and not a political or commercial obligation to write music for the masses ("forced and essentially anemic Ersatz-Musik"). He failed to entertain the possibility that one could write populist music out of inward necessity. In the 1930s, Sessions's attitude was a minority position, although it would gain traction in the postwar period, not least through the writings and teachings of his student Milton Babbitt.

Thomson's three groups—traditionalists, elitists, populists—match up neatly with the main musical parties of the Weimar Republic, the ones centered on Pfitzner, Schoenberg, and Eisler. As in Weimar, the possibility lingered of a "great fusion," an agglomeration of classical and popular inheritances. Weill's *Mahagonny* and Gershwin's *Porgy and Bess* both aimed for approximately the same synthesis. By cosmic coincidence, the composer of *Mahagonny* arrived on American soil in September 1935, the same month as *Porgy*'s premiere. Weill, who had been living in Paris and London since the Nazis took over, came to America to compose the score for a sort of Jewish pageant-opera titled *The Eternal Road*, with a libretto by Franz Werfel and a production by Max Reinhardt. The music carried on the incisive populist style of *Mahagonny*, its vigorous march rhythms again echoing the symphonies of Mahler. Weill came to New York to attend the premiere; the production was delayed for several months; and, as the situation in Europe worsened, Weill elected to remain on American soil. Once again, he was starting from scratch, this time in the real-life Mahagonny of Manhattan.

In quest of an American identity, Weill tested the waters at the Group Theatre, where, Harold Clurman told him, people passed the time by singing *The Threepenny Opera*. He did some work on an unrealized Federal Theatre Project production titled *The Common Glory*, about "the socialist idea in early America," and also on *Davy Crockett*, in which the hero of the Alamo would have battled capitalism in Tennessee. Weill's first big American score was for the 1936 Group Theatre production *Johnny Johnson*, which won respect less for its political message—it was antiwar, but in a wholesome way—than for its playful, propulsive style, its sharp use of the American vernacular.

Having had his fill of agitprop with Brecht in Berlin, Weill began to visualize himself as a mainstream theater composer. He had his first Broadway hit with *Knickerbocker Holiday* in 1938 and struck again with *Lady in the Dark* in 1941. Weill's hard-bitten Berlin style transferred to the

American stage with remarkable ease; the bittersweet added-sixth harmonies of "September Song," the big number in *Knickerbocker Holiday*, bear a family resemblance to "Mack the Knife." Weill's Americanization proceeded to the point where he could swear like Clark Gable in a 1940 interview: "I don't give a damn about writing for posterity . . . I have never acknowledged the difference between 'serious' music and 'light' music. There is only good music and bad music."

In this same period, the Broadway musical grew more ambitious. The grand new mode of music theater that Kern had set in motion with *Show Boat* and Gershwin had carried forward in *Porgy and Bess* achieved maximum commercial impact with Richard Rodgers and Oscar Hammerstein's *Oklahoma!*—whose legendary first run began in 1943 and ended in 1948. While Weill generally told New York stories, Rodgers and Hammerstein extolled the heartland. The work's "open-air spirit," as Rodgers called it, had much in common with Copland's "open prairie," and when Rodgers set about writing a dance sequence for farm boys and girls, he apparently looked to Copland's cowboy ballet *Rodeo* for inspiration.

The rapid advance of Broadway composers set in relief the fact that their counterparts in the classical world were writing relatively few operas or music-theater pieces, preferring to concentrate on orchestral writing. The Broadway musical was splitting off as a separate genre of American music, with its own language, its own styles of singing, its own schools and subgenres. The distinction between "opera" and "Broadway" was hardening into fact—a missed opportunity for the populist generation.

In the elections of 1938, the Republicans picked up a large number of seats in Congress and joined forces with conservative Democrats to mount an assault on the New Deal. The House Un-American Activities Committee, under the leadership of Congressman Martin Dies, launched an investigation of the WPA, and the arts programs proved a juicy target. Congressman J. Parnell Thomas charged that the Theatre Project was "one more link in the vast and unparalleled New Deal propaganda machine." The Music Project faced a separate challenge from the American Federation of Musicians, which saw government-funded performances as unfair competition for professional orchestras, opera companies, and bands. Roosevelt came to the conclusion—justified or not—that the broad American middle would not accept the burden of "encouraging art, music, and literature," as he put it in a letter to Nelson Rockefeller.

The death knell for the federal arts programs sounded on June 30, 1939, when Congress called for the abolition of the Federal Theatre Project and allowed the other arts projects to continue only under state and local sponsorship. Roosevelt made a show of decrying the way in which the FTP had been singled out for abuse, claiming that it could have carried on under the terms extended to the other divisions, but all that was a whitewash: as had been predicted in the House hearings, few WPA organizations were able to survive on local support alone.

A late efflorescence of WPA spirit took place at the New York World's Fair, which opened in Queens in April 1939. Money for this grand venture came largely from private sources, but New Deal idealism still filled the air, blending uneasily with the adspeak of corporate America. Millions of visitors gazed awestruck at the self-styled "World of Tomorrow"—the sleek forms of the Trylon and Perisphere at the center of the fairgrounds; the "Futurama" spectacular, with its radiant vision of suburban communities interconnected by superhighways; and, at the RCA pavilion, a device called television, which the ever-optimistic David Sarnoff hailed as "a new art." Roosevelt's Four Freedoms were monumentalized in sculptures that Mussolini might have found appealing.

Several prominent composers of Popular Front orientation contributed to the fair, struggling to reconcile their ideals with the requirements of big business. Weill wrote music for the historical pageant *Railroads on Parade*, in which fifteen working locomotives moved across a massive reinforced stage and blew their whistles on cue. Eisler, suspending his anticapitalist crusade, teamed with Joseph Losey on the puppet film *Pete Roleum and His Cousins*, which explained the oil industry to children.

Copland, for his part, wrote a score for a film documentary titled *The City*, which played every day on the fairgrounds. The narration, written by Lewis Mumford, advanced the thesis that the American city had become frenzied, oppressive, and inhumane. First, New England scenes illustrate a golden age before humanity and nature fell out of balance, Copland's music making liberal use of plainspoken melody and purehearted harmony. Then industry invades. "Smoke makes prosperity," the narrator intones, "no matter if you choke on it." Copland responds with brassy dissonance. A sequence depicting the congestion of the city inspires vamping repetitive music that anticipates the minimalism of Philip Glass. (*Koyaanisqatsi*, Glass's film symphony about the ruination of the planet, is essentially an update of *The City*.) Finally, we are given the solution—the model community of Greenbelt, Maryland, where modern convenience was joined to rural values, "where children play under trees and the people who laid out this place didn't forget that air and sun was what we need for growing." Despite the overlay of Popular Front rhetoric, the film was trumpeting the concept of the commuter suburb, which served the interests of the big automobile manufacturers. General Motors was a major investor in the fair.

The summer of 1939 was a somber time for leftist artists. News of the abrupt termination of the Federal Arts Projects coincided with the even more shocking news of Stalin's pact with Hitler. Some American Communists were beginning to realize that blood, prisons, ruin, and darkness, to paraphrase Joshua Kunitz, were very much part of Stalin's world. Copland, though, was in a buoyant frame of mind; long a force behind the scenes, he was now tasting real popularity. "Mr. Copland Here, There, and at the Fair" was *The New Yorker*'s headline for a column on his doings. If one avenue, the way of New Deal art, was blocked, others were opening up. In October 1939, Copland went west to Hollywood. Ever the optimist, he wrote to Koussevitzky: "Hollywood is an extraordinary place . . . It's like nothing else in the world. Thank heavens."

Hollywood Music

Schoenberg's epigram about his California exile—"I was driven into Paradise"—is sometimes used as the setup for a grim punch line, along the lines of "For émigré artists, the Hollywood paradise soon became a nightmare." Or, to quote a line from Brecht that Hanns Eisler set to music in his *Hollywood Elegies* of 1942: "Paradise and hell can be the same city."

Schoenberg, an Austro-German chauvinist turned American patriot, would never have condoned such a simplistic formula. Los Angeles, and Hollywood in particular, became a nightmare only for those who arrived with irrational expectations. Hollywood was in the business of generating maximum revenue from entertainment. Any composer—or writer or director—who came west with the intention of indulging his genius was bound to go away embittered. "The man who insists on complete self-expression had better stay home and write symphonies," Copland wrote in 1940. "He will never be happy in Hollywood."

Say this for the movie people: they were certainly mad for music. Lauritz Melchior and Kirsten Flagstad flirted with film stardom; Nelson Eddy became one of the biggest box-office draws of the period; there were biopics of Schubert (*Melody Master*), Chopin (*A Song to Remember*), Robert and Clara Schumann (*Song of Love*), even Rimsky-Korsakov (*Song of Scheherazade*). John Garfield played a violinist in *Humoresque*; Bette Davis played a pianist entangled with a cellist and a composer in *Deception*; Leopold Stokowski played Leopold Stokowski in the Deanna Durbin comedy *One Hundred Men and a Girl*. Each major studio assembled a symphony orchestra to record its scores, providing employment to the throngs of Jewish musical émigrés who had been driven out of the great ensembles of Central Europe. The director of music at Paramount Studios was a curious character named Boris Morros, who made it his mission to sign up famous composers for film work. He negotiated at various times with Schoenberg, Stravinsky, Copland, and Weill, and even tried to get Shostakovich on loan from the Soviet Union. All the while, he was serving as a KGB agent, with an assignment to generate pro-Soviet propaganda. Morros seems to have used his subversive activities mainly as an ingenious way of raising cash for his own projects and accounts.

Hollywood may have been hazardous territory for composers, but they at least felt *wanted* there, as they never did in American concert halls. The shift to talkies had created a mania for continuous sound. Just as actors in screwball comedies had to talk a mile a minute, composers were called upon to underline every gesture and emphasize every emotion. An actress could hardly serve a cup of coffee without having fifty Max Steiner strings swoop in to assist her. ("What that awful music does," Bette Davis once said to Gore Vidal, "is erase the actor's performance, note by note.") Early movie scores had a purely illustrative function, which composers called "Mickey-Mousing": if a British frigate sails into the frame, "Rule, Britannia" plays. Later, composers introduced techniques of musical distancing and irony, along the lines of Sergei Eisenstein's counterpointing of image and sound. Music could be used to reveal a hidden psychological subtext, to indicate absent figures and forces, to subvert whatever film reality the viewer was seeing.

In Alfred Hitchcock's thriller *Shadow of a Doubt*, Franz Lehár's "Merry

Widow Waltz" undergoes spooky variations by Dimitri Tiomkin, thereby tracing out the tortured psychology of Joseph Cotten's serial-killer character. As the film scholar Royal Brown writes, the tune stands in for Uncle Charlie's "loathing of the present day in favor of an idealized past." In Fritz Lang's *Hangmen Also Die* (co-written by Brecht), Hanns Eisler had the pleasant assignment of depicting the assassination of the SS leader Reinhard Heydrich, and marked the moment of death by writing rapid, sibilant string figures in the upper register, suggestive of a squealing rat. When a portrait of Hitler appears on-screen, Eisler responds with a cackling eruption of atonality.

Copland, when he came to Hollywood, had the luck to work with directors who let him write in his accustomed style. His favorite collaborator was the literate, left-wing, musically sensitive director Lewis Milestone, who hired him to score a film adaptation of John Steinbeck's *Of Mice and Men*. As the *Los Angeles Times* noted in wonder, there was no music director looking over the composer's shoulder as he worked. The setting for the novel, the agricultural valleys of California, elicited winsome stretches of music in the now familiar pastoral mode, while the later tragic twists in the drama prompted Copland to revive his "modernist" voice; the music for the climactic scene of Lennie's death is a near-recapitulation of the *Piano Variations*. What's distinctive about the score is its reticence; its commentaries tend to be subtle rather than obvious, and for long stretches it stays silent. It's as if the composer were watching the drama along with the audience. David Raksin, one of the most gifted native-born film composers, singled out the "absolutely clear and pure and wonderful style" in *Of Mice and Men*, noting that it set the tone for dozens of classic Hollywood Westerns.

The crown prince of the Hollywood music community was Erich Wolfgang Korngold. In his youth Korngold had been one of history's most remarkable composer-prodigies, astonishing both Mahler and Strauss with his prepubescent mastery of the Wagnerian orchestra. Back in 1920, at the age of twenty-three, he had conquered the opera houses of Central Europe with *Die tote Stadt*, or *The Dead City*, a tale of artistic and romantic obsession in the vein of Schreker's *Der ferne Klang*. As the twenties went on, the opulent style that Korngold had so easily mastered fell out of European fashion, although it remained in demand in thirties Hollywood, especially for social dramas and period pictures.

Korngold's first assignment, in 1934, was to arrange Mendelssohn's *Midsummer Night's Dream* music—banned in Nazi Germany—for a Max Reinhardt adaptation of the play. Korngold all but took over the production, telling the actors how to recite their lines and letting the cinematographer know how many feet of film would be needed to cover his musical cues. On a second visit the following year, Korngold scored the Errol Flynn picture *Captain Blood*, his muscular, flamboyant style transforming what might have been a run-of-the-mill adventure into the first of Flynn's box-office-smashing "swashbucklers." All told, Korngold won for film composing a degree of respectability that soon drew other international celebrities into the game.

Korngold was the flashiest, but the most original of Hollywood composers was Bernard Herrmann, who began with Orson Welles's *Citizen Kane*, reached his peak with Alfred Hitchcock's *Vertigo*, and ended his career with Martin Scorsese's *Taxi Driver*. Herrmann started out as a feisty youngster on the New York scene, a sometime member of Copland's "commando unit." Keenly aware of the possibilities of radio and film, he went to work as an arranger, conductor, and composer at the CBS network in 1934. It was at CBS that Herrmann met Welles, who, on the heels of his Federal Theatre Project successes, was presenting innovative radio productions under the title Mercury Theatre on the Air.

When Welles went to Hollywood to launch what promised to be a history-making film career, he took Herrmann with him. Welles remained a model Popular Front activist, as he had been in New York, and *Citizen Kane* was perhaps the supreme Popular Front work; it told of a great American who betrays the progressive ideals of his youth and becomes a decrepit capitalist relic. The right-wing newspaper mogul William Randolph Hearst, who was the main target of Welles's satire, tried to have the film suppressed, but it opened anyway, on May Day 1941.

Like his idol Sergei Eisenstein, Welles possessed exceptional musical instincts. An opera maven in his youth, he understood how music could amplify stage action, draw out hidden moods and emotions, even expose a lie. *Kane*'s opening two-and-a-half-minute sequence, showing the protagonist's last moments and death, is propelled entirely by Herrmann's score, the only nonmusical sound being Kane's whisper of "Rosebud!" The principal motif, a five-note phrase that drops down a tritone at the end, recalls, aptly, Rachmaninov's tone poem *Isle of the Dead*. Throughout the film those notes undergo variations and mutations; for example, in the rapid-fire sequence that describes Kane's early days in the newspaper business, they are heard sped up and in a major key.

The most amazing synergy of music and image comes when Kane's second wife, the would-be singer Susan Alexander, makes a disastrous debut on the opera stage that the tycoon has built for her. It is the turning point in Kane's transformation from hero to monster, and grand opera epitomizes his delusions. As Herrmann's gloriously overwrought French verismo aria plays, the camera pans up to show a stagehand holding his nose in disgust. Is he a working-class opera lover who knows a fake voice when he hears one? Or a pop-music devotee who rejects opera as upper-crust foolery? The viewer decides. Following Eisenstein's practice in *Alexander Nevsky* and *Ivan the Terrible*, Welles shot this sequence and also the final scene with Herrmann's music already composed and recorded. He later remarked that Herrmann was "50 percent responsible" for the success of *Kane*.

Herrmann's scores for *Citizen Kane*, *The Magnificent Ambersons* (mangled along with the film in release), *Vertigo*, and *Psycho* contain some of the century's most piercingly effective dramatic music, but film work was terminally unfulfilling for this arrogant, irascible, impassioned man, who dreamed of returning in triumph to concert music and opera. Korngold, likewise, yearned to reassert himself as a "serious" composer but could not shake the Hollywood tag. His Symphony in F-sharp, a valedictory utterance whose slow movement takes the form of a shatteringly eloquent funeral oration for FDR, met with dismissive shrugs after its 1954 premiere. Other Hollywood émigrés, such as Ernst Toch, Karol Rathaus, Miklós Rózsa, Franz Waxman, and Eric Zeisl, labored under the kitsch-composer stereotype. They were generally considered too serious for Hollywood and not serious enough for the concert hall. Most would have identified with Toch when he wrote, "I am the forgotten composer of the twentieth century."

Exile Music

Had there been a demand, the vendors who hawked maps of movie stars' homes on street corners in Beverly Hills could also have sold maps for the stars of European music. Schoenberg had a house on North Rockingham

Avenue in Brentwood, down the way from Tyrone Power. Stravinsky lived on North Wetherly Drive, up the hill from the Sunset Strip. Rachmaninov was on North Elm Drive, in the center of the movie colony. Bruno Walter was on North Bedford Drive, next door to Alma Mahler and Franz Werfel; Theodor Adorno on South Kenter Avenue in Brentwood, near the cellist Gregor Piatigorsky; Otto Klemperer, former head of the Kroll Opera, on Bel Air Road, up the street from the directors Otto Preminger and Ernst Lubitsch; and Eisler on Amalfi Drive, in Pacific Palisades, close to Thomas Mann and Aldous Huxley. Korngold, befitting his high station, lived in the elite Toluca Lake development, near Frank Sinatra, Bing Crosby, and Bob Hope. The more culturally attuned movie stars, such as Charles Chaplin and Charles Laughton, mixed comfortably with their impressive new neighbors. Others committed the occasional faux pas. At a dinner at Harpo Marx's, the comedienne Fanny Brice walked up to Schoenberg and said, "C'mon, Professor, play us a tune."

The most surreal thing about the Los Angeles music scene was that Schoenberg and Stravinsky, the twin giants of modernism, now lived just eight miles apart, each on a side street north of Sunset Boulevard. On four occasions the masters were within sight of each other: at Franz Werfel's funeral, in 1945; at the dress rehearsal for a multicomposer work called the *Genesis Suite*, for which both had written movements, in the same year; at a dinner for Alma Mahler at the Crystal Ballroom of the Beverly Hills Hotel, in 1948; and at a seventy-fifth-birthday concert in Schoenberg's honor, in 1949. They might have enjoyed speaking to each other, but in this imaginary Europe it was somehow inconceivable that they should meet.

Schoenberg had been living in the Los Angeles area since 1934, teaching first at the University of Southern California and then at UCLA. He adapted to his new surroundings with alacrity; the Weimar Republic, with its health fads and cult of sport, prepared him well for the Republic of California. He tooled around in his Ford sedan, followed UCLA football, and played a mean set of tennis. Welcome anytime on George and Ira Gershwin's court, he would show up almost every week, accompanied by a gaggle of pupils. He also played tennis with Chaplin, who enjoyed the sight of the "frank and abrupt little man" in a white T-shirt and cap. He took pride in the all-American lifestyles of his daughter, Nuria, and his sons, Lawrence and Ronald; the latter's victory in a junior tennis championship occasioned much celebration. Although the composer never fully mastered English, he did pick up a fair amount of American slang, which he would wield to lacerating effect. When one pupil presented a piece that had an exaggerated galloping rhythm, Schoenberg started to jump around like the Lone Ranger, shouting, "Hi-yo, Silver!" His dress grew funky. According to his student Dika Newlin, he came to one class at UCLA wearing "a peach-colored shirt, a green tie with white polka-dots, a knit belt of the most vivid purple with a large and ostentatious gold buckle, and an unbelievably loud gray suit with lots of black and brown stripes."

In his music Schoenberg experienced what he called an "upsurge of desire for tonality." With a series of more or less tonal works—the Suite in G for Strings, the Variations on a Recitative in D Minor for organ, *Kol nidre* for synagogue choir, and the Theme and Variations in G Minor for high-school band—he evidently hoped to create marketable "hits," whose profits would then allow him to carry on with *Moses und Aron* and other more advanced endeavors. Even the twelve-tone Violin and Piano Concertos were written in the hope that the classical virtuosos of the radio age would popularize them. These pieces proved no more financially rewarding in America than the comic opera *From Today Until Tomorrow* had been in the Weimar Republic.

As a teacher, Schoenberg remained tough as nails, but he did not foist his methods on students. He raised eyebrows by praising the tonal symphonic art of Sibelius and Shostakovich, which he might have been expected to deplore. When one of his pupils started attacking Shostakovich, Schoenberg cut him off, saying, "That man is a composer born." He once or twice caught his class off guard with the announcement that "there is still plenty of good music to be written in C major."

Schoenberg loved the movies and hoped to write a film score himself. In late 1934, Irving Thalberg, the frail, cultured head of production at Metro-Goldwyn-Mayer, heard Schoenberg's *Transfigured Night* or perhaps the Suite in G on the radio one day and asked the composer in for a meeting. The screenwriter Salka Viertel, who was present, described the scene unforgettably in her memoir, *The Kindness of Strangers*:

> I still see [Schoenberg] before me, leaning forward in his chair, both hands clasped over the handle of the umbrella, his burning

> genius's eyes on Thalberg, who, standing behind his desk, was explaining why he wanted a great composer for the scoring of the *Good Earth*. When he came to: "Last Sunday when I heard the lovely music you have written . . ." Schoenberg interrupted sharply: "I don't write 'lovely' music" . . . He had read the *Good Earth* and he would not undertake the assignment unless he was given complete control over the sound, including the spoken words. "What do you mean by complete control?" asked Thalberg, incredulously. "I mean that I would have to work with the actors," answered Schoenberg. "They would have to speak in the same pitch and key as I compose it in. It would be similar to *Pierrot lunaire* but, of course, less difficult."

Unfazed, Thalberg asked Schoenberg to think about what kind of music would best suit the screenplay. The composer prepared several sketches, again leaning in a tonal direction. The sticking point between composer and studio head was not style but money; at a follow-up meeting Schoenberg asked for no less than fifty thousand dollars, whereupon Thalberg lost interest. After hearing nothing from the executive for three weeks, Schoenberg wrote an uncharacteristically pleading letter: "I can not believe, this is your intention: to give me no answer at all. Maybe you are disappointed about the price I asked. But you will agree, it is not my fault, you did not ask me before and only so late, that I had already spent so much time, coming twice to you, reading the book, trying out how I could compose it and making sketches." But nothing more was heard from MGM. A few months later, Schoenberg called at Paramount to discuss a project called *Souls at Sea*, but it, too, came to nothing. The twelve-tone method finally reached the silver screen by way of Scott Bradley's inventive scores for Tom and Jerry cartoons in the forties, notably *Puttin' on the Dog* and *The Cat That Hated People*.

The crucial work of Schoenberg's "American" period was the String Trio of 1946, which hints at the conflicting pleasures, agonies, hopes, and regrets of life in California. On its surface, it is a piece of unapologetic difficulty, reminiscent of Schoenberg's wildest early atonal music. The score is full of distortion and noise, with the players asked to execute such eerie effects as *sul ponticello* (bowing the strings at the bridge) and *col legno* (bowing or tapping the strings with the wood of the bow). Yet the contrasting lyrical episodes radiate nostalgia for the former tonal world. By his own testimony, Schoenberg was depicting in musical terms a severe asthma attack he experienced in the summer of 1946, during which his pulse temporarily stopped and he was given an injection to the heart. Some passages represented the injections, he said, others the male nurse who treated him. The composer Allen Shawn, in a book about Schoenberg, notes that the String Trio is a kind of fantastic autobiography, "as if in his delirium he had reviewed his life." The ending is soft and wistful.

Ronald Schoenberg, the older of the composer's two American sons, still lives in the Brentwood house where his father spent the last part of his life. He recalls that in his childhood tour buses would regularly come up the street, and a voice on a loudspeaker would point out the home of Shirley Temple. The guide would never mention that the composer of *Erwartung* lived across the way. "My father was always a little sad about that," his son says. "But another time, we stopped at a juice bar out on Highway 1, and the radio was playing *Verklärte Nacht*, and I never saw him so happy."

Igor Stravinsky came to California in 1940. He had arrived on the East Coast the previous year, to deliver the Charles Eliot Norton lectures at Harvard. Not long after the final lecture, France fell, and Stravinsky again found himself a refugee from twentieth-century history.

Los Angeles naturally attracted him, not only for the pleasant climate but also for the opportunity to try his hand at film. Like Schoenberg, Stravinsky was a movie buff, enjoying Chaplin's classic silents, the comic masterpieces of Buster Keaton, the Hepburn-Tracy romantic comedies, and Disney's cartoons. The possibility of a Stravinsky-Disney collaboration particularly excited the press. "America may yet see Mickey Mouse liberating the princess in the *Firebird*," the *Cincinnati Enquirer* wrote in 1940. There were ambitious ideas for an entire Disney film built around a Stravinsky score. Stravinsky talked to other studios, and sketched music for the films *Commandos Strike at Dawn* (about the Nazi occupation of Norway), *The North Star* (about a Russian village under siege), *The Song of Bernadette* (based on the novel by his friend Franz Werfel), and *Jane Eyre* (starring Orson Welles, whose *Citizen Kane* Stravinsky admired).

In the end, Stravinsky's music appeared in only one Hollywood movie—Disney's animated magnum opus *Fantasia*, where dinosaurs danced in time to the rhythms of the *Rite*. Stravinsky later claimed to have been horrified by *Fantasia*, although there is no record of his saying anything negative at the time. "Igor appears to love it," Hindemith commented in a 1941 letter.

Why did Stravinsky have so little luck in Hollywood? The trouble wasn't money, as in Schoenberg's case. Studio heads were confident that Stravinsky's name would prove a box-office draw; Louis B. Mayer reportedly agreed to give the composer a whopping $100,000, which would be well over a million dollars in today's money. In a review of the composer's Hollywood activities, Charles Joseph observes that in almost every case Stravinsky demanded too much time to finish the music and too much control over the finished product. The studios may have revered Stravinsky as a cultural figure, but they could not bring expensive projects to a halt while the composer lined his paper and manipulated his colored pencils in pursuit of the perfect Norwegian commando sonorities. In other ways, Stravinsky happily played along with the culture industry, writing a *Tango* that was taken up by Benny Goodman's band; a *Circus Polka* that was danced by fifty young women and fifty elephants in pink tutus at the Ringling Bros. and Barnum & Bailey Circus (choreography by Balanchine); a *Scherzo à la russe* for Paul Whiteman; and an *Ebony Concerto* for Woody Herman.

Somewhat surprisingly, the main works of Stravinsky's first years of exile were symphonies: the Symphony in C (begun in Paris in 1938, finished in Los Angeles in 1940, premiered by the Chicago Symphony that year); *Ode* (three symphonic movements commissioned by the Boston Symphony, premiered in 1943); and the Symphony in Three Movements (New York Philharmonic, 1946). America's seemingly limitless hunger for symphonic utterances, whether by Beethoven, Brahms, Shostakovich, or Roy Harris, may have given Stravinsky incentive to explore a form that he had avoided since his studies with Rimsky-Korsakov (if the *Symphony of Psalms* is placed in a category by itself).

The Symphony in Three Movements became another peak in a mountain range of an output. It is unusual among Stravinsky's works in that it follows a quasi-Romantic narrative plan, one of struggle and resolution. The first movement is all dynamism and conflict, the pastoral

Andante provides respite, the finale carries on the conflict at a more strident pitch. Departing from his usual post-1918 line of defining music as a self-contained, anti-expressive art, Stravinsky later cited newsreel footage of goose-stepping soldiers as a source of inspiration. The piece begins with a striking, almost cinematic gesture—a swooshing upward rush of strings, lower winds, and piano, coupled with a four-horn fanfare, reminiscent of the columnar opening bars of *Oedipus Rex*. Then a rugged, foursquare march begins. Yet Stravinsky remains Stravinsky: the opening gesture is repeated in irregular fragments, as if the newsreels were being rearranged in a cubistic collage. Rhythms keep doubling back or springing ahead, plain chords bang against each other in unexpected ways. More warlike noises enliven the finale: trudging and swinging rhythms, exuberant whoops in the horns, and, at the end, a splashy, souped-up, self-confessedly Hollywoodish chord of victory—the sound of America on the march.

On August 7, 1945, the day after the atomic bomb destroyed Hiroshima, Stravinsky added an extra pulse to the final chord, perhaps by way of honoring the immense military might of the country of which he was about to become a permanent citizen.

On July 19, 1942, NBC broadcast Shostakovich's *Leningrad* Symphony, with Toscanini conducting the NBC Symphony. It was the most spectacular new-music event of the radio era, heralded by the *Time* magazine cover portrait of Shostakovich in his fireman's helmet.

Most of the émigré composers—Schoenberg, Stravinsky, Eisler, Rachmaninov, Hindemith, and Bartók—were listening, and almost all seem to have experienced a mass attack of envy and resentment. Schoenberg praised Shostakovich on other occasions, but this time he snapped, "With composing like this, one must be grateful that he has not already gone up to Symphony No. 77!" Hindemith condemned the trend toward "despicable rubbish" in orchestral music and sat down to write a set of fugues—the *Ludus tonalis*—in which he hoped to "remind those who have not completely succumbed what music and composition really are." None of the émigrés reacted more strongly than Bartók, who was listening at home in New York. When he wrote his Concerto for Orchestra the following summer, he included a savage reference to the *Leningrad*; in "Intermezzo interrotto," the fourth movement, the clarinet plays a sped-up, cartoonish version of the *Bolero*-ish "invasion" theme, accompanied by chortling trills and sneering trombone glissandos.

Bartók, like Hindemith, apparently believed that Shostakovich was indulging in oversimplified writing for cheap effect. Neither composer seemed to realize that the first movement of the *Leningrad* was a complicated act of parody, or that Shostakovich had little to gain, financial or otherwise, from American success. For Bartók, who had fled fascist Hungary in 1940 and endured periods of severe financial need in the first years of his American exile, a few high-profile performances by the likes of Toscanini and Koussevitzky would have made a world of difference. Fortunately, help was on the way; Koussevitzky commissioned the Concerto for Orchestra and gave it a brilliant premiere in Boston in December 1944.

The Concerto might be a tribute to the pluralism that Roosevelt's America in its ideal form embodied. There are folk melodies of the Hungarian, Romanian, and Czech peasant traditions, Gypsy dances, North African rhythms, echoes of both the impressionism of Debussy and the expressionism of Schoenberg (they are unified in the Elegy movement), Stravinsky's *Rite*, and, riding high above, pealing fanfares of all-American brass. Ridicule aside, the Shostakovich quotation adds to the polyglot diversity of the piece. Almost every instrument in the orchestra has a solo role, even as the collective emotion swells. Bartók's parting gift to his adopted country—he died on September 26, 1945—is a portrait of democracy in action.

Appalachian Spring

In Roosevelt's last years, the chief custodian of the rapidly fading New Deal spirit was Henry Wallace, who served as vice president from 1941 until January 1945. As Roosevelt's agriculture secretary, Wallace had presided over some of the New Deal's most ambitious and controversial programs, including the Agricultural Adjustment Act, whose demise provoked the Federal Theatre Project production *Triple-A Plowed Under*. As vice president, Wallace moved further to the left than any mainstream politician of the time, espousing radical economic measures and universal civil rights. In a November 1942 address to the Congress of American-Soviet Friendship—in whose parent organization Aaron Copland was later involved—Wallace disavowed what he called "political or Bill-of-Rights democracy" and praised the alleged "economic democracy" of the Soviet Union. On May 8 of the same year, he delivered a widely publicized speech in which he dared to criticize America's wartime mood of triumphalism. Henry Luce, the mightily influential publisher of *Time* and *Life*, had prophesied an "American Century," an age of American world domination. Wallace proposed instead the "century of the common man." "The people's revolution is on the march," he thundered, "and the devil and all his angels cannot prevail against it."

Left-wing intellectuals such as Orson Welles, Paul Robeson, Thomas Mann, and Aaron Copland thrilled to the soaring rhetoric of Wallace's speech, which was immediately published in book form. When, in the fall of 1942, Copland submitted a brief orchestral fanfare to the Cincinnati Symphony in response to a commission, he gave it the title *Fanfare for the Common Man*.

The source of the title should have been obvious to anyone who followed American politics, but Eugene Goossens, the English-born conductor of the Cincinnati orchestra, missed the reference and formed the impression that the *Fanfare* was a humorous tribute to the hardworking American taxpayer. He therefore programmed the premiere on March 15, which was tax day at the time. Copland wrote back: "The title was not meant to be funny. I got the idea from Vice-President Wallace's speech in which he talked about the next century being the century of the common man. Even so, I think it was a swell idea to have played it around March 15th." As ever, Copland declined to make his politics explicit. The *Fanfare* was soon enshrined alongside *Billy the Kid*, *Rodeo*, and *Lincoln Portrait* in Copland's gallery of "hits." Decades later, the rock group Queen incorporated part of the main melody and the stamping rhythm of the *Fanfare* into its 1977 stadium anthem "We Will Rock You."

In quick succession Copland manufactured another all-American music icon: the ballet score *Appalachian Spring*. The idea for the piece came from the choreographer Martha Graham, who wished to use her airy, athletic style of modern dance to create a mythic picture of life on the American frontier. Naturally, she went to Copland for the music.

The original scenario, which Graham had changed considerably by the time Copland finished composing, was set in western Pennsylvania before and during the Civil War, its cast of characters populated with nameless American archetypes. The Mother embodies the purity of the preindustrial American soul; the Daughter is a plucky pioneer type; the Citizen, who marries the daughter and carries her across the threshold of his newly built farmhouse, is a fighter for civil rights, perhaps something of an intellectual, certainly an abolitionist; the Fugitive represents the slaves; and the Younger Sister "suggests today." The central drama arrives in the "Fear in the Night" episode, when the Fugitive enters and brings with him all the pain and fear of the Civil War. Once the struggle is over, the music subsides toward a final Sabbath scene, which, according to Graham, "could have the feeling either of a Shaker meeting where the movement is strange and ordered and possessed or it could have the feeling of a negro church with the lyric ecstasy of the spiritual about it."

The title comes from Hart Crane's great, flawed poetic cycle *The Bridge*, and specifically from the section "The Dance":

O Appalachian Spring! I gained the ledge;
Steep, inaccessible smile that eastward bends
And northward reaches in that violet wedge
Of Adirondacks! . . .

Graham decided on the title only after Copland had completed the score, but according to Howard Pollack the idea of somehow using *The Bridge* as a source was present from the start. Crane and Copland had met in bohemian-modernist circles in the twenties, and although they had little contact, both were striving to create modern American myths. The bridge at the center of Crane's poem is the Brooklyn Bridge, which is said to "lend a myth to God." It is a sacred symbol in a city given over to flashing images and frantic movement. Elsewhere in the poem, Crane finds moments of transcendence variously in transient sexual connection—love, he says, is "a burnt match skating in a urinal"—and in the emptiness of the American wilderness. Lines from the section "The River" prefigure Copland's Popular Front vision in their simultaneously celebratory and critical evocation of modern American life:

RADIO ROARS IN EVERY HOME . . .
So the 20th Century—so
whizzed the Limited—roared by and left
three men, still hungry on the tracks . . .

This is the famous 20th Century Limited, the luxury train that whisked passengers from New York to Chicago in fifteen hours. Crane may have been thinking equally of the century itself, with its perennial sacrifice of superfluous human material to the idea of progress. He was one of the unlucky ones; beaten down by financial hardship, alcoholism, and guilt over his homosexuality, he committed suicide in 1932.

Appalachian Spring tries to stop the speeding train. Like so many other Copland works, it offers images of an ideal nation, the America that could have been or might still be. It begins with fifty bars in pure A major—white-key music, meaning that if it were transposed to the key of C it would use only the white keys of the piano. There are gentle pangs of dissonance as one simple strand is interwoven with another. A string of bucolic sketches culminates in variations on the Shaker hymn "Simple Gifts," whose words spell out Copland's aesthetic in brief: "When true simplicity is gained / To bow and to bend we shan't be ashamed."

In the "Fear in the Night" episode—which in Graham's final version becomes a fire-and-brimstone dance by a Revivalist—the idyll is cast in shadow. There are mechanical driving rhythms, icy passages for strings *sul ponticello* (as in the Schoenberg String Trio), percussive thuds like a fist rapping on a door. The finale brings reconciliation. A reprise of "Simple Gifts," stunningly harmonized over a descending scale, gives way to a bluesy passage marked "Like a prayer," whose phrases fall into the kinds of asymmetrical patterns that Copland identified with black music. This is perhaps the "negro church" of Graham's initial plan. In the final section, the frontier music of the opening alternates with the prayer music in evenly divided paragraphs—as if a divided country, black and white, were being made whole.

There is an affecting recording of the elderly Copland leading a rehearsal of *Appalachian Spring*. When he reaches the end, his reedy, confident Brooklyn voice turns sweet and sentimental: "Softer, very *sul tasto, misterioso*, great mood here . . . That's my favorite place in the whole piece . . . organlike. It should have a very special quality, as if you weren't moving your bows . . . That sounds too timid. It should sound rounder and more satisfying. Not distant. Quietly present. No diminuendos, like an organ sound. Take it freshly again, like an Amen." Copland conjures a perfect American Sunday, like the one at the end of Ives's *Three Places in New England*, when the music of all peoples streams from the open doors of a white-steepled church that does not yet exist.

9

DEATH FUGUE

Music in Hitler's Germany

Classical music was one of the few subjects, along with children and dogs, that brought out a certain tenderness in Adolf Hitler. In 1934, when the new leader of Germany appeared at a Wagner commemoration in Leipzig, observers noted that he spoke with "tears in his voice"—a phrase that appears infrequently in Max Domarus's twenty-three-hundred-page edition of the Führer's utterances. The previous year Hitler saluted the first Nuremberg Party Congress with a quotation from Wagner's *Meistersinger*—"*Wach' auf!*" ("Awake!"). Nor was Hitler the only Nazi who expressed reverence for the German musical tradition. Hans Frank, the governor-general of occupied Poland, said that his favorite composers were Bach, Brahms, and Reger. The Berlin Staatskapelle played Siegfried's Funeral Music at the funeral of SS Obergruppenführer Reinhard Tristan Eugen Heydrich, whose father had played in Hans von Bülow's orchestra and sung major tenor roles at Bayreuth. And Josef Mengele whistled favorite airs as he selected victims for the gas chambers in Auschwitz. There are many such anecdotes about music in the Third Reich, and they reinforce Thomas Mann's controversial but not easily refuted contention that during Hitler's reign as dictator of Germany great art was allied with great evil. "Thank God," Richard Strauss said after Hitler came to power, "finally a Reich Chancellor who is interested in art!"

In the nineteenth century, music, especially German music, was considered a sacred realm sufficient in itself, floating far above the ordinary world. In Nietzsche's caustic phrase, it became a "telephone from the beyond." Arthur Schopenhauer claimed in all earnestness that art and life had nothing to do with each other: "Beside the history of the world the history of philosophy, science, and art is guiltless and unstained by blood." Hans Pfitzner quoted those words as the epigraph to his 1917 opera *Palestrina*, which celebrated a composer's ability to rise above the politics of his time. Later, the composer used that same page of his score to write a dedication to Mussolini. That action made nonsense of the claim that music can achieve total autonomy from the society around it. Precisely because of its inarticulate nature, it is all too easily imprinted with ideologies and deployed to political ends.

In the wake of Hitler, classical music suffered not only incalculable physical losses—composers murdered in concentration camps, future talents killed on the beaches of Normandy and on the eastern front, opera houses and concert halls destroyed, émigrés forgotten in foreign lands—but a deeper loss of moral authority. During the war the Allies did their best to rescue the masterpieces of German tradition from Nazi propaganda, reappropriating them as emblems of the struggle against tyranny. The first notes of Beethoven's Fifth were matched to the Morse code signal for *V*, as in "Victory." As the years went by, however, classical music acquired a sinister aura in popular culture. Hollywood, which once had made musicians the fragile heroes of prestige pictures, began to give them a sadistic mien. By the 1970s the juxtaposition of "great music" and barbarism had become a cinematic cliché: in *A Clockwork Orange*, a young thug fantasizes ultraviolently to the strains of Beethoven's Ninth, and in *Apocalypse Now* American soldiers assault a Vietnamese village with the aid of Wagner's "Ride of the Valkyries." Now, when any self-respecting Hollywood archcriminal sets out to enslave mankind, he listens to a little classical music to get in the mood.

The ultimate correlation of music and horror is found in Paul Celan's 1944–45 poem "Death Fugue," in which a blue-eyed German instructs death-camp inmates in the art of digging their own graves. As he speaks, he mutates into a conductor urging his violin section to "bow more darkly," for "death is a *Meister* from Germany."

The aftermath of Hitler's corrosive love of music is unavoidable. Much

Richard Strauss, composer of *Salome*, expressionistically photographed by Edward Steichen in 1904. (Courtesy of the Library of Congress)

Gustav Mahler, known to Vienna cab drivers as "*Der Mahler,*" in the Netherlands in 1906. (Courtesy of the Amsterdam City Archives)

Mahler and Strauss outside the Graz opera house in May 1906. Strauss is in the boater hat. (Gilbert Kaplan)

Emancipator of the dissonance: Arnold Schoenberg circa 1915. (Arnold Schönberg Center)

Alban Berg strikes a pose in 1909, shortly before completing his apprenticeship with Schoenberg. (The Granger Collection, New York)

TOP LEFT: Master of the game: Igor Stravinsky in the 1920s. (Courtesy of the Library of Congress)

TOP RIGHT: Kurt Weill in 1935: "Once musicians obtained everything they had imagined . . . they started again from scratch." (Courtesy of the Weill-Lenya Research Center, Kurt Weill Foundation for Music, New York)

LEFT: George Gershwin photographed by the novelist and jazz enthusiast Carl Van Vechten. (Courtesy of the Library of Congress)

LEFT: Jean Sibelius: "Not everyone can be an 'innovating genius.'" (Courtesy of the Library of Congress)

BELOW: Aaron Copland, the archetypal New Deal composer, walks the open road on a trip to Mexico in the 1930s. (Courtesy of the Library of Congress)

Exiled in paradise: Schoenberg waters plants in the backyard of his home in Brentwood, California. (Arnold Schönberg Center)

Dmitri Shostakovich in a publicity photo used by the NBC network in the 1940s. (Courtesy of the Library of Congress)

Adolf Hitler listens to a rehearsal in the Luitpoldhalle in Nuremberg. (Photograph by Heinrich Hoffmann)

John Cage and Stockhausen take an imaginary flight. (Courtesy of the John Cage Trust at Bard College)

A conference of avant-garde minds at the International Summer Courses for New Music in Darmstadt in 1956: from left to right, Henri Pousseur, David Tudor, Heinz-Klaus Metzger, Karlheinz Stockhausen, and Pierre Boulez. (Copyright and photograph: Dr. Otto Tomek. Bildarchiv: Internationales Musikinstitut Darmstadt)

Anti-Communist demonstrations at the Soviet-sponsored Cultural and Scientific Conference for World Peace in New York in 1949. The previous year the schoolteacher Oksana Kasenkina had defected by jumping out a window. (George Silk/Getty Images)

Benjamin Britten at the Old Mill in Snape, where he wrote *Peter Grimes*. (Photograph by Enid Slater. Courtesy of the Britten-Pears Library, Aldeburgh)

Olivier Messiaen at Cedar Breaks in Utah in 1972, gathering material for his masterpiece *From the Canyons to the Stars . . .* (Yvonne Loriod-Messiaen/Nigel Simeone)

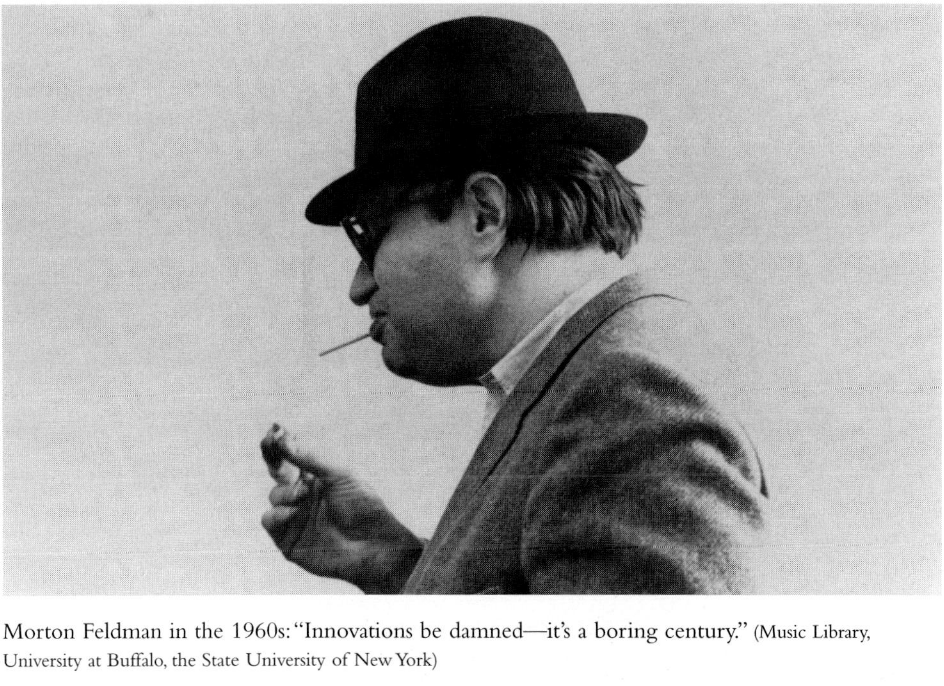

Morton Feldman in the 1960s: "Innovations be damned—it's a boring century." (Music Library, University at Buffalo, the State University of New York)

Steve Reich on the Brooklyn Bridge. (© Jeffrey Herman)

John Adams beneath the Golden Gate Bridge in 1987, around the time of *Nixon in China*.
(Photograph by Deborah O'Grady)

of subsequent twentieth-century musical history is a struggle to come to terms with it. Although there is no point in trying to restore Schopenhauer's separation of art and state, it is equally false to claim the opposite, that art can somehow be swallowed up in history or irreparably damaged by it. Music may not be inviolable, but it is infinitely variable, acquiring a new identity in the mind of every new listener. It is always in the world, neither guilty nor innocent, subject to the ever-changing human landscape in which it moves.

"There is too much music in Germany," Romain Rolland wrote, back in the heyday of Mahler and Strauss. Something was lurking, the French writer suspected, in these humongous Teutonic symphonies and music dramas—a cult of power, a "hypnotism of force." Germans themselves recognized the demonic strain in their culture. During the First World War, the not yet liberal-democratic Thomas Mann wrote a manifesto titled *Reflections of a Nonpolitical Man*, in which he praised all the backward German tendencies that he would later come to lament in the pages of *Doctor Faustus*. In the earlier work, Mann states that art "has a basically undependable, treacherous tendency; its joy in scandalous antireason, its tendency to beauty-creating 'barbarism,' cannot be rooted out . . ."

The melding of German music with reactionary politics goes back to Wagner. The composer's 1850 pamphlet *Das Judentum in der Musik*, or *Jewry in Music*, decried the "Jewification" of German music and demanded that the Jews undergo *Untergang* and *Selbstvernichtung*—destruction and self-annihilation.

"*Vernichtung*" is the word that the Nazis used to describe the mass murder of the European Jews, as Wagner's most astringent latter-day critics, such as Paul Lawrence Rose and Joachim Köhler, have emphasized. Jens Malte Fischer and other scholars have countered by pointing out that Wagner, in line with Hegel and other German thinkers, conceived "annihilation" not as a physical process but as a spiritual one, akin to Buddhist self-abnegation. Yet, even amid the chorus of nineteenth-century anti-Semitism, Wagner's rantings stood out for their malicious intensity. The Jews, he once said, were "the born enemy of pure humanity and all that is noble in man." They were also, he said, the "plastic demon of the ruin of mankind"—a phrase that Joseph Goebbels often employed in his speeches, and that appeared in the foul anti-Semitic film *The Eternal Jew*.

In Wagner's waning years, Bayreuth became a mecca for all manner of anti-Semites, Aryan priests, and social Darwinists. The monthly publication *Bayreuther Blätter* broadcast the racist theories of Paul de Lagarde, Arthur de Gobineau, and, most noxiously, Houston Stewart Chamberlain, who married Wagner's daughter Eva and became the intellectual leader of Bayreuth after Wagner's death. Although the composer feared that his disciples would make him look ridiculous, he failed to restrain them. Indeed, he singled out for praise several articles that delivered tendentious racial interpretations of his works.

Inevitably, anti-Semitism seeped into discussion of the music itself. Even in Wagner's lifetime the jabbering, gesticulating villains in the operas—the dwarves Alberich and Mime and the half-human Hagen in the *Ring*, the pedant Beckmesser in *Meistersinger*, the evil magician Klingsor in *Parsifal*—were sometimes understood as cartoons of Jews. Gustav Mahler believed that Mime embodied the "characteristic traits—petty intelligence and greed" of the Jewish race. "I know of only one Mime," he added, "and that is myself." The names of Wagner's villains could double as code words for Jews. When the right-wing composer Max von Schillings complained in a letter to Strauss that "Alberichs" in the Prussian Culture Ministry were undermining true German art, we can guess that the Jewishness of those agitators, chief among them Leo Kestenberg, prompted the Wagnerian association.

No work by Wagner acquired a more threatening aspect than *Parsifal*, which the composer created concurrently with his late prose writings on race and regeneration. According to Cosima, he once read aloud from Gobineau's *Essay on the Inequality of Human Races* and then went to the piano to play the opera's Prelude. The plot lends itself all too easily to racial exegesis. King Amfortas is suffering from an obscure wound, which appeared on his body after he succumbed to the mysterious Kundry; he would seem to be the modern German whose blood has mixed with inferior races, thus becoming "Jewified." Kundry is the female version of the Wandering Jew, who laughed at Christ on His way to the Cross and is now condemned to wander the earth; in a previous life she was Herodias, Salome's mother. Klingsor prepares to use her again to strike his final blow against the knights. Only Parsifal, the "pure fool," can resist the advances of Klingsor's slave. "*Verderberin!*" he shouts. "Corrupter! Stand away from me! Forever and ever, away from me!"

By remaining pure of blood, Parsifal is able to banish Klingsor, regain the lance that pierced Christ's side, and preside over the healing of the company of the Grail. As Parsifal holds the spear aloft, Kundry falls dead. Many anti-Semites wished that the Jews themselves could disappear so magically, with a stroke of the Meister's bow.

Richard Strauss, circa 1933, was the model of the Jewified German. His son, Franz, had married Alice von Grab, the daughter of the Czech-Jewish industrialist Emanuel von Grab. Writers of Jewish ancestry had contributed to almost all of his operas to date: Hedwig Lachmann had made the translation on which *Salome* was based; Hugo von Hofmannsthal had written the play *Elektra* and the librettos for *Der Rosenkavalier, Ariadne auf Naxos*, *Die Frau ohne Schatten*, *Die ägyptische Helena*, and *Arabella*; and Stefan Zweig was by then working on the libretto for Strauss's next opera, *Die schweigsame Frau*. Two years later the Propaganda Ministry would note in horror that the vocal score of *Die schweigsame Frau* displayed the names of no fewer than "4 Juden": Zweig; the publisher Adolph Fürstner; the composer Felix Wolfes, who made the piano arrangement; and, curiously, the Jacobean playwright Ben Jonson, who wrote *Epicoene; or, The Silent Woman*, on which the opera was based, and who was not Jewish in the least.

How Strauss became a prize exhibit of Nazi culture is a tangled tale. In his youth he had hardly been a political or cultural reactionary; his first opera, *Guntram*, unsettled conservative Wagnerians with its anti-collectivist message, and in following years he became Germany's foremost representative in the marketplace of international modernist decadence. In 1911, Siegfried Wagner, a composer far more modestly talented than his father, bemoaned the fact that *Parsifal* was being performed in theaters "contaminated by the misfortune-gestating works of Richard Strauss." The sardonic, anarchic side of Strauss's character persisted as late as 1921, when he proposed to the critic Alfred Kerr the idea of a "political operetta" set against the chaos of postwar Germany, featuring "workers and industrial councils, prima-donna intrigues, tenor ambitions, resigning directors of the old regime," together with "the National Assembly, war societies, party politicking while the people starve, pimps as Culture Ministers, criminals as War Ministers, murderers as Justice Ministers," and, somewhere in the middle, a "true German Romantic" composer who engages in uncouth behavior, flirts with conservatory girls, and, "as a respected anti-Semite, takes donations from rich Jews." Alas, nothing came of this promising plan.

The Weimar era brought many disappointments. While Krenek's *Jonny* and Weill's *Threepenny Opera* played to packed houses, Strauss's artful if sometimes overprecious operatic comedies—*Intermezzo*, *Die ägyptische Helena*, *Arabella*—met with mixed success. By the end of the twenties he had gone a long time without a hit, and insecurities were gnawing at him. Coincidentally or not, his politics slid to the right. When, in 1925, a young journalist named Samuel Wilder—soon to become Billy Wilder, director of *Sunset Boulevard* and *Some Like It Hot*—knocked on Strauss's door to ask his opinion of Mussolini, the composer expressed admiration for the dictator. Strauss met Mussolini more than once, and the two men evidently shared their disgust for artistic modernism. Later in the decade, Count Harry Kessler attended a luncheon at Hugo von Hofmannsthal's and recorded in his diary that Strauss had spoken in favor of a dictatorship. But the composer had little to say about Hitler himself. The name first crops up in Strauss's published utterances in November 1932, when, in the wake of the most recent German elections, he matter-of-factly wrote, "Hitler is apparently finished."

The protagonist of Alfred Döblin's novel *Berlin Alexanderplatz*, Franz Biberkopf, is a stubborn, tough-minded, self-reliant man who finds himself transformed into a Nazi stooge. In much the same way, Strauss's philosophy of self—"The laws of my mind determine my life," to quote *Guntram*—left him defenseless before Hitler's seductions. Nazism was itself the product of egoism, nihilism, cynicism, and amoral aestheticism. Hitler relished the role of the munificent prince: he displayed avid interest, made knowledgeable comments, behaved bashfully around his favorites. That the master of Germany should have assumed a servile air in Strauss's presence was thoroughly flattering. The two men first talked at length at the Bayreuth festival of 1933, when Strauss stepped in to conduct *Parsifal* after Toscanini had withdrawn in protest. The composer mentioned various matters that concerned him, including the idea of using film and radio revenues to support theater. He also put in a good word for the Jewish conductor Leo Blech. "I thank you," Hitler said simply.

Certain of Hitler's defining musical experiences took place against the familiar backdrop of Austria in the spring of 1906. He made his first trip to Vienna at the beginning of May, venturing forth from his hometown of Linz. On May 7 he sent his friend August Kubizek a postcard mentioning that he would see *Tristan* at the Court Opera the following night and *The Flying Dutchman* the night after. In a second card he gave his impression of the acoustics: "Powerful waves of sound flood the room, and the murmur of the wind gives way to a terrible frenzy of surging sound." The third card said: "Today 7:30–12 Tristan." Hitler stayed in Vienna for several more weeks, and he would have had time to go see *Salome* in Graz. Manfred Blumauer, the only scholar who has thoroughly investigated the matter, leaves open the unanswerable question of whether or not Hitler actually made the trip. Either way, he did tell Franz and Alice Strauss, in 1933 or 1934, that he had attended the Graz performance. Alice recounted the conversation to Blumauer decades later. At this meeting or another like it, Hitler apparently kissed Alice's hand, despite the fact that she was Jewish.

The *Tristan* that Hitler saw in Vienna in 1906 was the famous production that originated under Gustav Mahler. Alfred Roller, the painter and stage designer, used a semi-abstract, Symbolist interplay of color and light to heighten the mysteries of Wagner's score. Riveted by the spectacle, Hitler formed the ambition of studying painting and opera direction under Roller. He managed to obtain a letter of introduction from his mother's landlady, who had connections in Vienna. But when he moved to the imperial city, in February 1908, he failed to follow up on the invitation, even though Roller had spelled out where and when he could be found. Hitler later claimed that he had gone up to Roller's door before turning away in a state of anxiety. Images of *Tristan* stayed with him: in a sketchbook from the period 1925–26 he reproduced the image of the lovers huddled under a canopy of stars, and in 1934, when he finally met Roller, he could still recall the production in detail, including "the tower to the left with the pale light."

Biographies of Hitler have generally overlooked the fact that the conductor of *Tristan* on May 8 was Mahler himself. Kubizek, whose recollections can be used only with caution, states that his friend admired Mahler "because [he] concerned himself with the music dramas of Richard Wagner and produced them with a perfection that for its time literally shone." The story is partly confirmed by a comment that Hitler made to Goebbels in 1940, to the effect that he "did not contest the abilities and merits" of select Jewish artists such as Mahler and Max Reinhardt.

Hitler had worshipped Wagner from an early age. On various occasions he reported that a performance of Wagner's Roman drama *Rienzi* had inspired him to enter politics. In Vienna, Hitler became uneasy over the fact that masterpieces of Aryan culture were being performed in a city thronged with Jews. Once, in conversation with Hans Frank, he recalled hearing *Götterdämmerung* at the Court Opera and encountering "a couple of yammering Jews in caftans" on his way home. Hitler said: "It's impossible to think of a more irreconcilable combination. This glorious mystery of the dying hero and this Jewish filth!"

The spectral figure of the ghetto Jew also appears in *Mein Kampf*. Hitler claims to have met such a person during a long walk and asked himself: "Is this a Jew? . . . Is this a German?" At that moment, he said, hatred of Jews first welled up in him. There is a strange displacement going on here, given that a Jew occupied the podium during what may have been the most tremendous musical experience of Hitler's life. Was Mahler a tormenting symbol of Jewish power amid Hitler's failures? Or did the young man identify with Mahler's aura, his ability to command forces with a wave of his arms? In photographs, certain of the Führer's oratorical poses seem vaguely characteristic of Mahler's conducting—the right hand raised in a clenched, rotated fist, the left hand drawing back in a clawlike motion.

Hitler made his political reputation by bellowing out bilious speeches in Munich beer halls and soldiers' barracks, but his knowledge of music helped win him entrée to more rarefied circles. Edwin Bechstein, the renowned piano manufacturer, and Hugo Bruckmann, the publisher who printed the works of Houston Stewart Chamberlain, both welcomed Hitler into their salons. When Hitler met Carl von Schirach, the intendant of the National Theater in Weimar, he launched into a detailed analysis of *Die Walküre*, comparing recent Weimar performances with legendary ones that he had heard in Vienna. Schirach promptly invited him to tea. Such connections proved crucial in Hitler's rapid ascent from provincial to national fame.

The Wagner family fell deeply under Hitler's spell. Winifred Wagner opened the gates of Wahnfried for the man she considered Germany's savior. Hitler first visited the Wagners on October 1, 1923, as he was preparing his initial attempt at seizing control of Germany. The ailing Chamberlain rose from his sickbed, like Amfortas in *Parsifal*, to say that Hitler had come to save Germany in its "hour of highest need." In a later essay Chamberlain called Hitler a true man of the *Volk* who would rid Germany of the "ruinous, indeed poisonous influence of Jewishness on the life of the German people"—words echoing his own summary of Wagner's writings on "regeneration." Hitler was also told that he had a "Parsifal nature."

Hitler quickly absorbed the Bayreuth lifestyle—vegetarianism, agitation for animal rights, dabblings in Buddhism and Indian lore. Later, he would dote on the younger Wagners and served as a substitute father for the grandsons, Wieland and Wolfgang. When he came to Bayreuth, as he did every summer from 1933 until 1940, he became a different being. "He obviously felt at ease in the Wagner family and free of the compulsion to represent power," the Nazi architect Albert Speer observed.

The "Beer Hall Putsch" took place on November 8–9, 1923. Siegfried Wagner had planned to commemorate Hitler's victory by conducting his newest symphonic poem, *Glück*, at a concert in Munich. Defeat forced him postpone the premiere, but neither he nor his relations lost faith in the cause. Hitler, confined to Landsberg prison, wrote to express his gratitude. Bayreuth, he said, was "in the line of march to Berlin"; it was the place where "first the Master and then Chamberlain forged the spiritual sword which we are wielding today." The Wagners kept the prisoner well supplied, sending along recordings of Wagner excerpts, the libretto of Siegfried's opera *Der Schmied von Marienburg*, a variety of domestic items (blankets, jackets, stockings, foodstuffs, books), and writing materials, including typing paper of superior quality. A phonograph came from Helene Bechstein. Hitler set to composing *Mein Kampf*.

Hitler's speeches of the later 1920s often touched on cultural matters, displaying modest knowledge of the musical scenes of Berlin, Munich, and Vienna. One sign of Germany's decline, Hitler said, was its growing ignorance of the great musical tradition: "Only a couple hundred thousand know Mozart, Beethoven, Wagner, only some of them know Bruckner." Meanwhile, "little *Neutöner* [new-toners] come and unleash their dissonances." He made a knowing reference to Krenek's *Jonny spielt auf*: "In Germany one lets Jonny strike up and concerning South Tyrol one complains about the *Untergang* of German culture." In this same period he criticized the operetta *Das Dreimäderlhaus* for its travesties of Schubert songs and launched an extended assault on the conductor Bruno Walter, "alias Schlesinger." In Berlin, Hitler alleged, there were five opera conductors on the staff of the state-funded opera houses, all of them Jews. The reference to "*fünf Juden*" brings to mind the scene in *Salome* in which five Jews dispute among themselves in Herod's court.

Hitler took power in January 1933, and by the end of the year most of the German cultural apparatus had fallen under the control of Goebbels's Propaganda Ministry. But music did not become a direct instrument of the state. Hitler wanted the ministry to serve the "spiritual development of the nation," and Goebbels agreed. As the historian Alan Steinweis shows, the minister saw artists as "creating Germans" and organized them into semi-independent organizations. It was called "self-administration under state supervision." The Reichskulturkammer, or Reich Culture Chamber, had departments for each art form, including a Reich Music Chamber, whose first president was Richard Strauss. Musical life was not merely Nazified from above; to a great extent, it Nazified itself. Even the anti-Jewish clause in the Kulturkammer laws neglected to mention the Jews by name; cultural bureaucrats were left to decide which artists lacked "aptitude" for cultural life. Not surprisingly, all leading Jewish musicians were deemed inept. The April 7, 1933, law barring Jews from the public sector had already had a devastating impact, because so many had been employed by Weimar's arts programs. Weill left Germany on March 22, Klemperer on April 4, Schoenberg on May 17.

From the start, classical music blared in the background of Nazi life. Party rallies were so immaculately choreographed to Beethoven, Bruckner, and Wagner that the music seemed to have been written in support of the pageantry; it was through such sleights of hand that Hitler generated his authority. Unlike Stalin, who demanded that Soviet art mirror the ideology of the regime, Hitler wished to maintain the illusion of autonomy in the arts. Brigitte Hamann, in her biography of Winifred Wagner, reports that at the Bayreuth festival of 1933 the dictator asked audiences to refrain from singing the "Horst Wessel" song or from making other patriotic manifestations, on the grounds that "there is no more glorious expression of the German spirit than the immortal works of the Master." Like so many German music lovers, Hitler claimed that the classical tradition was an "absolute art" hovering above history, as in Schopenhauer's formulation.

Such was the import of Hitler's most ambitious statement on musical policy, his "cultural address" at the Party rally of 1938, in which he said that "it is totally impossible to express a scientific worldview in musical terms" and "nonsense" to try to express Party business. In contrast to Stalin, Hitler turned up his nose at sycophantic propaganda. In 1935, he directed that no more music should be dedicated to him, and three years later he complained that a group of works commissioned for the Reich Party Day paled in comparison to Bruckner. Politics aspired to the condition of music, not vice versa. Thus, when the Berlin Philharmonic played the finale of Bruckner's Seventh before that 1938 speech, the implication was that Hitler's rhetoric would follow the musical model. Goebbels wanted his propaganda efforts to stress, in Wagnerian fashion, key leitmotifs, renewed through ingenious variations.

Hitler, too, believed in "music for all." He demanded, for example, that new opera houses contain as many as three thousand seats. But in Nazi Germany, as in New Deal America, classical music could be sold to the masses only with pressure from above. German listeners had felt the pull of Americanized popular music in the Weimar era, and they kept demanding it under Nazism. Hitler's Wagner galas met with a tepid response from the Party rank and file. When Hitler walked into a mostly empty hall at the "official" *Meistersinger* of 1933, he sent out patrols to fetch high-ranking Party members from Nuremberg's beer halls and cafés. A *Meistersinger* at the 1938 Party congress drew so few Brownshirts that patrons of the Hotel Deutscher Hof around the corner were conscripted to fill the empty rows. During performances Hitler would shake his associates awake whenever they dozed off.

Great musicians occupied a special category, their ideological errors often overlooked or excused. Hitler deemed Wilhelm Furtwängler, the leader of the Berlin Philharmonic, Germany's supreme musician, and looked askance at charismatic younger artists who were rising through the ranks of Nazi culture. The podium virtuoso Herbert von Karajan, for example, may have joined the Party early on, but Hitler disliked him. Karajan's habit of conducting from memory was "arrogant," Hitler thought—Furtwängler would never do such a thing. Hans Knappertsbusch was also found wanting. His blue eyes and blond hair shouldn't fool anyone, Hitler said in one of his "table talk" monologues; this was a mere bandmaster with a poor feeling for tempo and "no ear for music." Conductors like Furtwängler and Clemens Krauss exhibited a more flexible, Romantic style, and in Hitler's opinion they probed the music more deeply. The critic John Rockwell has proposed that Hitler's youthful encounter with Mahler may have shaped his taste in conductors. Furtwängler's philosophical, anti-metronomic style would have naturally attracted one who had been swept away by Mahler's *Tristan*.

Despite his "apolitical" stance, Hitler did once or twice imply a link between his favorite music and his increasingly aggressive foreign policy. It happened with the symphonic orations of Bruckner. Derided in his lifetime as a naive country bumpkin who lacked Viennese sophistication, Bruckner apparently represented for Hitler the revenge of the "little" man on an uncomprehending world. In 1937, a bust of the composer was installed in the so-called Valhalla of German cultural heroes near Regensburg, and the Reich chancellor was photographed gazing raptly at it. The ceremony took place in conjunction with a major speech in which Hitler introduced the Nazi spiritual concept of *Gottgläubigkeit*—belief in God divorced from religious cant and wedded to national feeling. The scholar Bryan Gilliam suggests that the event was a kind of rehearsal for the annexation of Austria by the Reich, with Hitler using the composer as a metaphor for the synthesis of Austrian and German culture. As Bruckner's bust was installed in the German Valhalla, so would Austria be installed in the Reich.

After the *Anschluss* of March 1938, Hitler scheduled a plebiscite to confirm the takeover and took a campaign tour through smaller Austrian cities and towns. Many Austrian artists spoke in his favor. "Say a big YES to our Führer's action," urged the conductor Karl Böhm. On April 3, 1938, Hitler arrived in Graz, where twenty thousand Nazis had rioted against the Austrian government several weeks before. He had promised that Graz would be one of the first cities he would visit after the *Anschluss*. He drove down a two-and-a-half-mile-long *via triumphalis*, and the city that had cheered *Salome* three decades before thronged to greet the new leader. It was a "symphony of joy," said the *Völkischer Beobachter*, set against a white-blue sky. The pianist Alfred Brendel, who grew up in Graz, remembered the "mass hysteria" of the day.

On a return trip three years later, Hitler visited the Graz Opera and inspected the sets of a production of *The Magic Flute*. He did not mention having attended *Salome* in 1906; his entourage had the impression that he had never been in the city. He did, however, declare that the building would have to be rebuilt on account of its acoustical flaws—an odd thing for someone who had never heard a performance in the house to say.

Was there such a thing as a "Nazi sound"? Did a conservative style steeped in Wagner, Bruckner, and/or Strauss guarantee success in Hitler's world? Did more adventurous styles—those that had prospered in the free atmosphere of the Weimar Republic—guarantee failure? The answers to these questions are not as clear as is often assumed. The automatic equation of radical style with liberal politics and of conservative style with reactionary politics is a historical myth that does little justice to an agonizingly ambiguous historical reality.

By rights, the politically and aesthetically conservative composer Hans Pfitzner should have been the official genius of the Nazi period. He had long raged against the "Jewish-international spirit" in music and had admired Hitler from the earliest years. In 1923, when Pfitzner spent some time in the hospital, Hitler paid him a visit in the company of a mutual associate. The two men talked about Jewish war crimes, then fell into a discussion of the career of Otto Weininger, whose racial and sexual theories had fascinated Schoenberg and Berg. Pfitzner called Weininger the "greatest self-hater and anti-Semite who ever lived." Hitler replied that this man was "the one acceptable Jew" because he had "rid himself from the world." Pfitzner wondered aloud whether such a procedure would work for all Jews, whereupon Hitler became displeased. Pfitzner was at this time wearing a thin, faintly rabbinical beard, which gave Hitler the false impression that the composer was Jewish. "The Führer is very strongly opposed to Pfitzner," Goebbels wrote in his diary in 1943. "He considers him a half Jew, which, according to our records, is actually not the case."

When the Nazis took over, Pfitzner thought that his time had come. He said of Hitler in 1934, "Today there is no one beside him with the strength of body, spirit, or soul, him whom we have known as our German Führer for the past ten years." A pamphlet titled *Listen to Hans Pfitzner!* advertised the composer's relevance. But Pfitzner failed to gain hero status, and before long he was muttering that the cosmopolitan modernism of younger composers was being favored over his own pure German music—the same complaint that he had repeatedly made during the Weimar Republic. He pleaded in vain for another meeting with Hitler. In desperate need of a Nazi sponsor, he found one in Hans Frank, the Reger-loving governor-general of Poland, who had set up his own orchestra in Kraków. Pfitzner traveled there several times between 1942 and 1944, the last time bringing with him an overture titled *Krakau Greeting*. It was first heard thirty miles from Auschwitz, while the gas chambers were being dismantled.

In retrospect, it seems inevitable that Paul Hindemith should have been viciously criticized in the early Nazi era, to the point where he felt compelled to go into exile. Yet the former bad boy of Weimar Germany tried hard to find a place in Hitler's world and kept trying long after he had been made to feel unwelcome.

Nudged to the political right by his unhappy collaborations with Brecht, Hindemith struck up a relationship with the conservative poet Gottfried Benn, who penned for him an oratorio text entitled *The Unending*, a renunciation of politics, publicity, and worldly pleasure. From 1933 to 1935, Hindemith worked on the opera *Mathis der Maler*, which partook of the holy-German-art ethos of Wagner's *Meistersinger*. Based on the life of the Renaissance painter Matthias Grünewald, it described an artist's solitary struggle, amid political and religious chaos, to find roots in "the primal soil of your people," in the words of a peasant rebel leader. Nazi aestheticians took note of Hindemith's new tack, and mentioned him as a potential musical chieftain. In 1934, the composer told his publisher that he had talked to officials about instituting "the most ambitious program of popular musical education (together with appropriate composer training) the world has ever seen. One can literally have the musical enlightenment of millions in one's hands."

If Hindemith was politically on the right track, why did he fall from favor? Apparently, the prudish Hitler had been scandalized by the 1929 opera *News of the Day*, a rigorously up-to-date contribution to the *Zeitoper* genre in which a soprano sang nude in a bathtub. "It is obvious that [*News of the Day*] shocked the Führer greatly," Hindemith wrote to his publisher in November 1934. "I shall write him a letter (F. was very taken with this idea) in which I shall ask him to convince himself to the contrary and perhaps visit us sometime here in the school, where I would have the cantata from the Plöner Musiktag performed for him—no one has ever been able to resist that. F. is to give him my letter, also the text [of *Mathis*]." "F." is Furtwängler, who proceeded to make a major tactical mistake; instead of arguing his colleague's case behind the scenes, he defended him in a newspaper article, questioning the advisability of political controls on artists. Rather than achieving Hindemith's rehabilitation, Furtwängler doomed him.

Still, even as late as 1936, Hindemith was attempting to regain the trust of the authorities, promising to write a work in honor of the Luftwaffe. It was, he said, "an opportunity not to be missed," and he even hoped to "give them something really good." When the composer went to America in January 1939, he found himself sailing with a boatload of Jewish refugees—the sort of people, he wrote to his half-Jewish wife, whom one wouldn't want to see on a regular basis. The following year, he began teaching at Yale.

Other denizens of the Weimar music scene made a relatively smooth transition into the Nazi era. With some adroit maneuvering, they were even able to carry on in characteristic twenties styles. In January 1939, Hitler went to see Werner Egk's *Peer Gynt*, an eclectic piece steeped in Stravinsky, Weill, jazz, and Berg, and he liked it so much that he summoned the composer to his box, in the manner of Stalin at the Bolshoi. Hitler acclaimed Egk as a successor to Wagner; Goebbels praised him as a "really great, original talent." (Possibly, the Nazi leaders enjoyed *Peer Gynt* because it cleverly employed modern Western styles to satirize modern Western society; the anthem of the troll kingdom is "Do as you like.") Carl Orff, who had participated in Leo Kestenberg's socialistic education schemes in the Weimar period, scored a surprise hit in Nazi Germany with his cantata *Carmina burana*. With its exotic percussion writing (modeled on Stravinsky's *Les Noces*) and its syncopated "bounce," Orff's showpiece was far removed from Hitler's favorite Wagner operas. The review in the *Völkischer Beobachter*, the Nazi Party paper, identified it as "Bavarian *Niggermusik*." Once the work had demonstrated huge popular appeal, however, Nazi aesthetics were adjusted to accommodate it. By 1944 Goebbels was gushing in his diary that *Carmina burana* contained "extraordinary beauties."

One lonely force of noncompliance among German composers was Karl Amadeus Hartmann, who had connections to the anti-Nazi resistance, such as it was, and coded his music with messages of opposition. His orchestral score *Miserae* bore the inscription "To my friends, who had to die in the hundreds . . . Dachau 1933/1934." Historians have long honored Hartmann as the "good German" composer, the one who held fast against Nazification. But even this case becomes a little ambiguous on close inspection. As Michael Kater demonstrates in a painstaking study of German music under Nazi rule, Hartmann had the luxury of living off his father-in-law's ball-bearing fortune. And when *Miserae* had its first performance, in Prague in 1935, the inscription about Dachau was seen only by the conductor, Hermann Scherchen. The audience had no knowledge of it. Hartmann's anti-Nazism was equally invisible to Munich Nazi Party operatives, who noted in a report that he had greeted them with a Party salute.

Only in Mussolini's Italy—admittedly a less oppressive environment than Hitler's Germany—did a composer register an unmistakable public protest against totalitarian government in the form of a musical work. Luigi Dallapiccola, who found his personal style by synthesizing Stravinsky's neoclassicism with Schoenberg's dissonant language, initially thrilled to Mussolini's pseudo-heroic poses, as did many impressionable artists of the prewar years. Indeed, Dallapiccola believed in Fascism so fervently that he "sometimes annoyed us, his friends," as his colleague Goffredo Petrassi told the historian Harvey Sachs. Then, when the Italian-German Axis formed in the thirties, Dallapiccola, whose wife was Jewish, lost faith in Mussolini, and, unlike so many others, he wrote his disenchantment on the surface of his music. His *Canti di prigionia*, or *Songs of Imprisonment* (1938–41), a choral work of shadowy, secretive beauty, employs words of Mary Stuart, Boethius, and Savonarola to represent all those who had been thrown in prison for speaking their minds or for simply being who they were: "I implore you to set me free . . . Happy is the one who breaks the bonds of heavy earth . . . The world may press down, enemies may attack, I fear nothing." Dallapiccola found the first of these prayers in a book by Stefan Zweig, Strauss's former librettist. Two months after *Canti di prigionia* was first performed, Zweig committed suicide in Brazil, unable to see any hope in the deepening gloom.

Atonality and other modernist trends suffered an interesting fate in Nazi Germany. When an exhibition of Degenerate Music opened in Düsseldorf in May 1938, its organizer, Hans Severus Ziegler, decreed that atonal composition was a "product of the Jewish spirit" of Schoenberg. Yet, as Michael Kater points out, a committee led by Strauss had declared that "the Reich Music Chamber cannot forbid works of an atonal character, for it is up to the audience to judge such compositions." In the end, Ziegler's exhibition was poorly received, even in official circles. There was some embarrassment over the fact that Stravinsky had been included in the gallery of degenerates, and the German Foreign Affairs Office issued a quasi-apologetic explanation. (Stravinsky, who had yet to acquire the more or less liberal views that he would boast in America, grumbled back in 1933 that he was being unfairly neglected in the new Germany, in spite of his "negative attitude toward Communism and Judaism . . . not to put it in stronger terms.") Strauss made a particularly acid comment about the "degenerate music" concept; in a conversation with Ziegler, he asked, with a "half-bitter, half-mischievous" laugh, why the decadent operettas of Franz Lehár and his own "pure atonal" *Salome* had been omitted. The answer was implicit: Hitler liked them.

As it turned out, atonal and twelve-tone writing was sometimes tolerated, provided the composer assumed the right ideological stance. When Herbert Gerigk, a musicologist who headed the music section of Alfred Rosenberg's ideology bureau and worked tirelessly to identify all musical Jews, pondered the case of Arnold Schoenberg in 1934, he came to a startling conclusion: "Even so-called atonality can produce worthwhile art as long as the man standing behind it is racially and personally unobjectionable and creative."

Schoenberg's pupils Winfried Zillig and Paul von Klenau used twelve-tone technique throughout the Nazi period, softening its impact with tonal material. Zillig, in his opera *Das Opfer*, employed a row made up of major and minor triads, as in Berg's *Lulu*. Klenau, a reactionary Dane, justified the technique of his opera *Michael Kohlhaas* as follows: "In the opera *not one* note occurs that cannot be derived from one of seven underlying twelve-tone rows . . . The music of our time needs a new ordering regularity, which corresponds to ethical content. A future-oriented art appropriate to the National Socialist world requires ethical fellow feeling and a knack for craftsmanship that gets rid of all arbitrary individualistic activities in the realm of tones."

Ironically, Klenau's nationalistic spin on twelve-tone writing was not too far removed from his teacher's own conception of it. Although Schoenberg opposed the Nazis unstintingly, he was hardly free from authoritarian impulses, as his attack on the egalitarianism of the Weimar Republic shows. In 1931, as Germany was swinging politically rightward, Schoenberg described his music as "a living example of an art able most effectively to oppose Latin and Slav hopes of hegemony and derived through and through from the traditions of German music." Even in American exile, he had a hard time adjusting to the concept of "We the people," and in his 1938 essay "Four-Point Program for Jewry" he declared that democracy would be unsuitable for a mass Jewish movement. To illustrate the point, he provided an object lesson from his own biography; in the course of running the Society for Private Musical Performances in Vienna, he said, he had become "a kind of dictator," and on encountering internal opposition, he did something "which under other circumstances could be called illegal: I dissolved the whole society, built a new one, accepted only such members who were in perfect agreement with my artistic principles and excluded the entire opposition." This is precisely how Hitler took power in 1933.

Schoenberg sent the "Four-Point Program" to his fellow exile Thomas Mann, in the hope that the novelist would arrange to have it published. Mann wrote back in alarm, objecting to the document's "fascistic bent," its "will to terrorism." The seed of *Doctor Faustus* was planted.

Alban Berg lacked sympathy for Hitler's program, but he was not above tailoring his résumé in order to meet Nazi requirements. In 1933 he discussed the challenges of the new German marketplace with his pupil Adorno, who himself had no desire to leave Germany, despite his partly Jewish background. Adorno advised Berg to advertise his pure Aryan origins to the Reich Music Chamber, and also to distance himself from any notion of Jewish solidarity, "about which one can have so few illusions."

As for Webern, he forsook his onetime socialist views to become an unashamed Hitler enthusiast, greeting the invasion of Denmark and Norway with almost orgasmic prose: "This is Germany today! But the *National Socialist* one, to be sure! Not just any one! This is exactly the *new* state, for which the seed was already laid twenty years ago. Yes, *a new state it is*, one that has never existed before!! *It is something new!* Created by this unique man!!! . . . *Each day becomes more exciting*. I see such a good future. It will be different also for me."

No composer more painfully exhibited the moral collapse of German art than Richard Strauss, who served as president of the Reich Music Chamber from 1933 to 1935. The composer of *Salome* warmed to Hitler chiefly because he thought that under the aegis of this music-loving chancellor he would be able to enact a series of long-dreamed-of reforms—new royalty schemes favoring classical composers over popular ones; the extension of composers' copyrights; rules preventing spa orchestras from massacring Wagner overtures; guidelines discouraging young people from ruining their voices by bellowing patriotic songs.

The record is dismaying. Strauss appeared at Nazi functions and signed a meretricious denunciation of Thomas Mann. When the anti-fascist Toscanini canceled his Bayreuth engagements in 1933, Strauss replaced him, and in the same year he stepped in as a last-minute replacement for the racially unacceptable Bruno Walter in Berlin. On the relatively rare occasions when Strauss was in the capital, he socialized with Nazi leaders at the various stately mansions that they had commandeered. In February 1934, for example, he joined Hitler for a vegetarian meal at the home of Walther Funk; after dinner, the composer accompanied the singers Viorica Ursuleac and Heinrich Schlusnus in various of his Lieder. He offered the leadership birthday wishes, congratulated them on their speeches, and bestowed holiday gifts. For Christmas 1933 he gave Hitler a copy of Joseph Gregor's *World History of the Theater.*

Strauss's behavior was not always as contemptible as it seemed. In the case of the Bruno Walter affair, the outside world had no idea that Strauss accepted the assignment with reluctance, and only after a Jewish-owned concert agency, Wolff and Sachs, informed him—truthfully or not—that Walter himself had asked Strauss to step in. In general, Strauss refused to take part in the de-Jewification of musical life. He avoided signing papers that would have set in motion the removal of Jews from the Music Chamber. He resisted the ban on Jewish composers and announced that the symphonies of Mahler, among other things, should continue to be performed. Planning an international music festival in Hamburg in 1935, he became exasperated when the Propaganda Ministry demanded an "Aryan French" substitute for Paul Dukas's opera *Ariane and Bluebeard.* Strauss promptly declared his "total lack of interest in the Hamburg Festival from now on . . . I am not coming to Hamburg and, for the rest, *Götz v. B.*" *Götz von Berlichingen* is the Goethe play whose hero famously says, "Lick my ass."

Strauss also could not comprehend the banning of Felix Mendelssohn. Since his youth he had loved Mendelssohn's music—all his exalted horn solos are descended from the Nocturne of *A Midsummer Night's Dream*—and he ridiculed the "terrible, Aryan ersatz music" that German composers (including Orff) were hastily concocting to replace Mendelssohn's forbidden score.

When Stefan Zweig criticized his friend's accommodations with the Nazis, Strauss answered with a tortuously self-justifying letter. "Do you believe that I have ever let myself be guided in any act by the notion that I am Germanic (perhaps, *qui lu sa*)?" he asked Zweig. "For me there are only two kinds of people, those with talent and those with none, and for me the *Volk* does not exist until it becomes the public." The parenthetical remark is a fittingly cosmopolitan blending of French and Italian; Strauss probably meant to write "*Chi lo sa*" ("Who knows"). Which is to say, he neither knew nor cared whether he was a true Aryan.

For some time the Nazis had been keeping a file on Strauss's poor attitude. In February 1934, he and Furtwängler were denounced for failing to give the Fascist salute during a singing of the "Horst Wessel" song at a public event (reportedly, they were greeted with shouts of "Concentration camp!"). When it became known that several Jews had assisted in the creation of *Die schweigsame Frau, Der Stürmer* editorialized: "If [Strauss] wishes to use Jewish collaborators for his coming works we shall have to draw conclusions which are not very pleasant." And if later recollections by Albert Speer are to be believed, Hitler himself began to see Strauss as an "opponent of the regime," in league with "Jewish riff-raff."

But only when the Gestapo intercepted that remarkable letter to Zweig—"the *Volk* does not exist until it becomes the public"—did Strauss's situation as an "official" composer become untenable. He was immediately forced to resign his Reich Music Chamber post. In a private memorandum Strauss finally let down his cynical facade and issued a private cry of principled disgust: "I consider the Streicher-Goebbels Jew baiting as a disgrace to German honor, as evidence of incompetence, the basest weapon of untalented, lazy mediocrity against a higher intelligence and greater talent."

If Strauss had fled Germany in the wake of this fiasco, Hitler's regime would have suffered a severe embarrassment. But for various reasons the idea of leaving Germany probably never crossed his mind. By then well into his seventies, he could hardly have conceived of starting a new life on foreign soil. More important, if he had left by himself, his extended family would presumably have been sent to the concentration camps. Strauss had little choice but to undergo a humiliating process of self-rehabilitation. He began by writing an obsequious letter to Hitler, hailing him as "the great designer of German existence." In 1936 Strauss made a high-profile appearance at the opening ceremony of the Olympics in Berlin, conducting a trite ceremonial piece titled *Olympic Hymn*, whose manuscript he had presented to Hitler. Thousands of white pigeons were released into the air as the music played. The program also included "Deutschland, Deutschland, über alles," the "Horst Wessel" song, the "Hallelujah" Chorus, and the finale of Beethoven's Ninth. In Leni Riefenstahl's film *Olympia*, Strauss can be seen wearing the poker face that he displayed through the first half of the twentieth century.

Strauss wasn't merely trying to repair his wounded pride; he was also trying to protect his partly Jewish family. On Kristallnacht, in November 1938, Richard and Christian Strauss, the composer's beloved grandsons, were stopped on their way to school and forced to spit on a group of Jews who had been gathered in the village square; then they were spat on themselves. Later, Michael Kater relates, Franz and Alice Strauss were repeatedly harassed by the Gestapo, and on one occasion they were dragged from Richard's house in the middle of the night and interrogated for several days. All the same, Franz remained a Nazi supporter. An intelligence report from 1944 stated that he responded angrily when acquaintances expressed doubts about the progress of the war or about Party institutions. It was also reported that Alice did not contradict him. Inside the house, however, arguments raged. Franz generally spoke up for the Nazis, while Richard railed against them.

Music remained Strauss's refuge from politics, yet political issues shadowed the successor to *Die schweigsame Frau*—the one-act drama *Friedenstag*, or *Day of Peace*. The scenario for this work originated with Zweig; the libretto was written by the theater historian Joseph Gregor, who took over as Strauss's librettist when collaboration with Zweig became impossible. The story opens with a town starving under siege in the Thirty Years' War. Its commandant is determined to burn it to the ground rather than surrender, but he is released from his destructive mission by the abrupt arrival of the "day of peace." Some latter-day interpreters have tried to explicate the opera as a covert act of protest, but in truth the antiwar message blended all too well with Hitler's cynical manipulation of European pacifists; the Führer loved to twist the minds of democratic leaders by arguing that his territorial acquisitions would *prevent* war, not start it. ("Whoever lights the torch of war in Europe," Hitler said in 1935, "can only wish for chaos.") The emptiness of the sentiment bleeds through Strauss's blandly triumphant ending, a souped-up pastiche of the finales of Beethoven's Ninth and *Fidelio* with echoes also of Mahler's Eighth. The score comes to life only when Maria, the commandant's wife, complains about how dreary her life has become. As so often, Strauss identified most strongly with his lead female character.

Hitler confirmed Strauss's temporary return to grace by attending a gala performance of *Friedenstag* in Vienna in 1939. (The premiere had happened in Munich the previous year.) The Führer was awarded a stormy ovation when he appeared in his box. He then ceded the spotlight to Strauss, who was saluted with his own *Fanfare for the Vienna Philharmonic.* At a sort of press conference with Goebbels the next morning, Strauss delivered his thanks and expressed the hope that German art would prosper forever under the protection of the Third Reich. Then, in a two-hour-long private breakfast with Goebbels, he talked about various problems that beset him, including the effect of anti-Jewish measures on his family. "He is unpolitical, like a child," Goebbels wrote in his diary. Apparently, Strauss received assurances that his daughter-in-law and grandsons would have Hitler's official protection, although this was not forthcoming. Alice Strauss was given a passport in which she was assigned the middle name "Sara," like all the female Jews in Germany.

Two years later the composer suffered a public breakdown as a result of Goebbels's psychological games. Strauss had been heard to make dismissive remarks about the operettas of Lehár, whom, everyone knew, Hitler loved. Goebbels called Strauss in for a meeting, which he ironically recounted in his diary: "I say a few sweet nothings to him about his insolent letters. He cannot stop writing letters, and it has already brought him much misfortune. Next time I will show him." In fact, this intimate exchange took place in front of a large delegation of composers. Werner Egk described the scene in his memoirs. "Lehár has the masses, you do not!" the minister screamed. "Stop once and for all your chatter about the significance of 'serious music'! You are not helping your case! The art of tomorrow is different from the art of yesterday! You, Herr Strauss, are yesterday!"

Afterward, Egk reported, Strauss stood for a while on the steps of the Propaganda Ministry, tears streaming down his cheeks, his head buried in his hands. "If only I had listened to my wife and stayed in Garmisch," he murmured.

On January 30, 1939, Hitler celebrated the sixth anniversary of his regime by delivering a major address to the Reichstag. Since the burning of the Reichstag building in 1933, the German parliament had carried out its business, now purely ceremonial, in the Kroll Opera House—where, in the Weimar time, Otto Klemperer had conducted Hindemith's *News of the Day* and Stravinsky's *Oedipus Rex*. In the same hall in 1933, a crippled parliament had passed the Enabling Act, which granted the Reich chancellor dictatorial powers. Now, in 1939, Hitler gave notice that his dominion would in short order encompass much of Europe and that those who stood in the way of destiny would face destruction. Goebbels, in his diaries, described Hitler's speech as a "spacious" conception that built through an extended development of familiar themes to a potent climax. "Posterity must cherish his speech as a masterwork," Goebbels wrote. "The ending of the speech is gripping and devastating. All are totally enthralled by it. The Führer is a true genius."

This speech added two new themes to the familiar denunciation of the Jews: laughter and annihilation. "Very often in my life," Hitler said, "I have been a prophet, and have generally been laughed at [*ausgelacht*]." He announced that it was now finally time to bring the Jewish problem to a "solution" whose sheer scope might wipe the smiles from the faces of his enemies: "I believe that the formerly resounding laughter of Jewry in Germany has now choked up in its throat." Hitler made another prophecy: "If the international Jewish financiers inside and outside Europe should succeed in plunging the nations once more into a world war, then the result will not be the Bolshevization of the earth, and thus the victory of Jewry, but the annihilation [*Vernichtung*] of the Jewish race in Europe."

Hitler repeated these themes in subsequent speeches. In September 1942 he said, "The Jews in Germany once laughed [*haben einst . . . gelacht*] at my prophecies. I do not know if they are still laughing today, or if their laughter has not already died down. I can only affirm now: their laughter will everywhere die down." And in November of that year he said, "I have always been scorned [*ausgelacht*] as a prophet. Of those who formerly laughed [*die damals lachten*], untold numbers are no longer laughing today, and those who are still laughing may not be doing it for much longer."

Hitler was announcing in coded language that the Final Solution was under way. What makes these speeches especially disturbing from the musical angle is that they may contain a Wagner reference. The sound of laughter echoes all through *Parsifal*. Kundry tells Parsifal of how she mocked Christ's suffering on the way of the cross:

I saw—Him—Him—
and—laughed . . .
And He looked at me!

Otto Weininger, whom Hitler described in his monologues as the "one good Jew," said of the laughter in *Parsifal*, "The laughter of Kundry comes from Jewry. *The metaphysical guilt of the Jews is their grinning at God*." Later, in the scene of Good Friday Spell, the boy-messiah looks out over a blossoming meadow and thinks of the flower maidens who tempted him. "I saw them wither," he murmurs, "those who once smiled on me [*Ich sah sie welken, die einst mir lachten*]."

Hitler's obsession with *Parsifal* is well documented. Hans Frank, in his not always reliable autobiography, reported the following more or less believable scene, which took place in the Führer's private train car in 1935:

> The record player was pulled out and the Führer picked out some records. First the *Parsifal* Prelude, conducted by Muck in Bayreuth. We sat there in his car in the slowly rolling train, and in our lonely silence there sounded the sacred tones of the last work of Richard Wagner, his Master. As they died away, he said pensively: "On *Parsifal* I am building my religion—serving God in a solemn way without theological Party bickering. Over a brotherly pedal point of true love, without theatrical humility and empty formal babbling. Without these disgusting frocks and hag's skirts. Only in heroic garb can one serve God."

Parsifal became the subject of a tug-of-war among the Nazi leaders. Goebbels, Rosenberg, and Heinrich Himmler all wanted to have the opera removed from German stages on the grounds that its mystical Christianity traduced the Nazi spirit. According to a document that has been uncovered by Brigitte Hamann, Hitler laughed heartily when Wieland Wagner, the composer's grandson, told him that Rosenberg had deemed only the second act worthy of performance. *Parsifal* must remain, Hitler said, although directors would have to figure out a more modern setting for it. Wieland was instructed to "design a timeless Grail temple." As Wieland put it, "[Hitler] wants to have *Parsifal* performed so to speak *against* his own Party!!!!"

Back in 1934, Hitler had persuaded Winifred Wagner to hire Alfred Roller to design a new *Parsifal*, along the lines of the moody, semi-abstract *Tristan* that he had so admired in Vienna. The Bayreuth old guard rebelled against Roller's shadowy setting, calling it "an orgy from hell." The author Joachim Köhler has argued that Roller's conception of the Grail temple influenced some of the more grandiose spectacles of Nazi culture—for example, the "dome of light" at the Party rallies of the thirties and the "great dome" that was to have risen at the center of Albert Speer's Berlin. Six years after Hitler's death, Wieland Wagner unveiled a minimally furnished, poetically abstract version of *Parsifal*, which critics at the time hailed as a renunciation of the "Nazi" Bayreuth. One wonders how far it really was from Hitler's dream vision of the opera.

Richard Strauss's villa in Garmisch is still in the hands of the composer's family, and it remains much as he left it. Next to Strauss's desk is a small portrait of a Jewish boy by Isidor Kaufman, a painter of shtetl scenes. It belonged to Alice Strauss's grandmother Paula Neumann, who in 1942 was deported to the ghetto turned concentration camp at Theresienstadt, in former Czechoslovakia. After she had been sent there, Strauss made numerous attempts to have her released. One day he traveled to the camp by car, announced himself at the gates with his usual aplomb ("I am the composer Richard Strauss," he said), and declared that he wished to take Frau Neumann with him. The guards at the gate turned him away.

From around 1935 until his death in 1949, Strauss experienced an amazing creative resurgence. That his return to form should have happened against a backdrop of genocidal insanity is the kind of paradox that Thomas Mann addressed in *Doctor Faustus*. In the case of Strauss, there is no direct evidence that outer events had much effect on him, consciously or unconsciously. What does seem likely is that his humiliating dismissal from the Reich Music Chamber sent him back to first principles. So often in his operas and tone poems, he used his mighty apparatus to depict a lone figure stripped of worldly illusions, moving from braggadocio to resignation. In *Guntram* the hero walks away from his community into solitude. In *Rosenkavalier* the Marschallin looks past her furnishings to a cold, empty space where time is icily ticking down. In *Die Frau ohne Schatten* the fairy-tale emperor faces the threat of being turned to stone. Strauss began his late period with the mythological opera *Daphne*, in which a woman escapes her damaged life by turning into a tree. He signposted the work's autobiographical significance by making clear allusions to the harmonic structure and thematic material of *Guntram*, his painfully unsuccessful first opera: both works begin in the key of G major and end in F-sharp, and both are centered on melodies that weave gently around a triad and quicken into downward-falling triplets.

In a wider sense, *Daphne* bookended the entire history of music; the story, taken from Ovid's *Metamorphoses*, recalls the first opera for which music survives, Jacopo Peri's *Dafne* of 1597–98. Daphne, solitary nymph, daughter of the river god, prefers the company of nature to the company of men. She refuses the advances of her childhood friend, the shepherd Leukippos, only to fall into the arms of Apollo. When Leukippos persists in wooing her, Apollo kills him in a jealous rage. Daphne, distraught, promises to stand forever over her friend's grave, as a "symbol of never-ending love." The gods, taking pity, change her into a laurel tree that will stay forever rooted to that spot.

The metamorphosis itself is enacted almost entirely by the orchestra, with Daphne's voice returning just before the end to execute wordless arabesques. Scattered instruments, like trembling leaves, flicker around an F-sharp-major chord. As if in very distant echo of Ravel or Stravinsky, the orchestra takes up a delicate layering of rhythms, units of two against units of three, with occasional asymmetrical bursts of units of five. Even Apollo is lost in wonder at Daphne's song. "Are we still gods," he asks, "or were we overshadowed long ago by human emotion, obliterated long ago by such gentle greatness?"

The theme of indifference to the world resurfaced in Strauss's next opera, *Die Liebe der Danae*, or *The Loves of Danae*, in which the composer again lost himself in Greek mythology, though not without oblique references to his spiritual state. Jupiter, in the manner of Wagner's Wotan, eventually comes to grips with his powerlessness and renounces the dream of love. "The great restless one bids farewell as twilight falls," the god sings. He is presumably speaking also for the composer, who saw himself not only at the end of his life but at the end of history, the last in the procession of German masters that began with Bach.

Every time Strauss bade farewell, though, he found himself living a little longer. While the German Blitzkrieg was moving through Poland, in 1939, he conceived the peculiarly irrelevant notion of writing a short chamber piece about the art of opera itself, with the action or lack thereof set in the Paris of the ancien régime. It was eventually given the title *Capriccio*. After receiving inadequate ideas from the hapless Gregor, Strauss decided to write the libretto himself, although he called in the conductor Clemens Krauss to help.

Once more, a sophisticated, ambivalent, fascinating woman is at the center of the action. The countess Madeleine has commissioned an opera from the poet Olivier and the composer Flamand. The two men compete for her favor, and so, too, do the arts of poetry and music—which is more central to drama? At the end, the countess looks into a mirror, asking, "Can you help me to find the ending, the ending for their opera? Is there one that is not trivial?" At this moment her majordomo walks in to say, "Countess, dinner is served." A lovely irony colors Strauss's setting of that line. "The last words of the opera could not be more trivial," Michael Kennedy writes in his Strauss biography. "But they are set to an unforgettably touching, lyrical phrase, prolonged by the orchestra." The countess walks off humming the melody to herself (the orchestra hums for her), words forgotten.

It is at once touching and unsettling to picture Strauss immersed in the artifice of *Capriccio* in the early months of 1941, when German forces were gearing up for the invasion of Russia and Heydrich's *Einsatzgruppen* were set to slaughter Jews and Slavs in their wake. Touching, because one can sense Strauss's need to disappear into a realm of tones. Unsettling, because his work was so at odds with the surrounding reality. On August 3, 1941, the day that *Capriccio* was finished, 682 Jews were killed in Chernovtsy, Romania; 1,500 in Jelgava, Latvia; and several hundred in Stanisławów, Ukraine. On October 28, 1942, the day of the opera's premiere in Munich, the first convoy of Jews from Theresienstadt arrived at Auschwitz-Birkenau, and 90 percent of them went to the gas chamber.

The Holocaust accomplished the murder not only of millions of individuals but of entire schools of composition. The energetically middle-of-the-road, eclectic style that had prospered in Berlin, Vienna, and Prague between the wars was effectively wiped out. One of the more prominent victims was the Czech-Jewish composer Ervín Schulhoff, who died of tuberculosis in the Wülzburg concentration camp, in August 1942.

Schulhoff's career neatly maps the early twentieth century: he started off writing in a Romantic, folk-inflected style, then took up jazz piano and indulged in Dada provocations (his sardonic *Symphonia germanica* has a singer shrieking "*Deutschland über alles*" while a pianist bangs out dissonances). In the twenties he produced toughly lyrical chamber music in a Bartókian vein. In the next decade he embraced socialist realism and went so far as to set the *Communist Manifesto* to music. He was on the point of emigrating to the Soviet Union when the Nazis arrested him. Even in Wülzburg, he continued to compose, sketching a heroic Eighth Symphony in which the sayings of Marx, Lenin, and Stalin would have pointed the way to victory.

Several other Czech-Jewish composers ended up in the former prison of Theresienstadt, which had been converted into a "model camp" for wealthier and more notable Jews. Music flourished there for a time; the great Czech conductor Karel Ančerl led a performance of Beethoven's "Ode to Joy" as late as April 1944. The community of composers included Pavel Haas, a reserved but eloquent pupil of Janáček's; Viktor Ullmann, whose aesthetic overlapped in many ways with that of Alban Berg; Hans Krása, who showed the softer-edged influence of Alexander Zemlinsky and Albert Roussel; and Gideon Klein, who, in his early twenties, was already developing an individual voice.

The Theresienstadt composers became pawns in a grisly game when Nazi propagandists decided in 1944 to remodel the camp in preparation for a visit by the Red Cross. In the pseudo-documentary film *Theresienstadt*, a cast of children is seen singing Krása's opera *Brundibár*, and Haas takes a bow for his Study for Strings. It is practically unbearable to see the thin smiles on their faces. When the project was complete, the Nazis deported eighteen thousand Theresienstadt prisoners in eleven transports. On October 16, 1944, a train left for Auschwitz containing Klein, Ullmann, Haas, Krása, and the children who had performed in *Brundibár*. All but Klein were killed in the following days. The young composer was fit enough to survive Josef Mengele's selection process, and held on until January the following year.

Even in Auschwitz, music was still heard. Men's orchestras formed in 1941 and 1942 and played for the edification of members of the SS. An ambitious female SS officer decided to found a women's orchestra in 1943 and assembled a ragtag band of amateur and professional players. The quality of the women's group improved dramatically when the gifted Viennese violinist and conductor Alma Rosé—Gustav Mahler's niece—took over as director. As Richard Newman and Karen Kirtley recount in their biography of Rosé, she succeeded in putting together a disciplined ensemble of some fifty players and persuaded the SS to give her supplies, including a baton and a podium. The repertory included marches, Strauss waltzes, operatic excerpts, the first movement of Beethoven's Fifth, parts of Dvořák's *New World* Symphony, and Schumann's *Träumerei*, the last a special favorite of Mengele's.

"She lived in another world," a survivor said of Rosé. "Music to her meant her love and her disappointments, her sorrow and her joys, her eternal longing and her faith, and this music floated high above the camp atmosphere." One Polish cellist recalled how Rosé had violently upbraided her for playing an F-natural instead of an F-sharp. At the time, the young musician was furious; in retrospect, she thought that this seemingly futile insistence on perfection had saved her from insanity. Another time Rosé angrily halted a performance when she heard SS guards talking too loudly in the background. It was an eerie echo of her uncle's remonstrations of inattentive audiences in Vienna.

Alma Rosé fell ill in April 1944, apparently of botulism. She died quickly, despite Mengele's apparently sincere attempts to revive her. Many of her musicians survived, thanks in large measure to the special status that their conductor had obtained for them. Paula Neumann, Alice Strauss's grandmother, was not so lucky. One day the Strauss family received a package containing her death certificate; "spotted fever" was given as the cause of death, although in all probability she died in Auschwitz. The package also contained Isidor Kaufman's portrait of the Jewish boy, which Strauss hung next to his desk.

Thomas Mann's novel *The Magic Mountain*, an allegorical portrait of prewar Europe in the guise of a mountaintop sanatorium called the Berghof, has a scene in which Hans Castorp, the feckless young hero, falls in love with a phonograph and hears in its songs a "sympathy for death." Castorp goes on to fantasize about using a simple song to conquer the world: "One might even found whole empires upon it, earthly, all-too-earthly empires, very coarse, very progressive, and not in the least nostalgic." The young man appoints himself the operator of the gramophone, piloting his fellow inmates through the wonders of the record library. Both Hitler and Stalin liked to hold listening parties of the Magic Mountain kind. Stalin had a good American gramophone in his dacha and, according to an eyewitness, "changed the discs and entertained the guests." It was much the same with Hitler, who assembled an extensive record collection at his Berchtesgaden retreat—the Berghof—and subjected his guests to long disquisitions with phonographic accompaniment.

Typically, the evenings would revolve around Wagner excerpts, songs of Strauss and Hugo Wolf, and, of course, melodies by Lehár, whom Shostakovich had quoted mockingly in the *Leningrad* Symphony. The guests might hear, out of thousands of discs on hand, Karl Muck conducting *Parsifal*, Heinrich Schlusnus singing Strauss's "Heimliche Aufforderung," or Hermann Abendroth's recording of Sibelius's *Finlandia*. (The catalog of the Berghof record library fills three thick red-brown volumes; they can be seen at the Library of Congress.) Martin Bormann stood watch over the gramophone itself. Hitler habitually gave amateur music-appreciation lectures about each disc as it played, informing his captive audience that "Bruckner was the greatest organist of his time," that "Mozart was buried in a mass grave," that "*Tristan* is surely [Wagner's] greatest work. We have the love of Mathilde Wesendonck to thank for it."

A special warmth came over Hitler when *Tristan* appeared on the playlist. His mind would drift back to the Vienna of the prewar period. Heinrich Hoffmann, in his memoir *Hitler Was My Friend*, recalled one fireside monologue: " 'I would scrape and save every farthing,' he would tell us, gazing with a far-away look into the leaping flames, 'to get myself a seat in "the Gods" at the Imperial Opera. And the gala performances! What a superb spectacle of pomp and magnificence it was, to watch the members of the Imperial family arriving, and to see the Grand Dukes in their glittering gold uniforms and all the great ladies, adorned with their scintillating diadems, stepping out of their carriages!' "

Party officials began to entertain the notion that Hitler was losing his mind. "I had the impression that he had gone crazy in '43," Baldur von Schirach said during the period of Nuremberg trials. "I had that impression in '42," Hans Fritzsche replied. As the eastern front began to collapse, Hitler worked to perfect a music policy that no longer had meaning. One of his initiatives was to ship wounded soldiers to Bayreuth, so they could have their own Wagner epiphanies. The Führer also studied plans for a Bruckner Orchestra in Linz and for a Bruckner festival that would rival Bayreuth in magnitude. In the weeks following the Normandy invasion, Hitler feared for the safety of Furtwängler, his favorite conductor, and ordered that a bunker be built to protect him from bombs. Furtwängler, who was staying in a castle outside Berlin, told Hitler that such precautions were unnecessary. So workers were dispatched to the conductor's Berlin home to reinforce the cellar with bricks and beams.

Hitler also fretted over Strauss, who had committed a new outrage in 1943. When the local Garmisch government instructed Strauss to give over parts of his villa to evacuees and wounded soldiers, the composer replied that he wanted no strangers in his house. "No soldier needs to fall on my account," he supposedly said. "I did not want this war, it is nothing to do with me." He appealed to Hitler for assistance. "My achievements as composer and conductor," he wrote, "were last known to you, my Führer, in Bayreuth, where I had the honor of meeting you during *Parsifal*." Perhaps Strauss was trying to remind Hitler of his supposed attendance at *Salome* in Graz. Hitler was unmoved. The next day he ruled that Strauss would have to accommodate the refugees and that Nazi officials should have nothing more to do with him. When it came time to mark the composer's eightieth birthday, in June 1944, Hitler and Goebbels were at first inclined to snub him, but they relented under pressure from Furtwängler, who advised them, absurdly, that international opinion might turn against Germany if Strauss's birthday were ignored. Before the Garmisch fiasco, Hitler had intended to give the composer a new Mercedes along with a ration card for one thousand liters of fuel. Now he sent only a curt telegram. Goebbels mailed off a copy of Houdon's bust of Gluck.

Both Nazi officials and anti-Nazi émigrés made the same complaint about Strauss—that he acted like "a total bystander," in the words of a Reich Culture Chamber official. "His music, in particular his songs, is certainly wonderful," Hitler apparently said to Goebbels, "but his character is simply miserable." In an angrier mood, Hitler once announced to Speer that Strauss was "completely second-rate." Perhaps it is the ultimate insult to have one's morals impugned by Hitler, although the consternation that Strauss continuously created in the upper reaches of the Nazi hierarchy points up something stubborn and irreducible in his personality. He was a quantity that could not be controlled and could not be removed.

• • •

In the summer of 1944, Strauss began to plan a large-scale piece for string ensemble in the nature of a funeral oration or lamentation. It had been decades since he had written a major instrumental work; his last truly significant effort in that line had been the *Alpine Symphony*, composed in the wake of Mahler's death. The new piece would be called *Metamorphosen*—another homage to Ovid. Strauss had in mind the process by which souls revert from one state to another—though, as the scholar Timothy Jackson has suggested, the transformation may be a negative one, in which things devolve to their primordial state. The composer also took inspiration from a short poem by Goethe, whose complete works he read from beginning to end in his last years:

No one can know himself,
Detach from his self,
Yet he tries to become every day
What is finally clear from the outside,
What he is and what he was,
What he can and what he may.

Strauss sketched a choral work based on Goethe's text, and, as Jackson discovered, some of that material went into *Metamorphosen*. The composer was musing in some deep way on the course of his life, perhaps questioning the philosophy of individualism that had long guided him.

Metamorphosen, scored for twenty-three strings, begins with consecutive chords of E minor, A-flat major, B-flat major, and A major, anchored on a descending chromatic line. Dusky and doleful, the harmonies run through eleven of the twelve notes of the chromatic scale in just two bars, as if to acknowledge that Schoenberg might not have been so crazy after all. Contrapuntal lines intertwine like kudzu on a ruined mansion. As the movement unfolds, the music tries to settle into a more relaxed, lyrical voice, but at regular intervals a kind of drainage occurs and a *Tristan* mood of wounded desperation resumes. At a dramatic moment toward the end, most of the instruments drop out, leaving a sibilant G in the upper violas and cellos. The effect recalls the climax of the Adagio of Mahler's Ninth Symphony, when the ensemble falls away to expose a unison C-flat high in the violins. Strauss's high cry seems prepared to serve as a dramatic leading note to a brighter tonal region—something akin to Mahler's beatific resignation. Instead, it gravitates implacably to the deathly C minor that has been sounding throughout.

In the final section a new element enters: a quotation from the funeral march of Beethoven's *Eroica*. As the story goes, Beethoven had planned to dedicate the *Eroica* to Napoleon, but when Napoleon crowned himself emperor the composer crossed out the dedication and wrote instead, "To the memory of a great man." It has long been thought that Strauss was saying the same about Hitler, burying a man in whom he once believed. In light of the hidden citation of Goethe's line "No one can know himself," it is more likely that the hero being laid to rest is Strauss himself. There are anguished dissonances as Strauss's own funereal anthem falls in and out of sync with Beethoven's. Having seemingly reached bottom, it goes two more long steps down—a low G, then an even lower C. It is like the sunrise fanfare of *Thus Spake Zarathustra* moving in retrograde, the harmonic series rewinding to the fundamental. There is no "light in the night," only night.

Strauss finished *Metamorphosen* on April 12, 1945. Franklin Delano Roosevelt died the same day. Samuel Barber's Adagio for Strings, vaguely similar in tone to the music that Strauss had just composed, played on American radio. That afternoon in the ruins of Berlin, the Berlin Philharmonic presented an impeccably Hitlerish program that included Beethoven's Violin Concerto, Bruckner's *Romantic* Symphony, and the Immolation Scene from *Götterdämmerung*. After the concert, members of the Hitler Youth distributed cyanide capsules to the audience, or so the rumor went. Hitler marked his fifty-sixth birthday on April 20. Ten days later, he shot himself in the mouth. In accordance with his final instructions, the body was incinerated alongside that of Eva Braun.

Hitler possibly envisaged his immolation as a reprise of that final scene of the *Ring*, in which Brünnhilde builds a pyre for Siegfried and rides into the flames. Or he may have hoped to reenact the love-death of *Tristan*—whose music, he once told his secretary, he wished to hear as he died. Walther Funk thought that Hitler had modeled the scorched-earth policy of the regime's last phase on Wagner's grand finale: "Everything had to go down in ruins with Hitler himself, as a sort of false *Götterdämmerung*." Such an extravagant gesture would have fulfilled the prophecy of Walter Benjamin, who wrote that fascist humanity would "experience its own annihilation as a supreme aesthetic pleasure." But there is no evidence that the drug-addled Führer was thinking about Wagner or listening to music in the last days and hours of his life. Eyewitness reports suggest that the grim ceremony in the bombed-out Chancellery garden—two gasoline-soaked corpses burning fitfully, the one intact, the other with its skull caved in—was something other than a work of art.

Part III

1945–2000

We live in a time I think not of mainstream, but of many streams, or even, if you insist upon a river of time, that we have come to delta, maybe even beyond delta to an ocean which is going back to the skies.

—JOHN CAGE, KPFA RADIO, 1992

10

ZERO HOUR

The U.S. Army and German Music, 1945–1949

On April 30, 1945, the day of Hitler's suicide, "zero hour" in modern German history, the 103rd Infantry and Tenth Armored divisions of the U.S. Army took possession of the Alpine resort of Garmisch-Partenkirchen, which the war had hardly touched. Two hundred Allied bombers had been poised to lay waste to the town and its environs, but the strike was called off at the behest of a surrendering German officer.

Early in the morning a security detachment turned in to the driveway of a Garmisch villa, intending to use it as a command post. When the senior officer, Lieutenant Milton Weiss, went inside the house, an old man came downstairs to meet him. "I am Richard Strauss," he said, "the composer of *Rosenkavalier* and *Salome*." Strauss studied the soldier's face for signs of sympathy. Weiss, who had played piano at Jewish resorts in the Catskills, nodded his head in recognition. Strauss went on to recount his experiences in the war, pointedly mentioning the tribulations of his Jewish relatives. Weiss chose to install his post elsewhere.

At 11:00 a.m. on the same day, a squad of jeeps came up the drive, these led by Major John Kramers, of the 103rd Infantry Division's military-government branch. Kramers told the family that they had fifteen minutes to evacuate. Strauss walked out to the major's jeep, holding documents that declared him to be an honorary citizen of Morgantown,

West Virginia, together with part of the manuscript of *Rosenkavalier.* "I am Richard Strauss, the composer," he said. Kramers's face lit up; he was a Strauss fan. An "Off Limits" sign was placed on the lawn.

In the days that followed, Strauss posed for photographs, played the *Rosenkavalier* waltzes on the piano, and smiled bemusedly as soldiers inspected his statue of Beethoven and asked who it was. "If they ask one more time," he muttered, "I'm telling them it's Hitler's father."

All over Europe, young veterans were emerging from the rubble of the war into adulthood. Among them were several future leaders of the postwar musical scene, and they would be indelibly marked by what they had experienced in adolescence. Karlheinz Stockhausen was the son of a spiritually tortured Nazi Party member who went to the eastern front and never returned. His mother was confined for many years to a sanatorium, then killed in the Nazi euthanasia program. By the age of sixteen, Stockhausen was working in a mobile hospital behind the western front, where he tried to revive soldiers who had fallen victim to Allied incendiary bombs. "I would try to find an opening in the mouth area for a straw," he recalled, "in order to pour some liquid into these men, whose bodies were still moving, but there was only a yellow ball-like mass where the face should have been." On a given day Stockhausen and his comrades would haul thirty or forty corpses into churches that had been converted into morgues.

Hans Werner Henze trained as a radio operator for Panzer battalions and spent the first part of 1945 riding aimlessly around the ruined landscape. Bernd Alois Zimmermann fought on the front lines of Hitler's ill-fated invasion of the Soviet Union. Luciano Berio was conscripted into the army of Mussolini's Republic of Salò and nearly blew off his right hand with a gun that he did not know how to use. Iannis Xenakis joined the Greek Communist resistance, fighting not only the Germans but also the British, who, in an early demonstration of Cold War Realpolitik, made common cause with local Fascists when they occupied the country. At the end of 1944 a British shell landed on a building where Xenakis was hiding; after watching a comrade's brains splatter against a wall, he passed out and awoke to find that his left eye and part of his face were gone.

In July 1945, the young English composer Benjamin Britten, who had just scored a triumph in London with his opera *Peter Grimes*, accompanied the violinist Yehudi Menuhin on a brief tour of defeated Germany. The two men visited the concentration camp at Bergen-Belsen and performed for a crowd of former inmates. Stupefied by what he saw, Britten decided to write a cycle of songs on the Holy Sonnets of John Donne, the most spiritually scouring poetry he could find. On August 6 he set to music Sonnet 14, which begins, "Batter my heart, three person'd God." Earlier the same day, the first operational atomic bomb fell on Hiroshima. There is an eerie coincidence here, for J. Robert Oppenheimer, the head of the American nuclear program, cherished the same Donne poem, and evidently had it in mind when he gave the site of the first atomic test the name Trinity.

On August 19, Britten finished his cycle by setting Donne's sonnet "Death be not proud." The singer declaims the words "And death shall be no more" on a rising scale; fixates for nine long beats on the word "Death"; and finally, over a clanging dominant-tonic cadence, thunders, "Thou shalt die."

In 1945 Germany was a primitive society such as Europe had not known since the Middle Ages. The former citizens of Hitler's Thousand-Year Reich were living a hand-to-mouth existence, scavenging for food, drinking from drainpipes, cooking over wood fires, living in the basements of destroyed houses or in hand-built trailers and cabins. In 1948 the glamorous young American musician Leonard Bernstein arrived in Munich to conduct a concert and reported back home: "The people starve, struggle, rob, beg for bread. Wages are often paid in cigarettes. Tipping is all in cigarettes. It is all misery."

Millions of prisoners of war lived in camps; millions more roamed the roads, having fled the Soviet occupation in the east or been expelled from neighboring countries by policies of ethnic cleansing. No sooner had Hitler made his exit than Stalin replaced him as a threat. The collected might of Anglo-American industry, which had been used to obliterate one German city after another, now became the engine of reconstruction. Germany would be reinvented as a democratic, American-style society, a bulwark against the Soviets. Part of that grand plan was a cultural policy of denazification and reeducation, which would have a decisive effect on postwar music.

Germany and Austria broke apart into American, British, French, and Soviet zones. The head of the American occupation—the Office of Military Government, United States, or OMGUS—was an evenhanded, incorruptible, staggeringly efficient man named Lucius Clay. What made Clay interesting was that his background combined strict West Point training with a whiff of New Deal idealism; in the Army Corps of Engineers he had coordinated building projects with the WPA, and an early evaluation had called him "inclined to be bolshevistic." The military governor wanted to reshape and lift up Germany as Roosevelt had reshaped and lifted up America. At a conference in Berchtesgaden, near Hitler's old redoubt, Clay said, "We are trying to free the German mind and to make his heart value that freedom so greatly that it will beat and die for that freedom and for no other purpose."

The project of freeing the German mind went by the name "reorientation." The term originated in the Psychological Warfare Division of the Supreme Headquarters, Allied Expeditionary Force, which was led by Brigadier General Robert McClure. Psychological warfare meant the pursuit of military ends by nonmilitary means, and in the case of music it meant the promotion of jazz, American composition, international contemporary music, and other sounds that could be used to degrade the concept of Aryan cultural supremacy.

One key member of General McClure's staff was the émigré Russian composer Nicolas Nabokov. "He's hep on music and tells the Krauts how to go about it," one military man said of this ebullient, charming, and slippery personality. Back in the twenties and early thirties, Nabokov had belonged to Serge Diaghilev's cadre of composers at the Ballets Russes. His music was relatively negligible, his ability to cultivate high-level social and political connections positively virtuosic; in the postwar era he would show a Zelig-like ability to appear in the middle of any cultural imbroglio.

With the coming of OMGUS, Psychological Warfare evolved into Information Control, taking responsibility for all cultural activity in the occupied areas. In keeping with the reorientation paradigm, military and civilian experts were brought in to guide extant organizations and encourage new, forward-looking ones. Many in Information Control's Music Branches had thorough training and a progressive outlook on contemporary music. Two of the brightest were stationed in Bavaria, the birthplace of the Nazi Party. John Evarts, who served there from 1946 on, had taught at Black Mountain College in North Carolina, where Schoenberg's pupil Heinrich Jalowetz was on the faculty. Joining Evarts in 1948 was the Mississippi-born pianist Carlos Moseley, who had studied alongside Leonard Bernstein at Koussevitzky's music school in the Berkshires.

Moseley arranged for one of Information Control's triumphs—Bernstein's startlingly successful conducting engagement in Munich in May 1948, which led some experienced concertgoers to exclaim that this young American knew German music better than the Germans. In a letter home Bernstein exulted: "It means so much for the American military Government, since music is the Germans' last stand in their 'master race' claim, and for the first time it's been exploded in Munich."

Moseley's memories of his OMGUS service remained distinct more than five decades later, when he spoke to the author of this book at a restaurant in midtown Manhattan. Having arrived in Munich on a wet winter night, he had no time to dry his clothes before reporting to senior operatives for briefings. A senior general told him that one pressing task was to "look into that whole thing going on in Beulah." By this the general meant Bayreuth, where ideas for a possible revival of the Wagner festival were circulating. Moseley went to Bayreuth and walked up the Green Hill to the Festspielhaus. The roof was leaking and water dripped into the amphitheater. Down in the orchestra pit, Moseley saw instruments lying about, including a rack of bells. Remembering a recording of *Parsifal* that he had listened to many times in his youth—the one led by Karl Muck—he struck the notes C, G, A, and E, the Grail temple motif.

Afterward, Moseley went to Haus Wahnfried, Wagner's home, which Allied bombs had also damaged. Winifred Wagner, the widow of Wagner's son, Siegfried, had had to suffer the indignity of a denazification hearing, and she watched helplessly as the theater was used for Italian opera, light entertainment, and other "desecrations." Soldiers played jazz on the Wahnfried piano; doughnuts were baked in the festival restaurant. The Festspielhaus even served as a barracks for African-American troops—a circumstance that Winifred noted in her reminiscences with four exclamation points of horror. She gave Moseley a tour of the ruins and showed him the Meister's grave. "She began talking about '*unser*

Blitzkrieg'—'our Blitzkrieg'—and reminiscing fondly of the Hitler period. I froze up. I couldn't take it. I just walked away from her, feeling a definite terror in my veins."

OMGUS's music policies were summed up in a Psychological Warfare document titled "Music Control Instruction No. 1," which can be found at the National Archives in College Park, Maryland. "It is above all essential," the memo says, "that we should not give the impression of trying to regiment culture in the Nazi manner." Instead, "German musical life must be influenced by positive rather than by negative means, i.e., by encouraging the music which we think beneficial and crowding out that which we think dangerous." Only two men occupied the "dangerous" category: Richard Strauss and Hans Pfitzner. "We must not . . . allow such composers to be 'built up' by special concerts devoted entirely to their works or conducted by them." With this two-pronged approach, the document concludes, "we shall have little difficulty in giving a positive international direction to German musical life." The anonymous author also flagged Sibelius, deeming him likely to reawaken feelings of Nordic supremacy: hence, *Finlandia* was banned in Germany.

If not Strauss, Pfitzner, and Sibelius, which composers would be acceptable in the new Germany? The first order of business was to restore to the repertory music that the Nazis had banned on racial and ideological grounds. One early strategy had mixed results, as a report from August 1945 shows: "The rule of having to perform at least one 'verboten' work on each program has led to a stereotyped pattern of starting orchestral concerts with a Mendelssohn overture . . . The Mendelssohn situation has become critical, ridiculous, and urgent." The author of this memo, Edward Kilenyi, was the son of Gershwin's theory teacher.

Music Control also placed great emphasis on American music, promoting major works of Aaron Copland, Roy Harris, and Virgil Thomson along with more dubious fare such as Robert McBride's *Strawberry Jam Overture*. There was a sudden surge in performances of a symphony by the little-known Harrison Kerr, who happened to work in the Cultural Affairs Division's New York office. Censorship departments that were monitoring the German mails reported that on the whole American music was going down well, although symphonic works had less traction than popular songs. "I hear such nice American music over the radio," wrote a German woman to a friend in Philadelphia. "I really like it very much; I do not know why we were always told that it amounts to nothing. The fact is, that our music is heavier and everlasting, but your songs and hits are so jolly and light."

The extroverted, jazz-tinged music of the Weimar era, as embodied in *The Threepenny Opera*, had been condemned by the Nazis on political and racial grounds. It might have qualified as "safe" for the new Germany. By this time, though, Weill was entrenched as a composer on Broadway and uninterested in returning to Germany; his premature death in 1950 made the matter moot. Other young leftist composers who had thrived in twenties Berlin—the likes of Hanns Eisler and Stefan Wolpe—were evidently ruled out because of their Communist associations. The entire Weill-ish school of song-driven composition, whether because of its leftist leanings or because of its daring synthesis of classical and popular styles, figured little in the calculations of Music Control. Carl Orff, on the other hand, prospered, even though *Carmina burana* had been a hit with Goebbels. Orff misleadingly presented himself as an associate of the anti-Nazi resistance, and OMGUS gave him a clean ideological bill of health. It helped that Newell Jenkins, the local theater and music officer, had studied with Orff before the war.

The Americans placed highest confidence in musical progressives who lacked either Nazi or Communist affiliations. Karl Amadeus Hartmann, the Munich composer who dedicated his symphonic poem *Miserae* to the victims of Dachau in 1935, was extolled by Music Control as "a man of the utmost integrity [who] possesses a musical outlook which is astonishingly sound and fresh for a man who has survived the nazi [*sic*] occupation." Not long after the end of the war, Hartmann organized a series of Musica Viva concerts in Munich, with emphasis on "verboten" modernists. The OMGUS file dealing with Musica Viva is marked "Reorientation Project No. 1." The material is held in a stiff gray folder that had evidently been appropriated from a Nazi filing cabinet; under the American scrawl is a watermark reading "NSDAP."

Alas, Munich music lovers did not flock to Hartmann's series. John Evarts wrote, "They are extremely shy of any sort of art created in an idiom of a period later than, say, 1900." One event drew fewer than thirty people. Carlos Moseley decided to use OMGUS money to purchase

350 tickets, which he then distributed to young musicians and composers. Thus, the American occupation was not only providing funds for the concerts but also filling the seats—an exceptionally generous form of patronage.

The city of Darmstadt, most of which had been leveled in an incendiary bombing raid in September 1944, hosted another American-supported modern-music experiment. The music critic Wolfgang Steinecke proposed to set up a summertime institute so that young composers might familiarize themselves with music that the Nazis had banned. Steinecke persuaded the local city government to let him use the Kranichstein Hunting Castle, a picturesque pile outside of town. The American authorities warmly backed the venture, which was dubbed the International Summer Courses for New Music; the scholar Amy Beal estimates that OMGUS contributed about 20 percent of the budget. GIs even transported a Steinway grand up to the castle on the back of a jeep.

Instrumental to the growth of this soon-to-be-formidable institution was Everett Helm, the music officer for the Hesse region and a composer himself. Helm proudly noted that at Darmstadt "contemporary music <u>only</u> is taught and performed—and then only the more advanced variety. R. Strauss and J. Sibelius do <u>not</u> come into consideration." Hindemith was designated a "natural starting point," but Schoenberg quickly emerged as the shining beacon for young German composers.

Schoenberg had a prominent place in Darmstadt's programs from the beginning. The 1949 season coincided with his seventy-fifth birthday, and the organizers very much wanted the composer to attend. John Evarts, who had met Schoenberg in Berlin before the Nazi takeover, played a crucial role in the negotiations. To his apparently skeptical colleagues in New York Evarts wrote: "It would be both historically and personally an important final gesture for the U.S. to help make the trip possible before the old man makes his final exit." Red tape interfered with the plan. Coming to Germany as a visiting expert would have meant flying on an American military aircraft and passing a military examination. "In my former army service I was not very fortunate with military doctors," Schoenberg wrote to Evarts. In the end, he did not feel well enough to go.

All the same, Schoenberg's spirit loomed over Darmstadt in the summer of 1949; there were performances of the Five Pieces for Orchestra, the Variations for Orchestra, the Violin Concerto, the Fourth String Quartet, and the String Trio. Remarkably, the Trio appeared in an OMGUS-sponsored series devoted to *American* chamber works, alongside quartets by Charles Ives and Wallingford Riegger. Two summers later, just before Schoenberg's death, Darmstadt presented the "Dance Around the Golden Calf" from *Moses und Aron*, the first performance anywhere of music from the opera.

Some official observers were uneasy about the direction that Darmstadt was taking. Colonel Ralph A. Burns, the chief of the Cultural Affairs Branch of the Education and Cultural Relations Division of OMGUS, noted in a June 1949 memo that the summer school had "acquired a reputation for one-sidedness." The previous summer, the Polish-born, Paris-based composer and theorist René Leibowitz, the author of *Sibelius: The Worst Composer in the World*, had arrived to preach the gospel of twelve-tone music, and he caused great excitement among younger German composers. Leibowitz returned in 1949 in the company of the equally radical, though less doctrinaire, Olivier Messiaen. The French contingent had an unsettling effect, as Burns reported in his follow-up "Review of Activities for the Month of July 1949." After extolling the virtues of the Yale Glee Club, which had staged a successful German tour, he wrote the following:

> The Darmstadt Holiday Courses for New Music came to a close on 10 July with opinion as to their effectiveness sharply divided. The majority of students and faculty felt that the idea of the school—to foster new music through performances, lectures and courses—is splendid, but that the execution of the idea was faulty. During the concluding four days, five concerts were given under the title "Music of the Younger Generation." It was generally conceded that much of this music was worthless and had better been left unplayed. The over-emphasis on twelve-tone music was regretted. One critic (*Neue Zeitung*) described the concerts as "The Triumph of Dilettantism." A regrettable feature of the session was the tension created between the French group and the rest of the school. Led by their teacher Leibowitz, the French students remained aloof from the others and acted in a snobbish way. At one concert, their conduct led to open hostility. Leibowitz (an Austrian

> by birth [*sic*]) represents and admits as valid only the most radical kind of music and is openly disdainful of any other. His attitude is aped by his students. It was generally felt that next year's Holiday Course for New Music must follow a different, more catholic pattern.

Here was a sign of things to come. The aggressive tactics of Schoenberg's young French acolytes forecast the musical divides of coming years, when Pierre Boulez, the most "openly disdainful" of composers, would declare that any composer who had not come to terms with Schoenberg's method was "useless." Boulez himself did not attend that summer, but he had studied with Leibowitz and had already created a stink at a Stravinsky concert in Paris.

David Monod, in his history of music during the American occupation, writes that OMGUS inadvertently helped to bring about a "segregation of the modern and the popular." Darmstadt and similar organizations were wholly subsidized by the state, the city, and the Americans. They had no obligation to a paying public. Meanwhile, "classical music," in the pejorative sense of performances of well-known opera and symphonic repertory, carried on as it had during the Nazi period, with many of the same star conductors—Furtwängler, Karajan, Knappertsbusch—in charge, despite the various ceremonies of denazification to which they had been subjected. So there was, on the one hand, a classical establishment that eluded denazification, and, on the other, an avant-garde establishment that opposed itself so determinedly to the aesthetics of the Nazi period that it came close to disavowing the idea of the public concert. The middlebrow ideal of a popular modernism withered away, caught between extremes of revolution and reaction.

The worst mistake of the American occupation, from the musical point of view, was the accidental slaughter of Anton Webern, in Mittersill, Austria, on the night of September 15, 1945. As the American military were preparing to arrest a relative of Webern's, a black marketeer who was suspected of ties to the Nazi underground, a military cook named Raymond Bell collided with Webern in the dark, panicked, and shot him dead.

In the years that followed, the composer's reputation took an unexpected turn. Webern had long languished as the most obscure and arcane of the Second Viennese School composers, the one who made Berg sound like an over-the-top Romantic. After death, Webern acquired a saintly, visionary aura, the super-refined surfaces and intricate design of his works foreshadowing avant-garde constructions to come. Ernst Krenek, who had studied with Webern in Vienna, called him "the prophet of a new musical cosmos, torn from this world by a dastardly fate." When Webern's Piano Variations were performed at Darmstadt in 1948, young composers listened in a quasi-religious trance. That Webern had been possibly the most avid Hitlerite among major Austro-German composers was not widely known, or went unmentioned.

Richard Strauss remained in Garmisch. The "Off Limits" sign on his lawn protected his property but not his reputation. Klaus Mann, Thomas's son, serving as a correspondent for the U.S. Army newspaper *Stars and Stripes*, called on Strauss in mid-May 1945, identifying himself as "Mr. Brown." He had not forgotten that Strauss had signed a denunciation of his father in 1933. In a letter home Klaus wrote that Strauss "happens to be about the most rotten character one can possibly imagine—ingnorant [*sic*], complacent, greedy, vain, abysmally egotistic, completely lacking in the most fundamental human impulses of shame and decency." The *Stars and Stripes* article was scarcely less venomous, adorned with such headlines as "Strauss Still Unabashed About Ties with Nazis," "His Heart Beat in Nazi Time," and "An Old Opportunist Who Heiled Hitler." Some of the dialogue attributed to Strauss sounds implausible. Klaus claimed, for example, that Strauss showed no awareness of the destruction of German cities and opera houses; other sources indicate that the composer talked of little else. Incensed, Strauss wrote a letter of complaint to Klaus's father, but he never sent it, perhaps figuring that it would only add fuel to the fire.

Other visitors were friendlier, charmed by the old man's memories of America. When Private Russell Campitelli mentioned that he came from Poughkeepsie, Strauss nodded, and said, "Oh, yes, that is on the Hudson River."

Several soldiers happened to be skilled musicians. One day an intelligence operative named John de Lancie showed up at Strauss's door, not to conduct an interrogation but to express his admiration for the composer's woodwind writing; before the war he had played oboe in the Pittsburgh

Symphony. De Lancie boldly asked Strauss if he had ever thought of writing a concerto for oboe. "No," the composer answered. Several months later de Lancie was astonished to read in a newspaper that Strauss had indeed written an oboe concerto, at an American soldier's request. It was music of unexpected lightness, recalling the fleet-figured, Mendelssohnian scores that the composer had written in his youth, before he fell under Wagner's spell. Strauss's encounters with the Americans seemed to lift his spirits. In many later photographs he wears a dour expression, but in a snapshot taken by de Lancie his eyes are bright and his face is relaxed.

The long, strange career of Strauss faded out with the *Four Last Songs* of 1948. "Im Abendrot," or "At Sunset," out-Mahlers Mahler in the art of looking death in the face. The text paints the picture of an elderly couple walking into the twilight—"Through joy and need we have walked hand in hand"—and the E-flat-major music unfolds as one luminous arc above them. Friedrich Nietzsche might have been describing this greatest of Strauss songs when he wrote: "Masters of the very first order can be recognized by the following characteristic: in all matters great and small they know with perfect assurance how to find the end, whether it be the end of a melody or of a thought, whether it be the fifth act of a tragedy or the end of a political action. The very best of the second-in-rank grow restive toward the end. They do not plunge into the sea with a proud and measured tranquility, as do, for example, the mountains near Portofino—where the Gulf of Genoa sings its melody to the end."

Strauss died on September 8, 1949. Three weeks later, OMGUS was dissolved, and the American interregnum in German musical history was over.

11

BRAVE NEW WORLD

The Cold War and the Avant-Garde of the Fifties

"Everything begins in mystique and ends in politics," wrote the French poet Charles Péguy in 1910. Morton Feldman, the maverick modernist who loved Sibelius, applied this epigram to twentieth-century music, describing how grandiose ideas are made ordinary with the passage of time and become fodder for a power struggle among ideologues and pedants. "Unfortunately for most people who pursue art, ideas become their opium," Feldman said. "There is no security to be one's self."

The century began with the mystique of revolution, with the mind-bending harmonies and earthshaking rhythms of Schoenberg and Stravinsky. The process of politicization was already under way in the twenties, as composers competed to stay ahead of changing trends and accused one another of complicity in regressive tendencies. In the thirties and forties, the entire Romantic tradition was effectively annexed by the totalitarian state. But nothing could compare to what happened when the Second World War ended and the Cold War began. Music exploded into a pandemonium of revolutions, counterrevolutions, theories, polemics, alliances, and party splits. The language of modern music was reinvented on an almost yearly basis: twelve-tone composition gave way to "total serialism," which gave way to chance music, which gave way to a music of free-floating timbres, which gave way to neo-Dada happenings and collages, and so on. All the informational clutter of late-capitalist society, from purest noise to purest silence, from combinatorial set theory to bebop jazz, came rushing in, as if no barrier remained between art and reality. Strange bedfellows were the order of the day. Following in the footsteps of OMGUS, the CIA occasionally funded festivals that included hypercomplex avant-garde works. Cold War politicians such as John F. Kennedy promised a golden age of freethinking art, and twelve-tone composers at American universities were the indirect beneficiaries.

The Second World War was the war that never really ended. The Allied superpowers stayed on a military footing, and the introduction of atomic warfare and the discovery of the death camps in the summer of 1945 brought about a worldwide darkening of mood. The rhetoric of the early Cold War period crept into the musical discussion as into everything else. Composers exploited possibilities, annexed territory, neutralized the opposition, advanced, retreated, changed sides. When Stravinsky shocked his colleagues by giving up neoclassicism in favor of twelve-tone composition, Leonard Bernstein said that "it was like the defection of a general to the enemy camp, taking all his faithful regiments with him."

The dominant aesthetic, in European and American music alike, was one of dissonance, density, difficulty, complexity. The American composer Elliott Carter explained why he gave up Copland-style populism and Stravinsky-style neoclassicism: "Before the end of the Second World War, it became clear to me, partly as a result of rereading Freud and others and thinking about psychoanalysis, that we were living in a world where this physical and intellectual violence would always be a problem and that the whole conception of human nature underlying the neoclassic esthetic amounted to a sweeping under the rug of things that, it seemed to me, we had to deal with in a less oblique and resigned way."

The most formidable proponent of sweeping nothing under the rug was Theodor Adorno—Berg's old student, Sibelius's nemesis, Thomas Mann's musical adviser in the writing of *Doctor Faustus*. After the war Adorno acquired an intimidating reputation as a post-Marxist philosopher and deep-thinking musical analyst. He was an effective practitioner of the politics of style, using every device at his disposal to demean music that he considered retrogressive. One objective of his 1949 book *Philosophy of New Music* was to destroy the neoclassicism of Stravinsky: the very act of preserving tonality in the modern era, Adorno proposed, betrayed symptoms of the Fascist personality. He condemned Hindemith on similar grounds, arguing that the "New Objectivity" and "music for use" were tantamount to Nazi kitsch. In his book *Minima Moralia* Adorno mocked American composers of the populist persuasion, claiming that Copland's *Lincoln Portrait* could be found on the gramophone of every Stalinist intellectual.

The only possible path for Adorno was the one that Schoenberg had marked out at the beginning of the century. In fact, music would now carry its holy torch into abysses where even Schoenberg had not dared to go. All familiar sounds, all relics of convention, had to be expunged. The crucial passage in *Philosophy of New Music* was this:

> [New music] has taken upon itself all the darkness and guilt of the world. All its happiness comes in the perception of misery, all its beauty comes in the rejection of beauty's illusion. Neither the individual nor the collective wants any part of it. It dies away unheard, without echo. When music is heard, it is shot through with time, like a shining crystal; unheard music drops through empty time like a useless bullet. New music spontaneously takes aim at that final condition which mechanical music lives out hour by hour—the condition of absolute oblivion. It is the true message in a bottle.

Such language, reminiscent of the sermons of Thomas Mann's aesthetes ("Art is the sacred torch that must shed its merciful light into all life's terrible depths"), made perfect sense to the young composers who had recently witnessed oblivion at close range. Schoenberg, having been denounced by Hitler and Stalin alike, carried no taint from totalitarianism either on the left or on the right, or so it seemed. Ernst Krenek went so far as to suggest that he had converted to twelve-tone writing in order to distance himself from totalitarian aesthetics: "My adoption of the musical technique that the tyrants hated most of all may be interpreted as an expression of protest and thus a result of their influence." Many who abandoned neoclassicism and other between-the-war styles may have thought the same. René Leibowitz argued in his book *Schoenberg and His School* that atonality displayed "uncompromising *moral strength*."

Back on North Rockingham Avenue, Schoenberg delightedly witnessed the resurgence of his music and ideas. Yet the fanaticism of some of his adherents disturbed him. When Leibowitz criticized the persistence of tonal elements in works such as the *Ode to Napoleon Bonaparte*, Schoenberg replied, "I do not compose principles, but music." He explained that in earlier years he had avoided tonality in order to differentiate himself from what had gone before; now, he said, "I would not consider the danger of resembling tonality as tragically as formerly." Schoenberg disowned Adorno's attacks on Stravinsky ("One should not write like that") and found little more to like in the theorist's panegyrics to atonality ("this blathering jargon, which so warms the hearts of philosophy professors"). Schoenberg probably had both Adorno and Leibowitz in mind when he made a note to himself that the influence of the "Schbrg clique" would have to be broken before his music could gain a proper hearing. He repeated a remarkable prophecy that he had delivered back in 1909: "The second half of this century will spoil by overestimation, all the good of me that the first half, by underestimation, has left intact."

In his seeing-through-walls way, Schoenberg had mapped out the coming era. He understood that he was being elevated as the patron saint of a newly militant avant-garde mentality, with whose premises he did not agree. While he remained fiercely loyal to the nontonal language that he had pioneered at the beginning of the century, he was no longer so quick to condemn his rivals. Better than Adorno, Schoenberg understood the master dialectic of musical history, the back-and-forth between simplicity and complexity. "I cannot deny the possibility," Schoenberg once wrote, "that as often in the musical past, when harmony has developed to a certain high point, a change will occur which will bring with it entirely different and unexpected things."

Radical Reconstruction: Boulez and Cage

The avant-garde era may be said to have begun a few years early, on a cold winter night in 1941, when Olivier Messiaen's *Quartet for the End of Time* had its first performance, at the prisoner-of-war camp Stalag VIII A.

A composer of advanced ideas and strong religious feeling, Messiaen had been serving as a medical orderly when the Germans invaded France in 1940. He was captured near Nancy with two other musician-soldiers, the cellist Étienne Pasquier and the clarinetist Henri Akoka. While the three were being held with other French captives in an open field, Akoka played through a newly composed Messiaen piece titled "Abyss of the Birds"—a clarinet solo that took the form of precise yet disconnected gestures, slow, trancelike chanting lines intertwining with rapid runs and squawks and trills. When Messiaen was sent with his musician friends to Stalag VIII A, near Görlitz, Germany, he set about composing seven other movements for the unusual combination of clarinet, violin, cello, and piano, those being the instruments that he and his fellow inmates played. At the head of the finished score he wrote an inscription alluding to the book of Revelation: "In homage to the Angel of the Apocalypse, who lifts his hand toward heaven, saying, 'There shall be time no longer.'"

Stalag VIII A was staffed by several officers who lacked true devotion to the Hitler regime. As Rebecca Rischin reveals in a book about the *Quartet*, one of the guards, Karl-Albert Brüll, advised French-Jewish prisoners not to try to escape, on the grounds that they were safer in the camp than they would be in Vichy France. Brüll also took up the cause of Messiaen's music, giving the composer pencils, erasers, and music paper with which to work. The prisoner was relieved of his duties and placed in an empty barracks so that he could compose in peace, with a guard posted at the door to turn away intruders.

The premiere of the *Quartet* took place on January 15, 1941. Several hundred prisoners of many nations crowded into the camp's makeshift theater, with the German officers sitting up front. The work bewildered much of the audience, but a respectful silence prevailed. Messiaen returned to France shortly thereafter, Brüll having connived in the forging of documents in order to speed his release.

By this point in his career, Messiaen had worked out an idiosyncratic musical language, with an especially compelling conception of rhythm. The biblical phrase "There shall be time no longer" turned out to have a strict technical meaning: music would no longer keep to an unvarying meter. A steady beat, Messiaen liked to say, had no life in it; there had been enough of the old *one-two-three-four* during the war. For inspiration, he looked to *The Rite of Spring*, with its irregular, ever-changing rhythmic schemes, and also to the talas, or rhythmic patterns, of Hindustani Indian music. He showed how rhythmic cells—a simple telegraphic pulse of long-short, for example—could take on the character of musical themes, as the cells multiplied (long-short long-short long-short) or mutated (long-short-short-short). This, in essence, is the beat of Stravinsky's "Danse sacrale"—the sound of "implacable destiny," Messiaen said.

Such ideas won the respect of Messiaen's sharp-witted students at the Paris Conservatory, several future celebrities of postwar music among them. When the *Quartet* was played, they were impressed by the novel way it moved through time, in a succession of self-contained moments. What they tended to ignore, however, was the end point of the narrative: sweetly ringing chords in the key of E major. Like Britten in *The Holy Sonnets of John Donne*, Messiaen responded to the mechanized insanity of the Second World War by offering up the purest, simplest sounds he could find.

A few weeks after Allied forces landed at Normandy, a new student, nineteen years old, knocked at Messiaen's door. "M. Boulez (pupil of Pierre Jamet) at my house at 9:30," he wrote in his diary. "Likes modern music," he added. It was the understatement of the century. Pierre Boulez went on to become the perfect avatar of the postwar avant-garde, the one who permitted "no compromise, no concession, no half-way, no consideration of values," to quote Mann's story "At the Prophet's."

At first glance, Boulez was a kind of intellectual dreamboat, elegant in manner and dress, charming to men and women alike—"like a young cat," said the playwright Jean-Louis Barrault, for whom Boulez worked as musical director from 1946 to 1956. Yet, in feline fashion, he could turn ferocious in an instant, mastering the put-down as a way of ending arguments. He was a brilliant politician, equally skilled at persuasion and attack. At all times he seemed absolutely sure of what he was doing. Amid the confusion of postwar life, with so many old truths discredited, his certitude was reassuring. As Joan Peyser notes in her biography of Boulez, an early admirer was the literary socialite Suzanne Tézenas, formerly the companion of the novelist Pierre Drieu La Rochelle. Drieu had been an ardent fascist and had committed suicide shortly before the end of the war. Tézenas greeted Boulez as her new artist savior. She had no particular interest in music, but she liked the way the young man talked.

Unlike so many others of his generation, Boulez suffered little during the war. He was fifteen years old when Germany invaded, and was therefore too young to fight in France's brief war against Hitler. According to Peyser, he actually welcomed the infusions of German culture that were administered by the Nazi authorities. "The Germans virtually brought high culture to France," he was quoted as saying. The son of a prosperous factory engineer, he studied higher mathematics before turning to music. Upon enrolling in the Paris Conservatory, he made his presence felt almost immediately. "When he first entered class," Messiaen recalled, "he was very nice. But soon he became angry with the whole world. He thought everything was wrong with music." Messiaen also said that Boulez was "like a lion that had been flayed alive, he was terrible!"

In the spring of 1945, French radio organized a seven-concert survey of Stravinsky's works at the Théâtre des Champs-Élysées, where the fabled premiere of *The Rite of Spring* had taken place more than thirty years before. On March 15 a group of young composers, all of them students from the conservatory, disrupted a performance of Stravinsky's *Four Norwegian Moods* by booing, shouting, whistling, and, according to one report, banging with a hammer.

Afterward, the French musical world struggled to make sense of the episode. Francis Poulenc, a longtime Stravinskyite, wrote an article for *Le Figaro* titled "Vive Strawinsky," in which he lashed out against the "imitation Left" of "youths" and "pseudo-youths" who had insulted his hero. In a letter to Darius Milhaud, Poulenc described the troublemakers as a "fanatic sect" of "Messiaenistes." He apparently did not yet know the name of the ringleader: Boulez.

By this time Boulez was a Messiaeniste no longer. Messiaen had proved insufficiently ruthless in his methods, his sentimentality embarrassingly on display when, in a response to the Stravinsky booing affair, he decried "dry and inhuman" tendencies in contemporary music and called for "a little celestial tenderness." Instead, Boulez sought out lessons from René Leibowitz, who drilled him in twelve-tone procedures. After a year, Leibowitz, too, was found wanting. One day in 1946, Peyser tells us, Boulez brought in the manuscript of his First Piano Sonata, which he wished to dedicate to his teacher. When Leibowitz set about noting various procedural errors, Boulez threw a tantrum, shouted "*Vous êtes merde!*" and ran from the room. Later, while preparing the sonata for publication, Boulez saw Leibowitz's name at the top of the first page and stabbed it repeatedly with a letter opener. Boulez also showed animosity toward fellow composers who neglected to follow him on the high modern road. When, in 1951, Henri Dutilleux presented his vibrantly diatonic First Symphony, Boulez greeted him by turning his back.

In the First Sonata, Boulez's rage exploded into sound. Gone was the French taste for crisp construction. Gone too was Schoenberg's habit of couching his twelve-tone material in Classical forms and Romantic phrases. Webern was the chief model, although Webern's lyricism was minimized. Smatterings of pointillistic detail gave way to jabbing, crashing, keyboard-spanning gestures. Aided by Messiaen's researches, Boulez maximized rhythmic contrast, creating an asymmetry of pulse to match atonality in harmony. The first movement climaxes with an arpeggiated chord marked "violent and rapid," the second with a chord marked "very brutal and very dry."

Violence is the leitmotif of other Boulez works of this period: *Le Visage nuptial* for voice and orchestra, a setting of poems by René Char ("Take leave, my allies, my violent ones"); and *Le Soleil des eaux*, also based on poems by Char ("River with an indestructible heart in this mad prison-world, keep us violent"). Boulez wrote in 1948, "I believe that music should be collective hysteria and spells, violently of the present time." In the same year he finished his Second Piano Sonata, whose final movement builds through stepwise intensifications of expression—"more and more staccato and brutal," "still more violent"—to a passage in which the pianist is asked to "pulverize the sound; quick, dry attack, as if from bottom to top; stay *without nuances* at very high volume."

"Without nuances" is an apt phrase for a spate of polemical articles that Boulez began issuing in 1948. The essay "Trajectories: Ravel, Stravinsky, Schoenberg" cleared away extant compositional styles in anticipation of the next wave. Ravel was a gold mine of sounds, but circumscribed by "false discoveries," "impotence." The critique of Stravinsky resembled Adorno's in *Philosophy of New Music*; neoclassicism was "schematic, arbitrary, stereotyped." The attack on twelve-tone writing also echoed Adorno's sociological cant; Schoenberg used his technique "to enclose classic and preclassic forms in the elaboration of a world ruled by functions antagonistic to those very forms." The one bright light was Webern, whose orientation was "more virulent than that of his master's works of the same era, a position that in a sense would lead to their annihilation."

When Schoenberg died in the summer of 1951, Boulez penned a breathtakingly pitiless obituary. "The Schoenberg 'case' is irritating," he wrote. The old man had revolutionized the art of harmony while leaving rhythm, structure, and form untouched. He had displayed "the most ostentatious and obsolete romanticism." It was time to "neutralize the setback," to rectify the situation. "Therefore," Boulez concluded, "I do not hesitate to write, not out of any desire to provoke a stupid scandal, but equally without bashful hypocrisy and pointless melancholy: SCHOENBERG IS DEAD."

What could replace Schoenberg's antiquated paradigm? Messiaen supplied the beginning of an answer. Back in 1946 he had planned a "ballet on Time"—a piece in which he would "develop timbres, durations, and nuances according to the principles of serialism." In the summer of 1949, he set to work on a piano piece called *Mode de valeurs et d'intensités*, or *Scale of Durations and Dynamics*, which became the springboard for a new compositional technique known as "total serialism."

In the interest of cultivating rhythmic variety, Messiaen decided that the lengths of notes—sixteenth, eighth, quarter, and so forth—should be arranged in a scale parallel to the scale of pitches. He also made rows of dynamic levels (*ppp*, *fff*, *pp*, *ff*, and so on) and of attacks (accented, staccato, legato, and so on). A particular note is always assigned the same values. Thus, the high E-flat is always a thirty-second note, is always played *ppp*, and is (almost) always slurred. The idea of "scales of rhythm" was not new, having already been theorized by two American experimenters, Charles Seeger and Henry Cowell. Messiaen was, however, the first to coordinate all the variables in one system.

Scale of Durations and Dynamics, which appeared in the collection *Four Rhythm Études*, was the work that really electrified Messiaen's current and former students, among them Boulez, Jean Barraqué, and Karel Goeyvaerts. Here was the maximally differentiated music that they had been seeking. Barraqué, in fact, had already begun serializing rhythm and register, and would put the method into action in his sprawling, jaggedly eloquent Piano Sonata of 1952. But Boulez went furthest, organizing Messiaen's parameters—pitch, duration, volume, and attack—into sets of twelve, along the lines of twelve-tone writing. Pitches do not repeat until all twelve have sounded. Durations do not repeat until all twelve have been used. Dynamics and attacks vary from section to section. The result is a music in constant flux.

In 1950 and 1951, Boulez deployed his new procedures in *Polyphonie X*, for large ensemble, and *Structures 1a*, for two pianos. The latter piece begins grandiloquently, at maximum volume: an E-flat sounds in the topmost octave of the first piano, setting off two simultaneous twelve-tone rows, one in original form and one in inversion, unfolding in all registers and in rotating durations, with the lower end defined by a stentorian B-flat. One more heroic musical law is being graven in stone.

The emotional content of the music is elusive. The feeling of delirium wears off after a few minutes, giving way to a kind of objectified, mechanized savagery. The serialist principle, with its surfeit of ever-changing musical data, has the effect of erasing at any given moment whatever impressions the listener may have formed about previous passages in the piece. The present moment is all there is. Boulez's early works, notably the two Sonatas, *Structures*, and *Le Visage nuptial*, are perhaps best understood not as intellectual experiences but as athletic, even cerebrally sexual ones. Michel Foucault, the great theorist of power and sexuality, seemed almost turned on by Boulez's music, and for a time he was the lover of Boulez's fellow serialist Barraqué. "They represented for me the first 'tear' in the dialectical universe in which I had lived," Foucault said of the serialists. What drove Boulez's own rage for order remains unknown.

In the spring of 1949, John Cage, aged thirty-six, arrived in Paris with his professional and personal partner, the dancer Merce Cunningham. At the suggestion of Virgil Thomson, Cage went to see Boulez, and an unlikely, short-lived, but mutually influential friendship was born.

Already the most radical American composer of the time, Cage proceeded to unleash some of the most startling events and nonevents in musical history: tape and radio collages, works composed with rolls of dice, multimedia happenings, and, most famously, *4′33″*, during which the performer makes no sound. Some years later, in conversation with Calvin Tomkins, Cage defined himself in terms that Boulez would have readily understood: "I am going toward violence rather than tenderness, hell rather than heaven, ugly rather than beautiful, impure rather than pure—because by doing these things they become transformed, and we become transformed." And yet Cage's enterprise lacked the pitilessness of Boulez's assault on the past. In place of the term "avant-garde," which implied a quasi-military forward drive, Cage preferred "experimental," which, he said, was "inclusive rather than exclusive." In truth, Cage was capable both of great violence and of great tenderness, and his music wavers tensely between those extremes.

Cage was a Los Angeles native, the son of an inventor who built one of the earliest functioning submarines. He had a Roman nose, a gaunt face, and a reedy voice, like that of the actor Vincent Price. In the early fifties he assumed the look of a hip young physicist, cropping his hair short and dressing in stiff-collared white shirts. He had moved to New York in 1942, and by the end of the decade he was living on the top floor of a crumbling tenement on the East River, where he fashioned a bohemian-Zen utopia of white walls and minimal furnishings. He worked at a drafting table outfitted with a fluorescent lamp, etching his scores with German-made Rapidograph pens. Cage's personality was a curious mix of eccentricity and worldliness; even as he explored esoteric musical regions, his activities seldom went unrecorded in the press.

Cage began as an acolyte of Arnold Schoenberg. In 1935 and 1936 he audited several of the great man's classes at USC and UCLA. His attempts at twelve-tone writing were peculiar, featuring rows of up to twenty-five notes. From the start, he expressed disdain for the conventions of mainstream classical music and looked around for alternatives. In 1930, when he was only eighteen, he made a trip to Berlin and received stimulation from the culture of the Weimar Republic. He happened to attend a "phonograph concert" presented by Paul Hindemith and Ernst Toch, at which phonographs played prerecorded sounds onstage, including a "spoken music" of phonetic syllables. In 1939 Cage wrote a work in which a phonograph becomes a musical instrument—*Imaginary Landscape No. 1*, for muted piano, Chinese cymbal, and variable-speed turntables. Three years later came *Credo in Us*, which includes a part for a record player or radio; the score suggests, with apparent sarcasm, that the operator "use some classic: e.g. Dvořák, Beethoven, Sibelius, or Shostakovich."

For Cage, the classical tradition was worn-out kitsch ripe for deconstruction, in the manner of his intellectual hero, the conceptual artist

Marcel Duchamp. A record player squawking random bits of Beethoven or Shostakovich became the sonic equivalent of painting a mustache on the *Mona Lisa* or displaying a urinal as sculpture.

Also, Cage loved noise. In a 1937 manifesto he declared, "I believe that the use of noise to make music will continue and increase until we reach a music produced through the aid of electrical instruments which will make available for musical purposes any and all sounds that can be heard." He made his name as a composer for percussion, manufacturing instruments from brake drums, hubcaps, spring coils, and other cast-off car parts. At the same time, he was bewitched by soft sounds, rustlings on the border between noise and silence. The prepared piano, his most famous invention, never fails to surprise listeners expecting to be battered by some unholy racket; the preparation process, involving the insertion of bolts, screws, coins, pieces of wood and felt, and other objects between the strings, is conceptually violent, but the sounds themselves are innately sweet. Cage's prepared-piano pieces—among them *The Perilous Night*, *Daughters of the Lonesome Isle*, and the cycle *Sonatas and Interludes*—have some of the supernatural poignancy of Erik Satie, whose music Cage loved from an early age.

The same gentleness governs the *String Quartet in Four Parts* (1949–50), whose movements are titled "Quietly Flowing Along," "Slowly Rocking," "Nearly Stationary," and "Quodlibet." Underneath the ethereal surface, however, unsettling new processes are at work. In the quartet Cage gathers various kernels of musical sound and arranges them in a "gamut," a kind of chessboard of possibilities. He moves from one sound to another in a detached frame of mind, trying not to push them where they do not want to go. This abdication of control sets the stage for an enormous shock.

When Cage heard Boulez's Second Sonata, he was, in his own words, "stupefied by its activism, by the sum of the activities inherent in it." In his next works, *Sixteen Dances* and the Concerto for Prepared Piano and Chamber Orchestra, everything disintegrated. At first, Cage maintained the method of the *String Quartet in Four Parts*, making moves on a chart of sixty-four sounds, containing notes, chords, trills, and so on. Then, while writing the final movement of the Concerto, in late 1950 and early 1951, the composer began tossing coins in order to determine what should come next. He followed the rules of the Chinese divinatory practice of the *I Ching*, or *Book of Changes*, which uses random operations to generate any one of sixty-four hexagrams, each describing a different state of mind or being ("force," "radiance," and so on). The piano cycle *Music of Changes*, composed in 1951, depended on the *I Ching* throughout; successive rolls of the dice determined what sound would be heard, how long it should last, how loud it should be, what tempo should be observed, and how many simultaneous layers of activity should accumulate. When the dice called for maximum density, Cage wrote down what he acknowledged to be an "irrational" quantity of notes, leaving the execution to the performer's discretion.

Half the sounds on the charts were, in fact, silences. As James Pritchett writes in a study of Cage's music, the composer was becoming interested in the "interchangeability of sound and silence."

The use of chance—Cage would later make musical decisions based on imperfections in manuscript paper, star charts, and computer-generated numbers—strayed far outside European classical tradition. By downtown New York standards, however, it was nothing terribly outlandish. In these years Jackson Pollock, Willem de Kooning, Franz Kline, Barnett Newman, Mark Rothko, and Robert Rauschenberg were throwing down violent swirls of paint, stark monochrome patterns, and shiny geometric lines, or making canvases entirely black or entirely white. Pollock's "drip paintings" used a semi-chance process.

Cage consorted with the painters, following them from the Artists' Club on East Eighth Street to the Cedar Tavern. He also worked in tandem with Merce Cunningham, who had created the role of the Revivalist in Martha Graham's *Appalachian Spring* and later devised his own joltingly free and fluid choreographic language. Together, Cunningham and Cage invented a new kind of chance-driven dance in which sound and movement went their separate ways only to meet up again on a deeper conceptual level. Around this time, Cage browsed through the literature of Zen Buddhism, which supplied him with an all-accepting, "whatever happens will happen" approach to the creative process.

A few other New York–based composers were thinking along similar lines, and they gravitated into Cage's orbit. The most important of these was Morton Feldman, a New York native who had steeped himself in Bartók, Varèse, the Second Viennese School, and Abstract Expressionist painting. It was Feldman who set loose the imp of chance; one day at

Cage's apartment he offered up for inspection a draft of a piece titled *Projection 1*, whose score consisted not of notes on staves but of a grid of boxes, each box lasting a certain period of time and indicating a high, middle, or low range. This novel practice came to be known as graphic notation: the composer was no longer telling performers exactly which notes to play at any given time.

A laboratory atmosphere developed in Cage's apartment. Other frequent visitors were the teenage experimental prodigy Christian Wolff, whose early works drew on severely limited gamuts of three or four pitches; Earle Brown, whose open-form pieces imported some of the energy of bebop; and the pianist David Tudor, whose realizations of his friends' graphic and chance scores were compositions in themselves.

Cage launched his revolution at three historic concerts in the spring and summer of 1952. First came *Water Music*, at the New School for Social Research, in May. David Tudor not only played the prepared piano but shuffled cards, poured water from one receptacle to another, blew a duck whistle, and changed stations on a radio. Each action was plotted on a time continuum. Then came *Black Mountain Piece*, at Black Mountain College, the first true "happening." The boundary between artist and audience disappeared as participants stepped out of the crowd to perform musical or extramusical actions. Martin Duberman, in his history of the college, valiantly tried to determine what happened at the happening, but no two accounts agreed. Cage lectured on Zen Buddhism, perhaps standing on a ladder. Robert Rauschenberg exhibited artworks and/or played Edith Piaf records at double speed. Merce Cunningham danced. David Tudor played prepared piano. Movies of some kind were shown, boys or girls served coffee, a dog may or may not have barked. Black Mountain had always been a haven for adventurous spirits, but some of the faculty felt that Cage had gone too far. Stefan Wolpe, who had gone through his own Dada phase in 1920s Berlin, walked out in protest.

The final breakthrough was the premiere of *4′33″*, the so-called silent piece, on August 29, in the upstate New York town of Woodstock. Cage later said that he had been inspired to write *4′33″* after seeing a group of all-white Rauschenberg canvases at Black Mountain the previous year. "Music is lagging," he thought to himself, on encountering Rauschenberg's work. In fact, he had already experimented with spells of silence in *Music of Changes*, and, back in 1948, he had talked about writing a four-

and-a-half-minute soundless piece titled *Silent Prayer*. Rauschenberg simply emboldened him to do the unthinkable.

The original score was written out on conventional music paper, tempo = 60, in three movements. David Tudor walked onstage, sat down at the piano, opened the piano lid, and did nothing, except to close the lid and open it again at the beginning of each subsequent movement. The music was the sound of the surrounding space. It was at once a head-spinning philosophical statement and a Zen-like ritual of contemplation. It was a piece that anyone could have written, as skeptics never failed to point out, but, as Cage seldom failed to respond, no one else did.

The bourgeois piano having been silenced, the age of the machines could begin. On his European trip of 1949, Cage encountered several pioneering technicians of electronic music, who had set in motion the most sweeping of all postwar campaigns against the musical past.

The previous year, Pierre Schaeffer, an engineer at the French national radio network, had devised five electronic *Études of Noises*, one movement of which consisted of the huffing, chugging, and whistling of six locomotives that he had recorded in the Batignolles train station. Schaeffer worked initially with phonograph discs, but he soon realized that magnetic-tape recording, which German engineers had perfected during the war, allowed for the making of sound collages by way of cutting and splicing bits of tape. (His initial research into musical acoustics had actually taken place during the war, with the approval of the occupying German forces.) Schaeffer went on to create, in collaboration with another Messiaen pupil, Pierre Henry, an extended collage work titled *Symphony for a Solitary Man*. Schaeffer dubbed his work musique concrète and developed his tape fragments with contrapuntal intensity—playing them backward, speeding them up, slowing them down, slicing off the attack, or turning them into loops.

When Cage came to Paris, Boulez, knowing of his long-standing fascination with electronic gizmos, introduced him to Schaeffer. A few years later, in New York, Cage gained access to German-style magnetic-tape recorders, and, at the studio of Louis and Bebe Barron, he laboriously put together the four-minute tape collage *Williams Mix*, one of a group of pieces that emerged from the collaborative Project for Music for Magnetic Tape. The material came from an enormous heap of tape fragments, which were distributed in six categories: city sounds, country sounds, electronic sounds, manually produced sounds, wind sounds, and "small" sounds. Cage subjected these to *I Ching* manipulations, producing constant jumps from one sound to another or buzzing, scrambled textures of up to sixteen simultaneous layers. Notwithstanding the emotional detachment of the method, *Williams Mix* has the air of a world gone berserk, of modernity imploding on itself.

Imaginary Landscape No. 4 (1951), for twelve radios, partakes of the same madhouse atmosphere: two players are positioned at each radio, one switching stations according to patterns specified in the score, the other making adjustments to volume. A more pointed satire of media-saturated society could hardly be imagined, although, as ever, the composer's attitude is studiously deadpan. Some part of Cage longed for pretechnological, even preindustrial life. In his 1950 "Lecture on Nothing," he quoted a woman from Texas who told him, "We have no music in Texas." He then said, "The reason they've no music in Texas is because they have recordings in Texas. Remove the records from Texas and someone will learn to sing."

All this was too much for Boulez, who was soon speaking as witheringly of Cage as he had of so many others. By the seventies he was calling his former friend a "performing monkey" whose methods betrayed "fascist tendencies"—thereby putting Cage next to Strauss, Sibelius, and Stravinsky in the crowded room of composers who had been labeled fascist for one reason or another.

The divide that opened up between Cage and Boulez indicated sociological differences between the avant-garde cultures of America and Europe. Cage's audience was essentially a bohemian one, including like-minded artists, Greenwich Village eccentrics, and outsiders of every description. Boulez's audience, on the other hand, overlapped with traditional circles of connoisseurship and art appreciation. In 1954, with the assistance of Suzanne Tézenas, Boulez founded the concert series Domaine Musical, in the course of which he demonstrated his flair for programming, explicating, and conducting difficult scores. Its patrons consisted, in Tézenas's words, of "Nicolas de Staël, Mathieu, the great abstract painters, Michaux, Jouve, Char, Mandiargues, all the *grands amis*, gallery directors, society women." This was an extension of the crowd that had patronized Stravinsky and Les Six in the twenties. Indeed, none other than Jean Cocteau showed up for the first concert, swathed in a cape. Morton Feldman was not far off in dubbing Boulez's music a form of "hyperactive chic."

The irony of the broken Cage-Boulez friendship was that certain of Cage's chance pieces ended up sounding oddly similar to Boulez's total-serialist pieces. The young Hungarian composer György Ligeti pointed out the resemblance in two penetrating analytical articles of 1958 and 1960, concluding that Boulez and other serialist composers were not fully responsible for the outcome of their works. Their method obeyed a "compulsion neurosis" that effectively randomized their musical material.

In truth, there had always been an element of arbitrariness, of automatism, in atonal and twelve-tone music. When Schoenberg wrote *Erwartung* in seventeen days, he could hardly have known in advance exactly what each of his nine- and ten-note orchestral chords would sound like; he, too, was throwing paint on canvas. Cage brought this arbitrariness into the open. Of the *Concert for Piano and Orchestra*, a summary of his 1950s-era techniques, Cage said, "My intention in this piece was to hold together extreme disparities, much as one finds them held together in the natural world, as, for instance, in a forest, or on a city street." Back in 1949, on the eve of his most radical period, Cage had announced: "Any attempt to exclude the 'irrational' is irrational. Any composing strategy which is wholly 'rational' is irrational in the extreme."

Copland Under Fire

On May 8, 1945—V-E Day, or Victory in Europe Day—American city streets overflowed with jubilant throngs. On the same day, Aaron Copland received a Pulitzer Prize for *Appalachian Spring*. Prospects seemed bright for a long-term continuation of the populist style that Copland had helped to engineer. The following year Virgil Thomson crowed in the *New York Herald Tribune*, "We are producing very nearly the best music in the world." As evidence, the critic-composer listed most of the leading practitioners of the populist and/or neoclassical modes of American music—Copland, Harris, Barber, William Schuman, Walter Piston, Howard Hanson, and the boy wonder Leonard Bernstein, who had made a sensational conducting debut with the New York Philharmonic in 1943 and established himself as a composer with the oracular *Jeremiah* Symphony and the joyously hip musical *On the Town*.

Even as the confetti was being swept from Times Square, V-E exuberance faded into a darker, more volatile state of mind. America was surging toward unprecedented domestic prosperity and global influence, but the mood at home turned cynical and fearful. Roosevelt's spirit of "common discipline" was dissolving: even as middle-class Americans pursued material happiness in the form of television, rock 'n' roll records, cars, and tract homes, they fell prey to the overarching fear that Roosevelt had warned against in his first inaugural address. The fear focused, above all, on Communism. The year 1949 was pivotal: the detonation of the first Soviet nuclear device that summer and the subsequent unmasking of the physicist Klaus Fuchs as a KGB spy intensified the anti-Communist hysteria that was already sweeping the land.

In this same period, New Deal–style art for the masses began to acquire a dubious reputation. Excesses of populism in the "serious" arts counted as evidence of a politically compromised mind. Modernists, on the other hand, garnered admiring buzzwords such as "unyielding" and "uncompromising," their contrary stance imbued with political as well as aesthetic implications.

Clement Greenberg, who in his famous 1939 essay "Avant-Garde and Kitsch" had set up an Adorno-like antithesis between the avant-garde and commercial culture, trumpeted Abstract Expressionist painters as icons of a tough postwar spirit. In a March 1948 essay Greenberg announced that with the rise of Pollock and others "the main premises of Western art have at last migrated to the United States, along with the center of gravity of industrial production and political power." The mainstream media went along with this modernist morality play. In August 1949, *Life* magazine reproduced Jackson Pollock's "drip paintings" and asked in a headline whether Pollock was "the Greatest Living Painter in the United States." Given that *Life* was under the wing of the "American Century" mogul Henry Luce, Pollock's abstractions acquired political nobility.

Just as the country was tilting to the right, Copland introduced his Third Symphony—an ill-timed stab at heroic symphonism in the Shostakovich mode. Audience reactions were positive: Serge Koussevitzky, who commissioned the work for the Boston Symphony, called it "the greatest American symphony." But after the premiere in October 1946, *Time* magazine, Luce's other flagship publication, averred that Copland was now too popular for his own good ("too busy to be a great composer"). A few years later, the musicologist William Austin felt compelled to defend the symphony thus: "Nothing can persuade a listener to enjoy the piece if he is altogether out of sympathy with its rather New-Deal-ish spirit of hopeful resolution and neighborliness."

In the fourth movement, Copland quoted his own *Fanfare for the Common Man*, that muscular utterance modeled on Henry Wallace's speech "Century of the Common Man." By the fall of 1946 Wallace was no longer the nationally respected figure that he had been during the Roosevelt years. President Truman had fired him from the post of commerce secretary on account of a series of seemingly pro-Soviet remarks. This was the context for Austin's comment: to be associated with an unrepentant New Dealer such as Wallace had become a political risk. As Elizabeth Crist points out, Virgil Thomson made the subtext explicit in a review of the symphony the following year, in which he mocked its resemblance to "the speeches of Henry Wallace, striking in phraseology but all too reminiscent of Moscow." Thomson's enthusiasm for all-American symphonies was on the wane. In the same year he wrote a review headlined "Atonality in France," singling out Boulez for his virtuosity and noting the emergence of a "new international style."

Thomson's attack on the Third Symphony was a brilliantly manipulative feat of musical politics, and yet Copland himself was playing naive ideological games. His occasional commentaries on the international situation showed lamentably little awareness of what life inside the Soviet Union was really like. In April 1948, for example, he delivered the following analysis of Zhdanov's persecution of Shostakovich and Prokofiev: "[The composers] were rebuked for failing to realize that their musical audience had expanded enormously in the last several years . . . and that composers can no longer continue to write only for a few initiates." Such remarks brushed dangerously close to the Party line, and Copland was about to discover the consequences of clinging too long to the old spirit of American-Soviet solidarity.

In March 1949, Copland made the mistake of attending the Cultural and Scientific Conference for World Peace, at the Waldorf-Astoria Hotel in

New York. This was one of the first great propaganda battles in the cultural Cold War, and more than a few artistic reputations fell victim to the clash of ideologies. The martyr in chief was Dmitri Shostakovich, who had gone to America at Stalin's behest. Weird scenes surrounded Shostakovich from the moment he arrived on American soil. The Broadwood Hotel in Philadelphia canceled his dinner reservation on account of threats of violence. Demonstrators carried placards exhorting him to speak out or to defect:

SHOSTAKOVICH, WE UNDERSTAND

SHOSTAKOVICH! JUMP THRU THE WINDOW!

—the second slogan referring to the athletic defection of the schoolteacher Oksana Kasenkina the previous year. It was not in Shostakovich's nature to jump through the window. He read the speeches that were placed in front of him; he answered questions in accordance with instructions that were whispered in his ear. On the final night of the conference, he played a piano arrangement of the Scherzo of his Fifth Symphony at Madison Square Garden before an audience of eighteen thousand while two thousand picketers protested outside. All the while, Shostakovich maintained an indecipherable facade of nervous preoccupation. When Morton Gould sidled up to him in the hope of hearing some candid confession, Shostakovich muttered, "It's hot in here."

Left-leaning American artists of all disciplines and persuasions gathered at the Waldorf to greet their Soviet counterparts. Some attendees came in a spirit of political sympathy, others out of artistic fellow feeling or curiosity. Henry Wallace was there, and drew cheers as he entered. *Time* observed snidely that the event could have been mistaken for a Wallace rally. Clifford Odets, Lillian Hellman, and Arthur Miller also attended. Thomas Mann sent a message of support. Copland's role was especially prominent: he greeted Shostakovich at the airport and sat at the head table with Hellman and Wallace. Most of the attendees did not know to what extent the event had been engineered by Soviet propagandists, who were under the aegis of the Cominform organization.

Assembled on the other side of the political barricades was a coalition of disenchanted leftists who called themselves Americans for Intellectual Freedom. They holed up in the bridal suite at the Waldorf, trying to stem the tide of Communist and fellow-traveler propaganda. In the thick of the group was Nicolas Nabokov, the former Ballets Russes composer and OMGUS operative, whose career was taking a colorful new turn. After his stint in Berlin, Nabokov had applied for a position in the nascent Central Intelligence Agency, for which his sponsor was none other than George Kennan, one of the chief architects of American Cold War policy. Failing to receive security clearance—apparently J. Edgar Hoover nixed him—Nabokov decided to devote himself again to composition.

By various twists and turns, Nabokov ended up on the CIA's payroll all the same. Americans for Intellectual Freedom was receiving clandestine support from the CIA's Office of Policy Coordination, which had taken an interest in combating Soviet influence through the promotion of anti-Communist or pro-democratic cultural activities. Nabokov's subsequent protests that he had no knowledge of the CIA connection are difficult to credit. Surely, at about the time that the president of the International Ladies' Garment Workers' Union handed him a wad of cash to pay the hotel bill, it must have crossed his mind that all was not as it seemed.

The members of Americans for Intellectual Freedom fanned out to various speeches and panel discussions at the conference. Nabokov zeroed in on a Sunday-morning fine arts panel, where Shostakovich and Copland were scheduled to appear.

Shostakovich's contribution was a five-thousand-word speech that ranged from music to international politics and on to Soviet domestic policy. It would be too much to say that the composer "delivered" it; he sat in silence while his interpreter read it aloud. The speech attacked Stravinsky for betraying his native Russia and joining the ranks of the reactionary modernists: "His beginnings were promising, but . . . his moral barrenness reveals itself in his openly nihilistic writings, proclaiming the meaninglessness and absence of content in his creations. Stravinsky has no fear of that gaping abyss which separates him from the spiritual life of the people." The speech went on to denounce "new aspirants for world domination, now engaged in resurrecting the theory and practice of fascism." This "small clique of hatemongers"—presumably the cold warriors of the Truman administration—was engaged in developing weapons of mass destruction that stood in the way of world peace. The speech even criticized Hanson Baldwin, the military-affairs editor of the *New York Times*, for denigrating the economic status of Soviet Asian republics such as Uzbekistan and Tajikistan. The conceit that Shostakovich was an avid reader of military-affairs coverage in the *Times* added a slight comic note to the proceedings.

Copland responded with temperate, thoughtful remarks in which he declared himself independent of any political agenda. "I am going to start by saying that I wrote this paper myself," he said. "Nobody told me what to say, and if anybody had tried to tell me what to say, I wouldn't be here." At the heart of his speech was an affecting elegy for the lost idealism of the New Deal:

> Lately I've been thinking that the cold war is almost worse for art than the real thing—for it permeates the atmosphere with fear and anxiety. An artist can function at his best only in a vital and healthy environment for the simple reason that the very act of creation is an affirmative gesture. An artist fighting in a war for a cause he holds just has something affirmative he can believe in. The artist, if he can stay alive, can create art. But throw him into a mood of suspicion, ill-will and dread that typifies the Cold War attitude and he'll create nothing.

Unfortunately, the only part of Copland's speech that drew notice in the papers—the *Times*'s front-page article carried the headline "Shostakovich Bids All Artists Lead War on New 'Fascists' "—was this: "The present policies of the American Government will lead inevitably into a third world war."

Nabokov kept his gaze fixed on Shostakovich. The "culture generalissimo," as Stravinsky called him, had for many years been nursing a hatred of his Soviet counterpart. Like Bartók, he heard the *Leningrad* as musical kitsch, foisted by cynical maestros and impresarios on a "naively stupid, apathetic, and profoundly uncultivated American public" (as he put it in a letter to Stravinsky). In a 1943 article for *Harper's* magazine Nabokov declared that the fad for Shostakovich signaled a general decline in cultural values, a slide toward "absolute and immediate comprehensibility to large masses of people."

Despite his built-in hostility, Nabokov professed to feel a certain sympathy for the pathetic figure who stood before him in 1949. "Throughout the tumultuous conference," Nabokov recalled, "I watched [Shostakovich's] hands twist the cardboard tips of his cigarettes, his face twitch and his whole posture express intense unease. While his Soviet colleagues on the right and left looked calm and as self-contented as mantelpiece Buddhas, his sensitive face looked disturbed, hurt, and terribly shy . . . He seemed like a trapped man, whose only wish was to be left alone, to the peace of his own art and to the tragic destiny to which he, like most of his countrymen, had been forced to resign himself."

The knowledge that Shostakovich lacked freedom of speech did not prevent Nabokov from forcing him to speak. The émigré rose from his seat to ask whether Shostakovich really endorsed Zhdanov's condemnation of composers such as Stravinsky, Schoenberg, and Hindemith. Shostakovich had no choice but to say, "I fully agree with the statements made in *Pravda*." Decades later, Arthur Miller was haunted by the memory of Shostakovich's moment of humiliation: "God knows what he was thinking in that room, what splits ran across his spirit . . ."

If Shostakovich made any protest against the charade that he was required to conduct, it assumed a subtle, silent form. The night after the conference, he attended a Juilliard String Quartet concert of Bartók's First, Fourth, and Sixth quartets, works that fell into the formalist category. He congratulated the performers, and then, according to the *Times*, "slipped quietly out into the night." Bearing no apparent ill will for (or knowledge of) Bartók's parody of the *Leningrad*, he would incorporate Bartókian ideas into his own sublime late sequence of string quartets.

Several days later *Life* magazine opened fire on the entire world of Henry Wallace, the New Deal, the Popular Front, and the U.S. Communist Party. A sardonic photo essay on the Waldorf conference highlighted Wallace as the "standout fellow traveler," and a two-page photo gallery identified fifty "dupes and fellow travelers" who were said to be aiding the Communist cause. Copland, spelled "Copeland," appeared alongside Thomas Mann, Albert Einstein, Langston Hughes, Charles Chaplin, and all the above-mentioned attendees of the conference.

Among other things, Luce's attack indicated that the media's lionization of refugee intellectuals was at an end. A "strange rogue's gallery," Mann called the *Life* spread. The author of *Doctor Faustus* feared that

America was falling victim to the same totalitarian madness that had consumed his German homeland, and he began to think about emigrating once again. Three years later he moved to Switzerland, his final homeland. Mann had come to America looking for freedom from demonic politics, and he did not find it.

When the Waldorf debacle was over, Copland took a trip to Paris. Bearing no obvious scars from what he had endured, he busied himself with tracking down the latest musical trends in the city where, more than two decades before, he had got to know the work of Stravinsky and Les Six. In a letter to the composer Irving Fine and his wife, Verna, he reported that he was "ferreting out the dodecaphonistes."

In particular, he ferreted out Pierre Boulez. The two composers were apparently brought together by John Cage, who had met Boulez a few weeks earlier. Copland ascended the stairs to Boulez's apartment, which occupied two rooms on the top floor of a building in the Marais, and heard the young master play parts of his Second Sonata. "But must we start a revolution all over again?" Copland asked, when it was over. "*Mais oui*," Boulez replied, "*sans pitié*." The two composers met again a few days later, at a gathering of American expatriates that included the pianist Shirley Gabis and the gifted young composer Ned Rorem. Boulez once more banged out the Second Sonata, to the consternation of the neoclassical Americans. According to Rorem, Copland "stuck it out with a grin." Afterward, he went to the piano to play his own hard-driving *Piano Variations*, from 1930; he wanted to show that "he was just as hairy as Boulez," or so Rorem guessed.

That fall, the question of Copland's politics arose once more in the American media, and in a most bizarre way. Arnold Schoenberg, who usually limited his political utterances to Zionist issues, declared in a radio address: "You cannot change the natural evolution of the arts by a command; you may make a New Year's resolution to write only what everybody likes; but you cannot force real artists to descend to the lowest possible standards to give up morals, character, and sincerity, to avoid presentation of new ideas. Even Stalin cannot succeed and Aaron Copland even less."

Virgil Thomson reprinted Schoenberg's bellicose remarks in the *Her-*

ald Tribune and then allowed Copland to respond. Copland said: "Mr. Schoenberg must have seen my picture in the papers in company with Shostakovich on the occasion of his brief visit here last spring. In America it is still possible (I hope) to share a forum platform with a man whose musical and political ideas are not one's own without being judged guilty by association."

At the Federal Bureau of Investigation in Washington, D.C., someone went to the trouble to open a file on the composer ("Alias: Aaron Copeland," it said on one page). When Copland returned from a six-month tour of Europe and Israel in 1951, J. Edgar Hoover wrote a note to his counterpart at the CIA: "Copland has been abroad for some time and on June 25, 1951, he arrived in New York from Bombay, India, on TWA flight 6022-C. It would be appreciated if you would furnish this Bureau any information you have received concerning Copland's activities while abroad."

In 1951 and 1952 Copland delivered the Charles Eliot Norton lectures at Harvard, where he sketched an exceptionally clear and canny picture of the emergent ideological divide in postwar music. On the one hand, he said, you have the twelve-tone composer who "is no longer writing music to satisfy himself" but instead "is writing it *against* a vocal and militant opposition" of socialist realist composers. In other words, twelve-tone music had been politicized. On the other hand, you have the "composer of communist persuasion," who runs the risk of abandoning artistic quality for popular appeal.

Reading between the lines of Copland's flat-toned prose, you can sense his anxiety that he was falling too conspicuously into the second category. He had already been labeled a fellow traveler in the pages of *Life*. He had watched as old colleagues had been subjected to interrogation or driven out of the country. As a gay man, he had extra reason to worry: the FBI was conducting separate purges of homosexuals on the theory that they made easy targets for Soviet blackmail. One of them was John Evarts, the former music officer of OMGUS Bavaria, who lost his post as cultural attaché in 1951.

On January 20, 1953, Dwight D. Eisenhower was inaugurated as president of the United States. Copland's *Lincoln Portrait* had been scheduled for a preliminary Inaugural Concert by the National Symphony, but two weeks before the event Congressman Fred Busbey denounced Copland's work as Communist propaganda and demanded that it be removed from the program. Making the case for Copland as a "fellow traveler," Busbey read a long list of Copland's affiliations into the *Congressional Record*, including his appearance at the Waldorf-Astoria conference; his support of Hanns Eisler, who had been interrogated by the House Un-American Activities Committee in 1947 and then deported; and his relationships with such organizations as the American Committee for Protection of Foreign Born, the Artists' Front to Win the War, the Citizens Committee for Harry Bridges, the National Committee for the Defense of Political Prisoners, the National Council of American-Soviet Friendship, and the American Music Alliance of the Friends of the Abraham Lincoln Brigade. Busbey warned: "As the number of such activities or affiliations increase [*sic*], any presumption of the innocence of such a person must necessarily decrease."

Copland released a statement couched in the defensive jargon of the day: "I say unequivocally that I am not now and never have been a communist or member of the communist party or of any organization that advocates or teaches in any way the overthrow of the United States Government." Nonetheless, *Lincoln Portrait* was not played for President-elect Eisenhower at Constitution Hall.

Finally, on May 22, 1953, came the dreaded telegram: "YOU ARE HEREBY DIRECTED TO APPEAR BEFORE THIS COMMITTEE ON MONDAY MAY TWENTYFIFTH AT TWO THIRTY P M ROOM 357 SENATE OFFICE BUILDING WASHINGTON DC —JOE MCCARTHY CHAIRMAN SENATE PERMANENT SUBCOMMITTEE ON INVESTIGATIONS."

Fortunately, McCarthy did not treat Copland as brutally as he did other fellow travelers, perhaps because the senator was interested less in the composer's career than in his educational activities on behalf of the United States Department of State, which was supposedly riddled with Communists. "My impression," Copland wrote in a private memorandum, "is that McCarthy had no idea who I was or what I did." The composer claimed ignorance of the Communist affiliations of the organizations to which he had been linked. Sometimes, he said, his name had been used without his knowledge. In other cases the associations were tenuous; Copland's role in the Citizens Committee for Harry Bridges had amounted to a one-dollar check. Less sincere was Copland's claim that he had never knowingly consorted with a Party member. Fortunately, Roy Cohn's investigators did not learn of his 1934 speech to a rally of Communist farmers in Minnesota.

Having submitted his written response to the Permanent Subcommittee on Investigations, Copland waited to be called back for a public hearing. But none materialized. Apparently, he benefited from the unlikely support of the anti-Communist newspaperman George Sokolsky, who privately urged McCarthy to lay off "one of America's greatest living composers." Still, there were repercussions. For years Copland experienced hassles whenever he tried to travel abroad; the Passport Agency declined to renew his passport and repeatedly requested that he demonstrate affiliations with anti-Communist organizations. And in 1953, several of Copland's engagements were rescinded on political grounds.

Howard Pollack, in his biography of Copland, declares that the composer's political ordeal, grueling as it was, did not bring about a dramatic change in his style. He did not "convert" to twelve-tone writing, as is often stated. Only four certifiably dodecaphonic pieces ensued: the Piano Quartet of 1950, *Piano Fantasy*, *Connotations*, and *Inscape*. In other works, Copland still employed one form or another of his populist manner. His most ambitious project of the fifties was the opera *The Tender Land*, which applied the language of *Billy the Kid* and *Appalachian Spring* to a quietly moving tale of life on the open prairie. Erik Johns's scenario had undercurrents of social protest: the community becomes irrationally suspicious of two strangers in their midst, enacting in microcosm the paranoias of McCarthyite America. Open-interval melodies and spare instrumentation bathe the scene in the familiar Edenic light.

Copland hoped that *The Tender Land* would be broadcast on television, but the networks took no interest. New York City Opera presented it instead. Copland's thousand-dollar commissioning fee was a gift from Rodgers and Hammerstein, the creators of *Oklahoma!*

With *The Tender Land* overlooked, Copland's most conspicuous postwar statement was *Connotations*, whose first performance took place in September 1962. Hardly any American orchestral work had ever enjoyed such a heavy media glare: the occasion of the premiere was the opening of Philharmonic Hall, the flagship venue of the new Lincoln Center for the Performing Arts in New York. CBS broadcast the concert live to a television audience of twenty-six million people. Here was the mass public of which American composers had long dreamed.

But Copland was no longer in an ingratiating mood; some sudden rage welled up in him, some urge to confront the gala Lincoln Center audience with an old whiff of revolutionary mystique. *Connotations* is by some margin the most dissonant score of Copland's career, and it culminates in an apoplectically orchestrated sequence of chords encompassing all twelve notes of the chromatic scale. At intermission, the composer was greeted by none other than Mrs. John F. Kennedy, who had come up from Washington for the event. Ordinarily at ease in cultural settings, the First Lady was this time rendered more or less speechless. "Oh, Mr. Copland," she said. "Oh, Mr. Copland . . ."

After that barbaric yawp of a piece, Copland's output rapidly dwindled. *Inscape*, which Bernstein's Philharmonic played in 1967, was of more subdued, mysterious character. His last extended piece, the Duo for Flute and Piano from 1971, returns to a language of plainspoken eloquence, the flute's opening solo sounding like a pastoral version of the adamantine trumpet line that begins *Fanfare for the Common Man*. Around the same time, Copland published a poignant little piano piece called *In Evening Air*, reviving some music that he had written in 1945 for the Office of War Information documentary *The Cummington Story*, which showed how a group of Eastern European refugees were initially spurned and later embraced by a New England town. Some of the same material, including a Polish lullaby, appears in one of his very last works, *Midday Thoughts*, from 1982. It's as if Copland were dreaming back to a more hopeful time.

After a point, music stopped running through his head. "It was exactly as if someone had simply turned off a faucet," he told the critic Paul Moor. He began to suffer memory loss, the first sign of the onset of Alzheimer's disease. He lived until the age of ninety, fading into a tender silence. The epigraph for *In Evening Air*, from Theodore Roethke, told the story of his last years with heartbreaking simplicity: "I see, in evening air, / How slowly dark comes down on what we do."

Many leading lights of the New Deal period either fell silent in the postwar years or had difficulty carrying on as before. In some cases, politics had a chilling effect; in others, a general demoralization set in, as the mass audience disappeared into the television ether. Marc Blitzstein failed to capitalize on the success of *The Cradle Will Rock*; his first major opera, the torrid Southern tragedy *Regina,* fizzled on Broadway in 1949, and his most-talked-about achievement of the postwar period was his adaptation of *The Threepenny Opera*. He died in 1964 at the hands of three sailors on the isle of Martinique, the victim of a homophobic assault. Roy Harris never duplicated the triumph of his Third Symphony, despite many noble attempts. Virgil Thomson was much in demand, but mainly as a critic; there were few professional stagings of his Gertrude Stein operas, *Four Saints in Three Acts* and *The Mother of Us All,* and the Metropolitan Opera declined to produce his final effort, *Lord Byron*. Paul Bowles essentially stopped writing music and moved to Morocco, where he concentrated his talents on autobiographical fiction. Morton Gould was denied a commission by the Louisville Orchestra, which had a $400,000 grant from the Rockefeller Foundation to subsidize new music, on the grounds that his radio and pops work made him something other than a "serious composer." Samuel Barber subjected himself to debilitating self-criticism, intensified by alcoholism, and, in a Sibelian gesture, tried to destroy the score of his Second Symphony.

Copland provided the perfect epitaph for the era when he said, at the Waldorf-Astoria conference, that an artist who is forced to live in an atmosphere of "suspicion, ill-will and dread" will end up creating nothing.

Stravinsky Defects

Igor Stravinsky, who had long dismissed twelve-tone composition as so much Teutonic obscurantism, watched and brooded as Schoenberg's method spread across Europe and America in the late forties and early fifties. He received multiple reports of the 1945 Paris concerts at which Boulez and company jeered his *Danses concertantes* and *Four Norwegian Moods*, although he did not learn of Boulez's instigating role until many years later. "It seems that once the *violent* has been accepted," he grumbled in a letter, "the *amiable*, in turn, is no longer tolerable." He read with annoyance a Virgil Thomson column in which Webern was hailed as the new god of the young and the *Rite* was relegated to historical status. Meanwhile, the critic-philosopher Pierre Souvtchinsky, who a few years before had helped to write Stravinsky's neoclassical manifesto *Poetics of*

Music, was now denigrating his former idol and acclaiming Boulez as "a Mozart."

Stylistic politics affected the reception of the opera *The Rake's Progress*, on which Stravinsky had been working since 1947, in collaboration with W. H. Auden and Chester Kallman. After the 1951 Venice premiere, critics wrote of the composer's "worn out invention," his "artifice" and "impotence." Many of the younger generation were flatly contemptuous. "What ugliness!" Boulez wrote to Cage.

Commentators have periodically proposed that the Stravinsky of the late forties had run creatively aground, that twelve-tone writing saved him from obsolescence. In fact, between 1945 and 1951, the composer was at the very height of his abilities. The Symphony in Three Movements, picturing a world at war, proved to be his most potent music for orchestra since the *Rite*. *The Rake's Progress*, his first attempt at an evening-length theater work, glowed with a surprising new warmth of feeling. The ballet *Orpheus*, from 1947, maintained the classical equipoise of *Apollo*; the Mass of 1944–48 echoed the grave beauties of the *Symphony of Psalms*; the *Ebony Concerto* of 1945 was Stravinsky's craftiest tribute to jazz. Yet the quality of the music mattered little. What mattered was Stravinsky's perception of the music, and others' perceptions of it, and his perception of their perceptions.

Enter Robert Craft, a brash, young, Juilliard-trained conductor, who became Stravinsky's assistant, adviser, and intellectual guide. Craft began corresponding with Stravinsky in 1947, when he was only twenty-three, and met him the following year; almost immediately, the two men developed a remarkably close, almost father-son-like relationship. Craft facilitated the subsequent transformation of Stravinsky's style, though it would be too much to say, as some have done, that he cajoled the old man into writing twelve-tone music. He had the political advantage of being intimately familiar not only with Stravinsky's works but also with those of Schoenberg and Webern. Indeed, he was one of the very few who were welcome in both camps—*bei* Schoenberg on North Rockingham Avenue and *chez* Stravinsky on North Wetherly Drive.

When Schoenberg died, Stravinsky's attitude toward his old rival changed almost overnight. On July 19, 1951, while dining at Alma Mahler-Werfel's, he was shown Schoenberg's death mask, and according to Craft he was deeply moved. A methodical exploration of the Second

Viennese School began. During a German tour in the fall of 1951, Stravinsky heard tapes of Schoenberg's "Dance Around the Golden Calf," Webern's Variations for Orchestra (which, Craft excitedly noted, he listened to "*three times!*"), and Boulez's *Polyphonie X* (one audition apparently sufficed). The following February, Stravinsky looked on and asked questions as Craft rehearsed Schoenberg's Septet Suite.

One Saturday in early March, Craft joined the Stravinskys for an expedition to a barbecue restaurant in the Mojave Desert, and during the long drive back the old man suddenly broke down, lamenting that he had nothing more to say and that history was passing him by. "For a moment he actually seems ready to weep," Craft confided to his diary. "He is suffering the shock of recognition that Schoenberg's music is richer in substance than his own."

It is unlikely that Stravinsky thought any such thing. But he did know that Schoenberg mattered more at the present historical moment. And so, in this same period, he made his initial ventures into twelve-tone writing, or, more precisely, into composition using extended rows of mostly nonrepeating notes. He had been working on a Cantata based on old English texts, and on February 8, 1952, he started to set to music "To-Morrow Shall Be My Dancing Day," the source of the modern poem "Lord of the Dance." After some days of tinkering, he hit upon an eleven-note series as his main melody. The text reads, in part:

The Jews on me they made great suit,
And with me made great variance;
Because they lov'd darkness rather than light . . .
Before Pilate the Jews me brought,
Where Barabbas had deliverance,
They scourg'd me and set me at nought
Judg'd me to die to lead the dance.

Schoenberg would not have been flattered to know that Stravinsky's adventures in serial writing began with a song about the alleged Christ-killing machinations of the Jews.

In May 1952, Stravinsky returned to Paris for the first time since the war, to attend an elaborate, expensive, and incoherent festival called Masterpieces of the XXth Century. The organizer was Nicolas Nabokov, whom Stravinsky had known since the Diaghilev days. Now occupying the impressive-sounding post of general secretary of the Congress for Cultural Freedom, Nabokov was trying to counter the spread of Communism in Western Europe by producing model festivals of democratic culture.

The programming ranged from tonally oriented works such as Benjamin Britten's *Billy Budd* and Thomson's *Four Saints in Three Acts* to the expressionistic violence of Schoenberg's *Erwartung* and Berg's *Wozzeck* and onward to the futuristic bleeps of musique concrète. Although Nabokov never warmed to atonality and twelve-tone writing—in a 1948 article for the *Partisan Review* he spoke of Schoenberg's method as "a hermetic cult, mechanistic in its technique"—he appreciated its ideological value. "Advanced" styles symbolized the freedom to do what one wanted, which, as Nabokov wrote in an introduction to a special festival issue of the journal *La Revue musicale*, was the dominant theme of the festival—"the liberty to experiment . . . to be esoteric or familiar."

Funding for Masterpieces of the XXth Century was said to have come from the Farfield Foundation, a coalition of arts patrons under the leadership of a yeast-and-gin millionaire named Julius Fleischmann. In fact, Farfield was a front, its financing arranged entirely by the CIA.

Stravinsky had the lead role in Nabokov's jamboree. He conducted his Symphony in C and Symphony in Three Movements while Pierre Monteux led the Boston Symphony in the *Rite of Spring*. All performances took place at the Théâtre des Champs-Élysées. George Balanchine's New York City Ballet also came to town; Balanchine had wanted to stage the *Rite* with designs by Picasso, but Nabokov quashed the plan because "Comrade Picasso" had compromised himself with pro-Communist statements.

The climax of the festivities came with two staged performances of *Oedipus Rex*, but these were marred by yet another scandal. Nabokov had unwisely paired the second *Oedipus* with *Erwartung*, both under the direction of Hans Rosbaud. The Schoenberg came first, and a bevy of young people, presumably of the Boulezian type, applauded it. Then, at intermission, many of them walked out. Jean Cocteau delivered the *Oedipus* narration, and at one point he was interrupted by boos. When Cocteau asked the audience to respect the composer, the boos did not abate, though they were now mixed with bravos. Stravinsky got up from his seat and returned to his hotel. Once more the creator of the *Rite* was being booed on the avenue Montaigne, only now, instead of being too radical, he was considered not radical enough.

Boulez's *Structures 1a* figured in Masterpieces of the XXth Century as a sample of what the younger generation was doing. The composer and his erstwhile teacher Messiaen played it at 5:30 one afternoon, with Stravinsky and Craft in attendance. Boulez's involvement in Nabokov's festival was grudging; he could not have been pleased to be lumped together with the likes of Britten and Thomson. Two years later he would accuse Nabokov of creating a "folklore of mediocrity" and recommend that a future festival celebrate the twentieth-century condom.

Boulez also made his presence felt in the special Masterpieces of the XXth Century issue of *La Revue musicale*, contributing a lengthy essay titled "Eventually . . . ," which laid out the particulars of the total-serialist system. What got everyone's attention was a polemical section toward the beginning of the article, which started off with the ominous line "Why not play the sniper for a few moments?" and ended thus: "What to conclude? The unexpected: we assert for our part that any musician who has not experienced—we do not say understood, but experienced—the necessity of the dodecaphonic language is USELESS." A close reader might have guessed that the sniper's rifle was aimed straight at Stravinsky, who, in his *Poetics of Music*, had written that the artist should concern himself with the "*beautiful*" and the "*useful*."

As if emigrating yet again, Stravinsky set about learning a new language. In a score of *Structures 1a*, he dutifully noted each instance of the twelve-tone series, though he gave up after a couple of pages.

Over the next several years, Stravinsky absorbed Schoenberg's method, but on his own terms. Tone-row melodies appeared in the Septet of 1952–53. Full-blown dodecaphony became operational in the ballet *Agon*, which Stravinsky began in late 1953 and finished in 1957. Finally, by the end of the fifties, he was writing music from which nearly all traces of tonality have disappeared: the oratorio *Threni*, based on the Lamentations of Jeremiah, and the Movements for piano and orchestra. Nicolas Nabokov's well of funds helped to finance these adventures. The scholar Anne Shreffler has assembled evidence suggesting that the five thousand dollars that Stravinsky received for *Threni* came from the coffers of the CIA. The fifteen-thousand-dollar fee for the Movements appears to have been paid by a Swiss industrialist, although Nabokov had a hand in arranging the commission.

Knowing who held the power in the new postwar dispensation, Stravinsky cultivated a friendship with Boulez. The two met in New York in December 1952, at a party at Virgil Thomson's apartment in the Chelsea Hotel. The following year Stravinsky read Boulez's intermittently dismissive essay "Stravinsky Remains . . . ," but was still friendly at later meetings. When Boulez came to Los Angeles in early 1957, Stravinsky arranged for him to stay at the Tropicana Motor Hotel, just down the hill from his house. That summer the seventy-five-year-old composer made the ultimate gesture of respect—or self-abasement—when he walked up the long flight of stairs to Boulez's Paris garret.

Yet as the years went by Stravinsky found it increasingly difficult to ignore Boulez's ill-concealed contempt for everything he had written after *Les Noces*, whether neoclassical or twelve-tone. There were suggestions that Boulez's Domaine Musical series was using the great Stravinsky name mainly for its publicity value. In 1958 Stravinsky came to Paris to conduct *Threni* at the Domaine Musical; after the performance devolved into a near-fiasco, Boulez was blamed for failing to rehearse the ensemble adequately. In 1970, after sundry other ups and downs, Stravinsky finally came to grips with the younger man's "unforgivable condescension," as he or Craft put it in a letter to the *Los Angeles Times*.

If Stravinsky's twelve-tone writing failed to satisfy the implacable Boulez, it did restore the composer's faith in himself. Despite the change of technique, characteristic traits and tics remained. Like Berg before him, Stravinsky manipulated the series in order to generate whatever material, tonal or atonal, he required; and he delighted in the hidden continuities that emerge from repetitions of the twelve-tone row—"like so many changes in a peal of bells," to quote Stephen Walsh. In other words, Stravinsky's old bopping, bouncing patterns keep churning beneath the variegated surface.

The Movements and the Variations draw microscopic worlds from supercompressed material, in the manner of the later Webern. Atonal harmony lends a somber, solemn aura to a final series of religious works—*Threni*, *Canticum sacrum*, *A Sermon, a Narrative, and a Prayer*, *The Flood*, and

Abraham and Isaac—although even here the rows are stacked in favor of consonant chords: triads flicker like shafts of light in a darkened church. And the two late-period masterpieces, *Agon* and *Requiem Canticles*, synthesize all the voices of Stravinsky's long and varied career—the Russian-primitive, the Parisian-neoclassical, the American-modernistic—into works of untrammeled expressive urgency.

Agon came into being at the behest of George Balanchine and Lincoln Kirstein, the choreographer and impresario, respectively, of the New York City Ballet. Balanchine had been living in America since 1933, and, in the course of staging Stravinsky's *Jeu de cartes*, *Danses concertantes*, *Circus Polka*, and *Orpheus*, had formed a close-to-ideal partnership with a composer who had always thrived on cross-disciplinary collaboration. Stravinsky filled Balanchine's time slots down to the second; Balanchine invented moves that were organically related to Stravinsky's gestures, at once athletic and abstract.

The choreographer dreamed of summoning forth the definitive Stravinsky ballet—as Kirstein put it, "a ballet which would seem to be the enormous finale of a ballet to end all the ballets the world has ever seen." It would consist of a "contest" or vigorous interplay among informally dressed dancers on a blank stage. Kirstein had sent along a copy of François de Lauze's seventeenth-century manual *Apologie de la danse*; Stravinsky and Balanchine eventually decided to translate these ancient steps into modern forms, radically reinventing them in the process. Reading the manual, Stravinsky underlined passages that noted how certain dances had originated in pagan festivals, witch ceremonies, and ring dances around a stone representing the devil. In writing *Agon*, he was feeling his way back to energies that had lain dormant since the *Rite*.

This last great Stravinsky ballet, for twelve dancers in twelve sections, mixes sounds and styles from several centuries of musical history as well as from several decades of the composer's career. Regal, neo-Renaissance trumpet fanfares set the piece in motion and return several times as organizing punctuation. Driving *Rite*-like rhythms and creeping chromatic lines give shape to the Double and Triple Pas-de-Quatre. Stately Baroque rhythms decorate the Sarabande, surreal Renaissance twanglings animate the Gailliarde. Twelve-tone writing comes into play in the Coda of the First Pas-de-Trois, joined to scrappy violin solos that recall *Histoire du soldat*. Tensely expressive string lines, vaguely reminiscent of Berg's *Lyric*

Suite, make for a melancholy Pas de Deux. Finally, in the Four Duos and Four Trios, the archaic-modern ritual acquires a jitter of jazz.

All this is highly absorbing in itself, but the music really pulses with life when it is played alongside the Balanchine action that Stravinsky had in mind as he wrote: the streetwise look of the dancers in their rehearsal clothes; the four males standing stone-still at the outset of the piece, their backs turned to the audience; the acting out of the smallest details in the score, not just the rhythms but the placement of chords high or low, the differentiation of timbre, the lengthening or shortening of note values; the way the dancers register beats in every part of their bodies, with twitchings of the shoulder, snaps of the wrist, extensions or lashings of the arm; and the cohesiveness of the entire conception, reconciling brain and body, the cerebral and the sexual.

If *Agon* is a refined reprise of the visceral *Rite*, *Requiem Canticles* is the late-period counterpart of the *Symphony of Psalms*. It grew out of the most momentous experience of Stravinsky's last years—his return, after an absence of five decades, to his Russian homeland, in 1962. Inevitably, Cold War calculations were required to set the trip in motion, with Nabokov playing his usual rainmaker role. One day in 1961 Nabokov told Stravinsky, "Someone has said that you're going to Moscow." Two days later, an inquiry was made by the U.S. State Department. The following month a delegation of Soviet musicians, led by Tikhon Khrennikov, Shostakovich's sometime nemesis, showed up in Los Angeles and invited Stravinsky to Moscow.

Stravinsky, coolest of customers, was thunderstruck by the experience of going to Moscow and revisiting what used to be St. Petersburg. He saw old relatives, passed old haunts, soaked up the adulation of Russian crowds. Long-suppressed traits reappeared in his personality and in his music. *Requiem Canticles*, written in 1965 and 1966, makes systematic use, for the first time in decades, of Rimsky-Korsakov's octatonic scale and other devices that had anchored Stravinsky's youthful works. There are chords like the famous polytonal dissonances in the second section of the *Rite*, only now they move more slowly, as if in mourning. At the end, bell chords ring into the middle distance. In the one Romantic gesture of his career, the composer had written a Requiem for himself. He died in 1971, and was buried in Venice, near the grave of Serge Diaghilev.

Once the avatar of a primitivist-modernist Russia, Stravinsky ended up as the perfect cosmopolitan, everywhere and nowhere at home. "He wanted," Stephen Walsh writes, "to be thought of as a free spirit, a phenomenon without a history." Even as his music grew too recondite for the taste of general audiences, his fame increased to global proportions. The Kennedys invited him to dinner at the White House; Frank Sinatra and Pope John XXIII asked for his autograph. He was the living composer whom everyone professed to know; the premiere of the *Rite* was the measuring stick of artistic daring, inevitably cited in any encomium to a rock 'n' roll act or art film or fashion show that purported to shock the middle classes. But the man was more famous than his music.

Darmstadt

By the time Stravinsky began writing twelve-tone music, most of the younger composers considered the method out of date. Yesterday's revolt was today's status quo: music had entered a state of perpetual revolution.

The principal showplace of the avant-garde was the Darmstadt Summer Courses for New Music—the composers' institute that OMGUS had helped bring into existence in 1946. Nearly as important were two German radio stations, Northwest German Radio in Hamburg and Cologne and Southwest Radio in Baden-Baden, which commissioned, presented, and publicized the leading composers of the day. In 1950, Heinrich Strobel, the music director of Southwest Radio, relaunched the old Donaueschingen Festival, while in 1951 Northwest German Radio began building up an electronic-music studio in Cologne. Conditions were nearly as favorable in Italy, where socialist and Communist politicians generously funded the arts. In 1955, an electronic studio opened in Milan. By the end of the fifties, not only Europeans but also experimentalists from America and composers from Japan and South Korea were sharing in this generous apparatus of support. Boulez was sufficiently pleased with conditions in Germany that in 1959 he moved to Baden-Baden.

The former Fascist nations could thus demonstrate how far they had evolved from the days when Schoenberg's work had been labeled "degenerate music." In a larger sense, composers were creating a kind of esoteric mirror image of the emergent Western European economic and political community. Just as the proud old nation-states gave up certain of their cultural idiosyncrasies in order to assimilate themselves into the European Community, composers abandoned the national-folkish styles they had cultivated in former years in the name of joining a cosmopolitan conversation.

For a time, modern composition had the appearence of another form of high-tech, hush-hush Cold War work. Composers dressed like scientists, wearing thick black glasses and short-sleeve button-down shirts with pens in the pocket. Pierre Schaeffer, inventor of musique concrète, noted proudly that music had become a team effort rather than a labor of solitude, and went so far as to compare French composers to atomic physicists working together in a laboratory.

The advent of a pseudoscientific mentality is evident in the titles of works that were performed at Darmstadt from 1946 on. The first few years saw an abundance of neoclassical lingo—Sonatine, Scherzo, Concertino, and Sinfonietta. Then, after 1949, the archaic titles dropped from sight, replaced by phrases with a cerebral tinge: *Music in Two Dimensions*, *Syntaxis*, *Anepigraphe*. There was a vogue for abstractions in the plural: *Perspectives*, *Structures*, *Quantities*, *Configurations*. Audiences enjoyed *Spectrogram*, *Seismogramme*, *Audiogramme*, and *Sphenogramme*. Emblematic was the career of Hermann Heiss, who, back in the Nazi time, had written a *Fighter Pilot March*. At the first Darmstadt gathering, in 1946, he was represented by a Sonata for Flute and Piano. Ten years later, he showed up with *Expression K*.

The watchword at Darmstadt, as at Nabokov's festivals, was "freedom." After centuries of subservience to the Church, the aristocracy, the bourgeoisie, and the mass public, composers could finally do as they pleased—even embrace styles that took away freedom of choice. Stockhausen, the leader of the young German composers, put it this way: "Schoenberg's great achievement . . . was to claim freedom for composers: freedom *from* the prevailing taste of society and its media; freedom *for* music to evolve without interference. In other words, here was a composer who made it clear to society that he would not allow himself to be kicked about like Mozart who was kicked in the backside by a court official of the Archbishop of Salzburg when he was eight days late returning from a vacation in Vienna."

Yet not everyone felt free. There was the freedom to go forward, but not to go back. The young German composer Hans Werner Henze, who had been attending Darmstadt from the start, became frustrated with its more or less official ban on tonal writing, and, in his memoirs, he wrote in bitterly mocking terms of its faddish tendencies: "Everything had to be stylized and made abstract: music regarded as a glass-bead-game, a fossil of life. Discipline was the order of the day . . . The existing audience of music-lovers, music-consumers, was to be ignored . . . Any encounter with the listeners that was not catastrophic and scandalous would defile the artist, and would mobilize distrust against us . . . As Adorno decreed, the job of a composer was to write music that would repel, shock, and be the vehicle for 'unmitigated cruelty.'"

In 1953, feeling oppressed by the breathless forward march of German music, Henze fled to the island of Ischia, where, under the spell of the Mediterranean sun, he reincorporated tonal material, Stravinskyan neoclassicism, and Romantic textures. His nervously expressive operas caught the ear of the general public, but the new-music community regarded him as an apostate. The conductor Hermann Scherchen dismissed Henze's voluptuously neo-Romantic opera *König Hirsch* by saying, "But, my dear, we don't write arias today." When a smattering of triads in Henze's *Nocturnes and Arias* sullied the hall at Donaueschingen in 1957, Boulez and colleagues walked out, turning their backs in Schoenberg fashion.

By common consent, Stockhausen was the crown prince of the new-music kingdom. No composer was more tireless in inventing or appropriating new ideas, more ambitious in articulating the avant-garde's historical and spiritual mission, more adept at assembling the latest sounds into jaw-dropping spectacles. Stockhausen had the dash of a great colonial adventurer, proceeding through jungles of sound. He described himself as the purveyor variously of "serial music," "point music," "electronic music," "new percussion music," "new piano music," "spatial music," "statistical music," "aleatoric music," "live electronic music," "new syntheses of music and speech," "musical theatre," "ritual music," "scenic music," "group composition," "process composition," "moment composition," "formula composition," "multiformula composition," "universal music," "telemusic," "spiritual music," "intuitive music," "mantric music," and, last but not least, "cosmic music."

Bright, glib, fair-haired, collegial, Stockhausen exuded what would later be called positive energy, although deep-seated authoritarian tendencies made him a sometimes insufferable colleague. In later years he revealed a mystical streak, bordering on the hippie-dippy; it turned out that he had lived many past lives, and that he claimed to be extraterrestrial in origin.

Stockhausen was, in fact, born in a village outside Cologne, in 1928. At the Musikhochschule and the university in that city he received fairly conventional musical training. As the Second World War raged, he began opening his ears to new sounds; like many young Germans, he tuned in to American military broadcasts, and the bopping rhythms of Glenn Miller's band relieved the tedium of wartime discipline. Robin Maconie, Stockhausen's most assiduous chronicler, reports that the young composer took a particular interest in the semi-independent movement of jazz melodies, the way they floated above the beat in changing values.

On arriving in Darmstadt in 1951, Stockhausen heard a tape of Messiaen's *Scale of Durations and Dynamics* and immediately became excited by the idea of a totally organized serialist music. His first mature piece, *Kreuzspiel*, or *Cross Play*, is notable for its quasi-jazzy insouciance and quasi-sensuous appeal, beginning as it does with the sound of conga drums and tom-toms pattering quietly beneath three-note piano chords splayed across various registers. Stockhausen's first set of *Klavierstücke* (*Piano Pieces*), by contrast, exemplifies the reigning aesthetic of pulverization: sounds ricochet from the top to the bottom of the piano, as if the instrument were a pinball machine.

The new art of electronic music riveted Stockhausen from the start. His gurus were Werner Meyer-Eppler, an experimental physicist who specialized in the study of synthetic sound and speech, and the composer-theorist Herbert Eimert, who headed the nascent electronic studio in Cologne. Their vision of the musical future diverged from that of Pierre Schaeffer and Pierre Henry in Paris, and, not surprisingly, a familiar Franco-German cultural split defined the difference between the two electronic schools. Eimert deprecated French musique concrète as parasitical dilettantism, a facile rearrangement of familiar sonic objects. Instead, he said, electronic music must be generated entirely within the studio, thereby attaining a "pure" existence outside the known and the conventional. In 1951 and 1952, Eimert and Robert Beyer together created

Sound in Unlimited Space, which is more or less the first work of synthesized music—a bubbling, moaning landscape of sine tones.

Stockhausen, to his credit, refused to be blinkered by Meyer-Eppler and Eimert's purist ideology. Before establishing himself at the Cologne studio, in 1953, he spent an exploratory year in Paris, attending Messiaen's classes, exchanging ideas with Boulez, and working in Schaeffer's studio. Stockhausen's first electronic pieces, *Konkrete Etude* and *Electronic Studies*, neatly synthesized the Germanic and Gallic approaches to the brand-new medium. On the one hand, the composer made methodical use of serialist processes, arraying gradations of pitch, duration, and dynamics in series. On the other, he relished the exoticism of the medium, enveloping the listener in disordered images and sensations. "This music sounds indescribably pure and beautiful!" Stockhausen wrote excitedly to Karel Goeyvaerts, one of the co-inventors of the total-serialist language. He likened it to "raindrops in the sun."

Gesang der Jünglinge, or *Song of the Youths*, created in 1955–56, is Stockhausen's most original electronic creation and perhaps the most influential electronic piece ever composed. The youths in question are Shadrach, Meshach, and Abednego, from the book of Daniel, whom Nebuchadnezzar throws in the fiery furnace for refusing to worship a golden idol. The music is built up in layers from the recorded voice of a choirboy singing "Praise the Lord!" (from the canticle of praise that is included in Catholic and Orthodox versions of the tale). The boy's song is broken down into phonetic fragments and remixed in the style of musique concrète. All around is a flickering mass of electronic sound, which goes from eruptions of synthesized noise—Stockhausen was particularly proud of what he called "showers of impulses"—to hauntingly voicelike phrases. Boy and machine imitate each other, uniting natural and artificial worlds. Stockhausen heightened the impact of the work by recording it on five channels: at the 1956 Cologne premiere, the audience was placed inside a pentaphonic cauldron.

Two years later Stockhausen unveiled a new marvel, *Gruppen*, in which a 109-piece orchestra is divided into three "groups," each with its own conductor. The orchestration ingeniously duplicates electronic practice: a chord "pans" from one channel to another, instruments trade lines stereophonically, musical lines are "tracked" at independent tempos, one timbre dissolves into the next. Much of the time the work sounds improvised, even though serialist procedures apply. The climax is a wild squall of drumming and a great wall of noise for the three orchestras in tandem—a thirteen-bar freak-out, free jazz or avant-rock before the fact. At the same time, the sheer bombast of the design harks back to the tone painting of Mahler and Strauss and to Wagnerian spectacles such as Hagen's calling of the vassals in *Götterdämmerung*. What separates *Gruppen* from its monumental Romantic predecessors is its relative emotional neutrality; it lacks the grandeur and sorrow that Thomas Mann identified with Wagner. German music was renouncing its "special path," its Faustian urge, and joining the cosmopolitan frenzy of the postwar world.

Behind Darmstadt's hypermodern facade lurked some thoroughly traditional twentieth-century or even nineteenth-century obsessions: the revolutionary impulse, the urge to overthrow the bourgeois order, the age-old longing for sublimity and transcendence. Luigi Nono's defining move was to breach the wall that had been built up between "advanced" modern music and political music. In Weimar Berlin, the twelve-tone Schoenberg and the leftist-populist Weill had stood on opposite ends of the spectrum; in Nono, they were one and the same.

The scion of a notable old Venetian family, Nono dabbled in various media before settling on music at the age of twenty. He was second to none in his worship of the Second Viennese School, and went so far as to marry Schoenberg's daughter, Nuria. But he did not see composition as a withdrawal from the world; instead, he believed that radical sounds could serve as a vehicle for radical politics, awakening listeners' minds and preparing them for concerted action.

Nono's signature piece was the choral work *Il canto sospeso* (1955–56), whose title means "suspended song," and whose texts consists of letters from anti-Fascist resistance fighters who had been condemned to death. As in Stockhausen's *Gesang*, the vocal lines crumble under the pressure of serialist technique. In the ninth song, which sets the texts "I am not afraid of death," "I will be calm and at peace facing the execution squad," and "I go in the belief of a better life for you," words are broken into syllables and scattered through many parts. Stockhausen, when he heard the piece, congratulated Nono for having "composed the text as if to withdraw it from the public eye where it has no place." Nono was irritated by this assumption; by making the words less easily accessible to the casual listener, he intended them to matter more.

Iannis Xenakis was the other unclassifiable radical in the European avant-garde. In 1947 he fled from his native Greece, where the British and the Americans were propping up a right-wing, anti-Communist government, and sought asylum in Paris. There he sat in on Messiaen's classes at the conservatory and worked in Schaeffer's electronic studio. With Messiaen's encouragement, he began thinking about how instrumental sound could be "built" as a structure is built, without breaks or seams in the construction. He pursued a parallel interest in architecture and worked for a number of years as an engineer and later as a designer in the studio of Le Corbusier, specializing in complex architectural models with undulating convex and concave shapes.

Xenakis's masterstroke as a composer was to apply those models to musical space, writing out waveforms on graph paper and then translating them into conventional notation. As the fifties went on, he introduced an even more elaborate method known as "stochastic music," referring to the branch of mathematics that studies the random or irregular activity of particles. In other words, he began looking at the orchestra as a scientist looks at a gas cloud.

Yet Xenakis never quite fit the profile of the laboratory composer. He gave considerable thought to how his music would be perceived by the novice listener and wished to seize the attention with gestures of high impact. "The listener must be gripped," he once said, "and—whether he likes it or not—drawn into the flight path of the sounds, without a special training being necessary. The sensual shock must be just as forceful as when one hears a clap of thunder or looks into a bottomless abyss."

The title of Xenakis's first waveform composition, *Metastaseis* (1953–54), sets forth his intention of overcoming the stasis of total serialism: the Greek word translates as "beyond immobilities." It begins with a stupefying sound: forty-six string instruments playing the note G in unison, then sliding away from it in upward or downward glissandos, each glissando moving at a different rate. By the end of the process, the strings have become a buzzing mass of forty-six separate notes. The string clusters are soon infiltrated by sneering trombone glissandos and other razzing brass sounds. At the height of this meticulously planned bedlam, the listener is incapable of perceiving what any one instrument is doing; only the sum of the actions is apparent. Xenakis likened the effect to the sound of hail drumming on a hard surface or millions of cicadas singing in a field on a summer night.

In a rather more pointed metaphor, Xenakis cited memories of an anti-Nazi demonstration in Athens: a slogan is chanted by a crowd, another slogan comes forward to replace it, "the perfect rhythm of the last slogan breaks up in a huge cluster of chaotic shouts," machine guns are fired, and a "detonating calm, full of despair, dust, and death," settles. But the unison note at the end—one half step higher than at the beginning—suggests that some kind of battle has been won.

The collegiality of Darmstadt broke down as the fifties gave way to the sixties. Nono criticized Stockhausen and Cage for what he considered to be an excess of self-referential, hermetic activity. "Their freedom is spiritual suicide," Nono wrote. Xenakis faulted Stockhausen and Boulez on similar grounds. Boulez, the original agitator of the postwar era, sniped at almost all of his contemporaries for one reason or another.

There was a period when Boulez flirted in his fastidious way with Cagean ideas about "open form"; the score of his Third Piano Sonata (1955–57) gives the performers various options for how to proceed through the notated material. But the bigger story was his return to French roots, especially to the luminous language of Debussy and Ravel. His main work of the fifties was *Le Marteau sans maître*, or *Hammer Without a Master*, a seductive and menacing setting of René Char poems for soprano and ensemble. The voice appears in only four of the nine movements of the cycle; woven all around it is a glistening spiderweb of alto flute, viola, guitar, mallet percussion, bongos, maracas, claves, and other percussion. In the exotic instrumentation there are hints of Balinese, African, and Japanese music, but nothing so vulgar as a melody or a steady beat. This is ultramodern Orientalism that exploits world music at the highest remove and with the utmost refinement. A fabulous bit of instrumental theater enlivens the final pages of the score: as the flute traces deliquescing, faintly desperate-sounding patterns in the upper air, a trio of tam-tams and gong deliver booming tones in a descending pattern. It gives the impression of doors opening to the void—some immaculate Boulezian apocalypse.

Le Marteau remains a total-serialist composition, its title suggestive of a system operating under its own power. Yet Boulez was reclaiming control of his material, what he called "indiscipline—a freedom to choose, to decide, and to reject." Years later, in conversation with Joan Peyser, he casually dismissed his early ventures in total serialism, saying that *Structures 1a* had been not "Total but Totalitarian." He also brushed away the formerly dire necessity of the twelve-note composition. "I've often found the obligation to use all twelve tones to be unbearable," he said in 1999. In the end, the notion of musical progress proved to be contingent and subjective, its definition changing with the seasons. The philosophy of modern music was unmasked as the rhetoric of taste. All the same, Boulez adroitly maintained the illusion of being out in front—the signature of a master politician.

Kennedy's America: Twelve Tones and Show Tunes

President John F. Kennedy, the iconic Cold War leader, took office in January 1961, and from the start he endowed the White House with an unprecedented air of cosmopolitan sophistication. At Eisenhower's inaugural festivities, Copland's *Lincoln Portrait* had been canceled on account of the composer's Communist associations. At Kennedy's inauguration, Leonard Bernstein, even more vocally leftist, was commissioned to write a fanfare for a fund-raising gala. The Kennedys made it their mission to provide leadership in the arts in a way that had not been attempted since the early years of the Roosevelt administration. During the 1960 presidential campaign, Kennedy or a speechwriter took the trouble to write a letter to the magazine *Musical America*, declaring his intention to disclose a "New Frontier for American art" and to show "an openness toward what is new that will banish the suspicion and misgiving that have tarnished our prestige abroad."

In music, as in other cultural fields, Kennedy left the decision making to his wife—"The only music he likes is 'Hail to the Chief,'" Jacqueline Kennedy quipped—and it was she who created the illusion of the White House as a kind of endless Parisian salon. One evening, the great Spanish cellist Pablo Casals came to play, and the First Lady invited more or less the entire pantheon of American composers: Copland, Bernstein, Barber,

Thomson, Piston, Harris, Hanson, Sessions, William Schuman, Henry Cowell, Alan Hovhaness, Elliott Carter, and Gian Carlo Menotti. Another time, she arranged an intimate dinner for Igor and Vera Stravinsky, with Bernstein and Nicolas Nabokov in attendance. Stravinsky drank too much and went home early. "Nice kids," he said on the way out.

Americans were pouring millions of dollars of private and public resources into culture. Kennedy pushed for the creation of a national arts council, which in 1965 became the National Endowment for the Arts, and planned a major new cultural center in Washington, which became, after his assassination, the Kennedy Center. Lincoln Center began operations in 1962, with the opening of Philharmonic Hall, and grew to include the Metropolitan Opera, New York City Opera, Balanchine's New York City Ballet, and the Juilliard School, the final bill coming to $185 million. Across the country, the Ford Foundation was funding performing-arts centers, symphony orchestras, and cultural programs on television.

Anyone nostalgic for the vanished arts programs of the New Deal might have thought that the spirit of "music for all" was reawakening. But politics circumscribed this cultural largesse. Deteriorating relations between the superpowers, from the suppression of the Hungarian Revolution in 1956 to the construction of the Berlin Wall in 1961 and the Cuban missile crisis of 1962, created rivalries on every front; the arms race expanded into a science race and finally into a culture race. Each superpower had its agenda; the Soviets wished to demonstrate that they could tolerate a degree of freedom of expression—hence the publication of Aleksandr Solzhenitsyn's anti-Stalinist novella *One Day in the Life of Ivan Denisovich* in 1962—while America wished to prove that, contrary to Soviet propaganda, capitalism and high culture were not mutually exclusive. This would explain the ticker-tape parade that greeted the Texan pianist Van Cliburn when he returned home after winning the Tchaikovsky Competition in Moscow in 1958. This would also explain why President Kennedy would consent to spend an evening with twelve-tone composers when the Rat Pack was more his style.

New music played a very limited role in the Cold War arts bonanza. All the same, many American composers found themselves in a relatively happy situation. Money was plentiful, whether in the form of grants, prizes, commissions, or faculty salaries. American universities were growing at a rapid rate, their endowments fleshed out by wealthy contributors who feared that American education was falling behind the Russian. Colleges that once had only one or two composers on their faculty now had four or five. Dedicated ensembles such as Columbia University's Group for Contemporary Music were created to play their works and those of accredited predecessors. The institution of tenure gave the American composer unaccustomed feelings of financial and psychological security.

Of the multifarious strands of American music, one in particular began to prosper in the university environment: composition informed by twelve-tone technique. "Everyone started writing fat, Teutonic music again," Ned Rorem scornfully observed. "It was as though our country, while smug in its sense of military superiority, was still too green to imagine itself as culturally autonomous."

The conviction that political virtue resided in atonal and twelve-tone composition spread more slowly in America than in Europe, but it made headway all the same. In 1948 the anti-Communist journal *Partisan Review* invited René Leibowitz to air his views on the moral corruption of tonality and the righteousness of the twelve-tone method. In the same periodical, and in the same year, the critic Kurt List praised the dissonances of Charles Ives and Roger Sessions, saying, "This is the best that American music has to offer. The composer will finally have to shoulder the burden of the less popular, aesthetically more honest, style of atonal polyphony. He may, or may not, arrive at a solution. But if music is to exist as an artistic expression of modern America, atonal polyphony is really the only valid guide." Such rhetoric duplicated that of Adorno's *Philosophy of New Music*, not to mention Clement Greenberg's essay "Avant-Garde and Kitsch." Some years later Adorno would write, "No art at all is better than socialist realism." Or, as cold warriors liked to say, "Better dead than red."

Milton Babbitt, the emblematic Cold War composer, produced music so byzantine in construction that one practically needed a security clearance to understand it. Like Boulez and Xenakis, Babbitt was trained in mathematics as well as music, and during the war he performed secret intelligence work, the nature of which he demurely refused to disclose. He also taught math to operators of new radar and sonar technologies. Early on he was associated with Dwight Macdonald's magazine *politics*, another journal with an anti-Communist slant, although more radical and anarchist in orientation than the *Partisan Review*. In November 1945 *politics* published a defiant little poem by Babbitt that sounded like a rallying cry for the propaganda war:

A lie for a lie,
Untruth for untruth:
this can be read
in the book of the dead;
make it your maxim
and load it with lead.

Macdonald, in the following years, would inveigh repeatedly against middlebrow populism, or "Midcult," as he called it.

Babbitt first encountered Schoenberg's music in 1926, when a teacher showed him the Three Piano Pieces, Opus 11. He was only ten, but immediately fell in love with this "absolutely different world." Around the same time, he became bewitched by jazz and, as a high schooler, played in bands around Mississippi. His knowledge of early-twentieth-century American popular music was as encyclopedic as his knowledge of everything else, and at one point he tried his hand at writing a Broadway musical, called *Fabulous Voyage*. Had it reached the stage and found an audience, Babbitt's career might have taken a quite different course.

Instead, Babbitt committed himself single-mindedly to the Schoenberg legacy. In the late thirties, he studied composition at Princeton with Sessions, who by this time had turned against Copland-style populism. Babbitt inherited Sessions's belief that American composers had to "abandon resolutely chimerical hopes of success in a world dominated overwhelmingly by 'stars,' by mechanized popular music, and by the box-office standard, and set themselves to discovering what they truly have to say, and to saying it in the manner of the adult artist delivering his message to those who have ears to hear it. All else is childishness and futility."

Sessions was not at that time a twelve-tone composer, so Babbitt studied the method on his own. Independent of Boulez and Stockhausen, he came up with his own version of the total-serialist method. In 1948, a year before Messiaen's *Scale of Durations and Dynamics*, he created ordered sets of durations, applying them in *Composition for Four Instruments* and *Composition for Twelve Instruments*. Subsequently, he serialized all the parameters: pitch, dynamic level, register, duration, and timbre.

In the fifties, Babbitt laid claim to the electronic studio and early-model supercomputers, seizing the opportunity to engage in "complex, advanced, and 'problematical' activities," in his own words, without resorting to the "inapposite milieu of the public concert hall." The first American electronic pieces were made by Vladimir Ussachevsky and Otto Luening, two composers based at Columbia University; they used a magnetic-tape recorder to create dreamlike echo-chamber effects around voices and instruments. These efforts were primitive compared with what Stockhausen and company were accomplishing overseas, but leaps in Cold War technology soon allowed the Americans to catch up. In 1955, David Sarnoff, the chairman of NBC and RCA, unveiled the Electronic Music Synthesizer, which was intended to mimic the sounds of all extant musical instruments. Two years later, RCA's Mark II synthesizer was installed at Columbia, now equipped with a binary sequencer to program the sounds. The Columbia-Princeton Electronic Music Center grew around the Mark II apparatus, with Babbitt taking a leadership role.

Babbitt was not quite as difficult as he seemed. He may have been dealing in abstruse relationships among myriad elements, but his listeners didn't have to digest too many at once. From Webern, Babbitt learned the art of deriving a set from successive transformations of a group of just three notes ("trichord"), which becomes a microcosm of the series. With these tiny motives in play, the texture tends to be *less* complicated than in the average post-Schoenbergian work. *Composition for Four Instruments* gives the impression of economy, delicacy, and extreme clarity; flute, clarinet, violin, and cello play solos, duets, and trios, coming together as a quartet only in the final section, and even there the ensemble dissolves into softly questing solo voices at the end. Thick dissonances are rare; like Japanese drawings, Babbitt's scores are full of empty space. What's more, the harmonies are in many places surprisingly simple and sweet. Six bars into the second of the *Three Compositions for Piano* there is, out of nowhere, a loud B-flat-major triad. Before you can come to terms with the psychological effects of such "tonal puns," they disappear, like half-familiar faces in a crowd. This rigorously organized music ends up feeling mysteriously prankish, antic, loosey-goosey; it shuffles and shimmies like jazz from another planet.

The other giant of American modernism in the fifties and sixties was Elliott Carter, who made his name before the war as an expert if not exceptional practitioner of neoclassical styles. In the late forties, at around the same time that Babbitt was theorizing his version of total serialism, Carter renounced Copland-style populism and embraced the aesthetic of density and difficulty. At the beginning of the fifties, in a symbolic act of self-isolation, he spent a year in the lower Sonoran Desert in Arizona, writing a fully atonal First String Quartet that sounded something like Ives's Second Quartet with its hymns and popular melodies excised. "I decided for once to write a work very interesting to myself," Carter said, "and so say to hell with the public and with the performers too."

Carter's favorite strategy was to juxtapose independent streams of activity in overlapping, intersecting layers, each going at its own rate, each accelerating or decelerating like multiple lanes of traffic. Such effects were commonplace in jazz—the author Michael Hall compares Carter's rhythmic layering to the disjuncture between Art Tatum's left and right hands—and also in the most complex works of Ives. As it happens, Carter got to know Ives in his teens, and received from him a letter of recommendation to Harvard.

Carter worked slowly and meticulously, producing only seven major works between 1950 and 1970, his anticommercial, "uncompromising" stance made easier by the fact that he was independently wealthy. A lifelong New Yorker, he paid conscious homage to the disorganized intensities of urban life, and at times made oblique reference to the tensions of the Cold War era. The climax of his Double Concerto (1961)—a mad, jazzy piano cadenza, spastic harpsichord, shrill brass, and furious drums—gives way to a disintegrating fade-out; according to the composer's later commentary, the passage was inspired by the final lines of Alexander Pope's *Dunciad*: "Thy hand, great Anarch! lets the curtain fall; / And Universal Darkness buries All."

On one page of Carter's Piano Concerto (1964–65), the strings split Xenakis-style into fifty parts, none the same as any other, while the winds and brass go every which way above. Shostakovich had written music like this in the first section of his Second Symphony, but here no redemptive revolutionary anthems save the day. The piano drives a wedge into the molten mass, representing, the composer later said, the individual's struggle against the collective. Carter began writing the Piano Concerto in West Berlin, and the desperate vitality of that walled-in fragment of a city left audible traces on the music: rat-a-tat rhythms in the second movement echo the sound of machine guns at a U.S. Army target range.

The tireless mechanism of Cold War cultural politics gave Carter's international career an early boost. Although the First Quartet had little hope of charming American audiences of the period, it went over well in the new-music centers of postwar Europe. In 1954 the piece appeared on the program of a Congress for Cultural Freedom festival in Rome, Nicolas Nabokov having pulled the strings; as it happens, Nabokov and Carter had taught together at St. John's College during the war. The following year Carter's Cello Sonata was the only American work featured at the International Society for Contemporary Music festival in Baden-Baden, where Boulez's *Marteau* had its premiere. After breaking with Cage, Boulez came to consider Carter the only American composer consistently worthy of his attention.

Carter and Babbitt set the pace for a small army of American atonal and twelve-tone composers: Ralph Shapey, Charles Wuorinen, George Perle, Arthur Berger, Harvey Sollberger, Andrew Imbrie, Leon Kirchner, and Donald Martino, among others. Their ranks were augmented by émigré followers of Schoenberg, notably Stefan Wolpe, transplanted from Berlin to New York, and Ernst Krenek, transplanted from Vienna to Los Angeles. At one time or another the above-named taught at such leading universities as Harvard, Yale, Princeton, Columbia, the University of Chicago, and the University of California, Berkeley.

These composers thrived on campus because of the undeniable intellectual solidity of their project: behind the modernity of the language was a traditional emphasis on the arts of variation and counterpoint. Commentators tended to lump them into the uninviting category "academic atonal" or "academic twelve-tone," although each had a strong personality: Shapey, with his way of arranging jagged sonorities in a ritualistic procession; Wuorinen, with his flair for instrumental drama and his tonal surprises; Berger and Perle, with their love of clean melodic lines and euphonious chords. The average listener could, however, be pardoned for confusing them. Eschewing the audience-friendly gestures of the Copland era, they seemed concerned above all with self-preservation, with building a safe nest in a hostile world. Their theoretical essays could be interpreted as so much barbed wire to keep untrustworthy strangers at bay.

In 1958, Babbitt enlivened the pages of *High Fidelity* magazine with an essay notoriously headlined "Who Cares If You Listen?"—the original title was "The Composer as Specialist"—that sounded the signal for strategic withdrawal:

> I dare suggest that the composer would do himself and his music an immediate and eventual service by total, resolute and voluntary withdrawal from this public world to one of private performance and electronic media, with its very real possibility of complete elimination of the public and social aspects of musical composition. By so doing, the separation between the domains would be defined beyond any possibility of confusion of categories, and the composer would be free to pursue a private life of professional achievement, as opposed to a public life of unprofessional compromise and exhibitionism.

Schoenberg had stated back in the twenties that colleagues such as Hindemith and Weill would end up writing their "music for use" only for each other. Babbitt was saying the same thing to the leftover neoclassicists and populists of the fifties. But he got a little carried away. Even as the combative composer published his article, Broadway audiences were flocking to *West Side Story*, with music by Leonard Bernstein and lyrics by Stephen Sondheim, one of Babbitt's own students.

Bernstein was nearly John F. Kennedy's mirror image. Both men were Harvard graduates (Bernstein class of 1939, Kennedy class of 1940). Both overcame historically marginal ethnic backgrounds (Russian-Jewish and Irish) to reach the highest plateaus of American life. Both made for good TV (Bernstein delivered music-appreciation lectures on the Ford Foundation's *Omnibus* program starting in 1954). Both harbored sexual secrets (whether gay or straight). And the skeptics duly wondered whether the charisma was only skin-deep. Kennedy fell victim to an assassin's bullet before his promise could be measured against reality. Bernstein lived to a relatively grand old age, an aura of disappointment settling around him. Experts agreed that he had frittered away his gift amid glitzy conducting dates, media appearances, and "radical chic" parties at his apartment in Manhattan.

Yet Bernstein's failures outweighed many others' successes. For a brief, shining moment—to quote from Kennedy's favorite musical, *Camelot*—he took back the cultural middle ground that Gershwin had colonized in the twenties and thirties. Bernstein announced his grand project under the media glare of *Omnibus* in 1956. "We are in a historical position now similar to that of the popular musical theater in Germany just before Mozart came along," he said. "What we'll get will be a new form, and perhaps 'opera' will be the wrong word for it. There must be a more exciting word for such an exciting event. And this event can happen any second. It's almost as though it is our moment in history, as if there is a historical necessity that gives us such a wealth of creative talent at this precise time." The use of the phrase "historical necessity" was pointed; Bernstein was appropriating the jargon of new-music theorists such as Adorno and Leibowitz and deploying it to contrary ends.

A rising young American composer of the mid–twentieth century was expected to make his mark with a symphony. Bernstein made a formidable contribution to the genre with his *Jeremiah* of 1942, whose setting of the Lamentations of Jeremiah commemorated the suffering of the European Jews. But theater was his first and strongest love. In his undergraduate thesis at Harvard he envisaged an amalgam of all musical traditions—European and American, classical and popular, white and black. On moving to New York in 1942, he set about making that vision a reality. First in the Jerome Robbins ballet *Fancy Free*, then in the Betty Comden and Adolph Green musical *On the Town*, he applied his high-class training to the seemingly lowly subject matter of three sailors on leave in the city. "New York, New York," the signature number of *On the Town*, begins with a four-note rising figure that might have been lifted from the opening bars of Sibelius's Fifth Symphony. The same motif appears in the 1952 opera *Trouble in Tahiti*, where a jazzy, finger-snapping idiom conveys a savage satire of middle-class neurosis. The four notes now spell out the word "suburbia," puncturing the facade of America's postwar prosperity.

Bernstein's most dazzling transmutation of tradition took place in

"Somewhere," from *West Side Story*, where the main theme of the slow movement of Beethoven's *Emperor* Concerto becomes the love song of a white boy in love with a Puerto Rican girl in the gang-ridden neighborhoods of Manhattan's West Side. It was a theft with a political slant: Beethoven Americanized and miscegenated.

West Side Story is a beautifully engineered piece of pop theater, fueled by bebop melody, Latin rhythm, and old-school Tin Pan Alley lyric craft. It is also a sophisticated essay in twentieth-century style. The first bars of the prologue put forward a familiar complex of intervals: a fifth plus a tritone. This combination appears everywhere in the music of Schoenberg and his pupils, emblematic of eternal striving and conflict. Similarly charged, the two intervals form the kernel of Bernstein's score, and they are planted in its most famous melodies. Sometimes they express late-late-Romantic yearning: in Tony's love song "Maria," the first two notes spell out the tritone while the third goes one half step higher to reach the perfect fifth. But when this group of notes is arranged as a rising fourth plus a rising tritone it becomes a motif of "hate," of the endless gang conflict of the Sharks and the Jets. Later, in "Cool," something like a twelve-note series is used to propel a bebop fugue. All told, *West Side Story* has every right to be considered an uncompromisingly modern work: it is bold in language, unpredictable in its stylistic turns, politically engaged, steeped in contemporary American life.

Bernstein now made a fateful decision. Just as the musical had its out-of-town opening, in Washington, D.C., he accepted an offer to become music director of the New York Philharmonic, where an old friend—Carlos Moseley, ex–music officer of Bavaria—was rising to the top of the administrative hierarchy. Perhaps Bernstein thought that he could manage like his idol Mahler, conducting during the season and composing in the summer. But Mahler didn't do lectures, talk shows, quiz shows, parties, and political speeches. Bernstein certainly accomplished great things at the Philharmonic—his masterly Young People's Concerts, his promotion of fellow American composers, his rediscovery of Charles Ives—but in eleven years he produced only two major works, the immaculately crafted *Chichester Psalms* and the queasily preachy Third Symphony, *Kaddish*. Meanwhile, the tenement neighborhoods of *West Side Story* had been razed to make room for the high-culture colossus of Lincoln Center, the orchestra's new home. If Bernstein resigned himself to living out his days as an interpreter of other people's music, none other than Copland may have been responsible for implanting that idea in him. Back in 1943 Copland had written a letter saying, "Don't forget *our* party line—you're heading for conducting in a big way—and everybody and everything that doesn't lead there is an excrescence on the body politic."

Upon leaving the Philharmonic in 1969, Bernstein struggled to recommence his interrupted compositional career. For the opening of the Kennedy Center in 1971, Jackie Kennedy, now Mrs. Aristotle Onassis, commissioned from him the theater piece *Mass*, a kaleidoscopic blend of sacred settings, show tunes, and Beatles-era pop. As often in Bernstein's later music, cringe-inducing moments coincide with heart-filling ones: the crystalline setting of the words "I will sing the Lord a new song" would suffice to ensure the composer's immortality.

Mocked by critics for his presumption, Bernstein threw himself back into conducting. A promised opera on the Holocaust never surfaced. Ironically, Bernstein's successor at the Philharmonic was Pierre Boulez, who also had trouble maintaining his creative momentum amid a flurry of conducting dates. That Bernstein and Boulez should have ended up with the same job description—celebrity maestro with a major-label contract—neatly confirms Charles Péguy's dictum about everything ending in politics, or, as the case may be, economics.

Bernstein poured his unfulfilled ambition into stupefying powerful performances of the Mahler symphonies, freighting them with the themes that he should or would have addressed in his own music if only he had the time or the energy or whatever it was that he ultimately lacked:

> It is only after fifty, sixty, seventy years of world holocausts, of the simultaneous advance of democracy with our increasing inability to stop making war, of the simultaneous magnification of national pieties with the intensification of our active resistance to social equality—only after we have experienced all this through the smoking ovens of Auschwitz, the frantically bombed jungles of Vietnam, through Hungary, Suez, the Bay of Pigs, the farce-trial of Sinyavsky and Daniel, the refueling of the Nazi machine, the murder in Dallas, the arrogance of South Africa, the Hiss-Chambers travesty, the Trotskyite purges, Black Power, Red Guards, the Arab encirclement of Israel, the plague of McCarthyism, the Tweedle-

> dum armaments race—only after all this can we finally listen to Mahler's music and understand that it foretold all. And that in the foretelling it showered a rain of beauty on this world that has not been equaled since.

Bernstein's enthusiasm for Mahler was infectious, but his claims were exaggerated. In twentieth-century music, through all the darkness, guilt, misery, and oblivion, the rain of beauty never ended.

12

"GRIMES! GRIMES!"

The Passion of Benjamin Britten

Aldeburgh is a windswept fishing town on the east coast of the British Isles. "A bleak little place; not beautiful," the novelist E. M. Forster called it. He went on: "It huddles around a flint-towered church and sprawls down to the North Sea—and what a wallop the sea makes as it pounds at the shingle! Near by is a quay, at the side of an estuary, and here the scenery becomes melancholy and flat; expanses of mud, saltish commons, the marsh-birds crying."

Some decades later, the great German writer W. G. Sebald fell even more deeply in love with the oblique charms of Aldeburgh and neighboring villages, and devoted his book *The Rings of Saturn* to the geography and history of the region. "I had not a single thought in my head," Sebald wrote, describing one of his walks across the flats. "With each step that I took, the emptiness within and the emptiness without grew ever greater and the silence more profound . . . I imagined myself amidst the remains of our own civilization after its extinction in some future catastrophe."

There are ruins all around Aldeburgh. At Dunwich, a few miles up the coast from Aldeburgh, an entire medieval town has slid into the sea. Around Orford, to the south, the landscape is dotted with relics of two world wars and the Cold War that followed—gun emplacements, designed to impede a Nazi invasion that never came; radar masts, employing the technology invented by researchers in nearby Bawdsey Manor; Atomic Weapons Establishment facilities, looking like skeletons of palaces. When the weather changes, these wide-open vistas of sea and sky, with their stone and metal memories of the past, can have a somewhat terrifying effect. A mass of black cloud rears up behind a sunlit scene; the sea turns a dull, menacing green; an abandoned house groans in the wind. Then, in the next second, the light changes. The water assumes an iridescent color, as if lit from within. Anonymous jewels sparkle in the beach. The sun appears under the ceiling of cloud and floods the world.

In the Aldeburgh churchyard lies Benjamin Britten. He was born thirty miles up the coast, in Lowestoft, in 1913. His childhood home looked over the beach to the North Sea, or the German Ocean, as it was called before the First World War.

Britten lived for most of his life in the Aldeburgh area, and he once stated that all his music came from there. "I believe in roots, in associations, in backgrounds, in personal relationships," he said in a speech in Aspen, Colorado, in 1964. "I want my music to be of use to people, to please them . . . I do not write for posterity." Britten designed many of his pieces for performance in Aldeburgh's Jubilee Hall and in churches around the area. In 1948, with his companion, the tenor Peter Pears, and the writer-director Eric Crozier, he founded the Aldeburgh Festival, which featured his own music, contemporary works from Europe and America, and favorite repertory of the past; it was a kind of anti-Bayreuth, as intimate as Wagner's festival was grandiose.

Above all, Britten wrote *Peter Grimes*, an opera of staggering dramatic force that is soaked in Aldeburgh to its bones. First heard in June 1945, one month after the end of the European war, it tells of a fisherman who causes the death of his apprentices and loses his mind from guilt. The story comes from the poet George Crabbe, who grew up in Aldeburgh in the later eighteenth century, and apparently based the character of Grimes on a real-life case. Crabbe described the estuaries thus:

The dark warm flood ran silently and slow;
There anchoring, Peter chose from man to hide,
There hang his head, and view the lazy tide
In its hot slimy channel slowly glide . . .
Here dull and hopeless he'd lie down and trace

How sidelong crabs had scrawl'd their crooked race;
Or sadly listen to the tuneless cry
Of fishing gull or clanging golden-eye . . .

The first orchestral interlude in Britten's opera brings the coast to life. High grace notes mimic the cries of birds; rainbowlike arpeggios imitate the play of light on the water; booming brass chords approximate the thudding of the waves. It is rich, expansive music, recalling Debussy's *La Mer* and Mahler's more pantheistic moods. Yet it hardly ravishes the senses: the orchestration is spare, the melodic figures are sharply turned, the plain harmonies flecked with dissonance. The music is poised perfectly between the familiar and the strange, the pictorial and the psychological. Like the tone poems of Sibelius, it gives shape to what a wanderer feels as he walks alone.

In his Aspen speech Britten provocatively compared the regimentation of culture in totalitarian states to the self-imposed regimentation of the avant-garde in democratic countries. Any ideological organization of music, he said, distorts a composer's natural voice, his "gift and personality." Everything about Britten's style—his deliberate parochialism, his tonal orientation, his preference for classical forms—went against the grain of the postwar era. Luminaries of the avant-garde made a point of snubbing him; at the Dartington Summer School in 1959, Luigi Nono refused to shake his hand. Much else about Britten was at odds with Cold War social norms: his pacifism, his leftism, and especially his homosexuality.

Nonetheless, Britten succeeded in becoming a respected national figure, a focus of British pride. He was a little like Sibelius, a lonely, troubled man who became a patriotic icon. Even closer in temperament was Dmitri Shostakovich, whom Britten got to know in the 1960s. Despite the language barrier, the two composers formed a lasting bond. What they had in common was the ability to write elusive emotions across the surface of their music. Britten made his inner landscape as vivid as the rumble of the sea, the cries of the gulls, and the scuttling of the crabs.

Young Britten

Homosexual men, who make up approximately 3 to 5 percent of the general population, have played a disproportionately large role in composition of the last hundred years. Somewhere around half of the major American composers of the twentieth century seem to have been homosexual or bisexual: Copland, Bernstein, Barber, Blitzstein, Cage, Harry Partch, Henry Cowell, Lou Harrison, Gian Carlo Menotti, David Diamond, and Ned Rorem, among many others. In Britain, too, the art of composition skewed gay. The two young composers who seized the spotlight in the early postwar era were Britten and Michael Tippett, neither of whom made an effort to hide his homosexuality.

The nexus of classical music and gay culture goes back at least to the final years of the nineteenth century, when aesthetes of the Oscar Wilde type gathered at Wagner nights in London and wore green carnations in their lapels. "Is he musical?" gay men would ask of an unfamiliar newcomer. As the century went on, conservatories and concert halls filled up with introverted boys who had trouble fitting in with their fellows. Classical music appealed to some gay youngsters because of the free-floating power of its emotions: while most pop songs explicitly address love and/or sex between modern boys and girls, opera renders romance in an archaic, stylized way, and instrumental works give voice to unspoken passions. Already in the first years of the century, this music had the reputation of being a "sissy" culture—the association troubled Charles Ives, for one—and its cultural decline in the postwar era may have had something to do with the discomfort that the homosexual ambience caused in the general population.

Gay composers of the early twentieth century seldom hinted at their sexuality in their work, although Francis Poulenc, Henri Sauguet, and other composers associated with the Ballets Russes inhabited a recognizably gay subculture. One who trembled at the edge of disclosure was the Polish composer Karol Szymanowski, whose output included an unpublished, now mostly lost novel of pornographic tendencies, titled *Ephebos*. In the wake of sexually liberating travels to the south of Italy and North Africa between 1908 and 1914, Szymanowski fashioned a fiercely sensuous style that recalled Debussy at his most turbulent and Scriabin in his high mystic phase. His 1914 song cycle *The Love Songs of Hafiz* dives into the heady world of the fourteenth-century Persian poet Hafiz, who used the allure of young men's bodies as a metaphor for religious ecstasy, or perhaps the other way around. Szymanowski's Third Symphony (1914–16), based on a similarly charged text by Rumi ("Oh, do not sleep, friend, through this night . . ."), culminates in an orgasmic whole-tone chord for voices, orchestra, and organ. And in the daring and strange opera *King Roger* (1918–24), the royal hero struggles to resist the Dionysian magnetism of a young shepherd who proclaims, "My God is as beautiful as I am." The ending is ambiguous: the audience is unsure whether Roger has succumbed to the shepherd or overcome him. In the wake of the shepherd's final orgiastic ritual, Roger is left alone, holding his arms to the sun of Apollo, C-major harmony blazing around him.

The conflict between Dionysus and Apollo is a well-worn metaphor. Stravinsky often mused upon the divide; in the *Rite* he sided with the Dionysian, in *Apollon musagète* with the call to order. Britten understood the polarity much as Szymanowski did, not as an intellectual problem but as an acute personal dilemma, a choice between sexual exposure and sexual restraint. He ended his operatic career by setting to music Thomas Mann's novella *Death in Venice*, in which Dionysus and Apollo battle for the soul of a middle-aged man looking at a boy on a beach. What perplexed Britten was not his sexuality per se—he never concealed himself in a sham marriage, and sustained a loving relationship with Pears for more than half his life—but his longing for the company of underage males. Although that predicament places him outside most people's experience, the disordering power of desire is a universal theme, and Britten's music is a searing diary of its repercussions.

Britten grew up in an ordinary middle-class home. His father made a good living as a dentist, although he worried about money and took refuge in a late-morning glass of whiskey. Mrs. Britten, a gifted singer and a host of musical soirees, nurtured her son to excess, predicting that he would become "the fourth B," after Bach, Beethoven, and Brahms. Benjamin needed little prompting in the direction of the Bs; music was his native tongue, and he could harmonize before he could spell.

At the age of fourteen Britten began studying with Frank Bridge, an imaginative composer of Debussyish tendencies who quickly perceived the boy's potential. The first year of Britten's studies yielded, among other things, the orchestral song cycle *Quatre Chansons françaises*, which was not only amazingly accomplished in technical terms but disconcertingly mature in theme. One setting is of a Victor Hugo poem that depicts a five-year-old who plays outside a window behind which his mother lies dying; the juxtaposition of a childlike melody with shadowy harmonies prefigures many Britten works to come.

By the age of sixteen he was writing thorny, quasi-atonal pieces. The turn toward Viennese expressionism may have had something to do with the alienation he felt while at boarding school, where, according to ageless routine, older boys bullied younger ones. Britten marked his departure from Gresham's School with an Elegy for Viola that traces anguished nontonal circles around a tonal center of C.

Intellectual precocity often goes hand in hand with emotional immaturity. Into his twenties and beyond, Britten held on to an exaggerated boyishness, indulging in games, pranks, schoolboy slang, and baby talk. At age forty he was still writing in a School Boy's Diary. Adult realities scared him, most of all sex. As John Bridcut observes, in a book about Britten's relationships with children, the composer was in some ways emotionally frozen at the age of thirteen.

In 1930 Britten received a scholarship to study at the Royal College of Music in London. He also gained an informal education courtesy of the British Broadcasting Corporation, which, then as now, offered the finest classical radio programming in the world. At a time when David Sarnoff's NBC was playing Beethoven and little else, the BBC gave generous attention to living composers. Taking a dislike to Elgar and other mainstays of English music, Britten preferred the sharp new sounds coming out of Paris, Vienna, and Berlin, all of which could be sampled on the BBC's far-ranging programs. A radio broadcast in April 1930 prompted an interest in Schoenberg; he proceeded to program Schoenberg's Six Little Pieces at a musical soiree at his parents' home. A broadcast of Berg's *Wozzeck* in 1934 had him glued to his set, despite bursts of static. (He hoped to study with Berg in Vienna, but the idea was quashed on the grounds that Berg was "immoral" and "not a good influence.") That same year the BBC gave Britten his first national exposure by broadcasting his choral piece *A Boy Was Born.*

In the semi-socialistic spirit of the time, various divisions of the British government had their art and propaganda units, giving employment to artists who had lost work in the wake of the collapse of the consumerist twenties economy. The General Post Office had a film unit that was responsible for telling the public about the many uses of mail. In

1935 Britten went to work for the G.P.O. Film Unit as the house composer; his first assignment was to write music for a film about King George V's Jubilee stamp. Later projects included *Coal Face, Telegrams, Gas Abstract, Men Behind the Meters, How the Dial Works, Negroes,* and *Night Mail.*

Such English-style exercises in "music for use" sharpened Britten's ability to write on any subject and for any occasion, and they also brought him together with the young poet W. H. Auden, who was contributing witty texts to Post Office films. The two men went on to collaborate on a BBC feature, *Hadrian's Wall*; two song cycles, *On This Island* and *Our Hunting Fathers*; and the experimental operetta *Paul Bunyan*. Auden made it his mission to bring Britten out of his shell, socially, sexually, and intellectually. "Stand up and fold / Your map of desolation," he instructed, in a poem dedicated to the composer in 1936. "Strike and you shall conquer." Britten's literary taste moved into the twentieth century, and his political views veered toward socialism and pacifism (Bridge having already nudged him toward the latter). There was an obvious Popular Front flavor to such projects as the 1939 cantata *Ballad of Heroes*, dedicated to fallen British fighters in the Spanish Civil War; the texts were by Auden and by Randall Swingler, literary editor of the British *Daily Worker*. Auden had no stomach for agitprop, though, and his slogans fell short of Hanns Eisler's standards for proletarian song: "I must take charge of the liquid fire, / And storm the cities of human desire."

Young Britten assembled a personal language out of whatever pleased his uncommonly sharp ear. His harmonic vocabulary stemmed both from continental models such as Berg and Stravinsky and from the more adventurous British composers of the time, particularly Holst, composer of *The Planets*. From Holst, Britten seems to have picked up the device of the enharmonic change, in which one note holds steady while the harmony pivots to a distant chord—a trick much used by twentieth-century tonal composers, notably Shostakovich. Britten also developed the habit of wavering bluesily between major and minor modes by modifying the third degree of the scale. Greatly impressed by a 1936 London production of *Lady Macbeth of the Mtsensk District*, he mastered the Shostakovichian arts of parody and grotesquerie, and also took inspiration from operetta, vaudeville, and popular song.

Mrs. Britten died in 1937, and her will allowed Benjamin to purchase the Old Mill, in the tiny village of Snape, outside Aldeburgh—an eighteenth-century roundhouse with a view of the river and marshes and the sea beyond.

Britten was distraught by his mother's death, but he also felt liberated from the role of darling boy. For the first time he began seriously to explore his sexuality, and immediately felt torn between relationships with gay men his own age—in 1937 he got to know Peter Pears, the future love of his life—and romantically tinged attachments to teenagers. A friendship with the eighteen-year-old Wulff Scherchen, son of the conductor Hermann Scherchen, teetered on the edge of sexual contact. Eventually, Auden would confront Britten with his enthrallment to "thin-as-a-board juveniles, i.e. to the sexless and innocent." It was a way of evading the disorder of adulthood, Auden said, a false flight into memories of boyhood. Auden further criticized his friend's tendency to surround himself with a cocoon of caretakers and admirers—"to build yourself a warm nest of love . . . by playing the lovable talented little boy." Auden concluded: "If you are really to develop to your full stature, you will have, I think, to suffer, and make others suffer."

Britten ignored the advice. The sexless and the innocent attracted him to the end. He kept trying to build his warm nest of love, although some musicians and administrators who worked with him at the Aldeburgh Festival in later years found the love in short supply; the tenor Robert Tear recalled "an atmosphere laden with waspishness, bitterness, cold, hard eyes, with cabalistic meetings." Britten developed the unattractive habit of cutting off contact with devoted associates who disappointed him or outlived their usefulness. Ironically, Auden himself was among the first who suffered. That perceptive but intrusive letter he sent to Britten in 1942 derailed their friendship.

Over the years, the list of ex-friends grew long enough that Britten reportedly called them his "corpses." Yet he never ceased to think of himself as a vulnerable child: he acted not out of malice but out of a need to preserve the illusion of a boyish paradise. In the Thomas Hardy song cycle *Winter Words*, he set the poem "Before Life and After," which may be his most personal statement. Over a solemn procession of triadic harmonies, the singer recalls "a time there was . . . when all went well," a primal state before "the disease of feeling germed," and wonders whether such a time could come again. His plaint becomes a sob: "How long, how long, how long, how long, how long?"

In April 1939, Britten traveled to America in the company of his increasingly close friend Peter Pears, with the intention of settling there permanently. The main reason for this unexpected move was sexual-psychological: the ill-defined relationship with Wulff Scherchen had grown so fraught that Britten felt the need to leave the country. But there was also a political explanation. Auden had moved to America at the beginning of the year, seeking an exit from what he would call, in his famous poem "In Memory of W. B. Yeats," the "nightmare of the dark." America was a new land, a liberal land, a refuge from the Europe of Fascism and appeasement. On a practical level, Britten had received a tentative job offer from Hollywood, or "Holywood," as he called it in a letter to Scherchen. For the BBC he had composed some brawny music to accompany a King Arthur drama, and the director Lewis Milestone—for whom Aaron Copland later wrote *Of Mice and Men*—wanted Britten to score *The Knights of the Round Table*. Nothing came of that plan, and it's just as well, since Britten's sensitive ego would probably have suffered terrible scars in the movie business.

Much of what Britten knew of America came from Copland, whom he had befriended in England the previous year. On a visit to the Old Mill, Copland had played through his children's opera *The Second Hurricane*. Britten was charmed by the freshness of the vocal writing and by the harmonious picture of young comrades on a common mission. "It would be nice to keep in touch with your triumphs and 'problems,'" Copland subsequently wrote, "problems" being young males.

Britten rapidly disabused himself of the idea of becoming an American, although the outbreak of World War II and the attendant dangers of transatlantic travel prevented him from returning to England until 1942. He tried valiantly to adapt to the eccentric, bohemian lifestyle that Auden had cultivated in New York, but he could not find the cocoon of comfort he required. In the fall of 1940, he and Pears moved into a communal household at 7 Middagh Street, in Brooklyn Heights, overlooking the bridge. Living with them were Auden, Paul and Jane Bowles, the editor

George Davis, and, up in the attic, Thomas Mann's son Golo. The high-society stripper Gypsy Rose Lee was a frequent guest; Salvador Dalí, Christopher Isherwood, Leonard Bernstein, and Golo's brother Klaus also dropped by. When the Bowleses left, the novelist Carson McCullers moved in, with her alcoholic insanity.

Unable to work, Britten found asylum with the Mayers, German refugees on Long Island. "Everything here is crazes—crazes—crazes," he wrote to his brother-in-law back home. "I'm gradually realising that I'm English—& as a composer I suppose I feel I want more definite roots than other people."

Yet Britten gained much from his American experience. From Broadway shows he learned dramatic tricks that would serve him well in his operas from *Grimes* onward, and, with Auden as his librettist, he made his own beguiling if not entirely successful foray into musical theater with the archly surreal comedy *Paul Bunyan*. At the same time, isolation helped him to focus his voice, and he displayed new creative maturity in works from the years 1939 through 1943: the piercingly elegiac Violin Concerto, apparently inspired by the tragedy of the Spanish Civil War; the *Sinfonia da Requiem*, another bitterly eloquent lament in time of war; and, most important, three major song cycles written for Peter Pears, with whom Britten was now falling in love.

In the songs, homosexual themes make their first appearances in Britten's music. *Les Illuminations*, for high voice and strings, draws on poems by the bisexual Rimbaud—a "savage parade" populated by a "graceful son of Pan" (Wulff Scherchen, according to the dedication), a "Being Beauteous, tall of stature" (Pears), and "very sturdy rogues," among whom are "some young ones." The *Seven Sonnets of Michelangelo* play like love letters to Pears, who returned the love by singing them.

The third cycle, the *Serenade* for tenor, horn, and strings, was written in 1943, after the return to England. In this anthology-like setting of six English poems Britten confronted his central subject as composer, the corruption of innocence; the cycle turned out to be almost a dry run for *Peter Grimes*. At the beginning, the solo horn plays a broad theme in natural harmonics, which suggests, almost in the style of Copland's open-prairie music, a primordial realm untainted by human complexity. Then the cycle moves through a sequence of established forms, such as Pastoral, Nocturne, Elegy, and Dirge, and the "disease of feeling" germs. At the heart of the cycle is a brilliant, frightening setting of William Blake's "The Sick Rose":

O Rose, thou art sick.
The invisible worm,
That flies in the night
In the howling storm:

Has found out thy bed
Of crimson joy:
And his dark secret love
Does thy life destroy.

The strings begin with a "natural" open fifth on E and B, which pulses weirdly off the beat. The horn starts on the note G-sharp, forming a clean E-major triad, then falls to a G-natural, darkening the harmony to minor—a heart-sinking effect of a kind that appears often in Schubert and Mahler. The horn spirals through a circuitous, spasmodic pattern, creeping along in close semitone intervals and then leaping by fourths or fifths. The tenor recites the Blake text in the space of only eight bars, repeating the major-to-minor, light-to-dark shading of the opening. Afterward, the horn reprises its solo, and at the very end the first two notes are played in reverse order, G-natural to G-sharp. Thus, the piece closes in E major. But it is hardly an optimistic resolution; it is the worm's victory. Britten had discovered one of the core techniques of his dramatic language, the use of simple means to suggest fathomless depths.

Peter Grimes

George Crabbe's poem "Peter Grimes," part of the 1810 collection *The Borough*, is the story of a vile man. Even in boyhood, Grimes is a horror, spurning, berating, beating, and, it would seem, killing his own father. As a fisherman, he takes to drink and grows viler. He subjects his first apprentice to physical abuse—"He'd now the power he ever loved to show, / A feeling being subject to his blow"—and lets him die in bed, cause of death unknown. A second apprentice, gentle and slender, is abused in ways that sound sexual as well as physical: "Strange that a frame so weak could bear so long / The grossest insult and the foulest wrong." That boy falls from the mast of the boat. A third dies in a storm. Finally, the residents of Aldeburgh, who have averted their eyes from these incidents, forbid Grimes to hire more apprentices. He floats in his boat through the estuaries, driven mad by the ghosts of his victims. Raving but not contrite, he dies in a bed in the parish poorhouse. The epigraphs at the head of the tale, one from Walter Scott and two from Shakespeare, all contain the word "murder."

When Britten and Pears first talked about a *Grimes* opera, they imagined a character much like Crabbe's. In some early sketches for the libretto, which can be seen at the Britten-Pears Library in Aldeburgh, the death of the first boy apprentice is described as an "accidental murder"—meaning, presumably, manslaughter. Further, Grimes's relationship with the boy is given a sexual tinge. The fisherman is maddened by the boy's youth and beauty: "Love me darn you," he says in one draft. A later sketch has him exclaiming:

Your body is the cat o' nine
Tails' mincemeat. O! a pretty dish
Smooth-skinned & young as she could wish.
Come cat! Up whiplash! Jump my son
Jump (lash) *jump* (lash) *jump, the dance is on.*

A little later in the conceptual process, Britten and Pears brought in the playwright Montagu Slater to write the libretto, and Slater, an ardent Communist, cast Grimes as a more sympathetic type, the victim of a closed-minded society. Britten and Pears quickly accepted Slater's ideas. Pears later told the musicologist Philip Brett: "Once we'd decided to make it a drama of the individual against the crowd, then those things"—hints of Grimes's sexuality and sadism—"had to go." Pears wrote to Britten in the spring of 1944: "The more I hear of it, the more I feel that the queerness is unimportant & doesn't really exist in the music (or at any rate obtrude) so it mustn't do so in the words. P.G. is an introspective, an artist, a neurotic, his real problem is expression, self-expression."

In the final drafts of the score, the collaborators can be seen covering up traces of the original conception. More changes were made before publication, new lines drafted to fit the extant music. Grimes's line "You will soon forget your workhouse ways," addressed to the boy, becomes "She [the teacher Ellen Orford] will soon forget her schoolhouse ways."

Grimes's fitful evolution from villain to victim could easily have produced a confusing final impression. But the music is so richly layered that Grimes becomes a fully multidimensional character, whom singers have interpreted in strikingly different ways. Pears, the creator of the role, always portrayed Grimes as a man wounded by his status as a social outcast. The tenor might have agreed with Philip Brett, who read the opera as a "dramatic portrayal of the mechanics of oppression," and specifically as "an allegory of homosexual oppression." The Canadian tenor Jon Vickers, by contrast, played Grimes as a damaged brute, one who sways between heartbreaking lyricism and heartless violence. Britten obviously sided with Pears's portrayal, but Vickers's scalding performances pulled out hidden layers of the score.

Everything about *Grimes* is ambiguous. On first encounter, it looks to be an opera in the nineteenth-century tradition, stocked with arias, duets, choruses, and other set forms. Yet the inherited forms periodically splinter apart or stop short, as if overcome by emotions that the composer knows are too complex to be resolved in song. This is opera that presses constantly at the borders of the genre, whether high or low: it bursts with folk song, operetta and vaudeville tunes, and the vernacular punch of the American musical, and, at the same time, it erupts in twentieth-century dissonances. In many ways, *Grimes* is an English *Wozzeck*, extending sympathy to an ugly man, using his crimes to indict the society that sired him. Or, as Britten put it, in his no-nonsense way: "The more vicious the society, the more vicious the individual."

The scene is set with a bustling, businesslike Prologue. Grimes testifies at an inquest into the death of his first apprentice, who, in this version, dies of dehydration at sea. "Peter Grimes! Peter Grimes! Peter Grimes!" cries the village carrier—this tragedy will unfold against accusatory repetitions of the title character's name. Throughout the introductory scene, the music points up fractures beneath Aldeburgh's tidy surface: potential key centers jostle against each other, major and minor triads are clouded over extraneous notes, clotted chords appear in the lower brass.

Britten's psychological precision in setting the English language is obvious from the start. Like Janáček, he purposefully matches his vocal lines to the rhythms of conversation, oratory, and dispute. Notice how he treats a simple little question that the lawyer Swallow poses to Grimes—"Why did you do this?" A prosecutor throwing out this phrase in court would lift his voice a little after the "Why" and emphasize the "did" and the "do," which is just what Swallow does. As the scene goes on, the initial notes of the phrase—think of the first four notes of "Auld Lang Syne" in quick, even rhythm—take on a symbolic function, representing chatter, gossip, rumor. "How long were you at sea?" Swallow asks. "Three days," Grimes replies. At that, oboes and bassoons play the gossip motif twice, staccato and crescendo. Later, it is picked up by all the winds and becomes a driving ostinato, over which the chorus voices its growing suspicions of Grimes. Hatred of the outsider will be the moral focus by which these upright citizens organize themselves.

At first, Grimes is a blurry presence, trying to make himself heard above the din. But his pride, impatience, and belligerence soon show through. "Let me thrust into their mouths the truth itself," he sings. In a duet with Ellen Orford, the kindhearted schoolteacher, he reveals an alternate persona, one of keening vulnerability. There follows Britten's great orchestral evocation of the heaving ocean on a cold gray morning—the first of six interludes in the opera, illustrating different facets of the sea. Interestingly, some of the ocean's motifs have previously appeared in the courtroom scene, characterizing Grimes; he and the sea transmit the same primeval force.

The Borough's residents, seen going about their morning business after the interlude, are a motley lot, their peccadilloes more memorable than their virtues. Auntie, keeper of the Boar Inn, runs a part-time brothel, making her "nieces" available to the men of the town. The self-appointed lay preacher Boles is an incorrigible drunk. The prim, scolding Mrs. Sedley is addicted to laudanum and in need of a refill. When Ned Keene, the apothecary, offers Grimes a new apprentice, the townspeople begin their muttering again; and when Ellen offers to pick up the boy, they implicate her as well, accusing her of "fetching boys for Peter Grimes." Meanwhile, signs of an approaching storm gather in the orchestra, and all but Grimes scatter to safety.

Alone against the elements, Grimes dreams aloud of a future in which he will make a fortune, marry Ellen, and have his revenge on the town. He sings an abbreviated aria of desperate, upward-lunging fervor:

What harbour shelters peace
Away from tidal waves, away from storms,
What harbour can embrace
Terrors and tragedies?

An attempted A-major climax is broken apart by a three-note dissonance, starting *ppp* then growing in volume, in the trumpets and trombones. It moves like a wedge, and it has the effect of cracking the harmony open: we are hurled across the tritone into the E-flat-minor tonality of the second interlude, the music of the storm itself. Britten offers little in the way of realistic nature painting, instead whipping up a more abstract, contrapuntal tempest. The "What harbour" music dominates the second part of the sequence, reinforcing the impression that this is more a psychic storm than a physical one.

The townspeople have taken refuge at the Boar. Events follow a predictable trajectory from merriment to altercation. They unload their pent-up unease on Grimes, who comes blowing through the door with a vehement orchestral restatement of "What harbour shelters peace?" (The stylistically voracious Britten here borrowed from Gershwin, whose *Porgy and Bess* he saw in New York in 1942; as Donald Mitchell points out in his multivolume compendium of the composer's letters and diaries, Act II, Scene 4 of *Porgy* is structured in much the same way, with storm music blowing through an open door.) The hypocritically moralizing Boles accuses Grimes of the unspeakable: "His exercise is not with men but killing boys!" Ned Keene tries to restore good feeling with a round of the song "Old Joe Has Gone Fishing"—an ancient-sounding tune that Britten invented out of thin air—but the good feeling is washed away when the door swings open and Ellen enters with the new apprentice. Strings resume the "gossip" figure and harp on it maniacally until the end of the act.

The storm music flares up even when the door is closed, suggesting once again that Grimes is a storm unto himself. In the margins of Slater's first libretto draft for this scene, Britten wrote: "Climax of storm (+ boy's fear of murder?)." As chromatic scales crash downward in the orchestra—two parallel scales, a whole tone apart—Grimes takes the boy out of the inn and into his world.

Act II begins on a golden Sunday morning. The music is cast in the Lydian mode, with the fourth degree of the scale raised; in this context the flared note suggests an excess of radiance, light glittering on the surface of the water. As the curtain rises, the townspeople are streaming into church, and for once their chatter sounds wholesome. But in the middle of the D-major festivities a B-flat-major triad sounds low in the orchestra, creating a sudden, jarring dissonance. It is anchored on the rounded tone of a church bell. Off to the side of the Sunday procession, Ellen has appeared with Grimes's new apprentice, John.

A magnificent two-tiered sequence follows, worthy of Verdi. The churchgoers sing the hymns and responsories of their Sunday service in the church offstage, while Ellen sits with John by the beach, trying to assuage his fears. Noticing a bruise on the boy's body, she surmises that Grimes's violence is reawakening—"It's begun." She tells John that he has already discovered how near love is to torture. (In a last-minute revision, "love" was changed to "life," spoiling a chain of correspondences in the words and music.) In the background, the chorus sings such lines as "We have done those things which we ought not to have done." Indeed, Ellen shouldn't have let the boy anywhere near Grimes; her misplaced faith in human goodness sets the scene for the coming disaster.

When Grimes shows up, Ellen challenges him about the bruise, whereupon Grimes hits her, accompanied by an orchestral reminiscence of the storm. "God have mercy upon me!" he exclaims, in a downward-plunging, corkscrew-like musical line, and goes away with the boy. "Grimes is at his exercise," the churchgoers sing, to the same notes on which Grimes sang "God have mercy." Wagner, in the *Ring* cycle, established a leitmotif system in which recurring melodic figures cue the audience to recall certain concepts and characters. Britten, complicating the Wagnerian idea, attaches two distinct meanings to his leitmotif, one having to do with Grimes's feelings of guilt and the other having to do with the townspeople's condemnation. Their interpretation of the motif inevitably wins out—the church organ gives it moral gravity—and the corkscrew figure takes on percussive, propulsive energy. The townspeople resolve to send out a delegation to determine what is going on in Grimes's clifftop hut, and as they go, they are accompanied by a militaristic thudding of drums: "Now is gossip put on trial . . ."

Britten refrains from showing what happens between Grimes and the apprentice as they go back to the hut, but the fourth interlude, a fearsome passacaglia, lets us imagine what the boy is feeling.

Passacaglia form—variations over a bass ground—already had a distinguished history in twentieth-century opera. Berg, in *Wozzeck*, used it to depict the torturous experiments of the horrific Doctor. Shostakovich, in *Lady Macbeth*, employed a passacaglia to describe the aftermath of the killing of the kulak Boris. Britten introduced a passacaglia into the gravely sorrowing finale of his 1939 Violin Concerto, which obliquely memorializes the anti-fascist fighters of the Spanish Civil War.

In all these works, the passacaglia suggests murderous or destructive forces at work, and so it does in *Grimes*, where grim orchestral activity accumulates over repetitions of the "God have mercy upon me!" / "Grimes is at his exercise" leitmotif. When Britten prepared a stand-alone score for this interlude, he annotated it with more detailed associations, some of which are: "A crisis—a mistake? rough sea?," "the boy's guilt, depression, loneliness," "tears," "G's comforting," "G's encouraging" (spooky arpeggiated chords for trumpets and trombones), "Boy's efforts to work & please," "fe[ar?]" (fast, snaking figures for high winds and violins), "G threatens," "The walk up the hill, the boy's terror" (pushy figures in the horns, precipitate upward runs in the winds). The "boy himself" speaks through a halting song on the solo viola—an instrument that often carries autobiographical implications in Britten's music, the composer having played it in his youth.

What happens next is harrowing, particularly when the Passacaglia's programmatic indications are taken into account. John is thrust onstage, Grimes following behind. The boy's mental condition is indicated by the main viola theme and by the music denoting "tears" and "fear." Grimes insists on going ahead with the day's fishing expedition, and rants about marrying Ellen. The "crisis / mistake" music returns as Grimes shakes the boy, followed by a reprise of the uncomforting "comfort."

As the town procession nears, Grimes threatens further violence unless John makes a dangerous descent down the cliff: "Will you move or must

I make you dance!" (The original libretto reads, "Will you move if the cat starts making love"—as if Grimes is holding a whip.) The Passacaglia's "terror" figure shrieks in the strings. As John climbs down, he loses his grip, screams, and falls. Britten notates the scream with the phrase "*portamento lento*" (slowly sliding tone). The gesture of a descending shriek recalls the murder of Marie in *Wozzeck* ("*Hilfe!*"). That echo undermines the "official" interpretation of Grimes as "victim of society": the music comes close to accusing him of murder, in mind if not in deed.

The bloody-minded townspeople arrive, but they see nothing amiss. Commenting among themselves that Borough gossip might have got out of hand, they leave. Captain Balstrode, one of the few who want to understand Grimes rather than condemn him, stays behind to look around, and after a moment he makes a terrible discovery: the boy's Sunday clothes are lying on the floor. The solo viola melody of the Passacaglia is heard, but with its intervals inverted, so that it resembles the pattern to which Boles sang the fateful words "His exercise is not with men but killing boys!" It's as if the boy's ghost were talking.

Act III: night has fallen. A band is playing a barn dance in the Moot Hall—a tall-chimneyed sixteenth-century building that still stands in Aldeburgh. Outside, Swallow and Ned Keene are pursuing the coquettish nieces. The rector, sampling the racy atmosphere before going back to the cultivation of his roses, sings a brief but infectious song with the refrain "Good night, good people, good night." There is even a jokey cameo by Dr. George Crabbe, Grimes's creator. Amid the merrymaking, the awful Mrs. Sedley skulks in, trying to interest the townspeople in her theory that Grimes has murdered his apprentice:

In midnight's loneliness and thrilling quiet
The history I trace, the stifling secret
Murder most foul it is, and I'll declare it!

Mrs. Sedley is a great detective in her own mind, a sort of diseased Miss Marple who has been waiting for years for a crime to be committed on her doorstep. A chromatic bass line makes her sound like a ridiculous comic-opera villain, but a sliver of militant trumpet signals her ability to wreak havoc. The irony is that Mrs. Sedley is actually right: something is amiss with Grimes. But the justice that she seeks is vindictive rather than redemptive.

Ellen enters holding John's torn jersey, which Balstrode has found on the beach below the cliff. The schoolteacher knitted the garment herself, in an effort to create a perfect icon of childhood dreams. Now her handiwork tells a chilling tale—it is, she says, "the clue whose meaning we avoid." As she sings, she is accompanied by gauzy string chords and strummings on the harp, in the style of a Renaissance lament. The studied archaism of the aria suggests that Ellen is still averting her eyes from the truth about Grimes, even with the clue in her hand. Her role as an unwilling accessory in Grimes's actions is even hinted at in the music—when she and Balstrode declare, "We shall be there with him," they sing to the tune with which Grimes threatened the boy.

Having overheard Ellen and Balstrode's exchange, Mrs. Sedley goes victoriously to Swallow, bellowing, "This is official." She seizes control of B-flat major, the key of the introductory courtroom scene, and the others rapidly join her there, intending now not to investigate Grimes but to convict him: "Who holds himself apart, lets his pride rise / Him who despises us we'll destroy!" They are a kind of Un-Anglian Activities Committee, bent on personal destruction. The drunken vigor of the dance turns malevolent; Mrs. Sedley's formerly creaky chromatic line roars in the brass. To close, the chorus sings "Peter Grimes!" nine times *fortissimo*, eventually shortening it to a triple-*forte* "*Grimes!*" But they search in vain for their quarry. During the final sea interlude, the scene changes to the empty beach, where Grimes has fled.

But is he alone? At the beginning of this most mysterious of the interludes, a flute motif recalls a little flurry of notes that played as Ellen sat with the boy on Sunday morning. Other instruments join in with "Grimes is at his exercise" as the orchestra collectively plays a massive chord of E—the key in which the viola sang its ghostly song at the end of Act II. As in the original Crabbe poem, Grimes seems surrounded by the ghosts of his victims. Indeed, in the "mad scene" that follows, he sings fragments of his previous music and talks to the two boys who have died (and even to a third whom he has not yet met). Meanwhile, the chorus continues to chant his name offstage, seventy-nine times in succession: "Grimes! . . . Grimes! . . . Grimes! . . . Grimes! . . . Grimes! . . . Grimes! . . ."

The man's sense of self breaks down, and all he can do in the end is to sing his own name in response, in a drawn-out melisma. He sees himself only as the town sees him. Balstrode and Ellen appear, but Grimes does not hear them. Balstrode stops singing and simply talks: "Sail out till you lose sight of the Moot Hall. Then sink the boat. D'you hear? Sink her. Goodbye Peter."

As a new day dawns, the music of the first interlude returns. The residents of the Borough go about their tasks. Boles and Auntie watch a boat sinking out to sea. "What is it?" Auntie asks. "Nothing I can see," Boles replies. "One of these rumours!" Auntie replies, to the tune of "Grimes is at his exercise." With the outcast banished from its midst, the Borough appears to have forgotten all about him. The chorus sings again of the uncaring majesty of the sea: "In ceaseless motion comes and goes the tide . . . it rolls in ebb yet terrible and deep." Dense chords, like the ones that played when Grimes first walked into the courtroom, grunt in the bass. An ocean of sound, neither dark nor light, neither major nor minor, marks the fisherman's grave.

Britten's Cold War

The premiere of *Grimes* took place at the Sadler's Wells Opera Company on June 7, 1945. The ensuing triumph changed British music and Britten's life. Interest in the opera grew so intense that late in the run a London bus conductor entered the title into his litany of destinations: "Sadler's Wells! Any more for Peter Grimes, the sadistic fisherman!" European and American performances followed. In America the opera played first at the Tanglewood Festival and then at the Metropolitan Opera. The composer's face appeared on the cover of *Time*. Even Virgil Thomson was forced to admit that *Peter Grimes* was "not a bore."

From that storied first night onward, Britten was England's most celebrated living composer. He bore his national duties without difficulty, composing prolifically until his death a little over thirty years later. He went on to write thirteen more operas, equaling the output of Richard Strauss. His selection of literary sources was dauntingly ambitious, encompassing a Roman tragedy by the French playwright André Obey (*The Rape of Lucretia*, 1946); a social comedy by Guy de Maupassant (*Albert Herring*, 1947); a multilayered seafaring story by Herman Melville (*Billy Budd*,

1951, with a libretto by E. M. Forster); a historical drama of Elizabeth I's affair with the Earl of Essex (*Gloriana*, 1953); two tense and enigmatic stories by Henry James (*The Turn of the Screw*, 1954, and *Owen Wingrave*, 1971); a Shakespeare setting (*A Midsummer Night's Dream*, 1960); three church parables (*Curlew River*, *The Burning Fiery Furnace*, and *The Prodigal Son*, 1964–68); and, finally, *Death in Venice* (1973). Britten's songs drew variously on Donne, Blake, Wordsworth, Shelley, Coleridge, Goethe, Hölderlin, Pushkin, Thomas Hardy, T. S. Eliot, Edith Sitwell, Robert Lowell, and, most memorably, Wilfred Owen—the soldier-poet who supplied the core of the antiwar oratorio *War Requiem* of 1962.

Amid the raging paranoia of the Cold War era, however, Britten's position was never entirely secure. During the Second World War he had registered as a conscientious objector, and he remained committed to pacifism and other leftist causes throughout the anti-Communist witch-hunting era. Homosexuality also counted against him. If any whisper of those romantic friendships with boys had reached the press, Britten would have been destroyed in an instant. Furthermore, as in Cold War America, homosexuality was considered the mark of a duplicitous, anti-patriotic nature. After the defection of the gay spy Guy Burgess to the Soviet Union in 1951, Scotland Yard began hunting down homosexuals in the upper reaches of English society. Britten apparently submitted to an "interview" with Scotland Yard at the end of 1953, although no action was taken. Across the ocean, J. Edgar Hoover kept a file on Pears and Britten, listing them as "prohibited immigrants," which meant that every time they wanted to visit the United States they had to go through an elaborate visa-application process. A page from the composer's FBI file is so heavily redacted that only his name remains; the rest is blacked out.

As the Western world turned into the Borough writ large, a community of ill will, Britten kept pursuing his favorite themes: love among men, the beauty of boys, the endangerment of innocence, the pressure of society on the individual, the persistence of secret wounds, the yearning for unblemished worlds.

Homosexuality, implicit in *Grimes*, becomes more or less explicit in *Billy Budd*. The Melville story presents a kind of love triangle among male subjects: the beautiful sailor Billy, who loves all; the rapacious master-at-arms Claggart, who lusts after Billy and swears to destroy what he cannot possess; and Captain Vere, who hides his own sentiments for Billy behind an austere facade. Claggart falsely accuses Billy of fomenting a mutiny; Billy strikes him dead in a rage; military justice demands that Billy die. Vere, though, is torn. He summons Billy for a "closeted interview," presumably to explain why the death sentence cannot be reversed.

In Melville's telling, the interview between Billy and Vere is wrapped in "holy oblivion," in double negatives and circumlocutions, but the author lets slip that the captain may have "caught Billy to his heart"—words suggesting a physical embrace. In setting the interview to music, Britten brings the emotion, if not the action, into the open. Before an empty stage, the orchestra moves slowly through an array of thirty-four major and minor chords, each of which harmonizes a note of the F-major triad. The chord changes are often jarring: a tritone move from D minor to A-flat major, gentle C major in the strings giving way to rasping F-sharp minor in the brass, dynamics changing in almost every bar, as if in total-serialist fashion. But the tension slowly subsides, and the sequence ends in a peaceful alternation of F major and C major, with a muted D-major chord supplying one last gentle jolt at the end. This is the music of mute passion—"love that passeth understanding," as Vere says in the epilogue—and it nearly reverses the tragic momentum of the story.

The Turn of the Screw ventures into still riskier territory. The Henry James story tells of a governess who is hired to care for two children in a remote house and finds that they are seemingly under the spell of two ghosts, those of the former manservant Peter Quint and the former governess Miss Jessel. As in *Billy Budd*, Britten spells out what his nineteenth-century source merely implied. Quint becomes a fully supernatural presence, rather than a mental projection, while his designs on the boy, Miles, are given an erotic thrust: it is said that Quint "liked them pretty . . . and he had his will, morning and night." But the opera is really centered on the governess, who, like Ellen in *Grimes*, finds herself complicit in the children's fate even as she tries to rescue them. And, as in *Grimes*, the complexity of guilt is shown in the slippage of leitmotifs from one situation to another.

The opera takes the form of variations on a twelve-note theme, each of whose notes is sustained while the others enter, until all twelve are sounding. The score is hardly a riot of dissonance, though; all manner of melodies are teased out of the master matrix. We associate the theme with the malice of Quint, but it becomes clear as the opera proceeds that the theme also has much to do with the governess, and that Quint is slowly taking over her consciousness. When, at the climax of the opera, she urges Miles to say aloud the name of the specter haunting him, she finds herself singing through the "screw" theme. Unable to bear the shock of uttering Quint's name, Miles falls dead. The opera thus illustrates James's—and Britten's—favorite theme of characters thinking good and doing evil. It also shows how a child can be damaged by excesses of adult emotion, even if the emotion is not sexual.

The plots of *Peter Grimes*, *Billy Budd*, and *The Turn of the Screw* all pivot on the death of a boy or a young man. Each could be summarized with a line from Yeats's poem "The Second Coming," which Britten and his librettist Myfanwy Piper put into the mouth of Peter Quint: "The ceremony of innocence is drowned." Britten identified strongly with the victims, but he may also have seen something of himself in the predators. Even as he was rehearsing *The Turn of the Screw* for its 1954 premiere, he became infatuated with the twelve-year-old David Hemmings, who played the role of Miles.

Hemmings himself did not feel preyed upon; he later attested that although he and Britten slept in the same bed nothing overtly sexual happened. None of the boys whom Britten befriended over the years subsequently spoke ill of him, with one significant exception: Harry Morris, who had met Britten back in 1937, when he was thirteen, many years later told his family that Britten had made an apparent advance, which he fended off by screaming and throwing a chair. Then twenty-three, Britten may have understood the harm his desires could cause, and drawn a boundary that he did not cross again.

If *The Turn of the Screw* is the most comprehensively disturbing of Britten's operas, *A Midsummer Night's Dream* makes amends. In writing it, Britten possibly exorcised the darkest strains in his nature and found some semblance of the innocent haven that he had always sought. Working in the tradition of such twentieth-century "literature operas" as *Pelléas*, *Jenůfa*, *Salome*, and *Wozzeck*, Britten set Shakespeare to music directly, word for word, although, with Pears's help, he reduced the play to a manageable size. The mechanism of the "screw," the invasion of the supernatural and the unnatural, now turns in reverse: when troubling emotions arise in parallel human and fairy-tale realms, Puck's magic resolves them, mostly by undoing the mischief that it has caused. Britten casts his own spells, inventing a language of sweet noises, harmonic pratfalls, and supremely graceful melodies that vanish before they can be caught. At the end of Act II, Puck and a chorus of fairies send the four mortals into what the fairy king Oberon calls "death-counterfeiting sleep." As Puck prepares to squeeze juice on Lysander's eyes, the fairies sing:

On the ground,
sleep sound . . .
And the country proverb known,
In your waking shall be shown:
Jack shall have Jill;
Nought shall go ill;
The man shall have his mare again,
And all shall be well.

Britten describes the potion of sleep by way of sweet chords that add up to a twelve-note row: D-flat major, D major with B attached, E-flat major, and the notes C and E. Over iridescent orchestration, the boys sing a rising-and-falling melody in thirds, a lullaby from another world. Nothing more fragrant has ever emanated from Schoenberg's twelve-tone principle. Something equally magical happens in the coda, when the orchestra plays through the verse once more, violins taking the place of the voices. The sequence of four chords stops moving, instead coming to rest on warm D-flat, and utter peace seems at hand. Yet, as the thirds of the melody sink back down, their meaning changes: for the briefest instant, major turns to minor, and a shadow darts across the mind.

In November 1940, a German air raid nicknamed Operation Moonlight Sonata ravaged Coventry and made a ruin of a cathedral that had stood in the city since the Middle Ages. Twenty-two years later, on May 30, 1962, a new cathedral was dedicated next to the shell of the old, and Britten's *War Requiem* had its first performance. It is the composer's "official" work, his grandest public statement.

The complex literary and musical structure of the *War Requiem* may owe a debt to Michael Tippett, whom Britten respected as much as any colleague. The libretto for Tippett's oratorio *A Child of Our Time*, written during the early years of the Second World War, unfolds on two ingeniously intersecting levels—Tippett's own solemn, T. S. Eliot–like poetic meditations on the mid-century crisis and redemptive selections from James Weldon Johnson's *Book of American Negro Spirituals* ("Nobody Knows de Trouble I See," "Go Down, Moses," "Deep River"). In a similar vein, the *War Requiem* intersperses the Latin text of the Requiem Mass with antiwar poems by Wilfred Owen, which give rich new resonances to words that have been set to music thousands of times. Three soloists are positioned against two orchestras and two choruses, creating a multidimensional musical space which rivals that of Stockhausen's *Gruppen*. The complex architecture has the effect of folding the personal into the political, the secular into the sacred.

The climactic moment in the *War Requiem* comes in the "Libera me," where the composer pleads for peace, for liberation from "eternal death." After a mammoth choral-orchestral explosion, the tenor and the baritone recite to each other lines from Owen's poem "Strange Meeting," in which a freshly dead English soldier meets the German soldier he killed the day before. "It seemed that out of battle I escaped / Down some profound dull tunnel," the Englishman declares. "I am the enemy you killed, my friend," the German answers. By giving a tremor of eroticism to this meeting of strangers—sonorities marked "cold" give way to warm vibrato chords, the indications "expressive" and "passionate," a sense of a shivering midnight assignation—Britten cuts through the false complexities of politics. He could be echoing his ex-friend Auden's unforgettable cry of "We must love one another or die."

Britten and Shostakovich

In September 1960, Dmitri Shostakovich came to London to hear his Cello Concerto played by Mstislav Rostropovich. At that performance he was introduced to Britten. In the next several years Britten and Pears made several visits to Russia, usually in the company of Rostropovich and his wife, Galina Vishnevskaya. The friendship between the two composers blossomed in the summer of 1965, when Britten and Pears traveled to a Soviet composers' colony in Armenia, where the Rostropoviches and Shostakovich were staying. Despite obvious differences in temperament—

Britten was warm and affectionate with those whom he trusted, Shostakovich nervous to the end—the two quickly found sympathy with each other, and their connection may have gone as deep as any relationship in the life of either man.

Britten had long admired Shostakovich's music, as the *Lady Macbeth*–like Passacaglia in *Peter Grimes* shows. Shostakovich, for his part, knew little of Britten's music before the summer of 1963, when he was sent the recording and score of the *War Requiem*. He promptly announced to his old friend Isaak Glikman that he had encountered one of the "great works of the human spirit." In person he once said to Britten, "You great composer; I little composer." Britten's psychological landscape, with its undulating contours of fear and guilt, its fault lines and crevasses, its wan redeeming light, made Shostakovich feel at home.

Both men seem almost to have been born with a feeling of being cornered. Even in works of their teenage years, they appear to be experiencing spasms of existential dread. They were grown men with the souls of gifted, frightened children. They were like the soldiers in Wilfred Owen's poem, meeting at the end of a profound, dull tunnel.

Shostakovich met Britten only one week after he had experienced yet another in his seemingly endless series of political humiliations. He had been asked by Nikita Khrushchev, Stalin's successor as the general secretary of the Communist Party, to lead the Composers' Union of the RSFSR, and shortly after, he became a candidate member of the Party itself. Previously, Shostakovich had sworn to friends that he would never join an organization that used terror to carry out its aims. He now gave conflicting accounts of the train of events that led him to go back on this resolution, one being that he was drunk. "They've been pursuing me for years, hunting me down," he told Glikman, tears streaming down his face. Lev Lebedinsky claimed to have heard him say such things as "I am scared to death of them," "I'm a wretched alcoholic," and "I've been a whore, I am and always will be a whore."

Shostakovich would probably have suffered no serious consequences if he had turned down the RSFSR office or the membership. By the sixties younger musicians were actively resisting the Party's aesthetic strictures, studying twelve-tone composition and avant-garde techniques, aligning themselves with the dissident movement. They were aghast at Shostakovich's gesture of conformity. "Our disappointment knew no bounds," said the young composer Sofia Gubaidulina. "We were left wondering why, just at the time when the political situation had relaxed somewhat, when at last it seemed possible to preserve one's integrity, Shostakovich fell victim to official flattery." Later, Gubaidulina said, she understood better what Shostakovich had endured.

This latest crisis prompted Shostakovich to write his scathing, self-punishing Eighth Quartet, one of the most extraordinary autobiographical pieces in musical history. It was written in just a few days, following a visit to Dresden, where the director Lev Arnshtam was making *Five Days, Five Nights*, a film about the Allied bombings of February 1945.

No doubt the Dresden experience contributed to the Eighth Quartet's fraught tone, but Shostakovich's letters indicate that the dedication "to victims of fascism and war" was something of a cover for his own private anguish. To Glikman he wrote: "The title page could carry the dedication: 'To the memory of the composer of this quartet' . . . It is a pseudo-tragic quartet, so much so that while I was composing it I shed the same amount of tears as I would have to pee after half-a-dozen beers. When I got home, I tried a couple of times to play it through, but always ended up in tears. This was of course a response not so much to the pseudo-tragedy as to my own wonder at its superlative unity of form. But here you may detect a touch of self-glorification, which no doubt will soon pass and leave in its place the usual self-critical hangover."

The personal motto D S C H, which sounded pseudo-triumphantly in the finale of the Tenth Symphony, is woven into almost every page of the Eighth Quartet. It appears alongside quotations from previous Shostakovich works, including the Tenth Symphony, *Lady Macbeth*, and the youthful First Symphony, not to mention Tchaikovsky's *Pathétique*, Siegfried's Funeral Music from *Götterdämmerung*, and the revolutionary song "Tormented by Grievous Bondage." Was Shostakovich speaking ironically when he described the quartet as an exercise in "self-glorification"? The designation might apply to the ending of the Tenth, but it seems inappropriate for the Eighth Quartet, which trails off into a black, static chorale of lamentation. The final pages of the score resemble, in a curious way, the mad scene of *Peter Grimes*, in which the fisherman is reduced to singing his own name: "Grimes! Grimes! Grimes!" It is the ultimate moment of self-alienation.

The desolate psychological terrain of Shostakovich's late-period music overlaps everywhere with that of Britten's. Shostakovich busied himself with one of Britten's favorite forms, the song cycle. The *Seven Poems of Alexander Blok*, the *Six Poems of Marina Tsvetayeva*, and the *Suite on Verses of Michelangelo Buonarroti*—the last probably inspired by Britten's Michelangelo songs—show a newly economical approach to word setting, while the texts themselves resonate with the composer's life in the half-confessional style that Britten perfected with *Les Illuminations* and *Serenade*: villainous tartars, killings, and famine (Blok); the tsar as a murderer of poets (Tsvetayeva); Rome overrun by greed and bloodlust (Michelangelo).

Shostakovich's boldest political statement of the Khrushchev Thaw came in the Thirteenth Symphony, based on anti-Stalinist poems by Yevgeny Yevtushenko. The first movement, "Babi Yar," is ostensibly a lament for Jewish suffering under the Nazis, but it also remembers life under Stalin. Yevtushenko devotes one section to a depiction of Anne Frank cowering with her family in the attic: "Someone's coming!" "They're breaking down the door!" "No, it's the ice breaking." Shostakovich responds with a series of dissonant, hammering chords, which, in their peculiar hollowed-out voicing, suggest not only a murderous hand hammering at a door but also the terrified reactions of those waiting behind it.

Britten, meanwhile, resumed writing chamber and orchestral music, which he had largely ignored since his American period. Between 1964 and 1971 he composed three great suites for cello, which echo the taut language of Shostakovich's quartets while also honoring Bach. The beginning of the Second Suite quotes the opening cello theme of Shostakovich's Fifth Symphony almost note for note. The dedicatee was, of course, Rostropovich, for whom Britten also wrote, in 1962 and 1963, the Cello Symphony, the only major orchestral work of the latter part of his career. Here, too, Shostakovich's influence is perceptible, if not pervasive. The final movement is another passacaglia, this one roughly optimistic rather than tragic in tone. As Lyudmila Kovnatskaya points out, both Britten and Shostakovich used the recurring bass lines of the passacaglia to suggest the inescapable tensions of modern existence—"a chain of metamorphoses taking place within the confines of a closed circle of fate . . . a spiritual compass bridging the gap between the commonplace and the eternal."

In 1969 Shostakovich capped the friendship by placing Britten's name on the title page of his Fourteenth Symphony, a song cycle on poems by

Lorca, Apollinaire, Rilke, and Wilhelm Küchelbecker. The dedication is sealed by a quotation: in the last bars of the first movement, half of the double basses slide up a major seventh and then go back down, exactly as the same instruments do at the beginning of *A Midsummer Night's Dream*. But the Fourteenth goes some way toward revoking Britten's half-hopeful worldview. As in *Serenade* and *Nocturne*, the poems are organized around a common theme; here, the theme is death. In some prefatory remarks before the dress rehearsal, Shostakovich cited various works, Britten's *War Requiem* included, that aim to describe the "peculiar glow" or "supreme calm" of the experience of death. His own intention, he said, was to portray death without sentiment. "Death is in store for all of us," he told his audience, "and I, for one, do not see anything good about the end of our lives." The final measures of the symphony sound like nothing so much as a death rattle.

A strange event at the first performance underlined the symphony's uncanny character. During the fifth movement, Pavel Apostolov, a cultural functionary who had once denounced Shostakovich's "gloomy, introverted psychological outlook," left the hall in haste, his seat banging shut behind him. It was assumed that he was making his displeasure known. In fact, he was having a heart attack, and had to be carried off in a stretcher. "I didn't want *that* to happen," Shostakovich drily commented. Apostolov was dead within a month. The composer's colleagues noted that the fifth movement of the symphony contained the line "Now has struck the hour of death."

Yet this outwardly bleak work offers a kind of hope of life after death, in the form of an immortal solidarity between artists who transcend the stupidity of their time. At the heart of the symphony is a setting of Küchelbecker's poem "O Delvig, Delvig!":

O Delvig, Delvig! What is the reward
For noble deeds and poetry?
What solace for talent
Amid villains and fools? . . .
Free, joyous, and proud,
Our bond will not die!
Through joy and sorrow it will endure,
The union of those beloved by the eternal muses!

It does not take much guesswork to figure out who Delvig might be. When the Fourteenth was performed at Aldeburgh in 1970, Donald Mitchell speculated the movement portrayed the Britten-Shostakovich friendship, and Britten seemed to concur. Shostakovich's intentions are unknown, but the music affords some clues. The principal melody is set forth by a solo cello, with another cello moving in parallel sixths; it strongly resembles the double-stopped main theme of Britten's First Cello Suite.

For years, Britten and Pears had been hoping that their Russian friend would visit them at the Red House in Aldeburgh. Shostakovich finally made the trip in 1972, even though he was in constant pain from a complex of illnesses—heart trouble, lung cancer, and amyotrophic lateral sclerosis, or Lou Gehrig's disease. At the Red House, he went alone into the library, where Britten had laid out the material of a work in progress. It was a rare act of self-exposure from a composer who kept his creative process sacrosanct. Britten waited outside—Rosamund Strode recalled that he looked "very tense"—while Shostakovich pored over the music. Two hours later, he emerged, wearing a cryptic smile. In his mind, he had heard Britten's final opera.

Death in Venice

In late May 1911, a few days after Gustav Mahler died in Vienna, Thomas Mann arrived in Venice with his family. He had an assignment to write a brief essay about Richard Wagner, who had died in the city three decades before. Staying at the same beach hotel was a Polish boy named Władysław Moes, whom his friends called Adzio. Mann found his eyes drifting away from his writing paper and toward the boy, and a mental obsession took hold of him. He used the experience as the basis for *Death in Venice*, in which, true to life, a celebrated German author named Gustav von Aschenbach falls in love with a boy named Tadzio while vacationing in Venice.

Unlike his alter ego, however, Aschenbach carries his obsession to a comically self-debasing degree, chasing Tadzio around the city and painting his own face to look younger. Venice is in the grip of a cholera epidemic, and Aschenbach consciously risks his health in order to remain near the boy. He dies on the beach, in sight of his beloved.

At first encounter, Mann's novella would seem to be a solemn, somewhat overwrought story about an artist's struggle with the competing demands of the mind and the body, of Apollonian and Dionysian principles. Aschenbach's physical attributes were modeled on the mighty figure of Mahler, whose obituaries Mann had just read, and this association gives the fictional author a high-culture veneer. But there is something faintly ridiculous about his oeuvre of disciplined masterpieces, stocked with projects that Mann himself had contemplated and then set aside—a book about Frederick the Great, a novel titled *Maya*, an essay on "intellect and art." Aschenbach's blend of intellectual grandiosity and boy worship recalls Stefan George, with his circle of neomedieval adolescents, and also the nineteenth-century poet August von Platen, who extolled youth in formally perfect sonnets. In the end, *Death in Venice* makes devastating fun of an irretrievably high-minded artist who is overcome by the sexual energies that he has carefully repressed. Mann himself escaped that trap simply by writing the story, releasing his desire in harmless form.

It was not so easy for Britten to smile at Aschenbach's predicament, for his own situation was perilously similar. Venice had been the scene of Britten's embarrassing infatuation with David Hemmings, during the rehearsals for *The Turn of the Screw*. As work on *Death in Venice* progressed, life continued to mirror art in troubling ways. Britten ended up postponing a crucial heart operation in order to finish the opera; according to Donald Mitchell, "He talked quite calmly and dispassionately to us about the possibility of *not* having the operation, even though it had been made perfectly clear to him that following *that* path could have had only one outcome—the expectation of a very short future life." Pears was heard to say, "Ben is writing an evil opera, and it's killing him." The line might have come from Mann's story.

At the beginning of the opera, Aschenbach finds himself trapped inside a purely intellectual sphere—"My mind beats on, my mind beats on, and no words come"—and his twelve-syllable opening line is fixed symbolically on a twelve-note row. By the end of Act I, he has brought himself to the point where he can say "I love you" to Tadzio, although the boy is not close enough to hear him. But his profession of love is still pent-up and strangulated; although the setting of "I love you" ends on an E-major chord, it is threadbare tonality, with the E and the B deep in the bass and the G-sharp nothing more than an eighth note in the tenor part. (This is the same key through which Blake's "invisible worm" flies in the

Serenade.) From here on, Aschenbach's personality undergoes an audible dissolution; obsessive repetitions and self-quotations echo the final madness of Grimes. Yet when Aschenbach finally comes to terms with his condition and fate—"O Aschenbach . . . Famous as a master . . . Self-discipline . . . your strength . . . All folly, all pretense . . ."—the orchestra makes a final stab at Mahlerian splendor.

Tadzio's music comes from a different world. It is based on the Balinese gamelan, which Britten had first encountered as far back as his American days, via the composer Colin McPhee, and which he had experienced firsthand during a visit to Bali in 1956. One gamelan scale that he notated on that trip overlaps perfectly with Tadzio's theme in *Death in Venice*. Gamelan-like sounds had cropped up all over Britten's music from the late fifties onward: in the ballet score *The Prince of the Pagodas*, in the church parable *Curlew River*, in the music for Oberon in *A Midsummer Night's Dream*, and, significantly, in the "pacifist aria" of *Owen Wingrave*, in the course of which a young man rebels against his conservative military family. Britten's celebrations of the exotic have both a political dimension—the composer is reasserting his anti-establishment stance—and also an erotic one. He would have known from McPhee, a pioneer in gamelan-based composition, that Western visitors to Bali could purchase the favors of local boys for a modest price. Tadzio is no Anglican innocent; he is stereotyped as an Eastern Other, available and aware. Very likely, Aschenbach is the virgin in this scene.

Mann's story makes it clear that Aschenbach's "relationship" with Tadzio is a fever dream from beginning to end. Dying on the beach, the distinguished author hallucinates a moment of connection—"it was as if the pale and lovely soul-summoner out there were smiling to him, beckoning to him"—and then slumps over dead. The final sentence—"And later that day the world was respectfully shocked to receive the news of his death"—shows Mann's cold-eyed detachment from his alter ego.

In the opera, Tadzio beckons for real, and Aschenbach's air of fulfillment is allowed to stretch into the final bars. There is again a touch of Mahler in the surging of the strings. Tadzio's theme acquires new weight and wisdom. Yet it retains its non-Western aspect, ebbing and flowing like an Indian raga. The music of intellect fades, and what remains, a high violin and a glockenspiel, is the music of the Other. We are entering into Tadzio's consciousness, seeing the world through his eyes. With Aschenbach dead, he is no longer the object of desire but the voice of desire. He is like Szymanowski's King Roger, who rises from the "abyss of loneliness, of power" to bathe his body in the sun.

Like Aschenbach, Shostakovich and Britten died in middle age. On a last trip to America in 1973, Shostakovich spent a day with doctors from the National Institutes of Health, who could offer no solution to his myriad health problems. The composer took the news calmly, almost with a shrug, according to his American translator, Alexander Dunkel. He stopped in at a performance by Pierre Boulez and the New York Philharmonic and attended a postconcert banquet, which produced an awkward moment: the "arch-apostle of modernism," as Shostakovich called Boulez, bent down to kiss the hand of a composer about whom he had never had anything good to say. "I was so taken aback," Shostakovich reported to Glikman, "I didn't manage to snatch it away in time."

A more sincere gesture of respect greeted Shostakovich when he went to the Metropolitan Opera to hear *Aida*. During the final intermission, trumpet players in the orchestra saluted him by playing the opening phrase of the final movement of the Fifth Symphony. Now Shostakovich was the great man in the box, the focus of awe.

Somehow, Shostakovich went on writing music, even though he had trouble moving his right hand. Strains of Beethoven's "Moonlight" Sonata mysteriously infiltrate his final work, the Viola Sonata, written in June and early July 1975. He died on August 9, at the age of sixty-eight. At the premiere of the sonata Fyodor Druzhinin responded to the audience's ovation by holding the score over his head, as Mravinsky had done at the premiere of the Fifth.

Britten died in December of the following year, at the age of sixty-three, of complications brought on by bacterial endocarditis, the same condition that had killed Mahler. Michael Tippett wrote a remarkably generous obituary: "I want to say, here and now, that Britten has been for me the most purely musical person that I have ever met and I have ever known." Just as remarkable was the gesture made by Queen Elizabeth II, the head of the Church of England. When the news of Britten's decease reached her, she sent a telegram of condolence to Peter Pears.

((13))

ZION PARK

Messiaen, Ligeti, and the Avant-Garde of the Sixties

"I have found that *it is not to be*," Adrian Leverkühn declares, in his bloodcurdling meditation on Beethoven's Ninth Symphony. "The good and the noble, what they call the human, despite the fact that it is good and noble. What men have fought for, have stormed citadels for, and, in their moment of fulfillment, have jubilantly proclaimed—it is not to be. It will be taken back. I will take it back."

Thomas Mann's Faustian composer is alluding to a musical code that is written into Beethoven's last string quartet. In the introduction to the finale, the viola and cello play a sighing minor-key phrase to which are attached the words "Must it be?" The violins reply, swinging into the major: "It must be!" The little exchange was conceived as a joke, but it has a serious subtext; it expresses in miniature the spirit of cosmic affirmation that blares forth so triumphantly in Beethoven's "Ode to Joy." Leverkühn has no interest in embracing the millions. In the twentieth century, he might argue, affirmation has become banal. Only by striking the dark note can he achieve true seriousness and originality.

Leverkühn's aesthetic of denial and negation captures in somewhat exaggerated form one of the dominant strains of twentieth-century music. The fictional composer bears traces of Schoenberg and Webern, who professed to have killed tonality, and perhaps of Varèse, who fancied himself a "diabolic Parsifal." Leverkühn also foreshadows Boulez, with his aesthetic of "still more violent"; Cage, who said that he was "going toward violence rather than tenderness, hell rather than heaven"; the ironic, self-flagellating, death-obsessed Shostakovich; and even Britten, who made an arabesque of the words "The ceremony of innocence is drowned." (When Mann heard Britten's *Serenade*, he wrote, "Adrian Leverkühn might well have been very happy to have done some of these things.") More than a few canonical twentieth-century works—*Salome*, *Erwartung*, the *Rite*, *Wozzeck*, *Lulu*, *Lady Macbeth*, *Peter Grimes*—ride fateful currents toward scenes of violent or mysterious death. They are what Olivier Messiaen called "black masterpieces."

After the war, composers took up what might be called catastrophe style with a vengeance, history having justified their instinctive attraction to the dreadful and the dire. Krzysztof Penderecki one-upped his colleagues by producing, within one decade, *Threnody for the Victims of Hiroshima* and *Dies Irae (Auschwitz Oratorio)*. Not coincidentally, the fictional Leverkühn became something of a folk hero among postwar composers, most of whom read Mann's book at one time or another. Henri Pousseur's conceptual opera *Votre Faust* (1960–68) told of a Leverkühnish composer named Henri, who, in one scene, conducts an analysis of Webern's Second Cantata.

The twentieth century was unquestionably a terrible time in human history—"the century of death," Leonard Bernstein called it—but proximity to terror does not obligate the artist to make terror his subject. Theodor Adorno, who helped to write the musical passages in *Doctor Faustus*, saw modernism and kitsch as polar opposites, yet even he admitted that modernism can bring forth its own kind of kitsch—a melodrama of difficulty that easily degenerates into a sort of superannuated adolescent angst. Georg Lukács, in a critique of Adorno, remarked that the philosopher resided in a "Grand Hotel Abyss," from whose aestheticized security he gazed on the agony of man as if it were an Alpine vista.

There is much to be said for the artwork that answers horror by rejecting or transcending it. Think of the halo-like aura of Stravinsky's *Symphony of Psalms*, or of the weightless profundity of Strauss's *Four Last Songs*, or of the sacred song of Duke Ellington's "Come Sunday." As the fearful fifties gave way to the antic sixties, many European composers looked for a way out of the labyrinth of progress. One was György Ligeti, who witnessed the century of death at close range, having lost most of his family in Hitler's death camps and then suffered further under Stalinism in his native Hungary. Ligeti nonetheless found it in him to write music of luminosity and wit.

Messiaen, the composer of the *Quartet for the End of Time*, can be defined as the anti-Leverkühn. In the latter part of his career he wrote works titled *The Transfiguration of Our Lord Jesus Christ*, *From the Canyons to the Stars . . .*, and *Saint Francis of Assisi*, each of which ends with an explosive affirmation of a major key, outdoing even the coda of Beethoven's Ninth in unrestrained jubilation. Yet it is not harmony that Beethoven would readily have recognized. Messiaen's triads are suffused with surrealist, futurist energy. They are evidence of a deep investigation into sound itself, one that doubled as a quest for an all-encompassing language of the spirit. The composer once compared the Resurrection of Christ to an atomic detonation, and Christ's image on the Shroud of Turin to the human shadows that were supposedly seared on walls in Hiroshima. With utmost vehemence, he says, "It must be."

Messiaen

Saints are rarely as interesting as devils, and Messiaen, who was born in Avignon in 1908, led a fairly uninteresting life. His biography contains one very sad story—his first wife, the poet Claire Delbos, suffered from cerebral atrophy and had to be committed to a nursing home—and one intensely dramatic episode, the writing of the *Quartet for the End of Time* at Stalag VIII A. Otherwise, Messiaen kept to a steady routine—composing music, teaching classes at the Paris Conservatory, traveling to attend performances of his works, and, every Sunday, playing organ at the Church of the Holy Trinity in Paris. He held the latter job from 1931 until his death in 1992, playing *Messiah* at Christmastime and fulfilling other prosaic duties.

Fellow composers would sometimes drop by Holy Trinity to find out what kind of music Messiaen played for the parishioners on an ordinary Sunday. Aaron Copland wrote in his 1949 diary: "Visited Messiaen in the organ loft at the Trinité. Heard him improvise at noon. Everything from the 'devil' in the bass, to Radio City Music Hall harmonies in the treble. Why the Church allows it during service is a mystery."

For the last three decades of his life, Messiaen lived with his second wife, the pianist Yvonne Loriod, in an old building in the eighteenth arrondissement of Paris, in the area of Montmartre. As Peter Hill and Nigel Simeone report in their biography of the composer, the accommodations were fairly spartan, with one communal bathroom on each floor of the building. The main living quarters were decorated in devout Catholic style, plastic crucifixes all around. When the composer and conductor Esa-Pekka Salonen called on Messiaen, he looked to see what books and records were on the shelves, but could find only a copy of the Bible and various recordings of Messiaen's own works.

No one reported anything like a seamy underside to the composer's personality. The conductor Kent Nagano, who collaborated closely with Messiaen in his last years, was once pressed to tell some unflattering or otherwise revealing anecdote about his mentor, and all he had to offer was a story about how Messiaen and Loriod had once devoured an entire pear tart at one sitting.

God spoke to Messiaen through sounding tones, whether the mighty roar of the orchestra or the church organ, the clattering of exotic percussion, or the songs of birds. The Lord could manifest Himself in consonance and dissonance alike, though consonance was His true realm.

"The tonic triad, the dominant, the ninth chord are not theories but phenomena that manifest themselves spontaneously around us and that we cannot deny," Messiaen once said. "Resonance will exist as long as we have ears to listen to what surrounds us." He had in mind the fact that the major triad, on which tonality rests, is related to the lower intervals of the natural harmonic series, those that arise from any resonating string. Schoenberg, in his *Harmonielehre*, proposed to set aside consonances and to derive new chords from what he called "remote overtones." Messiaen believed that the ear could, and should, take in tones both near and remote—both the reassuring resonances of fundamental intervals and the obscure relationships among the higher tones.

In his 1944 textbook *Technique of My Musical Language*, Messiaen notated what he called "the chord of resonance," in which eight distinct pitches from the natural harmonic series sound together (C, E, G, B-flat, D, F-sharp, G-sharp, B-natural). Strongly dissonant in effect, it still has the C-major triad at its base—a "natural" foundation for an abstract form. Mahler placed a chord very much like this one at the roaring climaxes of his unfinished Tenth Symphony.

Technique of My Musical Language also set out a system of "modes of limited transpositions," analogous to the modes of ancient Greek music (Aeolian, Dorian, Lydian, and so on). They are based on the composer's study of early-twentieth-century music, especially Stravinsky and Bartók, as well as of folk and traditional music from Bali, India, Japan, and the Andes. The first mode is Debussy's whole-tone scale. Mode 2, made up of alternating semitones and whole tones, is the octatonic scale, on which Stravinsky built the *Rite*. Mode 3, in which one whole tone alternates with two semitones, slightly resembles the scale commonly associated with the blues. Mode 6 happens to be the same as the slithering clarinet scale that begins *Salome*. The three remaining modes are more eccentric scales of Messiaen's devising. What they have in common is that they are symmetrical in shape, dividing neatly along the fault line of the tritone. The *diabolus in musica* sounded divine to Messiaen's ears; it was the axis around which his harmony rotated. Messiaen's modes generate a fabulous profusion of major and minor triads, as Paul Griffiths points out in his study of the composer. But they do not—indeed, cannot—produce standard chord progressions of the kind that are found in hymnals. Instead, the harmony skids from one triad to another, following the sinuous contours of the modes. Messiaen called these effects "rainbows of chords."

The *Technique* might be read as Messiaen's answer to—and refutation of—*Harmonielehre*. Schoenberg, too, considered his harmonies emblems of the sacred; the wordless six-note chords in *Moses und Aron*, mimicking the voice of the burning bush, tremble with divine force. The difference between Schoenberg and Messiaen is ultimately theological. Schoenberg believed that God was unrepresentable, that His presence could be indicated only by placing a taboo on the familiar. Messiaen felt that God was present everywhere and in all sound. Therefore, there was no need for the new to supersede the old: God's creation gathered magnificence as it opened up in space and time.

Messiaen rejected the stereotype of French music as a poised, graceful, self-limiting art. From an early age, he favored the lavish, the opulent, the unashamedly grand. His 1932 organ piece *Apparition of the Eternal Church* intersperses velvety modal harmonies with pillar-like open fifths that the composer called "simple, almost brutal." There is an atmosphere of gradual ritual, incense, rustling robes, flickering candles in a shadowy space—a church of the mind as real as the one in which the listener is presumed to be seated.

While Messiaen took on a markedly more aggressive, even at times abrasive voice in the *Quartet for the End of Time*, he did not lose his flair for the simple, astounding gesture. The two most excruciatingly beautiful movements of the *Quartet*—the two "Louanges," or hymns of praise, to the eternity and immortality of Jesus—are in fact adaptations of pieces that he had written before the war. The first "Louange" is based on *Fêtes des belles eaux*, or *Festival of Beautiful Waters*, a work for six ondes Martenot (an early electronic instrument akin to the Theremin). The second comes from the 1930 organ piece *Diptyque*. Curiously, *Fêtes* was written in 1937 for a "festival of sound, water, and light" along the banks of the river Seine. Women in white dresses played Messiaen's music in conjunction with fireworks and fountains; the formal divisions of the piece were dictated by the requirements of the engineers. The first long, slow, searching phrase, which the cello plays in the *Quartet*, originally accompanied a tall jet of water, which, Messiaen said, was a "symbol of Grace and Eternity."

To know that such a spectacle lies behind the "Praise to the Eternity of Jesus" is to appreciate the many-sidedness of the composer's aesthetic, his ability to move in a flash from the mundane to the sublime. Messiaen expects paradise not just in a single awesome hereafter but also in the scattered ecstasies of daily life. In the end, his apocalypse—"There shall be time no longer"—may have nothing to do with the catastrophic circumstances under which it was conceived. Instead, it may describe the death and rebirth of a single soul in the grip of exceptional emotion.

Messiaen's early sacred pieces, the *Quartet* included, are like Christian surrealism. They have something in common with those later paintings of Salvador Dalí in which Christ floats above the earth like an astronaut or superhero. That image applies especially to the composer's next big works, *Visions of the Amen* for two pianos and *Three Small Liturgies of the Divine Presence* for chorus and instrumental ensemble, both written while the Germans still occupied France. The *Visions* indulges in what Paul Griffiths calls "ever splashier paroxysms of cheapened harmony . . . a further stage in Messiaen's abjuring of a sophisticated response to what is musically embarrassing." The text of the *Liturgies* scandalously intermingles sacred and erotic phrases, some culled from religious literature and some coined by the composer, all in the form of a love letter to God ("You are so complex and so simple, you are infinitely simple"). The harmony is plush and the orchestration picturesque, reminiscent in passing moments of the swashbuckling film scores of Erich Wolfgang Korngold and Max Steiner. Wailing in the middle of the ensemble are the sci-fi-ish tones of the ondes Martenot. Some critics balked—one compared the *Three Small Liturgies* to "an angel wearing lipstick"—but audiences cheered. Messiaen had the ability, Virgil Thomson noted, "to open up the heavens and to bring down the house."

The overflowing richness of the *Liturgies* and other works of this period belies the fact that Messiaen was at this time facing the greatest personal crisis of his life. His wife had suffered a sharp decline shortly before the end of the war, and after an unsuccessful operation she lost her memory. "She had to be put in a home, where everything was done for her," Yvonne Loriod told Peter Hill. "From that time Messiaen brought up his young son by himself. He did all the housework and all the cooking and he would get up at 5 o'clock in the morning to make the coffee and get breakfast for his son before he went to school." As Delbos's mind failed, Messiaen came to rely increasingly on Loriod, who was attending his classes. After a respectable interval, the two fell in love. Loriod played alongside the composer in the premiere of *Visions of the Amen*, her strong personality mirrored in the fresh extravagance of the music.

Three Messiaen works from the late forties—the song cycle *Harawi*, the *Turangalîla Symphony*, and the choral piece *Cinq rechants*—fall into what Griffiths calls the "Tristan trilogy." All address in one way or another the story of Wagner's doomed lovers, and *Tristan und Isolde* is directly cited along the way. At the same time, there are echoes of Indian talas, Balinese percussion ostinatos, and Peruvian folk song. In passing moments the harmony turns almost "pop"; Messiaen liked to sweeten his triads with added sixths, garnishing A major with an F-sharp, for example. At the end of the second "Chant d'amour" movement of *Turangalîla*, that chord is played as a slow, slinky arpeggio, in the manner of a cocktail-lounge pianist. There might as well be a chanteuse in a tight dress leaning to the side.

The jazzy tinge is felt even in the immense sacred landscape of the piano cycle *Twenty Aspects of the Infant Jesus*, written in 1944; one four-note motif in the tenth piece, depicting the "spirit of joy," sounds suspiciously like the jaunty four-note refrain of Gershwin's "I Got Rhythm," while the fifteenth, "The Kiss of the Infant Jesus," vaguely recalls the same composer's "Someone to Watch Over Me." Wagner, in *Tristan* and *Parsifal*, saw a fatal contradiction between body and spirit; Tristan and Isolde could complete their passion only in self-destruction, the Knights of the Grail could preserve themselves only by renouncing sex. Messiaen perceived no contradiction, indeed no difference, between the love of man and the love of God.

With the coming of the fifties, Messiaen went through his own "Cold War crisis"—a spell of experiment and self-doubt akin to Stravinsky's modernist maneuverings in the same period. Messiaen's faith in an "infinitely simple" God, as expressed in infinitely simple chords, wavered. "We are all in a profound night," he told his Paris Conservatory class one day, "and I don't know where I am going; I'm as lost as you."

Messiaen served as a mentor to many of the chief innovators of the postwar era. Boulez, Xenakis, and Stockhausen all studied with him at one time or another. Even before the end of the war, Messiaen's class had acquired the reputation of being a nest of radicalism. While the young revolutionaries learned much from their teacher's interest in non-Western music, his cultivation of new rhythmic processes, his early interest in electronic instruments, and, above all, his proto-serialist *Scale of Durations and Dynamics*, they were not persuaded of his more conservative ideas about harmony.

Boulez's high-handed, scornful treatment of Messiaen led to a situation in which the roles were almost reversed; for a while, it seemed as though Boulez were the master and Messiaen the disciple. "You know that Messiaen is developing wonderfully," Boulez wrote to Cage in 1951, in a schoolmasterish tone. He went on: "He has just written some organ pieces on 64 durations, with registration modes." These were part of the organ cycle *Livre d'orgue*, which contained perhaps the most intricately constructed, densely harmonized music of Messiaen's career.

From 1949 on, Messiaen made appearances at Darmstadt, where he proved as adept as any of his colleagues at filling up blackboards with quasi-scientific diagrams. But he soon took off on an unexpected tangent. One day in 1953, Antoine Goléa related, he showed his students a book containing colorful illustrations of birds. "Birds are my first and greatest masters," he announced. He then exhibited notebooks where he had transcribed birdsong heard on expeditions to different parts of France. "Birds always sing in a given mode," he said. "They do not know the interval of the octave. Their melodic lines often recall the inflections of Gregorian chant. Their rhythms are infinitely complex and infinitely varied, yet always perfectly precise and perfectly clear." Messiaen's students must have wondered whether he had lost his mind, or, alternately, whether he was satirizing the Darmstadt mentality.

But Messiaen was very much in earnest. He had first made deliberate use of birdsong in the *Quartet for the End of Time*, where the voices of the blackbird and the nightingale carry the solo clarinet movement "Abyss of the Birds." For the remainder of the fifties, Messiaen modeled nearly all of his instrumental lines on the contours of bird melodies, and they would reign over his music to the end. The first sustained demonstration came in *Réveil des oiseaux*, or *Awakening of the Birds*, for piano and ensemble, first performed at the Donaueschingen Festival in 1953. Dozens of birds are heard singing in turn, and in the "dawn chorus" twenty-one of them gather together in a charming polyphonic chaos. Then we go toward the silence of noon, and the birds fall asleep in the heat. In a way, this new technique could be compared to Cagean chance; Messiaen surrendered control of his music to outside forces. "I'm anxious to disappear behind the birds," he said before the premiere.

On the surface, Messiaen was indeed "developing wonderfully." In keeping with the aesthetic of the Darmstadt generation, his bird music of the fifties had an impeccably fragmented and pointillistic sound, as if the Cetti's warbler, the blue tit, and the great spotted woodpecker had propounded serialism in advance of Babbitt and Boulez. *Exotic Birds* (1956), *Chronochromie* (1960), *Seven Haikus* (1963), *Colors of the Celestial City* (1964), and *Et exspecto resurrectionem mortuorum* (1965) all duly appeared on Boulez's programs in Paris and elsewhere. Yet the opulent language of the *Quartet for the End of Time* and *Turangalîla* has not vanished completely. Messiaen's birds seem conversant with the modes of limited transposition, and unlike birds in nature they gravitate toward a tonal center; the nightingale at the beginning of *Réveil des oiseaux* sings unmistakably in the neighborhood of the key of D. Triads are tucked away in the innards of the harmony, submerged beneath layers of upper-harmonic tones, and melodies coalesce suddenly from clouds of timbre; the fourth of the *Seven Haikus*, for example, has a luxurious lyric solo for trumpet, doubled by winds and cossetted by strings. The reliance on birdsong allowed Messiaen to restore the primacy of a singing line. It showed him a way out of the "profound night."

Messiaen completed his great harmonic U-turn in the course of writing the almost three-hour-long piano cycle *Catalogue d'oiseaux*, or *Catalog of Birds* (1956–58). The music is built up from Messiaen's impressions of various scenic places in France and the birds that inhabit them. Faced with a teeming landscape of images and feelings, Messiaen realized that he no longer needed to choose among his various styles, the sensualism of his "Tristan" works and the thorniness of his early-fifties music; instead, he could, in a sense, have it all.

Thus, Boulezian piano effects become simply another "color" of the composer's palette; as Robert Sherlaw Johnson has observed, a twelve-note array is used to suggest the grittier aspects of the natural setting, such as the dirty ice of an Alpine glacier or the sinister hooting of owls in the dead of night. Triads delineate nature's brighter hues—the "joy of the blue sea," the broad movement of the river, the glow of the sunset. The birds are bustling, hyperactive, dissonant; sometimes they even sound like human tourists intruding on the mystery of nature. In the thirteenth and final piece, a mood of contemplative silence is broken several times by a shattering discord, which represents the foghorn of the Créac'h lighthouse, on the northwestern tip of France. The chord is a close cousin of the one that pounds repeatedly in "The Augurs of Spring" of the *Rite*. The closing bars are marked "tragic and desolate," with the call of the curlew ringing over a low D-minor chord and an arpeggio of surf fading into silence. Whether this is a tragic ending—man stamping his foot on the surface of nature—or a glimpse of some outer mystery is left for the listener to decide.

Having reclaimed his rainbow chords, Messiaen felt free to return to religious subjects, which he had generally avoided since 1950. *The Transfiguration of Our Lord Jesus Christ* (1965–69), a fourteen-movement work for chorus, seven instrumental soloists, and large orchestra, begins with a descending sequence of pitched gongs, in the manner of Boulez's *Marteau sans maître*. The chorus then unfurls an un-Boulezian ribbon of Gregorian chant. (The Second Vatican Council had just admitted vernacular music to the Mass, and, as the scholar Christopher Dingle notes, Messiaen declared his opposition to the change by filling the *Transfiguration* with Latin liturgical material.) In the first of eight "meditations," the music gravitates toward the key of E, the work's ultimate destination. Yet, as in *Catalogue d'oiseaux*, discord repeatedly crashes through the frame. The twelfth movement, "Terribilis est locus iste," ends with three gigantic chords of twelve notes each; the triads that follow in "Tota Trinitas apparuit" ("The Entire Trinity Appears") and the closing "Chorus of the Light of Glory" sound all the more brilliant for having been blasted out of dissonant ground. Indeed, the consonances are sometimes more terrifying than the dissonances that surround them. They are tonality transfigured, rising from the dead.

In 1970 the New York arts patron Alice Tully asked Messiaen to write a work in commemoration of the upcoming American bicentennial. It was an unlikely assignment, since Messiaen had little love for American culture and a special antipathy for New York. His reluctance gave way when Tully, well briefed on the composer's vulnerabilities, served him a sumptuous repast capped with "an immense cake crowned with pistachio frogs spewing *crème Chantilly*." Messiaen accepted under the condition that he could write in praise of the mountainous landscapes of the American West rather than the cities of the East.

In 1972, in the company of Loriod, Messiaen traveled to the canyons of Utah—Bryce Canyon, Cedar Breaks, Zion Park—and gazed for days at the boldly colored terrain, listening also to the songs of the local birds. Loriod photographed him standing alone in one of the crevasses of Cedar Breaks, reddish sandstone walls towering above him. In his sketchbook he wrote of the "immense solitude" of the place, of the whiff of terror and death in its hot and cold hues. He collected his impressions in a programmatic narrative that was variously ornithological, geological, astronomical, and spiritual. The piece would ascend "from the canyons to the stars and higher up to the resurrected souls in Heaven, so as to glorify God in all his Creation: the beauty of the earth (its rocks, its birdsong), the beauty of the physical sky, the beauty of the heavenly one."

From the Canyons to the Stars . . . , the result of Tully's commission, is perhaps Messiaen's greatest achievement. The majesty of the Utah canyons reawakened in the composer a songfulness that had long been missing from his music. The sound palette of *Canyons* is dominated by solo instruments singing out in a wide-open space—piano, horn, other solo winds, brass—with an ensemble of thirteen strings suggesting effects of resonance and reverberation. In a way, it is a colossal magnification of the instrumental drama of the *Quartet for the End of Time*. The clarinet solo in the *Quartet*, "Abyss of the Birds," has its counterpart in an extended movement for horn, "Interstellar Call." Other short movements in the first section depict the primordial desert out of which the canyons formed, the calls of the orioles, the glimmering of stars above. (In an early indication of the work's theological dimension, the last is titled "What is written in the stars"; the message in question is "*Mene, Mene, Tekel, Upharsin*," the writing on the wall in the book of Daniel.) The piano then takes over with a solo movement more or less in the style of *Catalogue d'oiseaux*, mimicking the calls of the white-browed robin.

At the heart of the work are movements celebrating the canyons themselves—"Cedar Breaks and the Gift of Awe," "Bryce Canyon and the Red-Orange Rocks," and "Zion Park and the Celestial City." "Cedar Breaks" is the music of the bedrock. Orations for brass in unison alternate with pulsing dissonant chords, rugged writing for piano, and quasi-jazzy episodes, replete with wah-wah trumpet and glissando trombone. "Bryce Canyon" recycles certain of those motifs of geological violence, but they give way to a series of mighty chorales, in which the silent splendor of the canyon resonates within the observer's mind. Messiaen, like his teacher Dukas, identified certain harmonies with certain colors; E major is red, and the final chords evoke not only the red-orange rock formations of Bryce Canyon but also the geology of the book of Revelation—the sardius, topaz, and amethyst stones embedded in the foundation of the celestial Jerusalem.

After "Bryce Canyon" comes a series of episodes in which the music swings back and forth between intricacy and purity. A euphoric song for strings depicts the reddish glow of the star Aldebaran; a second piano solo honors the mockingbird; a succulent instrumental intermezzo is based on the triadic call of the wood thrush; and, oddly, there's a busy fantasia on the birds of Hawaii.

Finally, the apotheosis of "Zion Park." Mormon settlers named the dazzling white and pink sandstone cliffs of this canyon "the natural temples of God"; Messiaen saw nothing less than celestial Jerusalem. He uses an elementary trick to create an atmosphere of enormous anticipation: several times he starts a progression in A major but does not complete it, and for the ten-minute span of the movement the cadence is withheld. It is as if the composer were afraid to finish his creation, preferring to take refuge one more time in his beloved birdsong, his disparate rhythms and modes. When the hunger for the missing chord becomes unbearable—the brass cry out for it three times, lustily, desperately—there is a supernova of A major, billowing into the lowest and highest reaches of the orchestra and whiting out in *fortissimo* strings.

The Avant-Garde of the Sixties

As Messiaen presided over the transfiguration of tonality, the European avant-garde was entering its carnivalesque, topsy-turvy, through-the-looking-glass period. These were the years of the great rock 'n' roll rebellion, of sexual liberation and drug experimentation and psychedelic culture. In the rambunctious spirit of the time, a second wave of avant-gardists rejected the previous generation's obsession with purity and abstraction. Chance, indeterminacy, graphic notation, and other forms of unconventionally notated music enjoyed a European vogue. Some gravitated toward the musical past, cutting it up by way of quotation and collage. Others pushed out into interstellar spaces, abandoning any pretense of an organizing system. There were Dada pranks, references to pop, a renewed fad for singable Communist ditties (this time in the name of Castro and Mao). A few composers in a dizzyingly self-referential vein made the situation of the international avant-garde their subject. Dieter Schnebel's 1961 work *Abfälle I/1* invited audience members to contribute to the performance by conversing among themselves, making noises of approval or disapproval, coughing, and moving chairs.

John Cage was entering his period of maximum influence. In 1958 he traveled to Germany to give a series of lectures at Darmstadt—substituting for Boulez—and European music was never quite the same afterward. Anyone who knew Cage's history should have been prepared for something unusual; back in 1950, his "Lecture on Nothing" at the Artists' Club had begun with the announcement "I am here and there is nothing to say," and the question period was derailed by Cage's decision to respond to all queries with a set of six fixed answers, one of which was "Please repeat the question . . . And again . . . And again . . ." Cage's Darmstadt lectures had episodes of coherence, but chance operations progressively took over, and by the third lecture he was lighting cigarettes at intervals specified by the *I Ching*. Most of the final talk took the form of a long string of questions, for example: "Do you agree with Boulez when he says what he says? Are you getting hungry? Twelve. Why should you (you know more or less what you're going to get)? Will Boulez be there or did he go away when I wasn't looking?"

Boulez was not there, but Stockhausen was, listening intently. The German visionary had first encountered Cage back in 1954, and had fallen under the spell of the American's ideas just as Boulez was becoming disenchanted with them. Early symptoms of Stockhausen's exposure to Cage can be detected in *Zeitmasse* (1955–56), in which five woodwinds periodically break free of a common tempo and buzz around one another in accelerating or decelerating patterns. Stockhausen also wrote a new series of *Klavierstücke* for David Tudor, Cage's favorite interpreter, tailoring them to the pianist's uninhibited style. *Klavierstück IX* (1954/61) begins with 139 repetitions of a strongly dissonant, Schoenbergian chord, fading slowly toward silence. *Klavierstück X* (1954/61) features cascades of cluster chords pounded out with the hands, fists, and forearms. In *Klavierstück XI* (1956), nineteen fragments are spread across the page, and the performer decides in what order they should be played; this is an obvious imitation of open-form pieces by Earle Brown and Morton Feldman.

Many young Darmstadt composers followed Stockhausen in flocking after Cage. One was Sylvano Bussotti, a flamboyant Florentine whose scores in graphic notation looked liked surrealist cartoons, with notes splattered all over and staves bent apart or tangled. (Tudor responded to these ambiguities by attacking the piano with boxing gloves.) Another mischief maker was the Argentine-German composer Mauricio Kagel, whose *Anagrama* (1957–58) offered up a new repertoire of vocal sounds—"stuttering, molto vibrato, with shaking voice, with a foreign accent, with almost closed mouth, quasi senza voce, speaking while inhaling, etc.," as the composer put it in the score.

In his 1960 work *Sur scène*, Kagel made Darmstadt itself the object of his sophisticated ridicule. An instrumental ensemble provides a ramshackle accompaniment to a spoken monologue on the crisis of modern music, which reads in part: "We cannot, with this never-ending talk about a crisis, lay bare all the problematic constituents of its problematic essence and simply bypass them, and yet we cannot get around the fact, to employ a consideration, again we take cognizance of the fact that this obscurity, impenetrability, this absence of resonance in extreme situations is something which—under these circumstances we cannot but reach a conclusion which sound common sense had indicated from the beginning: our perception at the end of the sound spectrum is by nature dim. I am sitting in the smallest room of my house."

The Italian composer Luciano Berio, who had been summering in Darmstadt since 1954, found a way out of the "crisis of modern music" by indulging in a touch of nostalgia: avant-garde practice was infused with age-old strategies of instrumental and vocal display. Berio's fantastic reconstructions of the art of singing owed much to the interpretive creativity of his wife, the American-born singer Cathy Berberian, who ran the gamut from primitive growls to angelically pure tone. For the 1958 electronic piece *Thema* (*Omaggio a Joyce*), Berio recorded Berberian reciting the opening of the "Sirens" chapter of Joyce's *Ulysses*, a passage that is itself a contrapuntal swirl of images, a literary approximation of serialism. Atomization of the voice leads not to a crisis atmosphere, as so often in Nono's music, but to an ecstatic, erotic, quasi-operatic frenzy. The extract begins with the words "A sail!" (Joyce's allusion to the first line of Verdi's *Otello*) and ends with whispered intonations of the name of Liszt. In the same year Berio wrote *Sequenza I* for flute, commencing a vivid series of *Sequenza* pieces—fourteen in all by the time of the composer's death in 2003—in which solo performers unloose a new kind of avant-garde virtuosity, exploiting every noise, tone, sound, and timbre that instruments can make. Later, Berio would criticize his colleagues for creating false dichotomies—between "style" and "expression," between virtuosity and structure, between the music of the daily world and the harmony of the spheres.

By the early sixties, the fascination with behind-the-scenes process—whether twelve-tone or chance-produced—had given way to a new appreciation of surfaces. The most-talked-about works of the period resembled a bubbling flow of timbres and textures, a sonic stream of consciousness. Xenakis had pioneered texture music in *Metastaseis* and *Pithoprakta*; Stockhausen, with his usual panache, made it his own by dubbing it "field composition" (which pointed toward a later category, "moment form"). The German trendsetter showed a new appreciation for continuous droning sounds, not unrelated to his American interests. On airplane flights to and from America in 1958, he listened intently to the propellers vibrating against the body of the plane, and reproduced those effects in a monster piece for four choirs and four orchestras titled *Carré*, which he composed with the help of his English assistant Cornelius Cardew.

In 1960, Stockhausen completed *Kontakte*, where live and electronic sounds bounce off each other or blur together. While writing it, the composer took advantage of a newly discovered method of generating tape loops by reversing the heads on a tape recorder. He also showed how tones are related to periodic beats; in the most electrifying passage of *Kontakte*, microscopic pulses are gradually lengthened until they form a pitch, which the piano confirms by playing a low E. Finally, in 1962, the world had its first glimpse of what would turn out to be the almost two-hour-long *Momente*, involving four choirs, a soprano soloist, a phalanx of trumpets and trombones, a pair of Hammond and Lowrey electric organs, and a percussion battery centered on an extra-large Japanese tam-tam. This was the bacchanalia of the avant-garde, a shouting, clapping, stamping liberation of the senses.

Several prizewinning samples of texture music turned up in Poland, from which little had been heard since Karol Szymanowski's death in 1937. In the early postwar years, Stalin's takeover of Eastern Europe had effectively stifled creative activity, but during the partial liberalization of the Khrushchev thaw the Soviet satellite nations found it convenient to encourage progressive artistic activity within their borders, knowing that the results could be exploited for propaganda purposes. The Warsaw Autumn festival, which began in 1956, was the Warsaw Pact's answer to Darmstadt and Donaueschingen; leading Western avant-gardists such as Stockhausen, Pierre Schaeffer, and David Tudor performed there, and younger Polish composers such as Krzysztof Penderecki, Henryk Górecki, Kazimierz Serocki, and Wojciech Kilar came to the fore, bringing with them a version of texture music that acquired the name sonorism.

The usual political issues arose. When Penderecki produced a floridly experimental piece called *8′37″*—an affair of shrieking cluster chords, sputtering streams of pizzicato, siren-like glissandos, and other Xenakis-like sounds—officialdom took a favorable view only when someone suggested that the work be retitled *Threnody for the Victims of Hiroshima.* It went on to have a successful career in the West.

The major figure in the Polish Renaissance was Witold Lutosławski, an older, established composer who, amid the relative freedom of the thaw, happily took possession of avant-garde methods that he had long studied in secret. In 1960 Lutosławski heard a radio broadcast of Cage's *Concert for Piano and Orchestra,* which sent him into a creative trance. As he later said, "Composers often do not hear the music that is being played . . . We are listening to something and at the same time creating something else." Lutosławski responded by reconciling chance and order: semi-improvisatory episodes alternated with passages in strict notation. "I could start out from chaos," the composer said, "and create order in it, gradually." Another time he spoke of looking down at a city from a great height and then descending until streets and buildings come into view. Lutosławski's chief works of the sixties—*Venetian Games, Three Poems of Henri Michaux, Paroles tissées,* the Second Symphony, the Cello Concerto—stand out for their explosively precise musical images and their clear-cut, surging narratives. Often they pivot on sudden epiphanies, akin to the discovery of a clearing in thick woods; one such moment occurs at the end of the Michaux settings, when delicately piercing F-sharps underpin the phrase "I let myself go." *Paroles tissées* was written for Peter Pears, and it combines *ad libitum* passages with spells of near-tonal lyricism. Benjamin Britten, no friend of the avant-garde, admiringly presented *Paroles* at the Aldeburgh Festival in 1965.

The improvised episodes in Polish sonorist works—"aleatory" was the approved European term for randomized activity—reflected a general trend toward collective and collaborative creation, which intensified in the last years of the decade. Amid the worldwide student protests of May 1968, Stockhausen sat down to write *Aus den sieben Tagen,* or *From the Seven Days,* whose score consisted of textual instructions for the composer's ensemble on the order of "Play a vibration in the rhythm of your body" and "Play a vibration in the rhythm of the universe." Musica Elettronica Viva, an improvisational collaboration among American composers based in Rome (Frederic Rzewski, Richard Teitelbaum, Alvin Curran, Allan Bryant, and others), jammed with the then brand-new Moog synthesizer. Cornelius Cardew, Stockhausen's former assistant, sat in with the London-based group AMM, which moved beyond notated composition, beyond the avant-garde, beyond even free jazz, into the spontaneous production of unanalyzably dense sonorities—noise so engulfing that the listener can neither hear nor imagine other sound. Cardew, for one, could go no further. In 1972, he denounced the avant-garde as a bourgeois luxury, wrote an incendiary essay titled "Stockhausen Serves Imperialism," and set about writing simple songs in praise of Mao Zedong.

In the central scene of *Doctor Faustus*, Leverkühn conducts a hallucinatory dialogue with the devil, who keeps changing guises and at one point assumes the form of "an intellectualist, who writes of art, of music, for vulgar newspapers, a theorist and critic, who is himself a composer, in so far as thinking allows"—Mann's wry portrait of Theodor Adorno. The critic-devil hands down judgments on the state of contemporary music, eliminating all possibilities except the Schoenbergian path, the one that follows "an implacable imperative of density." Leverkühn counters, "One could know all that and yet acknowledge freedom again beyond any criticism. One could raise the game to a yet higher power by playing with forms from which, as one knows, life has vanished." The devil dismisses such an approach as "aristocratic nihilism." Yet Leverkühn goes on to realize this possibility in his Violin Concerto. It is a self-aware, ironic work, its tenderness bordering on mockery. Leverkühn's oratorio *Apocalipsis cum figuris*, likewise, is enlivened by "parodies of the diverse musical styles in which hell's insipid excess indulges: burlesqued French impressionism, bourgeois drawing-room music, Tchaikovsky, music hall songs, the syncopations and rhythmic somersaults of jazz—it all whirls round like a brightly glittering tilting match, yet always sustained by the main orchestra, speaking its serious, dark, difficult language."

Music about music had always been part of twentieth-century discourse, going back to the neo-Baroque stylings of Strauss's *Ariadne auf Naxos* and Stravinsky's *Pulcinella*. But in the sixties games of parody and play caught on everywhere. Composers talked of "pluralistic sound composition," "polystylism," and "metacollage" (as the tirelessly neologistic Stockhausen called it). Works incorporated fragments of Beethoven and Mahler, imitated Renaissance masses and Baroque concertos, absorbed jazz, pop songs, and rock 'n' roll. Eastern European composers championed pluralism as a compromise position between tradition and the avant-garde: Penderecki, for one, introduced medieval organum and old church chorales into his *St. Luke Passion* (1963–65). Stockhausen weighed in with *Hymnen* (1966–67), a two-hour electronic-instrumental fantasy on the world's national anthems. Perhaps the ultimate collage work was the score that Kagel wrote for his own mind-bending film *Ludwig van* (1969), in which bits and pieces of Beethoven's piano sonatas and other works are transcribed for a ragtag band whose players seem to have incomplete mastery of their instruments.

Devices of collage, quotation, and pastiche efficiently performed the service of twitting the bourgeois audience, to the extent that such an entity still existed. Familiar classical strains run up against an abrupt noise, signaling a return to contemporary reality. But sometimes this music concealed a clandestine longing for the former tonal world. The modern European composer could commandeer tonal music without committing the sin of writing tonal music as such. This was the canny compromise that Berio presented in two of his most immediately appealing works: *Folk Songs* (1964), an imaginative arrangement-deconstruction of traditional tunes from France, Italy, Azerbaijan, Armenia, and America; and *Sinfonia* (1968–69), which reclaimed the late-Romantic symphony by annexing the music of Gustav Mahler. Throughout the third movement of *Sinfonia*, the Scherzo of Mahler's Second Symphony is heard playing in the background, its progress interrupted by quotations from more than a hundred other composers from Bach to Boulez, each one dovetailed ingeniously with Mahler's score. Over that grand collage, amplified voices enunciate fragments of Samuel Beckett's *The Unnamable*, and a speaker delivers a satirical text of the composer's devising. At one point the narrator announces in soothing tones that there is "nothing more restful than chamber music," implicitly mocking ordinary listeners' preference for cozy bits of Mozart and Brahms.

In sixties Britain, two radical youths, Peter Maxwell Davies and Harrison Birtwistle, used quotation and pastiche to thumb their noses at the conservatism of the English musical scene. Both came from northern working-class backgrounds and never identified with the sensibility of "Land of Hope and Glory." They met at the Royal Manchester College of Music, where experimentation reigned, and they resolved to catch up with the latest European developments. On moving to London in the late sixties, they organized a group called the Pierrot Players, which was modeled on the versatile ensemble for which Schoenberg wrote *Pierrot lunaire*.

The spirit of Swinging London mated with the European avant-garde. In Davies's *Revelation and Fall* (1965–66), the solo soprano shrieks poetry of Georg Trakl into a megaphone while the ensemble satirizes the operettas of Lehár. In the same composer's *Eight Songs for a Mad King* (1969), the madness of King George III is enacted as avant-garde street theater, the lead vocalist reciting the text in a gibbering delirium while sentimental Handelian, Victorian, and Edwardian musical strains are chewed to pieces by the players. In Birtwistle's *Punch and Judy*, likewise, mangled Baroque numbers limp through a dimly lit, indistinct, eerily groaning instrumental landscape. A wide gulf separated this stony music from the work of Britten, who had by this time become an establishment icon, somewhat against his will. Britten hosted the premiere of *Punch and Judy* at the 1968 Aldeburgh Festival, but, after a certain interval, he and Pears retired from the directors' box in search of drinks.

The collage works of Kagel, Berio, Davies, and Birtwistle have an exuberant, insolent tone. Those of the German composer Bernd Alois Zimmermann are, by contrast, tortured and tragic. Educated in a monastery school, Zimmermann came of age just before the Second World War and served in the cavalry both in France and on the Russian front. Circa 1945 he was still writing in a style that owed much to Hindemith, middle-period Stravinsky, even Anton Bruckner. At first, the hardened ex-soldier was reluctant to let go of German-nationalist attitudes that had been drilled into him; in his diary he denounced the Nuremberg trials and other anti-Nazi proceedings as "witch hunts." At the same time, he despaired of Germany's future: "O Germany, what has become of you? How your people have come to naught, have even destroyed themselves . . . Are not fear and anxiety, insecurity and terror standing on the horizon of our future like dark storm clouds in front of a setting sun? 'Abide with us; for it is toward evening.' " The diary bears an astonishing resemblance to passages in *Doctor Faustus*, which Mann was writing in Los Angeles at this time. Mann's narrator assumes the same biblical tone: "Watch with me . . . Forsake me not."

Zimmermann arrived at Darmstadt in 1948. Although he admired Schoenberg, he initially looked askance at twelve-tone writing as propagated by René Leibowitz, fearing that the technique would lead to an overintellectualized, technically overdetermined mode of composition. Still, the lure of progress proved irresistible. The composer's manuscripts, held at the Akademie der Künste in Berlin, show him steadily scrubbing out "backward" elements in his scores and installing devices more amenable to the temper of the times. In the second version of his unpublished Concerto for Orchestra, harp is replaced by piano, the texture is thickened with rapid-moving figuration, exotic percussion comes to the fore, octave doublings are eliminated, and heavy ostinato figures disappear.

Still, Zimmermann remained a recognizably German composer, exuding a Gothic-Romantic aura that was foreign to his compatriots Stockhausen and Henze. The opening bars of his opera *Die Soldaten* (1958–64) are a cataclysmic revision of Brahms's First Symphony, with the timpani pounding a single note against screaming cluster chords. When masterpieces of the German canon are directly quoted in his works, they flow seamlessly out of the "serious, dark, difficult" language beneath them.

In 1969 Zimmermann finished what would become his final major work, *Requiem for a Young Poet.* It calls for huge and varied forces, including orchestra, organ, three choruses, three solo voices, a jazz combo, and electronic elements. There are quotations from Prime Minister George Papandreou of Greece ("Democracy will triumph!"), Mao ("A revolution is no banquet, not like writing an essay or painting pictures or embroidering"), and Joyce's *Ulysses*; the sounds of tanks, jets, artillery; recordings of Wagner's *Tristan* and Messiaen's *Ascension*; poems of Mayakovsky ("My song rends the times with force"); and the voice of Hitler ("I lead you back into that homeland, which you have not forgotten and which has not forgotten you!"). In the climax of the piece, loudspeakers blare a collage of Beethoven's Ninth Symphony, the Beatles' "Hey Jude," the voices of Goebbels and Stalin, and radio transmissions by Allied bomber pilots. Soprano and bass sing from the Revelation of Saint John while the chorus chants, "Dona nobis pacem." The moral of all this seems to be that classical and popular music have bled together into cultural white noise obscuring imminent technological disaster. It all sounds very much like Leverkühn's "tilting match" of irreconcilable sounds, and in the middle is the Ninth, the work that Leverkühn had "taken back."

Zimmermann's despair over music's future was also despair over his own. On August 10, 1970, he committed suicide.

Ligeti

The predicament of the avant-garde composer seemed complete. To continue in pursuit of the "modern" was to go over the brink into absurdity; to retreat into the past was to admit defeat. In a talk delivered in 1993, György Ligeti put it this way:

> When you are accepted in a club, without willing or without noticing you take over certain habits of what is in and what is out. Tonality was definitely out. To write melodies, even nontonal melodies, was absolutely taboo. Periodic rhythm, pulsation, was taboo, not possible. Music has to be *a priori* . . . It worked when it was new, but it became stale. Now there is no taboo; everything is allowed. But one cannot simply go back to tonality, it's not the way. We must find a way of neither going back nor continuing the avant-garde. I am in a prison: one wall is the avant-garde, the other wall is the past, and I want to escape.

Ligeti escaped by not saying no. He opened himself to all music past and present, absorbing everything from the Renaissance masses of Johannes Ockeghem to the saxophone solos of Eric Dolphy, from the virtuoso piano writing of Liszt to the rhythmic polyphony of African Pygmy tribes. At the same time, he succeeded in imprinting his prickly, melancholy, ever-restless personality on whatever he caught in the web.

Many composers of the early avant-garde period witnessed horrific things in their youth. What Ligeti saw with his own eyes is practically unimaginable. He was born in 1923, in Transylvania, to a family of Hungarian Jews. Three years before he was born, Transylvania became part of Romania, and Ligeti went to study at the conservatory in Cluj, which had been called Kolozsvár. In 1940, the fascist government in Hungary regained control of Transylvania, and Cluj became Kolozsvár again. Ligeti was mobilized into a forced-labor gang in 1944, wearing the yellow armband required by anti-Semitic regulations, and carried heavy explosives on the eastern front. The Nazis took over the country later that year, and deportations to the death camps began. Calculating the likelihood of his being either killed in action, shot by the SS, or sent to the camps, Ligeti deserted from the front line. He immediately fell into the hands of Soviet troops, but once again managed to slip away. After a long walk home, he found that the Russians were now in control and that strangers were living in his parents' house. When the war ended, he learned of his family's fate: his father had been killed in Bergen-Belsen, his brother in Mauthausen, and his aunt and uncle in Auschwitz. His mother somehow survived.

The nightmare did not end in 1945. Ligeti went to study at the Franz Liszt Academy in Budapest, and he watched as the Soviets and their stooges took control of Hungary; the same thugs who had committed atrocities on behalf of the fascist Arrow Cross Party went to work for Mátyás Rákosi's Communists.

For the most part, Ligeti managed to avoid the odious task of creating Party propaganda. Instead, he buried himself in folk-music research, probably aware that Bartók had collected songs in the vicinity of a Transylvanian town where the Ligeti family had lived for a time. In secret, Ligeti dabbled in twelve-tone writing, though his understanding of the method was gleaned haphazardly from the pages of Mann's *Doctor Faustus*, which he read in 1952. The first movement of *Musica ricercata*, written from 1951 to 1953, consists of nothing more than the tuning note A arranged in various octaves, until a D enters at the end. The second movement uses three pitches, the third movement four, and so on. All twelve tones circulate in the final movement, but along the way the composer enjoys a rich diversity of material, including a sweet-sad folkish melody that he would revive decades later in his career-summarizing Violin Concerto. He later described some stabbing single notes in the second movement as "a knife in Stalin's heart."

In 1956, a reformist government in Budapest attempted to break away from Soviet control, and troops quickly moved in to put down the uprising. Ligeti, unable to face yet another wave of repression, escaped to the West, hiding under mailbags in a postal train and then dashing over the Austrian border by the light of military flares. He sought refuge in Vienna, where he formed alliances with leaders of the Western European avant-garde. Back in Hungary, he had cherished their works as symbols of creative freedom—on one bloody night in 1956 he stayed glued to a radio broadcast of Stockhausen's *Gesang der Jünglinge*—and from 1957 onward he showed up at Darmstadt in the company of his heroes. But his intimate knowledge of the totalitarian personality made him wary of any musical ideology that was too sure of its rectitude. "I don't like gurus," he said once in an interview, in a discussion of Stockhausen. Years later he gave a testy interview in which he compared the warring camps of Darmstadt to the power struggles within the Nazi and Stalinist regimes. "True, there were no people being liquidated," he said, "but there was certainly character assassination."

Ligeti naturally inclined toward the absurdist end of the avant-garde spectrum—the music about music of Kagel and Schnebel, the conceptualism of Cage. In his 1960 work *Apparitions*, bassoonists play their instruments without reeds, brass players smack their mouthpieces with their hands, and a percussionist is asked to smash a bottle into a crate lined with metal plates ("Be sure to wear protective goggles," the score advises). In 1961 Ligeti performed a Cagean conceptual piece titled *The Future of Music*, in which he stood in front of an unsuspecting audience and wrote instructions on a blackboard: "Crescendo," "più forte," "Silence." The resulting hubbub was the composition. And in 1962 Ligeti unveiled the *Poème Symphonique for 100 Metronomes*, which, true to the title, had one hundred windup metronomes ticking away in concert. Like many Ligeti jokes, this one had a serious undertow. The initial hilarity of the scene—a concert stage filled with inanimate antique machines—gives way to unexpected complexity: as the faster metronomes wind down and stop, spiderwebs of rhythm emerge from the cloud of ticks. As the last survivors wave their little arms in the air, they look lonely, forlorn, almost human.

Impatient with the clichés of musical pointillism, with what he called the pattern of "event - pause - event," Ligeti resolved to restore spaciousness and long-breathed lines to instrumental writing. He took inspiration from Xenakis's *Metastaseis*, Stockhausen's *Carré*, and other examples of late-fifties "texture music." Ligeti's version of the style is called micropolyphony; large structures are assembled from multiple layers of microcosmic contrapuntal activity. That sound first surfaces in the last part of *Apparitions* and crystallizes in the famous *Atmosphères* of 1961. The opening chord of the latter work has fifty-nine notes spread over five and a half octaves: the effect is mysterious rather than assaultive, a seductive threshold to an alien world. Later, half-familiar entities, quasi- or crypto-tonal chords, are glimpsed in the sonic haze. The dominant process in Ligeti's music is one of emergence—shapes come out of the shadows, dark cedes to light.

Raised an atheist, Ligeti never accepted a religious doctrine. Nonetheless, in the mid-sixties, he wrote two religiously inflected works of revelatory impact: *Requiem*, for two soloists, double chorus, and orchestra, and *Lux aeterna*, for sixteen solo voices. They are like no sacred pieces before them. *Requiem* is a twenty-five-minute battering of the senses—a black mass in which singers whisper, mutter, speak, shout, and shriek the Requiem text. In the "Kyrie," the overlapping of individual voices in micropolyphonic style creates the effect of a subhuman howling, of souls melting into a hellish mob. In the closing "Lacrimosa," the cluster harmonies lose their diabolical aspect and give intimations of the music of the spheres: the note G-flat fans out through a widening series of intervals to a primordially humming open fifth on D and A. Coincidentally or not, a similar transformation is said to happen in Adrian Leverkühn's *Apocalipsis cum figuris*, where a choral passage moves "through all the shades of graduated whispering, antiphonal speech, and quasi-chant on up to the most polyphonic song—accompanied by songs that begin as simple noise, as magical, fanatical African drums and booming gongs, only to attain the highest music."

The plateau of "highest music" is maintained in *Lux aeterna* and its companion orchestral piece, *Lontano*. Both works have the character of occult objects, or of dream landscapes in which sound becomes a tangible surface. In the opening section of *Lontano*, micropolyphonic lines creep upward into the very highest ranges of the orchestra, then stop at the edge of an abyss: a blistering high C gives way to an almost inaudibly low D-flat in the tuba and contrabassoon. In the middle section the harmony gravitates toward the key of G minor, and the orchestra plays a ghostly chorale, vaguely recalling the opening lament of Bach's *St. Matthew Passion*. There is a second desperate surge into the treble, followed by a second vertiginous collapse, but now the listener is led onward into a secret tonal paradise of near-resolutions and almost-cadences. Blissful Messiaen-like harmony seems within reach, but the brass push it away with a mournful, honking chord. Triads are scattered through the score in the final pages, but they are clouded and covered so that you can barely hear them. What happens at the end can almost be heard as an "Amen" cadence.

In early 1968, a few months after *Lontano*'s premiere, an American friend wrote to Ligeti with the news that the film director Stanley Kubrick had released a science-fiction epic titled *2001: A Space Odyssey*, in which no fewer than four Ligeti scores—*Requiem*, *Lux aeterna*, *Atmosphères*, and *Aventures*—were heard. Although the director had not asked permission, and paid a fee only after a protracted legal squabble, Ligeti expressed admiration for Kubrick's achievement. The *Requiem* accompanies the various apparitions of an inscrutable black monolith, which represents the invasion of a superior alien intelligence. When the astronaut played by Keir Dullea undertakes his final journey into the beyond, Ligeti's micropolyphony merges hypnotically with Kubrick's abstract light patterns and negative-exposure images of natural landscapes. Among other things, the film neatly brackets the entire arc of twentieth-century musical history. It begins with Strauss's *Thus Spake Zarathustra*, the music of nature's original majesty. In the final section, the movie is subsumed into Ligeti's alternate universe, spiraling through the outer limits of expression before returning to the point of origin. As the august *Zarathustra* chords sound again at the end, the cycle is ready to begin anew.

Saint Francis

Kubrick's *2001* exhilarated sixties-era audiences because Western culture was starved for sacred images. In Europe, churchgoing was in decline, and churches had lost their community-forming function and their ability to generate awe. In America, the theologian Harvey Cox made an improbable appearance on the bestseller lists with the book *The Secular City*, analyzing the rituals of desacralized man, and *Time* magazine ran a cover story asking, "Is God dead?" Temples of culture doubled as sites of spiritual transport—rock arenas no less than classical concert halls. This transference of roles goes back to the late nineteenth century, when Wagner's *Parsifal* created a new kind of sacred space in an industrial world. The bourgeois nineteenth century brought forth relatively few major works of a strictly religious nature; the requiems of Berlioz and Verdi, to name two obvious exceptions, are really Romantic concert spectacles with a Latin text. The godless twentieth century, by contrast, generated devotional masterpieces by the dozen. It seems no accident that both Stravinsky and Schoenberg responded to the decade of the twenties—the century's first extended bout of mass consumption, youth rebellion, and sexual liberation—with, respectively, the *Symphony of Psalms* and *Moses und Aron*.

French-speaking composers seemed particularly susceptible to religious reawakenings. Francis Poulenc, the former prodigy of Les Six, reverted in the thirties to the Catholicism of his childhood and made it his mission to bring "peasant devotion" into his music. First in *Litanies to the Black Virgin*, then in the Mass in G, the *Stabat Mater*, the *Gloria*, and the faith-based drama *Dialogues of the Carmelites*, Poulenc deftly converted his lighter-than-air twenties style into a medium of meditative simplicity, using the *Symphony of Psalms* as a model. (Poulenc's "peasant devotion" could be mistaken for Copland's "open prairie.") Arthur Honegger, Poulenc's comrade in Les Six, broke away from twenties frivolity even as the decade was still getting under way; in his 1921 oratorio *King David*, he told the biblical story ardently and gravely, without a trace of Cocteau-like irony. The French Swiss composer Frank Martin, the son of a Calvinist minister, saw faith as a path not of imminent revelation but of unending struggle. If Messiaen's consonances shine in triumph, Martin's waft enigmatically out of the fog, as in the final measures of each movement of his *Maria-Triptychon* (1968).

The European avant-garde was generally secular in orientation, but it had a few mystics in its midst. Stockhausen's *Gesang der Jünglinge* is the book of Daniel gone high-tech: the electronic fabric approximates the flames that surrounded the three boys in Nebuchadnezzar's furnace. Cage based his aesthetic partly on the precepts of Zen Buddhism. And the unswervingly eccentric Italian composer Giacinto Scelsi emerged from a long immersion in Eastern philosophy with the conviction that he could approximate in instrumental forms the sound of chanting Tibetan monks.

Tibetan chant generally consists of deviations around a fundamental tone, with droning pipes and ringing bells as an accompaniment. Scelsi tried to enact similar rituals on the piano, then made use of the ondiola, an electronic keyboard whose dials allowed him to vary pitch and tone quality. He hired a fellow composer, Vieri Tosatti, to help him shape his ondiola sketches and improvisations into full-fledged orchestral, chamber, and vocal scores, which began appearing in the late 1950s. They generally commence with a generative monotone, and as the central pitch shifts, splits apart, and spreads, novel landscapes open up before the ears. Orchestral works such as the *Four Pieces*, *Aion*, and *Anahit* build to crypto-Romantic climaxes worthy of Bruckner: horns leap up an octave, winds trill on high, timpani bang out thirds, and the heavens open. In *Konx-Om-Pax*, a chorus is added to the mix, chanting an apocalyptic "OM."

It was left to Messiaen to write a religious work on a scale that no composer had attempted since *Parsifal*. The five-hour sacred opera *Saint Francis of Assisi*, which he began sketching in 1975 and finished in 1983, served not merely as a pageant in honor of the humble friar but as a kind of live-action reenactment of the very process of sanctification. *Parsifal* enclosed sacred ritual within a theatrical frame; Messiaen, by contrast, was enclosing theater within religion, creating a new genre of operatic meditation. In the process, he made extraordinary demands on his audience. Act II stretches on for two hours and ends with a forty-five-minute version of Francis's sermon to the birds. *Saint Francis* harks back to those archaic liturgies in which spells of boredom give way to precisely staged epiphanies—as when, in the Greek Orthodox Easter service, the church goes dark and the light of a single candle remains.

Messiaen wrote the libretto himself, elaborating the standard legends of Francis with theology out of Saint Thomas Aquinas. Almost nothing in the text would have come as a shock to an audience of thirteenth-century Loire Valley villagers. There are eight tableaux, each recording a stage in the life of the saint. Francis kisses a leper, encounters a musician angel, speaks to the birds, receives the stigmata, and dies in a state of suffering joy. He is sung by a dramatic baritone voice and comes across as a flesh-and-blood figure. He might be the haggard Francis as depicted in paintings by Caravaggio and Zurbarán—a youngish man gazing ravenously toward the heavens, his mouth hanging open, his hands wrapped around a skull.

The central epiphany of the opera takes place in the fifth tableau, in which Francis meets the musician angel on the road. The episode is taken from Franciscan hagiography, according to which the friar once fainted after hearing an angel play a viol. He told his brethren, "If the Angel had played one more note—if, after down-bowing, it had made an up-bow—from unbearable sweetness my soul would have left my body." In Messiaen's version, the angel prefaces his concert with lines adapted from Aquinas: "God dazzles us by an excess of truth. Music carries us to God in default of truth." (Human reason, Aquinas wrote, is confounded equally by the elusiveness of poetic expression and by the superabundance of the Word of God.) The strings play a soft, unceasing C-major chord; over it, three ondes Martenot unwind a scarlet thread of melody that touches on ten of the twelve chromatic notes. The ears are teased by two textures—warm strings spreading out from the center, electronic tones pinging everywhere. In the space between them listeners can catch a glimpse of whatever they consider divine.

"Certain people are annoyed that I believe in God," Messiaen said in January 1992, three months before his death. "But I want people to know that God is present in everything, in the concert hall, in the ocean, on a mountain, even on the underground." In the end, *Saint Francis* is not as monumental as it appears; it is really a village mystery play on a Wagnerian scale. Anthony Pople got to the heart of the matter when he wrote of Messiaen's refusal to "play God." These reverberating triads exercise such power because they don't sound like the calculated gestures of a master plan; they crash in from a more elemental sphere. *Saint Francis*, true to form, ends in twelve bars of hyperbright C major, replete with rapidly gesticulating brass, trilling and groaning ondes Martenot, madly glissandoing mallet instruments, and a shimmering cascade of bells and gongs. It is the negation of the negation, the death of death.

(((14)))

BEETHOVEN WAS WRONG

Bop, Rock, and the Minimalists

One night in 1967, György Ligeti was sitting with several colleagues at the Darmstadt Schlosskeller, the favorite late-night hangout of teachers and students at the Summer Courses for New Music, when *Sgt. Pepper's Lonely Hearts Club Band*, a new album by the Beatles, started playing over the loudspeakers. Some of the sounds on the record bore a surprising resemblance to the Darmstadters' latest and most advanced experiments. The song "A Day in the Life" included two spells of *ad libitum* playing, the second of them leading into a gorgeously strange E-major chord played by three pianos and a harmonium. Players were given a score indicating what register they should have reached in any given bar. The last chord was executed in musique concrète fashion, the attack cut off and the decay amplified over a long duration.

The Beatles had first dipped into the Darmstadt sound in March of the previous year, while working on the album *Revolver*. Paul McCartney had been checking out Stockhausen's *Gesang der Jünglinge*, with its electronic layering of voices, and *Kontakte*, with its swirling tape-loop patterns. At his request, engineers at Abbey Road Studios inserted similar effects into the song "Tomorrow Never Knows." By way of thanks, the Beatles put Stockhausen's face on the cover of *Sgt. Pepper's Lonely Hearts Club Band*, in and among cutout pictures of other mavericks and countercultural heroes. The following year, for the White Album, John Lennon and Yoko Ono created the tape collage "Revolution 9," where, for a split second, the final chords of Sibelius's Seventh Symphony can be heard. Adventurous rock bands on the West Coast also paid heed to the classical avant-garde. Members of both the Grateful Dead and Jefferson Airplane attended Stockhausen's lectures in Los Angeles in 1966 and 1967, while the maverick rock star Frank Zappa spoke of his teenage love for the music of Edgard Varèse, whom he once looked up in the phone book and called out of the blue.

Even the most jaded veteran of twentieth-century musical upheaval must have been startled to find that the postwar avant-garde was now serving as mood music for the psychedelic generation. The wall separating classical music from neighboring genres appeared ready to crumble, as it had momentarily in the twenties and thirties, when Copland, Gershwin, and Ellington crossed paths at Carnegie Hall. Classical record labels made amusing attempts to capitalize on the phenomenon by marketing abstruse modern repertory to kids on LSD. An LP of Bengt Hambraeus's *Constellations II* and *Interferences* on the Limelight label carried this text on the jacket: "Listening to Bengt Hambraeus's fantastic sound—it's [*sic*] magnificent electronic and organ-organized electronic total sound experience should involve you as much as any music that you are capable of loving . . . be it the sound of The Beatles, Bach, Beethoven, Boulez, Beach Boys, or Belefonte [*sic*], Barbra Streisand, Pearl Bailey, Blue Cheer, or whatever. Hambraeus is really tuned in. Smashing!"

Even as Stockhausen and Ligeti brushed against the counterculture, several younger Americans—Terry Riley, Steve Reich, and Philip Glass—made a different kind of breakthrough. They simplified their harmonic language and rediscovered the pleasure of a steady pulse, devising a modern tonality that had nothing nostalgic about it. What Weill said in the twenties held true again: "Once musicians obtained everything they had imagined in their most daring dreams, they started again from scratch."

Riley, Reich, and Glass came to be called minimalists, although they are better understood as the continuation of a circuitous, difficult-to-name development in American music that dated back to the early years of the century, and more often than not took root on the West Coast. This alternative canon includes Henry Cowell and Lou Harrison, who drew on non-Western traditions and built up a hypnotic atmosphere through insistent repetition; Morton Feldman, who distributed minimal parcels of sound over long durations; and La Monte Young, who made music from long, buzzing drones. All of them in one way or another set aside a premise that had governed classical composition for centuries—the conception of a musical work as a self-contained linguistic activity that develops relationships among discrete thematic characters over a well-marked period of time. This music was, by contrast, open-ended, potentially limitless.

It was a purely American art, free of modernist angst and inflected with pop optimism. Reich said: "Schoenberg gives a very honest musical portrayal of his times. I salute him—but I don't want to write like him. Stockhausen, Berio, and Boulez were portraying in very honest terms what it was like to pick up the pieces of a bombed-out continent after World War II. But for some American in 1948 or 1958 or 1968—in the real context of tail fins, Chuck Berry, and millions of burgers sold—to pretend that instead we're really going to have the dark-brown *Angst* of Vienna is a lie, a musical lie . . ." Reich and his colleagues borrowed from popular music, especially from bebop and modern jazz, and they affected pop music in turn. The Velvet Underground adopted Young's drone aesthetic. Art rockers such as David Bowie and Brian Eno showed up at Reich's and Glass's shows. Minimalist influence radiated outward in the eighties and nineties, to the point where you could walk into any hip boutique or hotel lounge and sooner or later hear some distant, burbling cousin of Reich's *Music for 18 Musicians*.

Eno once summarized minimalism as "a drift away from narrative and towards landscape, from performed event to sonic space." Riley, Reich, and Glass spent their formative years in the urban wilds of New York and San Francisco, but their works have spiritual links to the capacious West. Unlike Copland's sepia-toned prairie, minimalist vistas are filtered through new ways of seeing and hearing that relate to the technology of speed. They evoke the experience of driving in a car across empty desert, the layered repetitions in the music mirroring the changes that the eye perceives—road signs flashing by, a mountain range shifting on the horizon, a pedal point of asphalt underneath.

Bebop

During the two-decade stretch from 1945 to 1965, when the minimalist composers were growing from childhood to maturity, American popular music exploded with creative energy. Jazz, blues, country, and gospel evolved into rhythm and blues, rock 'n' roll, soul, and funk. Hank Williams, a white singer with an ear for the blues, crafted country songs of gem-like beauty; Ray Charles and James Brown fused gospel elation with blues sensuality; Chuck Berry let loose the stripped-down anarchy of rock 'n' roll; Elvis Presley and the Beatles repackaged rock for a huge youth public.

For young American composers with open ears, the Cold War decades were, above all, the age of bebop and modern jazz. Dizzy Gillespie, Charlie Parker, Thelonious Monk, Miles Davis, John Coltrane, and Charles Mingus burst through the formal confines of swing and made music of ricocheting freedom and imperturbable cool. At the height of bop, electric strings of notes lashed around like downed power lines on wet pavement. Two sounds caught the ear of the fourteen-year-old Steve Reich: the punch-drunk rhythm of *The Rite of Spring* and the blindsiding beat of Kenny Clarke. Terry Riley was a bebop kid who later mastered ragtime piano. La Monte Young played excellent alto sax in his youth and probably could have had a major jazz career if he had wanted one. (When Young auditioned for a place in the top-notch Los Angeles City College jazz band, he beat out Eric Dolphy.) Philip Glass never played jazz, but listened avidly. The history of minimalism can't be written without a cursory look at postwar jazz.

It was at the end of the Second World War that many young jazz players began to think of themselves as "*serious* musicians," to quote Amiri Baraka's classic book *Blues People*. Bebop, the poet said, articulated the self-esteem felt by hundreds of thousands of black soldiers as they returned home from the Second World War. When Parker inserted the opening notes of *The Rite of Spring* into "Salt Peanuts," he was paying his respects while also declaring his freedom with a somewhat impudent air. You couldn't dance to "Koko"; you had to sit back and listen as Parker scribbled lightning in the air. Monk threw in angular lines and dissonant chords, softening them with the elegance of his touch. Coltrane relished Bartók's chords of fourths in the Concerto for Orchestra. "We had some fundamental background training in European harmony and music theory superimposed on our own knowledge from Afro-American musical tradition," Gillespie wrote. "We invented our own way of getting from one place to the next."

Ellington, in the twenties, had capitalized on the timbral possibilities of electrical recording. Bebop players took advantage of the next big advance, the long-playing record. The LP side allowed for the creation of half-composed, half-improvised works of mesmerizing breadth, the logical descendants of *Black, Brown, and Beige.* In March 1959, Miles Davis released *Kind of Blue*, which put the brakes on bop's forward drive. "So What," the nine-minute opening track, is a proto-minimalist piece, defined by the dreamlike slowness of the harmonic rhythm. As the melodies drift by and change color, the underlying harmony stays fixed on a D-minor seventh chord, with periodic sidesteps into E-flat minor. Mingus, Coltrane, and Ornette Coleman also abandoned standard progressions in favor of a more open-ended tonal language. Their writing had much in common with the expanded tonality of Debussy, Stravinsky, and Messiaen. When Mingus explicated his "pedal point" style in the notes to his 1963 album *The Black Saint and the Sinner Lady*, he could have been paraphrasing Messiaen's *Technique of My Musical Language*, with its schemes of multiple modes.

Jazz had entered its high-modern era, and assumed a modernist contempt for convention. Monk set the tone: "You play what *you* want, and let the public pick up what *you* are doing—even if it does take them fifteen, twenty years." Miles Davis, in performance, turned his back to the crowd in Schoenbergian fashion. Bebop and dissonant composition drew close enough that there was talk of a merger. In the early sixties the composer and scholar Gunther Schuller propagated the idea of "Third Stream," a confluence of jazz and classical energies. "It is a way of making music," Schuller later wrote, "which holds that *all musics are created equal*, coexisting in a beautiful brotherhood/sisterhood of musics that complement and fructify each other." Schuller brought in the likes of Coleman and Eric Dolphy to perform his brawny twelve-tone compositions, while Coleman asked Schuller for advice, notably while planning his epoch-making 1960 album *Free Jazz*. Anthony Braxton and Cecil Taylor, two other pioneers of free jazz, sounded like atonal composers in exile.

Even in its arcane phase, modern jazz hung on to its dynamism, its physical energy. That spirit proved irresistible to younger classical composers looking for a way out of Schoenberg's maze. Jazz was intuitive, intimate, collaborative; it was serious in thought but playful in execution. Steve Reich remembers attending composition classes where students showed off byzantine scores whose intellectual underpinnings could be discussed ad nauseam. Then he'd go to see Coltrane play with his quartet. He liked the idea that Coltrane could walk out with a saxophone, play freewheeling improvisations on just one or two harmonies, and then disappear into the night. "The music just comes out," Reich later said. "There's no argument. There it is. This presented me with a human choice, almost an ethical, moral choice."

The California Avant-Garde

Reich was living in northern California when he had his Coltrane revelation. A few years later, he created *It's Gonna Rain*, the first example of what he would call "music as a gradual process." Maybe this New York–born composer would have found his way even if he had never left the East Coast, but his move westward brought him into contact with alternative American traditions that had been developing in relative isolation since the second decade of the century, with sporadic infusions from the European émigrés who had come to Los Angeles in the thirties and forties. In fact, the circuitous chain of events that led to minimalism began with a kind of California mutation of the Second Viennese School.

The story begins, oddly and aptly, with Charles Seeger, the future dogmatician of American Popular Front music, who came out to the University of California at Berkeley in 1912 to start a music department. The idea of teaching music in a university was novel enough that Seeger's work fell under the purview of the Department of Agriculture. He held classes in a YMCA, in the Hearst Mining Building, and in a "smelly old house" on Bancroft Way. With no curriculum in place, Seeger felt free to introduce unorthodox ideas. He presented his theory of "dissonant counterpoint," with its anticipations of twelve-tone practice, and also exposed students to early music, folk music, popular music, and non-Western traditions.

The first student to receive a thorough grounding in Seeger's syllabus went on to become the godfather of the American experimental tradition. Henry Cowell was the son of a bohemian Irish poet who settled in San Francisco and hailed it as "an undefiled Eden." Young Henry attracted attention as a child prodigy and gave solo recitals of his piano compositions. One precocious teenage piece, *Adventures in Harmony*, included a flurry of cluster chords, dissonances produced by hitting groups of adjacent keys with the entire hand. Other pieces reduced music to a few essentials: for example, in *The Anaemic Rag* chains of thirds unwind over an open-fifth ostinato.

Cowell enrolled at the University of California in 1914 and studied with Seeger for two crucial years. He also joined a mildly cultish Pismo Beach community called Temple of the People, led by the Theosophist poet John Varian, who proclaimed, "There is a new race birthing here in the West. We are the germic embryonic seed of future majesties of growth." From Varian and other local visionaries Cowell inherited the idea that California would be the eastern frontier of a great Pacific Rim culture, an ecstatic commingling of far-flung peoples. His vision of a Pacific Rim utopia grew to embrace the entire globe. Indian music, Japanese koto and shakuhachi, Balinese gamelan, old American hymns, Gaelic airs, and Icelandic *rímur* all figured in his music at one time or another. He thought nothing of supplementing a string quintet with three Native American thundersticks.

In 1930, Cowell summed up his and Seeger's ideas in an astonishing little book titled *New Musical Resources*, a kind of American *Harmonielehre*, which anticipated many "big ideas" of the postwar avant-garde. One central concept of the book was that harmony and rhythm should be interdependent; since any resonating tone consists of a certain number of vibrations per second, the ratios among the notes in any given chord could be used to dictate the rhythms of any given bar. For example, a chord of G, C, and E would translate into simultaneous pulses of three against four against five. Back in 1917 and 1919, Cowell put these ideas into practice in his *Quartet Romantic* and *Quartet Euphometric*, although he acknowledged that the pieces were (at that time) unplayable.

On one page of *New Musical Resources* Cowell proposed in passing that "highly engrossing rhythmical complexes" could be punched out on the paper roll of a player piano. Conlon Nancarrow, an Arkansas-born composer of radical tendencies who had fought for the Communists during the Spanish Civil War and then gone into Mexican exile, saw a world of possibility in Cowell's suggestion, and relied on his mechanical instrument to execute insanely intricate rhythmic designs that only a many-armed robot pianist could have played. In the notorious *Study No. 33*, for example, tempos are superimposed according to the ratio $\sqrt{2}/2$. This music was maximal rather than minimal, but its jazzy, hyperkinetic energy put it far outside the postwar modernist mainstream.

Harry Partch, the other great West Coast nonconformist of the twenties and thirties, wanted to "find a way *outside*"—to jettison the entire discourse of European music as it had been practiced since at least the time of Bach.

Partch was a true child of the Wild West. He spent much of his childhood in the railway outpost of Benson, Arizona, where his father was a government inspector. According to Bob Gilmore's biography, young Harry caught glimpses of old-school outlaws on the edge of town. Moving to Los Angeles in 1919, Partch studied at the University of Southern California and made money as a movie-house pianist. Stylish, handsome, and gay—homosexuality is a common thread among composers of this time and place—Partch fell in love with a struggling actor named Ramón Samaniego, whom he met when both men were ushers at the Los Angeles Philharmonic. Samaniego ended the affair shortly after changing his name to Ramon Novarro and finding world fame as a silent-movie idol. That experience apparently cemented Partch's determination to reject the mainstream in favor of the companionship of outcasts.

One day Partch asked himself why there are twelve notes in an octave, and couldn't find a satisfactory answer. He buried himself in a study of the history of tuning, paying particular attention to Helmholtz's *On the Sensations of Tone*. He emerged with the conviction that the modern Western system of equal-tempered tuning had to go. In its place, Partch would revive the tuning principles of the ancient Greeks, who, at least in theory, derived all musical pitches from the clean integer ratios of the natural harmonic series.

To this end, Partch invented a scale made up not of twelve notes but of forty-three. Extant instruments were incapable of producing such microtonal shadings, so Partch invented his own; he started by building an Adapted Viola and eventually fashioned an entire private orchestra of bowed, plucked, and keyboard instruments, together with Cloud-Chamber Bowls (Pyrex carboys obtained from the Berkeley Radiation Laboratory), the Kithara (modeled on a harp-like instrument seen on Greek vases), and the awesome Marimba Eroica (whose lowest notes boom forth from five-foot-high blocks). By the same token, Partch rejected modern styles of singing, which he considered artificial. Like Leoš Janáček, he sought to close the gap between song and speech, and his annotations of overheard American conversations bear a striking resemblance to Janáček's transcriptions of Czech. A Western tradition clotted with studied abstractions—what Partch called the "Faustian" strain—would give way to "corporeal music," an art at one with the body and the soul.

On a trip to Europe in the early thirties, Partch aroused the interest of William Butler Yeats, who watched as the young American composer chanted Psalm 137, "By the Rivers of Babylon," while sawing on the Adapted Viola. Yeats was charmed, but the musical establishments of Europe and America ignored or mocked Partch's ideas. By the time he returned to America in 1935, the Great Depression was at its height, and prospects for a conventional career seemed poor.

Partch now made a momentous decision: instead of begging for assistance from patrons or the WPA bureaucracy, he dropped out of civilization entirely, and became a hobo. For several years he crisscrossed the country, riding trains, doing manual labor, sleeping in shelters or in the wild, contracting syphilis, working occasionally as a proofreader, and, all the while, rethinking every parameter of music. In the desert city of Barstow, California, he found a set of inscriptions on a highway railing, which he wrote down for future use. An excerpt:

Car just passed by,
Make that two more, three more.
Do not think they'll let me finish my story.
Here she comes, a truck, not a fuck, but a truck. Just a truck.
Hoping to get the hell out, here's my name—
Johnnie Reinwald, nine-fifteen South Westlake Avenue, Los Angeles

These words reappeared in the 1941 cycle *Barstow*, for baritone and Adapted Guitar. The landscape is nothing like Copland's idealized heartland, where the wheat is plentiful and golden. Partch's songs captured the roughness of life during the Great Depression—you can practically smell rye on the breath of the singer. A lot of people would be hard-pressed to identify *Barstow* as "classical music" at all. It comes closer to the twisted white blues of Frank Zappa, Captain Beefheart, and Tom Waits. The tenuous situation of classical music in America was, for this composer, not a deficit but an advantage. In one essay he wrote: "There is, thank God, a large segment of our population that never heard of J. S. Bach."

Harry Partch passed through the University of Southern California a few years too early to meet Arnold Schoenberg. This was probably just as well, because the grand old man of modern music would almost certainly have taken a dim view of Partch's crusade against equal-temperament tuning. In general, Schoenberg was poorly equipped to comprehend the emergent West Coast aesthetic. For him, the ultimate sin was to repeat an idea unnecessarily ("Hi-yo, Silver!"), whereas the California composers were discovering the joys of insistent repetition and gradual change. Yet Schoenberg became an unlikely mentor for two other major figures of the California avant-garde: Lou Harrison and John Cage.

Harrison, a gentle soul in a century of sacred monsters, was born in 1917, the son of a West Coast Chrysler salesman. His mentors were a formidable group: he studied first with Cowell in San Francisco and then with Schoenberg in Los Angeles, and, during a generally unhappy New York period, he worked closely with Charles Ives and Carl Ruggles. From the ultra-moderns, Harrison acquired a flair for stark, prophetic utterances—questing rivers of chant, machinelike ostinatos, erupting dissonances, enveloping silences. From Cowell he picked up a lifelong love of non-Western traditions, especially the Javanese gamelan. And a reading of Partch's *Genesis of a Music* in 1949 sparked an interest in just intonation, as pure-ratio tuning is known.

Ingrained in Harrison's personality was a love of musical merriment, of hummable song and rollicking dance. He managed to assimilate these diverse strains into forms of Baroque poise and precision; his favorite composer was Handel. "Use only the essentials," Schoenberg once said to his pupil. Harrison's career was a creative misinterpretation of that remark; it gave him permission to vacate the overcrowded city space of modern music and to camp out in a desert landscape of long drones and lulling patterns.

As for Cage, he found the seeds for many of his most extreme inspirations on the West Coast. Cowell passed along his cherished ideas about flexibility of form and the interchangeability of music and noise. Cage took Cowell's classes on non-Western music in New York in 1934 and drove across the country with him at the end of that year; American music was never the same afterward. Harrison helped Cage refine his writing for percussion; the two men organized annual concerts in the San Francisco Bay Area starting in 1939. The California spirit persists in the music that Cage wrote after moving permanently to New York—notably in the string-of-pearl sounds of the prepared-piano pieces and in the "nearly stationary" textures of the *String Quartet in Four Parts*.

Although Cage avoided tonality and repetition in his music from 1950 onward, he hovered over the radical end of American music as a liberating spirit. He had done the preliminary work of dismantling the European "vogue of profundity," as he called it. In 1952, he scandalized a crowd at Black Mountain College by saying that Beethoven had misled generations of composers by structuring music in goal-oriented harmonic narratives instead of letting it unfold moment by moment. At a New York gathering, he was heard to say, "Beethoven was wrong!" The poet John Ashbery overheard the remark, and for years afterward wondered what Cage had meant. Eventually, Ashbery approached Cage again. "I once heard you say something about Beethoven," the poet began, "and I've always wondered—" Cage's eyes lit up. "Beethoven was wrong!" he exclaimed. *"Beethoven was wrong!"* And he walked away.

Cage's definitive refutation of Beethoven came in the form of an epic, almost daylong performance of Erik Satie's piano piece *Vexations*. The original score is only a page long and would normally take just a minute or two to play, but at the top appears this instruction: "In order to play this motif 840 times, one would have to prepare oneself in advance, and in the utmost silence, through serious immobilities." Cage took this sentence at face value, and, on September 9 and 10, 1963, at the Pocket Theatre in New York, he presented *Vexations* complete. A team of twelve pianists played from 6:00 p.m. until 12:40 p.m. the following day. The *New York Times* responded by sending a gang of eight critics to cover the event, one of whom ended up performing. In the audience for part of the time was Andy Warhol, who remembered the experience when he made an eight-hour film of the Empire State Building the following year.

The venue was equipped with a time clock, which patrons punched on entering and leaving. Listeners were reimbursed five cents for each twenty minutes they spent in the hall. Those who saw the entire performance received a twenty-cent bonus. Karl Schenzer, an off-Broadway actor, was the only one to get a full refund, having sat in the hall for nearly nineteen hours. "I feel exhilarated, not at all tired," Schenzer told the *Times*. "Time? What is time? In this music the dichotomy between various aspects of art forms dissolves."

Feldman

It was after a New York Philharmonic performance of Anton Webern's Symphony, on January 26, 1950, that John Cage met a six-foot-tall, nearly three-hundred-pound Jewish guy named Morton Feldman. Both men had walked out of Carnegie Hall early—according to Feldman, because they were dismayed by the hostile response that Webern's music had inspired in Philharmonic listeners; according to Cage, because they wanted to avoid hearing Rachmaninov's *Symphonic Dances*, which ended the program. When their paths crossed by the door, Feldman turned to Cage and asked, "Wasn't that beautiful?" A lifelong friendship began.

The two composers were often mentioned in the same breath, as part of the New York experimental school that also included Christian Wolff and Earle Brown. But Feldman was a singular character—in Steve Reich's words, "an absolutely unforgettable human being." As a conversationalist, he was verbose, egotistical, domineering, insulting, playful, flirtatious, and richly poetic—one of the great talkers in the modern history of New York City. As a composer, he was inward and withdrawn, seldom raising his musical voice above a whisper. His preoccupation with vast, quiet, agonizingly beautiful worlds of sound opened up yet another unmapped space in American music.

Feldman, whom everyone called Morty, was born in 1926, the son of a manufacturer of children's coats. He came of age in the cosmopolitan New York of the thirties and forties, when Fiorello La Guardia championed high art for the working man and European émigrés crowded the streets. In these years a resourceful youth could pick up a world-class education simply by hanging out in seminars and bars across the city. In 1944, Feldman enrolled at NYU, but dropped out after a day or two. Instead, he took a job at his father's factory, and also worked part-time at his uncle's dry cleaners. He held one or another of these jobs until he was forty-four.

Two independent artists from Berlin and Paris—Stefan Wolpe and Edgard Varèse—served as Feldman's mentors. Wolpe had come to New York by way of Palestine, holding fast to his far-left political convictions even as he adopted a hard-driving form of twelve-tone writing. Teacher and student would have long arguments about music's role in society; once, when Wolpe pointed out the window of his Greenwich Village studio and exclaimed that one must write for the man in the street, Feldman looked down and saw, to his ironic delight, Jackson Pollock walking by. Feldman learned much from Wolpe's tensile, shape-shifting atonal scores, but he was closer in spirit to Varèse, the master sculptor of abstract sound. Varèse would tell his young admirer to think of music as an arrangement of objects in space, and to keep in mind how long it takes for any sound to travel through the hall.

Feldman's early works take off from Schoenberg and Bartók, but they move at an unpredictable, fitful pace; in accordance with Varèse's instruction, Feldman periodically stops to let his sonorities reverberate for a while in the listener's mind. Then came the galvanizing meeting with Cage, which led Feldman to invent graphic notation and thereby to inaugurate the age of chance, indeterminacy, and improvisation. More important for his own future development, he launched a parallel series of conventionally notated pieces called *Intermissions* and *Extensions*, which, in the spirit of works such as Webern's Symphony, find a world of meaning in a rigorously limited smattering of notes. In Europe at this time, twelve-tone writing was being used as the blueprint for a congested new serialist order. Feldman, like Cage, understood music of the Second Viennese School as an invitingly strange, quasi-sacred space from which everything extraneous has been scrubbed away. His music is inconceivable without the precedent of the "Colors" movement of Schoenberg's Five Pieces for Orchestra, with its rotating transpositions of one muted chord, or the funeral march of Webern's Six Pieces for Orchestra, with its misty layers of winds and brass over drumrolls.

What Feldman did was to slow the pace of events in the Viennese universe. Schoenberg was, above all, an impatient man, who had to keep scurrying on to the next combination of sounds. Feldman was patient. He let each chord say what it had to say. He breathed. Then he moved on to the next. The textures are daringly sparse. One page of *Extensions 3* has a mere fifty-seven notes in forty bars. In confining himself to so little material, Feldman releases the expressive power of the space around the notes. The sounds animate the surrounding silence. Rhythms are irregular and overlapping, so that the music floats above the beat. Harmonies dwell in a no-man's-land between consonance and dissonance, paradise and oblivion.

Feldman also emulated the New York painters of the forties and fifties, most of whom he knew personally. His scores are close in spirit to Rauschenberg's all-white and all-black canvases, Barnett Newman's gleaming lines, and Rothko's glowing fogbanks of color. Feldman said that New York painting led him to attempt a music "more direct, more immediate, more physical than anything that had existed heretofore." Just as the Abstract Expressionists wanted viewers to focus on paint itself, on its texture and pigment, Feldman wanted listeners to absorb the basic facts of resonant sound. Wilfrid Mellers, in his classic book *Music in a New Found Land,* eloquently summed up Feldman's early style: "Music seems to have vanished almost to the point of extinction; yet the little that is left is, like all of Feldman's work, of exquisite musicality; and it certainly presents the American obsession with emptiness completely absolved from fear."

Yet the unearthly sphere of Feldman's music was not entirely free of fears and memories. The Holocaust had a dominating effect on his consciousness. He once explained that the title of his percussion piece *The King of Denmark* was inspired by King Christian X, who occupied the Danish throne when the Germans invaded his country in 1940. Feldman proceeded to tell the story, now considered apocryphal, of King Christian responding to German anti-Semitism by walking the streets with a yellow star pinned to his chest. It was a "silent protest," Feldman said. All of his music was a silent protest, cutting loose from the ghost-ridden European world. Once, during a visit to Berlin, the American composer Alvin Curran asked him why he didn't move to Germany, since audiences there responded so avidly to his music. Feldman stopped in the middle of the street, pointed down, and said, "Can't you hear them? They're screaming! Still screaming out from under the pavements!"

Another time, when a German new-music expert asked Feldman whether his music was in mourning for the Holocaust, he said that it wasn't, but then he added, in sentences punctuated by long pauses, "There's an aspect of my attitude about being a composer that is like mourning. Say, for example, the death of art . . . something that has to do with, say, Schubert leaving me."

Feldman made his mourning palpable in the 1971 piece *Rothko Chapel*. The title comes from an octagonal array of Rothko paintings that had been installed in a nondenominational religious space in Houston. Rothko had committed suicide the previous year, and Feldman, a close friend, responded with the most personal, affecting work of his life. It is scored for viola, solo soprano, chorus, percussion, and celesta. There are voices but no words. Chords and melodic fragments float along like shrouded forms, surrounded by thick silence. The viola offers wide-ranging, rising-and-falling phrases. The drums roll and tap at the edge of audibility. Celesta and vibraphone chime gentle clusters. There are fleeting echoes of past music, as when the chorus sings distantly dissonant chords reminiscent of the voice of God in Schoenberg's *Moses und Aron*, or when the soprano sings a thin, quasi-tonal melody that echoes the vocal lines of Stravinsky's *Requiem Canticles*. That passage was written on the day of Stravinsky's funeral, April 15, 1971—another thread of lament in the pattern. But the emotional sphere of *Rothko Chapel* is too large to be considered a memorial for any individual.

Shortly before the end comes an astonishing shift. The viola begins to play a keening, minor-key, modal song, redolent of the synagogue. Feldman had written this music decades earlier, during the Second World War, when he was attending the High School of Music and Art, in New York. It is a gesture comparable to the moment in *Wozzeck* when Berg relies on his old student piece in D minor to provide the climax of the drama. Underneath the melody, celesta and vibraphone play a murmuring four-note pattern, which suggests Stravinsky's *Symphony of Psalms*. The song is heard twice, and both times the chorus answers with the Schoenbergian chords of God.

These allusions suggest that Feldman is creating a divine music, appropriate to the somber spirituality of Rothko's chapel. In a sense, he is fusing two different divinities, representative of two major strains in twentieth-century music: the remote, Hebraic God of Schoenberg's opera and the gentle, iconic presence of Stravinsky's symphony. Finally, there is the possibility that the melody itself, that sweet, sad, Jewish-sounding tune, speaks for those whom Feldman once heard crying beneath the cobblestones. It might be the chant of millions in a single voice.

No less than Messiaen, Feldman was in the business of creating places of spiritual otherness, which in his case may have had some connection to medieval kabbalistic thought. In his last years, from 1979 to 1987, he wrote a series of works that went on for an hour or two hours or even longer, straining the capabilities of performers to play them and audiences to hear them. Extreme length allowed Feldman to approach his supreme goal of making music a life-changing force, a transcendent art form that, as he once said, "wipes everything out" and "cleans everything away." To sit through performances of the two longest pieces—*String Quartet (II)* of 1983 and *For Philip Guston* of 1984, six and five hours long respectively—is to enter into a new consciousness. Some passages test the listener's patience—how long can a repeated note or a semitone dissonance be endured? Then, out of nowhere, some very pure, almost childlike idea materializes. Most of the closing section of *For Philip Guston* is in modal A minor, and it is music of surpassing tenderness, even if it inhabits a far-off place that few travelers will chance upon.

Feldman's music can be called "minimalist" if the word is understood to mean a minimum of notes on the page. He was not unlike Partch in his refusal to identify with what he called "Western civilization music." And his feeling for the positioning of music in space puts him in the company of West Coast composers from both early and late in the twentieth century. But, ultimately, he stands apart from his time. No twentieth-century composer, with the possible exception of Sibelius in his last years, achieved such imperturbable separateness; and no wonder Feldman fell in love with Sibelius's Fourth and Fifth symphonies.

Uptown, Downtown

Feldman once delivered a merciless sketch of the prospects of the American composer. He starts out as a romantic, Feldman said, a budding genius overflowing with original ideas, or at least with ideas about originality. Then he goes off to university and discovers that romanticism is defunct. He studies for six years at Princeton or Yale, learning about twelve-tone writing, total serialism, indeterminacy, and the rest. He goes to Darmstadt and samples the latest wares of the European avant-garde. "He writes a piece occasionally," Feldman wrote. "It is played occasionally. There is always the possibility of a performance on the Gunther Schuller series. His pieces are well made. He is not without talent. The reviews aren't bad. A few awards—a Guggenheim, an Arts and Letters, a Fulbright—this is the official musical life of America."

Essentially, Feldman pictured the life of an academic composer as a kind of living death. Since he himself taught for the latter part of his life at the State University of New York at Buffalo, his stance might be deemed hypocritical. But he insisted that composition could not actually be taught, and in his classes he meandered all over the map—one eccentric assignment being to analyze Sibelius's Fifth.

In the late sixties and early seventies, twelve-tone composers were reaching the height of their influence. By some accounts, they effectively took control of university composition departments across the country. Milton Babbitt, who was usually named as the mastermind of this conspiracy, later protested that reports of his omnipotence were exaggerated. "Would that I had known," Babbitt wrote, "over whom or what I held sway, for I surely couldn't infer it from the number or venues of my performances, publications, or recordings, or my inability to secure a mere Guggenheim fellowship."

No matter who was running the show, young composers with tonal yearnings found little happiness in academia, as colorful testimonials from composers and musicians in Michael Broyles's book *Mavericks and Other Traditions in American Music* suggest. George Rochberg said: "[Twelve-tone composers] have proclaimed an orthodox cultural church, with its hierarchy, gospels, beliefs, and anathemas." Michael Beckerman said: "Trying to write tonal music at a place like Columbia University in the 1960s and '70s was like being a dissident in Prague in the same period, with similar professional consequences." William Mayer used a homelier high-school metaphor: "To be a tonal composer in the '60s and '70s was a deeply dispiriting experience. One was shunned as the last teen-aged virgin."

By the end of the sixties, the youth were rebelling against what Babbitt called "complex, advanced, and 'problematical' activities." Rochberg, who had made his name with toughly argued abstract pieces, reverted to the harmonic vocabulary of late-period Beethoven in his Third String Quartet. David Del Tredici, another twelve-tone prodigy, indulged his Romantic inner self in a series of pieces inspired by Lewis Carroll's Alice in Wonderland stories, the later installments orchestrated somewhat in the manner of Strauss's *Symphonia domestica*. Others returned to tonality along the more roundabout path of collage. Lukas Foss, in his 1967 *Baroque Variations*, distorted Handel, Scarlatti, and Bach; George Crumb injected his sumptuously layered, timbre-driven pieces with quotations from Bach, Schubert, Mahler, and Ravel, not to mention all-American twangs of banjo and guitar. The boldest of neotonalists was William Bolcom, a devoted student of Milhaud, whose evening-length William Blake oratorio, *Songs of Innocence and of Experience* (1956–81), devoured everything from Shaker hymns to reggae.

These new American Romantics found common ground with surviving members of the old populist generation, who enjoyed the unfamiliar feeling of being au courant. Bolcom's wild eclecticism resembled Leonard Bernstein's in *Candide* and *Mass*, while his veneration for the French lyric tradition matched that of Ned Rorem, who had long been writing plainspoken, pensive music in uncompromising loyalty to his core principles.

For composers steeped in the experimental tradition of Cowell and Cage, this squabble between neo-Romantic and die-hard atonal composers meant nothing. From their vantage point, it was essentially a dispute over which aspect of the European inheritance—the late Romantic or the high modern—should hold sway. Such is the analysis set forward by the composer Kyle Gann in some trenchant commentaries on late-twentieth-century music. Gann lumps both "modernists" and "New Romantics" together in the "uptown" category, named for the Upper West Side of New York City, home of Lincoln Center, the Juilliard School, Carnegie Hall, Columbia University, and other richly endowed institutions. Downtown composers are those who, in Harry Partch's words, look for "a way *outside*"—anti-European, anti-symphonic, anti-operatic. They descend from the free spirits who had long gone their own way on the West Coast. In New York such composers have tended to congregate in loft spaces, art galleries, and rock clubs below Fourteenth Street.

"Downtown" as a musical construct dates back to the pioneer days of Edgard Varèse, who took up residence in Greenwich Village and wandered the lower end of Manhattan in search of musical noise. But it really got going after the Second World War, when Cage and Feldman unleashed chance in a tenement by the East River. By the late fifties, young Cageans were converging on New York from around the country. One of them, James Tenney of Silver City, New Mexico, moved to New York in 1961, and paid tribute to the city in the pathbreaking computer piece *Analog #1*, an oceanic surge of sound inspired by the noise of traffic in the Holland Tunnel. When Cage taught a class in experimental composition at the New School, the likes of Jackson Mac Low, Al Hansen, George Brecht, and Dick Higgins, all conceptual troublemakers who went on to co-found the neo-Dada movement Fluxus, were taking notes. In the name of Fluxus, violins were smashed (Nam June Paik's *One for Violin Solo*, 1962), pianos were dismantled (Philip Corner's *Piano Activities*, 1962), and Stockhausen concerts were picketed (Henry Flynt employed the slogan "STOCKHAUSEN—PATRICIAN 'THEORIST' OF WHITE SUPREMACY: GO TO HELL!" in 1964).

The spirit of "downtown" also crossed the flat spaces of the Midwest, touching down in the university towns of Oberlin, Ann Arbor, Champaign-Urbana, and Iowa City. Gann calls experimentalists in these places the "I-80 avant-garde," after the interstate highway that cuts across the upper Midwest. Their chief gathering place was the ONCE Festival in Ann Arbor, which ran from 1961 to 1965. Composers "took matters into their own hands," as ONCE's co-founder Gordon Mumma said, by creating a new-music center that relied on no single institution for support. The music tended from the difficult toward the freakish: Robert Ashley, Mumma's chief collaborator, made a virtue of howling feedback in his voice-and-tape piece *The Wolfman*. Media were mixed in inventive ways; ONCE pioneered an early version of the psychedelic light show.

The Interstate 80 composers later conspired with the Boston-based ex–neoclassical composer Alvin Lucier, who had fastened on to Cage and gone off the deep end while teaching on the relatively demure campus of Brandeis University. In *Music for Solo Performer* (1965), Lucier made himself a kind of mind-control test subject by attaching electrodes to his head and broadcasting his brain's alpha waves to loudspeakers around the room, the low-frequency tones causing nearby percussion instruments to vibrate.

For *I am sitting in a room* (1969), Lucier recorded himself reciting the following text: "I am sitting in a room different from the one you are in now. I am recording the sound of my speaking voice and I am going to play it back into the room again and again until the resonant frequencies of the room reinforce themselves so that any semblance of my speech, with perhaps the exception of rhythm, is destroyed." The piece simply enacts that process. Lucier had a pronounced stutter, and one result of the rerecording process was to systematically erase his vocal tic, leaving only wordless tones behind. Partch's idea of corporeal music, music rooted in the voice and the body, was going strong.

Out on the West Coast, the "downtown" aesthetic was headquartered in the San Francisco Bay Area, where Cowell had launched the experimental tradition decades before. The San Francisco Tape Music Center started up in 1961 under the aegis of the San Francisco Conservatory, but was thrown off the premises after a concert in which, as Gann writes, "dancers went around spraying the audience with perfume as a found tape was played of a woman talking to her minister about her out-of-wedlock baby." In 1966 the center found a home at Mills College. Its principal personalities were Pauline Oliveros, a Texas-born composer-accordionist who blended cool soundscapes with raw human voices, and Morton Subotnick, an Angeleno whose all-electronic works made products of the previous decade sound quaint. Subotnick's 1967 synthesizer rhapsody *Silver Apples of the Moon* became a surprise bestseller on the Nonesuch label, its alternately abstract and propulsive swirls of synthesized sound entrancing college kids of the Beatles generation. But perhaps the most significant of the Tape Center's activities was a performance that it hosted in 1964: the premiere of Terry Riley's *In C.*

West Coast Minimalism

Minimalism proper begins with La Monte Young, the master of the drone. He was born in 1935 in a tiny dairy community in Idaho, and spent his childhood listening to the secret music of the wide-open landscape—the microtonal chords of power lines, the harsh tones of drills and lathes, the wailing of far-off trains, the buzzing songs of grasshoppers, the sound of the wind moving over Utah Lake and whistling through the cracks of his parents' log cabin. In 1940 he moved to Los Angeles with his family. As he later said, he fell in love with California's "sense of space, sense of time, sense of reverie, sense that things could take a long time, that there was always time."

It took a while for Young to bring that spaciousness to his music. Early on he adhered to bebop jazz and twelve-tone music, which, as Gunther Schuller liked to say, often sounded like the same thing. Young's teacher at Los Angeles City College was Leonard Stein, who had long served as Schoenberg's personal assistant. Later, at UCLA and Berkeley, Young joined the international cult of Webern. But he interpreted Webern's twelve-tone pieces in a fresh, unexpected way. He noticed, for example, that any one note in a Webern row tended to come back in the same register (high, low, middle) and that those recurring notes created hidden through-lines in the music. He made it his mission to bring those continuities to light. Like Feldman, he slowed the pace of events in the twelve-tone cosmos, only in his case each note in the series became an extended tone, or "long tone," as he called it. Twelve-tone writing became something like Tai Chi, combat in slow motion.

Young wrote his first long-tone work, *for Brass*, in June 1957. The following summer, at Berkeley, he wrote a Trio for Strings, which has all the headlong momentum of continental drift. In a 1989 performance timed by Edward Strickland, the viola began with a sustained C-sharp and was joined fifty-one seconds later by a violin playing E-flat. The whole-tone interval lasted for more than a minute before the cello entered with a D. The three notes clashed for one minute and forty-two seconds before the instruments began dropping out at the same glacial pace.

To hear the piece is to enter into the same kind of waking dream state that is encouraged by Feldman's later music. Events move so slowly that you can no longer detect the twelve-tone motion of the piece, or even the identities of the tones themselves. You become accustomed to the rapid beats of clashing frequencies. And you wait for the revelatory moments when the composer rediscovers clear intervals such as the fourth and the fifth. The Trio ends with a C and a G on the cello, sounding for minutes on end and then dying away *ppppp*. That glowing open fifth points the way to minimalist tonality.

When Young presented his Trio to his Berkeley colleagues, they reacted with disbelief, although two of the younger composers, Terry Jennings and Dennis Johnson, picked up on the long-tone concept. In 1959

Young ventured to Stockhausen's composition seminar in Darmstadt, where he made contact with many kindred spirits, notably John Cage. Under Cage's influence Young veered toward conceptual art: works that involved furniture being dragged across floors, garbage cans thrown down stairwells, butterflies released in the performance space, and fires built onstage. Here are three scores in their entirety:

> *Composition 1960 #10*: Draw a straight line and follow it.
>
> *Composition 1960 #15*: This piece is little whirlpools out in the middle of the ocean.
>
> *Piano Piece for David Tudor #3*: Most of them were very old grasshoppers.

As these works were being written, the Berkeley music department awarded Young a travel fellowship—according to legend, to get him out of town. Downtown New York welcomed him. With the electronic composer Richard Maxfield, Young curated a series of concerts at the downtown loft of the expatriate Japanese artist Yoko Ono, who, at that time, was married to the avant-garde composer Toshi Ichiyanagi.

In a few short years Young went from being a Webern disciple to a sort of musical shaman. For some time he had been experimenting with drugs, especially mescaline; an Andy Warhol associate later described him as "the best drug connection in New York." But Young claimed that he would have followed the same path even if he had never dabbled in psychedelics. Just as important was his exploration of Indian music, in which the tambura drones the tonic note as the rest of the ensemble plays. (His guru in later years was the North Indian classical singer Pandit Pran Nath.) The drone took center stage in *Composition 1960 #7*, which takes off where Trio for Strings left off, with the sound of an open fifth. The score consists of the notes B and F-sharp, below which is the instruction "To be held for a long time."

By the early sixties Young had dropped notated composition in favor of evening-length ritual improvisations, which he dubbed the Theatre of Eternal Music. The first Eternal Music event happened in 1963, on a New Jersey farm, and in tribute to Young's childhood fascination with the sounds of power plants it was called *The Second Dream of the High-*

Tension Line Stepdown Transformer. This led to a tetralogy called *The Four Dreams of China*, each part of which was based on different arrangements of the pitches C, F-natural, F-sharp, and G. The performers were Young, who played sopranino saxophone; Young's companion Marian Zazeela, who sang or intoned; the musician-poet Angus MacLise, who beat African rhythms on bongos; and, particularly critical in the evolution of the sound, the violinist-composer Tony Conrad, who had studied up on the just-intonation music of Harry Partch, Lou Harrison, and Ben Johnston. Later in 1963 the group took in the young Welsh composer John Cale, who strung a viola with electric-guitar strings and let loose drones of incomparable roaring power. Nothing like this had been heard in notated music, because there was no way to notate it. Nothing like it had been heard in jazz, either, although the free jazz of Sun Ra and Albert Ayler came close. Young had reached the outer limits, and he remains there still, presiding in guru style over musical rituals in his Church Street loft.

Young has never written anything resembling conventional tonal music. For some reason, his ears have a strong aversion to the fifth partial of the harmonic series, which is tied to the interval of the major third. Without the major third, triads are impossible. Terry Riley's contribution was to add the sweet sound of triads to the long-tone process. This move completed the minimalist metamorphosis.

An easygoing character of the rural-hippie type, Riley grew up in the foothills of the Sierra Nevada. He met Young in 1958 while studying at Berkeley. "What La Monte introduced me to," Riley said, "was this concept of not having to press ahead to create interest." Young also introduced Riley to the postserialist tendencies of marijuana and mescaline. Feeling the pull of Young's shamanistic world, Riley wrote his own long-tone String Trio. In it the viola drones the notes A and C-sharp—the major third that Young preferred to avoid.

While working at the San Francisco Tape Music Center alongside Subotnick and Oliveros, Riley strung loops of tape between the reels of one or more tape recorders, elabroating techniques that Stockhausen had used in *Kontakte*. Riley's first tape-loop work was called *Mescalin Mix*. In 1962 he went to France, where he made a living playing lounge piano at

Strategic Air Command bases; in the off-hours he kept on tinkering with tape. One day in a French radio studio he said to the engineer, "I want this kind of long, repeated loop." The engineer—"a very straight guy in a white coat," Riley recalled—ran a piece of tape through two machines and set one on record and the other on play. When a sound was fed into this extended loop, it would replicate itself, building into a layered blur of beats and textures. Riley called the effect "time-lag accumulation technique" and he decided to mix it with live performance. He hooked up with the jazz trumpeter Chet Baker, who had just served time in jail for heroin possession. Riley, Baker, and others improvised an accompaniment to Ken Dewey's play *The Gift*. The tune they jammed on was, naturally, Miles Davis's "So What."

On returning to America in February 1964, Riley heard the Theatre of Eternal Music in New York and likened it to "the sun coming up over the Ganges." He then set to work on an instrumental piece that would unite static drones and busy loops, that would somehow move quickly and slowly at the same time. The score took the form of a chart of fifty-three "modules," or brief motivic figures. Each player in the ensemble is instructed to proceed from one module to the next at his or her own pace, tailoring the music to the needs of the instrument and the desires of the moment. The modules derive from the seven notes of the C-major scale, with a few F-sharps and B-flats thrown in for good measure. No matter what choices are made in performance, the harmony tends to move into E minor in the middle and into G major (the dominant of C) toward the end, with the B-flats supplying a touch of blues at the close. Tying the whole thing together is a pair of high Cs on the piano, pulsing without variation from beginning to end. Hence the title: *In C.*

The premiere took place on November 4, 1964. Alfred Frankenstein, the broad-minded critic of the *San Francisco Chronicle*, wrote a review that remains the best description of the piece: "Climaxes of great sonority and high complexity appear and are dissolved in the endlessness. At times you feel you have never done anything all your life long but listen to this music and as if that is all there is or ever will be."

Playing electric piano that night was the twenty-eight-year-old Steve Reich. He'd moved to northern California in 1961 and met Riley in the spring of 1964. It was Reich's idea to introduce the chiming Cs and thus to organize the piece around a crisp, unvarying pulse. The aesthetic tension at the heart of *In C*—between Riley's lust for liberation and Reich's liking for order—anticipated the divergent trajectories of the two composers in coming years. Riley threw himself into hippie culture, attracting throngs of tie-dyed fans with all-night improvisations on electronically enhanced saxophone and organ. Liner notes for his 1969 album *A Rainbow in Curved Air* look forward to the lamentably still unrealized moment when "the Pentagon was turned on its side and painted purple, yellow & green . . . The concept of work was forgotten." Reich, on the other hand, cast off psychedelic trappings and made minimalism a rapid-fire urban discourse. The endless highway led back to New York.

New York Minimalism

Circa 2000, you could ride the subway to the lower end of Manhattan, emerge onto a street within sight of the Brooklyn Bridge, walk for a minute or two, press a buzzer marked REICH, and hear a crisp voice say, "Come on up." The composer does not look the part of a musical revolutionist. Within his black button-down shirts and signature baseball cap, he fits the image of an independent film director, a cultural-studies professor, or some other out-in-the-world intellectual. Once he starts speaking, you feel the peculiar velocity of his mind. He is as much a listener as a talker, although he talks at blistering speed. He reacts swiftly to slight sounds in his midst—the soft buzz of a cell phone, a siren on the street outside, the whistle of a teakettle. Each sound contains information. The 1995 work *City Life* conveys what it would be like to experience the world through Reich's ears: the hidden melodies of overheard conversations and the rhythms of pile drivers melt together into a smoothly flowing five-movement composition, a digital symphony of the street.

Reich was born one year after Young and Riley, in 1936. His parents, of Eastern European and German-Jewish descent, separated when he was still a baby, and he spent much of his childhood riding trains between New York and Los Angeles, where his mother moved to pursue a career as singer and lyricist. He later said that the clickety-clack of wheels on rails helped shape his rhythmic sense. And he offered a melancholy reflection: "If I had been in Europe during this period, as a Jew I would have had to ride on very different trains." In one of his finest later works, *Different Trains*, he combined the voices of Pullman porters with those of

Holocaust survivors over a nervously mournful string-quartet accompaniment, joining American idyll to European horror.

Like many American teenagers of the fifties, Reich grew up listening to music on recordings. Bach's Fifth Brandenburg Concerto, Stravinsky's *Rite of Spring*, and bebop records featuring Charlie Parker, Miles Davis, and Kenny Clarke played nonstop on his turntable. After majoring in philosophy at Cornell, Reich switched to music and studied composition at Juilliard, where one of his fellow students was Philip Glass. Feeling the call of West Coast freedom, he moved to San Francisco and enrolled in the music school at Mills College. Although Darius Milhaud was then the dominant presence on the Mills faculty, the principal attraction for a jumpy young composer such as Reich was Luciano Berio, who was a visiting professor in the early sixties. Impressed by the intellectual force in the twelve-tone method, Reich spent his days analyzing Webern scores under Berio's tutelage. Yet tonal harmonies kept cropping up in his works, prompting the undogmatic Berio to say to him, "If you want to write tonal music, why don't you write tonal music?"

At night Reich haunted the jazz clubs, seeing John Coltrane at least fifty times. He also wore out 78-rpm recordings of polyrhythmic African drumming and studied A. M. Jones's classic treatise on African rhythm, which provided a blueprint for a music of multiple interlocking patterns. San Francisco prankster culture beckoned; starting in 1963, Reich was the house composer for various mess-with-your-head productions by the San Francisco Mime Troupe, the most notorious of which was a satire of racial stereotypes titled *Minstrel Show*. With two other Berio students, Phil Lesh and Tom Constanten, Reich formed an improvisation group of uncertain classification. He and Lesh also presented *Event III/Coffee Break*, blending live and tape music, street theater by the Mime Troupe, and a light show (the spirit of ONCE gone west). Having completed his master's at Mills, Reich bowed out of academic life and never looked back. Rather than seek a Guggenheim or an assistant professorship, he drove a taxi and worked at the post office.

In the fall of 1964, while the Free Speech Movement was flaring up on the Berkeley campus, Reich was pursuing his own tape-loop experiments. In San Francisco's Union Square, he recorded a Pentecostal preacher named Brother Walter, who was sermonizing on the subject of Noah and the Flood. The tape included the words: "[God] began to warn the people. He said, 'After a while, it's gonna rain, after a while, for forty days and for forty nights.' And the people didn't believe him, and they began to laugh at him, and they began to mock him, and they began to say, '*It ain't gonna rain!*'"

At the time, Reich was suffering through a painful divorce, and, along with the rest of the country, he felt spiritually battered by the Cuban missile crisis of 1962 and the Kennedy assassination of 1963. Brother Walter's anguished prophecy of "It's gonna rain!" articulated his free-floating feelings of panic and fear.

One day in January 1965, Reich was sitting in front of two tape decks with the words "It's gonna rain" cued up on each. His intention was to cut quickly from "It's gonna" on one machine to "rain" on the other. But he had lined up the tapes wrong, and when he hit play, they sounded in unison: "*It's gonna rain! It's gonna rain! It's gonna rain!*" He was reaching to shut them off when he became aware of an interesting phenomenon. One tape was playing slightly faster than the other, so that the unison began to break up into a phasing pattern: "*It's-s gonna-a rain-n! It's-'s gonn-nna rai-in! It's-t's gonna-onna rai-ain! It's-it's gonna-gonna rain-rain!*" Listening on stereo headphones, with one ear tuned to the left machine and the other to the right, Reich had a physical reaction to the sound. "It's an acoustical reality that if you hear one sound a fraction of a second after another it appears to be directional," he later said. "The feeling here was that the sound was going over to my left ear and coming down my left shoulder and down my leg and out on to the floor."

The remarkable thing about the tape piece *It's Gonna Rain* is not just the intricacy of the rhythmic patterns but the almost operatic power of the voice itself. Reich doesn't reduce Brother Walter's sermon to a found object in a collage; instead, he magnifies the emotion inherent in the voice to an almost unbearable degree. In 1964, that outsider black preacher probably caused passersby to wince and walk faster. Now his warning will ring out forever, or as long as recordings last.

By the summer of 1965, psychedelia was in full swing. The surreal provocations of the Mime Troupe gave way to Acid Tests, radical demonstrations, parties curated by the Hells Angels. Bill Graham, the business manager of the Mime Troupe, saw the commercial possibilities of new bands like Jefferson Airplane, the Warlocks, and the Mothers of Invention. Later that year he opened the Fillmore, which became the epicenter of the scene. Phil Lesh, his mind forever altered by a night during which he had tripped on LSD while listening to Mahler's Sixth Symphony at high volume, abandoned composition to play bass for the Warlocks, who later became the Grateful Dead.

Reich grew uneasy with the scene. Sidestepping a question about drugs, he told the writer Keith Potter: "In the group of people I seemed to form a contact with, I did not feel on solid psychic footing." In September 1965 he returned to New York, taking with him the sublime accident of *It's Gonna Rain*.

For most of 1966 Reich contemplated the mechanics of his phasing procedure. In one sense, all he'd done was to isolate a technological quirk: the machines essentially wrote *It's Gonna Rain* by themselves, and he was simply smart enough not to stop them. Many radical American works of the sixties and seventies were created this way, with the composer setting up a musical situation and sitting back to observe the outcome; it was an attitude that originated with Cage, the master of coordinated accidents. The English composer Michael Nyman, in his book *Experimental Music*, dubbed minimalism a subspecies of "process" music, classifying it alongside the chance processes of Cage, the "people processes" of Frederic Rzewski (players going through their parts at their own speeds), and the electronic processes of Lucier and Ashley. But minimalism was a different kind of process from the start. Composers immediately grasped all kinds of opportunities—temptations, the pure Cagean might say—to interfere with the playing out of the process, to bend it toward a more personal mode of expression.

In his next tape piece, *Come Out*, Reich made use of another angry African-American voice, that of Daniel Hamm, one of six African-American boys who were beaten up in a Harlem police precinct house in 1964. "I had to, like, open the bruise up and let some of the bruise blood come out to show them," Hamm said on tape.

Reich isolated the phrase "come out to show them." Again, the loops go out of phase, splitting onto four channels and then onto eight. After a while the words become unintelligible, although the pitches inherent in them—E-flat, C, D, C—persist. You are essentially listening to an electronic canon for eight seething voices in the key of C minor. Reich later extended this technique of generating pitch from speaking voices in *Different Trains*, and also in the "video operas" *The Cave* and *Three Tales*, co-created with Beryl Korot.

Reich now had another brainstorm: he decided to transpose the going-out-of-phase effect to instrumental music. He made an early attempt in the score to Robert Nelson's short film *Oh Dem Watermelons*, part of the Mime Troupe's *Minstrel Show* spectacle of 1965; that work, incidentally, makes ironic use of the Stephen Foster tune "Massa's in de Cold Ground," which figures hauntingly in the music of Charles Ives. Far more convincing was *Piano Phase* (1966–67), a twenty-minute work generated from various permutations of the first six notes of the A-major scale. As two pianists move in and out of sync with each other, an eventful narrative ensues, replete with modulations, transitions, and climaxes. The opening section uses only the notes E, F-sharp, B, C-sharp, and D, which, when run together in rapid patterns, suggest the key of B minor. Halfway in, the note A is added, nudging the harmony toward A major. As in *It's Gonna Rain* and *Come Out*, a cool process stealthily takes on emotion: when that A enters, it never fails to have a brightening, energizing, gladdening impact on the mind.

In 1968 Reich spelled out his new aesthetic in a terse essay titled "Music as a Gradual Process." "I am interested in perceptible processes," he wrote. "I want to be able to hear the process happening throughout the sounding music."

This philosophy differs starkly from the thinking inherent in Boulez's total serialism and Cage's *I Ching* pieces, where process works behind the scenes, like a spy network employing front organizations. Reich's music transpires in the open air, every move audible to the naked ear. Recognizable in it are multiple traces of the creator's world: modal jazz, psychedelic trance, the lyrical rage of African-American protest, the sexy bounce of rock 'n' roll. But there's no pretense of authenticity, no longing for the "real." Instead, sounds from a variety of sources are mediated by technology, broken down by repetition, folded into the composer's personal voice. As Reich once said, in an ingenious aphorism, "All music turns out to be ethnic music." The composer becomes an antenna receiving signals, a satellite gathering messages from around the globe.

• • •

In 1968 and 1969, the culture tilted toward chaos and madness. Violence filled the news—the assassinations of Robert Kennedy and Martin Luther King, the massacre at My Lai in Vietnam, riots on university campuses and in inner cities. Harry Partch's onetime lover Ramon Novarro was tortured to death by a hustler intent on finding money hidden in his home. Richard Maxfield, whose 1960 tape piece *Amazing Grace* anticipated minimalism in its use of intersecting loops, flung himself out of a San Francisco window, his mind undone by drugs. And, in August 1969, Charles Manson directed his followers to commit grisly murders in the canyons of Los Angeles, citing the Beatles' White Album as inspiration.

That same month Reich conceived *Four Organs*, in its own way a cruel, end-of-the-world piece. When the electric organs of the title are amplified at full volume, they become a crushing mass. Yet it seems that a musical center, if not a social one, can still hold. The piece is rooted in a set of six notes that sound like a big dominant-eleventh chord on E, one that longs for resolution to the key of A. As maracas provide a steady pulse in 11/8 meter, the notes of the chord are prolonged by degrees and the harmony rotates this way and that. After many changes, it comes to rest on E and A. As Reich commented to Edward Strickland, the ending of the piece is contained within the opening chord, so that it is a matter not of traveling from one place to another but of uncovering the destination inside the point of departure.

In the last years of the twentieth century, minimalism acquired a degree of popularity with mainstream audiences, saturating American music with its influence. But in the early years it caused a fair amount of distress. When *Four Organs* was played at Carnegie Hall in 1973—at a concert by the Boston Symphony under the direction of Michael Tilson Thomas—an elderly woman went to the front of the hall and repeatedly struck the edge of the stage with her shoe, demanding that the performance stop. Someone else shouted, "All right, I'll confess!"

Since the Schoenberg revolution began, audiences had been pleading for contemporary composers to return to the plain old major and minor chords. Now the minimalists were giving them more tonality than they could handle. Reich, a meticulous man with no urge to provoke, had the honor of setting off the last great scandal concert of the century.

• • •

Having invented a new kind of music, Reich needed to find a new breed of performers to play it, a new kind of space in which to present it, and, not least, a new audience to hear it. He elected to form his own ensemble, which came to be called Steve Reich and Musicians, and put on performances in whatever venues accommodated him—art galleries, warehouses, rock clubs, even discos. The group acted more like a jazz combo than a purebred classical ensemble. Like his hero Coltrane, Reich could rent a space, perform, pack up, and walk into the night.

The downtown New York arts scene embraced this new sound from the start, as it had Cage's and Feldman's music some years before. In March 1967 Reich put together a series of concerts at Paula Cooper's Park Place cooperative on West Broadway, and in 1969 he performed at the Whitney Museum as part of a multimedia show called Anti-Illusion. Practitioners of so-called minimal art—in particular, the conceptual artist Sol LeWitt and the sculptors Richard Serra and Donald Judd—responded instinctively to what Reich was doing. Perceived affinities between Reich's geometric arrays of musical modules, LeWitt's geometric arrays of white cubes, and Serra's geometric arrays of plates and rods brought the term "minimalism" into musical circulation.

As with most A-B comparisons between music and other arts, the linkage is partly a matter of intellectual convenience. Minimalist painting and sculpture remained arts of abstraction. Minimalist music, with its restoration of tonality, rejected abstraction and often came closer to the spirit of the Pop Art of Robert Rauschenberg, Roy Lichtenstein, and Andy Warhol. That resemblance was especially strong in the music of Philip Glass, which gives off a kind of Times Square neon glow.

Glass attended one of Reich's Park Place concerts and talked to his old schoolmate afterward. He, too, had been seeking his "way *outside*." He had absorbed neoclassical technique at Juilliard, taken Darius Milhaud's summer class in Aspen in 1960, and studied in Paris with Nadia Boulanger, who had taught Copland almost forty years earlier.

The European avant-garde did nothing for Glass. He later called it "a wasteland, dominated by these maniacs, these creeps, who were trying to make everyone write this crazy creepy music." Instead, he was drawn to the usual array of non-Western musics, and in particular to Indian music.

After working with the sitarist Ravi Shankar on a score for a hallucinogenic film titled *Chappaqua*, he began to think, as Indian improvisers do, in terms of recurring cycles of tones, of rhythmic pulses added and subtracted. His String Quartet of 1966 shows him working with drastically reduced means, often with motivic strands made up of only two notes.

Only when Glass encountered Reich's music, however, did his new style come into focus. His 1968 piece *Two Pages for Steve Reich* owes an obvious debt to *Piano Phase*: where the latter took off from the first six notes of the A-major scale, the former is based on rapid rearrangements of the first five notes of the C-minor scale. But Glass developed his own technique of variation: in place of patterns shifting in and out of phase, Glass introduced constant rhythmic change, adding or subtracting notes in the style of Indian music. Segments of a phrase would also repeat themselves by rising multiples—three times, four times, five times, six times—before contracting toward a more manageable size.

Like Reich, Glass made his living outside academia, driving taxis and doing odd jobs. The two minimalists briefly formed a company called Chelsea Light Moving and eked out a wage carrying furniture up and down the narrow staircases of New York walk-ups. Glass also worked as a plumber, and one day installed a dishwasher in the apartment of the art critic Robert Hughes, who could not understand why SoHo's composer laureate was crawling around the floor of his kitchen.

After Glass found fame, his up-by-the-bootstraps image put him in good stead with a wider public: there was nothing of the snob about him. If Steve Reich and Musicians had the detached cool of a bebop group, the Philip Glass Ensemble had the extrovert energy of a rock band. It traveled to art galleries, Upper East Side apartments, city parks, and nightclubs (the famous Max's Kansas City, among others). On the strength of his operas and film scores, Glass eventually vaulted to a level of popular recognition that no modern composer since Stravinsky had enjoyed.

But the spirit of camaraderie that infused New York minimalism in the late sixties did not last. Glass and Reich quarreled over who had done what first and eventually stopped speaking. Reich took offense at the fact that Glass shortened the title *Two Pages for Steve Reich* to *Two Pages*, as if to deny Reich's influence. Glass, for his part, seems to have resented Reich's lofty intellectual reputation, the tendency of critics to identify Reich as the serious one and himself as the more commercial artist.

In the early years Glass was as austere and severe as anyone. His amplified ensemble of winds and organs focused with almost maddening thoroughness on the basic mechanism of repetition, addition, and subtraction. Over the course of 1969, Glass added new components one by one. In *Music in Fifths*, two lines move exactly parallel to each other; in *Music in Contrary Motion*, two lines unfold as mirror images of each other, the mode indicating a key of A minor. In *Music in Similar Motion*, written at the end of 1969, four voices enter in staggered fashion, the arrival of the bass line four and a half minutes in triggering the sort of "Ah!" effect on which minimalism thrives. In *Music with Changing Parts*, from 1970, Glass and his ensemble stretched out to the spacey length of an hour, tracing limpid patterns around static harmonies.

Over the next four years, Glass assembled the monumental cycle *Music in Twelve Parts*, which in some performances went on for as long as four hours. Here he summed up his various methods to date, explored some new rhythmic and harmonic fields, and, in the final two parts, switched to a music of relatively quick chord changes. As the critic Tim Page notes, there's an inside joke in the final section of Part Twelve: a crazy creepy twelve-tone row snakes through the bass.

The end point of Glass's early phase was the theater event *Einstein on the Beach*, created in 1975 and 1976 in collaboration with the director Robert Wilson. It is opera without plot, a conceptual piece held together by recurring visual motifs and found-object texts. Singers chant numbers and "do re mi"; a Civil War–era locomotive inches across the stage; a cryptic courtroom scene features an elderly judge speaking poor French; an Einstein figure saws on a violin; a dancer soliloquizes about the "prematurely air-conditioned supermarket"; the lineup of the New York station WABC is recited; three of the four Beatles are named (no Ringo); a beam of light described as a bed tilts upward for twenty minutes; and some sort of spaceship arrives at the end. There are echoes of past musical styles, but from a cosmic distance: quasi-Bachian organ solos, nondenominational church choirs, Alberti bass accompaniments swirling around like lost pages of Mozart. Glass and Wilson discovered that minimal harmonic movement and minimal onstage action can together suggest a canyon of emotion behind the stage, a zone of nameless loss.

Four centuries into the history of opera, *Einstein* engendered a new kind of theater. It had its premiere in Avignon in the summer of 1976, and in November of that year it played for two nights at the Metropolitan Opera, which had been booked for the occasion. The performances were sold out, but the composer emerged from the experience ninety thousand dollars in debt, and for a while he went back to driving his cab.

Downtown music had entered a phase that might be called grand minimalism. Large-scale structures and modulatory schemes ascended toward moments of transcendence. Perhaps Beethoven wasn't so wrong after all.

In the summer of 1970 Reich went to Ghana to study with the master drummer Gideon Alorwoyie, who taught him to play the polyrhythms that he had read about in the writings of A. M. Jones. He returned to America with an urge to write a more spread-out kind of music for large ensemble, in which the participants could add their own energies to the action. The result was *Drumming*, a ninety-minute minimalist tour de force. Knowing that the phasing processes would not sustain a piece of such length, Reich added other devices to his armory, including a technique of setting up repeating patterns with alternating beats and rests and then slowly filling in the rests with beats. He also enriched his palette of timbres, supplementing an array of percussion with female voices and a piccolo. The drama of *Drumming* is the transfer of molten material from one group to another: the pummeling tones of bongo drums give way to the mesmerizing patter of marimbas, and then to the higher-pitched chiming of glockenspiels. In the final section, all come together in a blazing chorus, although the ending is admirably curt.

In his next piece, *Music for 18 Musicians*, Reich added strings, winds, and pianos to create a fine-tuned minimalist orchestra. The premiere took place at New York's Town Hall on April 24, 1976. Here the fascination of rhythm is joined to a comparably sophisticated drama of harmony: at the core of the piece is a cycle of eleven chords, each of which underpins a section from two to seven minutes in length. Early on, bass instruments touch repeatedly on a low D, giving the feeling that this is the work's fundamental level. But in Section V, the midpoint of the structure, the bass clarinets and cello lower the floor from D to C-sharp—a crucial alteration in the physical space of the music. The harmony sinks toward F-sharp or C-sharp minor, and rugged six-note figures burrow in. A similar change in the weather darkens Section IX, which is almost expressionistic in its stabbing intensity. Only at the very end do bright D- and A-major-ish chords clear the air. As in Feldman's *Rothko Chapel*, the seeming stasis of the sound encourages the listener to zero in on seemingly inconsequential details, so that the smallest changes have the force of seismic shocks and something as simple as a bass line going down a half step sends chills up the spine.

In the seventies the downtown Manhattan scene reached an apex of cool. Composers from around the country converged on the city to take part in it. Loft apartments were cheap, alternative performance spaces imposed no creative restrictions, audiences sat through the most far-out occurrences with an attitude of jaded calm. Phill Niblock worked with enormously amplified, slowly glissandoing electronic tones, which resonated with the surrounding acoustics to create soundscapes of mind-bending force. The singer-composer-dancer Meredith Monk manipulated the extremes of her voice to produce the illusion of an Ur–folk music, a ritual language of sensual chants. Frederic Rzewski wrote *The People United Will Never Be Defeated!*—a massive, hour-long sequence of variations on a Chilean revolutionary song, in heaven-storming, semi-Romantic, virtuoso style.

John Rockwell remembers a magic night when Glass and his ensemble played in Donald Judd's SoHo studio:

> The music danced and pulsed with a special life, its motoric rhythms, burbling, highly amplified figurations and mournful sustained notes booming out through the huge black windows and filling up the bleak industrial neighborhood. It was so loud that the dancers Douglas Dunn and Sara Rudner, who were strolling down Wooster Street, sat on a stoop and enjoyed the concert together from afar. A pack of teenagers kept up an ecstatic dance of their own. And across the street, silhouetted high up in a window, a lone saxophone player improvised in silent accompaniment like some faded postcard of fifties Greenwich Village Bohemia. It was a good night to be in New York City.

Rock 'n' Roll Minimalism

Minimalism is the story not so much of a single sound as of a chain of connections. Schoenberg invented the twelve-tone row; Webern found a secret stillness in its patterns; Cage and Feldman abandoned the row and accentuated the stillness; Young slowed down the row and rendered it hypnotic; Riley pulled the long tones toward tonality; Reich systematized the process and gave it depth of field; Glass gave it motorized momentum. The chain didn't stop there. Starting in the late sixties, a small legion of popular artists, headed by the Velvet Underground, carried the minimalist idea toward the mainstream. As Reich later said, there was "poetic justice" in this flipping of roles: just as he had once been transfixed by Miles Davis and Kenny Clarke, pop personalities in New York and London gawked at him in turn.

On the eve of his gradual revolution, Reich had a lot of pop ringing in his ears. He listened not only to modern jazz but to rock and R&B. In an interview he singled out two sixties songs that make the minimalist gesture of locking on one chord: Bob Dylan's "Subterranean Homesick Blues" and Junior Walker's "Shotgun." *It's Gonna Rain* has something in common with Dylan's "A Hard Rain's A-Gonna Fall," which combines biblical prophecy and atomic-age anxiety into an anthem of imminent doom: "And it's a *hard*, and it's a *hard*, and it's a *hard*, and it's a *hard*, and it's a *hard rain's* a-gonna fall."

The Velvet Underground essentially took the form of a musical conversation between Lou Reed, a poet turned songwriter with an achingly decadent voice, and John Cale, the droning violist of La Monte Young's Theatre of Eternal Music. Cale's early career gives a comprehensive tour of the late-twentieth-century musical horizon: he studied at Goldsmiths College in London with Humphrey Searle, a pupil of Webern's; moved on to conceptual composition in the vein of Cage, Fluxus, and La Monte Young; arrived in America by way of a scholarship to Tanglewood; reduced Mme. Koussevitzky to tears by performing a work that required the smashing of a table with an ax; rode to New York with Xenakis; made his debut by playing in John Cage's marathon performance of Satie's *Vexations*; and, finally, joined Young's ensemble. In his autobiography Cale states that one of his duties was to obtain drugs for Eternal Music performances. Transactions were allegedly conducted in musical code: "six bars of the sonata for oboe" meant "six ounces of opium."

Reed entered the picture in 1964. At the time he was writing kitsch songs for a company called Pickwick Records. For reasons that remain obscure, Pickwick hired three Eternal Music performers—Cale, Tony

Conrad, and the drummer-sculptor Walter De Maria—to assist Reed in performing a would-be novelty hit called "The Ostrich." It went nowhere, but the Eternal musicians got along with Reed, who was independently experimenting with novel tunings and modes. The first Reed-Cale band was called the Primitives. A little later, with Sterling Morrison on guitar and the Eternal Music percussionist Angus MacLise on drums, they became the Velvet Underground.

At first the Velvets specialized in art happenings and underground-film screenings. Then they began putting on conventional rock shows. MacLise quit, objecting to any format that would force him to start and stop at a specific time. Maureen Tucker, a drummer with a hard minimal touch, replaced him. A 1965 New Year's Eve show caught the ear of Andy Warhol, who plugged the band into a multimedia event called the Exploding Plastic Inevitable. An album finally emerged in 1967, with some of the songs sung by the doomy-voiced German model Nico. *The Velvet Underground & Nico* sold poorly at first but is now recognized as one of the most beautifully daring rock records ever made.

La Monte's everlasting fifth ("To be held for a long time") is all over *The Velvet Underground & Nico*. It hums in back of "All Tomorrow's Parties," stamps beneath the bluesy "I'm Waiting for the Man," flickers in the stream of consciousness of "The Black Angel's Death Song." Other songs gravitate to blues, rock 'n' roll, and Tin Pan Alley forms, but with a flat, unsentimental affect. Free dissonance periodically saturates the field, leaving the listener with the uneasy feeling that these often wistful songs survive at the whim of a cruel authority.

In the seven-minute onslaught of "Heroin," at the end of side A of the LP, a held note sets a deceptively calming tone. Maureen Tucker lays down a purring pattern of tom-tom and bass-drum beats. Cale's viola kicks in with an open fifth. Reed's lyrics evoke the eerie peacefulness of a junkie absorbed in the task of sending himself into oblivion. Later, the drone splinters apart into a storm of microtonal, electric-Xenakis noise, as Reed looks around with contemptuous sorrow at a world of "politicians making crazy sounds" and "dead bodies piled up in mounds." Three months before the release of *Sgt. Pepper's*, the Velvet Underground had closed the gap between rock and the avant-garde.

After the Velvets came Brian Eno, an art-school experimentalist who metamorphosed into one of the unlikeliest pop stars of the modern era.

Eno's early musical loves were John Cage and La Monte Young; he liked to unnerve audiences by smashing out the endless repeated chords of Young's *X for Henry Flynt*, which was also part of Cale's repertory. When the Philip Glass Ensemble played *Music with Changing Parts* in London in 1971, Eno was in the crowd, enthralled. He also attended a Steve Reich and Musicians concert in 1974. Reich remembers a trendy-looking Englishman with long hair and lipstick greeting him after the show, although at that time he had no idea who Eno was.

Eno acquired pop celebrity circa 1971, when he played keyboards and designed sound effects for the art-rock band Roxy Music, which shot to stardom on the strength of the song "Virginia Plain." Reichian phasing effects appear on the second Roxy Music album, *For Your Pleasure*, marking another slippage of minimalism into pop. Eno broke away to become a solo artist, superstar record producer, record-label entrepreneur, sound theorist, and freelance composer. Under the influence of the minimalists, he propagated the genre of "ambient" music—music that floats at the edge of the listener's consciousness, weightless and pristine.

The chain of influences continued. Standing next to Eno at Glass's 1971 performance in London was the rising rock star David Bowie. On his mid-seventies albums *Station to Station*, *Low*, and *Heroes*, Bowie abandoned A-B-A pop-song structure in favor of semi-minimalist forms characterized by dry attacks and rapid pulses. (Glass returned Bowie's homage by writing a *Low Symphony*.) Terry Riley got a nod from the Who, who learned tricks from his solo electronic improvisations and worked his name into the title of their teenage-wasteland anthem "Baba O'Riley." Swirling patterns out of Reich and Glass showed up in upbeat disco hits of the late seventies, then spread to the darker, druggier environs of techno, house, and rave music. The great New York post-punk band Sonic Youth has a distinguished minimalist ancestry; its two lead guitarists, Thurston Moore and Lee Ranaldo, first met while playing in an electric-guitar orchestra organized by the downtown composer Glenn Branca, a committed Reich and Glass fan.

Even hip-hop, the dominant end-of-century pop form, isn't immune to the minimalist virus. Lacking instruments of their own, rappers from America's ruined inner cities built up tracks by playing fragments on turntables, placing themselves in a circuitous line of descent that goes back, by way of Cage's *Imaginary Landscape No. 1*, to Wolpe and Hindemith's phonograph concerts in pre-Nazi Berlin. As technology grew more sophisticated, tracks became monstrously dense: Public Enemy's "Welcome to the Terrordome" is the *Rite of Spring* of black America. Hip-hop relies on the speaking voice, but, as Janáček, Partch, and Reich demonstrated at different times, the speaking voice has music in it. On Missy Elliott and Timbaland's antimaterialist anthem "Wake Up," a preacher or politician is heard angrily shouting, "Wake up! Wake up!" Then an ultraminimal three-note melody is extracted from the pitch content of the voice. This is much like Reich's *Different Trains*. Not since Wagner has a classical composer put so much of the outer world under his spell, whether or not the outer world knows it.

"Repetition is a form of change," Brian Eno once said, summing up the minimalist ethos. Repetition is inherent in the science of sound: tones move through space in periodic waves. It is also inherent in the way the mind processes the outside world. So, in a sense, minimalism is a return to nature. At the same time, repetition underpins all technological existence. Robert Fink, in a cultural study of the movement, acknowledges that minimalism often mimics the sped-up, numbed-out repetitions of consumer culture, the incessant iteration of commercial jingles on TV. But he argues that the minimalists deliver a kind of silent critique of the world as it is. They locate depths in surfaces, slowness in rapid motion. Borrowing a neologism from the musicologist Christopher Small, Fink writes: "Repetitive musicking rarely expresses a longing for authentic relationships that don't exist, and in this way has at least the virtue of honesty that more traditionally avant-garde musicking often lacks. More often repetitive music provides an acknowledgment, a warning, a defense—or even just an aesthetic thrill—in the face of the myriad repetitive relationships that, in late-capitalist consumer society, we all must face over and over (and over and over . . .). We repeated ourselves into this culture. We might be able to repeat ourselves out."

15

SUNKEN CATHEDRALS

Music at Century's End

As Highway 1, the California coastal highway, goes north of San Francisco, it holds the eyes like a work of art. The landscape might have been devised by a trickster creator who delights in grand gestures and abrupt transitions. Rolling meadows end in cliffs; redwood trees rise above slender patches of beach. Towers of rock rest on the surface of the ocean like the ghosts of clipper ships. A lost cow sits on the shoulder, looking out to sea. Side roads head up the inland hills at odd angles, tempting the aimless driver to follow them to the end. One especially beguiling detour, the Meyers Grade Road, departs from Highway 1 shortly after the town of Jenner. The grade is 18 percent, and the steepness of the ascent causes dizzying distortions of perspective. The Pacific Ocean rises in the rearview mirror like a blue hill across a hidden valley.

Not far from here is Brushy Ridge, the forest home of the composer John Adams. One way to describe his work is to say that it sounds like Highway 1. It is a cut-up paradise, a stream of familiar sounds arranged in unfamiliar ways. A glitzy Hollywood fanfare gives way to a trancelike sequence of shifting beats; billowing clouds of Wagnerian harmony are dispersed by a quartet of saxophones. It is present-tense American romanticism, honoring the ghosts of Mahler and Sibelius, plugging into minimalist processes, swiping sounds from jazz and rock, browsing the files of postwar innovation. Sundry sounds are broken down and filtered through an instantly recognizable personal voice, sometimes exuberant and sometimes melancholy, sometimes hip and sometimes noble, winding its way through a fragmentary culture.

Brushy Ridge is at the far end of the Meyers Grade Road, and the last part of the drive is a matter of guesswork. The Adams house, at the top of a rocky hill, is a comfortable, earthy, rural-hippie kind of place; not too long ago, it served as the headquarters for a pot farm. Walking in, you might find the composer asleep on the couch with the collected poems of Allen Ginsberg lying open in front of him. He has a youthful face, framed by a neat, silvery beard. His eyes are sometimes bright with curiosity, sometimes clouded with a slight sadness. There is an appealing innocence about him, but it is an innocence sharpened by confidence. He speaks in mild, unhurried tones, halting to look for the right words. On occasion, he breaks into an unexpectedly aggressive cackle, underscoring it with a clap of his hands and a merry roll of his eyes.

Adams makes his way across a ravine to a modern warehouse. "My composing shed," he calls it. There is a tradition of composers working in the woods; Sibelius's Ainola is surrounded by a stand of forest, and Mahler wrote most of his symphonies in rustic one-room studios constructed to his specifications. Adams can claim the largest composing hut in history. He raises the overhead door and walks through the space, part of which is rented out to a woodcutter neighbor. There is a sharp smell of freshly cut redwood. He goes into a smaller room, where sheets of music paper are scattered around an electronic keyboard and a computer terminal.

It is the year 2000, and Adams is writing an oratorio called *El Niño*—a latter-day, Spanish-inflected retelling of the Christmas story. He fiddles with the keyboard, commanding the computer to play an aria for mezzo-soprano and orchestra titled "Pues mi Dios ha nacido a penar," or "Because My Lord Was Born to Suffer." In meekly peeping tones, the computer sings a sinuous, long-breathed melody, twisting and turning over lullaby chords. After about fifty bars the music trails off into a single line. The composer stares at the floor, cupping his chin in his hand. Then he goes back to work, chipping away at the silence of everything that remains to be composed.

After the End

This has been a book about the fate of composition in the twentieth century. The temptation is strong to see the overall trajectory as one of steep decline. From 1900 to 2000, the art experienced what can only be described as a fall from a great height. At the beginning of the century, composers were cynosures on the world stage, their premieres mobbed by curiosity seekers, their transatlantic progress chronicled by telegraphic bulletins, their deathbed scenes described in exquisite detail. On Mahler's last day on earth, the Viennese press reported that his body temperature was wavering between 37.2 and 38 degrees Celsius. A hundred years on, contemporary classical composers have largely vanished from the radar screen of mainstream culture. No one whispers "*Der Adams!*" as the composer of *El Niño* walks the streets of Berkeley.

From a distance, it might appear that classical music itself is veering toward oblivion. The situation looks especially bleak in America, where scenes from prior decades—Strauss conducting for thousands in Wanamaker's department store, Toscanini playing to millions on NBC radio, the Kennedys hosting Stravinsky at the White House—seem mythically distant. To the cynical onlooker, orchestras and opera houses are stuck in a museum culture, playing to a dwindling cohort of aging subscribers and would-be elitists who take satisfaction from technically expert if soulless renditions of Hitler's favorite works. Magazines that once put Bernstein and Britten on their covers now have time only for Bono and Beyoncé. Classical music is widely mocked as a stuck-up, sissified, intrinsically un-American pursuit. The most conspicuous music lover in modern Hollywood film is the fey serial killer Hannibal Lecter, moving his bloody fingers in time to the *Goldberg Variations*.

Seen from a more sympathetic angle, the picture is quite different. Classical music is reaching far larger audiences than it has at any time in history. Tens of millions show up from night to night in opera houses, concert halls, and festival grounds. Huge new audiences have materialized in East Asia and South America. While the repertory is preternaturally resistant to change, it is being permeated by twentieth-century music. Stravinsky's *Rite*, Bartók's Concerto for Orchestra, and Shostakovich's Fifth Symphony are beloved orchestral showpieces; works of Strauss, Janáček, and Britten have joined Mozart and Verdi in the opera repertory.

Young audiences crowd into small halls to hear Elliott Carter's string quartets or Xenakis's stochastic constructions. Living composers such as Adams, Glass, Reich, and Arvo Pärt have acquired a semblance of a mass following. And a few farsighted orchestras have put modern repertory front and center: in 2003, the Los Angeles Philharmonic, under the visionary direction of Esa-Pekka Salonen, inaugurated Walt Disney Concert Hall with a program that included Ligeti's *Lux aeterna*, Ives's *The Unanswered Question*, and, naturally, the *Rite*. As the behemoth of mass culture breaks up into a melee of subcultures and niche markets, as the Internet weakens the media's stranglehold on cultural distribution, there is reason to think that classical music, and with it new music, can find fresh audiences in far-flung places.

There is little hope of giving a tidy account of composition in the second fin de siècle. Styles of every description—minimalism, postminimalism, electronic music, laptop music, Internet music, New Complexity, Spectralism, doomy collages and mystical meditations from Eastern Europe and Russia, appropriations of rock, pop, and hip-hop, new experiments in folkloristic music in Latin America, the Far East, Africa, and the Middle East—jostle against one another, none achieving supremacy. Some have tried to call the era postmodern, but "modernism" is already so equivocal a term that to affix a "post" pushes it over the edge into meaninglessness. In retrospect, modernism, in the sense of a unified vanguard, never existed. The twentieth century was always a time of "many streams," a "delta," in the wise words of John Cage. What follows is an aerial tour of an ever-changing landscape.

Composing remains, as Thomas Mann's Devil says, "desperately difficult." Although vast quantities of music are being written down day by day—national websites display lists of 450 composers in Australia, 650 composers in Canada, several thousand in the Nordic countries—few of them have found an audience outside a relatively limited clique of new-music fanciers. Some specialize in "music for use," writing for church choirs or collegiate wind bands or the soundtracks of video games. The majority make a living by teaching composition, and their students usually become teachers themselves. They may sometimes ask, with the title character of Hans Pfitzner's *Palestrina*, "What is it for?" They have read in books that their forebears humbled kings, electrified crowds, forged nations. Sooner or later they realize that modern popular culture has no place for a composer hero. The most celebrated composers are sometimes the unhappiest; György Ligeti, in his last years, was reportedly haunted by the feeling that he would be forgotten after his death, that he had outlived the age in which music mattered.

Perhaps Ligeti was right; perhaps classical composition is being sustained past its date of expiration by the stubborn determination of those who perform it, those who support it, and, above all, those who write it. More likely, though, a thousand-year-old tradition won't expire with the flipping of a calendar or the aging of a baby-boom cohort. Confusion is often a prelude to consolidation; we may even be on the verge of a new golden age. For now, the art is like the "sunken cathedral" that Debussy depicts in his Preludes for Piano—a city that chants beneath the waves.

After Europe

"The symphony must be like the world," Mahler said to Sibelius in 1907. "It must be all-embracing." Now music *is* the world; it has ceased to be a European art. You can use new works to draw a map of the globe—from the orchestral works of the Australian composer Peter Sculthorpe, which draw on the sounds and rhythms of the Australian outback, to R. Murray Schafer's radical music-theater cycle *Patria*, which can only be performed in the forests and lakes of the Canadian north. A comprehensive list of significant voices in contemporary music would include Franghiz Ali-Zadeh of Azerbaijan, Chen Yi of China, Unsuk Chin of South Korea, Sofia Gubaidulina of Russia, Kaija Saariaho of Finland, and Pauline Oliveros of the United States. Composition has also ceased to be exclusively male; the preceding six composers are all women.

In one of the primal scenes of modern music, Debussy fell in love with Javanese and Vietnamese ensembles at the Paris Universal Exposition of 1889. Appropriately, the first internationally renowned composer to emerge from Asia—Tōru Takemitsu—found his voice by listening to French music. Toward the end of the Second World War, soldiers and civilians on the Japanese home front constructed networks of underground bases, in anticipation of an invasion that never came. Takemitsu was stationed in one of these dugout fortresses in 1944, all of fourteen years old. Although no music aside from patriotic songs was permitted at the base, one day a kind-hearted officer ushered the child-soldiers into a back room and played them some records, using a windup phonograph with a bamboo needle. One disk had Lucienne Boyer singing "Parlez-moi d'amour." Takemitsu listened, he later said, in a state of "enormous shock." After so much sunless, soulless labor, that winsome chanson opened a world of possibility in his mind. Ever after, he honored the moment as the birth of his musical consciousness.

Largely self-taught, Takemitsu first studied Debussy and Messiaen, then moved on to Boulez and Cage. He refined his technique not only in concert works but in scores for various masterpieces of postwar Japanese cinema, including Akira Kurosawa's *Dodes'ka-den* and Hiroshi Teshigahara's *Woman in the Dunes*. In the former he seduced the ears with popular airs, in the latter he raised goosebumps with Xenakis-like string glissandos and electronic noise. Like Messiaen, Takemitsu felt no need to choose between the sweet and the harsh. In the sixties, inspired partly by his film work, he added Japanese instruments such as shakuhachi flute and biwa lute to his Western-based ensembles. By the time of his early death, in 1996, Takemitsu had forged a late style that was precise in design, rich in timbre, tonal on the surface, mysterious at the core. He compared his music to a "picture scroll unrolled."

Chinese music has been operating at a high level of sophistication for several thousand years. The bianzhong bells of Marquis Yi, which rested undisturbed in a tomb for twenty-four hundred years before being uncovered in 1978, are meticulously tuned in twelve-note octaves, close to the modern Western chromatic scale. Nonetheless, in the early decades of the twentieth century, Chinese composers defected from native traditions toward the West. They initially emulated Russian composers, and, a little later, Debussy, whose pentatonic harmony sounded as familiar to the Chinese as it did to Takemitsu in Japan. Sheila Melvin and Jindong Cai's absorbing history, *Rhapsody in Red: How Western Classical Music Became Chinese*, offers a telling anecdote about the conversation between East and West. Some years ago, an American visitor to China commented that one composer's music sounded like Debussy's. The composer answered in irritation, "No, this piece doesn't resemble Debussy! Not at all! Debussy resembles me! Debussy resembles China!"

When Mao Zedong and the Communists took power in 1949, composers found themselves in a recognizable predicament. Like Hitler and Stalin, Mao fancied himself a patron of the arts, and he meddled incessantly in the cultural sphere, zigzagging between liberalization and repression. In the "Let a hundred flowers bloom" period of the late fifties, Western-style orchestras, opera houses, and conservatories multiplied, and composers such as He Luting tentatively tried out early twentieth-century styles. Then, in late 1965, Jiang Qing, Mao's fourth wife, incited the anti-Western crusade of the Cultural Revolution, and a wave of terror engulfed every sector of society. Jiang Qing had strong ideas about music, although they added up to no coherent system. As *Rhapsody in Red* recounts, she expressed at various times a dislike of the sound of the trombone, a preference for Beethoven's Sixth Symphony over the unscientifically "fateful" Fifth, and an admiration for Aaron Copland's film score *The Red Pony*. In the spirit of proletarian solidarity, "bourgeois" artists were subject to vicious public humiliation, and some chose suicide as a way out.

An astonishing incident took place on Chinese television. He Luting, who had drawn fire from a proletarian-minded critic for defending the music of Debussy, was subjected to a physically abusive interrogation but refused to apologize. "Your accusations are false!" he shouted. "Shame on you for lying!" No composer ever made a braver stand against totalitarianism. He Luting lived to the age of ninety-six.

At the height of the madness, conservatories were closed and orchestras shut down. The few composers who continued working were confined to the task of perfecting Jiang Qing's "shining-star models" of Communist musical theater—ballets and operas such as *Red Detachment of Women*, *The Red Lantern*, and *Taking Tiger Mountain by Strategy* (a title later ironically appropriated by Brian Eno). These works were thuggishly simple in design, relying on a kitschy blend of pentatonic tunes and Tchaikovskyan Romanticism. Yet they hinted at a new direction for Chinese composition. At the same time that Takemitsu was mixing strings and taiko drums in the soundtrack for *Woman in the Dunes*, Wu Zuqiang and Du Mingxin, the composers of *Red Detachment of Women*, used makeshift but effective combinations of Western and Chinese timbres.

Mao died in 1976, and the conservatories reopened in 1978. The first classes in composition brought forth a remarkable roster of talent: Tan Dun, Chen Yi, Zhou Long, Bright Sheng, and Guo Wenjing, among others. All were children of the Cultural Revolution, and their ignorance of tradition turned out to be a sort of bliss: they could start with a blank slate. Tan spent much of his childhood in a remote village in Hunan Province, singing folk songs while planting rice in the fields and playing fiddle in a provincial Peking opera troupe. When, at his entrance exam at the Central Conservatory in Beijing, he was told to play something by Mozart, he innocently asked his examiners, "Who's Mozart?"

In the eighties the Chinese "New Wave" composers caught up fast, treading the progressive path from Debussy to Boulez to Cage. Yet they did not forget the rural musical traditions to which they had been exposed while doing compulsory labor on collective farms. Tan juxtaposed Cagean water and paper noises with lavish Romantic orchestration and humble folkish melodies that might have brought a smile to the face of Jiang Qing. The irony is that most of the New Wave composers ended up in America, practicing cultural interpenetration within the familiar university setting. Back home, Western music commanded an enormous audience, but the repertory tended to stop short at Tchaikovsky. If the Chinese classical business can accommodate new music in the coming century, the center of gravity may shift permanently eastward.

The term "classical music" changes meaning as it traverses the globe. It now connotes almost any ancient practice that has persisted into the modern era—the ritual opera of China, the imperial court music of Japanese *gagaku*, the *radif* or "order" of Persian melodies, the great classical traditions of India, and the polyrhythmic drumming of West African tribes, among a hundred others. Those who cherish the "classical musics" share a fear that the behemoth of mass-marketed pop will wipe out the wisdom of the centuries. To be "classical," in this sense, is to protect tradition from the ravages of passing time, to perpetuate the musical past. Not surprisingly, coalitions have recently formed among "classical music" practitioners around the world: the Persian master Kayhan Kalhor has performed at Lincoln Center's Mostly Mozart Festival; Yo-Yo Ma's Silk Road Project has convened American, European, East Asian, Central Asian, and Middle Eastern musicians in programs of ear-catching intercultural design.

All this activity renews the old folkish projects of Bartók, Janáček, the young Stravinsky, and de Falla—the quest for the real, the "dance of the earth." Folkishness went out of fashion in the high avant-garde era, its ideal of communal wholeness compromised by the bloodthirsty nationalism of the world wars, but by century's end it had regained its political virtue, counteracting the homogenizing force of corporate conglomerates.

In the year 2000, the Argentinean composer Osvaldo Golijov, a descendant of Russian and Eastern European Jews, unveiled his *St. Mark Passion*, which trumpeted from a different station the end of European hegemony over modern composition. It opens with a barrage of Latin-American sounds: a rustling of Brazilian shakers and musical bows; spooky accordion moans, representing the voice of God; the hot tones of a chorus braying in Africanized Spanish over a soft roar of Afro-Cuban drumming. The listener is thrown into the middle of a Lenten street festival, one whose celebratory mood is filigreed by tension and dread. The work falls halfway between ritual and opera, in the manner of Stravinsky's *Les Noces*. There are also mercurial minimalist canons in the manner of Steve Reich and timbral rustlings out of Luciano Berio and George Crumb. But Golijov transcends his models in repeatedly ceding creative control to his singers, players, and drummers, inviting them to improvise on given material.

At the same time, the composer of this *Passion* proceeds according to a cannily controlled plan; he coaxes his sounds into a strong narrative arc and places at the climax a softly lamenting Kaddish for the man on the cross. Suddenly the language is Aramaic, the cantillation is Jewish, and the centuries have slipped away like sand.

After Minimalism

In 1907, American music was almost invisible in listings of musical events in New York City. For the most part, concert life consisted of European musicians playing European composers either living or dead. One hundred years down the line, new music is omnipresent. On any given night at the height of the season, you can find up to a dozen competing new-music events in venues around the city, whether at Miller Theatre at Columbia, in Zankel Hall underneath Carnegie Hall, at downtown spaces such as the Kitchen and Roulette, or in Brooklyn warehouses. At Issue Project Room, a performance series temporarily located in an abandoned oil silo on the industrial Gowanus Canal, the composer-vocalist Joan La Barbara sings excerpts from Kenji Bunch's electronically enhanced chamber opera *Confessions of the Woman in the Dunes*, inspired by Teshigahara's movie. At Joe's Pub, the young composer Nico Muhly performs delicate minimalist-inflected pieces with the Icelandic sound artist Valgeir Sigurðsson, who's worked with the avant-pop star Björk. At the Stone, on Avenue C, the free-jazz saxophonist, klezmer aficionado, collage artist, and avant-garde composer John Zorn rallies all the sounds in his experience into music as coolly hectic as the city itself.

The geography of New York—downtown and uptown, youthful and mature, rebellious and established—still serves as a convenient organizing principle for American music, although rising real-estate prices have made the notion of a cheap Manhattan loft a movie fantasy. To track the disparate activities of downtown composers, Kyle Gann has coined the term "postminimalism." He describes it as a tonal, steady-pulsing kind of music that avoids defining itself through a controlling process, such as Reich's phase shifting or Glass's additive rhythm. Instead, repetition becomes a background grid on which a large variety of material can be plotted: everything from the Southern American shape-note singing in William Duckworth's *Southern Harmony* to the microtonal electric-guitar soundscapes of Glenn Branca.

Postminimalists tend also to be plugged-in composers. Each new technological advance—digital sampling, the MIDI interface for computers and synthesizers, computer music software, interactive Internet linkups—mandates a change in technique. The advent of laptop computers means that composers can carry their life's work in a backpack, and via the Internet they can send it around the world at the touch of a button. Downtown composers also show sympathy for pop. The original minimalists revivified tonality in part by studying jazz, R & B, and early rock. Postminimalists have taken cues variously from funk, punk, heavy metal, electronic and DJ music, and hip-hop.

In the 1980s, three composers from the Yale School of Music, Michael Gordon, Julia Wolfe, and David Lang, banded together under the name Bang on a Can. They summed up their thinking thus: "We had the simplicity, energy and drive of pop music in our ears—we'd heard it from the cradle. But we also had the idea from our classical music training that composing was exalted." As the new century began, Gordon created a score for Bill Morrison's film *Decasia*, a mind-altering cinematic collage in which pieces of archival footage melt before one's eyes. Letting his own harmonies "decay" by way of microtonal tunings and glissandos, Gordon split the difference between minimalist transparency and modernist density, to superbly ominous effect.

Refining his map of the musical city, Gann has introduced the category of "midtown" to cover the sizable number of composers who are still working in traditional orchestral, operatic, and chamber-music genres, their harmonies usually more tonal than not. The most successful members of this group—John Corigliano, Mark Adamo, Christopher Rouse, Joan Tower, and John Harbison, among others—have regained the confidence of mainstream classical listeners, who never quite got around to accepting Schoenberg, never mind Milton Babbitt. The challenge, as ever, is to honor the expectations of an audience weaned on Mozart without pandering or committing pastiche. A degree of wit often saves the day. Rouse's *Der gerettete Alberich*, or *Alberich Saved*, for percussionist and orchestra, begins with the sublime final measures of Wagner's *Ring* and goes on to answer the question of whatever became of Alberich, master of the Nibelungs, after the twilight of the gods. It turns out that the dwarf lord conquers the world at the head of a demonic high-school marching band playing covers of heavy-metal tunes.

Downtown and midtown composers are alike in rejecting the prophet-in-the-wilderness, who-cares-if-you-listen mentality that prevailed after the Second World War. They often speak in terms of an atonal nightmare ending, of a melodic morning dawning. By now, members of these formerly suspect camps have achieved positions of eminence in American academia, and young composers no longer fear intellectual ostracism if they dabble in tonality.

But the modernist impulse is by no means dead. For some years the British-born, American-based composer Brian Ferneyhough has been testing the outer limits of what players can play and listeners can hear, and he has become the somewhat unwilling figurehead for a movement known as the New Complexity. Ferneyhough may win the prize for inscribing more black dots per square inch than any composer in history: a characteristic bar of his Third String Quartet has the first violin setting forth jagged, double-stopped figures over a range of several octaves, replete with glissando, trills, and seven different dynamic markings; the second violin playing a stream of twenty-nine thirty-second notes; the viola playing a stream of thirty-*three* thirty-second notes; and the cello scrubbing out disjointed figures down below. Because not even the most expert performers can execute such notation precisely, it becomes a kind of planned improvisation, more akin to a free-jazz or avant-rock freak-out than to anything in the mainstream classical tradition—mutatis mutandis, a mosh pit for the mind.

The New Complexity is not exactly new. Henry Cowell layered rhythm upon rhythm back in 1917. But the pursuit of extreme musical situations has eternal appeal. For the young composer it becomes another tough-walled refuge within a hypercommercialized culture that dictates artistic choices by way of audience surveys and focus groups. And it intersects in surprising ways with the noncommercial end of rock and electronic pop. In sticky-floored basement clubs across the country, young people compare notes on Sonic Youth and Morton Feldman, seeking the sound that will annul the norm. In the empire of noise, formal distinctions disappear, just as the gaps between continents vanish under the Arctic ice.

After Modernism

In Europe the long heyday of modernism continues. Hidden beneath the plaza outside the Centre Pompidou, in Paris, is the Institute for the Research and Coordination of Acoustics and Music, or IRCAM, a subterranean electronic-music laboratory that opened in 1977 under the velvet-fist direction of Pierre Boulez. The mere existence of such a place, never mind its choice location, is testimony to the long-standing cultural largesse of the European welfare state, on which composers have for decades depended. Boulez formed IRCAM at the invitation of Georges Pompidou, the president of France from 1969 to 1974, and the financial outlay was huge: in the early years the institute and the allied Ensemble Intercontemporain consumed up to 70 percent of the government budget for contemporary music. Classical music may no longer be a European art, but composers from abroad almost invariably pass through Paris, London, Berlin, Vienna, or Munich at some point in their careers. They come because money is there, and the media attention, and the audience, and, perhaps most important, the continuity with the storied past. IRCAM's address is symbolic: 1 place Igor-Stravinsky.

The European modern-music utopia, which dates back to the founding of Darmstadt in 1946, will not last forever. In recent years, as welfare-state economies have struggled to stay afloat in the global free market, arts budgets have shrunk. European composers may soon be confronted with the interesting challenge, long familiar to American composers, of writing for a paying audience. In subtle ways this change is already under way, as younger composers modify or reject the classic avant-garde stance of the composer in opposition to society. Even Boulez has recalibrated a few of his more extreme positions. When, in 1999, he was asked why so few major works of the fifties and sixties had become repertory pieces, he blandly replied, "Well, perhaps we did not take sufficiently into account the way music is perceived by the listener."

Boulez's recent music has a cool, silvery sheen. Made up of lush surfaces, rapid swirls of interior activity, and generously swooping forms, it resembles the rippling facades that architects such as Santiago Calatrava and Frank Gehry have devised for civic structures in the wealthy urban centers of the European Union. Boulez's most formidable latter-day work is *Répons* (1980–84), which deploys various IRCAM technologies—electronic instruments, computerized sound synthesis, software for the instantaneous electronic manipulation of live sounds—to spectacular and satisfying effect. The big moment comes at the beginning of Section 1, when, after an extended instrumental introduction, bursts of electronically modified sound surge in from six separate stations that are distributed around the audience in a circle: thickly arpeggiated chords jump from one station to the next and build into a reverberating roar. On the whole, the music is closer to the ear-drenching aesthetic of Stockhausen's *Gruppen* and *Carré*, or of later Luciano Berio works such as *Coro*, than to the clipped violence of Boulez's youthful work.

Stockhausen spent the last twenty-three years of the twentieth century—and the first three years of the twenty-first—laboring on *Licht*, a meta-Wagnerian cycle of seven operas, each named for a day of the week. It tells a ritualistic, symbolic story of relationships among three archetypal characters: the birth-giving Eva, the wisdom-seeking Michael, and the freedom-seeking Lucifer. The score makes extravagant demands; as of this writing, no opera house has yet succeeded in staging *Wednesday*, whose third scene calls for four string players to take off in helicopters. *Friday* requires, according to the composer's prospectus, "twelve very different objects like rockets flying, a woman in the moon, a giant syringe moving towards a woman, a huge pencil sharpener about four meters high as a woman and a man who is a pencil pushing himself into the pencil sharpener; an enormous male raven flying around a woman nest." In *Sunday*, the finale to the cycle, scents representing the days of the week are released into the audience.

The plot may be nuts, but grand sounds crop up all over *Licht*—the pealing, quasi-tonal theme of Michael that resounds through *Thursday*; Lucifer's sneering glissandos in *Saturday*; the phantasmagoric ending of that opera, with boomings of the tam-tam, alternating chords of organ and trombones, ecstatic shouts and murmurs, and endless ringing bells. Stockhausen is going out in style.

When Terry Riley's *In C* was played at Darmstadt in 1969, it elicited lusty boos from the rank and file of the avant-garde. Only a few European composers understood that something revolutionary was happening in American music. One close listener was György Ligeti, who included in his 1976 piece *Three Pieces for Two Pianos* a playfully repetitive movement titled "Self-Portrait with Reich and Riley (and Chopin Is Also There)." Another was the radical-anarchist Dutch composer Louis Andriessen, who, after hearing *In C* in 1970, began working out his own emphatically pulsing, pop-inflected language, which, in the eighties, had a considerable impact on the composers of Bang on a Can.

Andriessen went on to become the only major European minimalist. In 1976, the year of *Music for 18 Musicians* and *Einstein on the Beach*, he finished a large-scale work for voices and ensemble titled *De Staat*, or *The Republic*, after Plato. The choice of texts gives ironic prominence to Plato's warnings about the dangers of free musical expression ("Any alteration in the modes of music is always followed by alteration in the most fundamental laws of the state"). The score itself embodies the loudness and lewdness that Plato feared: a swing-band wall of brass, a trio of electric guitars, riff-like themes, funky rhythms. All the same, Andriessen remains a recognizably European composer. The harmonies are thicker and more changeable than Reich's or Glass's, the off-kilter motor rhythms of Stravinsky lurk behind almost every bar. The music is nervous rather than mellow, not the kind of thing you can bliss out to.

If minimalism made hardly a dent on mainstream European music—its reliance on consonances and steady pulses broke all the modernist taboos at once—the younger generation of composers, those who came of age in the era of the student revolutions of May 1968, did find their own direction, distinct from that of Boulez. In the seventies, three composers working at IRCAM—Tristan Murail, Gérard Grisey, and Hugues Dufourt—used advanced computer software to analyze the spectra of overtones that accompany any resonating tone, and from the complex patterns that they found they extrapolated a new kind of music. Their common effort, which came to be called Spectralism, had an antiestablishment, back-to-nature aspect. It was, in a way, an oblique response to minimalism and to the predecessor movements of the West Coast American avant-garde, notably the work of Harry Partch and La Monte Young. If you are faithful to the material of the natural harmonic series, you will not neglect the intervals at the lower end of the spectrum of tone—the octave, the fifth, and the major third, whence comes major- and minor-key tonality. Grisey later said in an interview: "I have to acknowledge the differences [between consonance and dissonance] and avoid flattening everything. Making everything flat and equal. It's a way of recovering the hierarchy."

The exemplary Spectralist work is Grisey's *Les Espaces acoustiques*, a ninety-minute instrumental cycle whose material stems from a single low E on the trombone. This music is by no means easy on the ears; the overtone-derived material converges in forbiddingly thick, ultradissonant textures or goes spinning through hectic patterns dictated by ring-modulator technology. Yet there are arresting moments of simplification, as quasi-tonal harmonies rush to the fore. Spectralism is often just a step or two removed from the singing and shimmering textures of Debussy and Ravel. Floating through Murail's orchestral soundscape *Gondwana* is a citation of Sibelius, his time come around at last.

The Spectralists' cautious rapprochement with consonance—call it détente—stopped short at the German border. The reunification of East and West and the emergence of the new Germany as the dominant player in the European Union failed to distract the country's composers from their wary brooding over the past; indeed, Germans and Austrians seemed more conscious than ever before of the "danger of resembling tonality," as Schoenberg once put it. Sixty years after the Wagner-loving Hitler killed himself in Berlin, pundits could still be heard declaring that clear-cut repetition of material or a nonironic use of triads betrayed a fascist mentality. With Stockhausen no longer taken as seriously as before, the mantle of greatness fell on Helmut Lachenmann, who has said, "My music has been concerned with rigidly constructed denial, with the exclusion of what appears to me as listening expectations preformed by society." One analyst approvingly notes that Lachenmann's work is "uncontaminated" by the world around it. Familiar instruments are pushed to make unfamiliar sounds—flutes are blown without mouthpieces, cellos are bowed on the body or the tailpiece, piano pedals become instruments in themselves. Fragments of the musical past float by in mangled, scorched form; childish melodies sputter into futility. Frenzied blasts of flutter-tonguing brass alternate with passages of stasis and near-silence.

Lachenmann's fractured aesthetic is allied to political convictions of a far-leftist, insurrectionary character. The libretto of his opera *The Little Match Girl* (1990–96) augments the beloved Hans Christian Andersen tale with a quotation from Gudrun Ensslin, a leader of the Baader-Meinhof terrorist gang: "Criminal, madman, and suicide . . . Their criminality, their madness, their death express the revolt of the destroyed against his destruction."

We have heard this kind of talk before. The imagery of contamination recalls Schoenberg's theory of degeneration in *Harmonielehre*, while the citation of Ensslin smacks of the terrorist chic of Eisler's *The Measures Taken*. As usual in the German case, the music must be separated from the rhetoric: for all his head-banging verbiage, Lachenmann is a sensitive composer who places his cries and whispers with extraordinary care and keeps the listener in a tensely riveted state. After a century of noise, he still succeeds in delivering authentic, bracing shocks. In the most alarming section of *The Little Match Girl*, fragments of Mahler, Berg, Stravinsky, and Boulez flare out briefly from the orchestra, as if someone were flipping the dial of an all-twentieth-century radio station. Crashing in their midst is the A-minor chord that ends Mahler's Sixth Symphony.

Thrilling as the latest voyages in "novel spheres" may be, much contemporary music in Austria and Germany seems constricted in emotional range—trapped behind the modernist plate-glass window of Adorno's "Grand Hotel Abyss." The great German tradition, with all its grandeurs and sorrows, is cordoned off, like a crime scene under investigation.

After the Soviets

East of Berlin and Vienna, the landscape ages. In the years immediately following the fall of the Soviet Union, cities and towns all over Russia and Eastern Europe looked frozen in time. In Tallinn, the capital of Estonia, you could sit outside a church in the Old Town on a Sunday morning and see little evidence that the nineteenth century had ended. On the backstreets of East Berlin, faded lettering on storefronts in the old Jewish neighborhoods spoke of an annihilated world. And, backstage at the Mariinsky Theatre in St. Petersburg, the ghost of Chaliapin could be sensed lurking among the piles of decaying scenery. Valery Gergiev, the Mariinsky conductor, studied with the Soviet-era pedagogue Ilya Musin, who continued teaching five classes a week at the Petersburg Conservatory until a few days before his death in 1999, at the age of ninety-five. On the day that Musin first enrolled as a student at the conservatory, Shostakovich was standing behind him in line.

The Soviet era, for all its ravaging effects on the spirit, preserved prewar musical culture as if in amber. As late as the 1980s, composers were still lionized, opera houses and orchestras were generously funded, and an imposing music-education system funneled major talents from the provinces to the center. All that changed, of course, when the Communist Party fell from power. In the new plutocratic Russian state, institutions such as the Mariinsky are maintained as elite showplaces, but sponsorship of new music has all but disappeared. Composers who were long accustomed to dachas and honoraria now flounder in the open market. Others, mostly the younger ones, have embraced the creative freedom that comes along with relative poverty. American minimalism, pop and rock influences, and the ghosts of Russian tradition are colliding and combining to sometimes scandalous effect—as in Leonid Desyatnikov's opera *Rosenthal's Children*, in which an émigré German-Jewish geneticist establishes a secret biological laboratory at Stalin's behest and succeeds in cloning Mozart, Verdi, Wagner, Mussorgsky, and Tchaikovsky.

The death of Shostakovich, in 1975, left a temporary void at the heart of Russian music, but a new cohort of composers quickly filled it. Born around the same time as the American minimalists and the French Spectralists, the last major Soviet generation radiated a disruptive, nonconformist energy, openly defiant of official direction where their predecessors had been accommodating or ambivalent. Alfred Schnittke spiked his orchestra with electric guitars. Sofia Gubaidulina wrote a Concerto for Bassoon and Low Strings in which the soloist issues a bloodcurdling yell in the middle. Arvo Pärt, of Estonia, participated in a Cagean happening at which a violin caught fire. In later years provocation gave way to meditation: the long twilight of the Brezhnev regime brought a midnight harvest of religious music.

Schnittke, a man of haunted, sallow visage, Russian-Jewish and Volga German in origin, was Shostakovich's heir apparent. A master ironist, he developed a language that he called "polystylistics," gathering up in a troubled stream of consciousness the detritus of a millennium of music: medieval chant, Renaissance mass, Baroque figuration, Classical sonata principle, Viennese waltz, Mahlerian orchestration, twelve-tone writing, aleatory chaos, and touches of modern pop. Schnittke told a friend: "I set down a beautiful chord on paper—and suddenly it rusts." In his First Symphony of 1972, the opening theme of Tchaikovsky's First Piano Concerto fights like a wounded animal against a fusillade of sound.

Wandering deeper into the labyrinth of the past, Schnittke ceased to be an ironic commentator on Romantic style and instead became a phantom Romantic himself. He fell under the spell of the ultimate Romantic myth, the life and death of Faust, and, like so many postwar composers, he read Thomas Mann's novel, which, he said, "had an incredible influence on me." His unfinished magnum opus was the opera *Historia von D. Johann Fausten*, which, like Adrian Leverkühn's fictional *Lamentation of Doctor Faustus*, employed the original *Faust* text of 1587. In a late-twentieth-century twist, Schnittke's hero goes down to hell to the accompaniment of a satanic tango, with an amplified mezzo-soprano presiding like an Ethel Merman of the apocalypse.

Shostakovich looked askance at Schnittke, perhaps because the two composers were close in temperament. Toward Gubaidulina he extended a warmer hand. "I want you to continue along on your mistaken path," Shostakovich told her, presumably with an enigmatic smile. In a career that has gone from strength to strength, Gubaidulina has aimed at nothing less than "spiritual renewal" in the act of composing. An admirer of Cage among others, she fills her scores with far-out sounds—buzzing, throbbing textures, caterwauling glissandos in the wind and brass, scrapings and whisperings of strings, spells of improvisation (sometimes with Russian,

Caucasian, Central Asian, and East Asian folk instruments). Episodes of extreme quiet, in which serpentine chromatic figures curl through small groups of instruments, give way to roarings of tam-tams, tubas, and electric guitars. These free, wild, organic narratives often culminate in what Gubaidulina calls, in a Messiaen-like turn of phrase, "transfigurations," moments of radiant clarity. Her 1980 work *Offertorium*, for violin and orchestra, deconstructs the "royal theme" from Bach's *Musical Offering*, distributing the notes among different instruments in Second Viennese School style. By the end, Bach's theme has somehow mutated into an ancient-sounding liturgical melody, passing through a murmuring orchestra like an icon in a procession.

In the music of Pärt, the icon is all. The Estonian turned to religious subjects at the end of the sixties, defying the official atheism of the Soviet Union. In his 1968 cantata *Credo*, the words "*Credo in Jesum Christum*" are set to the tune of Bach's Prelude in C Major and beset with aleatory bedlam. After that, for a period of eight years, Pärt composed little, immersing himself in a study of medieval and Renaissance polyphony. Then, in 1976, the year of Reich's *Music for 18 Musicians* and of Glass's *Einstein on the Beach*, Pärt reemerged with a stunningly simple piano piece titled *For Alina*, which consists of just two voices, one moving by melodic steps and the other rotating through the pitches of a B-minor triad. The following year he wrote a *Cantus* in memory of Benjamin Britten, whose music haunted him in ways he could not quite put into words. The technique of *Cantus* is like that of Reich's phase-shifting music, with downward A-minor scales unfurling in different voices and at different speeds. In the two-violin concerto *Tabula Rasa*, also from 1977, Pärt goes from strict process to free expression; at the beginning of the second movement, "Silentium," a rustling arpeggio on a prepared piano, like the rustling of wings, ushers in icily beautiful chords of D minor. Both the invocation of silence and the use of a prepared piano acknowledge John Cage, who opened so many doors in colleagues' minds.

The quietude of Pärt's music did not mean that he had become a quietist. References to him as "monkish" miss the mark; behind his sad eyes and long beard is a steely will. In 1979 he performed the un-Shostakovich-like gesture of donning a long-haired wig and haranguing the Estonian Composers' Union on the subject of official restrictions. He defected to the West the following year; Schnittke, who had played the prepared-piano part in the first Western performances of *Tabula Rasa*, arranged for Pärt and his wife to stay in Vienna, and the couple ended up settling in Berlin.

A lonely exile might have awaited him; the German music establishment opposed minimalism in any form. But when the German label ECM began issuing recordings of Pärt's music in the eighties, they sold copies into the millions, unheard-of quantities for new music. It is not hard to guess why Pärt and several like-minded composers—notably Henryk Górecki and John Tavener—achieved a degree of mass appeal during the global economic booms of the eighties and nineties; they provided oases of repose in a technologically oversaturated culture. For some, Pärt's strange spiritual purity filled a more desperate need; a nurse in a hospital ward in New York regularly played *Tabula Rasa* for young men who were dying of AIDS, and in their last days they asked to hear it again and again.

When the Berlin Wall was broached on November 9, 1989, seventy-one years to the day after the proclamation of the Weimar Republic and fifty-one years after Kristallnacht, Leonard Bernstein rushed to the scene to conduct performances of Beethoven's Ninth on both sides of the crumbling wall. The grand old man of American music had less than a year to live, but he seized the world's attention one last time with a typically gaudy and soulful act; Schiller's "Ode to Joy" was rewritten as an "Ode to Freedom." Thomas Mann would have smiled at the gesture: the Ninth had been "taken back" again. All over Eastern Europe that fall, and in Russia in the years to come, peoples who had lived under the fear of the Soviet regime glimpsed freedom, and Bernstein's revision of the Ninth symbolized burgeoning hopes for the future. Freedom arrived quickly in some places, more slowly in others, and in more than a few former Soviet republics it never showed up at all.

As it happens, allusions to Beethoven crop up in several major late-period works by celebrated composers from Eastern European countries, although none delivered anything like an ode to joy. In 1981, just as the Polish Communist leadership was trying to shut down the Solidarity movement, Witold Lutosławski began writing his Third Symphony, and his point of departure was four sharp iterations of the note E—a martial signal that recalls the attention-grabbing opening of Beethoven's Fifth. For most of the symphony's half-hour duration, the orchestra seems to be trying to figure out how to respond to that initial blast of energy, testing pathways that in one way or another appear to be blocked. Only in the last few minutes does it find a resolution—a kind of magnificence without triumph. Cellos and basses intone a low E, and then match it with a B, forming a rock-solid perfect fifth. Arcs of melody extend from that foundation, intersecting into a convulsive twelve-note dissonance. Gleaming atop the tower of sound is the note B-flat, a tritone away from the original E. Then the music wheels back to the fundamental tone, which is blasted out four times to close. Lutosławski was in his late sixties when he wrote this music, but it has the dynamism of raging, blissful youth.

György Ligeti, in his last years, adopted an idiosyncratic language that he called "non-atonality"—a kind of harmonic kaleidoscope in which tonal chords, quasi-folkish melodies, natural tuning, and other relics of the past swirled around one another in fractured counterpoint. Ligeti's Horn Trio of 1982 begins with a distorted variation of the "farewell" motif from Beethoven's Piano Sonata Opus 81a. It ends with a Lamento, a ravaged landscape full of dying cries, in which the composer seems to gaze back on a century that killed off most of his family and his faith in humanity. But the harmony never turns as grim as it might. Faint triads, stretched over many octaves, provide a tremor of hope. At the end, three tones glow in the night: a G, low on the horn; a C, high on the violin; and an A, sounding weakly in the middle range of the piano. These same notes appear in reverse order at the start of the last movement of Beethoven's final string quartet, in F major—the music to which the composer attached the words "It must be!"

Ligeti's fellow Hungarian György Kurtág chose to remain in Budapest through the worst years of the Cold War. Kurtág, too, was a master of the art of neither-nor—a composer neither traditional nor avant-garde, neither nationalist nor cosmopolitan, neither tonal nor atonal. Every attempt at a description of Kurtág's music has to be qualified: it is compressed but not dense, lyrical but not sweet, dark but not dismal, quiet but not calm. In 1994, for the Berlin Philharmonic, Kurtág composed a piece titled *Stele* (Greek for "memorial slab"), in which Beethoven's ghost walks again. At the beginning, octave Gs make an unmistakable reference to the opening of Beethoven's *Leonore* Overture No. 3—a representation of the topmost step of the staircase that goes down to Florestan's dungeon. Kurtág, too, leads us into a subterranean space, but we never get out. The final movement, muted and maximally eerie, fixates on a spread-out chord that repeatedly quivers forth in quintuplet rhythm. At the very end the harmony shifts to the white-key notes of the C-major scale, all seven of them sounding in a luminous smear.

Beethoven's overture marches off to C-major jubilation. *Stele*, by contrast, limps through a parched, depopulated landscape. But the white-note chords at the end aren't quite hopeless; they fall short of the total desolation of Adrian Leverkühn's "I have found that *it is not to be*." Instead, as Kurtág himself once indicated, in conversation with the conductor Claudio Abbado, they have the rhythm of a gaunt figure staggering on.

After Britten

The East Anglian coast looks much as it did when Benjamin Britten passed his childhood writing moody settings of Verlaine and listening to the crash of the German Ocean. On the Aldeburgh beach you still see the old houses of the town sloping against the sky, the tall chimneys of the Moot Hall, an old fishing boat resting on its side, nets and buoys scattered about. The Aldeburgh Festival continues to present Britten's works in the local spaces for which he designed them. Yet the management has changed. The artistic director of Aldeburgh is the composer Thomas Adès, a worldly young man who was only five years old when Britten died. Adès has absorbed the full spectrum of twentieth-century possibilities and knows his way around pop. Yet he has a deep feeling for classical tradition, and as a pianist he plays Schubert as beautifully as anyone. He is, perhaps, Britten without the agony.

Adès embodies the virtues of a musical culture that has long been the envy of the world, to borrow the title of Humphrey Carpenter's history of the British Broadcasting Corporation. Nowhere are twentieth-century composers more central to the repertory: any British orchestra would offend its audience if it neglected the symphonies of Elgar and Vaughan Williams, while British opera houses give constant attention to the works of Britten and Tippett. The BBC itself has long promoted contemporary composers at the national level. A young composer such as Adès may lack the name recognition of an Elton John, but neither is he an invisible man on the margins of the culture: he has a reasonably broad and brightly lit platform on which to speak.

The assimilation of new work into the mainstream is helped by the fact that the internal politics of modern music has never been as fraught in Britain as in continental Europe or America. The dominant twentieth-century trends have all found a native following, but without the constant background noise of ideological disputation. This may be because British music has no tragic past attached to it, no stain of totalitarian aesthetics.

What results is a pragmatic, pluralistic musical culture where unexpected combinations are the rule. Michael Nyman's score for Peter Greenaway's indescribably bizarre film *A Zed & Two Noughts*, a comedy of genetics and decomposition, gives a courtly Baroque air to chugging minimalist patterns. George Benjamin's *Sudden Time* merges the canyon colors of Messiaen with the urban polyrhythms of Elliott Carter. Jonathan Harvey's *Ashes Dance Back*, for choir and electronics, uses spectral analysis in the IRCAM vein to shed an eerie new light on the centuries-old English choral tradition. The doleful D-minor chords that kick off Oliver Knussen's Horn Concerto smack of Gustav Mahler, although the helter-skelter instrumental writing that swarms all around has the effect of shoving Mahler into the middle of Piccadilly Circus.

Adès's own *Asyla*, a four-movement symphonic work from 1997, exemplifies pragmatism in action. It cobbles together Ligeti's crazy-quilt tonality, the player-piano polyrhythms of Conlon Nancarrow, the Nordic landscapes of Sibelius, and a dozen other choice sounds. The composer dramatizes his own struggle to define himself within and against modernity, seeking "asylums" of one kind or another. Splintered rhythms and microtonal tunings create disorder at the outset, but an old-fashioned, nobly expressive theme surfaces, sounding like the subject of Bach's Passacaglia and Fugue in C Minor. The studious "classical" character of the first movement gives way to spacious melancholy in the second: shades of Wagner and Mahler glide through the orchestration. In the third movement, "Ecstasio," the protagonist swears off solitude and ventures out on the town. The title comes from a favorite party drug of the nineties, and the orchestration reproduces the noise and ambience of a London club: big beats, chanting choirs, whoops, whistles, the buzz of the crowd, the thrill and danger of bodily contact.

After this scary hedonism comes an attenuated, cryptic finale, in which a sequence of meandering chorales leads to a grand, dark, imperious chord of E-flat minor. The music then tapers into silence. It's like a drunken shout in an empty street—Stephen Dedalus making his way home at the end of *Ulysses*, his mind spinning with epiphanies that he will forget in the morning.

Nixon in China

"I like to think of culture as the symbols that we share to understand each other," John Adams says, walking in the woods and fields around his composing hut. "When we communicate, we point to symbols that we have in common. If people want to make a point, they reach for a reference. It might be a Woody Allen movie, or a John Lennon lyric, or 'I'm not a crook.'" Adams wants his own music to play that role. His music floats the possibility of a twenty-first-century synthesis in which the dichotomy between tradition and avant-garde is given a well-deserved rest.

Adams is a child of the twentieth century in all its manifestations. He came of age in the swinging sixties, but his childhood had something anachronistic, almost nineteenth-century, about it. He grew up in a white-steepled village in New Hampshire, a place that could have been composed by Charles Ives. His parents didn't buy a record player until he was ten and never owned a television. Both were musicians—Adams's father played the clarinet, his mother sang with big bands. His grandfather ran a dance hall called Irwin's Winnipesaukee Gardens on the shores of Lake Winnipesaukee, where Adams would go in the summer with his family. Once, when Duke Ellington's band came to play at Irwin's, Adams got to sit for a moment next to the master on the piano bench.

Steeped in big-band swing, European classics, populist Americana, and Broadway musicals, Adams had a rude shock when he went to college—Harvard, 1965—and discovered that contemporary composers spoke a different language. His principal teacher was Leon Kirchner, a Schoenberg pupil. By day, Adams would study the Second Viennese School, avant-garde techniques, musique concrète, and the writings of Boulez, persuading himself that musical language had to keep going forward. Indeed, he became so militant in his views that he wrote a letter to Bernstein berating him for the stylistic backwardness of *Chichester Psalms*.

("What about Boulez?" he queried.) At night, Adams would listen to Beatles records with his friends and wonder, as Reich had wondered when he alternated between Webern and Coltrane, whether he could unify his daytime and nighttime worlds.

When Adams graduated from Harvard, his mother gave him a copy of John Cage's *Silence*, which led him to question most of the musical convictions that he had held since childhood. Dreaming of Cagean liberation, Adams moved to San Francisco, where he worked odd jobs, took up teaching, and diverted small audiences with happenings and conceptual pieces. One work, *Lo Fi*, called for a random assortment of scratchy old 78-rpm records to be played on antiquated audio equipment for an hour or more. After a while, Adams found Cage's aesthetic equally confining, and looked for a way out.

Minimalism gave Adams his individual voice. His defining move was to combine Reich-Glass repetition with the sprawling forms and grandiose orchestration of Wagner, Mahler, and Sibelius. In 1985 he finished a forty-minute symphonic work called *Harmonielehre*, its title taken from the famous textbook in which Schoenberg first declared that tonality was dead. Adams's *Harmonielehre* says, in essence, "Like hell it is." Forty triple-forte chords of E minor set the piece in motion, their durations gradually diminishing and then lengthening again. This colossal opening, Adams said, was an attempt to capture something that came to him in a dream—an image of a huge oil tanker levitating from the waters of San Francisco Bay, its rusty hull gleaming in the sun. Within minutes decadent Wagnerian chords are proliferating everywhere, although they are filtered through the sensibility of a child of the sixties who once tripped on LSD while listening to Rudolf Serkin play Beethoven's *Choral Fantasy*.

Nixon in China, Adams's first opera, brings about an even more dramatic transformation of European form. Nothing seems more inherently unlikely than the idea of a great American opera—possibly the greatest since *Porgy and Bess*—based on the events surrounding President Richard Nixon's visit to China in 1972. When the director Peter Sellars first proposed the subject, Adams assumed he was joking. At the premiere, which took place at the Houston Grand Opera on October 22, 1987, many critics thought the same. Yet Sellars knew what he was doing. By yanking opera into a universally familiar contemporary setting, he was almost forcing his composer to clean out all the cobwebs of the European past. Adams also had the advantage of an extraordinary libretto by the poet Alice Goodman. Many lines come straight from the documentary record—the speeches and poetry of Chairman Mao, the fine-spun oratory of Prime Minister Zhou Enlai, the convoluted utterances and memoirs of Nixon—but they coalesce into an epic poem of recent history, a dream narrative in half-rhyming couplets.

Each character is sharply sketched: Mao brittle and piercing in his high tenor tessitura; Zhou visionary and elegiac in his baritone flights; Nixon at once pompous and insecure, his attempts at oratorical grandeur defeated by the lower demons of his nature. He introduces himself with the bravura aria "News Has a Kind of Mystery," an exaltation of the electronically interconnected world. Nixon repeats his words as if caught in a loop—"News news news news news news news news news news has a has a has a has a kind of mystery"—and the orchestra chugs along in the manner of Duke Ellington's locomotive numbers. Then Nixon digresses into a meditation on the American heartland, although the motoric patterns churn on beneath him, in keeping with the fact that the open prairie is now drenched in television blue:

It's prime time in the USA.
It's yesterday night. They watch us now;
The three main networks' colors glow
Livid through drapes onto the lawn.
Dishes are washed and homework done,
The dog and grandma fall asleep,
A car roars past playing loud pop,
Is gone. As I look down the road
I know America is good
At heart . . .

Then the idyll crumbles. A D-minor chord gives a sinister resonance to the word "heart." Nixon's mental eye drifts to enemies and subversives:

The rats begin to chew
The sheets. There's murmuring down below.
Now there's ingratitude!

Rasping trombone chords hint at the paranoid malice that will shortly drag Nixon down into the ignonimy of Watergate.

Throughout, *Nixon* delivers a chilling overview of twentieth-century games of power. Many early viewers had no idea what to make of the studied ambiguity with which the creative team handled the main characters, and the complaints came from opposing points on the political spectrum: liberals protested the seeming romanticization of a criminal president while right-wingers disliked the emphasis on the poetic-philosophical side of the genocidal Mao. Are Adams and his collaborators besotted with the glamour of authority? Act I raises that suspicion, with its high-flown rhetoric, its giddy air of global camaraderie, its innocent shouts of "Cheers!" But Act II breaks the spell. After another ode to Americana, this one delivered by Pat Nixon, Chinese singers and dancers arrive to perform the ballet-opera *Red Detachment of Women*, which Goodman and Adams have reimagined on their own terms. It is a sadistic ideological entertainment from which the Nixons recoil in horror. The music mixes secondhand American pop with secondhand Strauss and Wagner, at one point mashing the Jochanaan theme from *Salome* into "Wotan's Farewell" from *Die Walküre*. It's a half-charming, half-repulsive simulacrum of totalitarian kitsch.

Finally, Jiang Qing takes the spotlight. The Chairman's wife exults in her ability to control culture and dominate people. As in Thomas Mann's Faustian nightmares, bloodless intellectuality meets bloody barbarism. Adams's music takes on an icy hardness: the amiable key of B-flat major is hammered into blue steel. On top is a limber vocal line that lies somewhere between the fateful choruses of Verdi and the bouncing operetta numbers of Gilbert and Sullivan:

I am the wife of Mao Tse-tung
Who raised the weak above the strong
When I appear the people hang
Upon my words, and for his sake
Whose wreaths are heavy round my neck
I speak according to the book.
. . . Let me be
A grain of sand in heaven's eye
And I shall taste eternal joy.

The people shout along with her: "Joy! Joy! Joy! Joy! Joy! Joy! Joy! Joy! Joy! Joy! Joy! Joy! Joy! Joy!" Shostakovich could not have said it better.

In the last act a mist of forgetfulness descends. The assembled potentates cease to be distinct historical characters and instead become vessels of one sadly remembering mind—perhaps the soul of the century itself. Nixon thinks back to his service in the Second World War, when good and evil were distinct. Mao recalls his idealistic youth. And Zhou, the conscience of the piece, falls into a reverie of doubt, asking himself whether reality had ever come close to what his high-flown rhetoric had promised:

How much of what we did was good?
Everything seems to move beyond
Our remedy. Come, heal this wound.
At this hour nothing can be done.
Just before dawn the birds begin,
The warblers who prefer the dark,
The cage-birds answering. To work!
Outside this room the chill of grace
Lies heavy on the morning grass.

No birds sing in Adams's setting of these lines—not on first hearing, at least. Winding slowly upward in the cello is a familiar-sounding strain of lament: the American cousin of the cello solos in Sibelius's *Swan of Tuonela.* A surreal image comes to mind: Mao, Jiang Qing, Zhou Enlai, the Nixons, and Henry Kissinger standing on a mythical island in a pitch-black river while the swan of death glides serenely around them.

EPILOGUE

Extremes become their opposites in time. Schoenberg's scandal-making chords, totems of the Viennese artist in revolt against bourgeois society, seep into Hollywood thrillers and postwar jazz. The supercompact twelve-tone material of Webern's Piano Variations mutates over a generation or two into La Monte Young's *Second Dream of the High-Tension Line Stepdown Transformer.* Morton Feldman's indeterminate notation leads circuitously to the Beatles' "A Day in the Life." Steve Reich's gradual process infiltrates chart-topping albums by the bands Talking Heads and U2. There is no escaping the interconnectedness of musical experience, even if composers try to barricade themselves against the outer world or to control the reception of their work. Music history is too often treated as a kind of Mercator projection of the globe, a flat image representing a landscape that is in reality borderless and continuous.

At the beginning of the twenty-first century, the impulse to pit classical music against pop culture no longer makes intellectual or emotional sense. Young composers have grown up with pop music ringing in their ears, and they make use of it or ignore it as the occasion demands. They are seeking the middle ground between the life of the mind and the noise of the street. Likewise, some of the liveliest reactions to twentieth-century and contemporary classical music have come from the pop arena, roughly defined. The microtonal tunings of Sonic Youth, the opulent harmonic designs of Radiohead, the fractured, fast-shifting time signatures of math rock and intelligent dance music, the elegiac orchestral arrangements that underpin songs by Sufjan Stevens and Joanna Newsom: all these carry on the long-running conversation between classical and popular traditions.

Björk is a modern pop artist deeply affected by the twentieth-century classical repertory that she absorbed in music school—Stockhausen's electronic pieces, the organ music of Messiaen, the spiritual minimalism of Arvo Pärt. If you were to listen blind to Björk's "An Echo, A Stain," in which the singer declaims fragmentary melodies against a soft cluster of choral voices, and then move on to Osvaldo Golijov's song cycle *Ayre*, where pulsating dance beats underpin multi-ethnic songs of Moorish Spain, you might conclude that Björk's was the classical composition and Golijov's was something else. One possible destination for twenty-first-century music is a final "great fusion": intelligent pop artists and extroverted composers speaking more or less the same language.

Sterner spirits will undoubtedly continue to insist on fundamental differences in musical vocabulary, attaching themselves to the venerable orchestral and operatic traditions of the Baroque, Classical, and Romantic eras or the now equally venerable practices of twentieth-century modernism. Already in the first years of the new century composers have produced works of monumental character that invite comparison to the symphonies of Mahler and the operas of Strauss. Thomas Adès's *The Tempest*, first heard at Covent Garden in 2004, shows that a composer can still write a grand opera of ornate design and airy power in an atomizing digital age. The following year saw the premiere of John Adams's *Doctor Atomic*, an opera about the testing of the first atomic bomb. Holding his lyricism in reserve, Adams marshals a ghoulish army of twentieth-century styles to summon the awe and dread of the atomic morning. Georg Friedrich Haas's sixty-five-minute ensemble piece *in vain* may mark a new departure in Austro-German music, joining spectral harmony to a vast Brucknerian structure.

If twenty-first-century composition appears to have a split personality—sometimes intent on embracing everything, sometimes longing to be lost to the world—its ambivalence is nothing new. The debate over the merits of engagement and withdrawal has gone on for centuries. In the fourteenth century, Ars Nova composers engendered controversy by inserting secular tunes into the Mass Ordinary. Around 1600, Monteverdi's forcefully melodic style sounded crude and libertine to adherents of rule-bound Renaissance polyphony. In nineteenth-century Vienna, the extroverted brilliance of Rossini's comic operas was judged against the inward enigmas of Beethoven's late quartets. Composition only gains power from failing to decide the eternal dispute. In a decentered culture, it has a chance to play a kind of godfather role, able to assimilate anything new because it has assimilated everything in the past.

Composers may never match their popular counterparts in instant impact, but, in the freedom of their solitude, they can communicate experiences of singular intensity. Unfolding large forms, engaging with complex forces, traversing the spectrum from noise to silence, they show the way to what Claude Debussy once called the "imaginary country, that's to say one that can't be found on the map."

NOTES

Abbreviations Used

ACLC: Aaron Copland Collection, Music Division, Library of Congress.

ACR: *Aaron Copland: A Reader: Selected Writings, 1923–1972*, ed. Richard Kostelanetz (Routledge, 2004).

ACVP: Aaron Copland and Vivien Perlis, *Copland: 1900 Through 1942* (St. Martin's, 1984).

AHRP: *Hitler: Reden und Proklamationen, 1932–1945*, ed. Max Domarus (Schmidt, 1962–65).

AMM: Alma Mahler, *Gustav Mahler: Memories and Letters*, ed. Donald Mitchell, trans. Basil Creighton (Viking, 1969).

ASC: Arnold Schönberg Center, Vienna.

ASL: *Arnold Schoenberg: Letters*, ed. Erwin Stein, trans. Eithne Wilkins and Ernst Kaiser (University of California Press, 1987).

ASSI: *Style and Idea: Selected Writings of Arnold Schoenberg*, ed. Leonard Stein, trans. Leo Black (University of California Press, 1984).

BDC: Berlin Document Center, microfilm copies at National Archives II.

BGFI: Bryan Gilliam, " 'Friede im Innern': Strauss's Public and Private Worlds in the Mid 1930s," *Journal of the American Musicological Society* 57:3 (Fall 2004), pp. 565–98.

BGRS: Bryan Gilliam, *The Life of Richard Strauss* (Cambridge UP, 1999).

DMBB1, 2, 3: *Letters from a Life: Selected Letters and Diaries of Benjamin Britten, 1913–1976*, vols. 1 and 2 (Faber, 1991), vol. 3 (University of California Press, 2004), ed. Donald Mitchell, Philip Reed, and Mervyn Cooke.

ETS1, 2, 3: Erik Tawaststjerna, *Sibelius, Volume I: 1865–1905* (University of California Press, 1976); *Volume II: 1904–1914* (University of California Press, 1986); *Volume III: 1914–1957* (Faber, 1997), all trans. Robert Layton.

EWS: Elizabeth Wilson, *Shostakovich: A Life Remembered*, 2nd ed. (Princeton UP, 2006).

FMP: Records of the Federal Music Project, RG 69, National Archives II.

GGLC: George Gershwin Collection, Music Division, Library of Congress.

GMRS: *Gustav Mahler, Richard Strauss: Correspondence, 1888–1911*, ed. Herta Blaukopf, trans. Edmund Jephcott (University of Chicago Press, 1984).

HHS: Hans Heinz Stuckenschmidt, *Arnold Schoenberg: His Life, World, and Work*, trans. Humphrey Searle (Schirmer Books, 1978).

HMAW: Hans Moldenhauer and Rosaleen Moldenhauer, *Anton von Webern: A Chronicle of His Life and Work* (Knopf, 1979).

HPAC: Howard Pollack, *Aaron Copland: The Life and Work of an Uncommon Man* (Holt, 1999).

IGSF: Isaak Glikman, *Story of a Friendship: The Letters of Dmitri Shostakovich to Isaak Glikman, 1914–1975*, trans. Anthony Phillips (Cornell UP, 2001).

JASR: Joseph Auner, *A Schoenberg Reader: Documents of a Life* (Yale UP, 2003).

JCS: John Cage, *Silence: Lectures and Writings by John Cage* (Wesleyan UP, 1973).

JGT: *Die Tagebücher von Joseph Goebbels*, ed. Elke Fröhlich (K. G. Saur, 1987–).

LFS: Laurel E. Fay, *Shostakovich: A Life* (Oxford UP, 2000).

LGM1, 2, 3: Henry-Louis de La Grange, *Mahler, Volume 1* (Doubleday, 1973); *Volume 2: Vienna: The Years of Challenge (1897–1904)* (Oxford UP, 1995); *Volume 3: Vienna: Triumph and Disillusion (1904–1907)* (Oxford UP, 1999).

MFS: *Morton Feldman Says: Selected Interviews and Lectures, 1964–1987*, ed. Chris Villars (Hyphen, 2006).

NG: *New Grove Dictionary of Music and Musicians*, 2nd ed., ed. Stanley Sadie (Macmillan, 2001).

NSM: Nicolas Slonimsky, *Music Since 1900*, 5th ed. (Schirmer Books, 1994).

NSPHM: Nigel Simeone and Peter Hill, *Messiaen* (Yale UP, 2005).

OMGUS: Records of the Office of Military Government, United States, RG 260, National Archives II.

RCSC: Robert Craft, *Stravinsky: Chronicle of a Friendship* (Vanderbilt UP, 1994).

RSC: Franz Trenner, *Richard Strauss: Chronik zu Leben und Werk*, ed. Florian Trenner (Verlag Dr. Richard Strauss, 2003).

RSRR: *Richard Strauss and Romain Rolland: Correspondence, Together with Fragments from the Diary of Romain Rolland and Other Essays*, ed. Rollo Myers (Calder and Boyars, 1968).

RTS1, 2: Richard Taruskin, *Stravinsky and the Russian Traditions: A Biography of the Works Through "Mavra,"* 2 vols. (University of California Press, 1996).

SRW: Steve Reich, *Writings on Music, 1965–2000*, ed. Paul Hillier (Oxford UP, 2002).

SSC1, 2, 3: *Stravinsky: Selected Correspondence*, ed. Robert Craft, 3 vols. (Knopf, 1982–85).

SWS1, 2: Stephen Walsh, *Stravinsky: A Creative Spring: Russia and France, 1882–1934* (Knopf, 1999), and *Stravinsky: The Second Exile: France and America, 1934–1971* (Knopf, 2006).

TMDF: Thomas Mann, *Doctor Faustus*, trans. John E. Woods (Vintage, 1999).

Epigraph

vii *"It seems to me"*: TMDF, p. 11.

Preface

xi *"Mr. Gershwin"*: Edward Jablonski, *Gershwin* (Da Capo, 1998), p. 167.

xii *"Wherever we are"*: JCS, p. 3.

1: The Golden Age

1 *"I am ready"*: Johann Wolfgang von Goethe, *Faust*, ed. Cyrus Hamlin, trans. Walter Arndt (Norton, 2001), pp. 19–20.

3 *"terribly cacophonous"*: *Puccini: 276 lettere inedite*, ed. Giuseppe Pintorno (Nuove Edizioni, 1974), p. 130.

3 *six of his pupils*: They were Alban Berg, Heinrich Jalowetz, Karl Horwitz, Erwin Stein, Viktor Krüger, and Zdzislaw Jachimecki. See "Fremden-Liste," *Grazer Tagespost*, May 18, 1906; and HHS, p. 67.

3 *"feverish impatience"*: Hermann Watznauer's unpublished biography of Berg, *Vom Barockpalais ins Zwölftongebäude*, as published in Erich Alban Berg, *Der unverbesserliche Romantiker: Alban Berg, 1885–1935* (Österreichischer Bundesverlag, 1985), p. 62.

3 *"young people"*: Richard Strauss, *Der Strom der Töne trug mich fort: Die Welt um Richard Strauss in Briefen*, ed. Franz Grasberger (Hans Schneider, 1967), p. 169.

4 *Hitler*: Ibid., p. 392. Whether or not Hitler attended is addressed in Chapter 9.

4 *news from Croatia . . .* Faust: *Grazer Tagespost*, May 16, 1906.

4 *Alma recounted*: AMM, p. 97. RSC, p. 277, indicates that the day trip happened on the sixteenth. For the photograph, see Gilbert Kaplan, ed., *The Mahler Album* (Kaplan Foundation, 1995), nos. 77 and 78.

4 *"Der Mahler!"*: Stephen Hefling, *Mahler, "Das Lied von der Erde"* (Cambridge UP, 2000), p. 90.

4 *"a pure kind of German"*: Gemma Bellincioni, *Io e il palcoscenico: Trenta e un anno di vita artistica* (R. Quinteri, 1920), p. 133.

5 *"All untrue"*: GMRS, p. 140.

5 *"Strauss and I tunnel"*: AMM, p. 98.

5 *Mahlerverein*: BGRS, p. 75. For "*Cacophony*," see *Musical Times*, July 1, 1906, p. 486.

5 *piano shop*: AMM, pp. 88–89.

5 *"You would not believe"*: GMRS, p. 92.

6 *"great excitement"*: Ernst Decsey, *Musik war sein Leben: Lebenserinnerungen* (Hans Deutsch, 1962), pp. 171–72.

6 *"tone-color world"*: Ernst Decsey, "Salome: Zur Einführung," *Grazer Tagespost*, May 16, 1906.

6 *nervous electricity*: Decsey, "Nachtrag," *Grazer Tagespost*, May 17, 1906.

6 *C-sharp minor*: Roland Tenschert, "Strauss as Librettist," in *Richard Strauss, "Salome,"* ed. Derrick Puffett (Cambridge UP, 1989), p. 47. See also BGRS, pp. 82–83.

8 *eight-note dissonance*: See the last chord of one bar before 361. The vocal score omits the B-sharp in the flutes and clarinets.
9 *"satanic and artistic"*: Ernst Decsey, "Nachtrag," *Grazer Tagespost*, May 17, 1906.
9 *"Me, too"*: Wilhelm Kienzl, *Meine Lebenswanderung: Erlebtes und Erschautes* (J. Engelhorns Nachf., 1926), pp. 149–50.
9 *"It is raining"*: Richard Strauss, *Strom der Töne*, p. 169.
9 *"I am sorry"*: Richard Strauss, *Betrachtungen und Erinnerungen*, ed. Willi Schuh (Piper, 1989), p. 227.
9 *"one of the greatest masterworks"*: *Gustav Mahler: Letters to His Wife*, ed. Henry-Louis de La Grange, Günther Weiss, and Knud Martner, trans. Antony Beaumont (Cornell UP, 2004), p. 258.
9 *voice of the people*: AMM, p. 98.
10 *at a restaurant*: Berg, *Der unverbesserliche Romantiker*, pp. 62–63.
10 *"What a gifted"*: Thomas Mann, *Doktor Faustus* (Fischer, 1971), pp. 155–56.
10 *"I have actually outlived"*: Kurt Wilhelm, *Richard Strauss: An Intimate Portrait*, trans. Mary Whittall (Rizzoli, 1989), p. 284.
11 *Tchaikovsky was captivated*: Robert W. Gutman, *Richard Wagner: The Man, His Mind, and His Music* (Harcourt Brace Jovanovich, 1968), pp. 347–48.
12 *"a democrat, a new man"*: Gerald D. Turbow, "Wagnerism in France," in *Wagnerism in European Culture and Politics*, ed. David C. Large and William Weber (Cornell UP, 1984), p. 152.
12 *"counter-religion"*: Charles Baudelaire, "Richard Wagner and Tannhäuser in Paris," in *The Painter of Modern Life and Other Essays*, trans. Jonathan Mayne (Phaidon, 1964), p. 128. For M. Carey Thomas, see Joseph Horowitz, *Wagner Nights: An American History* (University of California Press, 1994), pp. 227–28. For Herzl and *Tannhäuser*, see Carl Schorske, *Fin-de-Siècle Vienna: Politics and Culture* (Vintage, 1981), p. 163.
12 *"This Book contains"*: Jerrold Northrop Moore, *Edward Elgar: A Creative Life* (Oxford UP, 1999), pp. 172–73.
12 *"first English progressivist"*: Ibid., p. 369.
13 *"an oracle"*: Friedrich Nietzsche, *On the Genealogy of Morals and Ecce Homo*, trans. Walter Kaufmann and R. J. Hollingdale (Vintage, 1967), p. 103.
13 "Il faut méditerraniser": Friedrich Nietzsche, *The Birth of Tragedy and The Case of Wagner*, trans. Walter Kaufmann (Vintage, 1967), p. 159. For more on Nietzsche's "neoclassicism," see Walter Frisch, *German Modernism: Music and the Arts* (University of California Press, 2005), pp. 23–28.
13 *"I have felt the pulse"*: *Selected Letters of Richard Wagner*, ed. and trans. Stewart Spencer and Barry Millington (Norton, 1988), p. 210.
14 *"If we want thousands"*: Kurt Blaukopf and Herta Blaukopf, *Mahler: His Life, Work, and World* (Thames and Hudson, 2000), p. 138.
14 *"Richard III"*: BGRS, p. 1.
14 *"You can be certain"*: Max Steinitzer, *Richard Strauss: Biographie* (Schuster und Loeffler, 1922), p. 34.
14 *mocked a passage*: "Selections from the Strauss-Thuille Correspondence," trans. Susan Gillespie, in *Richard Strauss and His World*, ed. Bryan Gilliam (Princeton UP, 1992), p. 214.
14 *Strauss's parents*: For a revealing commentary, see Michael Kennedy, *Richard Strauss: Man, Musician, Enigma* (Cambridge UP, 1999), pp. 3–11.
15 *"immoral" and "the seeds of death"*: Willi Schuh, *Richard Strauss: A Chronicle of the Early Years, 1864–1898*, trans. Mary Whittall (Cambridge UP, 1982), pp. 282 and 285.
15 *"Dream on"*: Max Stirner, *The Ego and Its Own*, ed. David Leopold (Cambridge UP, 1995), p. 111.
16 *"apostles of moderation"*: Schuh, *Richard Strauss*, p. 401.
16 *"scourge of the Philistines"*: Ibid., p. 505.
16 *"crimes against religion" and "spiritual fodder"*: David Clay Large, *Where Ghosts Walked: Munich's Road to the Third Reich* (Norton, 1997), p. 10.
16 *"book of images"*: Claude Debussy, *Debussy on Music*, ed. and trans. Richard Langham Smith (Knopf, 1977), p. 160.
16 *Latter-day Strauss scholars*: See Walter Werbeck, *Die Tondichtungen von Richard Strauss* (Hans Schneider, 1996), esp. pp. 453–54; the work of Bryan Gilliam (BGRS, BGFI); and Charles Youmans, *Richard Strauss's Orchestral Music and the German Intellectual Tradition* (Indiana UP, 2005).
17 *"imbecile"*: RSRR, p. 155. See also *Richard Strauss–Stefan Zweig: Briefwechsel*, ed. Willi Schuh (Fischer, 1957), p. 128.
17 *court of Kaiser Wilhelm*: Chris Walton, "Beneath the Seventh Veil: Richard Strauss's *Salome* and Kaiser Wilhelm II," *Musical Times* 146 (Winter 2005), pp. 14–19.
17 *he indicated to Hofmannsthal*: BGRS, p. 86.

17 *"I was never"*: ASSI, p. 137.
18 *"music of Herr Richard Strauss"*: Wilhelm, *Richard Strauss: An Intimate Portrait*, p. 100.
18 *"More of a stock company"*: Karl Kraus, "Cultural Bankruptcy" (1924), trans. Susan Gillespie, in Gilliam, *Richard Strauss and His World*, p. 360.
18 Libre Parole: RSRR, p. 148.
18 *"If one of the two"*: Alma Mahler, *Mein Leben* (Fischer, 1963), p. 346.
19 *"from then on"*: Donald Mitchell, *Gustav Mahler, Volume II: The Wunderhorn Years* (University of California Press, 1995), p. 74.
19 *"Don't you compose"*: LGM2, pp. 371–72.
20 *"Is music such a serious"*: Jonathan Carr, *Mahler* (Overlook, 1997), p. 95.
20 *May Day*: Kurt List, "The Music of Soviet Russia," *politics,* May 1944, p. 106.
21 *"Down with programs!"*: LGM2, p. 522.
21 *"pure musician"*: ibid., p. 524.
21 *"satanic"*: LGM3, p. 425.
21 *"Krupp makes only cannons"*: ibid., p. 534.
22 *switch the middle movements*: Gilbert Kaplan, ed., *The Correct Movement Order in Mahler's Sixth Symphony* (Kaplan Foundation, 2004), demonstrates beyond a doubt that Mahler never went back on his decision, although Alma Mahler and the editor Erwin Ratz later claimed otherwise.
22 *"fully grown cow"*: LGM3, p. 413.
22 *"walked up and down"*: AMM, p. 100.
22 *"over-instrumented"*: Klaus Pringsheim's recollections, quoted in Norman Lebrecht, *Mahler Remembered* (Norton, 1988), p. 192.
22 *"reduced almost to tears"*: Bruno Walter, *Gustav Mahler*, trans. Lotte Walter Lindt (Quartet Books, 1990), p. 51.
23 *lightened the orchestration*: LGM3, pp. 810–11.
23 *"I extend to [Strauss]" and "very sweet"*: *Ein Glück ohne Ruh': Die Briefe Gustav Mahlers an Alma*, ed. Henry-Louis de La Grange and Günther Weiss (Siedler, 1995), pp. 306–8.
23 *"Tonio Kröger"*: GMRS, p. 142.
23 *"redeemed from"*: Peter Heyworth, *Otto Klemperer: His Life and Times, Volume 1, 1885–1933* (Cambridge UP, 1996), p. 60.
23 *"I am to find"*: Recollection of Bernard Scharlitt, *Neue Freie Presse*, May 25, 1911.
23 *"The time is coming"*: La Grange and Weiss, *Glück ohne Ruh'*, p. 129.
24 *"In his mature years"*: Leon Botstein, "Whose Gustav Mahler?" in *Mahler and His World*, ed. Karen Painter (Princeton UP, 2002), pp. 20–21.
24 *"had to return"*: *Musical Times*, July 1, 1906, p. 486.
24 *"gift to the nation"*: LGM3, p. 431.
24 *"Vorbei!"*: Ibid., p. 792.
25 *"the highest fee"*: Ibid., pp. 661–62.
25 *rehearsals took place in German*: Glenn Watkins, *Proof Through the Night: Music and the Great War* (University of California Press, 2003), p. 300.
25 *ten thousand people*: Ezra Schabas, *Theodore Thomas: America's Conductor and Builder of Orchestras, 1835–1905* (University of Illinois Press, 1989), p. 136.
25 *"electric sign"*: Horowitz, *Wagner Nights*, p. 210.
26 *two hundred dollars*: Roland Gelatt, *The Fabulous Phonograph: From Edison to Stereo* (Appleton-Century, 1965), p. 146.
26 *million copies*: Fred Bronson, *Billboard's Hottest Hot 100 Hits* (Billboard Books, 2003), p. 179.
26 *Telharmonic Hall*: Thom Holmes, *Electronic and Experimental Music*, 2nd ed. (Routledge, 2002), pp. 44–52.
26 *"anarch of art"*: James Huneker, *Overtones: A Book of Temperaments* (1904; Scribner's, 1922), dedication page.
26 *White House, Senate*: "Richard Strauss Meets the President," *New York Herald*, April 27, 1904.
27 *house of Agamemnon*: Arthur Schopenhauer, *The World as Will and Representation*, trans. E. F. J. Payne (Dover, 1966), vol. 2, p. 449.
27 *Wanamaker's*: RSC, p. 252.
27 *"They do things"*: "Dr. Strauss at Wanamaker's," *New York Times*, April 17, 1904.
27 *Strauss was promptly pilloried*: BGRS, pp. 81–82.
27 *Boxes 27 and 29*: "Strauss's 'Salome' the First Time Here," *New York Times*, Jan. 23, 1907.
27 *J. P. Morgan's daughter*: Jean Strouse, *Morgan: American Financier* (Random House, 1999), pp. 561–62.
27 *"man of middle life"*: " 'Salome' Condemned," *New York Times*, Jan. 24, 1907.
28 *"indefinable dread"*: "Strauss's 'Salome' the First Time Here."
28 *fogbank*: "Message from Out the Fog: Says Puccini Is Off the Hook and Hopes to Be in Town To-day," *New York Times*, Jan. 18, 1907.
28 *"Bret Harte's novels"*: "Puccini Just in Time," *New York Times*, Jan. 19, 1907.
28 *"coon songs"*: "Puccini Hears Coon Songs," *New York Times*, Feb. 25, 1907.
29 *black minstrel*: On the "exotic" sources of

The Girl of the Golden West, see Annie J. Randall and Rosalind Gray Davis, *Puccini and "The Girl": History and Reception of "The Girl of the Golden West"* (University of Chicago Press, 2005).

29 *"German atmosphere"*: Theresa M. Collins, *Otto Kahn: Art, Money, and Modern Time* (University of North Carolina Press, 2002), p. 83. See also "Conried Resigns as Opera Director," *New York Times*, Jan. 24, 1908.

29 *Philharmonic was reconstituted*: Joseph Horowitz, *Classical Music in America: A History of Its Rise and Fall* (Norton, 2005), pp. 185–88.

29 *"completely unprejudiced"*: *Selected Letters of Gustav Mahler*, ed. Knud Martner, trans. Eithne Wilkins, Ernst Kaiser, and Bill Hopkins (Farrar, Straus and Giroux, 1979), p. 319.

29 *On a good night*: AMM, p. 166.

29 *Philharmonic musician*: Recollections of Benjamin Kohon, in Lebrecht, *Mahler Remembered*, p. 294.

29 *"Wherever I am"*: Ibid., p. 300.

30 *"I see everything"*: Martner, *Selected Letters of Gustav Mahler*, p. 329.

30 *"I have found that people"*: Ferruccio Busoni, *Letters to His Wife*, trans. Rosamond Ley (Edward Arnold, 1938), p. 182.

30 *"victim of the dollar"*: "A Victim of Dollars," *New York Times*, May 21, 1911.

30 *"You cannot imagine"*: Zoltan Roman, *Gustav Mahler's American Years, 1907–1911: A Documentary History* (Pendragon, 1989), p. 475.

31 *"I have never worked"*: Ibid., p. 474.

31 *Charles W. Kruger*: Henry-Louis de La Grange, *Gustav Mahler: Chronique d'une vie*, vol. 3, *Le génie foudroyé* (Fayard, 1984), p. 247; see also "Thousands Mourn Dead Fire Chief," *New York Times*, Feb. 17, 1908.

31 *Strauss was stunned*: Wilhelm, *Richard Strauss, An Intimate Portrait*, p. 106.

31 *"antipode"*: Walter Thomas, *Richard Strauss und seine Zeitgenossen* (Langen Müller, 1964), p. 155.

31 *"this aspiring"*: GMRS, p. 153.

32 *"about" Mahler*: Tim Ashley, *Richard Strauss* (Phaidon, 1999), pp. 116–17.

2. Doctor Faust

33 *"Lies, Frau Marta"*: Lawrence Weschler, "Paradise: The Southern California Idyll of Hitler's Cultural Exiles," in *Exiles + Emigrés: The Flight of European Artists from Hitler*, ed. Stephanie Barron and Sabine Eckmann (Abrams, 1997), p. 346.

34 *"lost paradise"*: Thomas Mann, *The Story of a Novel: The Genesis of "Doctor Faustus,"* trans. Richard Winston and Clara Winston (Knopf, 1961), p. 229.

34 *"extremely difficult"*: Thomas Mann, *Tagebücher, 28.5.1946–31.12.1948*, ed. Inge Jens (Fischer, 1989), p. 56.

34 *"I have found"*: Thomas Mann, *Doktor Faustus* (Fischer, 1971), p. 477.

34 *"You will lead"*: Ibid., p. 244.

34 *"bloodless intellectuality"*: Ibid., p. 373.

34 *"I can see through walls"*: Oscar Levant, *The Memoirs of an Amnesiac* (Bantam, 1966), p. 120.

35 *"Great art"*: Hanns Eisler, "Notes on 'Dr. Faustus,'" in *Hanns Eisler: A Miscellany*, ed. David Blake (Harwood, 1995), p. 252.

36 *"Strange regions"*: Thomas Mann, *Stories of Three Decades*, trans. Helen T. Lowe-Porter (Knopf, 1936), p. 283.

36 *"Do you think"*: Thomas Mann, *Death in Venice and Other Stories*, trans. David Luke (Bantam, 1988), p. 87.

37 *Vienna was the scene*: On aspects of fin-de-siècle Vienna, see Carl E. Schorske, *Fin-de-Siècle Vienna: Politics and Culture* (Vintage, 1981); Allan Janik and Stephen Toulmin, *Wittgenstein's Vienna* (Touchstone, 1973); William M. Johnston, *The Austrian Mind* (University of California Press, 1972); Steven Beller, *Vienna and the Jews, 1867–1938: A Cultural History* (Cambridge UP, 1989); and Steven Beller, ed., *Rethinking Vienna 1900* (Berghahn Books, 2001).

37 *"truth-seekers"*: Carl Schorske, talk at the symposium "*Wozzeck*: The Play—The Opera—Past and Present," Princeton University, July 8, 2003.

37 *"critical modernists"*: Allan Janik, "Vienna 1900 Revisited: Paradigms and Problems," in Beller, *Rethinking Vienna 1900*, pp. 40–41.

37 *"Now with my murderer"*: Georg Trakl, *Dichtungen und Briefe*, ed. Walther Killy and Hans Szklenar (Müller, 1969), p. 132.

37 *Peter Altenberg*: Andrew Barker, "Berg and the Cultural Politics of 'Vienna 1900,'" in *The Cambridge Companion to Berg*, ed. Anthony Pople (Cambridge UP, 1997), p. 25.

38 *"If I must choose"*: Janik and Toulmin, *Wittgenstein's Vienna*, p. 91.

38 *"the greatest man"*: Otto Weininger, *Geschlecht und Charakter* (Braumüller, 1919), p. 456.

38 *Schoenberg and his pupils*: For Webern reading Weininger, see HMAW, p. 113.

38 *"Everything purely aesthetic"*: Wolfgang

Gratzer, *Zur "Wunderlichen Mystik" Alban Bergs: Eine Studie* (Böhlau, 1993), pp. 97–98.

38 *"Ethics and aesthetics"*: Ludwig Wittgenstein, *Tractatus Logico-Philosophicus*, trans. C. K. Ogden (Routledge, 1981), p. 183. Compare with Weininger, *Geschlecht und Charakter*, p. 320: ". . . alle Ästhetik doch ein Geschöpf der Ethik bleibt."

39 *84 percent*: William Weber, "The Rise of the Classical Repertoire in Nineteenth-Century Orchestral Concerts," in *The Orchestra: Origins and Transformations*, ed. Joan Peyser (Billboard Books, 2000), p. 376.

39 *"If it is art"*: ASSI, p. 124.

40 *"budding insanity"*: *Cosima Wagner's Diaries, Volume II: 1878–1883*, ed. Martin Gregor-Dellin and Dietrich Mack, trans. Geoffrey Skelton (Harcourt Brace Jovanovich, 1980), p. 963.

40 *"Everything that is sacred"*: Henry Weinfield, introduction to Stéphane Mallarmé, *Collected Poems* (University of California Press, 1994), p. xii.

40 *"Music really ought"*: *Debussy Letters*, ed. François Lesure and Roger Nichols, trans. Roger Nichols (Harvard UP, 1987), p. 52.

40 *Debussy at Mallarmé's gatherings*: See François Lesure, *Claude Debussy: Biographie critique* (Klincksieck, 1994), p. 115. For more on Debussy and the occult, see Robert Orledge, *Debussy and the Theatre* (Cambridge UP, 1982), pp. 14–17.

41 *Universal Exposition*: See Annegret Fauser, *Musical Encounters at the 1889 Paris World's Fair* (University of Rochester Press, 2005), pp. 165–95.

41 *"contained all gradations"*: Claude Debussy, *Correspondance, 1884–1918*, ed. François Lesure (Hermann, 1993), p. 107.

41 *Turner and Whistler*: See Leon Botstein, "Beyond the Illusions of Realism: Painting and Debussy's Break with Tradition," in *Debussy and His World*, ed. Jane F. Fulcher (Princeton UP, 2001), pp. 141–79.

41 *"clear . . . unclear"*: Christopher C. Hill, "Consonance and Dissonance," in *The New Harvard Dictionary of Music*, ed. Don Michael Randel (Harvard UP, 1986), p. 198.

41 *The interval of the octave*: Hermann von Helmholtz, *On the Sensations of Tone as a Physiological Basis for the Theory of Music*, trans. Alexander J. Ellis (Dover Books, 1954), pp. 188–89.

42 *Debussy and Helmholtz*: Gary W. Don, "Brilliant Colors Provocatively Mixed: Overtone Structures in the Music of Debussy," *Music Theory Spectrum* 23:1 (Spring 2001), pp. 61–73.

42 *"Long shall my discourse"*: Mallarmé, *Collected Poems*, p. 39.

43 *"I love you"*: See the passage from 42 to 44 of Act IV.

44 cante jondo: For Debussy's aptitude for Spanish music, see Carol A. Hess, *Manuel de Falla and Modernism in Spain* (University of Chicago Press, 2001), p. 176.

44 *The son of a publisher*: See Steven Moore Whiting, *Satie the Bohemian: From Cabaret to Concert Hall* (Oxford UP, 1999), p. 66.

45 *"Satie was"*: Notes to the recording *Erik Satie, Vol. 2: Early Piano Works* (Philips 420 472–2).

45 *"smell of the lamp"*: *Debussy Letters*, p. 117.

45 S *volume*: Dika Newlin, *Schoenberg Remembered: Diaries and Recollections, 1938–1976* (Pendragon, 1980), p. 316.

45 *Zemlinsky's parents*: Antony Beaumont, *Zemlinsky* (Cornell UP, 2000), pp. 3–10.

46 *desecration of* Parsifal: Erich Alban Berg, *Alban Berg: Leben und Werk in Daten und Bildern* (Insel, 1976), p. 89.

47 *"paradox of the most violent description" and "Take good care"*: AMM, p. 78.

47 *"Why am I still writing"*: Richard Specht, *Gustav Mahler* (Schuster und Loeffler, 1913), p. 29.

47 *"Thank you"*: Josef Bohuslav Foerster, *Der Pilger: Erinnerungen eines Musikers* (Artia, 1955), p. 681.

47 *"very talented"*: Roswitha Schlötterer, *Richard Strauss, Max von Schillings: Ein Briefwechsel* (W. Ludwig, 1987), p. 78.

47 *"blessedly light up"*: Nuria Nono-Schoenberg, ed., *Arnold Schönberg, 1874–1951: Lebensgeschichte in Begegnungen* (Ritter Klagenfurt, 1992), p. 45.

47 *"I would like to take"*: HHS, p. 66.

47 *"He was very friendly"*: Arnold Schoenberg, "Attempt at a Diary," trans. Anita Luginbühl, *Journal of the Arnold Schoenberg Institute* 9:1 (June 1986), p. 29.

48 *vocal score*: Schoenberg's *Salome* score can be seen at ASC.

48 *"Perhaps in twenty years' time"*: Willi Reich, *Schoenberg: A Critical Biography*, trans. Leo Black (Praeger, 1971), p. 25.

48 *"one of us"*: Robert E. Norton, *Secret Germany: Stefan George and His Circle* (Cornell UP, 2002), p. 73.

49 *"I must not"*: The translation is by Philip Miller, published in the booklet for Glenn Gould's recording of Schoenberg Lieder

(Sony Classical SM2K 52 667). Date comes from manuscript at ASC.

49 *affair with Gerstl*: Bryan R. Simms, " 'My Dear Hagerl': Self-Representation in Schoenberg's String Quartet No. 2," *Nineteenth-Century Music* 26:3 (Spring 2003), p. 267.

49 *Gerstl's suicide*: Klaus Albrecht Schröder, *Richard Gerstl, 1883–1908* (Kunstforum der Bank Austria, 1993), pp. 182–86; and Beaumont, *Zemlinsky*, pp. 164–66.

50 *"I have only one hope"*: Simms, " 'My Dear Hagerl,' " p. 276.

50 *"I have cried"*: JASR, pp. 53–55.

50 *four-note figures*: Stuckenschmidt identifies the notes A, D, G-sharp, and their various transpositions as the "primal cell" of Schoenberg's early music (HHS, p. 525), and he relates it to the four-note cell that appears in the Second Quartet's scherzo (F-sharp, F, C, B, and transpositions), throughout *The Book of Hanging Gardens*, and many times thereafter. The possible derivation of this cell from tritonally opposed tonalities can be glimpsed in the sketches for the Second Chamber Symphony—for example, in the juxtaposition of F-flat major and B-flat minor on p. 34 [Sk212] of Sketchbook 3, ASC.

50 *Maximilian Kronberger*: See Norton, *Secret Germany*, pp. 326–41.

53 *"I feel the heat"*: Nono-Schoenberg, *Arnold Schönberg*, p. 70.

53 *fistfight*: LGM3, pp. 608–609.

53 *"seat-rattling"*: Egon Wellesz, *Arnold Schönberg* (Heinrichshofen, 1985), p. 31.

53 *"Stop it!"*: Martin Eybl, *Die Befreiung des Augenblicks: Schönbergs Skandalkonzerte 1907 und 1908* (Böhlau, 2004), pp. 177–87. See also NSM, p. 87; and Willi Reich, *Arnold Schönberg; oder, Der konservative Revolutionär* (Fritz Molden, 1968), p. 54.

53 *Heinrich Schenker*: Egon Wellesz and Emmy Wellesz, *Egon Wellesz: Leben und Werk* (Zsolnay, 1981), p. 57.

53 *Liebstöckl*: For more on this character, see Julius Korngold, *Die Korngolds in Wien: Der Musikkritiker und das Wunderkind: Aufzeichnungen* (M & T, 1991), pp. 73–74.

53 *"I have your quartet"*: *Mahler's Unknown Letters*, ed. Herta Blaukopf, trans. Richard Stokes (Northeastern UP, 1987), p. 175. For Mahler's reactions to the Five Pieces, see Specht, *Gustav Mahler*, pp. 28–29; for "If I go," see AMM, p. 198.

54 *"There is no architecture" and "daring experiments"*: ASC.

54 *one hundred marks*: Anton Webern, *Briefe an Heinrich Jalowetz*, ed. Ernst Lichtenhahn (Schott, 1999), p. 163.

54 *"shoveling snow"*: Alma Mahler, *Mein Leben* (Fischer, 1963), pp. 223–24. For Erwin Stein's involvement, see Stein to Alma Mahler, March 28, 1914, in the Alma Mahler-Werfel Collection, University of Pennsylvania.

54 *Schoenberg snapped*: ASL, p. 51.

54 *"Schoenberg! Schoenberg!"*: For accounts of the *Gurre-Lieder* premiere, see Newlin, *Schoenberg Remembered*, p. 237; Reich, *Arnold Schönberg; oder, Der konservative Revolutionär*, p. 99; and Nono-Schoenberg, *Arnold Schönberg*, p. 120.

54 *"huddled in the most distant"*: Newlin, *Schoenberg Remembered*, p. 237.

54 *"rather indifferent"*: ASSI, p. 41.

55 Self-Portrait, Walking: See Esther da Costa Meyer and Fred Wasserman, eds., *Schoenberg, Kandinsky, and the Blue Rider* (Jewish Museum, 2003), p. 147.

55 *"Loud laughter"*: Foerster, *Der Pilger*, p. 682.

55 *"The public was laughing"*: *Neue Freie Presse*, April 22, 1913, p. 13.

56 *irritating flash of light*: Helmholtz, *On the Sensations of Tone*, pp. 168–70.

56 *"When a periodic"*: Fred Lerdahl, "Spatial and Psychoacoustic Factors in Atonal Prolongation," *Current Musicology* 63 (1999), p. 18.

57 *"the will to annihilate"*: Arnold Schoenberg, *Theory of Harmony*, trans. Roy E. Carter (University of California Press, 1983), p. 409.

57 *"Art belongs"*: JASR, p. 89.

57 *"I strive for"*: Ferruccio Busoni, *Selected Letters*, ed. and trans. Antony Beaumont (Faber, 1987), p. 389.

57 *"colors, noises"*: Letter to Alma Mahler, Oct. 7, 1910, in the Alma Mahler-Werfel 57, University of Pennsylvania.

57 *treated like idiots*: See David Josef Bach's sardonic riposte to Schoenberg's propaganda in "Der neuste Fall Schönberg," *Arbeiter Zeitung*, Jan. 2, 1909. For more, see Leon Botstein, "Habits of Listening and the Crisis of Musical Modernism in Vienna, 1870–1914" (Ph.D. diss., Harvard University, 1985), p. 1208.

57 *"emancipation of the dissonance"*: ASSI, p. 216.

57 *"We shall have no rest"*: Schoenberg, *Theory of Harmony*, p. 314.

57 *North Pole*: Radio lecture on the Variations for Orchestra, March 22, 1931, ASC.

58 *"MUSIC OF NOISE"*: NSM, p. 1021.
58 *"You are proposing"*: Busoni, *Selected Letters*, p. 391.
58 *tonal centricity*: For more on this point, see Ethan Haimo, "Schoenberg and the Origins of Atonality," in *Constructive Dissonance: Arnold Schoenberg and the Transformations of Twentieth-Century Culture*, ed. Juliane Brand and Christopher Hailey (University of California Press, 1997), p. 71.
59 *"We broke its neck!"*: Anton Webern, *The Path to the New Music*, ed. Willi Reich (Universal, 1960), p. 48.
59 *"Our age sees"*: Schoenberg, *Theory of Harmony*, pp. 1–2.
59 *"inbreeding and incest"*: Ibid., p. 314. For other quoted words, see pp. 195–96, 238, and 258.
60 *"[T]he end of the system"*: Ibid., p. 196.
60 *"Every living thing"*: Ibid., p. 29.
60 *"All that is born"*: Weininger, *Geschlecht und Charakter*, p. 324.
60 *"homeless phenomena"*: Schoenberg, *Theory of Harmony*, p. 258.
60 *"adapts himself"*: Weininger, *Geschlecht und Charakter*, p. 426.
60 *Ringer has argued*: Alexander Ringer, "Assimilation and the Emancipation of Historical Dissonance," in Brand and Hailey, *Constructive Dissonance*, pp. 23–34.
61 *"no more and no less"*: HMAW, p. 411. See also ASL, p. 92.
61 *"at the center of culture"*: Beller, *Vienna and the Jews*, pp. 216–17.
61 *"This book I have learned"*: Schoenberg, *Theory of Harmony*, p. 1.
61 *"Viennese school"*: Joseph Auner, "The Second Viennese School as a Historical Concept," in *Schoenberg, Berg, and Webern: A Companion to the Second Viennese School*, ed. Bryan R. Simms (Greenwood, 1999), p. 3.
62 *"raised to the tenth"*: Schoenberg, "Attempt at a Diary," p. 39.
62 *sometimes moved ahead*: See the opening section of the Quartet of 1905. For more speculation, see Allen Forte, *The Atonal Music of Anton Webern* (Yale UP, 1998), p. 372.
62 *"reached the farthest"*: Webern, *Path to the New Music*, p. 48.
62 *successive stages of grief*: HMAW, p. 126.
63 *Webern and* Pelléas: HMAW, p. 104.
63 *"Whereof one cannot speak"*: Wittgenstein, *Tractatus Logico-Philosophicus*, p. 189.
63 *Don't play the note*: HMAW, p. 484.
64 *"Such a dear person"*: Theodor W. Adorno, *Alban Berg: Master of the Smallest Link*, trans. Juliane Brand and Christopher Hailey (Cambridge UP, 1991), p. 17.
64 *"[Berg] wasn't lacking"*: *The Memoirs of Elias Canetti* (Farrar, Straus and Giroux, 1999), p. 760.
64 *"sex appeal"*: Soma Morgenstern, *Alban Berg und seine Idole: Erinnerungen und Briefe*, ed. Ingolf Schulte (Aufbau, 1999), p. 343.
64 *Anton Bruckner*: Erich Alban Berg, *Der unverbesserliche Romantiker: Alban Berg, 1885–1935* (Österreichischer Bundesverlag, 1985), p. 25.
64 *George Borgfeldt*: Rosemary Hilmar, *Alban Berg: Leben und Wirken in Wien bis zu seinen ersten Erfolgen als Komponist* (Böhlau, 1978), pp. 15–23. On Hermann Berg's discovery of the teddy bear, see www.teddybearfriends.co.uk/history-of-teddy-bears.php (accessed Jan. 5, 2007).
65 *His tasks in the year 1911*: See *The Berg-Schoenberg Correspondence: Selected Letters*, ed. Juliane Brand, Christopher Hailey, and Donald Harris (Norton, 1987), pp. 3–25.
65 *"Are you composing"*: Ibid., p. 44.
65 *He dismissed*: For more of Schoenberg's hostility to the Altenberg cycle, see ibid., p. 257; and Willi Reich, *Alban Berg*, trans. Cornelius Cardew (Harcourt, Brace and World, 1965), p. 41.
65 *steal a baton*: Reich, *Alban Berg*, p. 19.
65 *six more times*: Ibid., p. 20.
65 *"How I would like"*: Mosco Carner, *Alban Berg: The Man and the Work* (Holmes and Meier, 1983), p. 6.
65 *"rather too obvious"*: *Berg-Schoenberg Correspondence*, p. 143.
66 *"War!"*: "Gedanken im Kriege" (Nov. 1914, republished 1915), in Thomas Mann, *Politische Schriften und Reden* (Fischer, 1968), p. 10.
66 *"war psychosis"*: Nono-Schoenberg, *Arnold Schönberg*, p. 134.
66 *"Now comes the reckoning!"*: Aug. 28, 1914, letter, in Alma Mahler-Werfel Collection, University of Pennsylvania.
67 *diary of the weather*: "War Clouds Diary," trans. Paul A. Pisk, *Journal of the Arnold Schoenberg Institute* 9:1 (June 1986), pp. 53–77.
67 *"very shameful"*: Carner, *Alban Berg*, p. 42.
67 *"total material and intellectual"*: Barbara Tuchman, *The Guns of August* (Ballantine, 1994), p. 321.
67 *Richard Strauss refused*: RSRR, pp. 160–61.
67 *"It is sickening"*: *A Working Friendship: The Correspondence Between Richard Strauss and*

Hugo von Hofmannsthal, ed. Franz Strauss, Alice Strauss, and Willi Schuh, trans. Hanns Hammelmann and Ewald Osers (Random House, 1961), p. 216.

68 *Patricia Hall notes*: Patricia Hall, "Berg's Sketches and the Inception of *Wozzeck*: 1914–18," *Musical Times* 146 (Autumn 2005), pp. 3–24.

68 *"There is a bit of me"*: Alban Berg, *Letters to His Wife*, ed. and trans. Bernard Grun (St. Martin's, 1971), p. 229.

68 *Dr. Wernisch*: Hall, "Berg's Sketches and the Inception of *Wozzeck*," p. 15.

69 *Berg used both those operas*: For the *Salome* comparison, see Josef Gmeiner, "Ideal und Bête noire: Richard Strauss—Alban Bergs beschädigtes Leitbild," in *Musica conservata: Günter Brosche zum 60. Geburtstag* (Hans Schneider, 1999), p. 79. For *Pelléas*, see Hall, "Berg's Sketches and the Inception of *Wozzeck*," p. 10.

69 *Berg went so far as to conceal*: For mention of the unwritten biography, see *Berg-Schoenberg Correspondence*, p. 306. For Berg's urge to conceal the work on *Wozzeck* from Schoenberg, see Alban Berg, *Briefe an seine Frau* (Langen Müller, 1965), p. 457. For Schoenberg's opposition to the project, see George Perle, *The Operas of Alban Berg, Vol. 1: "Wozzeck"* (University of California Press, 1980), p. 192.

69 Salome *chord*: See the flute, trumpet, and harp figures in Act I, bar 370. For other occurences of this chord in *Wozzeck*, see Act III, bars 101 and 371, and, transposed, the sustained chord in Act III, bars 384–86. Helpful in tracking these down was Janet Schmalfeldt, *Berg's "Wozzeck": Harmonic Language and Dramatic Design* (Yale UP, 1983), pp. 125, 200, 205.

70 *a little Schoenberg*: Anthony Pople, "The Musical Language of *Wozzeck*," in Pople, *Cambridge Companion to Berg*, pp. 151–52, notices the quotation from the Five Pieces and speculates on other Schoenbergian subtexts in *Wozzeck*.

72 *"Like the murder"*: Robert Cogan, *New Images of Musical Sound* (Harvard UP, 1984), p. 95.

72 *"a confession"*: Alban Berg, "A Lecture on *Wozzeck*," in Douglas Jarman, *Alban Berg, "Wozzeck"* (Cambridge UP, 1989), p. 169.

72 *Sonata in D Minor*: For more, see Ulrich Krämer, *Alban Berg als Schüler Arnold Schönbergs: Quellenstudien und Analysen zum Frühwerk* (Universal, 1996), p. 165. For Helene's request, see Reich, *Alban Berg*, p. 229; and Berg, *Briefe an seine Frau*, p. 487.

72 *"worldwide festival of death"*: Thomas Mann, *The Magic Mountain*, trans. John E. Woods (Knopf, 1995), p. 706.

72 *Berg . . . pointed out*: Berg, "Lecture on *Wozzeck*," p. 156.

3. Dance of the Earth

74 *eighty-five degrees*: Truman Campbell Bullard, "The First Performance of Igor Stravinsky's *Sacre du Printemps*" (Ph.D. diss., Eastman School of Music, 1971), vol. 1, p. 136.

74 *"There, for the expert"*: *Le Coq et l'Arlequin*, in *Oeuvres complètes de Jean Cocteau* (Marguerat, 1946–51), vol. 9, pp. 46–47.

74 *zeppelin*: Thomas Forrest Kelly, *First Nights: Five Musical Premieres* (Yale UP, 2000), p. 277.

74 *"a new thrill"*: Bullard, "First Performance," vol. 3, p. 1.

75 *"a sacred terror"*: RTS2, p. 1000.

75 *mutterings, titters*: Alfredo Casella, *Music in My Time*, trans. Spencer Norton (University of Oklahoma Press, 1955), pp. 108–9.

75 *"Till the end"*: From an interview with the composer included with Sony Classical's *Igor Stravinsky Edition*, vol. 4 (SM2K 46 294).

75 *"The dancers trembled"*: Lynn Garafola, *Diaghilev's Ballets Russes* (Da Capo, 1998), p. 68.

75 *"Shut up, bitches"*: Igor Stravinsky and Robert Craft, *Expositions and Developments* (Doubleday, 1962), p. 164. See Doris Monteux, *It's All in the Music* (Farrar, Straus and Giroux, 1965), p. 90, for "*A bas des grues du 16ème!*" See also Igor Stravinsky, *An Autobiography* (Norton, 1962), p. 47.

76 *Jeanne Mühlfeld*: Garafola, *Diaghilev's Ballets Russes*, p. 294.

76 *"One literally could not"*: *Selected Writings of Gertrude Stein*, ed. Carl Van Vechten (Vintage, 1972), p. 129. Stein says that she attended the second performance, but it is more likely that her description applies to the May 29 premiere.

76 *applauding faction*: Bullard, "First Performance," vol. 2, pp. 31–32. For later performances, see ibid., pp. 91 and 107; SWS1, p. 232; and RTS2, p. 1032.

77 *"our slender bodies"*: Translation by Thomas Land, included with Pierre Boulez's recording of *Cantata profana* (DG 435 863-2).

78 *"The great thing"*: Herschel B. Chipp, *Theories of Modern Art: A Source Book by Artists and Critics* (University of California Press, 1968), p 44.

78 *"just as it is"*: Ibid., p. 45.
79 *Edison Bell cylinder*: John Bird, *Percy Grainger* (Oxford UP, 1999), pp. 121–22. See also Gwilym Davies, "Percy Grainger's Folk Music Research in Gloucestershire, Worcestershire, and Warwickshire, 1907–1909," *Folk Music Journal* 6:3 (1992), pp. 339–58.
79 *damp, rundown schoolhouse*: Mirka Zemanová, *Janáček: A Composer's Life* (Northeastern UP, 2002), p. 12.
80 *"Flashing movements"*: Ibid., p. 60.
80 *"Dobrý večer"*: Leoš Janáček, *Letters and Reminiscences*, ed. Bohumír Štědroň, trans. Geraldine Thomsen (Artia, 1955), pp. 94–95.
80 *"entire being"*: *Janáček and His World*, ed. Michael Beckerman (Princeton UP, 2003), p. 246.
81 *"Innumerable notes"*: Leoš Janáček, "How Ideas Come About," in *Janáček's Uncollected Essays on Music*, ed. and trans. Mirka Zemanová (Marion Boyars, 1989), p. 69.
81 *forty folk songs*: Malcolm Gillies, *Bartók Remembered* (Faber, 1990), pp. 6–7. For other details, see Kenneth Chalmers, *Béla Bartók* (Phaidon, 1995); and Halsey Stevens, *The Life and Music of Béla Bartók* (Clarendon, 1993).
82 *Maxim Gorky*: *Documenta Bartókiana* (Akadémiai Kiadó, 1964–81), vol. 4, pp. 38–40.
82 *"destructive urban influence"*: Béla Bartók, preface to *Rumanian Folk Music* (Martinus Nijhoff, 1967–75), vol. 1, pp. 4–5.
82 *contaminating influence*: Julie Brown, "Bartók, the Gyspies, and Hybridity in Music," in *Western Music and Its Others: Difference, Representation, and Appropriation in Music*, ed. Georgina Born and David Hesmondhalgh (University of California Press, 2000), pp. 119–42.
83 *strict tempo*: See "Béla Bartók Replies to Percy Grainger" (1934), in *Béla Bartók Essays*, ed. Benjamin Suchoff (Bison Books, 1992), p. 224.
83 *"hateful"*: Günter Weiss-Aigner, "The 'Lost' Violin Concerto," in *The Bartók Companion*, ed. Malcolm Gillies (Amadeus, 1993), p. 469.
84 *"The essence of art"*: Judit Frigyesi, *Béla Bartók and Turn-of-the-Century Budapest* (University of California Press, 1998), pp. 163–64. For the following quotations, see pp. 148, 121, and 204.
84 *"The Arabs"*: *Béla Bartók Letters*, ed. János Demény, trans. Péter Balabán and István Farkas (St. Martin's, 1971), p. 122.
84 *sizable library*: See Robert Orledge, "Evocations of Exoticism," in *The Cambridge Companion to Ravel*, ed. Deborah Mawer (Cambridge UP, 2000), pp. 30–31.
85 *"subtly authentic"*: Gerald Larner, *Maurice Ravel* (Phaidon, 1996), p. 12.
85 *Falla, in his writings*: As quoted in Federico García Lorca, "Deep Song," in *Deep Song and Other Prose*, trans. Christopher Maurer (New Directions, 1975), p. 26.
86 *money from the Romanov dynasty*: Garafola, *Diaghilev's Ballets Russes*, pp. 167–73.
87 *"few points of sympathy"*: "Busy Kaiser Wilhelm," *New York Times*, July 26, 1891.
87 *"gusto"*: Igor Stravinsky and Robert Craft, *Conversations with Igor Stravinsky* (Doubleday, 1959), p. 82.
87 *"beautiful, healthy"*: Romain Rolland, *Journal des années de guerre, 1914–1919* (Michel, 1952), p. 59.
88 *"His music reflects"*: Nicolas Nabokov, *Old Friends and New Music* (Little, Brown, 1951), p. 210.
89 *"This goes further"*: Jann Pasler, "Stravinsky and the Apaches," *Musical Times* 123 (June 1982), p. 404.
89 *"symphony" and "counterpoint"*: RTS1, pp. 672 and 682.
90 *"It suppresses"*: Jacques Rivière, "Petrouchka," *Nouvelle Revue Française* 33 (1911), p. 377.
90 *"Stravinsky is the only"*: Ezra Pound, "Tibor Serly, Composer," quoted in György Novák, "'I am a Vi====olerplayer' [*sic*]: Pound and Serly in the Early 1930s," *Americana* 2:1, www.arts.u-szeged.hu/american/americana/volIIno1/novak.htm (accessed July 20, 2006).
90 *folkloric sources*: RTS1, pp. 891–923.
91 *"a kind of apotheosis"*: *Béla Bartók Essays*, p. 360.
91 *"great fusion"*: RTS1, p. 965.
91 *"You are truly"*: See the chord combining a C-sharp dominant seventh and a D-major triad at 299 of *Salome*.
91 *"A silent accent"*: *A Virgil Thomson Reader* (Houghton Mifflin, 1981), p. 16.
92 *"Une musique nègre"*: Igor Stravinsky and Robert Craft, *Memories and Commentaries* (Doubleday, 1960), p. 77.
92 *"Salt Peanuts"*: Carl Woideck, *Charlie Parker: His Music and Life* (University of Michigan Press, 1996), p. 162.
92 *spill his Scotch*: Alfred Appel Jr., *Jazz Modernism: From Ellington and Armstrong to Matisse and Joyce* (Yale UP, 2002), pp. 59–60.
92 *As Bartók observed*: *Béla Bartók Essays*, p. 41.

93 *As Lynn Garafola points out*: Garafola, *Diaghilev's Ballets Russes*, pp. 72–73.
93 *"There are works"*: Jacques Rivière, "Le Sacre du printemps," *Nouvelle Revue Française* 59 (Nov. 1913), p. 730.
93 *"infiltrations funèstes"*: Jane Fulcher, "Speaking the Truth to Power," in *Debussy and His World*, ed. Jane Fulcher (Princeton UP, 2001), p. 207.
93 *"universal formula"*: Carol A. Hess, *Manuel de Falla and Modernism in Spain* (University of Chicago Press, 2001), pp. 67–69.
94 *Seal Harbor, Maine*: Glenn Watkins, *Proof Through the Night: Music and the Great War* (University of California Press, 2003), p. 304.
94 *Albéric Magnard*: Ibid., p. 433.
94 *"Both hands touch"*: Russell Wortley and Michael Dawney, "George Butterworth's Diary of Morris Dance Hunting," *Folk Music Journal* 3:3 (1977), p. 204.
94 *"I don't believe"*: Arbie Orenstein, ed., *A Ravel Reader* (Columbia UP, 1990), pp. 162–63. Also p. 168.
95 *fighter plane*: Watkins, *Proof Through the Night*, pp. 176–90.
95 *"the intolerable spirit"*: Rolland, *Journal des années de guerre*, p. 61.
95 *early performances of* Pierrot: Igor Stravinsky and Robert Craft, *Dialogues and a Diary* (Doubleday, 1963), p. 53; Vera Stravinsky and Robert Craft, *Stravinsky in Pictures and Documents* (Simon and Schuster, 1978), p. 91.
95 *Taruskin is right*: RTS2, pp. 988–1006.
95 *"sauce" and "atmosphere"*: Rivière, "Le Sacre du printemps," pp. 706–707.
96 *"each object"*: Jacques Rivière, "La saison russe," *Nouvelle Revue Française* 67 (July 1914), p. 155.
96 *"By imperceptible degrees"*: RTS2, p. 1006.
96 *"progressive abstraction"*: Ibid., title of part 3.
96 *"a machine to hit"*: Drue Fergison, "Bringing *Les Noces* to the Stage," in *The Ballets Russes and Its World*, ed. Lynn Garafola and Nancy Van Norman Baer (Yale UP, 1999), p. 185.
96 *"leaning dangerously"*: Claude Debussy, *Correspondance, 1884–1918*, ed. François Lesure (Hermann, 1993), p. 358.
96 "Cher *Stravinsky"*: Ibid., p. 361.
96 *As Taruskin shows*: RTS2, pp. 1486–99.
97 *"Austro-Boche miasmas"*: Debussy, *Correspondance*, p. 361.
97 *March 23, 1918*: Various articles in the *New York Times*, March 24–30, 1918.
98 *"hyper-alertness"*: Wolfgang-Andreas Schultz, "Avant-Garde and Trauma: Twentieth-Century Music and the Experiences from the World Wars" (unpublished English translation), p. 10.
98 *"Boches!"*: Francis Steegmuller, *Cocteau: A Biography* (Nonpareil Books, 1986), p. 186. Other details, pp. 175 and 187.
99 *"The Titanic"*: Frederick Brown, *An Impersonation of Angels: A Biography of Jean Cocteau* (Viking, 1968), p. 128.
99 *"That Mysterious Rag"*: See Nancy Perloff, *Art and the Everyday: Popular Entertainment and the Circle of Erik Satie* (Clarendon, 1991), p. 133; and Steven Moore Whiting, *Satie the Bohemian: From Cabaret to Concert Hall* (Oxford UP, 1999), pp. 477–79.
99 *"For the first time"*: Steegmuller, *Cocteau*, p. 185.
99 *"The nightingale sings badly"*: *Le Coq et l'Arlequin*, p. 16. For other quotations, see pp. 39 and 26.
100 *"lie of the grand style"*: Friedrich Nietzsche, *The Birth of Tragedy and The Case of Wagner*, trans. Walter Kaufmann (Vintage, 1967), p. 157.
101 *"Banana lou ito kous kous"*: Glenn Watkins, *Pyramids at the Louvre: Music, Culture, and Collage from Stravinsky to the Postmodernists* (Harvard UP, 1994), p. 105.
102 *"the steam-driven merry-go-rounds"*: Darius Milhaud, *Notes Without Music: An Autobiography*, trans. Donald Evans (Knopf, 1953), p. 98.
102 *Vance Lowry*: Jean Wiéner, *Allegro appassionato* (Belfond, 1978), p. 43.
102 *"a not unamusing place"*: *Selected Letters of Virgil Thomson*, ed. Tim Page and Vanessa Weeks Page (Summit, 1988), p. 54.
102 *"Against the beat"*: Milhaud, *Notes Without Music*, pp. 136–37. For Ellington at Capitol Palace, see Stuart Nicholson, ed., *Reminiscing in Tempo: A Portrait of Duke Ellington* (Northeastern UP, 1999), pp. 29–31.
103 *"Little melodies"*: Cocteau, *Le Coq et l'Arlequin*, p. 45.
103 *Antonio María Romeu*: Milhaud, *Notes Without Music*, p. 91.
103 *Villa-Lobos speculating*: See Gerard Béhague, *Heitor Villa-Lobos: The Search for Brazil's Musical Soul* (University of Texas at Austin, 1994), pp. 5–6; and Eero Tarasti, *Heitor Villa-Lobos: The Life and Works, 1887–1959* (McFarland, 1995), pp. 169–80.
103 *"unheard-of music"*: Claude Tappolet, ed., *Correspondance Ernest Ansermet–Igor Strawinsky (1914–1967)* (Georg, 1990–92), vol. 1, p. 48.
103 *Creole Band*: Lawrence Gushee, *Pioneers of*

Jazz: The Story of the Creole Band (Oxford UP, 2005), pp. 160 and 193.

103 *"Jelly Roll Blues"*: Gabriel Fournier, "Erik Satie et son époque," *La Revue musicale* 214 (June 1952), p. 130. The "*compositions de Jelly Roll Morton*" referred to here could only be "Jelly Roll Blues," which was published in Chicago in 1915; nothing else by Jelly Roll was in circulation at the time.

103 *"the musical ideal"*: Rolland, *Journal des années de guerre*, p. 852.

103 *"Dance must* express nothing": Steegmuller, *Cocteau*, p. 95.

104 *jazz ensembles*: RTS2, pp. 1301–4, argues against a jazz influence, saying that the instrumentation is close to that of Eastern European Gypsy and klezmer bands. See also Stravinsky and Craft, *Expositions and Developments*, pp. 103–104. For the makeup of the Creole Band, see the frontispiece photo of Gushee's *Pioneers of Jazz*. Buddy Bolden's pioneering group had the same makeup around 1900.

104 *"disappearance of the skyscraper"*: Steegmuller, *Cocteau*, p. 259.

104 *"Adieu New-York"*: Perloff, *Art and the Everyday*, pp. 173–75.

104 *"Already the influence"*: Darius Milhaud, *Études* (Aveline, 1927), p. 22.

104 *"period modernism"*: Garafola, *Diaghilev's Ballets Russes*, pp. 90–115.

105 *"reconstitutes the past"*: Sylvia Kahan, *Music's Modern Muse: A Life of Winnaretta Singer, Princesse de Polignac* (University of Rochester Press, 2003), p. 363.

105 *"the days of big orchestras"*: Ibid., pp. 177–78.

105 *"I would like"*: Stravinsky and Craft, *Conversations with Igor Stravinsky*, p. 83.

105 *high-backed chair*: Wiéner, *Allegro appassionato*, p. 57.

105 *"Madame la Princesse"*: Kahan, *Music's Modern Muse*, p. 235.

106 *asked to tone down*: Milhaud, *Notes Without Music*, p. 159.

106 "Le Train bleu": Paul Collaer, *Darius Milhaud*, trans. Jane Hohfeld Galante (San Francisco Press, 1988), p. 78.

106 *"What's good about Poulenc"*: Renaud Machart, *Poulenc* (Seuil, 1995), p. 18.

106 *"modern* fêtes galantes": Francis Poulenc, *My Friends and Myself* (Dobson, 1978), pp. 43–44. For more description, see Garafola, *Diaghilev's Ballets Russes*, pp. 129–32.

107 *"Defend me, Spaniards"*: Hess, *Manuel de Falla and Modernism in Spain*, p. 170.

107 *"You were a friend"*: Stravinsky and Craft, *Conversations with Igor Stravinsky*, pp. 94–101.

107 *"We're sinking"*: Calvin Tomkins, "Living Well Is the Best Revenge," *New Yorker*, July 28, 1962, pp. 44–46.

108 *"My Octuor"*: Eric Walter White, *Stravinsky: The Composer and His Works* (University of California Press, 1979), pp. 574–75.

108 *"Even in the early days"*: "Interview with Stravinsky," *Observer*, July 3, 1921.

108 *"I consider music"*: Igor Stravinsky, *Chroniques de ma vie* (Denoël/Gonthier, 1962), p. 63.

108 *"Art never expresses anything"*: Oscar Wilde, "The Decay of Lying," in *The Complete Works of Oscar Wilde* (Perennial Library, 1989), p. 991.

109 *Brunswick Records*: SWS1, p. 406.

109 *Each movement of the Serenade*: Ibid., p. 412.

109 *"open covenants"*: Margaret MacMillan, *Paris 1919: Six Months That Changed the World* (Random House, 2001), p. 57.

109 *"to shake the hands"*: Paul Op de Coul, "Modern Chamber Music at the 1920 Mahler Festival: A Prelude to the International Society for Contemporary Music," in *Gustav Mahler: The World Listens* (Het Concertgebouw, 1995), p. I.84.

109 *"Arnold Schönberg"*: Steegmuller, *Cocteau*, p. 247.

109 Pierrot lunaire: Wiéner, *Allegro appassionato*, pp. 50–51.

109 *"a nice person"*: ASL, p. 69.

110 *"an exquisite boy"*: Francis Poulenc, *Correspondance, 1910–1963*, ed. Myriam Chimènes (Fayard, 1994), p. 170.

110 *Hobsbawm writes*: Eric Hobsbawm, *The Age of Extremes: The Short Twentieth Century, 1914–1991* (Abacus, 1995), p. 90.

110 *Martinů*: Brian Large, *Martinů* (Holmes and Meier, 1975), pp. 39–40.

110 *"politics of style"*: Bernard Holland, "Bringing Sibelius out of Bleak Oblivion," *New York Times*, Dec. 8, 1997.

111 *"To be frank"*: David E. Schneider, "Bartók and Stravinsky: Respect, Competition, Influence, and the Hungarian Reaction to Modernism in the 1920s," in *Bartók and His World*, ed. Peter Laki (Princeton UP, 1995), p. 186.

111 *"Here I am"*: *Correspondance Ernest Ansermet–Igor Strawinsky*, vol. 2, p. 21.

111 *"Ravel, it's a masterpiece"*: Larner, *Maurice Ravel*, pp. 172–73.

112 *a bit of jazz*: See *Béla Bartók Essays*, p. 350, for a brief mention of jazz in 1941. As Benjamin Suchoff observes in his notes,

Mikrokosmos No. 151 is explicitly written in a Gershwin style. *Contrasts*, written for Benny Goodman in 1938, has jazzlike moments, as well as reminiscences of Balinese gamelan music.

112 *"racial impurity"*: See *Béla Bartók Essays*, p. 31; and Brown, "Bartók, the Gypsies, and Hybridity in Music," p. 132.

112 *"sufficiently modern"*: Jan Maegaard, "1923—the Critical Year of Modern Music," in *The Nielsen Companion*, ed. Mina Miller (Amadeus, 1995), p. 106.

112 *"'stylized' noise"*: *Béla Bartók Essays*, p. 456.

113 *"Peacock Melody"*: This resemblance was pointed out by members of the Hungarian folk-music group Muzsikás, which played Hungarian songs and dances alongside Bartók's Fourth Quartet at a concert by the Takács Quartet at Zankel Hall in New York on Feb. 13, 2004.

113 *"fascinating exchange"*: *Documenta Bartókiana*, vol. 3, p. 122. First meeting on Jan. 10, 1925, second on Oct. 16, 1927.

113 *opened the wrong door*: Zemanová, *Janáček*, pp. 201–2.

114 *"Lord have mercy"*: *Janáček's Uncollected Essays on Music*, pp. 111–13.

114 *Janáček dreamed of being a forester*: Zemanová, *Janáček*, p. 20.

115 *"Good and evil"*: John Tyrrell, *Janáček's Operas: A Documentary Account* (Princeton UP, 1992), p. 296.

115 *"You must play this"*: Zemanová, *Janáček*, p. 191; and Zdenka Janáčková, *My Life with Janáček*, ed. and trans. John Tyrrell (Faber, 1998), p. 238.

115 *"the demon that lurked"*: SWS1, p. 489.

116 *abscess was gone*: Vernon Duke, *Passport to Paris* (Little, Brown, 1955), p. 200.

116 *"out of extreme mental"*: SWS1, p. 431.

116 *"crisis of the concept"*: Jacques Rivière, "La Crise du concept de littérature," *Nouvelle Revue Française* 125 (Feb. 1924), pp. 159–70.

116 *"well made"*: Jacques Maritain, *Art and Scholasticism and The Frontiers of Poetry*, trans. Joseph W. Evans (University of Notre Dame Press, 1974), p. 104. For "art *for nothing*," see p. 92.

116 *"The choice"*: Stravinsky, *Autobiography*, p. 125.

117 *"The swing of the pendulum"*: Stravinsky, *Autobiography*, p. 136.

118 *"Logically"*: Garafola, *Diaghilev's Ballets Russes*, p. 140.

118 *private chapel*: SWS1, p. 499.

118 *"called to our mind"*: Paul Rosenfeld, *Discoveries of a Music Critic* (Vienna House, 1972), p. 196.

118 *"Do I adore Stravinsky"*: Ned Rorem, "Stravinsky at 100," in *Setting the Tone: Essays and a Diary* (Limelight, 1984), p. 191.

119 *"Here is the real core"*: William James, *The Varieties of Religious Experience* (Penguin, 1958), p. 149.

4: Invisible Men

120 *"the true grandfathers"*: Carl Van Vechten, "The Great American Composer: His Grandfathers Are the Present Writers of Our Popular Ragtime Songs," *Vanity Fair*, April 1917, pp. 75 and 140.

120 *"primitive birthright"*: Carl Van Vechten, *Nigger Heaven* (University of Illinois Press, 2000), p. 89.

121 *"I am now satisfied"*: "Real Value of Negro Melodies," *New York Herald*, May 21, 1893. This article was ghostwritten by James Creelman, as Michael Beckerman has established; see Beckerman, *New Worlds of Dvořák: Searching in America for the Composer's Inner Life* (Norton, 2003), pp. 100–106. But the sentiments in the article must have been Dvorak's own, for Creelman later distanced himself from them. In June 1894 he wrote that the composer's enthusiasm for Negro music was "almost pathetic" and that Negroes were nothing more than "hewers of wood and carries of water to the white race, originating melodies which can be transformed in other hands"; see Creelman, "Dvořák's Negro Symphony," in *Dvořák and His World*, ed. Michael Beckerman (Princeton UP, 1993), p. 180. The phrase "hewers of wood and carriers of water" comes from the book of Joshua and was a favorite of slavery apologists. W. E. B. Du Bois makes ironic use of it in *The Souls of Black Folk*; see *Three Negro Classics* (Avon, 1965), p. 215.

121 *Paris, Texas*: Dennis Brindell Fradin and Judith Bloom Fradin, *Ida B. Wells: Mother of the Civil Rights Movement* (Clarion, 2000), pp. 63–65.

122 *promoted blacks themselves*: John C. Tibbetts, ed., *Dvořák in America, 1892–1895* (Amadeus, 1993), p. 377.

122 *a paper titled*: Leonard Bernstein, "The Absorption of Race Elements into American Music," in *Findings* (Simon and Schuster, 1982), pp. 36–99, esp. 38–39.

123 *"The limited resources"*: Paul Lopes, *The Rise of a Jazz Art World* (Cambridge UP, 2002), p. 40.

123 *"I like Louis Armstrong"*: Ralph Ellison, *Invisible Man* (Penguin, 1965), p. 11.

123 *Wallingford Riegger*: Lawrence Jackson, *Ralph Ellison: Emergence of Genius* (John Wiley, 2002), pp. 172–73.

123 *Copland . . . pointed out*: ACR, p. xvi.

124 *Harry Lawrence Freeman*: On Freeman, see Elise K. Kirk, *American Opera* (University of Illinois Press, 2001), pp. 186–88.

124 *"the most promising"*: Thomas L. Riis, "Dvořák and His Black Students," in *Rethinking Dvořák: Views from Five Countries*, ed. David R. Beveridge (Clarendon, 1996), p. 270.

124 Humoresque: Maurice Peress, *Dvořák to Duke Ellington: A Conductor Explores America's Music and Its African-American Roots* (Oxford UP, 2004), pp. 46–47; and Maurice Peress, "Arnold, Maurice," in *International Dictionary of Black Composers*, ed. Samuel A. Floyd Jr. (Fitzroy Dearborn, 1999), pp. 43–45.

125 *"I would . . . remain"*: Will Marion Cook, "Autobiography," transcribed in Marva Griffin Carter, "The Life and Music of Will Marion Cook" (Ph.D. diss., University of Illinois at Urbana-Champaign, 1988), pp. 395–96. For "You are a stranger," see p. 418.

125 *"felt exceptionally free"*: David Levering Lewis, *W.E.B. Du Bois: Biography of a Race* (Holt, 1993), pp. 132 and 138.

126 *"A deep longing"*: Du Bois, *Souls of Black Folk*, pp. 369 and 215.

126 *"musical phenomenon"*: *New York Age*, Nov. 30, 1889.

126 *William Marion Cook Orchestra*: See *New York Age*, Sept. 27, 1890.

126 *Colored People's Day*: Carter, "Life and Music of Will Marion Cook," pp. 27–30; and William S. McFeely, *Frederick Douglass* (Norton, 1991), pp. 370–71.

126 *letter of introduction*: Beckerman, *Dvořák and His World*, pp. 198–99.

126 *free of charge*: "Real Value of Negro Melodies."

126 *"the world's greatest Negro violinist"*: Duke Ellington, *Music Is My Mistress* (Doubleday, 1973), p. 97. For the review, see Carter, "Life and Music of Will Marion Cook," pp. 176–77; but see Peress, *Dvořák to Duke Ellington*, p. 212, for a possible sighting of the review in question.

127 *"confrontational jabs"*: Marva Griffin Carter, "Removing the 'Minstrel Mask' in the Musicals of Will Marion Cook," *Musical Quarterly* 84:1 (Spring 2000), p. 209.

127 *A Negro composer*: Will Marion Cook, "Clorindy, the Origin of the Cakewalk," in *Readings in Black American Music*, ed. Eileen Southern (Norton, 1983), p. 228.

127 *"All you white folks"*: Thomas L. Riis, ed., *The Music and Scripts of "In Dahomey,"* Recent Researches in American Music, vol. 25 (A-R Editions, 1996), pp. 118–19.

128 *"Developed Negro music"*: "Will Marion Cook on Negro Music," *New York Age*, Sept. 21, 1918.

128 *"a new musical school"*: "Dvořák's Theory of Negro Music," *New York Herald*, May 28, 1893.

128 *"a genius," "a highway"*: Ernest Ansermet, "Sur un orchestre nègre," in *Écrits sur la musique* (Baconnière, 1970), pp. 173–78.

128 *Will Vodery*: See Mark Tucker, "In Search of Will Vodery," *Black Music Research Journal* 16:1 (Spring 1996), pp. 123–82.

129 *Fletcher Henderson*: See Gunther Schuller, *Early Jazz: Its Roots and Musical Development* (Oxford UP, 1968), p. 253; and Jeffrey Magee, *The Uncrowned King of Swing: Fletcher Henderson and Big Band Jazz* (Oxford UP, 2005), p. 24.

129 *Billy Strayhorn*: Magee, *Uncrowned King of Swing*, p. 31; David Hajdu, *Lush Life: A Biography of Billy Strayhorn* (Farrar, Straus and Giroux, 1996), pp. 16–7; Walter van de Leur, *Something to Live For: The Music of Billy Strayhorn* (Oxford UP, 2002), pp. 6–7.

129 *"black Beethoven"*: Maurice Peress, "My Life with *Black, Brown, and Beige*," *Black Music Research Journal* 13:2 (Fall 1993), p. 147.

130 *Ives's family*: *Charles E. Ives: Memos*, ed. John Kirkpatrick (Norton, 1972), p. 245; Frank R. Rossiter, *Charles Ives and His America* (Liveright, 1975), pp 9–10.

130 *eyewitness testimony*: Vivian Perlis, *Charles Ives Remembered: An Oral History* (Yale UP, 1974), p. 16; and David Eiseman, "George Ives as Theorist: Some Unpublished Documents," *Perspectives of New Music* 14:1 (Fall–Winter 1975), p. 141.

130 *"Old Folks at Home"*: *Ives: Memos*, p. 115. Ives calls it "The Swanee River" (alternate title).

130 *organist since his teens*: See J. Peter Burkholder, "The Organist in Ives," *Journal of the American Musicological Society* 55:2 (Summer 2002), pp. 255–310.

130 *"spirited and melodious"*: J. Peter Burkholder, ed., *Charles Ives and His World* (Princeton UP, 1996), pp. 275–77.

131 *"Damn rot"*: Jan Swafford, *Charles Ives: A Life with Music* (Norton, 1996), p. 161.

131 *"emasculated art"*: *Ives: Memos*, pp. 130–31.

131 *"pussies"*: Swafford, *Charles Ives*, p. 334. For sissies and pansies, see Burkholder, *Charles Ives and His World*, p. 237.
131 *"simple enough"*: Charles Ives, *Essays Before a Sonata, The Majority, and Other Writings*, ed. Howard Boatwright (Norton, 1970), p. 240.
131 *"knock some BIG"*: Henry Cowell and Sidney Cowell, *Charles Ives and His Music* (Oxford UP, 1969), p. 59.
131 *"Music may be yet"*: Ives, *Essays Before a Sonata*, p. 88.
132 *"one of those exceptional"*: Swafford, *Charles Ives*, pp. 411–12 (part of review reproduced).
132 *"There is a great Man"*: Dorothy Lamb Crawford, *Evenings On and Off the Roof: Pioneering Concerts in Los Angeles, 1939–1971* (University of California Press, 1995), p. 125.
132 *Solomon, Sherwood*: Maynard Solomon, "Charles Ives: Some Questions of Veracity," *Journal of the American Musicological Society* 40:3 (Fall 1987), pp. 443–70, detects a "systematic pattern of falsification" in Ives's datings of his compositions (p. 463). Gayle Sherwood, in "Questions and Veracities: Reassessing the Chronology of Ives's Choral Works," *Musical Quarterly* 78:3 (Fall 1994), pp. 429–47, concludes that Ives's dates for early experimental choral works such as *Psalm 67, Psalm 25*, and *Psalm 24* are more or less correct. Sherwood's revised dates are cited by J. Peter Burkholder in his *All Made of Tunes: Charles Ives and the Uses of Musical Borrowing* (Yale UP, 1995). Still, questions remain about the dates and markings on Ives's scores. For example, on the first page of the full manuscript of the "St. Gaudens" movement is written: "Return to Chas. E. Ives, 70 W 11." Ives lived on West Eleventh Street in New York from 1908 to 1911, but Sherwood says that the manuscript paper dates from between 1919 and 1923.
132 *"Why tonality as such"*: Swafford, *Charles Ives*, p. 338.
132 *J. Peter Burkholder*: Burkholder, *All Made of Tunes*, throughout. For the Second Symphony, see pp. 102–36.
133 *"cumulative form"*: Ibid., pp. 137–215.
133 *"exaggerated"*: *Ives: Memos*, p. 53.
133 *"does not 'represent the American nation' . . . tomato ketchup"*: Ives, *Essays Before a Sonata*, p. 94.
133 *"fervently, transcendentally"*: Ibid., p. 80.
133 *"an African soul"*: Ibid., p. 79.
133 *Anderson Brooks*: *Ives: Memos*, p. 53, and app. 14, pp. 250–52.
134 *Colored Peoples' Day*: Swafford, *Charles Ives*, pp. 73–76.
134 *spirituals on the piano*: Perlis, *Charles Ives Remembered*, p. 82.
134 The Abolitionists: James B. Sinclair, *A Descriptive Catalogue of the Music of Charles Ives* (Yale UP, 1992), p. 613.
134 *tune in "St. Gaudens"*: Burkholder, *All Made of Tunes*, pp. 317–22.
134 *"Black March"*: *Ives: Memos*, p. 87.
134 *Von Glahn has described*: Denise Von Glahn, "New Sources for 'The "St. Gaudens" in Boston Common (Colonel Robert Gould Shaw and His Colored Regiment),' " *Musical Quarterly* 81:1 (Spring 1997), pp. 13–50.
136 *"mobbed the lobbies"*: "Throng Hears Ornstein," *New York Times*, Dec. 8, 1918.
136 *"commuters"*: Oja, *Making Music Modern*, p. 176.
136 *"I became a sort"*: Malcolm MacDonald, *Varèse: Astronomer in Sound* (Kahn and Averill, 2003), p. 56.
137 *"skyscraper mysticism"*: Paul Rosenfeld, *Discoveries of a Music Critic* (Vienna House, 1972), p. 260.
138 *"matinee idol"*: Oja, *Making Music Modern*, p. 26.
138 *L'Herbier*: See George Antheil, *Bad Boy of Music* (Samuel French, 1990), pp. 131–37; and Lynn Garafola, *Diaghilev's Ballets Russes* (Da Capo, 1998), p. 354. The riot scene from *L'Inhumaine* can be seen at musicmavericks.publicradio.org/features/interview_lehrman.html (accessed May 1, 2007).
138 A Jazz Symphony: Daniel Albright, *Untwisting the Serpent: Modernism in Music, Literature, and Other Arts* (University of Chicago Press, 2000), pp. 234–35.
138 *"Expected Riots Peter Out"*: Oja, *Making Music Modern*, p. 93. See also Antheil, *Bad Boy of Music*, pp. 187–97.
139 *"catering to the public"*: Claire R. Reis, *Composers, Conductors, and Critics* (Detroit Reprints in Music, 1974), p. 7. For more on Ruggles, see Marilyn J. Ziffrin, *Carl Ruggles: Composer, Painter, and Storyteller* (University of Illinois Press, 1994).
140 *tonic-dominant*: Kathleen Hoover and John Cage, *Virgil Thomson: His Life and Music* (Sagamore, 1959), p. 157.
140 *Jimmy Daniels*: Virgil Thomson, *Virgil Thomson* (Dutton, 1985), p. 217.
140 *"Pigeons are definitely not alas"*: James Thurber, "There's an Owl in My Room," *New Yorker*, Nov. 17, 1934, p. 19.

141 *"Negroes objectify"*: Steven Watson, *Prepare for Saints: Gertrude Stein, Virgil Thomson, and the Mainstreaming of American Modernism* (Random House, 1998), p. 202.

141 *"Thomson gave black artists"*: Anthony Tommasini, *Virgil Thomson: Composer on the Aisle* (Norton, 1997), p. 227.

141 *"Jazz is not America"*: Olivia Mattis, "Edgard Varèse's 'Progressive' Nationalism: *Amériques* Meets *Américanisme*," in *Edgard Varèse: Die Befreiung des Klangs*, ed. Helge de la Motte-Haber (Wolke, 1992), p. 167.

141 *Scholars have tracked*: See, for example, Jack Gottlieb, *Funny, It Doesn't Sound Jewish: How Yiddish Songs and Synagogue Melodies Influenced Tin Pan Alley, Broadway, and Hollywood* (SUNY Press, 2004), p. 218; and Andrea Most, *Making Americans: Jews and the Broadway Musical* (Harvard UP, 2004).

141 *"link between the exiled"*: Constant Lambert, *Music Ho! A Study of Music in Decline* (Hogarth, 1985), p. 185.

142 *the creators could hardly*: See Raymond Knapp, *The American Musical and the Formation of National Identity* (Princeton UP, 2005), pp. 185–94.

143 *"I frequently hear music"*: Isaac Goldberg, *George Gershwin: A Study in American Music* (Ungar, 1958), p. 139.

143 *Dvořák's* Humoresque: Ibid., p. 58.

144 *favorite pianists and composers*: See Gershwin's scrapbooks in GGLC.

144 *Hambitzer*: David Ewen, *A Journey to Greatness: The Life and Music of George Gershwin* (Holt, 1956), pp. 47 and 61.

144 *Kilenyi . . . better chance of winning*: Ibid., p. 63. For Kilenyi and *Harmonielehre*, see Howard Pollack, *George Gershwin: His Life and Work* (University of California Press, 2006), p. 30.

145 *Gershwin regularly attended*: Vernon Duke, *Passport to Paris* (Little, Brown, 1955), p. 90.

145 *accompanying Gauthier*: "Jazz Throws Down the Gage to the 'Classicists,' Invading New York's Strongholds of Serious Music," *Musical America*, Feb. 2, 1924.

145 *Whiteman*: Don Rayno, *Paul Whiteman: Pioneer in American Music, Vol. 1: 1890–1930* (Scarecrow, 2003), p. 19.

145 *"the tremendous strides"*: Goldberg, *George Gershwin*, pp. 144–45.

146 *"out of the kitchen"*: Deems Taylor, "Words and Music," *New York World*, Feb. 17, 1924.

146 *glissando*: On this effect, see Goldberg, *George Gershwin*, p. 71. Interestingly, when Duke Ellington recorded the *Rhapsody* in 1960, he *removed* the glissando, returning to Gershwin's original sketch. See David Schiff, *Gershwin, "Rhapsody in Blue"* (Cambridge UP, 1997), p. 69.

146 *such classical celebrities*: Ewen, *Journey to Greatness*, p. 162.

146 *more high-level admirers*: Pollack, *George Gershwin*, pp. 139–45.

146 Lyric Suite: Alban Berg, *Letters to His Wife*, ed. and trans. Bernard Grun (St. Martin's, 1971), p. 363. For the Berg photo, see Edward Jablonski and Lawrence D. Stewart, *The Gershwin Years* (Doubleday, 1958), p. 197.

147 *"I should study with you"*: Edward Jablonski, *Gershwin* (Da Capo, 1998), p. 168. For the story featuring Ravel, see Oscar Levant, *Memoirs of an Amnesiac* (Bantam, 1965), pp. 116–17.

147 *Pollack shows*: See Pollack, *George Gershwin*, pp. 118–35.

147 *Gershwin's notebooks*: GGLC.

147 *"jazz grand opera"*: *New York Evening Mail*, Nov. 18, 1924, clipping at GGLC.

148 *only by a black cast*: Henrietta Malkiel, "Awaiting the Great American Opera: How Composers Are Paving the Way," *Musical America*, April 25, 1925.

148 *"appeal to the many"*: George Gershwin, "Rhapsody in Catfish Row," *New York Times*, Oct. 20, 1935.

149 *"Summertime"*: Allen Forte, "Reflections upon the Gershwin-Berg Connection," *Musical Quarterly* 83:2 (Summer 1999), p. 154, also proposes a connection between Marie's lullaby and "Summertime," but he chooses the more dissimilar chords that appear beneath *"Mädel, was fangst Du jetzt an?"*

149 *"Melodic. Nothing neutral"*: Jablonski and Stewart, *Gershwin Years*, p. 233.

149 *Gershwin and Bubbles*: Jablonski, *Gershwin*, p. 286.

149 *"not a very serious"*: Virgil Thomson, "George Gershwin," *Modern Music* 13:1 (Nov.–Dec. 1935) pp. 16–17.

150 *"Abraham Lincoln of Negro music"*: Pollack, *George Gershwin*, pp. 597–98.

150 *"Grand music"*: Mark Tucker, ed., *The Duke Ellington Reader* (Oxford UP, 1993), p. 115.

150 *"Folk-lore subjects . . . I don't mind"*: Thomson, "George Gershwin," p. 17.

150 *"I don't feel I've really scratched"*: Interview with Frances Gershwin Godowsky, included on companion CD to Vivien Perlis and Libby Van Cleve, *Composers' Voices from Ives to Ellington* (Yale UP 2005).

151 *Anderson explains*: Paul Allen Anderson,

Deep River: Music and Memory in Harlem Renaissance Thought (Duke UP, 2001), p. 177. For "hybridic fusion," see p. 163.

151 *in his musical commentaries*: See Alain Locke, *The Negro and His Music* (Associates in Negro Folk Education, 1936), p. 86; and Alain Locke, "Toward a Critique of Negro Music," *Opportunity*, Nov. 1934, pp. 328–30.

151 *"We build our temples"*: Langston Hughes, "The Negro Artist and the Racial Mountain" (June 1926), in *The Portable Harlem Renaissance Reader*, ed. David Levering Lewis (Penguin, 1994), p. 95.

151 *"Bach and myself"*: Richard O. Boyer, "The Hot Bach," pt. 1, *New Yorker*, June 24, 1944, p. 30.

151 *"To attempt to elevate"*: Tucker, *Duke Ellington Reader*, p. 247.

152 *"heterogenous sound ideal"*: Olly Wilson, "The Heterogeneous Sound Ideal in African-American Music," in *New Perspectives on Music: Essays in Honor of Eileen Southern*, ed. Josephine Wright (Harmonie Park Press, 1992), pp. 328–29.

152 *"The phonograph record"*: Albert Murray, *Stomping the Blues* (Da Capo, 2000), p. 183.

152 *"I'd sing a melody"*: Boyer, "The Hot Bach," pt. 3, *New Yorker*, July 8, 1944, p. 29.

152 *"You know you should go"*: Ellington, *Music Is My Mistress*, p. 97.

153 *"a rhapsody unhampered"*: Tucker, *Duke Ellington Reader*, pp. 49–50.

153 *Gershwin and Ellington*: See Pollack, *George Gershwin*, pp. 165–68.

154 Boola: Mark Tucker, "The Genesis of *Black, Brown, and Beige*," *Black Music Research Journal* 13:2 (Fall 1993), pp. 73–74.

154 *churches outnumber*: Howard Taubman, "The 'Duke' Invades Carnegie Hall," *New York Times*, Jan. 17, 1943.

154 *Rattenbury points out*: Ken Rattenbury, *Duke Ellington, Jazz Composer* (Yale UP, 1990), p. 106.

154 *"That's the Negro's life"*: Tucker, *Duke Ellington Reader*, p. 150.

155 *"not a song of great Joy"*: Tucker, "Genesis of *Black, Brown, and Beige*," p. 78.

155 *assist from Billy Strayhorn*: On Strayhorn's contribution, see van de Leur, *Something to Live For*, pp. 87–88.

155 *"formless and meaningless"*: Paul Bowles, "Duke Ellington in Recital for Russian Relief," *New York Herald Tribune*, Jan. 25, 1943.

155 *Hammond . . . complained*: John Hammond, "Is the Duke Deserting Jazz?" in Tucker, *Duke Ellington Reader*, pp. 171–73.

156 *"Anyone who writes music"*: *On the Road with Duke Ellington* (NBC, 1967).

156 *"I was struck by"*: Tucker, *Duke Ellington Reader*, p. 209.

5: Apparition from the Woods

157 *"Desperately difficult"*: TMDF, p. 254.

157 *"God opens his door"*: James Hepokoski, *Sibelius, Symphony No. 5* (Cambridge UP, 1993), p. 33.

158 *"Isolation and loneliness"*: ETS3, p. 283.

158 *seven volumes*: Kari Kilpeläinen, "Sibelius Eight: What Happened to It?" *Finnish Music Quarterly* 4 (1995), pp. 33–35.

158 *"I suppose one"*: ETS3, p. 328, with emendations by Jeffrey Kallberg.

158 *"In the 1940s"*: Ibid., p. 317.

159 *"The small nations"*: Milan Kundera, *Testaments Betrayed*, trans. Linda Asher (HarperCollins, 1995), pp. 192–94.

160 *"I feel like a ghost"*: Sergei Bertensson and Jay Leyda, *Sergei Rachmaninoff: A Lifetime in Music* (Indiana UP, 2001), p. 351.

160 *"Not everyone"*: Hepokoski, *Sibelius, Symphony No. 5*, p. 13.

160 *"The simplest"*: Carl Nielsen, *Living Music*, trans. Reginald Spink (Hutchinson, 1953), p. 75.

161 *"could not grasp"*: *The Kalevala*, trans. Francis Peabody Magoun Jr. (Harvard UP, 1963), p. 245.

162 "Kullervo, Kalervon": Translation by William Forsell Kirby, included in the notes to Osmo Vänskä's 2000 recording of *Kullervo* (BIS CD-1215).

163 *"most broken-hearted protest"*: ETS1, p. 244.

164 *"severity of form"*: ETS2, pp. 76–77.

164 Salome *and* Elektra: Santeri Levas, *Sibelius: A Personal Portrait*, trans. Percy Young (Dent, 1972), p. 74.

164 *Debussy*: ETS2, p. 107.

164 *"my most faithful companion"*: James Hepokoski, "Sibelius, Jean," NG 23, p. 336.

165 *"The Raven"*: ETS2 pp. 195–201.

166 *"People avoided our eyes"*: ETS2, p. 170.

166 *"A symphony is not"*: ETS2, p. 159. Emendations by Jeffrey Kallberg.

166 *"Freudvoll und leidvoll"*: Ibid., p. 161.

166 *"rotational form"*: Hepokoski, *Sibelius, Symphony No. 5*, pp. 23–26.

167 *"One of my greatest"*: Ibid., pp. 36–37.

168 *overtone series of a meadow*: Matti Huttunen, "The National Composer and the Idea of Finnishness," in *The Cambridge Companion to Sibelius*, ed. Daniel M. Grimley (Cambridge UP, 2004), p. 14.

168 *"dissolution" and "decay"*: James Hepokoski,

"Rotations, Sketches, and the Sixth Symphony," in *Sibelius Studies*, ed. Timothy Jackson and Veijo Murtomäki (Cambridge UP, 2002), esp. pp. 328 and 345.

169 *"Where the stars dwell"*: Hepokoski, "Sibelius, Jean," p. 338.

169 *"deep acoustic throbbing"*: Julian Anderson, "Sibelius and Contemporary Music," in Grimley, *Cambridge Companion to Sibelius*, p. 198.

170 *"I have bedimmed"*: William Shakespeare, *The Tempest*, ed. David Lindley (Cambridge UP, 2002), p. 200.

171 *"It's strange"*: ETS3, p. 308.

172 *"the last of the heroes"*: Glenda Dawn Goss, *Jean Sibelius and Olin Downes: Music, Friendship, Criticism* (Northeastern UP, 1995), pp. 105 and 57.

173 *"My mother and I"*: Ibid., p. 202.

173 *"boring Nordic dreariness"*: ETS3, p. 293.

173 *"could not afford"*: Ibid., p. 291.

173 *"vulgar, self-indulgent"*: Virgil Thomson, *Music Reviewed, 1940–1954* (Vintage, 1967), p. 4.

173 *"The work of Sibelius"*: "The Sibelius Problem," subsection of "Memorandum: Music in Radio," pp. 59–60, Princeton Radio Research Project, Paul Lazarsfeld Papers, Columbia University.

174 *"the tone is more apt"*: *Selected Letters of Virgil Thomson*, ed. Tim Page and Vanessa Weeks Page (Summit Books, 1988), p. 182.

174 *correspondence with Koussevitzky*: Letters dated Jan. 2, 1930, Aug. 16, 1930, Aug. 20, 1931, Jan. 15, 1932, June 6, 1932, June 14, 1932, Dec. 31, 1932, and Jan. 17, 1933, in Serge Koussevitzky Archive, Music Division, Library of Congress.

175 *Sibelius Society*: Árni Ingólfsson, " 'This Music Belongs to Us': Scandinavian Music and 'Nordic' Ideology in the Third Reich," paper delivered at the American Musicological Society New England Chapter meeting, March 23, 2002.

175 *"I wish with all my heart"*: Harold E. Johnson, *Jean Sibelius* (Knopf, 1959), p. 213.

175 *"How can you"*: ETS3, p. 327.

175 "The tragedy begins": Jean Sibelius, *Dagbok, 1909–1944* (Svenska litteratursällkapet i Finland, 2005), pp. 325 and 338. Translation by Jeffrey Kallberg.

175 *"All the doctors"*: Levas, *Sibelius*, p. 20.

175 *"It is very painful"*: Ibid., p. 123.

176 *"Every day"*: ETS1, p. 289.

176 *"Here they come"*: ETS3, p. 330.

176 *Stravinsky and Sibelius*: See SWS2, p. 443; Eric Walter White, *Stravinsky: The Composer and His Works* (University of California Press, 1979), p. 143; and RCSC, pp. 170 and 242.

176 *"antimodern modernism"*: Milan Kundera, "Die Weltliteratur," trans. Linda Asher, *New Yorker*, Jan. 8, 2007.

176 *New-music luminaries*: See Brian Ferneyhough, *Collected Writings* (Harwood, 1995), p. 205; Hans Gefors, "Make Change Your Choice!" in *The Music of Per Nørgård*, ed. Anders Beyer (Scolar, 1996), p. 37; and, for many other examples, Anderson, "Sibelius and Contemporary Music."

177 *Lindberg*: For Lindberg on *Tapiola*, see Peter Szendy's interview in *Magnus Lindberg* (FMIC/IRCAM, 1993), p. 11.

177 *"The people who you think"*: MFS, p. 192.

6. City of Nets

178 *"The blood stains looked"*: Klaus Mann, *The Turning Point* (Fischer, 1942), pp. 257 and 260.

179 *"Music is no longer"*: Alexander Ringer, "Schoenberg, Weill, and Epic Theater," *Journal of the Arnold Schoenberg Institute* 4:1 (June 1980), p. 86.

180 *"I've had indescribable"*: David Farneth, Elmar Juchem, and Dave Stein, eds., *Kurt Weill: A Life in Pictures and Documents* (Overlook, 2000), pp. 20–21.

180 *champagne reception*: Klaus Kreimeier, *The Ufa Story: A History of Germany's Greatest Film Company, 1918–1945*, trans. Robert Kimber and Rita Kimber (Hill and Wang, 1996), pp. 46–47.

180 *Strauss had conducted*: BGFI, p. 571.

180 *four hundred political murders*: Emil Julius Gumbel, "Four Years of Political Murder," in *The Weimar Republic Sourcebook*, ed. Anton Kaes, Martin Jay, and Edward Dimendberg (University of California Press, 1994), pp. 100–104.

180 *Gustav Landauer*: See Joan Weinstein, *The End of Expressionism: Art and the November Revolution in Germany, 1918–19* (University of Chicago Press, 1990), pp. 177–205. The film director Mike Nichols is Landauer and Lachmann's grandson.

180 *"Nothing was so mad"*: Bernd Widdig, *Culture and Inflation in Weimar Germany* (University of California Press, 2001), pp. 10–11.

181 *Rockwell has shown*: John Rockwell, "The Prussian Ministry of Culture and the Berlin State Opera, 1918–1931" (Ph.D. diss., University of California at Berkeley, 1972); and

John Rockwell, "Kurt Weill's Operatic Reform and Its Context," in *A New Orpheus: Essays on Kurt Weill*, ed. Kim H. Kowalke (Yale UP, 1986), pp. 55–58.

181 *"This is not the true"*: Joseph Goebbels, "Around the Gedächtniskirche" (1928), in Kaes, Jay, and Dimendberg, *Weimar Republic Sourcebook*, p. 561.

181 *Count von Kielmannsegg*: Paul Hindemith, "Notizen zu meinen 'Feldzugs-Erinnerungen,'" *Hindemith Jahrbuch* 18 (1989), p. 88; and Andres Briner, Dieter Rexroth, Giselher Schubert, eds., *Paul Hindemith: Leben und Werk im Bild und Text* (Atlantis, 1988), p. 36; *Selected Letters of Paul Hindemith*, ed. and trans. Geoffrey Skelton (Yale UP, 1995), p. 21.

182 *"neither Impressionistically"*: Stephen Hinton, "Aspects of Hindemith's Neue Sachlichkeit," *Hindemith Jahrbuch* 14 (1985), p. 26.

183 *Orff and Brecht*: Kim H. Kowalke, "Burying the Past: Carl Orff and His Brecht Connection," *Musical Quarterly* 84:1 (Spring 2000), pp. 58–83.

183 *"hunger for wholeness"*: Peter Gay, *Weimar Culture: The Outsider as Insider* (Harper and Row, 1968), p. 96.

183 *Adorno and Hindemith*: Theodor W. Adorno, "Kritik des Musikanten," in *Gesammelte Schriften* (Suhrkamp, 1973), vol. 14, pp. 67–107.

184 *photomontage*: See the notes to the 1993 recording of *Jonny spielt auf* (London 436 631–2).

184 *"Fiftieth Avenue," Max Brand*: NSM, pp. 304 and 311.

186 *78-rpm recording*: See Susan C. Cook, "Flirting with the Vernacular: America in Europe, 1900–45," in *The Cambridge History of Twentieth-Century Music*, ed. Nicholas Cook and Anthony Pople (Cambridge UP, 2004), p. 179.

186 *Sam Wooding's jazz revue*: John L. Stewart, *Ernst Krenek: The Man and His Music* (University of California Press, 1991), p. 81.

186 *"Despite the infusions"*: Hanns Eisler, *Musik und Politik*, ed. Günter Mayer (VEB, 1973), p. 35.

186 *"relative stabilization"*: Ibid., p. 80.

186 Scheindasein: Ibid., p. 33.

186 *"The big music festivals"*: Hanns Eisler, "On the Situation of Modern Music" (1928), in *A Rebel in Music: Selected Writings*, ed. Manfred Grabs (International Publishers, 1978), p. 29.

186 *"Remember that"*: Ibid., pp. 30–31.

187 *"Hindemith has already"*: Jürgen Schebera, *Kurt Weill: An Illustrated Life*, trans. Caroline Murphy (Yale UP, 1995), p. 46.

187 *"pandering to the taste"*: Ibid., p. 47.

188 *"Do not be afraid"*: Kurt Weill, *Musik und musikalisches Theater: Gesammelte Schriften*, ed. Stephen Hinton and Jürgen Schebera (Schott, 2000), p. 489.

188 Schlagwort: The debt to Busoni is detailed in Michael Morley, " 'Suiting the Action to the Word': Some Observations on *Gestus* and *Gestische Musik*," in Kowalke, *A New Orpheus*, pp. 187–88.

188 *"in which pantomime"*: Daniel Albright, *Untwisting the Serpent: Modernism in Music, Literature, and Other Arts* (University of Chicago Press, 2000), p. 112.

189 *"cool, withdrawn"*: Ronald Taylor, *Kurt Weill: Composer in a Divided World* (Northeastern UP, 1992), p. 58.

189 *"She can't read music"*: *Speak Low (When You Speak Love): The Letters of Kurt Weill and Lotte Lenya*, ed. and trans. Lys Symonette and Kim H. Kowalke (University of California Press, 1996), frontispiece.

189 *"composer of atonal"*: Morley, " 'Suiting the Action to the Word,' " p. 189.

190 *"Is here no telephone?"*: Taylor, *Kurt Weill*, pp. 115–16.

190 *"ugly, brutal"*: John Willett, ed. and trans., *Brecht on Theatre: The Development of an Aesthetic* (Hill and Wang, 1964), p. 3.

191 *"Just as Wagner"*: Walter Benjamin, *Selected Writings, Volume 2, 1927–1934*, ed. Michael W. Jennings, Howard Eiland, and Gary Smith, trans. Rodney Livingstone et al. (Harvard UP, 1999), p. 369.

191 *"intimately the countermorality"*: Walter Benjamin, *Selected Writings, Volume 3, 1935–1938*, ed. Howard Eiland and Michael W. Jennings, trans. Edmund Jephcott, Howard Eiland, et al. (Harvard UP, 2002), p. 257.

192 *"style of willful"*: Stephen Hinton, "Misunderstanding 'The Threepenny Opera,'" in *Kurt Weill, "The Threepenny Opera,"* ed. Stephen Hinton (Cambridge UP, 1990), p. 189.

192 *twenty-three different instruments*: Stephen Hinton, *"Die Dreigroschenoper*: The 1928 Full Score," in *Die Dreigroschenoper: A Facsimile of the Holograph Full Score*, ed. Edward Harsh (Kurt Weill Foundation for Music, 1996), p. 8.

193 *"When I tell you"*: As recorded in Los Angeles on Oct. 30, 1986, released on

Frank Sinatra: The Reprise Collection (9 26340-2)

193 *Armstrong said*: Will Friedwald, *Stardust Melodies: The Biography of Twelve of America's Most Popular Songs* (Pantheon, 2002), p. 88.

193 *"The audience was"*: Bob Dylan, *Chronicles, Volume 1* (Simon and Schuster, 2004), pp. 273–75.

194 *direct quotation*: The song in question is "Lied von der Moldau," from *Schweyk im zweiten Weltkrieg*, a 1943 Brecht-Eisler revue. For more on the link between Brecht and Dylan, see Esther Quin, "Stumbling on Lost Cigars of Bertolt Brecht: Bob Dylan's Rebellion," *PN Review* 30:2 (Nov.–Dec. 2003), pp. 47–53.

194 *"You have betrayed"*: Translation by Allen Forte in the libretto to Pierre Boulez's 1995 recording of *Moses und Aron* (DG 449 174-2), p. 63.

194 *"method of composing"*: ASSI, p. 218.

194 *Pupils and friends*: HMAW, p. 252.

194 *"extreme emotionality"*: ASSI, p. 217.

194 *"The bourgeois God"*: Josef Rufer, *Das Werk Arnold Schönbergs* (Bärenreiter, 1959), p. 101. See also Arnold Schoenberg, *Texte* (Universal, 1926), pp. 23–28.

195 *twelve-tone patterns in* Salome: At the end of the opera, after Herod shouts, "Kill that woman!," the orchestra runs through eleven different tones in rapid, kaleidoscopic succession—a minatory chord in the brass (D, F, A), a skewy trumpet fanfare (C, G-flat, B-flat, D-flat, G), a rumbling trombone arpeggio (A-flat, C-flat, E-flat). See also a perfect twelve-tone aggregate at 3 before 255: arpeggiated chords of E-flat minor, D-flat major, G dominant seventh, and A minor. On quasi-twelve-tone writing in *Elektra*, see Tethys Carpenter, "The Musical Language of *Elektra*," in *Richard Strauss, "Elektra,"* ed. Derrick Puffett (Cambridge UP, 1989), pp. 74–106.

196 *"When all twelve notes"*: Anton Webern, *Path to the New Music*, ed. Willi Reich (Universal, 1960), p. 51.

196 *copied out rows*: HMAW, pp. 309–10.

196 *"used twelve tones"*: HHS, p. 442.

197 *"completely undifferentiated"*: Joseph Auner, "Proclaiming the Mainstream: Schoenberg, Berg, and Webern," in Cook and Pople, *Cambridge History of Twentieth-Century Music*, pp. 253–54.

197 *next hundred years*: HHS, p. 277.

197 *"Recognition does one good"*: ASL, pp. 117–18.

198 *"Art is from the outset"*: JASR, p. 212.

198 *"But who's this"*: As translated in JASR, p. 188. For other terms of derision, see Leonard Stein, "Schoenberg and 'Kleine Modernsky,'" in *Confronting Stravinsky: Man, Musician, and Modernist*, ed. Jann Pasler (University of California Press, 1986), p. 319.

198 *"want to apply"*: JASR, pp. 186–87.

198 *"They betray their God"*: ASSI, pp. 258–59.

198 *"Jo-Jo-Foxtrot"*: HHS, p. 306.

199 *"one after the other"*: From Susan Marie Praeder's translation in the booklet for Michael Gielen's 1997 recording of *Von heute auf morgen* (cpo 999 532-2), p. 35. See also Juliane Brand, "A Short History of *Von heute auf morgen* with Letters and Documents," *Journal of the Arnold Schoenberg Institute* 14:2 (Nov. 1991), p. 259.

199 *"wishes for only whores"*: JASR, p. 196. For Krenek's remark, see p. 194.

199 *"Modern music bores me"*: HHS, pp. 311–12.

199 *"treason"*: ASL, p. 120.

199 *"who, filled with disdain"*: Kurt Weill, "Verschiebungen in der musikalischen Produktion" (Oct. 1927), in *Musik und musikalisches Theater*, p. 61.

200 *"understandable"*: Ringer, "Schoenberg, Weill, and Epic Theater," pp. 85–86.

200 *"In the end"*: Ibid., p. 89.

200 *"I do not believe"*: ASSI, p. 96.

201 *Stresemann . . . attended*: Wolfgang Stresemann, *Zeiten und Klänge: Ein Leben zwischen Musik und Politik* (Ullstein, 1994), pp. 102–103.

201 *"It's the beginning of the end"*: Mann, *Turning Point*, p. 230.

201 *Beethoven's Fifth*: Thomas Phelps, "Stefan Wolpe: Eine Einführung," in Stefan Wolpe, *Lieder mit Klavierbegleitung, 1929–1933* (Peer, 1993). p. 5; Austin Clarkson, "Lecture on Dada by Stefan Wolpe," *Musical Quarterly* 72:2 (1986), pp. 209–10.

202 Zeus und Elida: Austin Clarkson, "Stefan Wolpe: Broken Sequences," in *Music and Nazism: Art Under Tyranny, 1933–1945*, ed. Michael H. Kater and Albrecht Riethmüller (Laaber, 2003), p. 222.

202 *failed to satisfy*: Ibid., p. 224.

202 *postwar recordings*: Ernst Busch, *Lieder der Arbeiterklasse & Lieder aus dem spanischen Bürgerkrieg* (Pläne CD 88 642).

202 *400,000 members*: Clarkson, "Stefan Wolpe: Broken Sequences," p. 223.

202 *balled-up fist*: Jürgen Schebera, *Hanns Eisler:*

Eine Biographie in Texten, Bildern, und Dokumenten (Schott, 1998), p. 68.

203 *"Better to make music"*: Stephen Hinton, "*Lehrstück*: An Aesthetics of Performance," in *Hindemith Jahrbuch* 22 (1993), pp. 80–81.

203 *"willingness to act"*: Ibid., p. 88.

204 *Gerhart Eisler*: See Herbert Romerstein and Eric Breindel, *The Venona Secrets: Exposing Soviet Espionage and America's Traitors* (Regnery, 2000), pp. 71–73 and 526; Raymond W. Leonard, *Secret Soldiers of the Revolution: Soviet Military Intelligence, 1918–1933* (Greenwood, 1999), p. 41; and John Willett, "Production as Learning Experience: *Taniko, He Who Says Yes, The Measures Taken*" in *Brecht and East Asian Theatre*, ed. Antony Tatlow and Tak-Wai Wong (Hong Kong UP, 1982), pp. 157–58.

204 *"What shall we do"*: Bertolt Brecht, *The Measures Taken and Other Lehrstücke*, trans. Carl R. Mueller (Arcade, 2001), pp. 33–34.

204 *"The I is disappearing"*: Ludwig Bauer, "The Middle Ages, 1932," in Kaes, Jay, and Dimendberg, *Weimar Republic Sourcebook*, p. 385.

204 *"phony Richard Strauss"*: John Fuegi, *Brecht and Company: Sex, Politics, and the Making of Modern Drama* (Grove, 1994), p. 267.

206 "Deutschland erwache!": Farneth, Juchem, and Stein, *Kurt Weill*, p. 115; and NSM, p. 325.

206 *"The great retaliation"*: Karl Kraus, "Die Büchse der Pandora," in *Grimassen: Ausgewählte Werke, Band I, 1902–1914* (Langen Müller, 1971), p. 54. See also Patricia Hall, *A View of Berg's "Lulu" Through the Manuscript Sources* (University of California Press, 1996), pp. 94 and 73–75.

207 *"I was with him"*: Theodor W. Adorno, *Alban Berg: Master of the Smallest Link*, trans. Juliane Brand and Christopher Hailey (Cambridge UP, 1991), p. 10.

207 *"Schoenberg envied Berg"*: Ibid., p. 29.

207 *new kinds of tonality: Theodor W. Adorno, Alban Berg: Briefwechsel, 1925–1935*, ed. Henri Lonitz (Suhrkamp, 1997), p. 108.

208 *"Alban invented"*: George Perle, *The Operas of Alban Berg, Vol. 2: Lulu* (University of California Press, 1985), p. 28.

209 *get his orchestration right*: Hall, *A View of Berg's "Lulu,"* pp. 39 and 167.

209 *Berg saw in Vienna*: David Drew, *Kurt Weill: A Handbook* (University of California Press, 1987), p. 184.

210 *noting the triads*: Hall, *A View of Berg's "Lulu,"* pp. 120–21. For more on *Lulu*'s row technique, see Douglas Jarman, *Alban Berg, "Lulu"* (Cambridge UP, 1991), pp. 67–71.

211 *"I always had the impression"*: Willi Reich, *Alban Berg*, trans. Cornelius Cardew (Harcourt, Brace and World), p. 30.

212 *"We saw tears"*: TMDF, p. 527.

212 *Mann thought often of Berg*: Mann seems to have read Willi Reich's book *Alban Berg* (Reichner, 1937) as a source. See Thomas Mann, *Tagebücher, 1944–1.4.1946* (Fischer, 1986), p. 14; and Thomas Mann, *The Story of a Novel: The Genesis of Doctor Faustus* (Knopf, 1961), p. 72. Only one Berg book existed in 1944. The Mann library in Zurich does not have Reich's book in its collection; perhaps Mann returned the volume to Adorno when he was done with it. For the *Lulu* premiere, see Thomas Mann, *Diaries, 1918–1939*, ed. Hermann Kesten, trans. Richard Winston and Clara Winston (Abrams, 1982), p. 278. For the inclusion of the final scene in the 1937 performance, see Perle, *Operas of Alban Berg, Vol. 2*, p. 266.

212 *"One instrument after another"*: Adorno, *Alban Berg*, p. 113. The original German, from Reich, *Alban Berg* (1937), p. 101: "*Ein Instrument schweigt nach dem anderen.*" Compare *Doktor Faustus* (Fischer, 1971), p. 490: "*Eine Instrumentengruppe nach der anderen tritt zurück.*"

212 *"One instrumental group"*: TMDF, p. 515.

7. The Art of Fear

213 *"Along the legendary"*: *The Complete Poems of Anna Akhmatova*, ed. Roberta Reeder, trans. Judith Hemschemeyer (Zephyr, 1997), p. 562.

215 *Box A*: Details of Stalin's visit to *Lady Macbeth* are drawn from Dmitri Volkogonov, *Stalin: Triumph and Tragedy* (Forum, 1996), p. 148; Galina Vishnevskaya, *Galina: A Russian Story*, trans. Guy Daniels (Harcourt Brace Jovanovich, 1984), p. 94; Krzysztof Meyer, *Dimitri Chostakovitch* (Fayard, 1994), pp. 201–202; and LFS, pp. 84–85.

215 *"make use of all"*: Boris Schwarz, *Music and Musical Life in Soviet Russia, 1917–1970* (Norton, 1972), p. 144.

216 *"sick at heart"*: EWS, p. 129.

216 *"From the first moment"*: LFS, pp. 84–85.

216 *New Year's Eve*: Harlow Robinson, *Sergei Prokofiev: A Biography* (Northeastern UP, 2002), pp. 309–10.

218 *"official" or dissident*: The main controversy

around Shostakovich is the debate set off by Solomon Volkov's book *Testimony: The Memoirs of Dmitri Shostakovich* (Harper and Row, 1979), which purports to be the composer's autobiography and portrays him as a dissident or "holy fool." That thesis was expanded in Ian MacDonald, *The New Shostakovich* (Northeastern UP, 1990); and in Allan B. Ho and Dmitry Feofanov, *Shostakovich Reconsidered* (Toccata, 1998). But two essays by Laurel E. Fay—"Shostakovich Versus Volkov: Whose *Testimony*?" (1980), reprinted in *A Shostakovich Casebook*, ed. Malcolm Hamrick Brown (Indiana UP, 2004), pp. 11–21; and "Volkov's *Testimony* Reconsidered," also in *Shostakovich Casebook*, pp. 22–66—have established that *Testimony* is a fraudulent document. For more information, see www.therestisnoise.com/2004/07/the_case_of_the.html.

218 *"There are those"*: Brecht wrote these lines in 1930 for G. W. Pabst's film of *The Threepenny Opera*.

218 *May Day colors*: Sheila Fitzpatrick, *The Commissariat of Enlightenment: Soviet Organization of Education and the Arts Under Lunacharsky, October 1917–1921* (Cambridge UP, 1970), p. 126.

218 *"I can't listen"*: Robert Payne, *The Life and Death of Lenin* (Simon and Schuster, 1964), p. 249.

219 *"old aesthetic junk"*: Fitzpatrick, *Commissariat of Enlightenment*, p. 121.

219 *"Spit on rhymes"*: Vladimir Mayakovsky, "Order No. 2 to the Army of the Arts" (1921), in *The Bedbug and Selected Poetry*, trans. Max Hayward and George Reavey (Indiana UP, 1975), pp. 147–48.

219 Symphony for Factory Whistles: Amy Nelson, *Music for the Revolution: Musicians and Power in Early Soviet Russia* (Penn State UP, 2004), pp. 27–28.

220 *"Let the worker hear"*: Fitzpatrick, *Commissariat of Enlightenment*, p. 134. Said in 1918.

220 *Bulgakov and Zoshchenko*: See Edvard Radzinsky, *Stalin*, trans. H. T. Willetts (Doubleday, 1996), pp. 261 and 524.

220 *fine tenor voice*: Simon Sebag Montefiore, *Stalin: The Court of the Red Tsar* (Weidenfeld and Nicolson, 2003), p. 73.

220 *"good," "so-so"*: Roy A. Medvedev and Zhores A. Medvedev, *The Unknown Stalin: His Life, Death, and Legacy*, trans. Ellen Dahrendorf (Tauris, 2003), p. 92.

220 *"sharp, unbearably explicit"*: Nadezhda Mandelstam, *Hope Against Hope: A Memoir*, trans. Max Hayward (Atheneum, 1970), p. 4.

220 *"Our mysterious awe"*: Ibid., p. 85.

221 *"It seemed to you"*: LFS, p. 121.

221 *Glazunov*: Ibid., p. 292.

221 *Funeral March*: Ibid., p. 12.

222 *burst out laughing*: Ibid., p. 36.

222 *" 'Art belongs' "*: Michael Ardov, *Memories of Shostakovich*, trans. Rosanna Kelly and Michael Meylac (Short, 2004), pp. 88–89.

222 *poison gas*: See Arno J. Mayer, *The Furies: Violence and Terror in the French and Russian Revolutions* (Princeton UP, 2000), p. 395; and Alexander Yakovlev, *A Century of Violence in Soviet Russia*, trans. Anthony Austin (Yale UP, 2002), p. 90.

222 *"a man of great"*: IGSF, p. 216.

222 *Moscow offer*: "Shostakovich: Letters to His Mother," trans. Rolanda Norton, in *Shostakovich and His World*, ed. Laurel E. Fay (Princeton UP, 2004), p. 16.

222 *Yavorsky*: See Gordon D. McQuere, "The Theories of Boleslav Yavorsky," in *Russian Theoretical Thought in Music*, ed. Gordon D. McQuere (UMI Research Press, 1983), pp. 109–64.

222 *Berg letter*: LFS, p. 39.

222 *commission of Second Symphony*: Ibid., pp. 39–40.

223 *Berlin influence*: In "Responses of Shostakovich to a Questionnaire on the Psychology of the Creative Process" (1927), trans. Malcolm Hamrick Brown, in Fay, *Shostakovich and His World*, pp. 29–30, Shostakovich mentions the influence of Schoenberg, Bartók, Hindemith, and Krenek.

223 New Babylon: See Richard Taylor and Ian Christie, eds., *Inside the Film Factory: New Approaches to Russian and Soviet Cinema* (Routledge, 1991), p. 180.

224 *"The first experiments"*: Sergei Eisenstein, Vsevolod Pudovkin, and Grigori Aleksandrov, "Statement on Sound," in *The Film Factory: Russian and Soviet Cinema in Documents, 1896–1939*, ed. Richard Taylor and Ian Christie (Harvard UP, 1988), pp. 234–35.

224 *"The Song of the Counterplan"*: For more on Shostakovich's film music, see John Riley, *Dmitri Shostakovich: A Life in Film* (Tauris, 2005).

225 *flute to his buttocks*: EWS, p. 93.

225 *Union of Soviet Composers*: Ibid., pp. 79–81, and LFS, p. 65.

225 *"engineers of human souls"*: Tovah Yedlin,

Maxim Gorky: A Political Biography (Praeger, 1999), p. 199.

225 *"tragedies and conflicts"*: Pauline Fairclough, "The 'Perestroyka' of Soviet Symphonism: Shostakovich in 1935," *Music & Letters* 83:2 (May 2002), p. 262.

226 *"typical master kulak," "future kulak"*: Dmitri Shostakovich, "About My Opera," in Victor Seroff, *Dmitri Shostakovich: The Life and Background of a Soviet Composer* (Knopf, 1943), pp. 254 and 253.

226 *"In* Lady Macbeth *I wanted"*: David Fanning, notes to Myung Whun-Chung's recording of *Lady Macbeth* (DG 437 511–2), p. 15.

226 *"petty," "vulgar"*: Shostakovich, "About My Opera," pp. 250–55.

226 *three million people*: Robert Conquest, *The Harvest of Sorrow: Soviet Collectivization and the Terror-Famine* (Oxford UP, 1986), pp. 305–306.

227 *Katerina and Nina*: Vishnevskaya, *Galina*, p. 351.

227 *"[Shostakovich] was thirsting"*: EWS, p. 110.

227 *Gavriil Popov*: Laurel E. Fay, "Found: Shostakovich's Long-Lost Twin Brother," *New York Times*, April 6, 2003; Pauline Fairclough, *A Soviet Credo: Shostakovich's Fourth Symphony* (Ashgate, 2006), pp. 43–45; and Victor Tsaritsyn, "This Strong, Brilliant Gift . . . ," *Neva*, September 2004. The author is grateful to Chris Lovett for bringing Tsaritsyn's article to his attention and for making a translation.

227 *"rebuses and riddles"*: Leonid Maximenkov, "Stalin and Shostakovich: Letters to a 'Friend,'" in Fay, *Shostakovich and His World*, p. 48.

228 *"We had to begin"*: Joshua Kunitz, "The Shostakovich 'Affair,'" *New Masses*, June 9, 1936, p. 18.

228 *"It has to be there"*: LFS, p. 87; IGSF, p. 214.

229 *"There's no need"*: Andrei Artizov and Oleg Naumov, eds., *Vlast' i khudozhestvennaia intelligentsiia: Dokumenty TsK RKP(b)-VKP(b), VChK-OGPU-NKVD o kul'turnoi politike, 1917–1953 gg.* (Demokratiia, 1999), pp. 290–95. Translation by Alex Abramovich. Abram Lezhnev was the pen-name of Abram Garelik.

230 *Meyerhold's defense*: LFS, p. 91. For Meyerhold attending *Lady Macbeth*, see Meyer, *Dimitri Chostakovitch*, p. 201.

230 *"All that the* Pravda*"*: *Maxim Gorky: Selected Letters*, ed. and trans. Andrew Barratt and Barry P. Scherr (Clarendon, 1997), p. 366.

230 *"as a gardener cultivates"*: Joseph Stalin et al., *Soviet Union, 1935* (Co-operative Publishing Society of Foreign Workers in the U.S.S.R., 1935), p. 13.

230 *"To my question"*: Memo from Kerzhentsev to Stalin and Molotov, Feb. 7, 1936, in Artizov and Naumov, *Vlast' i khudozhestvennaia intelligentsiia*, p. 289. Translation by Alex Abramovich.

230 *waiting by the phone*: LFS, p. 91.

230 *"I am living"*: Lyudmila Mikheyeva-Sollertinskaya, "Shostakovich As Reflected in His Letters to Sollertinsky," in *Shostakovich in Context*, ed. Rosamund Bartlett (Oxford UP, 2000), p. 76.

230 *Tukhachevsky sweating*: IGSF, p. 215.

231 *other relatives*: LFS, p. 98; EWS, pp. 145–46.

231 *bloodstains on several pages*: Robert Conquest, *The Great Terror: A Reassessment* (Oxford UP, 1990), p. 200.

231 *"enemies of the people"*: For the use of this phrase in connection with Shostakovich, see Henry Orlov, "A Link in the Chain," in Brown, *Shostakovich Casebook*, p. 197.

232 *"The authorities tried"*: IGSF, p. 194.

232 *Bukharin*: For more on the Fourth's relationship with the less restrictive, Gorky-Bukharin definition of socialist realism, see Fairclough, "'Perestroyka' of Soviet Symphonism," p. 262.

232 *Fairclough hears*: Fairclough, *Soviet Credo*, p. 205.

233 *Taruskin points out*: Richard Taruskin, *Defining Russia Musically: Historical and Hermeneutical Essays* (Princeton UP, 1997), p. 493.

233 *set to work on the finale*: LFS, p. 93; second movement is finished on Jan. 6, 1936.

233 *"I didn't like the situation"*: Ibid., p. 96. For "diabolical complexity," see IGSF, p. xxiii.

233 *"If I have really succeeded"*: Taruskin, *Defining Russia Musically*, pp. 523–24.

234 *"'Heroic' Symphony"*: Maxim Shostakovich, "Six Lectures on the Shostakovich Symphonies," trans. John-Michael Albert, in Ho and Feofanov, *Shostakovich Reconsidered*, p. 408.

234 *Benditsky*: EWS, p. 153.

234 *"separation call"*: Jaak Panksepp and Günther Bernatzky, "Emotional Sounds and the Brain: The Neuroaffective Foundations of Musical Appreciation," *Behavioural Processes* 60 (2002), p. 143.

235 *"An artist-barbarian"*: Translation by Alex Abramovich. Ironically, the quotation was first pointed out by the Soviet writer David

Rabinovich, who cited the final lines as evidence that Shostakovich was depicting his own rebirth in the arms of Soviet society. See David Rabinovich, *Dmitry Shostakovich* (Lawrence and Wishart, 1959), p. 49.

236 *"remarkable," "bad," "D-major," "tedious"*: LFS, pp. 99 and 103.

236 *"expressionist etching"*: Taruskin, *Defining Russia Musically*, pp. 527–28.

236 *"determination of a strong man"*: Shostakovich, "Six Lectures on the Shostakovich Symphonies," p. 409.

236 *Lyubov Shaporina*: For Shaporina's diary, see Véronique Garros, Natalia Korenevskaya, and Thomas Lahusen, eds., *Intimacy and Terror: Soviet Diaries of the 1930s*, trans. Carol A. Flath (New Press, 1995), p. 356; for other details, see EWS, p. 126.

236 *"You know"*: Taruskin, *Defining Russia Musically*, p. 482.

237 *football guard*: Robinson, *Sergei Prokofiev*, p. 145.

237 *St. Petersburg Conservatory*: For more, see *Prokofiev by Prokofiev*, ed. David H. Appel, trans. Guy Daniels (Doubleday, 1979), pp. 99–318.

238 *"sensation you get"*: Bruno Monsaingeon, *Sviatoslav Richter: Notebooks and Conversations*, trans. Stewart Spencer (Princeton UP, 2001), p. 71.

238 *David Nice notes*: See David Nice, *Prokofiev: From Russia to the West, 1891–1935* (Yale UP, 2003), p. 135.

238 *"in Russia we also"*: Stephen Press, "Prokofiev's Vexing Entry into the USA," *Three Oranges Journal* 6 (Nov. 2003), pp. 22–26.

239 *Christian Science*: Nice, *Prokofiev*, pp. 206–207.

239 *"frightfully desires"*: Ibid., p. 200.

240 *"new simplicity"*: Interview with *Los Angeles Evening Express*, Feb. 19, 1930, quoted by Alexander Ivashkin in his notes to Valeri Polyansky's recording of *On the Dnieper* (Chandos 10044), p. 5.

240 *OGPU and Prokofiev*: Radzinsky, *Stalin*, pp. 229–30.

241 *signs of surveillance*: See Sergei Prokofiev, *Soviet Diary 1927 and Other Writings*, ed. and trans. Oleg Prokofiev (Northeastern UP, 1992), pp. 43–44.

241 *five main lines*: Ibid., pp. 248–49.

242 Songs of Our Days: Robinson, *Sergei Prokofiev*, p. 341.

242 *the opening melody*: Philip Taylor, liner notes to Valeri Polyansky's recording of *On the Dnieper* and other works (Chandos 10056).

242 *"Daddy!"*: Robinson, *Sergei Prokofiev*, p. 370.

242 *Working with Eisenstein*: See Yon Barna, *Eisenstein* (Indiana UP, 1973), p. 215; Léon Moussinac, *Sergei Eisenstein* (Crown, 1970), p. 99; Marie Seton, *Sergei M. Eisenstein* (Dennis Dobson, 1978), p. 385.

243 *346 death sentences*: Montefiore, *Stalin*, p. 287.

243 *"behind this mask"*: Nabokov, *Old Friends and New Music*, p. 180.

244 *"That's nice bait"*: Vernon Duke, *Passport to Paris* (Little, Brown, 1955), p. 367.

244 *"I ought to have gone"*: Fyodor Dostoevsky, *The Gambler*, trans. Constance Garnett, in *Great Short Works of Fyodor Dostoevsky* (HarperCollins, 2004), p. 400.

244 *"Should I forget"*: Prokofiev, *Soviet Diary*, pp. 8 and 9.

244 *"A blizzard is raging"*: IGSF, p. 23. See also *Pis'ma k drugu : Dmitrii Shostakovich—Isaaku Glikmanu* (DSCH/Kompositor, 1993), p. 62.

245 *means the opposite*: IGSF, p. 249.

245 *"Everything is so fine"*: Ibid., p. 39.

245 *"I'm feeling fine"*: Ibid., p. 293.

245 *fire brigade*: Dmitri Sollertinsky and Ludmilla Sollertinsky, *Pages from the Life of Dmitri Shostakovich*, trans. Graham Hobbs and Charles Midgley (Harcourt Brace Jovanovich, 1980), p. 98; Manashir Yakubov, preface to *Dmitri Shostakovich, Symphony No. 7, "Leningrad," Op. 60 (1941): Facsimile Edition of the Manuscript* (Zen-On Music Company, 1992), pp. 7–8; Seroff, *Dmitri Shostakovich*, p. 236.

245 *staging of the photo*: LFS, p. 123.

245 *"Our art is threatened"*: Harrison E. Salisbury, *The 900 Days: The Siege of Leningrad* (Pan, 2000), pp. 283–84; and LFS, p. 125.

246 *For several composer friends*: Salisbury, *900 Days*, p. 298.

246 *Talk of the Town*: "Symphony," *New Yorker*, July 18, 1942.

246 *"Amid bombs"*: "Fireman Shostakovich," *Time*, July 20, 1942.

246 *August 9, 1942*: Details drawn from LFS, pp. 132–33; Galina Stolyarova, "Remembering an Orchestra That Played on Through the Horrific Siege of Leningrad," *St. Petersburg Times*, Feb. 5, 2004; and Ed Vulliamy, "Orchestral Manoeuvres," *Observer*, Nov. 25, 2001.

246 *"The exposition"*: Yakubov, preface to *Dmitri Shostakovich, Symphony No. 7*, pp. 8–9, dated Oct. 9, 1941. See also "Leningrad Calling," *New Masses*, Oct. 28, 1941.

247 *"all forms of terror"*: EWS, p. 185.

247 *"invasion episode"*: Yakubov, preface to *Dmitri Shostakovich, Symphony No. 7*, p. 81.

247 *"One had the feeling"*: Fyodor Dostoevsky, *The Devils*, trans. David Magarshack (Penguin, 1971), pp. 326–27.

247 *"Surely it is"*: *Beyond the Stars: The Memoirs of Sergei Eisenstein*, ed. Richard Taylor, trans. William Powell (Seagull, 1995), pp. 345–46. Some time later the literary critic Abram Gozenpud asked Shostakovich whether he had the Dostoevsky episode in mind in writing the *Leningrad*, and the composer answered that he was not thinking of it consciously but did not reject the possibility. See EWS, p. 520.

248 *"And over forests"*: *Complete Poems of Anna Akhmatova*, pp. 575–76. See also explanatory notes on pp. 580 and 847. Although Akhmatova's notes can be taken as saying that the poet herself carried out a manuscript of the symphony—"the first part [movement] of the symphony was taken by the author in a plane from the besieged city (1.X.1941)"—Laurel Fay doubts that such a thing happened (communication to author). It seems more likely that the "author" is Shostakovich.

249 *"Ivan . . . was very cruel"*: Montefiore, *Stalin*, p. 483.

250 *"When Prokofiev stood up"*: Monsaingeon, *Sviatoslav Richter*, p. 89. See also "Composer, Soviet-Style," *Time*, Nov. 19, 1945.

250 *"A very pleasant place"*: Harrison E. Salisbury, "Visit with Dmitri Shostakovich," *New York Times*, Aug. 8, 1954.

251 *"All of this made me"*: Maximenkov, "Stalin and Shostakovich," p. 43.

251 *anthem:* Ibid., p. 51.

251 *Order of Lenin*: See LFS, p. 153, for some of these other posts and prizes. For the conservatory, see David Fanning, "Shostakovich and His Pupils," in Fay, *Shostakovich and His World*, p. 278.

251 *plush lifestyle*: For more on the economic roots of the 1948 campaign, see Maximenkov, "Stalin and Shostakovich," pp. 51–52; and Kiril Tomoff, *Creative Union: The Professional Organization of Soviet Composers, 1939–1953* (Cornell UP, 2006), pp. 97–151.

252 *gone on vacation*: LFS, p. 152; and IGSF, pp. 241–42.

252 *"The Pianist"*: Montefiore, *Stalin*, pp. 122 and 482. But Shostakovich denied the story that Zhdanov played the piano for the composers.

253 *Quotations from Zakharov, Khrennikov, and others*: Alexander Werth, *Musical Uproar in Moscow* (Turnstile, 1949), pp. 54, 57, 55, 73, 69.

253 *Prokofiev is said*: For some of these accounts, see Robinson, *Sergei Prokofiev*, p. xvi; Meyer, *Dimitri Chostakovitch*, pp. 306–307; Alfred Schnittke, "On Prokofiev," in *A Schnittke Reader*, ed. Alexander Ivashkin, trans. John Goodliffe (Indiana UP, 2002), p. 63.

253 *"Comrade Zakharov"*: Werth, *Musical Uproar in Moscow*, p. 62.

253 *"I envy him"*: EWS, p. 260.

254 *forty-two works*: Order No. 17 of the Chief Directorate for Inspection of Programs and Repertory of the Committee for Artistic Affairs of the U.S.S.R. Soviet of Ministers Moscow, Feb. 14, 1948. Translation courtesy of Laurel Fay.

254 *insincerity was obvious*: EWS, p. 235; and Werth, *Musical Uproar in Moscow*, pp. 95–96.

254 *"unwittingly"*: NMS, p. 1065.

254 *"I am prepared"*: Robinson, *Sergei Prokofiev*, p. 458.

254 *chilling coincidence*: Simon Morrison's communication to author. Morrison has assembled evidence showing that Prokofiev was in reasonably good health in February 1948, contrary to the claim in his letter.

254 *"All the resolutions"*: NMS, p. 1063.

255 *"conspiracy of silence"*: LFS, p. 161.

255 *thrust into his hands*: EWS, p. 335; and LFS, pp. 320–21 n. 70.

255 *"I read like the most"*: EWS, p. 335.

256 *"O Lord, if only"*: Christopher Barnes, *Boris Pasternak: A Literary Biography, Volume 2: 1928–1960* (Cambridge UP, 1998), p. 252.

256 *"The violin played semiquavers"*: EWS, p. 245.

256 *"Thank you"*: See EWS, pp. 212–14; Ardov, *Memories of Shostakovich*, pp. 69–73; and LFS, p. 172.

256 *"You supported me"*: Maximenkov, "Stalin and Shostakovich," p. 55.

256 *breathe again*: Nelly Kravetz, "A New Insight into the Tenth Symphony of Dmitri Shostakovich," in Bartlett, *Shostakovich in Context*, p. 170.

257 *"most successful"*: NSM, p. 545.

257 *"ultimate Stalinist film"*: Peter Kenez, *Cinema and Soviet Society from the Revolution to the Death of Stalin* (Tauris, 2001), p. 232.

257 *burst into tears*: LFS, p. 175.

258 *"an extraordinarily good opera"*: See Lion Feuchtwanger, *Moskau 1937: Ein Reisebericht für meine Freunde* (Aufbau, 1993), p. 48.

258 Pathétique: Compare bars 221ff. of Tchaikovsky's third movement with Shostakovich's finale after bar 204.

258 *Sabinina*: EWS, p. 336.

259 *Prokofiev's body*: Monsaingeon, *Sviatoslav Richter*, p. 4; Rostislav Dubinsky, *Stormy Applause: Making Music in a Worker's State* (Hill and Wang, 1989), pp. 34–44; Ardov, *Memories of Shostakovich*, p. 92; Michel Dorigné, *Serge Prokofiev* (Fayard, 1994), pp. 712–13; Georges Bartoli, *The Death of Stalin* (Praeger, 1975), p. 162; and Schnittke, "On Prokofiev," pp. 65–66.

259 *"I wish you"*: "Prokofiev's Correspondence with Stravinsky and Shostakovich," trans. Natalia Rodriguez and Malcolm Hamrick Brown, in *Slavonic and Western Music: Essays for Gerald Abraham*, ed. Malcolm Hamrick Brown and Roland J. Wiley (UMI Research Press), p. 285. See also Rostropovich's interview with Manashir Yakubov, in Brown, *Shostakovich Casebook*, p. 147, for Shostakovich's admiration for the Sinfonia Concertante.

8: Music for All

260 *"I was driven"*: ASSI, p. 502. For the Ford car, see Schoenberg to W. D. Dunham, Nov. 2, 1934, ASC.

260 *"IF HITLER"*: Meyer Weisgal, . . . *So Far: An Autobiography* (Random House, 1971), p. 116.

261 *"highbrow" and "lowbrow"*: James Hoopes, *Van Wyck Brooks: In Search of American Culture* (University of Massachusetts Press, 1977), pp. 99–100.

261 *ninety-five million people*: Report of Mr. Hopkins, April 4, 1938, Correspondence of Harry L. Hewes, 1936–40, FMP.

261 *"The great mass of people"*: Marc Blitzstein, "Coming—the Mass Audience!," *Modern Music* 13:4 (May–June 1936), pp. 23 and 25.

262 *ten million*: Donald C. Meyer, "The NBC Symphony Orchestra" (Ph.D. diss., University of California at Davis, 1994), p. 157.

263 *twenty million records*: Joseph Horowitz, *Understanding Toscanini: A Social History of American Concert Life* (University of California Press, 1994), p. 277.

263 *film of* Don Juan: Donald Crafton, *The Talkies: American Cinema's Transition to Sound, 1926–1931* (University of California Press, 1999), pp. 72–82.

263 *government takeover*: See Hugh Richard Slotten, *Radio and Television Regulation: Broadcast Technology in the United States, 1920–1960* (Johns Hopkins UP, 2000), pp. 1–67.

263 "radio music box": *Looking Ahead: The Papers of David Sarnoff* (McGraw-Hill, 1968), pp. 31–33. For more on Sarnoff, see Carl Dreher, *Sarnoff: An American Success* (Quadrangle, 1977); and Evan I. Schwartz, *The Last Lone Inventor: A Tale of Genius, Deceit, and the Birth of Television* (HarperCollins, 2002).

263 *"I regard radio"*: Schwartz, *Last Lone Inventor*, p. 66.

264 *Ohio State . . . Lotte Lehmann*: See broadcasts of Oct. 1 and 2, as reported in *Time*, Oct. 3, 1938.

264 *"Toscanini's Hep Cats"*: Donald C. Meyer, "Toscanini and the NBC Symphony Orchestra: High, Middle, and Low Culture, 1937–1954," in *Perspectives on American Music, 1900–1950*, ed. Michael Saffle (Garland, 2000), p. 306.

264 *"Wagner, Beethoven, Bach"*: "The Messenger Boy," *New York Times*, March 7, 1938.

264 *six native works*: Horowitz, *Understanding Toscanini*, p. 133.

264 *"Dee next Beethoven"*: HPAC, p. 122.

264 *85 premieres*: H. Earle Johnson, *Symphony Hall, Boston* (Little, Brown, 1950), p. 163.

265 *would not be renewed*: Horowitz, *Understanding Toscanini*, p. 176; Virgil Thomson, *Music Reviewed, 1940–1954* (Vintage, 1967), p. 111; and Meyer, "The NBC Symphony Orchestra," pp. 242–44.

265 *"It is highly doubtful"*: Theodor W. Adorno, in *Essays on Music*, ed. Richard Leppert, trans. Susan H. Gillespie (University of California Press, 2002), p. 268.

266 *Ott & Pfaffle's*: "Early Dallas Hotels," free pages.history.rootsweb.com/~jwheat/adairtoc.html (accessed Dec. 1, 2003).

266 *Jesse James*: ACVP, p. 3. A possible problem with this tale is that Frank James worked in Dallas only from about 1885 on, after his criminal career had ended.

266 *"simply drab"*: ACR, p. xix.

266 *"When we were finally"*: ACVP, p. 130. For more on the relationship between Gershwin and Copland, see Carol J. Oja, "Gershwin and American Modernists of the 1920s," *Musical Quarterly* 78:4 (Winter 1994), pp. 656–58.

266 *Swedish Ballet*: Copland, in ACVP, p. 44. For other events attended, see ACVP, p. 91; "My First Trip Abroad," ACLC; and Gail Levin and Judith Tick, *Copland's America: A*

Cultural Perspective (Watson-Guptill, 2000), pp. 136–77. For Joyce and Le Boeuf, see ACVP, p. 75.

267 *hearing Copland bang out*: Aaron Copland, *Copland on Music* (Doubleday, 1960), p. 74; Léonie Rosenstiel, *Nadia Boulanger: A Life in Music* (Norton, 1982), p. 162.

267 *"The day of the neglected"*: "America's Young Men of Promise," in Copland, *Copland on Music*, p. 151.

268 *"filthy bunch of Juilliard Jews"*: Olivia Mattis, "Edgard Varèse's 'Progressive' Nationalism: *Amériques* Meets *Américanisme*," in *Edgard Varèse: Die Befreiung des Klangs*, ed. Helge de la Motte-Haber (Wolke, 1992), p. 169.

268 *"commando unit"*: Virgil Thomson, *Virgil Thomson* (Dutton, 1985), p. 254.

268 *"It began, I suppose"*: Aaron Copland, "Jazz Structure and Influence," in ACR, p. 84.

268 *Pollack observes*: HPAC, pp. 129–30.

268 *"harsh and solemn"*: Paul Rosenfeld, *Discoveries of a Music Critic* (Vienna House, 1972), p. 334.

268 *$6.93*: HPAC, p. 90.

268 *"I might force myself"*: Diary of 1927, ACLC.

269 *"How does one deepen"*: Diary, Christmas Day 1930, ACLC.

269 *without indoor plumbing*: David M. Kennedy, *Freedom from Fear: The American People in Depression and War, 1929–1945* (Oxford UP, 1999), p. 16. On populism, see Michael Kazin, *The Populist Persuasion: An American History* (Cornell UP, 1998).

269 *"open mind"*: Michael Denning, *The Cultural Front: The Laboring of American Culture in the Twentieth Century* (Verso, 1997), p. 4.

270 *"Communism is"*: Ibid., p. 129.

270 *Denning argues*: Ibid., p. 10.

270 *"Don't worry"*: Joshua Kunitz, "Stairway That Leads Nowhere," *New Masses*, May 5, 1936, p. 21.

270 *"Based not on my words"*: Andrew Hemingway, *Artists on the Left: American Artists and the Communist Movement, 1926–1956* (Yale UP, 2002), p. 105.

271 *"foremost revolutionary"*: Hanns Eisler, *A Rebel in Music: Selected Writings*, ed. Manfred Grabs (International Publishers, 1978), p. 15.

271 *"dealers in narcotics"*: Ibid., p. 115.

271 *"the modern composer"*: Ibid., p. 112.

271 *"dissonant counterpoint"*: Charles Seeger, "Manual of Dissonant Counterpoint," in *Studies in Musicology II, 1929–1979*, ed. Ann M. Pescatello (University of California Press, 1994), pp. 163–228. On Crawford, see Joseph N. Straus, *The Music of Ruth Crawford Seeger* (Cambridge UP, 1995); David Nicholls, *American Experimental Music, 1890–1940* (Cambridge UP, 1990); and Judith Tick, *Ruth Crawford Seeger: A Composer's Search for American Music* (Oxford UP, 1997).

272 *"combination of simplicity"*: Tick, *Ruth Crawford Seeger*, p. 254.

272 *"can't compose symphonies"*: Ibid., p. 200.

272 *"first great individualist"*: Margaret Brenman-Gibson, *Clifford Odets, American Playwright: The Years from 1906 to 1940* (Atheneum, 1981), p. 171.

273 *"the corruption of legal systems"*: ACVP, p. 234.

273 *Clurman plausibly heard*: Harold Clurman to Copland, Oct. 25, 1947, ACLC.

273 *"from ivory tower"*: Ibid., p. 223.

273 *"We learned to know"*: Sept. 1934 letter to Israel Citkowitz, ACLC.

274 *"At last I have found"*: Sept. 5, 1932, letter to the Koussevitzkys, ACLC.

274 *José Vasconcelos*: David Craven, *Art and Revolution in Latin America, 1910–1990* (Yale UP, 2002), pp. 25–32.

274 El Salón *and* Variations: Michael Tilson Thomas, lecture/recital at Zankel Hall, Nov. 19, 2003. Compare the music at 6 in *Piano Variations*, and also bar 10 of the Coda.

274 *"rural peasants"*: Elizabeth Crist, *Music for the Common Man: Aaron Copland During the Depression and War* (Oxford UP, 2005), p. 59.

275 *"workers' music"*: ACVP, p. 224.

275 *"Shake the midtown towers"*: "Into the Streets May First," *New Masses*, May 1, 1934, pp. 16–17.

275 *balalaikas and mandolins*: Ashley Pettis, "Second Workers' Music Olympiad," *New Masses*, May 22, 1934, pp. 28–29. ACVP, p. 226, implies that the entire eight-hundred-strong complement of choruses performed the piece, but according to Pettis they were not able to come together to rehearse.

275 *advised David Diamond*: HPAC, p. 190.

275 *"plain unpretentious person"*: Charles Seeger, "Grass Roots for American Composers," *Modern Music* 16:3 (March–April 1939), p. 148.

275 *"Those young people"*: Aaron Copland, "A Note on Young Composers," in ACR, p. 216.

276 *Walter Noble Burns*: HPAC, pp. 316–17; Walter Noble Burns, *The Saga of Billy the Kid* (University of New Mexico Press, 1999).
276 *Scottsboro Boys*: See Beth E. Levy, "From Orient to Occident: Aaron Copland and the Sagas of the Prairie," in *Aaron Copland and His World*, ed. Carol J. Oja and Judith Tick (Princeton UP, 2005), pp. 307–49. In 1967 Copland renamed the piece *Prairie Journal*.
277 "Roosevelt was willing": Richard D. McKinzie, *The New Deal for Artists* (Princeton UP, 1973), p. x. See also Joseph P. Lash, *Eleanor and Franklin* (Norton, 1971), p. 407.
277 *"responsibility toward art"*: Allida M. Black, ed., *Courage in a Dangerous World: The Political Writings of Eleanor Roosevelt* (Columbia UP, 1999), p. 26.
277 *"Gospel Train"*: Allan Keiler, *Marian Anderson: A Singer's Journey* (University of Illinois Press, 2002), p. 165.
278 *funding for WPA, FMP*: George Foster, Record of the Operation and Accomplishments of the Federal Music Project, June 1943, FMP.
278 *quantities for FMP*: Report on FMP, March 17, 1939, Hearings on H.J. Res. 83, Subcommittee of the Committee on Appropriations, House of Representatives, 76th Cong., 1st sess., *Congressional Record*, pp. 113–14. For more on the FMP, see Kenneth J. Bindas, *All of This Music Belongs to the Nation: The WPA's Federal Music Project and American Society* (University of Tennessee Press, 1995).
278 *"When the arts flourished"*: Eleanor Roosevelt, My Day, Nov. 1, 1939.
278 *"social revolution"*: George Biddle, *An American Artist's Story* (Little, Brown, 1939), p. 268. For Biddle's background, see Hemingway, *Artists on the Left*, p. 60.
278 *"despondent theme"*: "Public Buildings May Get New Deal Art; Roosevelt Favors Murals Instead of Scrolls," *New York Times*, April 26, 1934.
278 *"both slavery"*: McKinzie, *New Deal for Artists*, p. 31.
278 *"Through the program"*: Feb. 1, 1937, release, Correspondence of Harry L. Hewes, project supervisor, with the division liaison officer of the Division of Professional and Service Projects, July 1936–Dec. 1939, box 29: 1936–1937, entry 815, FMP.
278 *"This was opera"*: Quoted in Hewes's memo of Aug. 20, 1936, box 29, as above.
279 *"sissy stuff"*: *New York Evening Journal*, Nov. 30, 1936, box 29, as above.
279 *"For the first time"*: Dean Richardson to Nikolai Sokoloff, April 8, 1938, Monthly Narrative Reports, box 5: MI–RI 1938, entry 805, FMP.
279 *"The highlight"*: Report of the Federal Music Teaching Project of Oklahoma, May 1 to 31, 1938, Monthly Narrative Reports, box 5: MI–RI 1938, entry 805, FMP.
279 *"A technic has been perfected"*: Oct. 6, 1936, press release on Composers' Forum-Laboratories, Correspondence of Harry L. Hewes with the division liaison officer of the Division of Professional and Service Projects, July 1936–Dec. 1939, box 29: 1936–1937, entry 815, FMP.
280 *"a very great virile music"*: Transcript dated Oct. 30, 1935, NYC Composers' Forum, box 1 General, F1-Y, Composers' Forum Records, FMP.
280 *"hewed by hand"*: "Log Cabin Composer," *Time*, Nov. 11, 1935.
280 *"If I had pitchers"*: Nicolas Slonimsky, "Roy Harris: The Story of an Oklahoma Composer Who Was Born in a Log Cabin on Lincoln's Birthday," in *A Celebration of American Music: Words and Music in Honor of H. Wiley Hitchcock*, ed. Richard Crawford, R. Allen Lott, and Carol J. Oja (University of Michigan Press, 1990), p. 314.
280 *"the conception of art"*: "Is This the Time and Place?," speech delivered Oct. 8, 1935, Records of the Federal Theatre Project, Library of Congress. For more on Flanagan, see her memoir *Arena* (Duell, Sloan and Pearce, 1940).
281 *"Franco-Russian pretty music"*: Eric A. Gordon, *Mark the Music: The Life and Work of Marc Blitzstein* (St. Martin's, 1989), p. 28.
282 *"little more than drivel"*: Ibid., p. 41.
282 *"write a piece"*: Ibid., p. 113. For good readings of *The Cradle Will Rock*, see Geoffrey Block, *Enchanted Evenings: The Broadway Musical from "Show Boat" to Sondheim* (Oxford UP, 1997); and Raymond Knapp, *The American Musical and the Formation of National Identity* (Princeton UP, 2005).
282 *feared outbreaks of violence*: Frank Brady, *Citizen Welles: A Biography of Orson Welles* (Scribner, 1989), p. 114; Gordon, *Mark the Music*, pp. 140–41.
283 *"You can't imagine"*: Barbara Leaming, *Orson Welles: A Biography* (Limelight, 1995), p. 130.
283 *"It don't sound wicked"*: Anthony Tom-

masini, *Virgil Thomson: Composer on the Aisle* (Norton, 1997), pp. 276–77.

283 *violently percussive*: Thomson, *Virgil Thomson*, p. 264. For "hysterical," see Denning, *Cultural Front*, p. 369. See also Brooks Atkinson, "WPA Journalism," *New York Times*, July 25, 1936.

284 *hostile judicial rulings*: In May 1936, the Court of Appeals for the District of Columbia ruled the Resettlement Administration unconstitutional. See "Jersey Housing Halted," *New York Times*, May 19, 1936.

284 *"The water comes"*: Pare Lorentz, "The River," in *The New Deal: A Documentary History*, ed. William E. Leuchtenburg (University of South Carolina Press, 1968), pp. 131 and 135.

284 *"The German Führer"*: Tommasini, *Virgil Thomson*, p. 288.

284 *five men*: Thomson, *Virgil Thomson*, p. 254.

284 *"The luxury-trade"*: "In the Theatre," *Modern Music* 15:2 (Jan.–Feb. 1938), p. 114.

285 *Toscanini was listening*: Barbara B. Heyman, *Samuel Barber: The Composer and His Music* (Oxford UP, 1992), p. 122. See also p. 539 n. 4.

285 *"grotesque harlequinade"*: R. D. Darrell, "Sights and Sounds," *New Masses*, April 27, 1937.

285 *" 'authentic,' dull"*: "From the Mail Pouch," *New York Times*, Nov. 13, 1938.

285 *absolute sincerity*: Heyman, *Samuel Barber*, p. 174.

285 "essential innerlich notwendig": Nov. 1932 letter, in *The Correspondence of Roger Sessions*, ed. Andrea Olmstead (Northeastern UP, 1992), p. 191.

286 *"the socialist idea"*: David Drew, *Kurt Weill: A Handbook* (University of California Press, 1987), p. 295.

287 *"I don't give a damn"*: David Farneth, Elmar Juchem, and Dave Stein, eds., *Kurt Weill: A Life in Pictures and Documents* (Overlook, 2000), p. 196.

287 *"open-air spirit"*: Richard Crawford, *America's Musical Life: A History* (Norton, 2001), p. 680. The resemblance to *Rodeo* was noted by Harold Clurman in a June 24, 1943, letter in ACLC, box 251: "dance by Agnes de Mille à la Rodeo."

287 *"one more link"*: "Theatre Project Faces an Inquiry," *New York Times*, July 27, 1938.

287 *American Federation of Musicians*: See "Teachers Fear Socialization of Music by WPA," *New York Herald Tribune*, April 17, 1936.

288 *"encouraging art"*: McKinzie, *New Deal for Artists*, p. 186.

288 *"a new art"*: David Gelernter, *1939: The Lost World of the Fair* (Free Press, 1995), p. 167.

289 *"Mr. Copland Here"*: Robert A. Simon, "Mr. Copland Here, There, and at the Fair," *New Yorker*, June 3, 1939, pp. 69–71.

289 *"Hollywood is an extraordinary"*: ACVP, p. 298.

289 *"Paradise and hell"*: *Fünf Elegien*, No. 4.

289 *"The man who insists"*: Aaron Copland, "Second Thoughts on Hollywood," in ACR, p. 111.

290 *mad for music*: For a good commentary on Hollywood's movies about classical composers and musicians, see John C. Tibbetts, *Composers in the Movies: Studies in Musical Biography* (Yale UP, 2005).

290 *Boris Morros*: See Allen Weinstein and Alexander Vassiliev, *The Haunted Wood: Soviet Espionage in America—the Stalin Era* (Random House, 1999), pp. 118–25; and Boris Morros, *My Ten Years as a Counterspy* (Viking, 1959).

290 *"What that awful music"*: Gore Vidal, *Point to Point Navigation* (Doubleday, 2006), p. 107.

291 *"loathing of the present"*: Royal S. Brown, *Overtones and Undertones: Reading Film Music* (University of California Press, 1994), p. 71.

291 *squealing rat*: Theodor W. Adorno and Hanns Eisler, *Composing for the Films* (Athlone, 1994), pp. 27–28.

291 *noted in wonder*: "Copland Given Free Hand in Scoring Picture," *Los Angeles Times*, Nov. 19, 1939. Milestone was a cousin of the violinist Nathan Milstein (HPAC, p. 340).

291 *"absolutely clear"*: HPAC, p. 347.

292 *how many feet of film*: Brendan Carroll, *The Last Prodigy: A Biography of Erich Wolfgang Korngold* (Amadeus, 1997), p. 240.

292 *tried to have the film suppressed*: Simon Callow, *Orson Welles: The Road to Xanadu* (Viking, 1996), pp. 530–59.

293 *"50 percent responsible"*: Steven C. Smith, *A Heart at Fire's Center: The Life and Music of Bernard Herrmann* (University of California Press, 1991), p. 84.

293 *"I am the forgotten composer"*: Diane Peacock Jezic, *The Musical Migration and Ernst Toch* (Iowa State UP, 1989), p. 17.

294 *"C'mon, Professor"*: Oscar Levant, *A Smattering of Ignorance* (Doubleday, 1940), p. 65.

294 *On four occasions*: See Dorothy Lamb Crawford, *Evenings On and Off the Roof: Pioneer-*

ing Concerts in Los Angeles, 1939–1971* (University of California Press, 1995), p. 127; and SWS2, pp. 183 and 251.

294 *Gershwins*: Levant, *Smattering of Ignorance*, p. 187.

294 *"frank and abrupt"*: Sabine M. Feisst, "Arnold Schoenberg and the Cinematic Art," *Musical Quarterly* 83:1 (Spring 1999), p. 110.

295 *"Hi-yo, Silver!"*: Dika Newlin, *Schoenberg Remembered: Diaries and Recollections* (Pendragon, 1980), p. 146.

295 *"a peach-colored shirt"*: Ibid., p. 58.

295 *"upsurge of desire"*: ASL, p. 255.

295 *Sibelius and Shostakovich*: ASSI, p. 136.

295 *"That man is a composer"*: Author's interview with David Raksin, Feb. 23, 2001.

295 *"there is still plenty"*: Dika Newlin, "Secret Tonality in Schoenberg's Piano Concerto," *Perspectives of New Music* 13:1 (Fall–Winter 1974), p. 137; Roger Sessions, "Schoenberg in the United States" (1944), in *Schoenberg and His World*, ed. Walter Frisch (Princeton UP, 1999), p. 335.

295 *"I still see"*: Salka Viertel, *The Kindness of Strangers* (Holt, Rinehart, and Winston, 1969), pp. 207–208. For more, see www.therestisnoise.com/2007/07/schoenberg-thal.html

296 *"I can not believe"*: Schoenberg to Thalberg, Dec. 6, 1935, ASC.

296 Souls at Sea: Dorothy Lamb Crawford, "Arnold Schoenberg in Los Angeles," *Musical Quarterly* 86:1 (Spring 2002), pp. 17 and 41.

296 *Tom and Jerry cartoons*: Daniel Goldmark, *Tunes for 'Toons: Music and the Hollywood Cartoon* (University of California Press, 2005), pp. 70–73; and Roy M. Prendergast, *Film Music: A Neglected Art* (Norton, 1992), p. 194.

297 *male nurse*: See JASR, pp. 313–14; and HHS, p. 479.

297 *"as if in his delirium"*: Allen Shawn, *Arnold Schoenberg's Journey* (Farrar, Straus and Giroux, 2001), p. 265.

297 *"My father was always"*: Author's interview with Ronald Schoenberg, Feb. 22, 2001.

297 *Stravinsky and Disney*: Charles M. Joseph, *Stravinsky Inside Out* (Yale UP, 2001), pp. 108–11. For more on Stravinsky's attempts at film scoring, see ibid., pp. 100–31; and SWS2, pp. 143–44. For Stravinsky's admiration for *Kane*, see Orson Welles and Peter Bogdanovich, *This Is Orson Welles* (HarperCollins, 1992), p. 175.

298 *no record of his saying anything negative*: Joseph, *Stravinsky Inside Out*, p. 111. Compare Igor Stravinsky and Robert Craft, *Expositions and Developments* (Doubleday, 1962), pp. 166–67.

298 *"Igor appears"*: *Selected Letters of Paul Hindemith*, ed. and trans. Geoffrey Skelton (Yale UP, 1995), p. 177.

298 *$100,000*: Joseph, *Stravinsky Inside Out*, p. 117.

299 *goose-stepping soldiers*: Igor Stravinsky and Robert Craft, *Dialogues and a Diary* (Doubleday, 1963), pp. 83–84.

299 *added an extra pulse*: SWS2, p. 180.

299 *"With composing like this"*: Soma Morgenstern, *Alban Berg und seine Idole: Erinnerungen und Briefe* (Aufbau, 1999), p. 297.

299 *"remind those who have not"*: Giselher Schubert, preface to Paul Hindemith, *Ludus tonalis* (Schott, 1989), p. iii. On Bartók's Shostakovich quotation, see Peter Bartók, *My Father* (Bartók Records), pp. 174–77.

301 *"economic democracy"*: John C. Culver and John Hyde, *American Dreamer: A Life of Henry A. Wallace* (Norton, 2000), pp. 291–92. For "century of the common man," see ibid., pp. 275–78.

301 *"The title was not meant"*: Copland to Goossens, April 12, 1943.

302 *"could have the feeling"*: HPAC, p. 396. For Crane and Graham, see HPAC, p. 402. For Crane and Copland, see *The Letters of Hart Crane, 1916–1932*, ed. Brom Weber (Hermitage House, 1952), p. 195.

303 *"Softer, very* sul tasto": Recording session of May 9–11, 1973, released on *A Copland Celebration Vol. 1* (Sony Classical SM2K 89323).

9. Death Fugue

305 *"tears in his voice"*: AHRP I:1, p. 369.

305 "Wach' auf!": JGT I:2, p. 462. For more on Hitler's citations of *Meistersinger*, see Hans Rudolf Vaget, "Hitler's Wagner: Musical Discourse as Cultural Space," in *Music and Nazism: Art Under Tyranny, 1933–1945*, ed. Michael H. Kater and Albrecht Riethmüller (Laaber, 2003), p. 27. For Hans Frank, see Leon Goldensohn, *The Nuremberg Interviews*, ed. Richard Gellately (Knopf, 2004), p. 19. For Heydrich, see Günther Deschner, *Reinhard Heydrich: Statthalter der totalen Macht* (Bechtle, 1977), p. 300; Lina Heydrich, *Leben mit einem Kriegsverbrecher* (Ludwig, 1976), p. 16; and Edouard Calic, *Reinhard Heydrich: The Chilling Story of the Man Who Masterminded the Nazi Death Camps*, trans. Lowell Bair

(William Morrow, 1982), p. 16. For Mengele, see Robert Jay Lifton, *The Nazi Doctors* (Basic Books, 2000), p. 344.

305 *"Thank God"*: Paul Ehlers, "Die Musik und Adolf Hitler," *Zeitschrift für Musik*, April 1939, p. 361.

306 *"Beside the history"*: From the title page of *Palestrina* (Schott score). For the Mussolini dedication, see Sabine Busch, *Hans Pfitzner und der Nationalsozialismus* (J. B. Metzler, 2001), p. 422.

307 "There is too much music": RSRR, p. 215. For "hypnotism," see p. 209.

307 *"has a basically"*: Thomas Mann, *Reflections of a Nonpolitical Man*, trans. Walter D. Morris (Ungar, 1983), p. 289.

307 Untergang: Jens Malte Fischer, *Richard Wagners "Das Judentum in der Musik"* (Insel, 2000), p. 173. For varying interpretations of "annihilation," see Joachim Köhler, *Wagner's Hitler: The Prophet and His Disciple*, trans. Ronald Taylor (Polity, 2000), p. 86–88; Paul Lawrence Rose, *Wagner: Race and Revolution* (Yale UP, 1992), pp. 78–88; and Fischer, *Richard Wagners "Das Judentum in der Musik,"* pp. 85–87.

307 *"the born enemy"*: *Selected Letters of Richard Wagner*, ed. and trans. Stewart Spencer and Barry Millington (Norton, 1988), p. 918.

307 *"plastic demon"*: Richard Wagner, "Erkenne dich selbst," in *Gesammelte Schriften und Dichtungen* (Siegel's Musikalienhandlung, 1907), vol. 10, p. 272. For Goebbels, see "Why Are We Enemies of the Jews?" (1930), in *The Weimar Republic Sourcebook*, ed. Anton Kaes, Martin Jay, and Edward Dimendberg (University of California Press, 1994), p. 138; and John Hallowell, *Main Currents in Political Thought* (Holt, 1950), p. 740 (quoting Nuremberg speech of 1937).

308 *singled out for praise*: See Annette Hein, *"Es ist viel 'Hitler' in Wagner": Rassismus und antisemitische Deutschtumsideologie in den "Bayreuther Blättern" (1878–1938)* (Niemeyer, 1996), p. 120.

308 *"characteristic traits"*: LGM1, p. 482.

308 *"Alberichs"*: *Richard Strauss, Max von Schillings: Ein Briefwechsel*, ed. Roswitha Schlötterer (W. Ludwig, 1987), pp. 203–204.

308 *Gobineau and* Parsifal: *Cosima Wagner's Diaries, Volume II: 1878–1883*, ed. Martin Gregor-Dellin and Dietrich Mack, trans. Geoffrey Skelton (Harcourt Brace Jovanovich, 1980), p. 666.

309 *"4 Juden"*: Hans Hinkel to Karl-Theodor Zeitschel, Sept. 24, 1935, memo, Richard Strauss file, BDC. On the friendship of Strauss and Wolfes, see Günther Weiß, "Richard Strauss und Felix Wolfes," *Jahrbuch der Bayerischen Staatsoper 1988/89* (Bruckmann, 1988), pp. 77–92.

309 *"contaminated by"*: Brigitte Hamann, *Winifred Wagner; oder, Hitlers Bayreuth* (Piper, 2002), p. 18.

309 *"political operetta"*: "Der Briefwechsel zwischen Alfred Kerr und Richard Strauss," ed. Marc Konhäuser, *Richard Strauss–Blätter* 39 (June 1998), p. 38.

310 *Billy Wilder*: Kevin Lally, *Wilder Times: The Life of Billy Wilder* (Holt, 1996), p. 11. For Strauss's admiration of Mussolini, see Robert Scherwatzky, *Die grossen Meister deutscher Musik in ihren Briefen und Schriften* (Deuerlichsche Verlagsbuchhandlung, 1939), p. 358. For his advocacy of dictatorship, see Harry Kessler, *In the Twenties: The Diaries of Harry Kessler*, trans. Charles Kessler (Holt, Rinehart, and Winston, 1971), p. 346.

310 *"Hitler is apparently finished"*: RSC, p. 531.

311 *"I thank you"*: Ibid., pp. 539–40.

311 *postcards*: Adolf Hitler, *Sämtliche Aufzeichnungen, 1905–1924*, ed. Eberhard Jäckel with Axel Kühn (Deutsche Verlags-Anstalt, 1980), pp. 44–45.

311 *Hitler in Graz*: See Manfred Blumauer, *Festa teatrale: Musiktheater in Graz* (Edition Strahalm, 1998), pp. 68–82, for a thorough discussion of the issue. Two other scholars conclude that Hitler did not go to Graz: see Brigitte Hamann, *Hitler's Vienna: A Dictator's Apprenticeship* (Oxford UP, 1999), p. 411; and Frederic Spotts, *Hitler and the Power of Aesthetics* (Overlook, 2003), p. 230. For Alice's testimony, see Blumauer, *Festa teatrale*, p. 76. For the kissing of the hand, see Kurt Wilhelm, *Richard Strauss persönlich: Eine Bildbiographie* (Kindler, 1984), p. 311—although Hamann, *Winifred Wagner*, p. 285, says it was a "handshake."

311 *up to Roller's door*: Hamann, *Hitler's Vienna*, pp. 38–40 and 61; John Toland, *Adolf Hitler* (Anchor Books, 1976), p. 31; and Adolf Hitler, *Monologe im Führer-Hauptquartier, 1941–1944*, ed. Werner Jochmann (Knaus, 1980), p. 200.

311 *"the tower to the left"*: Hamann, *Hitler's Vienna*, p. 61.

312 *Mahler conducting* Tristan: Wiener Staatsoper to author, June 5, 1998.

312 *"because [he] concerned himself"*: Hamann, *Hitler's Vienna*, p. 66. This is from the unpublished first draft of Kubizek's memoir,

which Hamann uses as a source in *Hitler's Vienna*. That draft seems more reliable than the published version, which was concocted after the war, probably with the help of a ghostwriter, as Frederic Spotts points out in *Hitler and the Power of Aesthetics*, pp. xv–xviii. In the book, Hitler is said to have had "greatest admiration" for Mahler (August Kubizek, *Adolf Hitler, mein Jugendfreund* [Leopold Stocker, 1953], p. 229). The practically useless English translation, *The Young Hitler I Knew*, trans. E. V. Anderson (Tower, 1954), uses the first-person plural (p. 173), implying that Kubizek, too, heard Mahler, which was impossible.

312 *"did not contest"*: JGT I:9, p. 62.

312 *Hitler and* Rienzi: Henry Picker, *Hitlers Tischgespräche im Führerhauptquartier, 1941–1942*, ed. Percy Ernst Schramm (Seewald, 1963), p. 95.

312 *"a couple of yammering Jews"*: Hans Frank, *Im Angesicht des Galgens* (Friedrich Alfred Beck, 1953), p. 213. This is in 1935.

312 *"Is this a Jew?"*: Adolf Hitler, *Mein Kampf* (NSDAP, 1943), p. 59.

312 *Bechstein and Bruckmann*: David Clay Large, *Where Ghosts Walked: Munich's Road to the Third Reich* (Norton, 1997), p. 152.

312 *Schirach*: Baldur von Schirach, *Ich glaubte an Hitler* (Mosaik, 1967), p. 27.

312 *Germany's savior*: Friedelind Wagner, *The Royal Family of Bayreuth* (Eyre and Spottiswoode, 1948), p. 9.

312 *"hour of highest need"*: Hartmut Zelinsky, *Richard Wagner—ein deutsches Thema* (Zweitausendeins, 1976), p. 169.

312 *"ruinous, indeed poisonous"*: Ibid., p. 170.

312 *"Parsifal nature"*: Hamann, *Winifred Wagner*, p. 119.

312 *"He obviously felt"*: Albert Speer, *Inside the Third Reich*, trans. Richard Winston and Clara Winston (Macmillan, 1970), p. 149.

312 Glück: See Hamann, *Winifred Wagner*, pp. 86–87.

312 *"in the line of march"*: Hitler, *Sämtliche Aufzeichnungen*, pp. 1231–32. For recordings in Landsberg, see Henriette von Schirach, ed., *Anekdoten um Hitler: Geschichten aus einem halben Jahrhundert* (Türmer, 1980), p. 50. For *Schmied*, see Winifred's Dec. 9, 1923, letter, reproduced in the illustrations to Toland's *Adolf Hitler*. For domestic items, see Hamann, *Winifred Wagner*, p. 97. For paper, see Friedelind Wagner, *Royal Family of Bayreuth*, p. 17; and Toland, *Adolf Hitler*, p. 197. For the phonograph, see Hamann, *Winifred Wagner*, p. 98.

314 *"Only a couple"*: *Hitler: Reden, Schriften, Anordnungen, Februar 1925 bis Januar 1933*, II:2 (K. G. Saur, 1992–2003), p. 652.

314 *"In Germany one lets"*: Ibid., III:2, p. 267.

314 *"alias Schlesinger"*: Ibid., pp. 130 and 177–78.

314 "fünf Juden": Ibid., p. 179. Erich Kleiber, the chief conductor of the Staatsoper, was not Jewish, but there were in fact five Jewish conductors on the staff of the Staatsoper and the Kroll: Leo Blech, Otto Klemperer, George Szell, Alexander Zemlinsky, and Fritz Zweig.

314 *"spiritual development"*: Alan E. Steinweis, *Art, Ideology, and Economics in Nazi Germany: The Reich Chambers of Music, Theater, and the Visual Arts* (University of North Carolina Press, 1993), p. 33.

314 *"self-administration"*: Ibid., pp. 39–40 and 42.

315 *"there is no more glorious"*: Hamann, *Winifred Wagner*, p. 256.

315 *"it is totally impossible"*: "Die grosse Kunstrede des Führers," *Völkischer Beobachter*, Sept. 7, 1938.

315 *no more music should be dedicated*: Michael H. Kater, *The Twisted Muse: Musicians and Their Music in the Third Reich* (Oxford UP, 1997), p. 13.

315 *paled in comparison to Bruckner*: JGT I:3, p. 491. For Bruckner at the 1938 rally, see JGT I:6, p. 76. For Goebbels's leitmotif metaphor, see JGT II:7, p. 53.

315 *three thousand seats*: AHRP I:2, p. 984.

315 *mostly empty hall*: See Speer, *Inside the Third Reich*, p. 60. For the Deutscher Hof, see Fritz Wiedemann, *Der Mann, der Feldherr werden wollte* (Blick + Bild, 1964), p. 207. For Hitler shaking concertgoers awake, see Traudl Junge, *Until the Final Hour*, trans. Melissa Müller (Arcade, 2002), p. 81.

316 *Karajan's arrogance*: Nicolaus von Below, *Als Hitlers Adjutant, 1937–45* (Hase and Koehler, 1980), p. 166. On Knappertsbusch, see Picker, *Hitlers Tischgespräche*, p. 303.

316 *John Rockwell*: Communication to author.

316 *Hitler and Bruckner*: See Christa Brüstle, "The Musical Image of Bruckner," in *The Cambridge Companion to Bruckner*, ed. John Williamson (Cambridge UP, 2004), p. 258.

316 *kind of rehearsal*: See Bryan Gilliam, "The Annexation of Anton Bruckner: Nazi Revisionism and the Politics of Appropriation," *Musical Quarterly* 78:3 (Fall 1994), p. 584.

316 *"Say a big YES"*: Fred K. Prieberg, *Trial of Strength: Wilhelm Furtwängler in the Third Reich*, trans. Christopher Dolan (Northeastern UP, 1994), p. 231. On Hitler's triumphal entry into Graz, see Stefan Karner, *Die Steiermark im Dritten Reich, 1938–1945* (Leykam, 1986), p. 62.

317 *"symphony of joy"*: "Volk den Führer," *Völkischer Beobachter*, April 5, 1938.

317 *"mass hysteria"*: Alfred Brendel, *Me of All People: Alfred Brendel in Conversation with Martin Meyer*, trans. Richard Stokes (Cornell UP, 2002), p. 8.

317 *visited the Graz Opera*: Percy Ernst Schramm, "Adolf Hitler: Anatomie eines Diktators," *Der Spiegel*, Jan. 28, 1964, pp. 47–48; and Werner Maser, *Hitler: Legend, Myth, and Reality*, trans. Peter Ross and Betty Ross (Harper and Row, 1973), pp. 57 and 360.

317 *"Jewish-international spirit"*: Busch, *Hans Pfitzner und der Nationalsozialismus*, p. 73.

317 *"the one acceptable Jew"*: Hans Pfitzner, "Glosse zum II. Weltkrieg," in *Sämtliche Schriften*, ed. Bernhard Adamy (Schneider, 1987), vol. 4, pp. 339–41. Hitler had a habit of bringing up Weininger in conversation; see Hitler, *Monologe im Führer-Hauptquartier*, p. 148; and Frank, *Im Angesicht des Galgens*, p. 313. For Hitler's impression of Pfitzner as Jewish, see Kater, *Twisted Muse*, p. 218.

317 *"The Führer is very strongly"*: JGT II:8, p. 448.

318 *"Today there is no one"*: Kater, *Twisted Muse*, p. 219. For Pfitzner attacking Orff and Egk, see ibid., p. 192. For the *Kraków Greeting*, see Fred K. Prieberg, *Musik im NS-Staat* (Fischer, 1982), p. 225.

318 *"the most ambitious program"*: *Selected Letters of Paul Hindemith*, ed. and trans. Geoffrey Skelton (Yale UP, 1995), p. 77.

319 *"It is obvious"*: Ibid., p. 85.

319 *"an opportunity"*: Ibid., pp. 92–93.

319 *Jewish refugees*: Ibid., p. 125.

319 *"really great"*: Michael H. Kater, *Composers of the Nazi Era: Eight Portraits* (Oxford UP, 2000), p. 10; JGT I:3, p. 567.

320 *"Bavarian* Niggermusik*"*: Kim Kowalke, "Burying the Past: Carl Orff and His Brecht Connection," *Musical Quarterly* 84:1 (Spring 2000), p. 70.

320 *"extraordinary beauties"*: Kater, *Composers of the Nazi Era*, pp. 122–25 and 132; and JGT II:13, p. 466.

320 *"To my friends"*: Kater, *Composers of the Nazi Era*, p. 89.

320 *Party salute*: Ibid., pp. 93–96.

320 *"sometimes annoyed us"*: Harvey Sachs, *Music in Fascist Italy* (Norton, 1987), p. 146.

321 *"product of the Jewish spirit"*: "Die Düsseldorfer Reichsmusiktage," *Völkischer Beobachter*, May 27, 1938.

321 *"the Reich Music Chamber cannot"*: Kater, *Twisted Muse*, p. 19.

321 *poorly received*: Albrecht Dümling and Peter Girth, eds., *Entartete Musik: Zur Düsseldorfer Ausstellung von 1938: Eine kommentierte Rekonstruktion* (Düsseldorf, 1988), pp. xxx–xxxi; JGT I:5, p. 323.

321 *"negative attitude"*: Peter Heyworth, *Otto Klemperer, His Life and Times, Volume 2: 1933–1973* (Cambridge UP, 1996), p. 13. For more, see Joan Evans, "Stravinsky's Music in Hitler's Germany," *Journal of the American Musicological Society* 56:3 (Fall 2003), pp. 525–94.

321 *"half-bitter, half-mischievous"*: Prieberg, *Musik im NS-Staat*, p. 212.

321 *"Even so-called atonality"*: Herbert Gerigk, "Eine Lanze für Schönberg!," *Die Musik* 27:2 (Nov. 1934), p. 89. On Gerigk's catalog of musical Jews, see Pamela M. Potter, *Most German of the Arts: Musicology and Society from the Weimar Republic to the End of Hitler's Reich* (Yale UP, 1998), pp. 142–61.

322 *Zillig's* Das Opfer: See Erik Levi, "Atonality, 12-Tone Music, and the Third Reich," *Tempo* 178 (Sept. 1991), pp. 17–21.

322 *"In the opera"*: Paul von Klenau, "Zu Paul von Klenaus 'Michael Kohlhaas,'" *Zeitschrift für Musik*, May 1934, p. 530.

322 *"a living example"*: ASSI, p. 173.

322 *"a kind of dictator"*: Alexander L. Ringer, *Arnold Schoenberg: The Composer as Jew* (Clarendon, 1990), p. 235.

322 *"fascistic bent"*: Mann to Schoenberg, Jan. 9, 1939, ASC.

323 *"about which one can have"*: *Theodor W. Adorno, Alban Berg: Briefwechsel, 1925–1935*, ed. Henri Lonitz (Suhrkamp, 1997), p. 286.

323 *"This is Germany today!"*: HMAW, p. 527.

323 *Strauss's reform ideas*: BGFI, p. 577; Kurt Wilhelm, *Richard Strauss: An Intimate Portrait*, trans. Mary Whittall (Rizzoli, 1989), p. 220; and Michael Kennedy, *Richard Strauss: Man, Musician, Enigma* (Cambridge UP, 1999), p. 284.

323 *home of Walther Funk*: RSC, p. 546.

324 *gave Hitler a copy*: Ibid., p. 544.

324 *Bruno Walter affair*: See Kater, *Composers of the Nazi Era*, pp. 220–25; and Erik Ryding

and Rebecca Pechefsky, *Bruno Walter: A World Elsewhere* (Yale UP, 2001), pp. 220–23.

324 *avoided signing papers*: Steinweis, *Art, Ideology, and Economics*, p. 52.

324 *Mahler should be performed*: Wilhelm, *Richard Strauss: An Intimate Portrait*, p. 219.

324 *"Aryan French"*: *Ihr aufrichtig Ergebener*, vol. 2 of *Richard Strauss im Briefwechsel mit zeitgenössischen Komponisten und Dirigenten*, ed. Gabriele Strauss and Monika Reger (Henschel, 1998), p. 286.

324 *"total lack of interest"*: Ibid., p. 285.

324 *"terrible, ersatz"*: Kater, *Composers of the Nazi Era*, p. 127.

324 *"Do you believe"*: Strauss to Zweig, June 17, 1935, BDC. See also Albrecht Riethmüller, "Stefan Zweig and the Fall of the Reich Music Chamber President, Richard Strauss," trans. Sherri Jones, in Kater and Riethmüller, *Music and Nazism*, pp. 277–78.

324 *"Concentration camp!"*: Gerhard Splitt, *Richard Strauss, 1933–1935: Ästhetik und Musikpolitik zu Beginn der nationalsozialistischen Herrschaft* (Centaurus, 1987), pp. 110–11.

324 Der Stürmer: Donald A. Prater, *European of Yesterday: A Biography of Stefan Zweig* (Clarendon, 1972), p. 231.

325 *"opponent of the regime"*: Joachim Fest, *Albert Speer: Conversations with Hitler's Architect*, trans. Patrick Camiller (Polity, 2007), pp. 45–46.

325 *"I consider . . . Jew baiting"*: *A Confidential Matter: The Letters of Richard Strauss and Stefan Zweig, 1931–1935*, trans. Max Knight (University of California Press, 1977), p. 119.

325 *"the great designer"*: Josef Wulf, *Musik im Dritten Reich: Eine Dokumentation* (Mohn, 1963), p. 184.

325 *whose manuscript he presented to Hitler*: Albrecht Dümling, "Zwischen Autonomie und Fremdbestimmug: Die *Olympische Hymne* von Robert Lubahn und Richard Strauss," *Richard Strauss-Blätter* 38 (Dec. 1997), p. 80; and RSC, p. 559. For accounts of the performance, see Richard D. Mandell, *The Nazi Olympics* (University of Illinois Press, 1987), p. 152; and Frederick T. Burchall, "100,000 Hail Hitler; U.S. Athletes Avoid Nazi Salute to Him," *New York Times*, Aug. 2, 1936.

325 *Richard and Christian*: Kater, *Composers of the Nazi Era*, p. 253.

326 *Franz and Alice interrogated*: Ibid., p. 256.

326 *Franz defends Nazis*: Feb. 21, 1944, report, Franz Strauss file, BDC.

326 *arguments in the house*: Kater's communication to author.

326 Friedenstag: Gerhard Splitt, "Oper als Politikum: 'Friedenstag' (1938) von Richard Strauss," *Archiv für Musikwissenschaft* 55:3 (1998), pp. 220–51, paints *Friedenstag* as a political opera, but Gilliam gives a different picture in BGFI, p. 587, noting that Strauss described one political interpretation of the opera as an example of a "kindergarten" mentality.

326 *"Whoever lights"*: AHRP I:2, p. 514. The playing of the Fanfare can be heard on the Koch Schwann recording Edition Wiener Staatsoper Live, vol. 15 (3-1465-2), containing the entire performance of *Friedenstag* on June 10, 1939.

326 *Strauss and Goebbels*: RSC, p. 597.

327 *"He is unpolitical"*: JGT I:6, p. 375.

327 *Strauss received assurances*: BGRS, p. 160.

327 *"I say a few sweet nothings"*: JGT I:9, p. 165.

327 *"Lehár has the masses"*: Werner Egk, *Die Zeit wartet nicht* (R. S. Schulz, 1973), pp. 342–43.

328 *"Posterity must cherish"*: JGT I:6, pp. 244–45.

328 *"Very often in my life"*: AHRP II:1, p. 1058.

328 *"The Jews in Germany"*: AHRP II:2, p. 1920.

328 *"I have always been scorned"*: Ibid., p. 1937.

328 *"The laughter of Kundry"*: Otto Weininger, *Über die letzten Dinge* (Braumüller, 1918), p. 91.

329 *"The record player was pulled out"*: Frank, *Im Angesicht des Galgens*, p. 213.

329 *"design a timeless"*: Hamann, *Winifred Wagner*, pp. 440–41.

329 *"an orgy from hell"*: Ibid., pp. 284–85.

329 *Joachim Köhler*: See his *Wagner's Hitler*, pp. 230–31.

330 *Paula Neumann*: Wilhelm, *Richard Strauss: An Intimate Portrait*, p. 264; Hamann, *Winifred Wagner*, p. 454.

332 *"The last words"*: Kennedy, *Richard Strauss*, p. 333.

332 *August 3, 1941, . . . October 28, 1942*: www.holocaustchronicle.org/StaticPages/254.html and www.holocaustchronicle.org/StaticPages/381.html (accessed Nov. 11, 2006).

333 *Schulhoff's Eighth*: Josef Bek, *Erwin Schulhoff: Leben und Werk* (Bockel, 1994), p. 152.

333 *Karel Ančerl*: Viktor Ullmann, *26 Kritiken über musikalische Veranstaltungen in Theresienstadt*, ed. Ingo Schultz (Bockel, 1993), pp. 66–67. For the "Ode to Joy" being sung by the children's chorus of the There-

sienstadt family camp at Auschwitz, see Joža Karas, *Music in Terezín, 1941–1945* (Beaufort, 1985), pp. 158–59. For the deportations, see Lubomír Peduzzi, *Pavel Haas: Život a dílo skladatele* (Muzejní a vlastivědná společnost v Brně, 1993), p. 165.

333 *biography of Rosé*: See Richard Newman and Karen Kirtley, *Alma Rosé: Vienna to Auschwitz* (Amadeus, 2000).

334 *Rosé's repertory*: Ibid., pp. 249–55 and 262–66.

334 *"She lived in another world"*: Reminiscence of Manca Svalbova, in Hermann Langbein, *People in Auschwitz*, trans. Harry Zohn (University of North Carolina Press, 2004), p. 127.

334 *other recollections*: Ibid., p. 128.

334 *Rosé's death*: Newman and Kirtley, *Alma Rosé*, pp. 305–6.

334 *Neumann's death*: Hamann, *Winifred Wagner*, p. 454, says that Neumann was deported east in 1943.

334 *"sympathy for death"*: Thomas Mann, *The Magic Mountain*, trans. John E. Woods (Knopf, 1995), p. 643.

334 *"changed the discs"*: Simon Sebag Montefiore, *Stalin: The Court of the Red Tsar* (Weidenfeld and Nicolson, 2003), p. 73.

335 *Berghof playlist*: Junge, *Until the Final Hour*, pp. 80–81.

335 *catalog of the Berghof*: *Schallplatten-Verzeichnis*, Third Reich Collection, Rare Book and Special Collections, Library of Congress.

335 *"Bruckner was the greatest"*: Hitler, *Monologe im Führer-Hauptquartier*, p. 198 (Bruckner and Mozart) and p. 224 (Wesendonck).

335 *" 'I would scrape' "*: Heinrich Hoffman, *Hitler Was My Friend*, trans. R. H. Stevens (Burke, 1955), pp. 189–90.

335 *"I had the impression"*: G. M. Gilbert, *Nuremberg Diary* (Da Capo, 1995), p. 71.

335 *Bruckner Orchestra*: JGT II:7, p. 619.

335 *Furtwängler's bunker*: Prieberg, *Trial of Strength*, pp. 307–9.

336 *"No soldier needs to fall"*: Wilhelm, *Richard Strauss: An Intimate Portrait*, p. 256.

336 *"My achievements"*: Strauss to Hitler, Jan. 15, 1944, BDC.

336 *Furtwängler advised*: Prieberg, *Musik im NS-Staat*, p. 214.

336 *gifts from Hitler and Goebbels*: John Deathridge, "Richard Strauss and the Broken Dream of Modernity," in *Richard Strauss und die Moderne*, ed. Bernd Edelmann, Birgit Lodes, and Reinhold Schlötterer (Henschel, 2001), pp. 84–85.

336 *"a complete bystander"*: Heinz Ihlert to Hans Hinkel, May 22, 1935, BDC.

336 *"miserable"*: JGT II:12, p. 527.

336 *"completely second-rate"*: Fest, *Albert Speer*, p. 45.

337 *Jackson has suggested*: See Timothy Jackson, "The Metamorphosis of the *Metamorphosen*: New Analytical and Source-Critical Discoveries," in *Richard Strauss: New Perspectives on the Composer and His Works*, ed. Bryan Gilliam (Duke UP, 1992), pp. 199–201.

338 *cyanide capsules*: Joachim Fest, *Speer: The Final Verdict*, trans. Ewald Osers and Alexandra Dring (Harcourt, 2001), p. 261.

338 Tristan: Christa Schroeder, *Er war mein Chef*, ed. Anton Joachimsthaler (Langen Müller, 1985), p. 189.

338 *"Everything had to go down"*: Goldensohn, *Nuremberg Interviews*, p. 99.

339 *"experience its own annihilation"*: Walter Benjamin, *Selected Writings, Volume 4, 1938–1940*, ed. Howard Eiland and Michael W. Jennings, trans. Edmund Jephcott et al. (Harvard UP, 2003), p. 270.

339 *Hitler's death*: H. R. Trevor-Roper, *The Last Days of Hitler* (Macmillan, 1947).

10. Zero Hour

341 *"We live in a time"*: Interview with Charles Amirkhanian, Jan. 14, 1992, quoted in *Writings Through John Cage's Music, Poetry, and Art*, ed. David W. Bernstein and Christopher Hatch (University of Chicago Press, 2001), p. 1.

343 *bombing of Garmisch*: See Ian Sayer and Douglas Botting, *Nazi Gold* (Grove, 1984), p. 77.

343 *Strauss's meetings with Americans*: See Peter Bloom, "History, Memory, and the Oboe Concerto of Richard Strauss," *Pendragon Review* 2 (2001), p. 4; author's interview with Milton Weiss, Aug. 7, 1997; Meyer Levin, "We Liberated Who's Who," *Saturday Evening Post*, July 21, 1945 (on Kramers); Michael H. Kater, "Jupiter in Hell," *New York Times*, Jan. 6, 2002; and Walter Panofsky, *Richard Strauss: Partitur eines Lebens* (Piper, 1965), p. 331.

344 *"Hitler's father"*: Kurt Wilhelm, *Richard Strauss persönlich: Eine Bildbiographie* (Kindler, 1984), p. 363.

344 *several future leaders*: See *Stockhausen on Music*, ed. Robin Maconie (Marion Boyars, 1989), pp. 15–23; Michael Kurtz, *Stockhausen: Eine Biographie* (Bärenreiter, 1988), p. 37; Hans Werner Henze, *Bohemian Fifths: An Autobiography*, trans. Stewart Spencer

(Princeton UP, 1999), pp. 43–45; David Osmond-Smith, *Berio* (Oxford UP, 1991), p. 3; and Nouritza Matossian, *Xenakis* (Taplinger, 1986), p. 26.

345 *Britten at Bergen-Belsen*: See DMBB2, pp. 1272–74. For the dates of *Holy Sonnets*, see *Benjamin Britten: A Catalogue of the Published Works*, ed. Paul Banks et al. (Britten-Pears Library, 1999), pp. 75–76. For Oppenheimer, see Kai Bird and Martin J. Sherwin, *American Prometheus: The Triumph and Tragedy of J. Robert Oppenheimer* (Knopf, 2005), p. 304.

345 *"The people starve"*: Bernstein to Helen Coates, May 5, 1948, Leonard Bernstein Collection, Library of Congress. For a good description of Germany's "year zero," see Patricia Meehan, *A Strange Enemy People: Germans Under the British, 1945–1950* (Peter Owen, 2001), pp. 31–43.

346 *"inclined to be bolshevistic"*: Jean Edward Smith, *Lucius D. Clay: An American Life* (Holt, 1990), p. 42.

346 *"We are trying"*: Proceedings of the Berchtesgaden Conference, Oct. 8–12, 1948, Education and Cultural Relations (hereafter E&CR), OMGUS.

346 *"He's hep"*: Nicolas Nabokov, *Old Friends and New Music* (Little, Brown, 1951), p. 258.

346 *Music Branches*: For more on OMGUS's music officers, see David Monod, *Settling Scores: German Music, Denazification, and the Americans, 1945–1953* (University of North Carolina Press, 2005).

347 *Moseley at Tanglewood*: Humphrey Burton, *Leonard Bernstein* (Doubleday, 1994), p. 94. For Moseley's report on Bernstein's visit, see Monthly Summary, May 24, 1948, E&CR, OMG Bavaria, OMGUS.

347 *"It means so much"*: Bernstein to Helen Coates, May 11, 1948, Leonard Bernstein Collection, Library of Congress.

347 *Moseley's visit to Bayreuth*: Author's interview with Carlos Moseley, Aug. 30, 2002.

347 *four exclamation points*: Walter Schertz-Parey, *Winifred Wagner: Ein Leben für Bayreuth* (Stocker, 1999), p. 181.

348 *"It is above all"*: "Music Control Instruction No. 1," June 19, 1945, Supreme Headquarters of the Allied Expeditionary Force, Psychological Warfare Division, OMGUS.

348 *"The rule of having"*: Edward Kilenyi, Report to Chief, Theater and Music, Aug. 10, 1945, E&CR, OMG Bavaria, OMGUS. For Kilenyi's background, see Monod, *Settling Scores*, pp. 21–22.

349 *"I hear such nice"*: Oct. 31, 1948, Civil Censorship Division, USFET (GERMAN), OMGUS.

349 *Newell Jenkins and Orff*: See Monod, *Settling Scores*, p. 65; and Michael H. Kater, *Composers of the Nazi Era*, pp. 133–40. Jenkins had the added distinction of being the grandson of Richard Wagner's dentist.

349 *"a man of the utmost"*: Arthur C. Vogler, "Daily Report," June 15, 1945, E&CR, OMG Bavaria, OMGUS.

349 *"They are extremely shy"*: Participation of Music Section in Reorientation Activities, May 9, 1947, E&CR, OMG Bavaria, OMGUS.

350 *Moseley's patronage*: Semi-annual Report, July 1–Dec. 31, 1948, E&CR, OMG Bavaria, OMGUS.

350 *piano on jeep*: Amy C. Beal, *New Music, New Allies: American Experimental Music in Germany from Zero Hour to Reunification* (University of California Press, 2006), pp. 40 and 38.

350 *"contemporary music only"*: Everett Helm, "Letter from Germany," undated manuscript (apparently 1948), Theater and Music, E&CR, OMGUS.

350 *"It would be both"*: Evarts to Harrison Kerr, April 23, 1949, Theater and Music, Education, Records of the Cultural Affairs Branch, E&CR, OMGUS.

350 *"In my former army service"*: Schoenberg to John Evarts, April 23, 1949, ASC.

351 *"acquired a reputation"*: Ralph A. Burns, "Review of Activities for the Month of June 1949," Theater and Music, Education, Records of the Cultural Affairs Branch, E&CR, OMGUS.

351 *excitement over Leibowitz*: Henze, *Bohemian Fifths*, p. 74.

351 *"The Darmstadt Holiday Courses"*: Burns, "Review of Activities for the Month of July 1949."

352 *"segregation of the modern"*: Monod, *Settling Scores*, p. 198.

353 *"the prophet of a new"*: Hans Moldenhauer, *The Death of Anton Webern: A Drama in Documents* (Philosophical Library, 1961), p. 5. Moldenhauer notes that the cook died of alcoholism in 1955 in Mount Olive, North Carolina, adding that the Mount of Olives was "the scene of the agony and betrayal of Jesus Christ" (p. 98).

353 *"happens to be about"*: See Klaus Mann, *Briefe und Antworten, Band II: 1937–1949*, ed. Martin Gregor-Dellin (Edition Spangenberg, 1975), p. 226. See also Klaus

Mann, *Der Wendepunkt: Ein Lebensbericht* (Nymphenburger, 1969), p. 488; and Gertrud Maria Rösch, "'I thought it wiser not to disclose my identity': Die Begegnung zwischen Klaus Mann und Richard Strauss im Mai 1945," *Thomas Mann Jahrbuch* 14 (2001), pp. 233–48. For the unsent letter to Mann, see Walter Thomas, *Richard Strauss und seine Zeitgenossen* (Langen Müller, 1964), p. 283; Richard Strauss, *Briefwechsel mit Willi Schuh* (Atlantis, 1969), p. 81; and Hans Rudolf Vaget, "The Spell of Salome: Thomas Mann and Richard Strauss," in *German Literature and Music: An Aesthetic Fusion, 1890–1989*, ed. Claus Reschke and Howard Pollack (Fink, 1992), p. 46.

353 *"Oh, yes"*: Russell Campitelli to author, June 10, 2003.

354 *photograph of Strauss*: Included in John de Lancie's letter to the author, Dec. 23, 1999.

354 *"Masters of the very first"*: David Farrell Krell and Donald L. Bates, *The Good European: Nietzsche's Work Sites in Word and Image* (University of Chicago Press, 1997), p. 217. Originally in *The Gay Science*, sec. 281.

11. Brave New World

355 *"Everything begins"*: Charles Péguy, *Notre jeunesse* (Gallimard, 1933), p. 30.

355 *"for most people"*: Morton Feldman, "An Interview with Robert Ashley, August 1964," in *Contemporary Composers on Contemporary Music*, ed. Elliott Schwartz and Barney Childs (Da Capo, 1998), pp. 363 and 365.

356 *"it was like the defection"*: Leonard Bernstein, *The Unanswered Question: Six Talks at Harvard* (Harvard UP, 1976), p. 419.

356 *"Before the end"*: Allen Edwards, *Flawed Words and Stubborn Sounds: A Conversation with Elliott Carter* (Norton, 1971), p. 61.

357 *Adorno on Copland*: Theodor W. Adorno, *Minima Moralia: Reflections from Damaged Life*, trans. E.F.N. Jephcott (Verso, 1978), p. 207.

357 *"has taken upon itself"*: Theodor W. Adorno, *Philosophie der neuen Musik* (Suhrkamp, 1976), p. 126.

357 *"My adoption"*: Ernst Krenek, "A Composer's Influences," *Perspectives of New Music* 3:1 (Fall–Winter 1964), p. 38.

357 *"uncompromising"*: René Leibowitz, *Schoenberg and His School: The Contemporary Stage of the Language of Music*, trans. Dika Newlin (Da Capo, 1975), p. xvi.

358 *"I do not compose principles"*: ASL, pp. 236–37. On Adorno, see JASR, p. 335.

358 *"Schbrg clique"*: Robert Craft, *Stravinsky: Glimpses of a Life* (St. Martin's, 1993), p. 40.

358 *"The second half"*: JASR, p. 333. For the original utterance, see ibid., p. 66.

358 *"I cannot deny"*: ASSI, p. 286.

359 *"Abyss of the Birds"*: Nigel Simeone, *Olivier Messiaen: A Bibliographical Catalogue of Messiaen's Works* (Schneider, 1998), p. 72; and Rebecca Rischin, *For the End of Time: The Story of the Messiaen Quartet* (Cornell UP, 2003), pp. 9–12.

359 *Rebecca Rischin reveals*: Rischin, *For the End of Time*, pp. 27–31 and 72–73. For other details, see Antoine Goléa, *Rencontres avec Olivier Messiaen* (Juilliard, 1960), p. 62.

359 *steady beat*: Claude Samuel, *Olivier Messiaen: Music and Color*, trans. E. Thomas Glasow (Amadeus, 1986), p. 68.

359 *rhythmic cells*: Olivier Messiaen, *The Technique of My Musical Language*, trans. John Satterfield (Leduc, 1956), p. 14.

360 *"implacable destiny"*: Olivier Messiaen, "Le rythme chez Igor Strawinsky," *La Revue musicale* 191 (1939), pp. 91–92.

360 *"M. Boulez"*: Nigel Simeone's communication to author. See also NSPHM, p. 138.

360 *"like a young cat"*: Jean-Louis Barrault, "Travailler avec Boulez," *Résonance* 8 (1995), reprinted at mediatheque.ircam.fr/articles/textes/Barrault95a (accessed Dec. 17, 2006).

360 *Peyser on Tézenas*: Joan Peyser, *Boulez: Composer, Conductor, Enigma* (Schirmer Books, 1976), pp. 54 and 246.

361 *"The Germans virtually"*: Ibid., p. 25.

361 *"When he first entered"*: Ibid., p. 31.

361 *"like a lion"*: "Entretien avec Claude Samuel," booklet included with the 1988 Erato box-set recording of Messiaen's works (ECD 75505), p. 27.

361 *booing, shouting*: See Antoine Goléa, "La Musique," *Esprit*, May 1945; Guy Bernard-Delapierre, "Musique d'un autre monde," *Confluences*, April 1945; Guy Bernard-Delapierre, "Post-scriptum: Le Cas Strawinsky," *Confluences*, May 1945, p. 439; Antoine Goléa, *Rencontres avec Pierre Boulez* (Julliard, 1958), pp. 9–10; Peyser, *Boulez*, p. 33; Peter Heyworth, "Taking Leave of Predecessors," pt. 1, *New Yorker*, March 24, 1973, p. 45; and, for the most thorough account, SWS2, pp. 175–77.

361 *"pseudo-youths"*: Francis Poulenc, "Vive Strawinsky," *Le Figaro*, April 7, 1945. For "fanatic sect," see Francis Poulenc, *Correspondance, 1910–1963*, ed. Myriam Chimènes (Fayard, 1994), p. 585.

361 *"dry and inhuman"*: NSPHM, p. 153.
361 "Vous êtes merde!": Peyser, *Boulez*, p. 39.
362 *turning his back*: *Henri Dutilleux: Music—Mystery and Memory: Conversations with Claude Glayman*, trans. Roger Nichols (Ashgate, 2003), p. 36.
362 *"I believe that music"*: Pierre Boulez, *Notes of an Apprenticeship*, trans. Herbert Weinstock (Knopf, 1968), p. 71.
362 *"false discoveries"*: Ibid., p. 244.
362 *"schematic, arbitrary"*: Ibid., p. 250.
362 *"to enclose classic"*: Ibid., pp. 255–56.
362 *"more virulent"*: Ibid., p. 264.
363 *"The Schoenberg 'case'"*: Ibid., pp. 268–76.
363 *"develop timbres"*: NSPHM, p. 169.
363 *Seeger and Cowell*: Henry Cowell, *New Musical Resources* (Cambridge UP, 1996), pp. 98–108 and 83.
364 Structures 1a: For the classic analysis, see Györgi Ligeti, "Pierre Boulez: Decision and Automatism in Structures 1a," trans. Leo Black, *Die Reihe* 4 (Presser, 1960), pp. 36–62. The duration series at the opening are RI(5) and R(12).
364 *"They represented"*: James Miller, "Michel Foucault: The Heart Laid Bare," *Grand Street* 39 (1991), p. 60.
364 *"I am going toward violence"*: Calvin Tomkins, *The Bride and the Bachelors: Five Masters of the Avant-Garde* (Penguin, 1976), p. 144.
365 *"inclusive rather than exclusive"*: JCS, p. 13.
365 *Cage and Schoenberg*: For an account of Cage's studies with Schoenberg, the extent of which is sometimes exaggerated, see Michael Hicks, "John Cage's Studies with Schoenberg," *American Music* 8:2 (1990), pp. 125–40. See also David Revill, *The Roaring Silence: John Cage: A Life* (Arcade, 1992), pp. 47–49.
365 *"phonograph concert"*: See Mark Katz, *Capturing Sound: How Technology Has Changed Music* (University of California Press, 2004), pp. 99–113.
366 *"I believe that the use"*: JCS, pp. 3–4.
366 *"stupefied by its activism"*: *For the Birds: John Cage in Conversation with Daniel Charles*, trans. Richard Gardner, Tom Gora, and John Cage (Boyars, 1995), p. 180.
367 *"interchangeability of sound"*: James Pritchett, *The Music of John Cage* (Cambridge UP, 1993), p. 71.
368 *Black Mountain*: Martin Duberman, *Black Mountain: An Exploration in Community* (Dutton, 1972), pp. 348–62.
368 *"Music is lagging"*: Quoted in Douglas Kahn, *Noise Water Meat: A History of Sound in the Arts* (MIT Press, 1999), p. 168.
369 *five* Études of Noises: Pierre Schaeffer, *À la Recherche d'une musique concrète* (Seuil, 1952), pp. 18–23. For Schaeffer under the German occupation, see Peter Manning, *Electronic and Computer Music* (Oxford UP, 2004), p. 20.
369 Williams Mix: See Larry Austin, "John Cage's *Williams Mix* (1951–3)," in *A Handbook to Twentieth-Century Musical Sketches*, ed. Patricia Hall and Friedemann Sallis (Cambridge UP, 2004), pp. 189–213.
370 *"We have no music"*: JCS, p. 126.
370 *"performing monkey," "fascist tendencies"*: *The Boulez-Cage Correspondence*, ed. Jean-Jacques Nattiez, trans. Robert Samuels (Cambridge UP, 1993), p. 23.
370 *"Nicolas de Staël"*: Pierre-Michel Menger, *Le Paradoxe du musicien: Le compositeur, le mélomane, et l'État dans la société contemporaine* (Flammarion, 1983), p. 223. For Cocteau in a cape, see Dominique Jameux, *Pierre Boulez*, trans. Susan Bradshaw (Faber, 1991), p. 67.
371 *"hyperactive chic"*: MFS, p. 226.
371 *"compulsion neurosis"*: See Ligeti, "Pierre Boulez"; and Ligeti, "Metamorphoses of Musical Form," in *Die Reihe* 7 (Presser, 1965), p. 10.
371 *"My intention"*: From Cage's notes to *The 25-Year Retrospective Concert of the Music of John Cage*, May 15, 1958 (Wergo 6247-2).
371 *"Any attempt"*: JCS, p. 62.
371 *"We are producing"*: Virgil Thomson, *Music Reviewed, 1940–1954* (Vintage, 1967), p. 170.
372 *"the main premises"*: Charles Harrison and Paul Wood, eds., *Art in Theory, 1900–2000: An Anthology of Changing Ideas* (Blackwell, 2003), p. 579.
372 *"the greatest American . . . too busy"*: "Copland's Third," *Time*, Oct. 28, 1946, p. 55.
373 *"Nothing can persuade"*: HPAC, p. 411.
373 *"the speeches of Henry Wallace"*: Elizabeth Crist, *Music for the Common Man: Aaron Copland During the Depression and War* (Oxford UP, 2005), p. 193.
373 *"new international style"*: Thomson, *Music Reviewed*, p. 183.
373 *"were rebuked"*: HPAC, p. 283.
374 *Broadwood Hotel*: *New York Herald Tribune*, March 25, 1949.
374 *"SHOSTAKOVICH, WE UNDERSTAND"*: *New York Herald Tribune*, March 27, 1949.

374 *"SHOSTAKOVICH! JUMP"*: "Red Visitors Cause Rumpus," *Life*, April 4, 1949.

374 *"It's hot in here"*: Peter W. Goodman, *Morton Gould: American Salute* (Amadeus, 2000), p. 196.

374 *Wallace rally*: "Tumult at the Waldorf," *Time*, April 4, 1949, p. 23. For Copland's seating, see Aaron Copland and Vivien Perlis, *Copland Since 1943* (St. Martin's, 1989), p. 183.

375 *Hoover and Nabokov*: Peter Coleman, *The Liberal Conspiracy: The Congress for Cultural Freedom and the Struggle for the Mind of Postwar Europe* (Free Press, 1989), pp. 43–44, says that J. Edgar Hoover's FBI evidently had files on the composer's "bohemian private life."

375 *Office of Policy Coordination*: Frances Stonor Saunders, *The Cultural Cold War: The CIA and the World of Arts and Letters* (New Press, 1999), pp. 45–56.

375 *wad of cash*: Saunders, *Cultural Cold War*, pp. 47 and 54–55.

375 *"His beginnings were promising"*: "Shostakovich Hits Stravinsky As 'Betrayer,' " *New York Herald Tribune*, March 28, 1949, and "Shostakovich Bids All Artists Lead War on 'New Fascists,' " *New York Times*, March 28, 1949.

376 *"I am going to start"*: ACR, pp. 128–29.

376 *"The present policies"*: "Shostakovich Bids All Artists."

376 *"culture generalissimo"*: SSC2, p. 365.

376 *"naively stupid"*: Ibid., p. 376.

376 *"absolute and immediate"*: Nicolas Nabokov, "The Case of Dmitri Shostakovich," *Harper's*, March 1943, p. 423.

377 *"Throughout the tumultuous"*: Nicolas Nabokov, *Old Friends and New Music*, expanded ed. (Hamish Hamilton, 1951), p. 204.

377 *"I fully agree"*: Nicolas Nabokov, *Bagázh: Memoirs of a Russian Cosmopolitan* (Atheneum, 1975), pp. 237–38.

377 *"God knows what"*: Arthur Miller, *Timebends* (Grove, 1987), p. 239.

377 *"slipped quietly"*: "Bartok's Modern Music Soothes Shostakovich," *New York Times*, March 29, 1949.

377 *"standout fellow traveler"*: "Red Visitors Cause Rumpus."

377 *"strange rogues' gallery"*: Thomas Mann, *Tagebücher, 1949–1950*, ed. Inge Jens (Fischer, 1991), pp. 45 and 657.

378 *"ferreting out"*: Copland to Irving Fine and Verna Fine, June 6, 1949, ACLC.

378 "Mais oui": "European Diary," 1949, ACLC.

378 *"stuck it out"*: Ned Rorem, *Knowing When to Stop* (Simon and Schuster, 1994), p. 283. In *Setting the Tone: Essays and a Diary* (Limelight, 1984), p. 168, Rorem repeats the anecdote of Boulez playing the Second Sonata at his apartment, adding that the music caused Shirley Gabis (now Shirley Perle) to throw up. In a conversation with the author on May 17, 2004, Perle vigorously denied throwing up, although she may have wanted to.

378 *"You cannot change"*: Schoenberg's attack was printed in Thomson's Sunday column in the *New York Herald Tribune*, Sept. 11, 1949. Copland's protest appeared in the *Herald Tribune* on Sept. 25.

379 *"Alias: Aaron Copeland"*: Copland's FBI file was released in May 2003 under the Freedom of Information Act. The Hoover memo is dated July 13, 1951.

379 *"Copland has been abroad"*: Hoover to director of CIA, ibid., p. 10.

379 *"is no longer writing"*: Aaron Copland, *Music and Imagination* (Harvard UP, 1952), p. 75.

379 *Evarts's fate*: Amy C. Beal, *New Music, New Allies: American Experimental Music in Germany from Zero Hour to Reunification* (University of California Press, 2006), p. 31.

380 *Busbey read*: *Congressional Record*, 83rd Cong., 1st sess., app. A169. See also *Congressional Record*, 83rd Cong., 1st sess., July 30 and 31, 1953, pp. 2793, 3609, 3680.

380 *"I say unequivocally"*: "Statement of Aaron Copland," box 427, House Un-American Activities, ACLC.

380 *"YOU ARE HEREBY"*: The telegram can be found in ACLC. The date was subsequently changed to May 26.

380 *"My impression"*: "Impressions (May 27, 1953) of the Hearing Before the Senate Subcommittee on Investigations," ACLC. For Copland's claims in his testimony, see Executive Sessions of the Senate, Permanent Subcommittee on Investigations of the Committee on Government Operations, *Congressional Record*, 83rd Cong., 1st sess., pp. 1288 and 1283. The one-dollar check can be found in Copland's personal file on the Un-American Committee experience.

381 *"one of America's"*: Martin Merson, "My Education in Government," *Reporter*, Oct. 7, 1954. Clipping in ACLC.

381 *Pollack declares*: HPAC, pp. 446–47.

381 *fee from Rodgers*: HPAC, p. 470.

382 *CBS audience*: Edgar Young, *Lincoln Center, the Building of an Institution* (NYU Press, 1980), p. 170.

382 *"Oh, Mr. Copland"*: Copland and Perlis, *Copland Since 1943*, p. 136.
382 *Copland's decline*: HPAC, pp. 409–10.
382 *"It was exactly"*: Ibid., p. 516.
383 *"serious composer"*: Goodman, *Morton Gould*, p. 210.
383 *multiple reports*: SSC2, p. 347.
383 *"It seems that once"*: Ibid.
383 *read with annoyance*: RCSC, p. 42.
384 *"a Mozart"*: Peyser, *Boulez*, p. 66.
384 *"worn out invention"*: SWS2, p. 271.
384 *"What ugliness!"*: *Boulez-Cage Correspondence*, p. 118.
384 *Craft and Stravinsky*: Craft produced six books of "conversations" with Stravinsky. Charles Joseph, who has studied differences between the raw material of these volumes and the finished product, concludes, as many always suspected, that the books are an erratic mix of Stravinsky's own voice and Craft's approximation of it. See Joseph, *Stravinsky Inside Out* (Yale UP, 2001), p. 262: "The charges [that Craft scripted Stravinsky] are frequently unsubstantiated or exaggerated, yet in other places justified." I have chosen to rely mostly on Craft's diaries and firsthand recollections.
384 *Schoenberg's death mask*: RCSC, p. 54.
385 "three times!": Ibid., pp. 66–67.
385 *"For a moment"*: Ibid., pp. 72–73.
385 *"To-Morrow Shall Be"*: Vera Stravinsky and Robert Craft, *Stravinsky in Pictures and Documents* (Simon and Schuster, 1978), p. 422.
386 *"a hermetic cult"*: Nicolas Nabokov, "The Atonal Trail: A Communication," *Partisan Review*, May 1948, p. 581.
386 *"the liberty to experiment"*: Nicolas Nabokov, "Introduction à l'oeuvre du XXe siècle," *La Revue musicale* 212 (April 1952), p. 8. For the funding, see Saunders, *Cultural Cold War*, pp. 125–28.
386 *"Comrade Picasso"*: SSC2, p. 381.
386 *youths walk out*: RCSC, p. 82.
387 *Stravinsky at* Structures 1a: RCSC, p. 77; Mark Carroll, *Music and Ideology in Cold War Europe* (Cambridge UP, 2003), pp. 1–3.
387 *"folklore of mediocrity"*: Saunders, *Cultural Cold War*, p. 224.
387 *"Eventually . . . "*: Pierre Boulez, "Éventuellement . . .," *La Revue musicale* 212 (April 1952), p. 119: "*Que conclure? L'inattendu: affirmons, à notre tour, que tout musicien qui n'a pas ressenti—nous ne disons pas compris, mais bien ressenti—la nécessité du langage dodécaphonique est INUTILE.*" Compare Stravinsky, *Poetics of Music in the Form of Six Lessons*, trans. Arthur Knodel and Ingolf Dahl (Harvard UP, 1970), p. 98: "*Le bon artisan, dans ces époques bénies, ne songe lui-même qu'à atteindre le* beau *à travers les catégories de l'*utile." There would appear to be other references to the *Poetics* in the first section of Boulez's essay.
387 *he dutifully noted*: Joseph, *Stravinsky Inside Out*, p. 251.
388 *Shreffler has assembled*: See Anne C. Shreffler, "Ideologies of Serialism: Stravinsky's *Threni* and the Congress for Cultural Freedom," in *Music and the Aesthetics of Modernity*, ed. Karol Berger and Anthony Newcomb (Harvard UP, 2005), p. 229. Information about Movements comes from Shreffler's communication to the author, with reference to Nabokov's letter to Stravinsky of March 11, 1958. Shreffler does not believe that Karl Weber, the industrialist in question, was a "front."
388 *Boulez meets Stravinsky*: Virgil Thomson, *Virgil Thomson* (Dutton, 1985), pp. 402–3. For Stravinsky reading Boulez's essay, see SSC2, p. 348. For the Tropicana, see ibid., p. 350. For Stravinsky's visit to the garret, see RCSC, p. 167.
388 *"unforgivable condescension"*: Martin Bernheimer, "Igor Stravinsky Has Another Tiff with the Times," *Los Angeles Times*, July 5, 1970.
388 *"like so many changes"*: Stephen Walsh, *The Music of Stravinsky* (Clarendon, 1988), p. 233.
389 *"a ballet which would seem"*: SSC1, p. 287.
389 *François de Lauze*: Charles M. Joseph, *Stravinsky and Balanchine: A Journey of Invention* (Yale UP, 2002), pp. 228–30.
389 *the devil*: Ibid., pp. 233–34.
390 *"Someone has said"*: SWS2, p. 440.
390 *octatonic scale*: See RTS2, p. 1674.
391 *"He wanted"*: SWS1, p. 53.
391 *autographs*: For Sinatra, see Stravinsky and Craft, *Stravinsky in Pictures and Documents*, p. 476; for the Pope, see RSC, p. 280.
392 *Schaeffer noted*: Schaeffer, *À la Recherche d'une musique concrète*, p. 198.
392 *Sonatine, Scherzo, Concertino*: These titles belong, respectively, to works by Teuscher, Françaix, Jarnach, Roussel, Maderna, Maderna again, Herbert Brün, Bernd Alois Zimmermann, Boulez, Nilsson, Heiss (and Zimmermann), Hambraeus, Pousseur, Nilsson again, and Mayuzumi. See "Neue Musik in Darmstadt, 1946–1958," in *Darmstädter Beiträge zur neuen Musik* (1959), pp. 75–94.

392 *"Schoenberg's great achievement"*: Anders Beyer, *The Voice of Music: Conversations with Composers of Our Time*, ed. and trans. Jean Christensen and Anders Beyer (Ashgate, 2000), p. 178.

393 *"Everything had to be stylized"*: Hans Werner Henze, *Music and Politics: Collected Writings, 1953–81*, trans. Peter Labanyi (Faber, 1982), pp. 40–41.

393 *"my dear"*: Hans Werner Henze, *Bohemian Fifths: An Autobiography*, trans. Stewart Spencer (Princeton UP, 1999), p. 140.

393 Nocturnes and Arias: Ibid., p. 146.

393 *He described himself*: These terms can be found at the composer's website, www.stockhausen.org.

394 *Glenn Miller's band*: Robin Maconie, *Other Planets: The Music of Karlheinz Stockhausen* (Scarecrow, 2005), pp. 18–19.

395 *"This music sounds"*: Robin Maconie, *The Works of Karlheinz Stockhausen* (Clarendon, 1990), pp. 51–53.

395 *"showers of impulses"*: Karlheinz Stockhausen, "Music and Speech," *Die Reihe* 6 (Presser, 1964), p. 59.

396 *"composed the text"*: Stockhausen, "Music and Speech," p. 48.

397 *gas cloud*: For more, see James Harley, *Xenakis: His Life in Music* (Routledge, 2004), pp. 10–18.

397 *"The listener must be gripped"*: Notes to *40 Jahre Donaueschinger Musiktage, 1950–1990* (col legno AU-031800), p. 130.

398 *"the perfect rhythm"*: Iannis Xenakis, *Formalized Music: Thought and Mathematics in Composition* (Pendragon, 1992), p. 9. See also Nouritza Matossian, *Xenakis* (Kahn and Averill, 1986), p. 58, where similar images are used and the connection to the anti-Nazi demonstration is made explicit.

398 *"Their freedom"*: Luigi Nono, "Geschichte und Gegenwart in der Musik von heute," *Darmstädter Beiträge zur neuen Musik* (1960), p. 47.

399 *"indiscipline"*: Lev Koblyakov, *Pierre Boulez: A World of Harmony* (Harwood, 1990), p. 117.

399 *"Total but Totalitarian"*: Peyser, *Boulez*, p. 102.

399 *"I've often found"*: Wolfgang Fink's interview with Boulez, in the liner notes to *Pli selon pli* (DG 289 471-2).

399 *"New Frontier for American art"*: John F. Kennedy to Theodate Johnson, Sept. 13, 1960, *Musical America*, Oct. 1960, p. 11.

399 *"The only music he likes"*: Donna M. Binkiewicz, *Federalizing the Muse: United States Arts Policy and the National Endowment for the Arts, 1965–1980* (University of North Carolina Press, 2004), p. 49.

400 *composers at White House*: Harold C. Schonberg, "Casals Plays at White House; Last Appeared There in 1904," *New York Times*, Nov. 14, 1961.

400 *"Nice kids"*: RCSC, p. 285.

401 *"Everyone started writing"*: Rorem, *Knowing When to Stop*, p. 283.

401 *"This is the best"*: Kurt List, "Music Chronicle: The State of American Music," *Partisan Review*, Jan. 1948, p. 90.

401 *"No art at all"*: Theodor W. Adorno, *Aesthetic Theory*, ed. Gretel Adorno and Rolf Tiedemann, trans. C. Lenhardt (Routledge, 1984), p. 79.

402 *"A lie for a lie"*: Milton Babbitt, "Battle Cry," *politics*, Nov. 1945, p. 346.

402 *"absolutely different world"*: Milton Babbitt, *Words About Music*, ed. Stephen Dembski and Joseph N. Straus (University of Wisconsin Press, 1987), p. 31.

402 *"abandon resolutely"*: Roger Sessions, "Vienna—Vale, Ave," *Modern Music* 15:4 (May–June 1938), pp. 207–208.

403 *"complex, advanced"*: Milton Babbitt, "The Revolution in Sound: Electronic Music," in *The Collected Essays of Milton Babbitt*, ed. Stephen Peles et al. (Princeton UP, 2003), pp. 74–75.

403 *trichords*: See Andrew Mead, *An Introduction to the Music of Milton Babbitt* (Princeton UP, 1994), pp. 55–123.

404 *"I decided for once"*: David Schiff, *The Music of Elliott Carter*, 2nd ed. (Cornell UP, 1998), p. 55.

404 *Art Tatum*: Michael Hall, *Leaving Home: A Conducted Tour of Twentieth-Century Music with Simon Rattle* (Faber, 1996), p. 70.

404 *"Thy hand"*: Schiff, *Music of Elliott Carter*, p. 240.

405 *Piano Concerto in Berlin*: Ibid., p. 254.

406 *"I dare suggest"*: Milton Babbitt, "Who Cares If You Listen?," *High Fidelity* 8:2 (Feb. 1958), p. 126.

407 *"We are in"*: Leonard Bernstein, "American Musical Comedy," Oct. 7, 1956, reprinted in *The Joy of Music* (Simon and Schuster, 1959), p. 179.

409 *"Don't forget"*: Humphrey Burton, *Leonard Bernstein* (Doubleday, 1994), p. 102.

409 *"It is only after fifty"*: Leonard Bernstein, *Findings* (Simon and Schuster, 1982), p. 257.

12: "Grimes! Grimes!"

411 *"A bleak little place"*: E. M. Forster, "George Crabbe: The Poet and the Man,"

in *Benjamin Britten: Peter Grimes*, ed. Eric Crozier (John Lane/Bodley Head, 1946), p. 9.

411 *"I had not a single"*: W. G. Sebald, *The Rings of Saturn*, trans. Michael Hulse (New Directions, 1998), pp. 234 and 237.

412 *childhood home*: Beth Britten, *My Brother Benjamin* (Kensal Press, 1986), illustrations.

412 *"I believe in roots"*: Benjamin Britten, "On Winning the First Aspen Award," in *Contemporary Composers on Contemporary Music*, ed. Elliott Schwartz and Barney Childs (Da Capo, 1998), p. 122.

412 *"The dark warm flood"*: *The Poetical Works of George Crabbe* (Oxford UP, 1932), p. 198.

413 *"gift and personality"*: Britten, "On Winning the First Aspen Award," p. 118.

413 *Nono refused to shake*: John Amis, *Amiscellany: My Life, My Music* (Faber, 1986), p. 199.

414 *Tippett*: For one of Michael Tippett's commentaries on his sexuality, see his memoir, *Those Twentieth Century Blues* (Hutchinson, 1991), p. 52.

414 *"Is he musical?"*: Philip Brett, "Musicality, Essentialism, and the Closet," in *Queering the Pitch: The New Gay and Lesbian Musicology*, ed. Philip Brett, Elizabeth Wood, and Gary C. Thomas (Routledge, 1994), p. 11.

414 The Love Songs of Hafiz: See Stephen Downes, *Szymanowski, Eroticism, and the Voices of Mythology* (Ashgate, 2003); and Stephen O. Murray and Will Roscoe, *Islamic Homosexualities: Culture, History, and Literature* (NYU Press, 1997).

415 *glass of whiskey*: Humphrey Carpenter, *Benjamin Britten: A Biography* (Faber, 1992), pp. 3–4.

415 *"the fourth B"*: DMBB1, p. 12.

415 *harmonize before he could spell*: Imogen Holst, *Britten* (Crowell, 1965), p. 19.

415 *Victor Hugo setting*: David Matthews, *Britten* (Haus, 2003), p. 10.

416 *School Boy's Diary*: John Bridcut, *Britten's Children* (Faber, 2006), pp. 1–8.

416 *BBC*: For more on the early history of the BBC's modern-music programming, see Humphrey Carpenter, *The Envy of the World: Fifty Years of the BBC Third Programme and Radio 3, 1945–1996* (Weidenfeld and Nicolson, 1996); and Jennifer Doctor, *The BBC and Ultra-Modern Music, 1922–1936: Shaping a Nation's Tastes* (Cambridge UP, 1999).

416 *Schoenberg soiree*: DMBB1, pp. 127–28.

416 Wozzeck *on radio*: Carpenter, *Benjamin Britten*, p. 51.

416 *study with Berg*: DMBB1, p. 395; Carpenter, *Benjamin Britten*, p. 52. It seems possible that Britten's parents thought that Berg was homosexual and would corrupt their son; see DMBB1, p. 506.

417 *"Stand up and fold"*: *The English Auden: Poems, Essays, and Dramatic Writings, 1927–1939*, ed. Edward Mendelson (Faber, 1977), pp. 160–61.

417 *literary taste*: See Paul Kildea, "Britten, Auden, and 'Otherness,'" in *The Cambridge Companion to Benjamin Britten*, ed. Mervyn Cooke (Cambridge UP, 1999), pp. 38–39.

417 *enharmonic change*: Carpenter, *Benjamin Britten*, p. 16.

418 *Snape*: DMBB1, pp. 495–96.

418 *"thin-as-a-board juveniles"*: Ibid., pp. 1015–16.

418 *"waspishness, bitterness"*: Carpenter, *Benjamin Britten*, p. 501.

418 *"corpses"*: Ibid., p. 243.

419 *Britten traveled to America*: On the decision to leave, see DMBB1, pp. 619 and 634.

419 *"Holywood"*: Ibid., p. 610.

419 *Milestone*: Ibid. and DMBB2, pp. 692–95.

419 *"It would be nice"*: DMBB1, p. 567.

419 *7 Middagh*: Paul Bowles, *Without Stopping* (Ecco, 1985), pp. 233–35.

419 *"Everything here"*: DMBB2, p. 794.

420 *Violin Concerto and Spanish Civil War*: Matthews, *Britten*, p. 52.

421 *"He'd now the power"*: *Poetical Works of George Crabbe*, p. 197.

422 *"accidental murder"*: *Peter Grimes* materials, Britten-Pears Library, Aldeburgh. See Draft Scenario (Brett's L5), Johnson Line notes (L6), and Pears's list of scenes (L7).

422 *"Once we'd decided"*: Philip Brett, "'Peter Grimes': The Growth of the Libretto," in *The Making of "Peter Grimes": Notes and Commentaries*, ed. Paul Banks (Boydell, 2000), p. 67.

422 *"The queerness"*: DMBB2, p. 1189.

423 *"You will soon forget"*: *Peter Grimes* materials, Britten-Pears Library.

423 *"dramatic portrayal"*: Philip Brett, "'Peter Grimes': The Growth of the Libretto," p. 73; Philip Brett, "Salvation at Sea: *Billy Budd*," in *The Britten Companion*, ed. Christopher Palmer (Faber, 1984), p. 136.

423 *"The more vicious"*: "Opera's New Face," *Time*, Feb. 16, 1948, p. 63.

424 *"Why did you do this?"*: For more on Britten's use of conversational rhythms, see

Philip Rupprecht, *Britten's Musical Language* (Cambridge UP, 2001).

425 Porgy and Bess: DMBB2, pp. 637–38.

427 *Passacaglia's programmatic indications*: Banks, *Making of Peter Grimes*, p. 205.

430 *"Sadler's Wells!"*: DMBB2, p. 1264.

430 *"not a bore"*: Thomson's review of Feb. 13, 1948, reprinted in DMBB3, p. 378.

431 *Scotland Yard interview*: Carpenter, *Benjamin Britten*, p. 335.

431 *FBI file*: Donald Mitchell, "Violent Climates," in Cooke, *Cambridge Companion to Benjamin Britten*, pp. 211–16.

431 *homosexuality and* Billy Budd: The erotic implications of the scenario had already been noticed by the critic F. O. Matthiessen, who in 1941 took note of Claggart's "soft yearning" for Billy and the "sexual element in Claggart's malevolence." See Matthiessen, *The American Renaissance: Art and Expression in the Age of Emerson and Whitman* (Oxford UP, 1941), pp. 506–7. Matthiessen, incidentally, committed suicide in 1950, just as Britten was starting work on *Billy Budd*.

432 *interview chords*: For a discussion of their erotic implications, see Clifford Hindley, "Eros in Life and Death in *Billy Budd* and *Death in Venice*," in Cooke, *Cambridge Companion to Benjamin Britten*, pp. 151–53.

433 *David Hemmings*: Carpenter, *Benjamin Britten*, p. 357.

433 *Harry Morris*: Bridcut, *Britten's Children*, pp. 46–53. The two authors who have studied Britten's relationships with boys come to different conclusions. Humphrey Carpenter portrays a would-be pedophile who plies boys with martinis and encourages them to swim nude in his swimming pool (*Benjamin Britten*, pp. 350–58). Bridcut tells the same stories but puts them in a less sinister light, concluding that "whatever shadows may have lurked in Britten's mind, his effect on these boys was benign, wholesome, and inspiring" (*Britten's Children*, p. xii). The truth is probably somewhere in between, or unknowable.

435 A Child of Our Time: For more, see Kenneth Gloag, *Tippett, "A Child of Our Time"* (Cambridge UP, 1999).

435 *Shostakovich and Britten meeting*: LFS, p. 219.

436 *"great works of the human spirit"*: IGSF, p. 114.

436 *"You great composer"*: Michael Oliver, *Benjamin Britten* (Phaidon, 1996), p. 170.

436 *"They've been pursuing me"*: IGSF, pp. 91–92.

436 *"I am scared"*: EWS, p. 377.

436 *"Our disappointment"*: Ibid., p. 348.

437 *"The title page"*: IGSF, p. 91.

438 *"a chain of metamorphoses"*: Lyudmila Kovnatskaya, "Shostakovich and Britten: Some Parallels," in *Shostakovich in Context*, ed. Rosamund Bartlett (Oxford UP, 2000), p. 187.

439 *"peculiar glow"*: "Editor's Note," Symphonies nos. 14 and 15 (State Publishers "Music," 1980).

439 *"gloomy, introverted"*: EWS, p. 305.

439 *"I didn't"*: Ibid., p. 470.

439 *"Now has struck"*: IGSF, pp. 165 and 306–7.

440 *Donald Mitchell speculated*: See his notes to Britten's live recording of Symphony No. 14 and his own *Nocturne* (BBC 8013-2).

440 *Lou Gehrig's disease*: EWS, pp. 441–42.

440 *"very tense"*: Carpenter, *Benjamin Britten*, p. 541.

440 *Władysław Moes*: " 'I Was Thomas Mann's Tadzio,' " in *Benjamin Britten: Death in Venice*, ed. Donald Mitchell (Cambridge UP, 1987), pp. 184–85.

441 *Mann's unfinished works*: Donald Prater, *Thomas Mann: A Life* (Oxford UP, 1995), p. 88.

441 *"He talked quite calmly"*: Carpenter, *Benjamin Britten*, p. 543.

441 *"Ben is writing"*: Ibid., p. 546.

442 *gamelan scale*: Mervyn Cooke, "Britten and the Gamelan," in Mitchell, *Benjamin Britten: Death in Venice*, pp. 122–23. See also Mervyn Cooke, *Britten and the Far East: Asian Influences in the Music of Benjamin Britten* (Boydell, 1998); and Mervyn Cooke, "Distant Horizons: From Pagodaland to the Church Parables," in Cooke, *Cambridge Companion to Benjamin Britten*, pp. 167–87.

442 *known from McPhee*: Cooke, *Britten and the Far East*, pp. 27–28.

442 *"it was as if"*: Thomas Mann, *Death in Venice and Other Stories*, trans. David Luke (Bantam, 1988), p. 263.

443 *Alexander Dunkel*: Author's interview, July 19, 2004.

443 *"I was so taken aback"*: IGSF, p. 193.

443 *salute at Met*: David J. Baker, " 'It *Vas* Premiere: The Night Shostakovich Came to the Met," *Opera News*, Dec. 10, 1994, p. 17.

443 *Viola Sonata*: EWS, pp. 528–32; LFS, p. 286.

443 *"I want to say"*: DMBB2, p. 1154.

13. Zion Park

444 *"I have found"*: Thomas Mann, *Doktor Faustus* (Fischer, 1971), p. 477.

445 *"Adrian Leverkühn might"*: *Letters of Thomas Mann, 1889–1955*, trans. Richard Winston and Clara Winston (Knopf, 1971), pp. 549–50. Golo Mann once wrote to Britten: "My father, incidentally, used to say, that if it ever came to some musical illustration of his novel, *Doctor Faustus*, you would be the composer to do it." See Patrick Carnegy, "The Novella Transformed: Thomas Mann as Opera," in *Benjamin Britten: Death in Venice*, ed. Donald Mitchell (Cambridge UP, 1987), p. 168. Britten and Leverkühn both set William Blake's "The Sick Rose" and Verlaine's "Chanson d'automne"; both had a taste for archaic folk poetry and medieval subjects; both composed a Shakespeare comedy. *Doctor Faustus* can be seen on the shelves of the library of the Red House in Aldeburgh, but, according to Donald Mitchell, Britten probably never read it.

445 *"black masterpieces"*: "Entretien avec Claude Samuel," booklet included with the 1988 Erato box-set recording of Messiaen's works (ECD 75505), p. 16.

445 *Pousseur*: Paul Griffiths, *Modern Music: The Avant Garde Since 1945* (Braziller, 1981), p. 258. There are also references to the fictional composer in Henze's Third Violin Concerto; Peter Maxwell Davies's *Resurrection* (see John Warnaby, "Peter Maxwell Davies's Recent Music, and Its Debt to His Earlier Scores," in *Perspectives on Peter Maxwell Davies*, ed. Richard McGregor [Ashgate, 2000], pp. 76–77; and notes to recording of *Resurrection* [Collins Classics 70342]); Poul Ruders's *Corpus cum figuris*; Bengt Hambraeus's *Apocalipsis cum figuris secundum Dürer*; and Alfred Schnittke's *Historia von D. Johann Fausten*, among others.

445 *"the century of death"*: Leonard Bernstein, *The Unanswered Question: Six Talks at Harvard* (Harvard UP, 1976), p. 313.

445 *"Grand Hotel Abyss"*: Georg Lukács, *The Theory of the Novel*, trans. Anna Bostock (MIT Press, 1971), p. 22.

446 *Resurrection as Hiroshima*: NSPHM, p. 337.

446 *playing* Messiah: Ibid., p. 333.

446 *"Visited Messiaen"*: "European Diary," 1949, ACLC.

447 *communal bathroom*: NSPHM, p. 340.

447 *Esa-Pekka Salonen*: Author's interview, March 25, 2003.

447 *Kent Nagano*: Author's interview, Oct. 8, 2002.

447 *"The tonic triad, the dominant"*: Claude Samuel, *Olivier Messiaen: Music and Color*, trans. E. Thomas Glasow (Amadeus, 1986), pp. 51–52.

447 *"remote overtones"*: Arnold Schoenberg, *Theory of Harmony*, trans. Roy E. Carter (University of California Press, 1983), p. 318.

447 *"the chord of resonance"*: Olivier Messiaen, *The Technique of My Musical Language*, trans. John Satterfield (Leduc, 1956), p. 50 and ex. 208.

448 *Messiaen's modes generate*: See Paul Griffiths, *Olivier Messiaen and the Music of Time* (Cornell UP, 1985), pp. 38–39. See also Messiaen, *Technique of My Musical Language*, ex. 366.

448 *"rainbows of chords"*: Antoine Goléa, *Rencontres avec Olivier Messiaen* (Julliard, 1960), p. 30.

449 Fêtes des belles eaux: See Nigel Simeone, *Olivier Messiaen: A Bibliographical Catalogue of Messiaen's Works* (Schneider, 1998), pp. 192 and 194.

449 *"ever splashier paroxysms"*: Griffiths, *Olivier Messiaen and the Music of Time*, p. 110.

450 *"an angel wearing lipstick"*: NSPHM, p. 151.

450 *"to open up"*: Virgil Thomson, *Music Reviewed, 1940–1954* (Vintage, 1967), p. 160.

450 *"She had to be put"*: "Interview with Yvonne Loriod," in *The Messiaen Companion*, ed. Peter Hill (Faber, 1995), p. 294.

450 *"Tristan trilogy"*: Griffiths, *Olivier Messiaen and the Music of Time*, p. 124.

451 *"We are all in a profound"*: NSPHM, p. 214.

451 *"Messiaen is developing"*: *The Boulez-Cage Correspondence*, ed. Jean-Jacques Nattiez, trans. Robert Samuels (Cambridge UP, 1993), p. 126.

452 *"Birds are my first"*: Goléa, *Rencontres avec Olivier Messiaen*, pp. 218–19.

452 *"I'm anxious"*: NSPHM, p. 208.

453 *Johnson has observed*: See Robert Sherlaw Johnson, *Messiaen* (University of California Press, 1975), p. 135.

454 *Dingle notes*: See Christopher Dingle, "'La statue reste sur son piédestal': Messiaen's *La Transfiguration* and Vatican II," *Tempo* 212 (April 2000), pp. 8–11.

454 *"an immense cake"*: Samuel, *Olivier Messiaen: Music and Color*, p. 160.

454 *"immense solitude"*: Catherine Massip, ed., *Portrait(s) d'Olivier Messiaen* (Bibliothèque National de France, 1996), pp. 20–21.

456 *"I am here"*: JCS, pp. 109 and 126.

457 *"Do you agree"*: Ibid., p. 48.
457 *boxing gloves*: David Osmond-Smith, "Bussotti, Sylvano," in NG 4, p. 678.
458 *"We cannot"*: Paul Attinello, "Imploding the System: Kagel and the Deconstruction of Modernism," in *Postmodern Music, Postmodern Thought*, ed. Judy Lochhead and Joseph Auner (Routledge, 2002), p. 271.
458 *Berio would criticize*: See, for example, his Harvard lectures of 1993–94, collected in Luciano Berio, *Remembering the Future* (Harvard UP, 2006), esp. p. 21.
459 *"field composition"*: Karlheinz Stockhausen, ". . . how time passes . . . ," *Die Reihe* 3 (Presser, 1959), pp. 32–33.
459 *propellers vibrating*: Robin Maconie, *The Works of Karlheinz Stockhausen* (Clarendon, 1990), p. 94.
459 *sonorism*: See Adrian Thomas, *Polish Music Since Szymanowski* (Cambridge UP, 2005), pp. 83–109.
460 *"Composers often"*: Charles Bodman Rae, *The Music of Lutosławski*, 3rd ed. (Omnibus, 1999), p. 75.
460 *"I could start"*: Bernard Jacobson, *A Polish Renaissance* (Phaidon, 1996), p. 92.
460 *from a great height*: Ibid., p. 99.
460 *"Play a vibration"*: Jonathan Harvey, *The Music of Stockhausen* (University of California Press, 1975), p. 113.
461 *an incendiary essay*: Cornelius Cardew, *Stockhausen Serves Imperialism* (ubuclassics, 2004), pp. 47–75.
461 *"an intellectualist"*: TMDF, p. 253. Other quotations are on pp. 256–57 and 395.
461 *"metacollage"*: Jonathan Cott, *Stockhausen: Conversations with the Composer* (Picador, 1974), p. 174.
463 *in search of drinks*: Humphrey Carpenter, *Benjamin Britten: A Biography* (Faber, 1992), pp. 482–83.
463 *"witch hunts"*: *Bernd Alois Zimmermann: "Du und Ich und Ich und die Welt": Dokumente aus den Jahren 1940 bis 1950*, ed. Heribert Henrich (Wolke, 1998), p. 72.
463 *"O Germany"*: Ibid., pp. 74–75.
463 *"Watch with me"*: TMDF, p. 516.
463 *looked askance*: "Kompositionstechnik und Inspiration" (1949), in *"Du und Ich und Ich und die Welt,"* pp. 124–25.
464 *steadily scrubbing out*: Archives of the Akademie der Künste, Berlin.
465 *"When you are accepted"*: György Ligeti, lecture at the New England Conservatory, March 10, 1993.
465 *Ligeti's wartime experiences*: Richard Toop, *György Ligeti* (Phaidon, 1999), pp. 19–22; "Interview with the Composer," in Paul Griffiths, *György Ligeti* (Robson Books, 1983), pp. 16–18; Richard Steinitz, *György Ligeti: Music of the Imagination* (Northeastern UP, 2003), pp. 19–21; György Ligeti, *"Träumen Sie in Farbe?": György Ligeti im Gespräch mit Eckhard Roelcke* (Paul Zsolnay, 2003), pp. 46–60.
466 *Ligeti reads Mann*: Wolfgang Burde, *György Ligeti: Eine Monographie* (Atlantis, 1993), p. 43.
466 *"a knife in Stalin's heart"*: Steinitz, *György Ligeti*, p. 57.
466 *escape from Hungary*: Ibid., pp. 70–71.
466 *Stockhausen broadcast*: Griffiths, *György Ligeti*, p. 22.
466 *"I don't like gurus"*: Richard Dufallo, *Trackings: Composers Speak with Richard Dufallo* (Oxford UP, 1989), p. 333.
467 *"True, there were"*: Ligeti, *"Träumen Sie in Farbe?"* p. 98.
467 *"event - pause - event"*: Ligeti, "Metamorphoses of Musical Form," in *Die Reihe* 7 (Presser, 1965), p. 10.
468 *moves "through all the shades"*: TMDF, p. 393.
470 *"peasant devotion"*: Francis Poulenc, *Entretiens avec Claude Rostand* (Julliard, 1954), p. 109.
471 *Aquinas wrote*: Vincent P. Benitez, "Simultaneous Contrast and Additive Designs in Olivier Messiaen's Opera, *Saint François d'Assise*," *Music Theory Online* 8:2 (Aug. 2002), note 45.
472 *"Certain people are annoyed"*: Interview with Jean-Christophe Marti, in notes to Kent Nagano's recording of *Saint François d'Assise* (DG 445 176-2).
472 *refusal to "play God"*: Anthony Pople, "Messiaen's Musical Language: An Introduction," in Hill, *Messiaen Companion*, p. 46.

14. Beethoven Was Wrong

473 Sgt. Pepper's *at the Schlosskeller*: Richard Toop, *György Ligeti* (Phaidon, 1999), p. 155.
473 *"A Day in the Life"*: Allan Kozinn, *The Beatles* (Phaidon, 1995), p. 153; Mark Hertsgaard, *A Day in the Life: The Music and Artistry of the Beatles* (Delacorte, 1995), pp. 7–8; Mark Lewisohn, *The Beatles Recording Sessions* (Harmony, 1988).
473 *"Tomorrow Never Knows"*: See Ian MacDonald, *Revolution in the Head: The Beatles' Records and the Sixties* (Pimlico, 1998), p. 169; April 6 and 7, 1966, entries,

in Lewisohn, *Beatles Recording Sessions*; and Bob Spitz, *The Beatles: The Biography* (Little, Brown, 2005), p. 601.

474 *Grateful Dead and Stockhausen*: Derek Beres, *Global Beat Fusion: The History of the Future of Music* (iUniverse, 2005), p. 32.

474 *Zappa calls Varèse*: Frank Zappa, "Edgard Varèse: Idol of My Youth," *Stereo Review* 26:6 (June 1971), pp. 62–63.

474 *"Listening to Bengt"*: Recording of Hambraeus's *Constellations II* and *Interferences* (Limelight 86052).

475 *"Schoenberg gives"*: Edward Strickland, *American Composers: Dialogues on Contemporary Music* (Indiana UP, 1991), p. 46.

475 *"a drift away from narrative"*: Brian Eno, foreword to Mark Prendergast, *The Ambient Century: From Mahler to Trance—the Evolution of Sound in the Electronic Age* (Bloomsbury, 2000), p. xi.

476 *Young and Dolphy*: Interview with Young in Strickland, *American Composers*, pp. 56–57.

476 *Glass and jazz*: Ev Grimes, "Interview: Education," in *Writings on Glass: Essays, Interviews, Criticism*, ed. Richard Kostelanetz (University of California Press, 1999), p. 16.

476 "serious *musicians*": LeRoi Jones [Amiri Baraka], *Blues People: Negro Music in White America* (Quill, 1999), p. 188.

476 *Bartók's chords of fourths*: Lewis Porter, *John Coltrane: His Life and Music* (University of Michigan Press, 1998), p. 125.

476 *"We had some fundamental"*: Dizzy Gillespie, with Al Fraser, *To Be, or Not . . . to Bop* (Da Capo, 1985), pp. 140–41.

477 *"pedal point"*: From Mingus's notes to *The Black Saint and the Sinner Lady* (Impulse!/MCA IMPD-174).

477 *"You play what* you *want"*: Grover Sales, *Jazz: America's Classical Music* (Da Capo, 1992), p. 127.

477 *"It is a way"*: Gunther Schuller, "Third Stream" (1961) and "Third Stream Revisited" (1981), in *Musings: The Musical Worlds of Gunther Schuller* (Oxford UP, 1986), pp. 114–20. The quotation comes from the second essay, p. 119. For Schuller and *Free Jazz*, see Whitney Balliett, *Collected Works: A Journal of Jazz, 1954–2000* (St. Martin's, 2000), pp. 114–17.

478 *"The music just comes out"*: Author's interview with Reich, April 14, 2003.

478 *"smelly old house"*: Ann M. Pescatello, *Charles Seeger: A Life in American Music* (University of Pittsburgh Press, 1992), p. 53.

479 *"an undefiled Eden"*: Michael Hicks, *Henry Cowell, Bohemian* (University of Illinois Press, 2002), p. 13.

479 *"There is a new race"*: Carol J. Oja, *Making Music Modern: New York in the 1920s* (Oxford UP, 2000), p. 128. See also Hicks, *Henry Cowell*, p. 39.

479 *Native American thundersticks*: See Cowell's *Ensemble*, composed 1924/56.

479 *Nancarrow*: Cowell's suggestion about the player piano is found in his *New Musical Resources* (Cambridge UP, 1996), p. 65. For more, see Kyle Gann, *The Music of Conlon Nancarrow* (Cambridge UP, 1995), esp. pp. 5–7.

480 *"find a way* outside*"*: Bob Gilmore, *Harry Partch: A Biography* (Yale UP, 1998), p. 21.

480 *Gilmore's biography*: See ibid., p. 18.

480 *Ramon Novarro*: Ibid., p. 47.

481 *"Faustian" strain*: Harry Partch, *Genesis of a Music: An Account of a Creative Work, Its Roots and Its Fulfillments*, 2nd ed. (Da Capo, 1974), pp. 8 and 16.

482 *"There is, thank God"*: Philip Blackburn, ed., *Harry Partch: Enclosure 3* (American Composers Forum, 1997), p. 93.

482 *a reading of Partch's*: Leta E. Miller and Fredric Lieberman, *Lou Harrison: Composing a World* (Oxford UP, 1998), pp. 44–45.

482 *"Use only the essentials"*: Ibid., p. 23.

483 *Cage and Cowell*: Leta E. Miller, "Henry Cowell and John Cage: Intersections and Influences, 1933–1941," *Journal of the American Musicological Society* 59:1 (Spring 2006), pp. 47–111.

483 *"vogue of profundity"*: JCS, p. 130.

483 *Beethoven had misled*: Calvin Tomkins, *The Bride and the Bachelors: Five Masters of the Avant-Garde* (Penguin, 1976), p. 102. See also Martin Duberman, *Black Mountain: An Exploration in Community* (Dutton, 1972), p. 288.

483 *"Beethoven was wrong!"*: John Ashbery, discussion at Guggenheim Museum, May 14, 2001.

483 Vexations *performance*: Harold C. Schonberg, Richard Shepard, Raymond Ericson, Brian O'Doherty, Sam Zolotow, Anon., Howard Klein, and Marjorie Rubin, "A Long, Long, Long Night (and Day) at the Piano," *New York Times*, Sept. 11, 1963.

483 *Warhol*: Steven Watson, *Factory Made: Warhol and the Sixties* (Pantheon, 2003), pp. 108 and 136.

483 *Feldman's height and weight*: B. H. Friedman, "Morton Feldman: Painting Sounds," in

Give My Regards to Eighth Street: Collected Writings of Morton Feldman, ed. B. H. Friedman (Exact Change, 2000), p. xi.

483 *"Wasn't that beautiful?"*: *Morton Feldman Essays*, ed. Walter Zimmermann (Beginner, 1985), pp. 36–37. See also Tomkins, *The Bride and the Bachelors*, p. 107; MFS, p. 30; and "Hisses, Applause for Webern Opus," *New York Times*, Jan. 27, 1950.

483 *"an absolutely unforgettable"*: SRW, p. 202.

485 *Wolpe, Varèse*: MFS, pp. 31 and 257.

486 *"more direct, more immediate"*: Zimmermann, *Morton Feldman Essays*, p. 38.

486 *"Music seems to have"*: Wilfrid Mellers, *Music in a New Found Land: Themes and Developments in the History of American Music* (Knopf, 1965), p. 191.

486 *"silent protest"*: MFS, p. 152.

487 *"Can't you hear"*: Alvin Curran's communication to author, May 14, 2006.

487 *"There's an aspect"*: "Morton Feldman, Earle Brown, and Heinz-Klaus Metzger in Discussion" (1972), as heard on the LP set *Music Before Revolution* (German EMI/Odeon 1C 165-28954/57Y).

488 *kabbalistic thought*: For informed speculation on this topic, see Raphael Mostel, "The Tale of a Chance Meeting That Set the Music World on Its Ear," *Forward*, Feb. 2, 2001.

488 *"wipes everything out"*: MFS, p. 136.

488 *"Western civilization music"*: "Morton Feldman, Earle Brown, and Heinz-Klaus Metzger in Discussion."

489 *"He writes a piece"*: *Give My Regards To Eighth Street*, p. 48.

489 *Sibelius assignment*: See Morton Feldman Papers, Music Library, SUNY Buffalo. One exam question reads as follows: "By means of a Schenkerian sketch or other method familiar to you, analyze the first movement of the Sibelius Symphony No. 5. In a brief essay, comment on Sibelius's use of orchestration to highlight aspects of the formal and harmonic structures of this composition."

489 *"Would that I had known"*: Milton Babbitt, "On Having Been and Still Being an American Composer," in *Perspectives on Musical Aesthetics*, ed. John Rahn (Norton, 1994), pp. 146–47.

489 *colorful testimonials*: See Michael Broyles, *Mavericks and Other Traditions in American Music* (Yale UP, 2004), pp. 169–71. Discussion of the alleged atonal, twelve-tone, and/or serialist domination of American composition departments in the fifties and sixties can be found in Joseph N. Straus, "The Myth of Serial 'Tyranny' in the 1950s and 1960s," *Musical Quarterly* 83:3 (Fall 1999), pp. 301–43; and Anne C. Shreffler, "The Myth of Empirical Historiography: A Response to Joseph N. Straus," *Musical Quarterly* 84:1 (Spring 2000), pp. 30–39.

490 *trenchant commentaries*: See Kyle Gann, *Music Downtown* (University of California Press, 2006), pp. 1–15.

491 *Fluxus*: For documentation of the works and manifestos mentioned, see the websites www.medienkunstnetz.de and www.artnotart.com.

491 *ONCE Festival*: For the definitive account, see Leta E. Miller, "ONCE and Again: The Evolution of a Legendary Festival," essay included with the box set *Music from the ONCE Festival, 1961–1966* (New World 80567-2). See also Kyle Gann, "I-80 Avant-Garde," *Village Voice*, Nov. 17, 1987.

491 *"took matters"*: Gordon Mumma, "The ONCE Festival and How It Happened" (1967), reprinted at brainwashed.com/mumma/writing.html (accessed July 17, 2006).

491 Music for Solo Performer: See N. B. Aldrich, "What Is Sound Art," at emfinstitute.emf.org/articles/aldrich03/lucier.html (accessed July 17, 2006).

492 *"dancers went around"*: Kyle Gann, *American Music in the Twentieth Century* (Schirmer Books, 1997), p. 262; see also Joel Chadabe, *Electric Sound: The Past and Promise of Electronic Music* (Prentice Hall, 1997), p. 86.

492 *Young's childhood*: William Duckworth, *Talking Music: Conversations with John Cage, Philip Glass, Laurie Anderson, and Five Generations of American Experimental Composers* (Schirmer Books, 1995), p. 218. See also Keith Potter, *Four Musical Minimalists: La Monte Young, Terry Riley, Steve Reich, Philip Glass* (Cambridge UP, 2000), p. 23.

493 *"sense of space"*: Potter, *Four Musical Minimalists*, p. 23.

493 *In a 1989 performance*: See Edward Strickland, *Minimalism: Origins* (Indiana UP, 1993), p. 119. The description of the Trio is also based on a performance of the just-intonation version at Young's MELA Foundation on Sept. 24, 2005. See also Potter, *Four Musical Minimalists*, p. 39.

493 *Terry Jennings and Dennis Johnson*: Strickland, *Minimalism*, p. 129; and Michael Nyman, *Experimental Music: Cage and Beyond* (Cambridge UP, 1999), pp. 140–41.

494 *Young's* Composition *and* Piano Piece: Potter, *Four Musical Minimalists*, pp. 51–52.

494 *according to legend*: Strickland, *Minimalism*, p. 137.
494 *"the best drug connection"*: Testimony of Billy Name, in Legs McNeil and Gillian McCain, *Please Kill Me: The Uncensored Oral History of Punk* (Penguin, 1996), p. 4.
494 *Indian influence*: Strickland, *American Composers*, p. 65. See also Terry Riley, "The Trinity of Eternal Music," in *Sound and Light: La Monte Young and Marian Zazeela*, ed. William Duckworth and Richard Fleming (Bucknell UP, 1996), pp. 98–103.
494 *"To be held"*: Dave Smith, "Following a Straight Line: La Monte Young," *Contact* 18 (Winter 1977–78), p. 5.
495 *Cale's drones*: Victor Bockris and Gerard Malanga, *Up-Tight: The Velvet Underground Story* (Omnibus, 2002), p. 13; Potter, *Four Musical Minimalists*, p. 71.
495 *"What La Monte"*: Duckworth, *Talking Music*, p. 282.
495 *marijuana and mescaline*: Ibid., p. 269.
496 *"I want this kind"*: Interview with Riley in notes to the recording *Music for The Gift, Bird of Paradise, Mescalin Mix* (Organ of Corti 1).
496 *"a very straight guy"*: Strickland, *American Composers*, p. 112.
496 *"So What"*: Ibid., p. 113.
496 *"the sun coming up"*: K. Robert Schwarz, *Minimalists* (Phaidon, 1996), p. 39.
496 *"Climaxes of great sonority"*: Alfred Frankenstein, "Music Like None Other on Earth," *San Francisco Sunday Chronicle*, Nov. 8, 1964.
496 *chiming Cs*: Strickland, *American Composers*, p. 113.
497 *"the Pentagon was turned"*: Riley's notes to the recording of *A Rainbow in Curved Air* (CBS MK7315).
497 *"REICH"*: The composer moved out of Manhattan in 2006.
497 *wheels on rails*: Author's interview with Reich.
497 *"If I had been"*: SRW, p. 151.
497 *Reich's favorite records*: Reich's communication to author, May 4, 2006.
497 *"If you want"*: SRW, p. 203.
497 *Coltrane fifty times*: Strickland, *American Composers*, p. 38.
497 *A. M. Jones*: SRW, p. 10.
497 Event III/Coffee Break: Phil Lesh, *Searching for the Sound: My Life with the Grateful Dead* (Little, Brown, 2005), pp. 37–38.
499 *"It's an acoustical reality"*: Author's interview with Reich.
500 *Mahler blows Lesh's mind*: See Dennis McNally, *A Long Strange Trip: The Inside History of the Grateful Dead* (Broadway Books, 2002), p. 69; and Lesh, *Searching for the Sound*, p. 35.
500 *"In the group of people"*: Potter, *Four Musical Minimalists*, p. 170.
500 *Michael Nyman*: See his *Experimental Music*, pp. 1–9.
501 *"I am interested"*: SRW, p. 34.
501 *"All music turns out"*: Ibid., p. 35.
502 *commented to Strickland*: Strickland, *Minimalism*, pp. 222–23.
502 Four Organs *scandal*: For various accounts, see ibid., p. 222; Schwarz, *Minimalists*, pp. 70–71; Alan Rich, "Surging Forward by Standing Still," *LA Weekly*, March 15, 2006; and Harold C. Schonberg, "Concert Fuss," *New York Times*, Jan. 20, 1973.
503 *"a wasteland"*: John Rockwell, *All American Music: Composition in the Late Twentieth Century* (Knopf, 1983), p. 111.
504 *Chelsea Light Moving*: Potter, *Four Musical Minimalists*, pp. 260–61.
504 *Robert Hughes*: Schwarz, *Minimalists*, pp. 122–23.
505 *twelve-tone row*: Tim Page, "Music in 12 Parts," in Kostelanetz, *Writings on Glass*, p. 101.
506 *ninety thousand dollars*: Tim Page, "Philip Glass," in ibid., p. 7; Philip Glass, *Music by Philip Glass* (Harper and Row, 1987), p. 54.
507 *"The music danced"*: Rockwell, *All American Music*, pp. 109–10.
508 *"poetic justice"*: Author's interview with Reich.
508 *Cale and Young*: Smith, "Following a Straight Line," pp. 4 and 7.
508 *Cale shocks Mme Koussevitzky*: John Cale and Victor Bockris, *What's Welsh for Zen: The Autobiography of John Cale* (Bloomsbury, 1999), p. 53.
508 *"six ounces of opium"*: Ibid., p. 64.
509 *MacLise quit*: Bockris and Malanga, *Up-Tight*, p. 28.
510 *Eno's early musical loves*: Prendergast, *The Ambient Century*, pp. 116–18.
510 *greeting him*: Author's interview with Reich.
510 *techno, house, and rave*: See Simon Reynolds, *Generation Ecstasy: Into the World of Techno and Rave Culture* (Routledge, 1999), pp. 36 and 200, for this crossover.
510 *turntable lineage*: For more, see Mark Katz, *Capturing Sound: How Technology Has Changed Music* (University of California Press, 2004).
511 *"Repetition is a form"*: Brian Tamm, *Brian*

Eno: His Music and the Vertical Color of Sound (Da Capo, 1995), p. 25.

511 *"Repetitive musicking"*: Robert Fink, *Repeating Ourselves: American Minimal Music as Cultural Practice* (University of California Press, 2005), pp. 21–22.

15. Sunken Cathedrals

512 *Adams at Brushy Ridge*: This description is based on the author's visit in June 2000. A new house has since been built.

514 *Mahler's temperature*: "Das Befinden Gustav Mahlers," *Neue Freie Presse,* May 18, 1911.

517 *"Parlez-moi d'amour"*: Peter Burt, *The Music of Tōru Takemitsu* (Cambridge UP, 2001), p. 22; and Tōru Takemitsu, "Contemporary Music in Japan," *Perspectives of New Music* 27:2 (1989), pp. 199–200.

517 "*picture scroll unrolled*": Yoko Narazaki, "Takemitsu, Tōru," in NG 25, p. 23.

517 *"No, this piece"*: Sheila Melvin and Jindong Cai, *Rhapsody in Red: How Western Classical Music Became Chinese* (Algora, 2004), p. 333.

518 *Jiang Qing's musical tastes*: Ibid., pp. 254, 266–67, 252.

518 *He Luting's interrogation*: Ibid., pp. 236–39.

519 *"Who's Mozart?"*: Ibid., p. 293; and "Tan Dun on the International Stage," *Sinorama,* July 2001.

521 *"We had the simplicity"*: www.redpoppymusic.com/artists.html (accessed Jan. 16, 2007).

522 *Ferneyhough*: The bar described is II/40.

523 *IRCAM budget*: Georgina Born, *Rationalizing Culture: IRCAM, Boulez, and the Institutionalization of the Musical Avant-Garde* (University of California Press, 1995), p. 85.

524 *"Well, perhaps"*: Stephen Johnson, "When the Wall Came Down," *BBC Music Magazine,* Nov. 2002, p. 20.

524 *"twelve very different"*: Malcolm Ball, "Licht aus Stockhausen," www.stockhausen.org/licht_by_malcolm_ball.html (accessed Aug. 13, 2006).

525 In C *at Darmstadt*: Richard Toop, *György Ligeti* (Phaidon, 1999), p. 146.

525 *Andriessen*: For more, see Maja Trochimczyk, ed., *The Music of Louis Andriessen* (Routledge, 2002).

526 *"I have to acknowledge"*: David Bundler, 1996 interview with Gérard Grisey, www.angelfire.com/music2/davidbundler/grisey.html (accessed Aug. 13, 2006).

527 *"My music has been concerned"*: Andrew Clements, "Helmut Lachenmann: Truth, Beauty, and Relevance," notes to recording of *Streichtrio, TemA, Trio fluido* (Auvidis Montaigne MO 782023).

527 *"uncontaminated"*: Ulrich Mosch, "Lachenmann, Helmut," in NG 14, p. 93.

528 *Ilya Musin and Shostakovich*: Martin Anderson, obituary for Ilya Musin, *Independent,* June 10, 1999.

529 *"I set down"*: Alex Ross, "The Connoisseur of Chaos," *New Republic,* Sept. 28, 1992.

529 *"had an incredible influence"*: Author's interview with Schnittke, Feb. 5, 1994.

529 *Shostakovich and Schnittke*: See Alexander Ivashkin, *Alfred Schnittke* (Phaidon, 1996), pp. 60–72.

529 *"I want you"*: Karen Campbell, "A Russian Composer's Path to Freedom," *Christian Science Monitor,* Aug. 27, 1997.

530 *"transfigurations"*: Laurel E. Fay, program notes for a concert of Gubaidulina's music at Carnegie Hall, Dec. 6, 2006.

530 *Pärt's study of polyphony*: Paul Hillier, *Arvo Pärt* (Oxford UP, 1997), p. 65.

531 *ECM sales*: Tina Pelikan's communication to the author.

531 *Pärt in AIDS ward*: Patrick Giles, "Sharps & Flats," *Salon,* Nov. 18, 1999.

535 *Adams's childhood and college experiences*: Details from the author's interviews with Adams in June 2000 and from a forthcoming memoir by Adams.

Epilogue

543 *"imaginary country"*: *Debussy Letters,* ed. François Lesure and Roger Nichols, trans. Roger Nichols (Harvard UP, 1987), p. 118.

SUGGESTED LISTENING

Ten Recommended Recordings

Schoenberg, Berg, and Webern, Pieces for Orchestra, Levine / Berlin Philharmonic (DG/ArkivMusic.com)

Stravinsky, *Rite of Spring* and *Petrushka*, Stravinsky / Columbia Symphony (Sony)

Bartók, Concerto for Orchestra and Music for Strings, Percussion, and Celesta, Reiner / Chicago Symphony (RCA)

Sibelius, Symphonies Nos. 4–7, Karajan / Berlin Philharmonic (DG)

Britten, *Peter Grimes*, Davis / Royal Opera House (Philips)

Copland the Populist, Tilson Thomas / San Francisco Symphony (RCA)

Shostakovich, Symphonies Nos. 5 and 9, Bernstein / New York Philharmonic (Sony)

Messiaen, *Quartet for the End of Time*, Tashi (RCA)

Ligeti, *Atmosphères* and *Lontano*, Nott / Berlin Philharmonic (Teldec)

Reich, *Music for 18 Musicians* (ECM)

Twenty More

Panorama: Claude Debussy (DG)

Mahler, Sixth Symphony, Abbado / Berlin Philharmonic (DG)

Strauss, *Salome*, Karajan / Vienna Philharmonic (EMI)

Berg, *Wozzeck*, Abbado / Vienna Philharmonic (DG)

Janáček and Schulhoff, String Quartets, Talich Quartet (Calliope)

Prokofiev and Ravel, Piano Concertos, Argerich / Abbado / Berlin Philharmonic (DG)

Stravinsky, Symphonies, Stravinsky / Columbia Symphony (Sony)

Ives: An American Journey, Tilson Thomas / San Francisco Symphony (RCA)

Gershwin, *Porgy and Bess*, Rattle / Glyndebourne Opera (EMI DVD)

Weill, *The Threepenny Opera* ("Berlin 1930" edition, Teldec)

Shostakovich, String Quartets Nos. 3, 7, 8, St. Lawrence Quartet (EMI)

Strauss, *Metamorphosen* and *Four Last Songs*, Karajan / Berlin Philharmonic (DG)

Xenakis, Orchestral Works and Chamber Music (col legno)

Stockhausen, *Elektronische Musik, 1952–1960* (Stockhausen Edition No. 3)

Cage, *The Seasons* (ECM)

Feldman, *Rothko Chapel* (New Albion)

Pärt, *Tabula Rasa* (ECM)

Adams, *Harmonielehre*, de Waart / San Francisco Symphony (Nonesuch)

Lutosławski, Third Symphony, Salonen / Los Angeles Philharmonic (Sony)

Golijov, *Ayre*, and Berio, *Folk Songs*, Dawn Upshaw (DG)

ACKNOWLEDGMENTS

For assistance with research I would like to thank Therese Muxeneder and Eike Fess at the Schoenberg Center in Vienna; Pia Hadl and Alexander Moore at the Graz Opera; Nancy Shawcross at the Alma Mahler-Werfel collection at the University of Pennsylvania; Werner Grünzweig at the Akademie der Künste, Berlin; Maria Wilflinger at the Austrian National Library in Vienna; Gabi Hollender at the Thomas Mann Archive in Zurich; Sven Friedrich at the Richard Wagner Museum; Noëlle Mann at the Sergei Prokofiev Archive; John Bewley at the Music Library of the State University of New York at Buffalo; Suzanne Eggleston Lovejoy at the Yale University Music Library; and staff members of the Britten-Pears Library in Aldeburgh, the Music Division and the Rare Book and Special Collections Division of the Library of Congress, the Wiener Library at Columbia University, the Music Division of the New York Public Library for the Performing Arts, and, especially, National Archives II in College Park, Maryland.

Thomas Adès, Milton Babbitt, Osvaldo Golijov, the late György Ligeti, Arvo Pärt, Steve Reich, and the late Alfred Schnittke generously spoke to me about their music. John Adams served both as a subject of the book and as an inspiration for its style. Judge Ronald Schoenberg, of Brentwood, California, and Dr. Christian Strauss, of Garmisch-

Partenkirchen, Germany, graciously showed me the homes of their forebears. Donald Mitchell, Carlos Moseley, the late David Raksin, the late John de Lancie, Russell Campitelli, and Milton Weiss told stories of a fading century. Frances Stonor Saunders guided me toward documents in the National Archives. Sylvia Kahan shared the Princesse de Polignac's correspondence with Stravinsky. Douglas Yeo of the Boston Symphony answered questions about the trombone glissando.

I leaned heavily on the scholarly advice of Amy Beal, Marva Griffin Carter, Donald Daviau, Chris Dempsey, Richard Giarusso, Lydia Goehr, Chris Grogan, Donald Meyer, Simon Morrison, Severine Neff, Rebecca Rischin, Malcolm Rowat, and Marc Weiner. Walter Frisch at Columbia, Mark Katz at Peabody, Karen Painter at Harvard, Steven Stucky at Cornell, Jeffrey Kallberg at the University of Pennsylvania, and Peter Bloom at Smith let me road-test sections of the book in academic settings. I am desperately grateful to a brilliant group of scholars and experts who read and commented on parts of the manuscript: Joseph Auner, Michael Beckerman, Peter Burkholder, Louise Duchesneau, Laurel Fay, Robert Fink, Kyle Gann, Bryan Gilliam, James Hepokoski, Peter Hill, Ethan Iverson, Gilbert Kaplan, Michael Kater, Kim Kowalke, Howard Pollack, James Pritchett, Anne Shreffler, Judith Tick, Hans Rudolf Vaget, and Pamela Wheeler. Christopher Hailey, Eric Bruskin, and Charles Maier went through the entire manuscript with great care, writing mini-essays on each chapter. Richard Taruskin, a major influence on my writing, performed merciless surgery to merciful effect.

I owe more than I can say to my piano teacher, the late Denning Barnes, who indoctrinated me into modernity by way of Berg's Piano Sonata, and also to my teachers Paul Barrett, Paul Piazza, Ted Eagles, Robert Kiely, and Alan Lentz. For help of all kinds I thank Charles Amirkhanian, William Berger, Björk, Will Cohen, Alvin Curran, the Goldstines (Danny, Hilary, Josh), Colin Greenwood and Molly McGrann, Dave Grubbs, Bob Hurwitz, Laura Kuhn of the John Cage Trust, Chris Lovett, Raphael Mostel, Kent Nagano, Esa-Pekka Salonen, Barry Shiffman, Michael Tilson Thomas, and John McLaughlin Williams. Part of the book was written under the auspices of the American Academy in Berlin, where Gary Smith created a Café Museum atmosphere and Yolande Korb braved an ice storm to bring me nineteen volumes of the diaries of Goebbels. Some late-stage work was done courtesy of a Fleck

Fellowship at the Banff Centre in Canada. The precocious Patrick "Pack" Bringley fetched documents from all over Gotham and offered astute advice. Tiffany Kuo spent a long hot summer checking every page of the manuscript in its monster incarnation, bringing to bear her own deep knowledge of the field. Jens Laurson commented incisively on German matters. Alex Abramovich took time off from his massive music history to make some translations from the Russian. Nigel Simeone kindly supplied the photograph of Messiaen in Utah.

The book grew out of fifteen years of work as a music critic. For the chance to practice that peculiar calling I thank David Elliott at WHRB; the great Leon Wieseltier at *The New Republic*; Edward Rothstein and James Oestreich at the *New York Times*; Joel Flegler at *Fanfare*; Louis Menand and Henry Finder at *The New Yorker*; and Tina Brown, who brought me to *The New Yorker* full time. Much of this material emerged from richly meandering conversations with Charles Michener, my longtime *New Yorker* editor. Daniel Zalewski, my virtuosic current editor, was hugely helpful in the later stages and somehow read the book in his nonexistent spare time. Martin Baron is the greatest fact-checker that ever was and ever will be. (Leave on author.) Aaron Retica, Liesl Schillinger, Dan Kaufman, and Marina Harss also checked parts of this book over the years. David Remnick, the Mahler/Strauss of magazines, gave me permission to pilfer my *New Yorker* articles, time to finish the book, and freedom to indulge my passions.

Tina Bennett, my agent, pushed me to write this book when the twentieth century was not yet dead and gave me hope whenever I felt lost. Eric Chinski, another recovering teenage *Doctor Faustus* addict, bushwhacked through the manuscript countless times; without his precision-targeted editing and moral support it would never have assumed readable form. In a phrase, he and Tina brought the noise. The project first took shape at Houghton Mifflin, and I am extremely grateful for their interest. Jonathan Galassi honored me by acquiring the book for Farrar, Straus and Giroux when Eric moved there. Christopher Potter, while at Fourth Estate, showed keen sympathy. David Michalek did me a great favor by taking the author's photo. Various people at FSG labored zealously on my behalf: Gena Hamshaw smilingly took care of innumerable hassles, especially with respect to the photos; Zachary Woolfe affably handled text permissions; Ingrid Sterner copyedited the manuscript with brilliant attention to detail; John McGhee oversaw production (and a panicky author) with a punctilious eye, knowledge of the avant-garde, and vast patience; Laurel Cook vigorously and enthusiastically undertook the intricate task of publicizing the book; Charlotte Strick designed a beautiful cover.

None of the above would have happened as it did without the generosity of Alex Star. Jason Royal, Jack Ferver, Sean O'Toole, Paula Puhak, Michael Miller, and various friends around New York kept me on the road toward sanity. Malcolm and Daphne Ross gave me, with so much else, their love of music; I owe them everything. My brother, Christopher, has been my expert listening companion for as long as I can remember. Penelope and Maulina, my personal assistants, lent feline expertise. My wonderful husband, Jonathan Lisecki, has been with me from the beginning of this saga to the end, enduring seven years of distraction with love, and I dedicate the book to him and my parents together.

INDEX